THIS ISSUE OF
DEDICATED TO TH
MR. TULSI

Author Shamya Dasgupta Remembers
Tulsi Ramsay
(1944-2018)

The Ramsay family made their movies in a manic burst between 1972 and 1993, seven brothers obsessed with the idea of making movies but not quite sure what sort: genre, treatment or budget. They ended up making a series of films, formulaic, yes, but outstanding in their thrills and chills. Made on shoestring budgets, with largely unknown leading men and women. All the films were made in locales that looked pretty much the same— because they *were* almost all shot in the hill station of Mahabaleshwar near Bombay (now Mumbai). Horror films with comedy tracks, songs and dances, little stretches of romance and a hint of skin-show.

What did Tulsi Ramsay, who passed away at 74 in mid-December last year, bring into all this?

The fourth of nine children born to Fatehchand and Kishni Ramsay, Tulsi was the one who brought commercial concerns to their productions, weaving these elements into the movies themselves. He was also one half of the two-brother directorial team along with the much-younger Shyam.

In many ways, he was the brains behind the brand. Tulsi was always the outgoing one, the one that fought hard to get film magazines and trade journals to write about the Ramsays and their films, advertise their releases.

A story which Komal Nahta, editor of *Film Information*, told me was illuminating: "I used to meet Tulsi Ramsay often when they were trying to sell their films. He would go all-out to project it as *the film*. Very pushy. I'm not saying it's a bad quality, because in our industry you have to look out for yourself. But, yes, he was very pushy."

When the movie was made, it was time to tell the world about it; tell the world in the pre-internet and pre-social media era, make it relevant, find a way to screen it in Bombay, jostle for space with the mainstream behemoths. So, it was Tulsi, out there, doing the marketing, the selling.

"When one of their films would be out, Tulsi Ramsay would come in and sometimes demand and sometimes plead for the reports to be good," remembers Nahta with a laugh.

During the filmmaking process, too, the brothers usually had very clearly-defined roles. It was collaborative, sure, but Kumar was the main man for the stories, Tulsi and Shyam were the directors, and Gangu the cinematographer. As for the scripts, there was the main storyline, involving the monsters and the terrors, and then there was the 'Tulsi-line'.

Ajay Agarwal, the massive monster-man of the Ramsays' biggest hit, **PURANA MANDIR** *[1984]*, refers to Shyam as a 'good director' and Tulsi as an 'excellent businessman'. How did that work? Well, Shyam focused on the horror. And Tulsi breathed sunshine into the scripts. With comedy. With songs. With a hint of sex and romance.

"Tulsi always kept the business in mind, the commercial aspect. Entertainment—music, action and comedy. He always insisted on that, and took care of it," says Shyam.

Tulsi elaborated on this: "When you show horror, it has an impact on the audience. But, after that, you need to give them a break. Have a song, or a comedy track, or something light. If you have a long sequence in the night, show some daylight. People will feel that, fine, things are all right. You can't scare people constantly for two, three hours!"

It certainly worked. **PURANA MANDIR**, the second-highest-grossing film of 1984, had a brilliant horror track with a significant backstory, spanned generations, and was epic-ish in its storyline. But the film also had memorable songs, perhaps the Ramsays' most elaborately created love story, and a spoofy take on **SHOLAY** *[1975, D: Ramesh Sippy]* that seemed to almost exist as a second film within the same film.

All Tulsi. He had leeway to work the non-horror aspect, and he totally got his teeth into it. Comedy, especially, was always a big part of the films, and looking at the success they achieved in their two-decade run, it did make sense. Yes, *you can't scare people constantly*.

He was an odd man. Often talking about money and "sexy girls" (in the context of casting heroines) in a way that might be perceived as crass by some people. But, at the same time, disarmingly candid and at times hilarious.

The "DNA" monster (actor Om Shivpuri under heavy makeup) flanked by two of the Ramsay Bros.—Tulsi at right and Shyam at left—on the set of their film **DAHSHAT** (1981)

While I was working on my book *Don't Disturb the Dead*, Tulsi was my first port of call when I started reaching out to the family. More than one trip to Mumbai, however, was wasted, because Tulsi was always busy with something or other or wasn't well. When we finally met, he said, "No, my health was fine, and I didn't have any work." Erm, *then*?! "I didn't want to meet you. What's the point of a book anyway? Who reads all this? Will we get any money? How will it help me?"

I tried answering him to the best of my ability, and he warmed up, gradually. And when he did, Tulsi sat back, thought hard, and remembered old, untold stories, some of which found their way into the book. He was a fantastic storyteller too, embellishing his tales with sound effects, the whooshing of the wind, the creaking of doors, the growls of the monsters… scary music, too.

We spoke often after the book was out, and had created a bit of a buzz. He was happy about it. His health wasn't at its best, clearly, but he wanted to make another film before finishing-up. "Find me a good story, and I'll do it—not the same thing anymore." He ran out of time.

Shamya Dasgupta is the author of Don't Disturb the Dead: The Story of the Ramsay Brothers *(Harper-Collins India, 2017)**

*Available to order on Amazon.com (@ *https://www.amazon.in/Dont-Disturb-Dead-Ramsay-Brothers/dp/9352644301*)

DON'T DISTURB THE DEAD:
THE STORY OF THE RAMSAY BROTHERS

By Shamya Dasgupta
(India: HarperCollins Publishers, 2017)

When Tulsi Ramsay (1944-2018) passed away in Mumbai this past December 13th, there was little in the way of coverage in the Indian press—neither in print nor on TV, or even online either. My friend and *Monster!* contributor Kinshuk Gaur (whose appraisal of the new Hindi/English Netflix horror series *Ghoul* [2018, India] can be found on p.274) wrote to me the day after he learned of the director/producer's passing, "I am shocked that there was *nothing* about Tulsi Ramsay on the news channels. The Ramsays were not liked by most film critics, but they did make blockbuster movies". That mere fact alone should have generated at least *some* kind of media buzz, you'd think. However, it wasn't until after Ramsay movie fans began posting their own obituaries / In Memoria on the man at blogs and on social media and such that some praise—however *faint* at times—was finally duly given to Mr. Ramsay (by such local newspapers as *The Hindustani Times*, for one).

What the press reported was the oft-told tale—albeit a highly-abridged/homogenized one, the likes of which most articles had been telling about The Ramsays for however many years prior—of the family's rise to become India's most influential horror movie powerhouse ever. To get the *real* dirt on the rise-and-fall and how-and-why (etc.) of the Ramsay Horror Dynasty, you need to read Shamya's must-have book.

The late '70s/early '80s period was one when Bolly-

wood, as well as the rest of India's various regional film industries too, were beginning to experiment with new cinematic forms. It was a time when the horror genre—which had marginally been explored by other Indian directors prior to that—was now ripe to be exploited to the max by the seven brothers: Tulsi, Shyam, Kumar, Keshu, Kiran, Gangu and Arjun. Much to the horror of India's censors, who subjected each new Ramsay Bros. film to severe edits (sometimes delaying their release for months; in the case of **VEERANA** [1988], for almost *two years*!), it was The Ramsays' shared no-nonsense, low-budget approach to unflinchingly gory chills 'n' thrills that produced films of a like never before seen in India's theatres: gruesome horror movies… made *by* Indians, *for* Indians!

Through extensive research and interviews (not to mention a fabulous color section of rare photos of The Ramsays and assorted related movie memorabilia), Shamya—this dude can *write!*—really delivers the goods, and his book is not to be missed.

– **Tim Paxton**

MONSTER!
contains photos,
drawings, and illus-
trations included for
the purpose of criticism
and documentation. All
pictures copyrighted by
respective authors,
production com-
panies, and/
or copyright
holders.

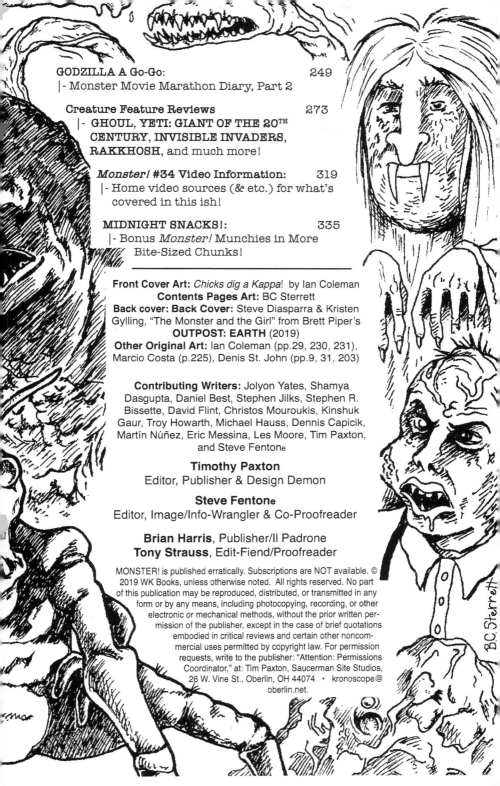

Front Cover Art: *Chicks dig a Kappa*! by Ian Coleman
Contents Pages Art: BC Sterrett
Back cover: Back Cover: Steve Diasparra & Kristen
Gylling, "The Monster and the Girl" from Brett Piper's
OUTPOST: EARTH (2019)
Other Original Art: Ian Coleman (pp.29, 230, 231),
Marcio Costa (p.225), Denis St. John (pp.9, 31, 203)

Contributing Writers: Jolyon Yates, Shamya
Dasgupta, Daniel Best, Stephen Jilks, Stephen R.
Bissette, David Flint, Christos Mouroukis, Kinshuk
Gaur, Troy Howarth, Michael Hauss, Dennis Capicik,
Martín Núñez, Eric Messina, Les Moore, Tim Paxton,
and Steve Fentone

Timothy Paxton
Editor, Publisher & Design Demon

Steve Fentone
Editor, Image/Info-Wrangler & Co-Proofreader

Brian Harris, Publisher/Il Padrone
Tony Strauss, Edit-Fiend/Proofreader

MONSTER! is published erratically. Subscriptions are NOT available. ©
2019 WK Books, unless otherwise noted. All rights reserved. No part
of this publication may be reproduced, distributed, or transmitted in any
form or by any means, including photocopying, recording, or other
electronic or mechanical methods, without the prior written permission of the publisher, except in the case of brief quotations
embodied in critical reviews and certain other noncom-
mercial uses permitted by copyright law. For permission
requests, write to the publisher: "Attention: Permissions
Coordinator," at: Tim Paxton, Saucerman Site Studios,
26 W. Vine St., Oberlin, OH 44074 • kronoscope@
oberlin.net.

MAKE MINE A MONSTER 2

There were some obvious reasons for me to visit India. Its culture and primary religion have always fascinated me and, over the past ten years or so, I have been diligently collecting, watching, and writing about Indian cinema for both *Monster!* digest and our "big sister" megazine, *Weng's Chop*. So, this memorable past October, I treated myself to a little month-long 'sabbatical' overseas to broaden my horizons; for research and study…and to see what I could find that was cool, interesting and novel. Without much planning (as per usual!) other than for booking planes, trains (if not automobiles!) and hotel rooms weeks and months in advance—*surprise, surprise!*—I landed in India; a truly fateful day for me, having spent so much time there already, if only vicariously, in my imagination…and at the movies, of course.

While I tried to keep my advance preconceptions of what I was expecting from the real—as opposed to 'reel'—India to a minimum, what I hadn't expected (not) to find there beforehand was the surprising scarcity of physical media for sale in the shops, bazaars and other such places where you might expect to find such things; which isn't to say that much of what *was* there wasn't *fantastic*, mind you. It all depends on what you're looking for, I guess. Commerce in India is very different from what we would expect if we were to go shopping at a mall or market here in the USA. While I got some limited exposure to the subcontinent's commercial aspects, being that I travelled to seven different cities and numerous smaller towns while there, I did glean at least some basic sense of how the Indian mercantile trade system works.

In the States, we typically have one localized neighborhood shop that sells everything you could need for a particular project—like, say, going to your local hardware store to buy nine-inch nails, a hammer, lightbulbs, a garden hose, etc.—you know, the wide variety of goods that smaller local chain-stores stock. Unlike here, however, I learned that Indian communities typically have individual merchants' stalls, where a certain vendor would have the nails you want… but *only* nails. While another seller would carry garden hose…but *only* that specific type of tubing. And so on…Want a new handlebar for your bike, say, or a piston for your car? There are shops in India that specialize *exclusively* in those types of items. If you need a screwdriver to go with your bag of newly-purchased #7 screws, then Santosh will send you on to his buddy Anil, who sells that particular kind of tool; Anil's stall being right next door, a block further along, or whatever. There are also shops that stock *solely* lightbulbs, and nothing but. Shops exclusively for electrical cords. You name it! (But you get the idea.) Yes indeed, it was both fascinating and at the same time sometimes frustrating to go shopping in India.

That isn't to say I didn't find any "hyperstores" there like we have here in the U.S. of A. Just out of curiosity, I popped my head in the doors of some (e.g., D-Mart, Big Bazaar, Bilka and Laxmi Mart branches), but their sparklingly orderly and uncluttered organization was a lot less appealing to me, more due to their air of careful compartmentalization and predictable familiarity than anything else. Meh. *Blah!*

If footwear is your thing, then the blocks of shops in Mumbai that sell nothing but shoes may be your personal Nirvana. (…Or, in my case, sheer *Hell*!) Trying to navigate through the crush of bodies as both men and women alike push 'n' shove their way to popular clothing stalls frantically waving cash at sellers for the saris, shirts, pants, or what-have-you in their clutches was unnerving. Luckily, I wasn't there for any of those items. Food stalls, clothing markets, bike or car parts, *tuk-tuk* parts, plastic junk, kitchen needs made of brass or aluminum (yes, there were stalls that *only* sold pot and pans. If you wanted any kind of utensils to go with them, go see ol' Vinod two stalls down!), and everything else you could imagine could be found at the weekend *chor* bazaars.

Everything? But what I was really looking for were VCDs and/or DVDs. Which isn't to say that the market for movies on physical media hasn't almost totally dried-up in India, although I was told there are shops that specialize in such goods (more on that below).

But anyway, I did manage to score *one* (1!) movie on disc (at right) during my entire Indian trip, so it wasn't a complete write-off on that score…

Upon examination of the CBFC certificate which usually appears just before a film's opening credits, turned out that this was a Kannada-language dub of the Tamil film VELLOKKIZHA-MAI 13AAM THEYTHAI (2016). And, lucky me, it happens to be a genre-crossover horror flick. That is to say, it has elements of ghostly possession, along with 'Goddess intervention', within a horribly unfunny 'comedic' framework. This begs the question: do I *want* to even bother reviewing VELLOKKIZHAMAI 13AAM THEYTHAI for *Monster!*, considering it's a so-called comedy? Those of you who may have read my numerous articles on / reviews of Indian cinema in the past may be able to guess the answer to the above question, since I can rarely abide such drivel and have said so many times! Nevertheless, as a hardcore enthusiast of Indian horror movies, I chose to throw all caution to the four winds (the East one especially) and steel myself for what might well be a dreadfully *dull* event… Here goes nothing!

The film begins with the usual drawn-out and utterly witless 'spooky' pre-credits sequence—that so many of these wannabe horror comedies

seemingly feel obligated to toss out—wherein a man is haunted by his own ghost…and now, with that out of the way (along with a title sequence involving other dumb shenanigans), a cleaning crew arrives at a very old and very haunted house. Here, after losing his protective lemon talisman, one of the workmen shortly unwittingly slices his finger on a rusty gate. Before you can say, "Better get a tetanus shot for that, buddy," both these ominously-foreshadowing actions awaken a whole gaggle of ghosts—including a highly pissed-off female one…

What follows *could* have been a decent film had the director credited only as Pugalmani (full name Pugalmani Kannan) removed all the dopey comedic elements and played things straight instead. There is sufficient substance in the basic story for a potential full-blooded horror movie (albeit a derivative one, as most of these films tend to be nowadays virtually anywhere around the globe that has a film industry). Instead, we get a 'light-and-breezy'— if exceedingly LOUD!—farce full of nonstop stupidity accompanied by Taj Noor's horrible soundtrack; much of which is, at times, so boisterously overbearing and filled with blaring strings and goofy sound effects as to drown-out the histrionic chittering (thank goodness for small mercies!) of everyone who has a line. The four goofballs in VELLOKKIZHA-MAI 13AAM THEYTHAI encounter thirteen ghosts who try to stop a young man (lead actor Rathan Mouli) from getting married on a Friday the 13th. Not unlike in William Castle's gimmicky tongue-in-cheek spook-a-thon 13 GHOSTS ([1960] and its utterly unrecognizable 'reimagining'-in-name-only, THIR13EN GHOSTS [2001, D: Steve Beck]), in V13AT there are a variety of spooks inhabiting the old mansion, including a headless man, a horrid old hag, and so forth. Most-prominent of this baker's dozen of restless spirits is that of the female lead (Suza Kumar), who confronts the human interlopers and is eventually put to rest by an act of divine intervention. The final ten minutes are what held me fascinated, and ultimately kept this single movie purchase while I was in India from being a total loss.

Oddly enough, two years prior to making **VEL-LOKKIZHAMAI 13AAM THEYTHAI**, Pugalmani Kannan directed another ghost movie, this one with the title **13 AAM PAKKAM PAARKKA**. Yet again therein, the 'unlucky' "Friday the 13th" trope was made use of, but this time there is little comedy involved other than the usual monkey shines which are often inserted into films of this genre to, 'give the audience a break from the horror,' as I have been told (something which the late Tulsi Ramsay alludes to in guest contributor, author Shamya Dasgupta's, opening tribute to the man in this very ish). **13 AAM PAKKAM PAARKKA** is the superior film of the two discussed here, and one which I have no need to discuss any deeper other than by wondering *why* Pugalmani Kannan ditched this preferable serious former format for a 'comedy'? One final note, and something truly sad to report, he also directed (this time credited as Pugazhmani) **PASAI VEETU AMMAN** in 2004, which is a wonderfully entertaining Tamil Goddess devotional film starring Meena as the twin deities Padai Veetu Amman / Muthu Mariamman. *Man oh man!* First there were the superior **PASAI VEETU AMMAN** then **13 AAM PAKKAM PAARKKA**, followed by the far-inferior (other than for its last act) **VELLOKKIZHAMAI 13AAM THEYTHAI**. My, how the mighty have fallen! I covered the 'goddess' film genre at some length in *Weng's Chop* #4 (pp.126-154), and should I ever have the cash (it's a little pipedream of mine), I would *love* to include **PASAI VEETU AMMAN** in a ten-movie disc set entitled *The Fierce Aspect: The Best of Angry Goddess Cinema*. Seriously. It's *that* good.

All this being said, I spent an entire month in India, yet, as mentioned above, only found just this single film on my travels. Sad, but true! There's a good reason for that current lack of physical media in India, though.

In my travels throughout the subcontinent, I stayed in Bengaluru ("Bangalore") for a couple of days. This was to give a badly-sprained ankle time to heal, and also a chance to explore various open-air markets. I had *hoped* to find a street-seller who had what I was looking for (i.e., movie-related merchandise), but no such luck… any more than that damned ankle injury I suffered was lucky! Oh well.

After three hours or more on my second trip out to a market, I concluded that, at least in India, physical media is fast becoming extinct. *Why?* Basically, it's because, as is virtually everywhere else, the omnipresent Internet has as-good-as supplanted DVDs or VCDs as a medium in the public's favor. For example, I stopped by no less than three small shops that each had banners advertising movies for sale. Each storefront—which were little more than stalls, really—had posters for new movies and TV shows plastered all over their interiors, along with ads for cellphones, SIM cards, service plans and what-have-you. The first shop's proprietor had no idea what I was talking about, although he did know some English. This clerk shook his head at my mention of VCDs, then pointed emphatically at his cellphone promos, so I thanked him and moved on... The second gentleman just laughed and said, "No VCDs no more!" and again attempted to interest me in his cellphones instead, even though there were posters for movies stuck all over his stall. The last husker made everything plain to me: he *did* have boxes of DVDs, which were, for the most part, older titles. I asked about buying them, and he informed me that these discs were not for sale, but that he could rip them and sell me a USB stick with the movies on it; or, better yet, he would simply sell me a code that I could use at his YouTube account to watch whatever movie(s) I wanted. Not exactly what I was looking for!

Just as I was leaving the market, feeling rather disappointed, I spotted a motley array of dingy DVDs and VCDs spread out on the ground in front of a man who was sitting in the dirt, attempting to sell them. That's where I found my copy of the above-discussed **V13AT**. Granted, it was a bootleg, but at least it was on an actual physical disc rather than merely a nebulous 'soft' copy.

As it stands these days, fewer and fewer new movies are currently making their way from the various Indian studios and onto the local theatre circuits, as the market is fast becoming an increasingly digital one. The trend now is to produce product for sale via online streaming services, or, at least if you can't find a physical distributor, to sell-off the product outright to a service. It's happening in India, and is slowly becoming a reality here in the USA (etc.) as well. The flipside to this sad sub-cinematic fate is that, while your film may not ever actually get seen by anyone in a theatre, it might possibly be viewed any number of times—depending on its popularity or lack thereof, of course—on Amazon or Netflix, or whatever other services bought the rights. Yes indeed, it appears as though the only 'butts in seats' for most movies soon will not be in actual theatre chairs but on comfy sofas in viewers' homes!

Bummer. What sorta crappy karma is that?

– **Tim Paxton**

Art by Denis St. John

SHIGERU MIZUKI

by Jolyon Yates

Introduction

Manga artist and *yōkai* scholar Shigeru Mizuki (1922-2015) is a key figure in any discussion of *yōkai* in Japanese pop culture. Hopefully this article serves as an introduction to Mizuki and the depiction of *yōkai* in print. I shall start with *yōkai* to introduce terms, and a bit of history up to the early 20th Century, then switch to a history of the medium in which Mizuki began to draw *yōkai* professionally, before concentrating on Mizuki himself and the *yōkai* boom he set-off in the 1960s.

Film titles are given in Japanese and English, with release dates, in *References*.

1: Yōkai

The *kanji* are 鴈 / "bewitching", and 挋 / "mysterious". *Yōkai* can be a broad term for all supernatural beings and monsters, or Japanese creatures in particular. Other catch-all terms are *kaii gensho* (怪異現象 / "bizarre phenomenon"), *mononoke* (琲肥挋 / "spirit of a thing"), *bakemono* (化物 / "changing thing") and *obake* (お化 / "changing thing" also), reminding us of the mutability of the world. They can be malign or friendly, grotesque and/or cute, sometimes embody natural threats or punishment for transgressions, and tend to be free of the repressions of normal society.

Since *Yōkai* are creatures of the animist *Shintō* culture, many of them are non-human objects, which are referred to as *onbake* (牧邸 / "grateful spirit", an inanimate object so adored by humans that it comes to literal life) and *tsukumogami* (嬾莋蜺 / "mourning attachment deity", an object which acquires a haunting spirit after 100 years of use). This belief has been dated as far back as the Muromachi Period (1336-1573, Rubin, p.1).

Yōkai have been infused with Japan itself ever since water dripped from Izanagi. According to the *Kojiki*, the "Record of Ancient Matters" compiled in the early 8th Century by O no Yasumaro, Izanagi ventured into the *Yomi-no-kuni*, the Underworld, to see his sister-wife Izanami, with whom he had raised the Japanese archipelago. She was so enraged by his seeing her in her corrupted state that she sicced Yakusa-no-ikazuchi-no-kami ("Eight Thunders God") and Yomotsu-shikome ("Underworld Hag") upon him. Izanagi escaped,

Eekosystem! Animistic Shintō spirits infest Japan; from *Gaki-zoshi* ("Scroll of the Hungry Ghosts") *[in the Tokyo National Museum]*

declared he was now divorced, and took a bath. Amaterasu the Sun Goddess sprang from his left eye, Tsukuyomi the Moon from his right, and wild man Susanoo the Tempest God from his nostrils. Water dripping from Izanagi soaked into the land so that, with the right concentration of the right energy, a *yōkai* might spring forth from anywhere and anything.[1]

Those which appear to be humans—albeit with unruly hair and missing feet—are closer to the Western idea of vengeful ghosts, and are known as *yūrei* (幽霊 / "otherworldly spirit"). *Yūrei* can also be referred to as *borei* (亡霊 / "deceased spirit") and *shiryo* (死霊 / "death spirit"). Peak *yūrei* viewing time is The Hour of The Ox, in the early hours after midnight. If a person's *reikon* (霊魂 / "spirit") is unable to join their ancestors because of a botched funeral or trauma, it becomes a *yūrei*. As *kaidan* (怪談 / "tales of the strange") became more popular in the 17th Century, *yūrei* took on more features which distinguished them from living humans, such as being dressed in white (the color of death); then, in the 18th Century, missing legs, demonstrating their disconnectedness from the spirit of the earth. Once the proper rites have been observed, or vengeance taken, the *yūrei* finds peace.

---

1 In the movie **NIHON TANJO**, Susanoo and Yamato Takeru are played by Toshirō Mifune, Izanami by Shizuko Muramatsu and Amaterasu by Setsuko Hara.

A lethal spirit can even originate from the living. Such is the fury of The Lady Rokujo in the early 11th Century story "Genji Monogatari" that it becomes an *ikiryo* (生霊 / "living spirit") and kills two of Genji's wives, without the knowledge of Rokujo, carrying her grudge even after the anger has left her. On the other hand, a spirit born of vengeful anger reaching from beyond death is an *onryō* (怨霊) The *onryō* is written-of in the historical record *Shoku Nihongi*, completed in 797.

Perhaps the earliest illustration of *yōkai* is the *Gaki Zoshi* ("Hungry Spirit Scroll"), in which greedy humans who have been reincarnated as grotesque creatures condemned to feeding on corpses, excrement and spilled water are saved by the actions of Buddhist priests. The scrolls date from the late 12th Century, a time of other instructional art, such as "Hell Scrolls" (*Jigoku Zoshi*), "Hell Pictures" (*Jigokuhen*) and "Disease Scrolls" (*Yamai Zoshi*). Scenes from the *Gaki* and *Yamai Zoshi* were used in the manga "Ashura" by Joji Akiyama (1970), and a hell picture is painted in the story *"Jigokuhen"* by Ryunosuke Akutagawa (published 1918), filmed in 1969. Heaven and Hell pictures were displayed at a local temple, Shofukuji, near Mizuki's hometown, and were apparently of great interest to him as a child.

Shiguro Mizuki 　　　　　　　　　*Jolyon Yates*

Even more *directly* influential on Mizuki was the *Hyakki Yako* (百鬼夜行 / "100 Spirit Night Parade"), a procession of *yōkai* led by a *nurarihyon* (ぬらりひょん), a slippery fellow dressed in Buddhist robes and sporting a distended, gourd-shaped head.[2] The parade was depicted in scrolls as far back as the 15th Century. Famous examples include the *Hyakki Yagyo Zu* of the 16th Century, now on display in Kyoto, and the 19th Century *Hyakki Yagyo* by Kawanabe Kyosai, shown in the British Museum. The spectacle also appears in book form in the *Gazu Hyakki Yagyo* by Toriyama Sekien, published in 1776, ostensibly a bestiary of 'actual' *yōkai*, although at least 80 of Sekien's creatures are of his own invention, and 14 are Chinese in origin. Mizuki himself has produced several *yōkai* guides, such as *Yōkaiden* (Kodansha, 1985). The *nurarihyon* and his fellow phantoms can be seen in Daiei's *Yōkai Monsters* movies of 1968-69 (see pp.225-248) and 2005 (see p.33), amongst the shape-shifting *tanuki* in **POM POKO** (平成狸合戦ぽんぽこ / *Heisei Tanuki Gassen Ponpoko*, 1994, D: Isao Takahata [which gives special thanks to Mizuki]), and a *nurarihyon* is one of Kitaro's arch enemies in Mizuki's works.

In the 17th Century, *yōkai* appeared in another format, *Otsu-e* ("Otsu pictures"), souvenir paintings sold at Otsu, just northeast of Kyoto, to travelers along the Tokaido, the coastal road from Kyoto to Tokyo, as immortalized in Utagawa Hiroshige's prints "The 53 Stations of the Tokaido" (parodied by Mizuki as "The 53 Stations of the Yokaido") and the setting for **THE GHOST OF YOTSUYA** (東海道四谷怪談 / *Tōkaidō Yotsuya kaidan*, 1959, D: Nobuo Nakagawa) and the third Daiei *yōkai* film, **ALONG WITH GHOSTS** (*Tōkaidō ōbake dōchu*, 1969, D: Yoshiyuki Kuroda, Kimiyoshi Yasuda) *[see p.245]*, 17th-Century samurai tested their mettle by taking part in the telling of one hundred ghost stories (百物語怪談会 / "Hundred Strange Tales Gathering"). As each tale was told, the narrator went into a room where he extinguished one more candle and looked into a mirror. Once the

hundredth story was done, and the last candle snuffed-out, a spirit was said to manifest in the darkness. This spooky game, the *Hyakumonogatari Kaidankai*, soon spread to other classes, and can be seen in the film **100 MONSTERS** (妖怪百物語 / *Yōkai hyaku monogatari*, 1968, D: Kimiyoshi Yasuda) *[see p.234]*.

In the latter half of the 18th Century, grandmasters of woodblock printing such as Katsushika Hokusai (1760-1849), Maruyama Okyo (1733-1795) and Kuniyoshi Utagawa (1797-1861) created some of the best-known images of *yōkai*. In 1814, Hokusai used the term *manga*, using the *kanji* 漫 / "unrestrained" and 画 / "picture", to describe

Gen Kuroki as the impish Kappa, on a Japanese tie-in book cover for **SPOOK WARFARE** (1968)

his drawings of everyday life, objects and whimsy, as opposed to proscribed subjects, such as landscapes, warriors and beautiful women (*manga* had been in usage as a term for picture books since the 1770s, and would not become synonymous with comics and cartoons until *c.*1930). His *yōkai* manga include a few depictions of *rokurokubi* (轆轤首), people with necks which, like the *kanji* of their name suggests, stretch

---

2 A *nurarihyon* dynasty is at the center of a manga and anime series by Shiibashi Hiroshi (born 1980): *Nurarihyon no Mago* (ぬらりひょんの孫, 2006), published in the US as *Nura: Rise of the Yōkai Clan*. In the *yōkai* movies, the parade is led by another slippery spirit, *abura sumashi* (油すまし / "Oil Wringer"; the ghost of an oil thief).

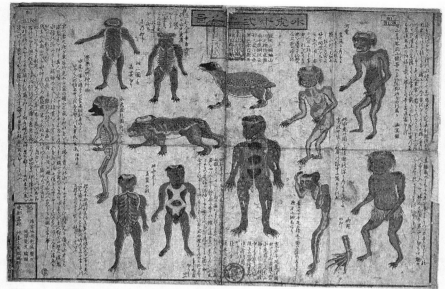

Above: *Suiko juni-hin no zu* ("Guide to 12 Types of Water-Children"), a mid-19th- Century *Kappa* woodcut print

like those of a clay pot being cast. The Edo period (1603-1868) was also the time when *karuta* (card) games became popular; one version being *obake karuta*, where players competed to collect cards illustrated with *yōkai*, and the winner was the one with the most ghost-lore knowledge and the fastest hand. *Yōkai* playing cards (面子 / *menko*) would again appear in the 1960s. The first half of the 18th Century had seen the increase of theatrical presentations of ghost stories, first as puppet shows then live-action on the stage in Osaka and Edo, and by the end of the century they had become a mainstay of Kabuki (歌舞伎), as they already were in No (能) drama, which had arisen in the 14th Century.

The 19th Century continued the production and refinement of woodblock printing, as well as the adoption of Western technology following the Treaty of Kanagawa in 1854. Magazines illustrated by pen drawings and influenced by Britain's *Punch* and America's *New York World* appeared, featuring anthropomorphic animals in cartoons and comic strips. Traditional print artists included Yoshitoshi Tsukioka (1839-1892),

infamous for his astoundingly gory series *28 Famous Murders With Verse* (英名 二十八 衆 句), also known as the *Muzan-e* (無残絵 / "Cruelty Pictures", 1866-68), a major influence on the *ero-guro* artists to come (see **2: Kamishibai**), although he also created pictures of conventional beauty, plus two *yōkai* series, *Wakan Hyaku Monogatari* (和漢 百 物語 / "One Hundred Stories of Japan & China", 1865) and *Shinkei Sanjuroku Kaisen* (新形 三十六 怪撰 / "New Forms of 36 Ghosts", 1889-92). In 1890, the Greek-Irish writer Patrick Lafcadio Hearn moved to Japan. Hearn had already described Louisiana Voodoo and compiled *Some Chinese Ghosts* (1887). His books, such as *Glimpses of Unfamiliar Japan* (1894) and *Kwaidan* (1903), brought Japanese folklore and ghost tales to the West, as well as recording them for readers of their home country. Four of Hearn's transcripts were adapted in the film **KWAIDAN** (怪談 / *Kaidan*, 1964, D: Masaki Kobayashi), while the *yuki-onna* (雪女 / "snow woman") story was again filmed as **THE SNOW WOMAN** (怪談雪女郎 / *Kaidan yuki-jorō*, 1968, D: Tokuzō Tanaka). The oft-filmed *yūrei* story "Tōkaidō Yotsuya Kaidan" (東海

道四谷怪談) was first staged in an Edo kabuki theatre in 1825, and "Kaidan Botan Doro" (怪談牡丹燈籠)—adapted from a Chinese story by Qu You translated into Japanese in the 17th Century—in 1892. Of their movie adaptations, I would recommend, for "Yotsuya Kaidan", the 1959 version directed by Nobuo Nakagawa, and the 1994 version directed by Kinji Fukasaku, although I have only seen half-a-dozen versions. Of the three films of "Botan Doro" seen to date, I would definitely pick the 1968 version directed by Satsuo Yamamoto. Lafcadio Hearn recorded the kabuki story of "Botan Doro" as "Passional Karma" in his book *In Ghostly Japan* (1899).

It is fortunate that Hearn rescued the *yōkai* from obscurity, because by this point native Japanese sentiment had turned against such superstitious, rural folk beliefs in the rush to be seen as modern. Enryo Inoue (1858-1919) dedicated himself to debunking the stories, apparently in order to separate them out from Buddhism and thus legitimize it as the modern state religion. Ironically, in founding the *Fushigi Kenkyukai* ("Paranormal Research Society") and the *Yōkai Kenkyukai* ("Yōkai Research Society"), he became known as "Dr. Yōkai", and his cataloguing of the stories remains a major resource for *yōkai* scholars. Indeed, the very use of the term has been credited to his scholarship (Natsuhiko Kyogoku, *Yōkai To Iu Kotoba Ni Tsuite*, Pt.2).

A few years before Inoue's death during a lecture tour, another influential *yōkai* study was published, *Tono Monogatari* (遠野物語 / "Tales from Tono", 1910), Kunio Yanagita's record of folktales from that town in the northeast of Honshu. Yanagita (1875-1962) was concerned with including everyday people and their beliefs in history, and his book spread the local stories of *kappa* and *zashiki-warashi*. *Kappa* (河童 / "river child") have many regional variations, but generally look like amphibious apes with a turtle shell, and an indentation in the cranium for holding water, without which they cannot survive long on land. *Zashiki-warashi* (座敷童子 / "Tatami room child") is a ruddy-faced child who may be a little mischievous but is good to have around a home, so be sure to take care of it because, if it leaves, disaster surely follows. On the 100th anniversary of *Tales from Tono*, a translated edition was released by Lexington Books and, in a Japanese

edition from Shogakukan, 29 of the stories were illustrated by Shigeru Mizuki.

There were numerous *yōkai* bestiaries published in the 20th Century, including *Yōkai Gadan Zenshu* ("Complete Discussions of Yōkai", 1929) by Fujisawa Morihiko, and *Nihon Yōkai Zukan* ("Japanese Yōkai Picture-book", 1972), text by Sato Arifumi, with glorious illustrations by Gojin Ishihara and, of course, several books and print series by Mizuki too.

2: Kamishibai

Kamishibai (紙芝居 / "Paper Theatre") is a street performance where the narrator, the *kamishibaiya*, slides illustrated boards into a miniature wooden proscenium, the *butai*, which is mounted on his

"Visiting the Backstreets of Edo/Tokyo", a guide to historical *yōkai* sightings, was based on the work *Mimibukuri* (literally "Ear Muffs"), a 10-volume collection of stories compiled by a late-Edo period samurai warrior named Negishi Yasumori (1737-1815). The stories ranged from local customs to folk medicine and urban legends

Top: A street performance of 紙芝居 / *Kamishibai* ("paper theatre"), for which the narrator, known as the *kamishibaiya*, slides illustrated boards into a miniature wooden proscenium known as a *butai*. **Above:** A *Kamishibai* title card for "Golden Bat", one of the earliest known examples

During the first *kamishibai* boom in the Depression years of the 1930s, a 1933 survey reported that there were 83 production companies and 1265 *kamishibaiya* in Tokyo alone. To feed the demand, writers and artists belonged to a bullpen of up to 200 employees called *kai* ("society"). Dealers (*kashimoto*) rented the artwork in the hope of making a profit from the candy.

To play to the crowd, art was produced with heavy India ink line work with layers of watercolor and tempera, protected with a coat of clear lacquer and a layer of rainproof wax. Heroes, often based on screen idols, were rendered quite realistically, with supporting characters drawn more cartoonishly, and backgrounds painted as vivid blurs or carefully constructed drawings, depending on the needs of the story. Boys could identify both with the heroes, who were often close to their age, although able to drive, fly and deal-out death with swords and guns, and the victims of the mayhem, who were also often children. At the time, children had freedom in the afternoons, and as dusk settled the show might also include evening news for adults.

A *yōkai* superhero was one of the most popular heroes of the medium. Debuting in 1931, *Ōgon Batto* (黄金 バット / "Golden Bat"), scripted by Ichiro Suzuki with art by Takeo Nagamatsu, was a creepy cross between the Lon Chaney Phantom of the Opera and Superman, who would make his print debut in 1938. Batto gave a chilling laugh as he clobbered arch-enemy Nazo and his minions. He transcended *kamishibai* to star in manga (from 1948), movies (in 1950 and 1966),[3] records (at least one, in 1956) and anime (1967). His second artist, from 1932, was Koji Kata, who studied the montage technique of Sergei Eisenstein. This approach really bore fruit as manga gradually took over from *kamishibai* in the 1940s, intercutting action shots with reaction close-ups and extending certain events over several pages; referred to as "decompression" in the manga-impacted US comics of the 1990s. Like *kamishibai*, manga are written to be taken in at speed; according to an editor of *Shōnen Magazine*, each page is read in an average of 3.75 seconds.

bicycle and fitted with a satin curtain, and tells the stories as he presents each picture. Notes on the story and suggested dialogue are on the back of the boards, and the *kamishibaiya* is also expected to provide sound effects and a variety of voices, much like the *benshi* or *katsuben* who narrated silent movies in Japan into the 1930s. The itinerant storyteller would travel a local circuit, announcing his presence by clapping together *hiyogoshi* sticks. Admission bought the crowd a treat, which could be roasted sweet potatoes or chestnuts, rice crackers smeared with plum jam, ice cream or other sticky sweets. The more sweets you bought, the closer you were allowed to the stage!

The format of a show was generally a funny story or a quiz, followed by a melodrama for girls (*shōjo*) and an adventure for boys (*shōnen*), which might involve superheroes, ninja, robots, dinosaurs, monsters and/or *yōkai*. The dramas were serials of 10-to-20 pictures a day, ending on a cliffhanger to be resolved on the next visit.

---

3 Apparently there was also a live-action comedy film in 1972, **ŌGON BATTO GA YATTEKURU**, and a Korean film in 1992, **YOUNG-GUWA HWANGGEUM BAKJWI** ("Yuong-gu and the Golden Bat").

As with the pulp magazines and comics of the United States, *kamishibai* was attacked. It was criticized for its lurid colors, the unsanitary candy passed between unsanitary hands, the crowds which blocked traffic and the corruption of youth, especially in the late 1930s when the government was grooming the youth of Japan for war. In 1937, the Japanese Home Ministry (内務省 / *Naimu-sho*) declared, "*kamishibai* and other amusements for the masses are debasing themselves to the lowest common denominator... social morals are not being heeded" (quoted in Nash, p.167). Eight years later, the attacks were more physical; many companies were destroyed by American air raids. However, being a relatively cheap and mobile art form, *kamishibai* arose again for a brief new boom during the postwar occupation.

The Civil Information and Education Section (CIE, 1945-1952) under Col. Kermit Dyke succeeded the Information Dissemination Section, itself a successor to the Psychological Warfare Branch. Among the CIE's concerns was "the presentation of unscientific notions", (quoted in Hirano, p.86), directed mostly at film production, but, I venture, a threat to the depiction of the supernatural in any medium. It also tried to control smut. Pulp magazines known as *kasutori zasshi* ("dregs magazines", the very word for magazine uses the *kanji* 雑 / "coarse" and 誌 / "record") sprang-up in late 1946, catering to a populace suddenly freed from repression, opened to American culture and forced into prostitution to survive. An early taboo to fall was kissing, a 'decadent' Western expression unseen during Japan's war years,[4] but *kasutori zasshi* included "pornography, crimes, grotesquerie and exposés" (Hirano, p.162).

These magazines soon died-out in the late 1940s, but by that time striptease and *ero-guro* films were on the rise. *Ero* (-tic) -*guro* (-tesque) *nansensu* was a term coined in the 1920s during the urban vogue for Western fashion and jazz, depicted by cartoonists such as Saseo Ono.[5] *Ero-*

guro is applied to the fiction of Edogawa Rampo, the pen name of Taro Hirai (based on a mangled pronunciation of Edgar Allan Poe), whose stories were adapted in many crime, horror and pink films to come. It can refer to the erotic, decadent, corrupt, malformed and deviant, and combinations thereof.

Kamishibai had been dragged into court during the International Military Tribunal for The Far East (1946-48) due to their use in the war effort. A report to the Supreme Commander for the Allied Powers (SCAP) had noted that, in the struggle against the good guys, "the exploits of the evil are too minutely explained, so that children are more deeply impressed with outrageous or immoral acts rather than the fact that the evil are conquered at last" (quoted in Nash, p.232), but their potential for propaganda was noted, too. Five million people a day gathered at the shows, including adults unable to afford radios or newspapers. In the Kansai and Kanto regions of central Japan, there were 40 production houses and 50,000 *kamishibaiya*.

movie **HORRORS OF MALFORMED MEN** (江戸川乱歩全集 恐怖奇形人間 / *Kyōfu kikei ningen: Edogawa Rampo zenshū*, 1969, D: Teruo Ishii), which was released on R1 DVD by Synapse Films in 2007; Arrow Video issued a RA BD edition in 2018.

Eric P. Nash's book *Manga Kamishibai: The Art of Japanese Paper Theatre* is highly recommended by *Monster!* co-editor Tim P

---

4   With one exception, **ONNA WA ITSUNO YO MO** ("Women Are in Every World", 1931).

5   And current artists such as Suehiro Maruo. His 2007 manga adaptation of Edogawa Rampo's *The Strange Tale of Panorama Island* was published in the US in 2013. The 1926 novella was the main source for the

Detail of a board from *Hakaba Kitarō* ("Graveyard Kitaro"), *circa* 1933; art by Kei Tajimi

SCAP-approved *kamishibai* were distributed nationally to explain such concepts as democracy and the need to consume goods. Censorial pressure on the industry prompted the introduction of a self-policing regulation committee in 1951, and creators learned it was safer to stick with tales of the fantastic, futuristic and horrific. However, despite the formation of a *kamishibai* union in 1953, the art form's days as a massively-popular entertainment medium were about to end. The first television broadcasts began that year and, to really twist the knife, not only were they set-up in the public spaces used by the *kamishibaiya*, but they were referred to as *"denki* ('electric') *kamishibai."* As society recovered, children's late afternoons were now occupied by cram schools. Artists jumped ship to manga, although educational *kamishibai* continues to this day in schools, and crime and horror shows (from companies like Nakayoshi-kai) remained popular throughout the decade.

3: Mura & Mizuki

Shigeru Mura was born in Sakaiminato, Tottori Prefecture[6] on the north coast of Honshu, March 8th, 1922, the middle son of three. As shown in his manga *Nonnonba*, when he was not being drawn into local boys' fights, he loved to spend his time drawing the natural and supernatural worlds, learning folklore from his neighbor (whose nickname provides the manga's title), eating, and building model ships. His first job was at a printer's, from which he was fired for being too slow, so he enrolled for art studies at the Seika Art School and a trade school in Osaka, but soon quit both and attended middle school until he was 20. By then it was 1942, and Mura was drafted. "You feel death already when you receive the call-up papers" (quoted in Otake).

Mura's poor showing as a soldier-in-training landed him a non-combat position in the bugle corps in Tottori. However, he could not play (!), so he was instead made to run around the grounds. When he asked to be released from his misery, the personnel officer asked him, "North or South?" Mura said "South", and found himself a private in the 229th Infantry Regiment, 38th Division, on his way to Rabaul, capital of the Territory of New Guinea.[7] The ship which took him there, *Shinanomaru*, was sunk with all hands on its way back.

New Guinea had become the battleground between Australia, which had administered the territory since 1920, and Japan, which invaded in 1942, turning Rabaul into a fortified base central to the Southwest Pacific Area. Australia's supplies could be cut off, perhaps leading to its invasion. For many Japanese troops in the early months of occupation, Rabaul was surprisingly delightful, well-supplied with food, drink and entertainments from home, and thousands of women forced into brothels.

Beyond Rabaul was not so inviting. There was anemia, beriberi, dysentery, smallpox, black-

---

6 Tottori is known for its dunes, the only ones in Japan. They were the location for **WOMAN IN THE DUNES** (砂 の女 / *Suna no onna*, 1964, D: Hiroshi Teshigahara) and the climax of **LONE WOLF & CUB: BABY CART AT THE RIVER STYX** (子連れ狼 三途の川の乳母車 / *Kozu-*

---

re *Ōkami: Sanzu no kawa no ubaguruma*, 1972, D: Kenji Misumi). Tottori was the birthplace of Nobuko Otowa, star of **ONIBABA** (鬼婆 / 1964) and **KURONEKO** (薮 の中の黒猫 / *Yabu no naka no kuroneko*, 1968 [see *M!* #10, p.42]), both directed by Kaneto Shindō. Regarding this period, the first volume of Mizuki's manga *Showa 1926-1939* was published in the US in October 2013.

7 The 1954 film **FAREWELL RABAUL** (さらばラバウル / *Saraba Rabauru*), directed by Ishirō Honda shortly before **GODZILLA**, blends romance in the city with anti-war sentiments.

water, dengue, scarlet and yellow fevers, hookworm, scrub typhus from chiggers, leishmaniasis from sandflies and malaria from mosquitoes;[8] Japanese defense trenches filled waist-high with rainwater and trench foot were also problems. New Guinea, the second-largest island after Greenland, was hot, wet and covered in thick jungle. There were only a few miles of roads. Soldiers who scaled the central mountain ranges, over 16,000 ft. high, were threatened with hypothermia. Once shipping lanes from Japan were cut-off in late 1943, it got worse. Cannibalism by Japanese soldiers was recorded as early as October 1942 (Milner, p.104).

Mura was often beaten for laziness and talkingback to officers, and sent on guard duty out in the jungle. On one such night he was late returning to his unit, because he had been off watching *parrots* instead of looking-out for enemy ships! His unit was attacked by Australian and local Melanesian forces, and he found himself the only survivor, (except for two or three men who escaped with injuries), fleeing local villagers. He escaped them—although they might have only been offering help—and swam back to camp. However, once there he was punished for not only losing his rifle, but for surviving. Mura was placed in a *kesshitai*, a unit determined to die in a suicide charge. At this point he was felled by malaria and sent to a hospital in the Zungen area. The hospital was then hit by a US air raid, and Mura, up until then a southpaw, had his left arm so badly damaged it had to be amputated on-site—badly, as it turned out. He recalls watching maggots feeding on his stump.

While he was recovering, the unit he had been attached to was sent on its final charge. Soldiers were taught about *gyokusai* (玉砕 / "Jade Shard"): "a man would rather be a shattered jade than be an intact roof tile" (from a Chinese text, *History of North Qi*). Their glorious death was reported, but somehow, some of the unit survived. Headquarters ordered them to commit suicide or charge again. This incident would be recorded in Mizuki's 1973 manga *Soin Gyokusai Seyo!* (published in the US in 2011 as *Onward Toward Our Noble Deaths*).

Yōkai Shishinroku ("Yokai Bluebook")

Mura was, like an *obake*, transformed inside and out. He walked the hill paths around Toma, above Rabaul, sometimes dodging strafing runs from Allied fighters, and came upon a Tolai village. They were hardly friendly towards the Japanese, who had killed a local chief, and yet, an old woman, Ikarian, returned his smile. "But I think now that she just sympathized with me, because I had only one arm" (from an interview with Mizuki by Iwamoto, September 5th, 2000). After several visits, Mura was invited to escape the army and stay in the village, where they grew potatoes for him and invited him to become part of Ikarian's family.[9]

When the war ended, Mura was ecstatic, even though it meant being a prisoner. He told an

8 Malaria was even more of a problem for the Allies. Quinine was scarce once the Japanese seized its sole source, Java, in 1942.

9 There are several Mizuki books on his experiences in the area, including his postwar visits: the manga *Topetoro Tono 50-nen* (2002), and as part of his Showa history series (see note #6), as well as *Mizuki Shigeru no Rabaul Senki* (1994) and *Mizuki Shigeru no Musume ni Kataru Otosan no Senki* (1995). There was also a 2008 film, **KITARŌ GA MITA GYOKUSAI: MIZUKI SHIGERU NO SENSOU** (鬼太郎が見た玉砕 〜水木しげるの戦争〜). Mizuki vowed to return in seven years, but didn't make it back until the mid-1960s. A road in Rabaul was named after him in 2003.

Mizuki's Kitaro and Medama Oyaji in "Graveyard Kitaro" (1959), a Kashihon era work that was written before Gegege no Kitarō

army surgeon about his wish to stay in the village, but was told to go back to Japan first, both to ask his parents' permission and to receive proper surgery. When he eventually returned, however, he had a long wait for treatment, and a hard scrabble to survive, working as a beggar, a fishmonger, a black market rice vendor, also at a pedicab company and as a cinema projectionist. His elder brother, an anti-aircraft artillery officer in the war, had been imprisoned as a Class B war criminal for ordering the execution of prisoners, which cannot have helped. Mura (武良 / "Martial Virtue") took the less-militaristic pen name Mizuki (水木 "Water Wood").[10]

10 "Shigeru" is written in *hiragana* as しげる, which is how his name appears on Japanese books, and it possibly took this form since his name change. The *kanji* of Shigeru, 茂, means "Thick Growth". According to Hideki Ozaki's afterword in *Showa: A History of Japan*, in around 1950 the artist came across Mizuki Manor, in Mizuki Street, Kobe, bought the place on loan and took its name for his pen-name. His early work with Koji Kata was produced here.

4: Mizuki in the 1950s: Eeking a Living

Mizuki attended Musashino Art University in Tokyo, but dropped out in 1949 and fell in with Golden Bat's Koji Kata, scraping a bit of money in the *kamishibai* market. At the time, his work was painted in a quite naturalistic style, and he illustrated domestic dramas for girls' stories. Contemporaries in the business included others who would go on to manga success: Sanpei Shirato (忍者武芸帳 / *Ninja Bugeichō*, 1959) and Kazuo Koike (*Lone Wolf & Cub* [子連れ狼 / *Kozure Ōkami*, 1970]). Mizuki also created books for the *kashi-bon* (貸本) market, rental libraries which had been around since the Edo Period (1603-1868) to provide literature for those who could not afford to buy it. With the coming of more regular libraries and greater, more affordable print runs, *kashi-bon* went into sharp decline in the early 1960s. Mizuki recalls it being a brutal business for artists, who had to provide 100-150 pages per book and, if their debut failed to sell, they were fired. However, with the high turnover and little concern from the publishers beyond the bottom line, subject matter was wide-ranging and sometimes shocking for some parents. Similar to the US outcry of the time, there was a "Campaign to Banish Bad Reading Matter", with the slogan "*Uranai Kawanai Yomanai!*" ("Don't Sell! Don't Buy! Don't Read!"), but dissimilarly, publishers and readers ignored it and comics continued to thrive.

Mizuki's debut book was *Rocketman*, published in February 1957. The painted cover depicts a superhero in the Superman mold[11] against a background of a rocket and a flying saucer in space. Others released in this decade include *Yūrei Ikka* ("Ghost Family"), *Kyofu no Yusei Majin* ("Horror of the Planet Demon"), *Plastic Man*, who looks just like the Jack Cole character in his stripey outfit, *Kaijū Ravan* ("Monster Ravan", a giant monster story), *Jigoku* ("Hell"), *Jigoku no Mizu* ("Hell Water", about a Himalayan water demon, which shares its title with

11 *The Adventures of Superman* teleseries (1952-58, USA) was first broadcast in Japan in 1956. The theatrical series *Supergiant* (鋼鉄の巨人 / *Kotetsu no Kyojin*) began in December 1957. Japan's first TV superhero, *Moonlight Mask* (月光仮面 / *Gekkō Kamen* [see M! #32, pp.40-67]), debuted in February 1958.

an episode of the 1970s Kitaro anime) and *Aya-kashi-den* (1960, a *yōkai* story anthology series featuring early appearances of Kitaro and his companion Nezumi Otoko). I have not been able to ascertain if all these books were entirely Mizuki's work, or if he merely supplied the covers for some.

In 1954, a publisher asked Mizuki to continue the *kamishibai* series *Hakaba no Kitarō* / 墓場の鬼太郎, which had first appeared in 1933 with a story about an orphaned boy ghost by Masami Ito. This was based on the Edo Period folk tale *Ame-kai Yūrei* ("The Sweets-Buying Ghost"), recorded by Lafcadio Hearn: a thin, pale young woman buys *midzu-ame* ("malt syrup") at a sweets shop night after night. The concerned owner decides to follow her, but she disappears at a Buddhist temple. The next day, he talks to the temple monk, who tells him a pregnant woman was recently buried there. The men decide to open her grave, and inside they find a child eating some candy. Mizuki and Ito created four stories, "Karate Kitaro", the most popular, "Galois", "Yūrei Hand" and "Snake People", which introduced Medama Oyaji (see below).

The *kamishibai* "Kitaro" was not a big hit, but Mizuki returned to the story in 1959 with the *kashi-bon* of *Hakaba no Kitarō*. A man named Mizuki working at a blood bank discovers their supply comes from a diseased *yōkai* mummy couple, who are expecting a child. As the parents die and decompose, their son emerges. Mizuki detests *yōkai*, so when he finds the boy crawling around in a cemetery, he hurls him against a gravestone, smashing the baby's left eye. The father's decaying body retains enough of his spirit that one eyeball pops out, grows limbs, then takes up residence in the boy's empty socket. This first story, *Okashi-na yatsu* ("Strange Guy") continues with the introduction of another Kitaro regular, Nezumi Otoko (Rat Man), a smelly, untrustworthy half-*yōkai*. Kitaro, Nezumi Otoko and Medama Oyaji (Eyeball Dad) help out a student haunted by the spirit of an ancient sorcerer. The artwork for the first run of Kitaro stories mixes realistic drawing with stylization for Kitaro and his *yōkai* friends, like the later manga, but the tone is darker and the humans less cartoonish, in the style of *gekiga*

Mizuki art for "Graveyard Kitaro", from the anthology *Yokiden* (October 1959), published by Usagitsugi Shobo

(劇画 / "drama pictures") which had emerged from the *kashi-bon* market in 1957 to appeal to older readers, spearheaded by Yoshihiro Tatsumi (several Tatsumi books have been released in the US, including the autobiographical *A Drifting Life*). Mizuki did three volumes for Togetsu Shobo, argued with the publisher over money, then took his character over to Sanyo-sha under the title *Kitarō no Yawai*. The original publisher continued *Hakaba no Kitarō* for another sixteen books, drawn by Mizuki's assistant Kanko Takeuchi (1907-1995, a fellow graduate of *kamishibai*), and still scripted by Masami Ito. Takeuchi started his run by killing-off two regular characters, Nezumi Otoko and Kineko ("Tree-Cat-Girl") but did not really make the series his own until number seven. In the final volume, Kitaro has his eyeball-father surgically implanted into his socket. Meanwhile, Mizuki's Kitaro ended after just three more books. Adults were certainly turning-out to horror films in the late '50s (there were four versions of *Yotsuya Kaidan* [四谷怪談] alone made from 1956-61), but the sales of *Kitarō* were disappointing. Perhaps adults found the *yōkai* too childishly cute; perhaps children found the story too morbid?[12]

---

12 *Hakaba Kitarō*, a TV anime series of the first Kitaro stories, aired from January 11th to March 21st, 2008. In the late '50s, children could see the theatrical series *Akado Suzunosuke* and *Seishun Kaidan*, which contained *yōkai* elements.

Mizuki's mighty tyke *Akuma-kun*, sat upon his throne!

1959 was also the debut of Kodansha's *Shōnen Magazine* (週刊少年マガジン), the first weekly to carry manga stories (it would later become all-manga), and remained the bestseller for a decade. As the *kamishibai* and *kashi-bon* artists' markets dried-up, they moved into the weeklies; creators from the *gekiga* titles brought their more realistic, grimmer takes on violence and horror into the magazines—as well as their leftist politics. *Shōnen Magazine* eventually picked up *Kitarō*, but in the meantime, Mizuki introduced two more series teaming *yōkai* with a spooky child…

5: Mizuki in the 1960s: The Kids Are All Fright

Kappa no Sanpei (河童の三平 / "Sanpei of the Kappa") *kashi-bon* ran from 1961-62. Sanpei Kawahara is a country boy living with his grandfather. He not only swims for his school, but also has a peculiarly *kappa*-like haircut, so understandably, when he is floating around in a river, *kappa* 'rescue' him and take him below to their world. Upon realizing he is human, the elders sentence him to death, but he convinces

them he can bring useful knowledge from the modern world. Not fully trusting Sanpei, they send along a young *kappa*, Kanpei, who bears a close resemblance to him, and remove his belly button, where they believe his soul resides.[13] Like Kitaro and Mizuki, Sanpei acquires his identity through *yōkai* and loss of a body part. Death stalks Sanpei, literally. The skull-headed Shinigami (死神 / "Death God") is after him and his grandfather throughout the series. Amidst all the slapstick and scatology, this is a story of abandoned children facing life and mortality and searching for their parents. It seems that, in Mizuki's life—at least as he tells it—death, the macabre and comedy are inseparable.

Wanting to explore the *yōkai* of the West, Mizuki's next *kashi-bon* series was *Akuma-kun* (悪魔くん / "Devil Boy", 1963-64). Ichiro Matsushita is nicknamed "Akuma-kun" because of his onion-like hairstyle and his bulging eyes. He is destined to save the world from evil by uniting The Twelve Apostles. He is aided in this by Dr. Faust, who has been waiting several centuries

---

13 Sanpei gets off lightly. Some *kappa* suck out the *shirikodama* (尻子玉 / "Anus Gem" [!?]), or life-force ball, then haul out his liver and eat it!

to pass-on his secrets to a special child from the East. This Faust does, then dies. The series was planned to run for five volumes, concluding the Apostle arc and featuring conflicts with various Western monsters and demons, but sales were poor on the first two books, so it was cut off at just three, leaving Akuma-kun dead at the hands of the Judas character, Yamoribito.[14] Later manga would bring Akuma-kun back from Heaven with enhanced powers, and conclude the Apostle story. *Akuma-kun* was the first of Mizuki's manga to criticize the war.

Mizuki's next magical boy was more successful commercially, especially since it was his move from *kashi-bon* to the number-one weekly, *Shōnen Magazine*. Asked to deliver a Science Fiction series, Mizuki combined *yōkai* and technology in *Terebi-kun* ("TV Kid", 1965). Yamada can enter televisions to steal products shown in commercials and give them to impoverished children in the real world. Only Yamada's best friend knows his secret. Again, there is familial loss and childhood hardship; the friend's father is dead and his mother is sick, and he has to sell newspapers to support his family. Television sets were then enjoying a huge rise in sales because of the unprecedented scale of telecasts of the 1964 Summer Olympics held in Tokyo,[15] so the character benefitted from catching some of the *zeitgeist*, but perhaps its very topicality kept it from becoming another one of Mizuki's recurring series. However, *Terebi-kun* won the Kodansha Manga Award in 1966, and thus drew further interest to the artist. As far as I know, this is the first *yōkai*, in the broadest definition, to inhabit modern electronic media, which they would later exploit with a vengeance in films like **RING** (リング / *Ringu*, 1998, D: Hideo Nakata),[16] et cet-

Screen grabs from *Yabu no Naka no Kuroneko* (1968)

era. The manga magazine *Terebi-kun*, published by Shogakukan since 1976, is an anthology of comics starring television superheroes.

The switch in manga releasing from monthly to weekly brought the experience of reading episodes closer to the viewing of television series and, if a manga story became popular, a television version was sure to follow. I speculate that if a series was seen as being a possible hit for children, in both media, there would be the motivation (if not pressure) to lighten things up. Kitaro had faltered in his ghastly first incarnation, and Mizuki was unable to sell "Graveyard Kitaro" to animation studios, so the boy got a makeover. Kitaro quit smoking, for one thing, and his irregular buckteeth gave way to curiously pursed lips. He became a friend of humans instead of an agent of supernatural punishment. Grue was scaled back. Still, this *was* a story

14 This description is most untrustworthy, due to my poor Japanese, lack of information on the original manga, and my confusion: storylines and characters differ in each of the subsequent runs of *Akuma-kun* as manga, anime and live-action.

15 The '64 Olympics served as backdrop for **WALK, DON'T RUN** (1966, USA, D: Charles Walters), a comedy starring Cary Grant and Samantha Eggar, which shows some glimpses of newly-transformed Japan. The event itself was the subject of a great documentary, **TOKYO OLYMPIAD** (東京オリンピック / *Tōkyō Orinpikku*, 1965), directed by Kon Ichikawa.

16 **RING**'s *yūrei* ghost-girl-from-the-well echoes an oft-told

tale, *Bancho Sarayashiki* (番町皿屋敷 / "The Dish Mansion of Bancho"). By the way, Ryoichi Ikegami, one of the first manga artists I fell for, was assistant to Mizuki in 1966.

Kitaro and chums reach Bone Mountain in *Kitarō no Jigokumeguri* ("Kitaro's Hell Tour", *Gekkan Shōnen Magazine*, August 1987)

---

about a one-eyed ghostboy with an eyeball father and a farting ratman friend! Sponsors were leery of being associated with graveyards and ghosts.

However, 1966 was the year of hit live-action monster shows like *Ultra Q* (ウルトラQ / *Urutora Kyū* [running since January]), and six *daikaiju* (大怪獣) movies,[17] so sponsors did pull the trigger on *Akuma-kun*, starring Mitsunobu "Johnny Sokko" Kaneko as the hero and Yoshio Yoshida as Mephisto, a devil whom Akuma-kun keeps in line with Solomon's Flute, an ocarina

given to him by Faust. The series ran for 26 episodes and pitted the team against Japanese *yōkai* like the hundred-eyed *ganma* and a *yuki-onna*, plus Western monsters like a mummy and a wolfman; acceptable to Japanese sponsors, but I doubt the devil-conjuring and bloody eye damage seen in episode 1 would have gotten airtime on children's hour in the West.

Akuma-kun's success spurred new interest in Mizuki and Graveyard Kitaro. A producer friend at Toei, Akira Watanabe, suggested a name change, and Mizuki came up with *Ge-GeGe no Kitaro* (ゲゲゲの鬼太郎).

There are several takes on an English rendering of "*GeGeGe*": "Brrr!", "Spooky Ooky", "The Spooky" and "Boo Boo Boo". In the manga, "GeGeGe…" is the chorus of frogs, birds and insects singing Kitaro's praise when he wins a battle. "*Ge!*" is also a cry of startled repulsion. Etymologically, as a child Shigeru Mizuki had a speech impediment, and pronounced his name as "Gegeru", so his nickname was "Ge-ge". The title change matched the manga with a new Kitaro series, this time an anime, which began on the January 3rd, 1968, directed by Isao Takahata (co-founder of Studio Ghibli). Episodes were adapted from the new manga, which itself reworked stories from the *kashi-bon* days; for example, the anime would be a third outing for the "Daikaiju" / 大海獣 tale (entitled "Creature from the Deep" in the 2013 US *Kitaro* book). The 65-episode anime ran from January 3rd, 1968 to March 30th, 1969. Its catchy theme song includes the lyrics, roughly translated, "In the morning I sleep / *Zzz Zzz Zzz* / *Yōkai* don't have to go to school", which I imagine delighted children, if not their parents. Anime series of "Kitaro" have been made in every decade since, as well as twelve animated movies (including the four edited from television episodes) so far.

In the manga, Kitaro lives in poverty on the outskirts of town—with his father Medama Oyaji, of course—and associates with Nezumi Otoko, Neko Musume (猫娘 / "Cat Girl", the new version of Kineko from the 1950s stories), Ittanmomen (一反木綿: literally "One Tan [29cm x 10m] Cotton", a flying strip of cotton), Sunakake Baba (砂掛け婆 / "Sand-spreading Crone"), Konaki Jiji (子泣き爺 / "Baby-Crying

---

17 Toho with **THE WAR OF THE GARGANTUAS** (フランケンシュタインの怪獣 サンダ対ガイラ / *Furankenshutain no kaijū Sanda tai Gaira*, D: Ishirō Honda [see *M!* #12, p.24]), Daiei with **GAMERA VS. BARUGON** (大怪獣決闘 ガメラ対バルゴン / *Daikaijū kettō Gamera tai Barugon*, D: Shigeo Tanaka) and the three *Majin* (大魔神 / *Daimajin*) films, and Toei with **THE MAGIC SERPENT** (怪竜大決戦 / *Kairyū daikessen*, D: Tetsuya Yamanouchi). All four major studios would release monster movies in 1967.

Old Man") and Nurikabe (塗壁 / "Coated Wall", a mobile wall). Kitaro can mentally control his *geta* shoes and detachable hand, and his hair can pop up like antennae to measure "spirit energy" or shoot from his skull like needles. He can blend into backgrounds like a chameleon, flatten himself like a rug and take on other shapes, much like Plastic Man. He can even talk to the fleas living in his ragged clothes and send them out on missions! He wears a stripy *chanchanko* vest woven from the spirit hairs of his ancestors, which can fly about and strangle enemies by itself. In a pinch, he can generate an electric shock. And of course, Kitaro and his dad have deep knowledge of *yōkai* lore.

The stories are eerie, often funny, and *VERY* weird. Mizuki's works from his mid-'60s breakout onward seem gentler, nostalgic for a magical, bucolic, mythical past, than the desperate horrors of the early "Kitaro" years when Mizuki was living hand-to-mouth/month-to-month, not knowing if he would be able to afford to eat, but perhaps the new stories *are* more subversive. "Kitaro" achieves much of its power through the blending of the ordinary, often rural and impecunious everyday world with the fantastic. Our mundane experience, easily recognizable as it is so meticulously rendered in photorealistic detail, is viewed with ironic detachment through Kitaro's eye. Mortal humans come across as blinkered, ignorant fools briefly materializing in the world of ancient elemental spirits. Are *we* haunting them? Compare Mizuki's stories with those of contemporary Horror manga maestro Kazuo Umezu (born 1936),[18] in which the viewpoint is that of ordinary human children who find themselves in a malevolent universe.

Antagonists can be human criminals or monsters of the West, like Dracula and others familiar from Universal Horror films, but in most cases they are local *yōkai*, although; like Sekien, the 18th-Century cryptozoologist, Mizuki feels free to embellish and reinvent his own versions, or simply make up 'all-new' creatures. The American master-monster Backbeard in *Yōkai Daisenso* (妖怪大戦争 / "Great Yōkai War", exactly the same title as the 1968 *yōkai* movie, and included in the 2013 Kitaro book) is a giant

Kappa no Sanpei anime (1993) movie

black eyeball with spidery limbs, looking like something out of an Odilon Redon drawing. The characters are usually drawn with smooth, clean lines, as if they were ready for an animation cel, although large *yōkai* can be rendered in a lot of detail with hatching and dotted shading to suggest textures and ghostly light. There is little use of screentones, except here and there as an extra layer of shade. Backgrounds are usually very detailed and heavily photo-referenced. I imagine Mizuki's assistants did the calorie-burning on those.[19] In the following years, the detailing would become even more intricate.

Not that he had time to enjoy it, but Mizuki was now the epicenter of the *yōkai* boom of 1968. *Shōnen Magazine* was selling over a million copies a week. On television, the *Kitarō* anime was joined by another live-action adaptation of his work, the 26-episode *Kappa no Sanpei: Yōkai Dai Sakusen* (河童の三平 妖怪大作戦 /

---

18 In Japan, he is also known as a successful comedy manga creator for series like *Makoto-chan* (まことちゃん, 1976).

19 In the aforementioned "Great Yōkai War" story, I reckon one of the panels in the "Brigadoon" sequence is based on a shot of the spaceship in **IT CAME FROM OUTER SPACE** (1953, USA, D: Jack Arnold). I wish I could credit the assistants by name, but manga tend not to list them.

"Hiderigami" (ひでりがみ) is a *Gegege no Kitarō* chapter-story that was first published in *Shōnen Magazine* (1968)

"Kappa Sanpei: Yōkai Great Strategy", October 4th, 1968 to March 28th, 1969), starring Yoshinobu Kaneko (**WATARI, NINJA BOY** [ワタリ / *Daininjutsu eiga Watari*, 1966, D: Sadao Nakajima]) as Sanpei and Ushio Kenji from the *Akuma-kun* show (Kenji is a familiar face, usually villainous, in *Kamen Rider*, *Lone Wolf* and *sentai* productions of the 1970s) as Itachi Otoko ("Weasel Man"), a character much like Nezumi Otoko from *Kitarō*.

Other television monster and horror series running or begun in 1968 were *Kamen no Ninja Akakage* (仮面の忍者 赤影 / "Masked Ninja Red Shadow"), also starring Yoshinobu Kaneko, *Ninja Hattorikun + Ninja Kaiju Zippo* ("Ninja Hattori + Ninjamonster Zippo"), *Ultra Seven* (ウルトラセブン / *Urutora Sebun*), *Kaiju Oji* (怪獣王子 / "Monster Prince"), *Giant Robo* (ジャイアントロボ / *Jaianto robo*, a.k.a. *Johnny Sokko and His Flying Robot* [see *Monster!* #1 & #18]), *Kaiki Daisakusen* (怪奇大作戦 / "Operation Mystery") and two seasons of *Mighty Jack* (マイティジャック / *Maiti Jakku*), the second of which featured monsters. Anime on television included the anime of *Ōgon Batto* (黄金 バット / "Golden Bat"), *Yōkai Ningen Bem* (妖怪人間ベム / "Yōkai Human Bem"),[20] *Bōken Shōnen Shyadaa*

("Adventure Boy Shudder"), *Mahotsukai Sally* ("Sorcerer Sally"), Osamu Tezuka's *Vampire* (バンパイヤ / *Banpaiya*), which mixed anime with live-action, the pilot of Tezuka's *Dororo*, *Chibiko Kaiju Yadamon* (ちびっこ怪獣ヤダモン / "Li'l Monster Yadamon"), *Oraa Guzura Dado* (おらぁグズラだど / "Hey, I'm Guzura!") and *Kaibutsu-kun* (怪物くん / "Monster Boy").

In the theatres, Daiei's **100 MONSTERS** (妖怪百物語 / *Yōkai Hyaku Monogatari*, D: Kimiyoshi Yasuda; released March 20th, 1968 on a double-bill with **GAMERA VS. VIRAS** [ガメラ対宇宙怪獣バイラス / *Gamera tai uchu kaijū Bairasu*, D: Noriaki Yuasa]) and **SPOOK WARFARE** (妖怪大戦争 / *Yōkai daisensō*, D: Yoshiyuki Kuroda [December 14th]) clearly show the influence of Mizuki's *yōkai* revival. Released by Daiei along with **SPOOK WARFARE** was **SNAKE GIRL AND THE SILVER-HAIRED WITCH** (蛇娘と白髪魔 / *Hebi-Musume to hakuhatsuma* ["Snake Girl and Grey-Haired Demon"], D: Noriaki Yuasa), from Kazuo Umezu stories, and the same studio released **THE SNOW WOMAN** (怪談雪女郎 / *Kaidan yukijorō*, 1968, D: Tokuzō Tanaka [April 20th]), a *yuki-onna* movie, and a double bill of **THE GHOSTLY TRAP** (怪談おとし穴 / *Kaidan otoshiana* ["Kaidan: Pit"], D: Koji Shima; a *yūrei* film) and **THE BRIDE FROM HADES** (牡丹燈籠 / *Botan-dōrō*, D: Satsuo Yamamoto; June 15th). Kindai Eiga Kyokai released the beautiful **KURONEKO** (藪の中の黒猫 / *Yabu no naka no kuroneko* ["Black Cat in a Grove"], 1968, D: Kaneto Shindō [see *Monster!* #10, p.42], February 24th), a *kaibyō* (怪猫 / "ghost cat" film), Toei released **BAKENEKO: A VENGEFUL SPIRIT** (*Kaibyō nori no numa* ["Ghost Cat: Cursed Pond"], D: Yoshihiro Ishikawa; more *kaibyō* action), **THE SNAKE WOMAN'S CURSE** (*Kaidan: hebi-onna*, ["Kaidan: Snake Woman"], D: Nobuo Nakagawa) and **THE GREEN SLIME** (ガンマー第3号 宇宙大作戦 / *Gamma dai-san-go: uchu daisakusen* ["Gamma 3: Operation Space"], D: Kinji Fukasaku; December 19th), Ōkura Eiga released **THE DISMEMBERED GHOST** (怪談バラバラ幽霊 / *Kaidan: barabara yurei* ["Kaidan: Dismembered Ghost"], a.k.a. **A GHOST STORY: BARABARA PHANTOM**, D: Kinya Ogawa), Shochiku released **GOKE, BODYSNATCHER FROM HELL** (*Kyuketsuki Gokemidoro* ["Bloodsucker Gokemidoro"], D: Hajime Satō; August 14th), **THE LIVING SKELETON** (*Kyūketsu dokuro-sen*, ["Bloodsucking Skeleton Ship"], D: Hiroshi Matsuno) and **GENOCIDE** (*Konchū daisensō* ["Insect War"], D: Kazui Nihonmatsu; both November 9th), and Toho rolled-out **KAIJŪ SŌSHINGEKI** (literally "Monster Charge", but

---

20 "Bem", used in several *kaijū* names, is adopted from the American SF acronym for "Bug-Eyed Monster" (i.e., B.E.M.). See the following article for more on this series.

known and loved as **DESTROY ALL MON-STERS** [怪獣総進撃], D: Ishirō Honda; August 1ˢᵗ) and a rerelease of 1963's **ATRAGON** (海底軍艦 / *Kaitei gunkan* ["Undersea Warship"], D: Ishirō Honda; featuring the *ayakashi* Manda ["Ten-Thousand Serpent"]).

Why was 1968 the peak year of *yōkai*? It was a tumultuous decade in Japan across the board. Old neighborhoods in Tokyo had been razed. The bullet train now whisked past where not that long ago people had walked the haunted footpath of Tōkaidō. Did Mizuki's ghosts speak to both anxiety and a sense of nostalgia for a simpler, mythical time now gone? In regard to *yōkai* films, there is a clear development of giant monster movies from dark horrors for all ages towards more child-oriented fare. Perhaps by this time the Mizuki-style *yōkai* were seen by studios as creatures they could market to children whilst parents continued to shudder at the bloodier horrors of *yūrei* and *kaibyō*. Kids were lapping-up monsters and ghosts on television and in manga, so might it have been the time when movie *yōkai*—which took more money and effort to create than the merely disfigured ghosts of stories like "Yotsuya Kaidan"—were seen as worth the risk? The bestiaries of the old scrolls and *yōkai* guides had rarely been plundered. In fact, I can only think of two films which brought them to the big screen before 1968,[21] and both of them were takes on the Edo Period *kaidan* "The Seven Wonders of Honjo" (本所七不思議). This is a group of nine stories (but the mystical number 'seven' just has more *kaidan* coolness than nine does!). In Shinko Kinema's 1937 version (本所七不思議 / *Honjo Nanafushigi*), such entries as "*Ashiarai Yashiki*" (足洗邸 / "Foot-washing Mansion", about a giant phantom leg, of all things), "*Oitekebori*" (置行堀 / "'Leave-It-and-Go' Moat", a place where fishermen shouldn't linger at the end of a rainy day), and "*Tanukibayashi*" (狸囃子 / "Tanuki Procession"; the haunting sounds of a parade of *tanuki*) are included. The 1957 Shintoho version, **GHOST STORIES OF WANDERER AT HONJO** (怪談本所七不思議 / *Kaidan Honjo Nanafushigi*, a.k.a. **SEVEN MYSTERIES**, D: Gorō Katano) *[see p.232]*, takes elements from the Honjo stories, such as the haunted moat and *tanuki* stories, but it is more of a '*yōkai*-on-parade' movie than an actual adaptation. *Tanuki* gather various creatures to foil a scheming samurai. There is a *yūrei*, ghost snakes, a *rokuro-*

Japanese B2 poster for **KURONEKO** (1968)

kubi, a *chochin obake* (提灯お化 / "paper lantern *obake*"), a *hitotsume kozu* (一つ目小僧 / "one-eyed Apprentice", a bald Cyclopean boy), a *mitsume otoko* (三つ目男 / "three-eyed man"), a *nopperabo* (のっぺら坊 / "blank-faced one") and the ever-delightful *karakasa obake* (から傘お化 / "from-umbrella *obake*"). Honjo, once a dark and sparsely-populated area, is now part of the Sumida ward of Tokyo.

Although *yōkai* movies—and the Japanese film industry in general—were in decline, Mizuki's fortune has continued up to the present day. Kitaro is a merchandising phenomenon, the star of manga, games, anime and two live-action movies (2007 and 2008). He was the mascot of the Gainare Tottori soccer team, although there seems to be a new mascot named Gainaman in recent years. Takashi Miike's entertaining **THE GREAT YOKAI WAR** (妖怪大戦争 / *Yōkai daisensō*) *[see p.33]*, his 2005 remake of Yoshiyuki Kuroda's aforementioned **SPOOK WARFARE** (1968), includes a cameo by Mizuki as the "Great Yōkai Elder". Mizuki won numerous awards in Japan and abroad, where translations have started to appear more widely; *Nonnonba* won "Best Comic Book" at the Angouleme International Comics Festival in 2007, and *Onward Towards Our Noble Deaths* an Eisner Award in 2012. He travelled to several countries gathering tales of local *yōkai* for his bestiaries, and created several award-winning manga on modern Japanese history and warfare. The 2008 autobiography by his wife Nunoe, called *GeGeGe no Nyobo* ("Ge-

---

21 A poster for 1967's **GHOST STORY OF TWO TRAVELERS AT TENAMONYA** (*Tenamonya yurei dochu* ["Tenamonya Ghost Journey"], D: Shūe Matsubayashi) shows what seem to be two monster statues, but I think they're just props used to scare off people from a counterfeit scheme. It's a period comedy which follows **TENAMONYA TŌKAIDŌ** (てなもんや東海道, 1966, D: Shūe Matsubayashi) and **BAKUMATSU: TENAMONYA DAIZŌDŌ** (1967, D: Kengo Furusawa).

Here seen at age 93, Shigeru Mizuki was truly a living legend in Japan; he passed away on November 30th, 2015

studied Hell paintings as a child. Tourists can ride the ghost train decorated with *yōkai* from Yonago Station to Sakaiminato, and spend a little time in the Mizuki Shigeru museum built in 2003, posing for photos with cut-outs of his ghostly creations, and admiring the collection of masks and carvings collected from his trips to Africa and New Guinea. Outside the station is a statue of Shigeru Mizuki at his desk, pen in hand, watched closely by Medama Oyaji, Nezumi Otoko—and, of course, Kitaro. Mizuki's mouth is open. Is he yawning, or hungry, or telling his children another *yōkai* tale…?

GeGe's Wife") was adapted as a television series and a movie in 2010.

In his hometown of Sakaiminato, one can walk the Mizuki Shigeru Road, set out in 1993, admiring the 134 bronze statues of his characters and shopping for Medama Oyaji balloons and Kitaro toilet paper by the light of 'eyeball' streetlamps. A statue of Mizuki stands at the temple where he

Above: The city of Sakaiminato, master manga artist Shigeru Mizuki's birthplace, has a whole street, including a museum, dedicated to the ghosts and monsters that populate his stories. Seen hard at work above is a sculpted impression of Mizuki, accompanied by two of his most-popular creations, The Rat Guy and Kitaro. Cast in bronze and mounted upon base-blocks of black granite, some 134 'life-size' statues of his beloved *yōkai* characters line both sides of the street. **Upper Right:** A *kasa-obake* from Mizuki's 1974 illustrated two-volume set *The Yōkai Encyclopedia* (妖怪事典)

References

Books & Periodicals

Ryunōsuke **Akutagawa**, *Kappa* (Tuttle, 1971). Originally published in *Kaizo* magazine, March 1927.

Frederick Hadland **Davis**, *Myths & Legends of Japan* (Graham Brash [Pte.] Ltd., 1913).

Hashimoto, Osamu *et al*, *Bakumatsu No Shura Eshi Kuniyoshi* (Shinchosha, 1995).

Lafcadio **Hearn**, *Kwaidan: Stories and Studies of Strange Things* (Tuttle, 1971). First published 1904.

Kyoko **Hirano**, *Mr. Smith Goes to Tokyo: Japanese Cinema Under The American Occupation, 1945-1952* (Smithsonian Institution, 1992).

John **Miller,** Jr., *The War in the Pacific: Cartwheel: The Reduction of Rabaul* (Center of Military History, 1990).

Samuel **Milner**, *The War in the Pacific: Victory in Papua* (Center of Military History, 1989).

Shigeru **Mizuki**, *Akuma-kun* volumes I-III (Tasugawa [?], 1995). Collection of the 1993 revival of the series.

Shigeru **Mizuki**, *Kitaro* (Drawn & Quarterly, 2013). Stories selected from the 1967-9 period. Introduction on Mizuki and *Yokai*, by Matt Alt. Yokai glossary by Zach Davisson.

Shigeru **Mizuki**, *Mizuki Shigeru Collection I: Kitaro no Jigoku Meguri* (Kadokawa, 1996). Stories selected from the 1984-7 period.

Shigeru **Mizuki**, *Nonnonba* (Drawn & Quarterly, 2012). Prose memoir of Nonnonba originally published as *NonNonBa to Ore* (Mizuki Productions, 1977). Edited, translated version of the essay 'A Japanese Yōkai Expert in Search of British Fairies' by Kimie Imura from *Chikuma Shonen Toshokan 37* (1977).

Shigeru **Mizuki**, *Onward Towards Our Noble Deaths* (Drawn & Quarterly, 2011). Originally published as *Soin Gyokusai Seyo!* (Mizuki Productions, 1973). Introduction by Frederik L Schodt. Afterword by and interview with Mizuki.

Shigeru **Mizuki**, *Showa: A History of Japan* (Drawn & Quarterly, 2013), Originally published as *Komikku Showa-shi* (Mizuki Productions/Kodansha, 1988). The English edition will run to four volumes. Volume 1 covers Japan and Mizuki's life from 1926 to 1939. Introduction by Frederik L Schodt, afterword by Hideki Ozaki. Nezumi Otoko serves as a commentator on the narrative.

Maurice **Horn** (ed.), *The World Encyclopedia of Comics* (Chelsea House, 1999).

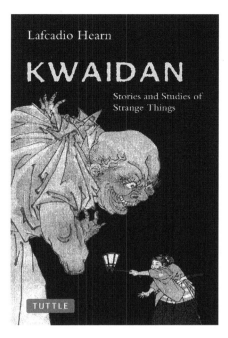

Eric P **Nash**, *Manga Kamishibai: The Art of Japanese Paper Theater* (Abrams Comicarts, 2009). Includes 4 panels of Mizuki's illustrations of the *kamishibai* "Kuruma the Cat".

Tomoko **Otake**, *Drawing On Experience* (The Japan Times, February 6th, 2005). Interview with Mizuki.

Frederik L **Schodt**, *Dreamland Japan: Writings on Modern Manga* (Stone Bridge Press, 1996).

Frederik L **Schodt**, *Manga! Manga! The World of Japanese Comics* (Kodansha, 1986).

Tim **Screech**, *Japanese Ghosts* (2002). Article in *Mangajin #40*.

Richard Gordon **Smith**, *Ancient Tales & Folklore of Japan* (A&C Black, 1918).

Yoshikatsu **Takeuchi**, *Nihon no Tokusatsu Kaijū Daizenka* (Akita Shoten, 1985)

Takeo **Udagawa**, *Manga Zombie* (Ota Shuppan, 1997). Information on Kanko Takeuchi and the first Kitaro books.

Various, *The Gamera Chronicles: The History of Daiei Fantastic Movies, 1942-1996* (Takeshobo, B Media Books Special, 1996).

Various, *Gamera Kara Dai Majin Made Daiei Tokusatsu Eiga No Subete 'Screen' Tokuhenban* (Kindaieigasha, 1995).

Various, *Geijutsu Shincho #9* (Shinchosha, 1994).

Various, *Nihon no Yokai Dai Hyakka* (Keibunsha, 1985).

Various, *Nippon Discovering Japan #4: Japan, Global Headquarters of Manga* (2010).

Various, *The Super Heroes Chronicles: The History of Japanese Fantastic Televisions, Movies and Videos, 1957-1995* (Takeshobo, B Media Books Special, 1995).

Various, *Toho Haikyu Sakuhin: Tokusatsu Eiga Daizenshyu* (Kindaieigasha, 1994).

Various, *TV Anime Daizenka* (Akita Shoten, 1979).

Various, *Zen Kaijū Kaijin Dai Hyakka* (Keibunsha, 1977).

Hiroko **Yoda** & Matt **Alt**, *Yōkai Attack! The Japanese Monster Survival Guide* (Kodansha, 2008). Illustrated by Mizuki understudy Tatsuya Morino ("*Kibakichi*").

Films & Television

Kinji **Fukasaku** (director), **CREST OF BETRAYAL** (忠臣蔵外伝　四谷怪談 / *Chūshingura gaiden: Yotsuya kaidan*, 1994, Shochiku).

Kazuo **Hara** (photography & direction), *The Emperor's Naked Army Marches On* (Facets Video, 2006). Incredible documentary following New Guinea veteran Kenzo Okuzaki as he tracks down, and sometimes beats on, fellow veterans in the 1980s. Originally released as *Yuki Yukite Shingun*, (Shisso Productions, 1987).

Hiroshi **Inagaki** (director), **THE THREE TREASURES** (日本誕生 / *Nihon tanjō*, Toho, 1959).

Gorō **Katano** (director), **GHOST STORIES OF WANDERER AT HONJO** (怪談本所七不思議 / *Kaidan Honjo Nanafushigi*, a.k.a. **SEVEN MYSTERIES**, 1957, Shin-Toho).

Masaki **Kobayashi** (director), **KWAIDAN** (怪談 / *Kaidan*, 1964). Released on R1 DVD by Criterion (2000).

Yoshiyuki **Kuroda** & Kimiyoshi **Yasuda** (co-directors), **JOURNEY WITH GHOST ALONG YOKAIDO ROAD** (東海道お化け道中 / *Tōkaidō ōbake dōchu*, 1969, Daiei). Released on R1 DVD as **YOKAI MONSTERS: ALONG WITH GHOSTS** by ADV Films (2003).

Yoshiyuki **Kuroda** (director), **SPOOK WARFARE** (妖怪大戦争 / *Yōkai daisensō*, 1968, Daiei). Released on R1 DVD as **YOKAI MONSTERS: SPOOK WARFARE** by ADV Films (2003).

Takashi **Miike** (director, co-screenplay), **THE GREAT YOKAI WAR** (妖怪大戦争 / *Yōkai daisensō*, 2005, Kadokawa Pictures). Released on R1 DVD by Tokyo Shock (2006).

Nobuo **Nakagawa** (director), **THE GHOST OF YOTSUYA** (東海道四谷怪談 / *Tōkaidō Yotsuya kaidan*, 1959, Shintoho).

Hajime **Sato** (director), **GOLDEN BAT** (黄金バット / *Ōgon Batto*, 1966, Toei).

Toshio **Shimura** (director), **ŌGON BATTO: MATENRŌ NO KAIJIN** (黄金バット 摩天楼の怪人 / 1950, Shin Eiga-sha). I've not seen this one.

Isao **Takahata** (director, co-writer), **POM POKO** (平成狸合戦ぽんぽこ / *Heisei tanuki gassen Ponpoko*, 1994, Studio Ghibli). Released on R1 DVD by Disney (2005).

Tokuzō **Tanaka** (director), **THE SNOW WOMAN** (怪談雪女郎 / *Kaidan yukijorō*, 1968, Daiei).

Shiro **Toyoda** (director), **PORTRAIT OF HELL** (地獄変 / *Jigokuhen*, 1969, Toho). Released on R1 DVD by Animeigo (2006).

Various directors, *Akuma-kun* (悪魔くん / Toei Productions, 1966, 26 episodes). TV series based on the Shigeru Mizuki manga *Akuma-kun*.

Satsuo **Yamamoto**, **THE BRIDE FROM HADES** (牡丹燈籠 / *Botan-dōrō*, 1968, Daiei).

Kimiyoshi **Yasuda**, **100 MONSTERS** (妖怪百物語 / *Yōkai hyaku monogatari*, 1968, Daiei). Released on R1 DVD as **YOKAI MONSTERS: 100 MONSTERS** by ADV Films (2003).

Websites

Keith **Aiken**, Melanie **Bourgeois**, Dan **Ross**, *Sci-Fi Japan*. Especially "*Kitaro* on Region 1 DVD and Blu-ray" (2008), "The Legends of Tono 100th Anniversary Edition" (2010) and "Yokai University: Matt Alt Interview" (2009).

Matt **Alt**, *AltJapan*. The February 18th, 2008 page "GeGeGe no Go", an interview between Go Nagai and Mizuki, was especially useful.

Anime News Network: Kitaro (manga).

Anime Picture Collections: Spooky Classic Anime (2011).

Shoriya **Aragoro**, *Kabuki 21*.

J Noel **Chiappa** & Jason M. **Levine**, *Yoshitoshi*. A *catalogue raisonne* of the artist's works, with useful links.

Jonathan **Clements**, *Schoolgirl Milky Crisis: Spooky Ooky* (2010). Blogspot on Mizuki and the live action *Kitaro* movies.

Zack **Davisson**, *Hyakumonogatari Kaidankai*. Excellent resource for the ghost game, *yōkai* and Mizuki.

Delphiessential.comicgenesis. Essay on *kamishibai*.

Masayuki **Eshita**, *Laboratoire Eshita Masayuki*. The January 28th, 2007 page shows covers of 1950s Mizuki books.

Dr Hiromitsu **Iwamoto**, *Remembering the War In New Guinea*, 2013. Resource for several details, including Mizuki quotes.

JZ, *Japanzine: Poor Little Ghost Boy* (2007). Page on Mizuki and *Kitaro*.

Katsuhiko **Komatsu** (supervisor), *Kaii, Yokai Denshu Database* / 怪異・妖怪伝承データベース (2002).

Manga Wiki: Shigeru Mizuki.

Matthew **Meyer**, @ *MatthewMeyer.net* (2012). Author/artist of *The Night Parade of 100 De-* mons. Features *A-Yokai-A-Day*.

MizukiPro Japanese site.

SH **Morgan**, *The Obakemono Project*.

Matthew **Penney**, *The Asia-Pacific Journal: Japan Focus, War & Japan: The Non-Fiction Manga of Mizuki Shigeru*, 2008. Mr. Penney also kindly gave me further details on Mizuki & his brother's 1940s experiences.

Pink Tentacle: Macabre Kids' Book Art by Gojin Ishihara (2010).

Norman A **Rubin**, *Asianart: Ghosts, Demons and Spirits in Japanese Lore*.

Sakaiminato: The City of Fish & Kitaro. English-language site with illustrated features on *yōkai*, the Shigeru Mizuki Road and Shigeru Mizuki Museum.

Mark **Schumacher**, *A-Z Photo Dictionary: Japanese Buddhist Statuary: Kappa*, updated 2013. Great *kappa* resource!

TSOTE, *Three Steps Over Japan: Manga Review: Kitaro, #1 and #1*. Shows pages from the adult and children's Kitaro debuts.

Roy **Ware**, *Black Sun 1987: Anime, Tokusatsu, Manga, Sci-Fi, Horror* blogspot. Pages on all of Mizuki's series.

Wikipedia, English & Japanese pages.

Below: *M!* #34 cover artist Ian Coleman's rendering of a bony *yōkai* known as *Gashadokuro* (餓者髑髏), or "starving skeleton"

Top: Japanese tie-in book for **THE GREAT YOKAI WAR** (2005). **Above Left:** The internal workin's of a *kappa*, by Shigeru Mizuki. **Above Right:** "*Oni* and child"; detail of a hand-painted wall scroll. *[Scan courtesy of Saucerman Site Studios Archive.]* **Left:** Japanese souvenir program for **SAKUYA** (2000)

Art by Denis St. John

by Jolyon Yates

SAKUYA, SLAYER OF DEMONS

(さくや 妖怪伝 / *Sakuya Yōkaiden,* 2000)

D: Tomo'o Haraguchi

Late in the 4th Year of Hoei (1707), the Great Hoei Earthquake was soon followed by the last eruption of Mount Fuji. This is the time of the stories in the first two *yōkai* films here, both directed by Tomo'o Haraguchi, whose work as a creature and makeup effects creator you may have seen in **SPIRAL** (うずまき / *Uzumaki,* 2000, D: Higuchinsky) and the Gamera movies from 1995 and '96. As director he helmed **MIKADROID** (ミカドロイド / *Mikadoroido,* 1991) and **DEATH KAPPA** (2010, Japan/USA).

SAKUYA blames the eruption of Japan's spiritual centerpiece on the loss of honor in the nation. *Yōkai* are unleashed, and fought by Sakaki (Hiroshi Fujioka, the original Kamen Rider) wielding the *Muramasa katana,* or Vortex Sword, as the subtitles would have it. The drawback of the sword is it drains the user's life every time it is employed. When Sasaki keels-over facing a *kappa,* his daughter Sakuya (Nozomi Ando) takes up the blade and finishes the job, but spares the *kappa*'s child, adopting the boy as her brother. A sage (veteran star Tetsuro Tanba) and wizard (**TETSUO** director Shin'ya Tsukamoto) send her on a mission to slay the top *yōkai,* the Queen Earth Spider (土蜘蛛 / *tsuchi-gumo*), played by Keiko Matsuzaka, accompanied by two disrespectful ninja and the *kappa* boy Taro, who has rapidly aged ten years (Shuichi Yamauchi). On their way to the spider's lair they encounter a man who can turn girls into dolls, a ghost cat

Hong Kong DVD cover for **SAKUYA**

with a forked tail (猫股 / *nekomata*) and a group of ghost soldiers (*yōkai musha*). They also witness a dance of various friendly *yōkai,* including the good old umbrella ghost, *karakasa obake.* Eventually they reach the blasted slopes of Mt. Fuji and defeat the Queen's spider women (絡新婦 / *jorogumo*), but the Queen becomes a *kaijū*-sized monster and it is up to Taro to unleash the power of the *Muramasa* sword...

This is a fairly amusing film with plenty of creatures and a good cast. It suffers a little from the trend of Japanese fantasy movies since the 1980s to have the characters strike postures and declaim dia-

RYUJI HARADA MIKI TANAKA MUBU NAKAYAMA

KIBAKICHI

WHEN MONSTERS
MEED WITH HUMANS,
THE SKY WILL SPLIT
AND ETERNAL DARKNESS
WILL COVER THE EARTH.

50071

DVD

KIBAKICHI: US DVD and tie-in figurine

logue, which might be intended to remind the viewer of manga imagery, but merely turn action films into waxwork shows. Not too bad here, though, and when fights erupt they are proficiently handled by the Japan Action Club (JAC), which was founded by Shin'ichi "Sonny" Chiba and supplied stuntwork for many a movie and television show.

2001 saw the release of perhaps the best *yōkai* film ever: Hayao Miyazaki's **SPIRITED AWAY** (千と千尋の神隠し / *Sen to Chihiro no Kamikakushi*), a great *anime* from Studio Ghibli—but let us stick with live-action for now.

A *sorta* similar wolfish *yōkai* appears in the classic film **SPOOK WARFARE**

KIBAKICHI

(跋扈妖怪伝 牙吉 / *Bakko-yōkaiden Kibakichi*, a.k.a. **WEREWOLF WARRIOR**, 2004)

D: Tomo'o Haraguchi

The *yōkai* hero Kibakichi—literally, "auspicious fang"—is one of the last survivors of the Inugami village massacre. *Inugami* (犬神) are dog-headed *yōkai*, although here the villagers are werewolves and are referred to as *hito okami* ("people-wolves"). Kibakichi (Ryuji Harada, veteran of TV samurai dramas) is a homeless wanderer with a mass of unkempt hair and a Native American-styled poncho. He finds a village run by Onizo and his *yakuza* mob, who are all *yōkai* sheltering from persecution, with the exception of a human girl whom Onizo has taken in, named Kikyo (Nozomi Ando, from **SAKUYA**). Most of the creature suits on display are recycled from **SAKUYA**, including the *kappa*, although there are a couple of new faces, like the *onbake* ghost dice, with which the gang fleeces 80% of humans who come to gamble. Their favorite targets are other *yakuza*, and those that kick up a fuss are fed to skeleton (*kyokotsu*) or spider-women *yōkai*. Onizo's grand dream is to establish a safe region for *yōkai*, and to achieve it he is in league with Yamaji Osuke, a young lord planning a takeover of his clan. However, Yamaji acquires a new source of power—machine-guns from England—and turns these weapons on the village. Kibakichi is so distraught at the battle that he transforms into a full-on wolfman, battling both the samurai and a treacherous one-eyed *yōkai* man (山童 / *yamawarawa*, "mountain child"). What with all the monster-dueling and running through explosions, things feel a little like the climax of a *Kamen Rider* episode, and for some reason the creatures are given sound effects right out of Toho *kaiju* films; I think the wolfman was dubbed by Titanosaurus!

Haraguchi again delivers a moderately entertaining film. Harada moves well in the action scenes but, except for being a werewolf, this lone-warrior-with-a-heart-of-gold character is an over-familiar one from samurai movies of the last 50 years (as well as the Italian Westerns they inspired), and his characterization is not helped any by his face being mostly hidden throughout. You can see more of it when he is a wolfman than in his human form.

Based on a manga by Takao Shimamoto and Tatsuya Morino. The latter was an assistant of Shigeru Mizuki and illustrated the excellent book *Yokai Attack!*

KIBAKICHI 2

(跋扈妖怪伝 牙吉 2 / *Bakko-yōkaiden Kibakichi 2*, 2004)

Ds: Tomo'o Haraguchi, Daiji Hattori

Yōkai are still being hunted-down by a government fearful of turmoil amongst the lower classes. However, the biggest threat posed to a town Kibakichi comes across is by a wild swordsman, Sakuramaru (professional wrestler Masakatsu Funaki), who turns out to be the bastard son of a Spaniard who raped and murdered his way through the region. The duels between Kibakichi and Sakuramaru are interrupted (until the end, of course) by the reappearance of Anju, the other survivor of the Inugami massacre—who blames Kibakichi's trust in humans for the tragedy—and a group of *yōkai*-hunting warriors under the thrall of Dogan, a one-horned demon (一角大王). Anju, a wolfwoman with a boomerang sword, turned-up for one scene in the first film, but here she takes up a lot more screen-time, as her fearlessness earns her the unwelcome fascination of Sakuramaru. Eventually the wolfpeople and the wildman have their showdown with the demons and, immediately afterwards, with each other, including a slow-motion werewolf duel on a stage set complete, with a full moon and falling cherry blossom petals, that really puts the 'kitsch' in kibakichi.

For this movie, Daji Hattori, assistant director on **SAKUYA**, took the reins. Previously he had been a writer and director on the *Kunoichi Nimpoden* series of 2000s ninja sex comedies known in the West as *Ninja Vixens*. **KIBAKICHI 2** is well-photographed and played, but light on *yōkai*, outside of the demons and werewolves. Given the intrigues and other challenges faced by the characters, this might have played better as a straightforward non-supernatural samurai film; it is difficult to maintain a sense of gravitas when a fateful duel is fought with a boomerang!

THE GREAT YOKAI WAR

(妖怪大戦争 / *Yōkai Daisensō*, 2005)

D: Takashi Miike

This shares its title with the 1968 *yōkai* classic, but goes its own way. Yasunori Kato, a character created in the *Teito Monogatari* novel (serialized from 1983) by Hiroshi Aramata, is a long-lived soldier, mystic, demonic man who tries to enact an ancient grudge against the Japanese who took the islands from his people. Kato has appeared on screen several times, and here he is portrayed by the elegant Etsushi Toyokawa. Kato is gathering-up *yōkai* and turning them into bio-mechanical monsters called *kikai* in a factory which itself becomes a colossal beast of the apocalypse, the Yomotsumono. However, the latest incarnation of the Kirin Rider, Champion of Peace, is found—a boy named Tadashi (Ryunosuke Ka-

Toronto Chinatown bootleg DVD-R. *[Image courtesy of The Fentonian Institution]*

Jolyon Yates   *Shiguro Mizuki*   **33**

Japanese DVD sleeve for **KITARO AND THE MILLENNIUM CURSE** (ゲゲゲの鬼太郎 千年呪い歌 / *Ge Ge Ge no Kitarō: Sennen Noroi Uta*), the second live-action film based on the comics by Shigeru Mizuki

miki)—and, with the aid of an army of *yōkai*, confronts Kato in his factory as it attacks the center of Tokyo…

This is the ultimate assemblage of *yōkai*. In the longest shots there are over *20 million* on-screen! Not only are there nods to the *yōkai* movies of the 1960s (from Daiei Studios, now owned by Kadokawa Pictures, which produced this movie with Shochiku), but there are direct references to Shigeru Mizuki and an appearance by the man himself in the role of Yōkai Dai-O, "King of Yōkai", delivering his judgment of war. At one point we visit the Mizuki Shigeru Road and the Mizuki Shigeru Museum in Sakaiminato. The creatures are designed along traditional lines, by Takayuki Takeya, but given a twist by showing them afflicted by Kato's toxic attack on the natural world; some of them are played by researchers from the World Yōkai Association.

Deftly-directed by Takashi Miike, the film also benefits from an excellent cast that features members of Miike's stock company, such as Shiro Sano, veteran actors like Bunta Sugawara (leading man in several outstanding gangster movies) and fresh faces like Chiaki Kuriyama as Kato's henchwoman.

The DVD extras include footage of the 10th World Yōkai Conference, with Guest of Honor Shigeru Mizuki.

KITARO

(ゲゲゲの鬼太郎 / *Ge Ge Ge no Kitarō*, 2007)

D: Katsuhide Motoki

Although there are a lot of *yōkai* on display here, the first live-action movie based on the 50-year-old manga is somewhat disappointing, with bland photography and a dull lead.

Several plot threads and characters are scattered before us: Construction disturbs a fox shrine. Apartment block dwellers are harassed by *yōkai*. These spooks are overseen by the flatulent Nezumi Otoko (Yo Oizumi, entertaining here, and a voice actor on several Ghibli films, including **SPIRITED AWAY**). One group of residents is the Miura family, their mother deceased, their dad an alcoholic. The Miura children are a boy named Kenta (Ruka Uchida) and his older sister Mika (Mao Inoue, in Hideo Nakata's **KAIDAN** [怪談] the same year). Kenta summons Kitaro (Eiji Wentz), who boots-out the *yōkai*. However, the Miura father, Haruhiko (Go Riju), becomes possessed by the Evil Stone sought by Nezumi Otoko, and a band of foxes led by Kuko, a nine-tailed fox (九尾狐 / *kyubi kitsune*, played by Satoshi Hashimoto).

Eiji Wentz does not seem committed to the role here. Unlike the manga, wherein Kitaro is the compelling center of attention, whenever Kitaro shares the screen with his colorful friends he is the least-interesting character. There is also little atmosphere, nor no sense of lurking fear and death, as in the comics. Even the afterworld is a letdown; just a slow walk through a national park. There are amusing moments and it is fun to see the Kitaro characters, but overall this feels like the first couple of *Harry Potter* movies. Fortunately, like in that series, things would pick up…

KITARO AND THE MILLENNIUM CURSE

(ゲゲゲの鬼太郎 千年呪い歌 / *Ge Ge Ge no Kitarō: Sennen Noroi Uta*, 2008)

D: Katsuhide Motoki

Tagline: *"Half Monster, Half Human, All Hero!"*

This immediately sets a darker tone with a scene of a mob descending on a woman in the past and a spooky *yūrei* scene in the present, where the eerie song of Kagome sucks the souls out of girls. Kaede Hiramoto (Kii Kitano) is marked by Kagome as her next victim. With the aid of Kitaro and his friends—and a trip to the Y*ōkai* Library—she discovers that Kagome can be banished by the performance of five instruments of a mountain sect called the Kidoshu, so the gang splits-up to retrieve them, encountering more *yōkai*, such as a tribe of *tanuki* (狸 / "raccoon dog"). However, a human-hating *nurarihyon* (Ken Ogata, who died in 2008) turns out to be using Kagome, actually a corrupted water *yōkai* known as a *nure onna* (濡女; played by Shinobu Terajima), to gather the souls of the descendants of the Kidoshu sect which had tried to kill her long ago. With the capture of the last soul, Kaede's, he can unleash a giant skeleton monster, *gashadokuro* (餓者髑髏) *[see Ian Coleman art on p.29]* upon the human world.

I liked Wentz much better in this movie; he seems more committed and expressive, and throws himself into some great fight scenes. The Kitaro gang returns, including Rena Tanaka as Cat Girl (*Neko Musume*), in more subdued colors. The production benefits from a higher budget, with moodier photography, more varied locations and greater spectacle. It is quite often funny, with ribald humor including a feces-blasting *yōkai*, a huge fart scene from Nezumi Otoko, and two gags about old women's breasts. Like **SAKUYA**, it suffers a little from scenes where characters stand around while one reels-off exposition, and there are a few climaxes too many. Like the previous film, it assumes a familiarity with the Kitaro characters, although his origin is shown during the credits. Both *Kitarō* films were directed by Katsuhide Motoke. This was very enjoyable, but disappointingly the last Kitaro film to date.

Yōkai Ningen Bem

(妖怪人間ベム / "Yōkai Human Bem" or "Humanoid Monster Bem" 1968-69/2011)

D: Noboru Ishiguro

Yōkai on Japanese television are so pervasive, I avoided more than a glance their way, because then this article would become a HUGE, obsessive undertaking, and *Monster!* is no place for that sort of thing. *[Sez who?! ☺ —eds.]* However, a friend sent me this series, so I feel obliged to give it at least a mention, and it *is* clearly a close relative of Kitaro, so...

The first series was a 26-episode anime running from October 7th, 1968 to March 31st, 1969, directed by Noboru Ishiguro, who would go on to *Space Battleship Yamato* (宇宙戦艦ヤマト / *Uchū Senkan Yamato*, 1974), co-directed by Hideo Wakabayashi, and created by Akira Adachi. Another 26-episode anime ran April 1st to October 7th, 2006, directed by Hiroshi Harada. The latest series was live-action, with 10 epi-

Above: The live action *[left]* and anime *[right]* versions of **Yōkai Ningen Bem** (妖怪人間ベム / "Yōkai Human Bem")

sodes broadcast between October 22nd and December 24th, 2011 on NTV, followed by a theatrical feature from Toho released December 15th, 2012. The director was Shunsuke Kariyama (and Noriyoshi Sakuma for some episodes), with scripts by Masafumi Nishida. An entertaining series, something of a splice of *Kitarō* and *X-Men*, with a good cast and involving drama.

The heroes are creatures born of experiments conducted sometime back in the 20th Century. They spring from a single cell in an oozing green culture developed from a certain leaf by Prof. Shinsaku Ogata. The trio is led by Bem (Kazuya Kamenashi of boy band Kat-Tun), the even-prettier Bela (Anne Watanabe, daughter of the actor Ken Watanabe) and Belo (Fuku Suzuki, who was just 7 years old at the time), whose toy collection includes dolls of Ōgon Batto and the television superhero Silver Mask. They never age and can regenerate wounds, but they wish to become human. When under duress, they become bulbous-skulled monsters! Bem struggles to maintain his faith in humanity, despite suffering persecution over the years, Bela has a cynical façade, although she also aids humans in danger, and Belo is so guileless he threatens their exposure, in which case they'll have to move on to another town. Their arch enemy is a mysterious man (Akira Emoto from 2005's **THE GREAT YOKAI WAR** (see above) and Takeshi Kawamura's eccentric **THE LAST FRANKEN-STEIN** (ラスト・フランケンシュタイン / *Rasuto Furankenshutain*, 1991 [see *Monster!* #14,

p.59]), who looks a lot like Bem in the initial anime. Their ally is Detective Aki Natsume (Kazuki Kitamura of **GODZILLA: FINAL WARS** [ゴジラ ファイナルウォーズ / *Gojira – Fainaru uōzu*, 2004, D: Ryūhei Kitamura]; see *Monster!* digest #11, p.12) and his family. Throughout the series and the movie, the mysterious man uses the green liquid to bring out the dark sides of tormented people.

As mentioned before, Japanese supernatural creatures may be called *obake* / "changing thing", a reminder of transformation as the essence of nature. Characters in *Yōkai Ningen Bem* yearn for yet fear transformation, physically and psychologically, and of course they cannot avoid it as a condition of being alive. Whether they can become enlightened or destructive is the conflict of the series. Although there is a lot of humor, including the opening, which includes comic book-style credits and a recreation of the anime's origin scene, the tone is often melancholic, a 'Monster-of-the-Week' show wherein each monster is a lonely, frustrated, frightened soul. Monster fans might prefer the movie, where the victim of the green stuff is Sayuri Ueno (Arisa Mizuki, **PSYCHIC GIRL REIKO** [超少女玲子超少女REIKO / *Chō shōjo Reiko*, 1991, D: Takao Okawara]), another *yōkai ningen*, who becomes a giant plant creature.

FOR MORE YOKAI ACTION, CHECK OUT PAGE 225!

Shiguro Mizuki   *Jolyon Yates*

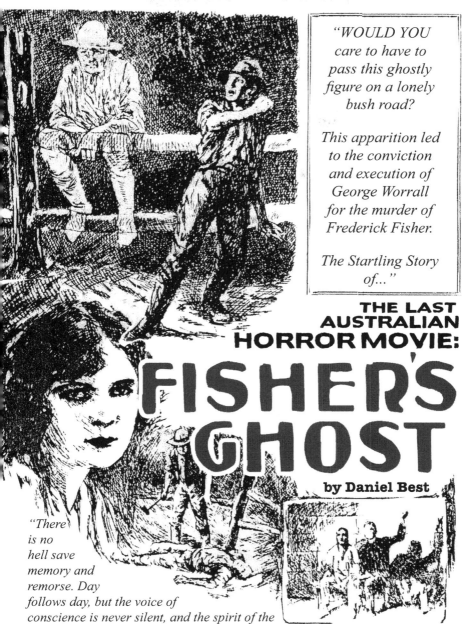

"WOULD YOU care to have to pass this ghostly figure on a lonely bush road?

This apparition led to the conviction and execution of George Worrall for the murder of Frederick Fisher.

The Startling Story of..."

THE LAST AUSTRALIAN HORROR MOVIE: FISHER'S GHOST

by Daniel Best

"There is no hell save memory and remorse. Day follows day, but the voice of conscience is never silent, and the spirit of the man I killed follows relentlessly. When I stand alone before the judgment throne of death, may God, in His everlasting mercy, grant my soul the peace it can never know on earth.' Thus spoke George Worrall, as he unburdened his soul in the sensational story of a tragedy of the early days of New South Wales."

DO YOU BELIEVE IN GHOSTS?

[with Endnotes on p.56] |- original press ad-copy for the film

A period etching of Fisher's Ghost, from *Professor Pepper*

Raymond Longford's and Lottie Lyell's 1924 silent film **FISHER'S GHOST**, took a classic well-known Australian ghost yarn and, combined with a professional film crew, 'known' producers and director and a professional cast, mixed them all together to make possibly *the finest* of all the silent horrors that Australia produced. Sadly, though, not only was it the *last* Australian silent horror, but it was also the last *real* horror movie produced in in this country until the belated resurgence of the genre in the early '70s.

"Une cause célèbre en Australie"; a French illustration of Fisher's Ghost dating from 1856, artist unknown

The legend of "Fisher's Ghost" dates back to the 19th Century. In 1826, in Campbelltown, New South Wales (N.S.W.), a settler named Farley was walking home, well in his cups, and spotted an apparition sitting atop a bridge. Addressing the drunken Farley, the ghost claimed to be the spirit of Frederick Fisher,[1] a prospector who had gone missing months prior after striking it rich with another man, George Worrall.[2] Worrall claimed that Fisher, after making his fortune, simply left the area in search of other adventures and, although much suspicion was cast upon Worrall, in the absence of any corpse, nothing could be done towards having the suspect charged and tried for murder.

The ghost pointed to the creek, leading Farley to a spot where Fisher's missing body was found. Farley took this in and contemplated, out loud, as to what he should do with the information, upon which the ghost screamed of bloody vengeance for his murder at the hands of George Worrall. That was enough for Farley, who took off down the dirt road back into town like a scalded cat. Upon returning to town, he flew into the pub babbling about ghosts and murder most foul. Taking no notice of his ravings, the locals merely assumed Farley, a habitual boozer, was drunk—as usual!— but this time he was so insistent that the townsfolk decided to humor him. Farley then led a group of men towards the 'haunted' bridge, whereupon he pointed to the spot where the ghost had allegedly been sitting. He then headed down to the creek, leading the group of locals to the submerged body of Fisher, which had been dumped in the water. The hilarity of Farley's story abruptly vanished, and the finders of the dead man's body quickly turned from happy drunks into a lynch mob. They promptly proceeded to hunt down Worrall and accuse him of Fisher's murder, which, naturally, he denied. However, faced solely with the damning testimony of a local drunk and the word of a ghost that nobody but the accused had (allegedly) seen, Worrall broke-down, confessed to murdering Fisher, was duly arrested, placed on trial, sentenced and then executed.

As a legend, the story had it all for 19th Century audiences: drama, murder, theft, ghosts, revenge and justice in the form of an execution. It was one of the first mythological stories to enter the annals of White Australian folklore. It was also a *ridiculous* story whose details constantly changed depending on who was telling it, with certain elements added and others removed, and before long almost every rural town—and a lot of cities too—each had its own regional 'legend' of a ghost sitting on a bridge, usually over a creek with a name such as "Dead Man's Creek" or the like. Like most legends, the story contained some germs of truth and, in the case of Fisher's murder, the truth was no less dramatic than the myth. Fred Fisher *did* exist and George Worrall actually *did* rob and murder him before dumping his body into the creek. Worrall twisted in the wind for his crimes, this after confessing on the morning of his date with the hangman. Really, the only thing missing was the ghost. *And* Farley…

The first mention of Frederick Fisher came when an announcement was placed on the front page of the *Sydney Gazette* on the 22nd of September, 1826 offering a substantive reward of £20 for information leading to the discovery of Fisher's body[3] and thus prove that he had met with foul play, as most suspected was the case. All anyone knew was that Fisher had mysteriously vanished following a night out drinking. He had bought a bottle of rum then left the pub intending to walk home, but hadn't been seen since. An additional sum of £5 was offered to anyone who could provide proof that Fisher had left Campbell Town (as Campbelltown was then known).

By the time the reward was posted, Fisher had been missing for some three months, and suspicion fell on George Worrall (or Worral), who had been the last person Fisher was seen in the company of. Worrall had lived with Fisher in a

Period newspaper item (from *The Sydney Gazette and NSW Advertiser* for September 23rd, 1826)

hut with four other men and, tellingly, had been seen with some of Fisher's property in his possession after the other's disappearance. Worrall had provided a cover story to explain Fisher's absence, saying that he (Fisher) had left the colony. However, the ship Worrall named, the *Lord Saint Vincent*, had never docked at nor ever even sailed into the local harbor. Worrall had seized Fisher's horses, clothing, property and monies—the then-fabulous sum of £300—and began to systematically sell it all off (except for the money, of course; that he *drank*!) because, he said, Fisher owed him for various debts. Worrall was already a suspect, and was brought into custody when a receipt for one horse, allegedly signed by Fisher, proved to be an exceedingly crude forgery.

The reward—a small fortune back in colonial days!—saw a frantic search for the body, led by Aboriginal trackers. One such search was led by an Aborigine named Gilbert. Gilbert walked along a wooden fence on the Worrall (formerly Fisher) property and, noticing either a tooth or a bone fragment and some blood, stopped at a nearby watering-hole. He noticed that the water was discoloured with a greasy film on the surface. Gilbert waded in and, using a leaf, scraped some of the film up and tasted it. He then turned to the people with him and stated simply, "This is the fat of a white fellow."[4]

The waterhole was connected to a small creek. The searchers followed this creek, which led to a swamp. Gilbert announced that the body was in the swamp, so everybody starting digging and searching until Fisher's body was duly recovered. The colony's physician, a certain Dr. Hill, examined the body and discovered that the skull had suffered several fractures, meaning that Fisher's head had been bashed-in with a blunt object, most likely a bottle. Faced with this damning physical evidence, Worrall, who was already in custody on suspicion of foul play, was charged with the crime of murdering Frederick Fisher on June 17th, 1826. He entered a plea of not guilty.

Justice was swift in colonial days. Worrall was found guilty by a jury on Friday, February 2nd, 1827, and he was sentenced to hang the following Tuesday. He continued to maintain his innocence, but at 5:00 a.m. on the morning of his execution, Worrall finally confessed while talking to a Reverend.[5] According to Worrall, he had met Fisher on his way home. The men were drinking from a bottle of rum and passed by a paddock where a horse was resting. For whatever reason, Worrall and Fisher took offense at the horse's behavior, and decided to teach it a lesson. Both men jumped the fence, whereupon Worrall noticed that Fisher had left the rum behind. The latter proceeded to grab a fence post, intending to beat the horse, but instead 'accidentally' bashed Fisher's skull in with it instead. Realizing that the penalty for causing death—even by drunken accident—meant the gallows for Worrall, he'd panicked and hid the body after doing the dirty deed. Two other men who were also in custody and suspected to be involved in the crime were exonerated by Worrall's admission of committing the crime, and they were thus set free.

This 'confession', such as it was, was more-than-likely just another of Worrall's many lies. It was well-known that he was just as much of a drunkard as Fisher was. The police believed that Worrall had met Fisher while the latter was heading home, and asked him for a drink. Fisher either handed Worrall an empty bottle, or denied his request. Either way, Worrall had then used the bottle to bash Fisher's brains out. Still, the evidence was sufficient enough. Be it by accident or otherwise, Worrall had admitted to killing Fisher. Case closed.

Execution.

George Worrall, who was convicted on Friday last of the murder of Frederick Fisher, yesterday suffered the dreadful sentence of the law. Till about 5 o'clock on the morning of his execution, he persisted in asserting his innocence, when he was at length induced to acknowledge to a gentleman, who had sat up with him during the night, that he, alone had perpetrated the murder, but positively affirmed that it was not his intention at the time to do so.

Period newspaper item (from *The Sydney Gazette and NSW Advertiser* for February 6th, 1827)

His 'confession' complete, a calmness settled over Worrall. His last moments were described as being "manly and becoming", which meant he did not embarrass himself during his last moments on Earth by either weeping, fainting or soiling himself. The condemned man approached the gallows steadily and without hesitation, and was observed to be absorbed in contemplation about his fate.[6] Minutes after the drop fell, Worrall was pronounced dead.

The first mention of Fisher's Ghost came nearly ten years later. In 1836 the *Sydney Gazette* published an account of the Fisher case, complete with mention of the ghost.[7] In this account the ghost was witnessed by a friend of Fisher's, one Mr. John Hurley. The report stated that Hurley had affirmed the ghost's existence to the court. It took five years for the myth to be debunked by Hurley himself, who wrote to the editor of the *Sydney Herald* denying any such affirmation and, although he had known Fisher, Hurley claimed to have been over 200 miles from Campbelltown when the body was discovered.[8]

It made no difference. Hurley's name was simply changed to "Farley", Worrall's to "Wurrell", while Fisher curiously became "Fredro" (?!) when a poem, written by one "Felix",[9] was published in *Bell's Life*. Because *Bell's Life* was a literary newspaper, the poem should have been taken in the spirit it was intended: as a simple work of fiction. Titled "The Sprite of the Creek," the poem bore a disclaimer that it was based on the murder of "poor F***** at Campbell Town".[10]

From that point on, the legend(s) of Fisher's Ghost has taken precedence over any truths in the case, and the story of the spook sitting on the bridge-rail has always been reported as incontrovertible fact. The city of Campbelltown quickly grasped upon the legend to promote the town for the tourism trade, and it still holds celebrations in commemoration of it to this day. Although the myth has been soundly re-debunked in every succeeding generation since, it still holds a special place in Australian folklore.

As early as 1879, a stage production of *Fisher's Ghost*[11] was being performed, and the story had been passed down, 'evolving' in its various reinterpretations. Even as late as the 1920s, *Fisher's Ghost* was still a popular Australian ghost story, and the cinematic possibilities were obvious (and still are today). One man who saw the obvious appeal in bringing the myth to the screen was Raymond Longford (1878-1959).

Longford[12] was a prolific Australian film director, writer, producer and actor of both the silent and sound eras, who had started out in theatre at the beginning of the century, then made the move to cinema in the early 1900s. It was while he had been on stage that he met Lottie Lyell (1890-1925), the woman with whom he would form a partnership for the next decade-and-a-half.

Lyell[13] is often described as being Australia's first real film star. She gained her celebrity status as an actress, and was a daredevil who often did her own—at times breathtaking—stunts. She first met Raymond Longford when she was only 19, after Edwin Geach chose her to play the lead, Maggie Brown, in a stage adaptation of *An Englishman's Home* (1907-1909). Also appearing in the play, as Mr. Brown, was Raymond Longford. Lyell's parents, who had connections with the Longford family, placed young Lottie in the care of Longford for the duration of the play's run.

Although young, Miss Lyell was already an experienced and highly capable actor. She had studied Shakespeare under the eminent thespian Harry Weston, whereafter her stage career flourished, with tours across Australia and New Zealand. Longford moved to acting in films under the tutelage of film pioneer Charles Cozens Spencer, appearing in the now-lost silent adventure, **CAPTAIN MIDNIGHT, THE BUSH KING** (1911, D: Alfred Rolfe; released in the

ORIGINAL POETRY.

—oo-oo—

THE

SPRITE OF THE CREEK !

An Australian Tale, founded on the Murder at Campbell Town, of a Sheriff's Bailiff, named F*****.

Period newspaper item (from *Bell's Life* for June 27th, 1846)

USA as **THE BUSHRANGER'S BRIDE**). In 1910, Longford was put in charge of production for Spencer, and it was he who first brought Lyell to the then-still-embryonic silver screen. Longford and Lyell acted in films together[14] before Longford moved into directing; Lyell remained the lead actress on his films. On the surface, Longford directed and Lyell acted. However, their partnership ran far deeper than that. While Longford and Lyell lived openly as a couple, they were never able to marry.

That the couple deeply loved each other has never been in dispute, but Longford had been married since 1900, and his wife, Melena, was a strict Catholic. Melena knew of the relationship between Longford and Lyell but, due to her religion, she would not agree to a divorce. Longford

Lottie Lyell as Eileen Shannon in Raymond Longford's **THE CHURCH AND THE WOMAN** (1917)

Daniel Best   *Fisher's Ghost*   **41**

and Lyell were discreet with their relationship, but after Lyell's father passed away, Longford moved into the Lyell family home. Longford and Lyell were inseparable from 1910 until Lyell's premature death just a few days before Christmas in December 1925.

Longford would consult with Lyell, and it was during one of these consulting sessions that Longford asked for Lyell's opinions on adapting C.J. Dennis' Australian literary classic *The Songs of a Sentimental Bloke* to the cinema. Longford would later say, "She had nothing but praise for the contents, and was positively certain it would prove a great success on the screen." Lyell was right. Costing £2000—a then-not-inconsiderable, if not exactly princely sum—to produce, the movie, released in 1919, was a roaring success, and it is considered to be Longford's best film, as well as an Australian si-

Lottie Lyell, Australia's first movie star! Promo art for **THE SENTIMENTAL BLOKE**

lent classic (which was remade locally in 1932 by F.W. Thring; the same original work was adapted for Australian television in 1976). Titled **THE SENTI-MENTAL BLOKE**, the 1919 filmization went on to gross an estimated £33,000 by 1922.[15]

From that point on, Longford and Lyell were partners in every way. Whatever one did, the other was also deeply involved. This copacetic arrangement saw Lyell become one of the first-ever female filmmakers, having her hand in almost every aspect of the craft. She was an actor, a writer and an editor. She also produced, co-directed and directed feature films. She worked on costume designs and, just to complete the picture, she handled all of the pair's financial business, too.

Lyell wasn't merely a backseat partner, by any means. Marjorie Osborne, the leading lady of

Lottie Lyell and director Raymond Longford on the set of their film **A MAORI MAID'S LOVE** (1916)

Fisher's Ghost   *Daniel Best*

Longford and Lyell's (lost) melodrama **THE BLUE MOUNTAINS MYSTERY** (1921), talked about Lyell in an interview at the time of the film's release: "I like brains in a woman, and she has them. She assists Mr. Longford, and the two of them have plenty of healthy arguments when their ideas about a scene are different."

Longford and Lyell quickly followed up **BLOKE** with **GINGER MICK** (1920), another feature based on a C.J. Dennis property. **ON OUR SELECTION** (1920), **RUDD'S NEW SELECTION** (1921) and aforementioned **THE BLUE MOUNTAINS MYSTERY** (1921) quickly followed, with each turning a healthy profit.

Despite the health of the filmmaking couple's arguments, Lyell herself was not a healthy woman, physically speaking. In 1920, she suffered a debilitating bout of tuberculosis, which saw her off the screen for a period, although she did recover sufficiently to appear in **GINGER MICK**. The long-term strain was too much for her, however, and by 1922 Lyell had all-but-retired from acting, preferring to work behind the screen instead.

In 1922, Longford and Lyell formed a new production company called Longford-Lyell. They raised *£50,000 by public subscription*, and seemed set for bigger and better things. This wasn't to be, however. Within a year, the company was faltering. The first Longford-Lyell production, **THE DINKUM BLOKE** (1922), cost £4,846 and had grossed only £5,831 after sixteen months. This was a disaster. Longford quickly found work directing three films, **AUSTRALIA CALLS**, **AN AUSTRALIAN BY MARRIAGE** and **AUSTRALIA, LAND OF SUNSHINE**, all of which were produced for the Australian government in 1923. Behind the scenes, Lyell attempted to save the company, all the time dealing with her ever-decreasing physical state. As her health continued to fade, she managed to write the scenarios/scripts for **FISHER'S GHOST** (1924), **THE BUSHWHACKERS** (1925), **THE PIONEERS** and **PETER VERNON'S SILENCE** (both 1926), while preparing the production of **FISHER'S GHOST**.

On May 26th, 1924, Longford-Lyell Australian Picture Productions Ltd. went out of business. The great experiment had failed, and Longford would long blame exhibitors for the company's collapse, often alluding to monies being taken off the books where **A DINKUM BLOKE** was shown.

The pair was still working, though. Longford later claimed to have spent a substantial amount of time studying papers relating to the case of Fish-

Top: A scenic view of Fisher's Ghost Creek Bridge in Campbelltown, New South Wales, circa 1945 *[photo by E.W. Searle]*.
Center: Fisher's remains are reputedly interred in the graveyard of St. Peter's Anglican Church, Campbelltown.
Above: Modern-day Campbelltown's picturesquely rustic Fisher's Ghost Restaurant *[photo by Simon Bullard]*

er's Ghost at Sydney's Mitchell Library, which dated back to 1826 when the library was founded, and wrote the scenario, with Lyell's input, based upon the true, accurate, historic record. As he was intending on showing the ghost therein, it's obvious that Longford and Lyell intended to make a film of the legend of Fisher's Ghost, and

Filmmaker Raymond Longford, looking just as dapper as can be

ford-Lyell were better able to film there. Frederick Fisher becomes John Fisher, George Worrall becomes Edward Smith and Farley becomes two people, John and Jim Weir.

Immediately following is the plot of **FISHER'S GHOST**, as detailed in the original shooting synopsis used by Longford-Lyell.[17]

The film opens with a shot of Longford himself, visiting the Mitchell Library in Sydney, whereupon he opens a book upon which are imprinted the words, "In the year 18-- there lived in the little town of Penrith, a farmer by the name of John Fisher". Fisher is then shown on his farm, working with Edward Smith. The next scene shows the pair at Dean's Country Pub, sharing a drink and talking about England. Smith suggests that Fisher should go back to the mother country to visit his family. Fisher isn't so sure, and recounts the tale of why he was transported in the first place—he killed a man with a stone by accident. As such, he believes his family would be ashamed to see him, even if he is a rich man with £100,000 in cash stashed at his farm. Smith then tells the landlord of the pub, Dean, that Fisher is intending to visit England. Fisher agrees, and the pair head off into the night.

Six weeks later, Smith visits the pub and tells Dean that Fisher has indeed gone back to England. Dean is surprised, as Fisher never said farewell to him; odd, considering they were close friends. Smith then tells Dean that Fisher left abruptly due to problems with a woman. Dean understands. Smith returns to the Fisher farm and tells all the workers about Fisher's leaving and him taking over in his stead. He promotes the head hand, Mr. Thompson, and tells him that he, Smith, will be moving into the main house and that Thompson can move into Smith's old house on the farm, with a raise in pay. This delights Thompson, who runs home to tell his family, including his daughter, Nell Thompson. This news causes dismay for Nell, as she is in love with her neighbor, Jim Weir. She tells the news to Weir, who is just as disappointed as she is.

Jim has a vision of he and Nell raising children, but, although they love each other, they are poor folk who cannot afford to marry. That's not the only hurdle they face, as Mr. Thompson can't stand the urchin Weir. It matters not, they duly move onto the farm.

One evening Smith makes a move on Nell, only to be interrupted by Thompson. Thompson notices Smith's interest in his daughter and encourages it. Smith is a man of wealth, so it'd be good for the entire family if Nell would just give in to

not portray the 'actual reality'. Longford later admitted this to be the case. "I took my facts from the Mitchell Library," Longford told the Royal Commission in 1927, "and upon them I made the picture, although I do not believe they are accurate."[16]

Once complete, the scenario for **FISHER'S GHOST** was filed for copyright on June 4th, 1924, and shooting began shortly thereafter. Longford-Lyell needed capital, and this was raised by the couple joining forces with exhibiter Charles Perry, who would share production credits with the company. Between them, they raised a modest sum of £1000, all of which was spent on the film. The film was shot on location just outside of Penrith. Unlike the still-standing sites used in **THE GUYRA GHOST MYSTERY** (1921 [see *Monster!* #31 {November 2016}, pp.100-113]), the actual location of the Fisher's Ghost Creek bridge and the spot nearby it where the corpse was found were by then long-lost to time.

Running for 55 minutes, the film's plot was a simple one, but in telling his version of the story, Longford changed details and inserted a love story for dramatic effect, further muddying the legend. The movie is set in Penrith, a town approximately 50 kilometers from Campbelltown. The reason for the change of location is unknown, but it's more than likely due to the fact that Long-

Hoyt's De-Luxe Theatre
SYDNEY

thought so much of this sensational Australian-made picture that they booked it as their A Grade Feature, and will advertise it on an unprecedented scale.

This amazing story of something that really happened, filmed by way of a change, and taken on the spot where it actually occurred.

Do You Believe in Ghosts?

'FISHER'S GHOST'

Produced by Raymond Longford who personally is convinced it is the supreme photoplay achievement of his eminently successful picture producing career.
BETTER THAN "SENTIMENTAL BLOKE"

Released by
LONGFORD-LYELL PRODUCTIONS.
29 BATHURST ST
SYDNEY

On an equity basis to all showmen, which means we don't demand a high price, but will stake our existence on the picture's exceptional merit.

Spook Ahoy! Newspaper ad (*circa* October 1924) for the film which we now have less than a ghost of a chance of ever seeing

him. Nell refuses and tells her parents she doesn't like Smith, and that she wants to marry Jim Weir. They refuse to give their consent, with Mr. Thompson banging the tabletop for emphasis.

A year after Fisher's disappearance, a local asks after him. Smith produces a letter supposedly written by Fisher in which he asks Smith to sell all his property, pay off any debts and send the rest over to England. He then tells Nell he has done all of this and wants to sail to England with her as his bride. Nell tells him she has no love to give him, and refuses.

Smith tells Mr. Thompson that Nell has turned him down. This means that Thompson is now out of work. He has one week to gather his family and leave the farm, along with his well-paying job. The family holds a crisis meeting and pressure Nell into accepting the proposal, which she does, the following morning. She then travels to the Weir farm to tell Jim the news. He isn't there, so she leaves a letter with the youngest Weir, Fred.

Weir rushes to the Fisher farm after he reads the note, but, alas, although they love each other, they can never be together. They cry.

A week later, John Weir comes home from the pub. "Well, Mother," he tells his wife, "a strange thing happened coming home tonight; I've either seen Mr. Fisher or his Ghost." Mrs. Weir puts this down to the effects of the grog, as everyone knows Fisher is away in England. In a flashback we then see Weir riding home and spotting Fisher sat on a fence post. He greets him, but gets no reply. Weir goes on to tell the same story to Jim, who advises him to lay off the booze.

A week later, and John Weir is again at Dean's pub. This time he refuses a drink, prompting jokes about Weir taking the Pledge. Weir laughs, but says he's not drinking, but won't say why. He leaves the pub and gives a lift to two men, Bob Hamilton and Ted Williams. They drive along and come to the bridge by Fisher's farm, whereupon all three see Fisher's Ghost, sitting on the bridge rail. They notice that the moonlight is shining through Fisher's body. Weir stops his horses and approaches Fisher, greeting him. Fisher does not reply. He touches Fisher on the shoulder and announces that foul play has happened, so all three men head towards the house of Mr. Cox, the Magistrate.

Cox listens to Weir and speaks to Hamilton and Williams. The next morning Cox, Weir, Williams, Hamilton, along with three Black trackers, visit the bridge and are excited when one tracker discovers what he calls "White man's blood." They then track through the creek and discover the remains of Fisher's body in a waterhole behind Fisher's farm. The body, although it is now just bones, is identified as Fisher via a buck knife found in the pocket with the initials "J.F." carved into it. Cox tells the trackers to place what's left of the corpse in back, and they all then ride on to Fisher's farm.

Smith is surprised to see the men, and even more surprised to see the remains of Fisher. Upon being accused by Cox, Smith maintains his innocence. Old man Weir talks about seeing the ghost; Smith gives a knowing wink at Cox, signaling that Weir is well-known as the town drunk. Weir is indignant, claiming he *wasn't* drunk. Smith produces the letter from Fisher and hands it to Cox. Cox

reads it and places Fisher under arrest for the crime of murder.

A month later all are in court. Smith is on trial, but the captain of the ship which the victim supposedly sailed on gives evidence that Fisher had indeed traveled to England aboard his vessel. Fisher's solicitor also backs-up Smith's story. Incriminating evidence is given against Smith by the three men who sighted the victim's ghost. The jury retire to consider their verdict. Smith is found guilty, and sentenced to hang.

Despite petitions calling for Smiths' release, the day of his execution is upon him. He writes a letter, hands it to the Reverend who is giving him comfort, and heads off to the gallows. Hours after he is dead, the editors of the local newspaper are readying to publish Smith's letter: it was a confession of guilt. He murdered Fisher. He arranged for a double to sail to England in Fisher's place. It's all true.

Six months later, Nell and Jim are married, and live happily ever after.

Fade out…

****

The film starred Robert Purdie as Edward Smith, Fred Twitcham as John Fisher and Lorraine Esmond as the tragic Nell Thompson, the girl whom Worrall is about to marry when he meets his unenviable fate. The film featured special effects, including those showing the ghost atop the fence, which required shooting a double exposure, and Longford later claimed that the production had used two tonnes (i.e., tons) of Fuller's earth with which to whip-up a dust storm for a sequence that was a dramatic highlight of the picture.[18]

FISHER'S GHOST has the distinction of being co-directed, albeit uncredited, by Lottie Lyell,[19] who also co-wrote the script ("scenario"), again uncredited. As the film came from the Longford-Lyell production company, this makes Lyell one of the first women ever to write, produce and direct (even in a collaborative manner) a horror film.

Shooting had wrapped by August of 1924, and the film was slated for release that coming October, some 98 years after the original events had taken place. It was then that Longford-Lyell ran into difficulties with release…

Although both Longford and Lyell were by then well established within the movie and stage industries, they were stymied by Stuart Doyle (then in charge of Union Theatres[20]), who flatly refused to allow the movie to be shown, because he considered it too gruesome for public consumption. If he dared show it in any of his theatres, he knew people would get up and walk out in disgust. Furthermore, just watching the film made him physically sick. As the New South Wales state censor, well-known for banning and censoring movies on lesser grounds, had already cleared the film for the release, with no cuts, Doyle's decision was censorship on a whole new level. So Longford, Lyell and Perry now had a film, fully-paid-for and in the can, complete with an official okay from the censor board, yet the main cinema chain, Union Theatres, wasn't willing to screen it!

The real dispute happened behind the scenes. Longford and Doyle hated each other with a passion. Longford had long rallied against Doyle and his Union Theatre chain, accusing them of collusion with other theatres, namely Hoyt's, in order to run independent Australian producers out of the business by using unfair monopolistic practices. Doyle, and Union Theatres, had a sizeable interest in the production company Australasian Films Limited, and any film produced by that company was guaranteed to gain an instant release. Longford further accused Doyle of running what he called "The Combine". The Combine, he claimed, had secured control of the local markets and made it virtually impossible for producers and backers to earn full value for their movies when they were released.

Even worse, Doyle had screened the film and then made Longford-Lyell wait two weeks before giving them his response, which was relayed impersonally through a company secretary. Incensed by the tone of his belated reply, the lack of respect shown and the lengthy wait, Longford and Perry insisted on meeting with Doyle in person. Upon eventually granting an audience, Doyle told them to their faces that Union Theatres would not be releasing **FISHER'S GHOST**.

Doyle denied all of this. In his eyes, Longford was complaining about nothing. If Longford-Lyell films made little money, then it was because they were simply not up to par with the quality of imported American or British films.

The long-standing animosity between Longford and Doyle went back over a decade. The so-called 'combine' was born out of a series of mergers which resulted in the formation of Union Theatres and Australasian Films on January 6th, 1913. The Combine's initial move was to merge Johnson & Gibson and J. & N. Tait into

Contemporaneous newspaper ad (from *The Queensland Times* for June 3rd, 1925)

Amalgamated Pictures. This began in September 1912, when the directors of West's Pictures, Spencer's Pictures and Amalgamated Pictures voted to merge into one under the banner of the General Film Company of Australasia. The addition of Greater J.D. Williams Amusement Co. brought the centralizing of four partners under Union Theatres and Australasian Films. These mergers, by The Combine, would create a monopoly in regards to film production/distribution in Australia and New Zealand.

Spencer had been out of the country on holiday when these mergers took place. The board of his company had voted to merge in his absence, and he opposed the merger of his own company. The Combine were now assured of a steady supply of imported films, and felt that there was no longer a need for Australasian Film or Spencer's Pictures to make films other than for *The Australasian Gazette* and *Spencer's Gazette*. The Combine then refused to invest in any of Spencer's productions. Longford, in his role as head of production at Spencer's, was privy to the machinations of The Combine first hand. Spencer, now gone from the company that bore his name, left for Canada in late 1914.[21] He never made another film.

Longford never forgot how Spencer was run out of the country. He also faced issues with obtaining financing for his own films, and The Combine often refused his requests to use the film studio at Rushcutters Bay (in New South Wales), which had, ironically enough, been funded and built by Spencer. Union Theatres also refused to release **THE SENTIMENTAL BLOKE**. This came on top of The Combine refusing permission for Longford and Lyell to film at their studios, so instead they filmed 'on location'. Over the years there were other slights and insults from Union, none of which were forgotten by Longford. Doyle likewise had a long memory, and he wasn't above using his powerful position to make people's lives difficult, if need be.

The dispute between Doyle, as head of The Combine, and Longford, long kept behind closed doors, erupted at the 1927 Royal Commission on the Moving Picture Industry of Australia.

When called before the commission on June 16th, 1927, Longford went straight on the attack. He first claimed that he had been subjected to many attacks by Australasian Films Limited, and that The Combine was doing their best to crush the Australian film industry. The Combine had taken over the major filming studios located in Sydney and had flatly refused all of Longford's requests to film there, meaning he had to shoot his films in back yards, fields and such places. He then outlined the failure of Longford-Lyell.

"My next effort," he told the Commission, "was to float a public company termed the Longford-Lyell Australian Picture Productions Limited with a capitol of £50,000. The promoters (Miss Lottie Lyell, Raymond Longford and Stephen Perry) received 6,000 fully paid shares—2,000 each. The first year's programme contemplated four pictures at a total cost of £20,000. The first production was **THE DINKUM BLOKE**, and

was made at a cost of £4,846. The picture was completed in November, 1922. Of the total cost of production the sum of £2,147 was paid to The Combine for film, camera man and studio. Despite this, The Combine refused to release the picture."[22]

Longford then related how it took seven months before **DINKUM** was released, through Hoyt's, and how it grossed just over £300 in three days, then being sold into the British market. The total profit to Longford-Lyell was £5,831. The relative failure of the film had seen the Motion Picture Distributors Association declare that they would not book any more Longford-Lyell films. This caused the directors of Longford-Lyell to order that the firm be folded.

"The Longford-Lyell Company had apparently no desire to continue production," said Longford. "Their threat to close down meant a lot to my reputation, and I was induced to surrender over 3,000 fully-paid-up shares without any payment or compensation of any kind. To further save the company's liquidation I offered to produce a picture for the company at a cost of £2,400."[23]

That picture was **FISHER'S GHOST**. Longford brought the picture in well under budget and took it to Doyle in order to obtain a release in The Combine's theatres. It was here that Longford came up against Doyle, still smarting over Longford's attacks, both in public and private.

"After viewing the picture several times, Mr. Doyle informed us that if he screened this picture in any of his theatres the public would walk

Merrymaking ghost hunters convene around a bonfire near to Fisher's Ghost Creek during the '50s

out. His reason was that the picture was too gruesome, this despite the fact that the picture had been passed without any trouble or cutting by the State Censor."[24] It had taken Doyle a fortnight to finally get around to screening the film, and he dispatched his decision to Longford via his secretary, flatly refusing to see Longford.

Doyle, appearing before the same Royal Commission on July 1st, 1927, outright denied all of Longford's charges. When handed a list of Longford-Lyell films, Doyle stated that they were mediocre, even though he had never even heard of some of them, let alone actually seen them. As for **FISHER'S GHOST**, Doyle, under oath, labelled Longford a liar. "We showed it everywhere except where Hoyt's or other opposition showed it."[25]

Doyle, while not admitting that he had kept Longford waiting two weeks for an answer, or that he had relayed his answer only through his secretary, didn't deny all the charges. Instead, he kept his answers non-committal. "I saw the picture," and "I spoke with Mr. Longford," he claimed. He was more forthright as to why he had refused to allow the movie to play in Union Theatres.

"I admit I said the picture was gruesome. I still say it is. I do not admit that I refused to release it. As a matter of fact, I released it in many theatres throughout Australia."[26] The Commission asked if the reason why Doyle booked the film for cities such as Melbourne and Adelaide was due to its success in Sydney. Doyle refused to give a straight answer, instead sticking to his mantra of, "The picture was booked for several theatres around Australia."

Doyle's evidence, in regards to **FISHER'S GHOST**, was full of contradictions, which angered Longford further. He appeared before the Royal Commission again, on November 28th, sticking stubbornly to his line that The Combine had refused to show **FISHER'S GHOST**, and that Doyle was a liar. The film, even with its distribution problems, had nevertheless been a success around the country. It was *not* "gruesome", nor was it "mediocre", either.

Desperate to get the movie properly released, Longford-Lyell accepted a highly unfavorable deal from Hoyt's. The managers of Hoyt's informed Longford how they knew, all too well, that The Combine had refused to take the film on, as well as the reasons why.[27] If Hoyt's took the film, they argued, Hoyt's would have to pay Paramount, as per their contract, for the film that **FISHER'S GHOST** would be replacing. Hoyt's

then laid their deal on the table: they would take the film, for one week, at a flat cost of £30, paid, in full, at the end of the week. If the film grossed over that amount, then Hoyt's would keep all the money. They would also have no control over when and where it would be shown, or how it would be exhibited. In a further insult, Longford was responsible for paying Hoyt's *£10 for all newspaper* advertising and another £10 per week for printing.[28]

Longford was apoplectic, but he had no choice. He had the investors and directors of the Longford-Lyell Company braying for money and blood, and a rapidly ailing Lottie Lyell to care for. So he signed the deal.

The film premiered at Hoyt's De-Luxe Theatre in Sydney on October 4th, 1924. It then moved to New Zealand in February of 1925.

Both the critics and public alike raved about the movie. The bringing to life of a classic ghost story appealed to everyone (in the early 20th Century, virtually every city in Australia had its own regional variation of the Fisher legend). The generally positive reaction their film garnered more than vindicated Longford-Lyell's judgement, but the film's woes didn't end there. Despite drawing large audiences, resulting in record profits for Hoyt's and the film industry newspaper, *Everyone's*, talking-up both the movie and Longford-Lyell's impressive production values, other cities refused to show it on the same grounds as Doyle had previously stated: that the movie was far too horrific for public consumption. It would take another two years more before the movie was finally screened in Perth, where, again, it did a roaring trade.

FISHER'S GHOST was shown at His Majesty's Theatre in Hobart. The theatre's manager, Cecil Shannon, later described how the film was promoted: "We exploited it in a rather novel fashion. It lent itself to exploitation. Outside the theatre we erected a fence with a mark on it showing where the ghost stood. Many people had heard of Fisher's Ghost, and that assisted us to put it over." [29]

In most cities, including in New Zealand, a similar set of fence posts were set up in the theatres, or in a neighboring window, most purporting to be the actual fence that Fisher's ghost had sat on way back in 1826. However, these were simply old wooden posts, sourced by promoters wherever the film went. The 'real' fence whereupon Fisher's ghost sat was, even by then, long-gone.

At the end of the first week in Sydney, **FISH-**

FISHER'S GHOST

Words and Music by
GEORGE DAVEY

Recorded by
JOHNNY ASHCROFT
on Columbia

FISHERS GHOST CREEK

Castle Music Pty. Limited
200-204 Castlereagh Street
SYDNEY

3/-

LEGEND OF
FISHERS GHOST
Souvenir Copy.
Jimmie McFarlane.

ER'S GHOST grossed £1,200, of which £1,170 went to Hoyt's and a mere *£30 went to Longford-Lyell*, minus the aforementioned costs. In reality, Longford-Lyell realized a sum total of just £10 from that first week. Hoyt's were keen to release to the film in England, and offered Longford £500 for the rights. Disillusioned, he took it.

FISHER'S GHOST was shown at a trade show in London in late February 1925, but it didn't impress. "Since the film was an attempt to boost Australian-made films, it was a pity that the picture was not more free of experiment," wrote the London representative of the Melbourne newspaper, *The Herald*. "It lacked vitality and the actors were unconvincing. It would have been an immense success, if taken in England, as an Englishman's idea of outback life, the alleged cocky's *[sic]* temperament and the personality being more reminiscent of a Devonshire farmer."[30]

Despite this negativity, the film scored a general release and did reasonable business. However another review raised the ire of Longford and his fellow Australian filmmakers, which, despite giving the film praise, was seen as a slur upon the industry. "Considering that the film was made in Australia the technical standard of the production as a whole is surprisingly high,"[31] wrote a critic in *The Bioscope*.

The incredibly patriotic *Everyone's* immediately went on the defensive, slamming the review as being condescending and, in the process, openly attacking Australia House (located in London) for not leaping to the defense of the film when the review appeared by pointing-out that the Australian film industry was *not* the boonies backwater that the English might think it was.

Eventually the fuss settled down and the movie was still being screened in rural locations even as late as 1931; no mean feat considering that it had been shot without sound and by that time "talkies" were all the rage, while silents were old hat. Despite its long-lasting popularity, the movie appears to have gone the way of the dodo at some point in the mid-1930s; more than likely prints were simply destroyed to regain the silver nitrate

Ghostly Grooves!

Top: Sheet music for a folk recording made by Johnny Ashcroft, *circa* 1961 *[image courtesy of The National Library of Australia].* **Center:** Picture sleeve to Aussie C&W singer Jimmie McFarlane's obscure souvenir 7" 45, *circa* 1970s. **Above:** McFarlane sat upon the rail of Fisher's Ghost Bridge

contained in the film stock. **FISHER'S GHOST** is now on listed the "Lost Films" register.

Sadly, Lottie Lyell wouldn't live to see the film achieve any real success. A long-time sufferer of TB, she passed away on December 21st, 1925, when she was just 35 years young. The first female Australian movie star, and a pioneer of Australian filmmaking, Lyell succumbed, having never been able to become Longford's lawfully-wedded wife. Although they had once come close to marrying. In August 1925, Melena Longford had finally given in to her husband's requests for a divorce, and she petitioned the court, on the grounds of desertion. The magistrate had given the then-typical decree that, after six months had passed, Longford would be free to remarry. Sadly, Lyell didn't have that long.

A three-act opera by John Gordon on the theme was performed in 1963

In their obituary, *Everyone's* referred to her death as, "…a distinct blow to the motion picture industry of this country, and the loss of one who has left the mark of her genius on Australian progress."[32]

Longford was heartbroken by the loss, and Lyell's death really affected his work. He would make other films, including **THE BUSHWHACKERS, THE PIONEERS** and **PETER VERNON'S SILENCE**—all of which were co-written by the late Lyell, the last two posthumously—but none of his 'post-Lyell' films ever reached the heights of their other work. After filing for bankruptcy in 1929, he quietly left the country and spent the next eighteen months traveling around Europe. Upon his return, he went to work (in both credited and uncredited capacities) for Frank Thring's Eftee Films. His heart wasn't in filmmaking anymore, he had been beaten down by industry attacks and the loss of Lyell, and his last film as a director was 1934's **THE MAN THEY COULD NOT HANG** (not to be confused with the 1939 US horror film of the same title starring Boris Karloff). Longford married one Emilie Elizabeth Anschutz in 1933. He later returned to acting, his last role coming in the homegrown production **THE POWER AND THE GLORY** (1941, D: Noel Monkman).

In 1957 Longford was asked, if he could make a film, *any* film, what it would be. He didn't hesitate with his answer. He hurried off to another room in the house and came back with a new synopsis entitled… *Fisher's Ghost*.[33] Longford had revised the script in 1934 and registered it again; keen to make a new version of the classic spook tale. Unfortunately, funding wasn't forthcoming, so his vision was never to be realized. In his final years, Longford was reduced to working

on the wharfs of Sydney as a nightwatchman. He slipped away in his sleep on April 2nd, 1959, at the age of 80.

His old enemy Doyle had gone nearly fifteen years before him. In 1929, Doyle formed the Australian Broadcasting Company, which was later taken over by the Australian Government and retitled the Australian Broadcasting Commission. The ABC is still active today. He flaunted his wealth often. In 1925, he bought himself a 44-foot, built-to-order luxury yacht, the *Miramar*, and became a yachtsman, often entering and winning races. In 1928, *Miramar* caught fire at its moorings at Rose Bay and sank, whereafter Doyle collected £5,000 in insurance for his loss. He quickly purchased a brand new 75-foot yacht, also christened the *Miramar*, in 1929.

Union Theatres, faced with massive debts to producers and the Government, was forced into liquidation in 1931. A simple thing like bankruptcy didn't stop Doyle: he simply formed a new company, called Greater Union Theatres Ltd., and bought up all of Union Theatres' assets as soon as the liquidator offered them for tender. The price he paid was £400,000, which 'just happened' to be the amount of the new company's overdraft. Greater Union then dumped Australasian Films and moved into radio, newspaper publishing and the direct importation of films. After two years of competing, Hoyt's gave up the ghost and were forced into a merger with Greater Union. The Royal Commission was bent on loosening the stranglehold over Australia's cinema, but, within five years, Stuart Doyle and Greater Union had a stronger grip on it than ever.

In 1936, under increasing pressure from the board of Greater Union, Doyle traveled overseas in search of capital. Upon his return in 1937,

Doyle found himself voted out of the company that he had ruled over, to be replaced by Sir Norman Rydge. Even his fancy showboat, the *Miramar*, was taken from him when the Royal Australian Navy commandeered it and pressed it into service during WWII.

Doyle suffered a heart attack at his home on October 20th, 1945. He died, a rich man... if nowhere near as rich as people *thought* he was. His estate was valued at £69,002.[34] For all of his career's professional/personal conflicts with Longford and others, he had nonetheless left his mark.

****

Three questions now must be asked: First, who wrote and directed **FISHER'S GHOST**? Was it Longford, alone, as credited, or was it Longford and Lyell, working in tandem?

In all the interviews he gave, Longford gave full credit to Lottie Lyell. His best work had been done in conjunction with her.

Although not fully credited for her work, it is accepted that Lottie Lyell was an equal partner with Raymond Longford. In her will, written in the

mid-1920s, Lyell gave her professional occupation as "Motion Picture Producer", not actress. In 1958, Longford penned an unpublished memoir about **THE SENTIMENTAL BLOKE**. In it, he wrote, "The scenario, preparation, exteriors and interiors of the film were carried out in its entirety by Longford Lyell Film Productions—Lottie Lyell was my partner in all our film activities."[35] There is enough contemporary and anecdotal evidence to back up the claim that Lyell not only co-wrote and co-produced, but that she also edited and even co-directed films with Longford. For instance, Longford gave testimony at the 1927 Royal Commission as to how Lyell reedited **MUTINY ON THE BOUNTY** (1916) for its UK release. Jack Moller, an extra on **BOUNTY**, recalled (in 1985) how he had observed Lyell first-hand directing scenes for that film.[36]

A publicity photo from **THE BLUE MOUNTAINS MYSTERY** (1921) shows Lyell on-set, standing between cinematographer Arthur Higgins and Longford, her hands firmly on the script as she intently regards the action being filmed. A contemporaneous newspaper report,[37] describes in detail Lyell directing scenes with Longford on the streets of Sydney for **THE DINKUM BLOKE** (1923). As Longford stated to the 1927 Royal Commission about Lyell editing **MUTINY** and insistently claimed that she became his

Young folks visit Fisher's Ghost Bridge sometime in the 1950s *[photo courtesy of The Campbelltown Macarthur Advertiser]*

"Australian in Story! Sentiment! Scenery!" Herald for a 1926 Longford-Lyell production

equal partner from the moment she recommended **THE SENTIMENTAL BLOKE** to him in 1915, it can be assumed that she was co-directing with him from that film through to **FISHER'S GHOST**.

With this in mind, Lottie Lyell can rightfully take her place as one of the first female horror film directors and producers.

Our second question is harder to answer: Was **FISHER'S GHOST** truly a "gruesome" movie?

Stuart Doyle certainly thought it was (or was he only *pretending* he did as a handy excuse to sabotage its theatrical release, perhaps?). "I admit that I said the picture was too gruesome. I still say it is," was the way he described it to the Royal Commission, and he rejected it on those grounds. As related above, the NSW State censor had no issue with its contents, and cleared it, uncut. Longford, also speaking to the Royal Commission, was adamant: "There was nothing gruesome in the picture; unless a ghost on a fence is gruesome," he told the Royal Commission, adding, "I was very careful about that." Longford was also careful to ensure that the murder of Fisher was not actually seen (it was only insinuated in the film, with a bloody knife and a body shown after-the-fact).

The above-given synopsis of the film, which correlates with contemporary reviews, certainly suggests that, outside of the ghost and possibly a shot or two of some bones in ragged clothing representing Fisher's earthly corporeal remains, there is nothing overly untoward in the film. Changes might have happened during filming, but Longford and Lyell, both of whom had years of experience both on the stage and in film under their belts, would have known the limits of what could be shown.

As the film is now seemingly irretrievably lost, it is hard to judge who was right and who was wrong. The mutual loathing between Doyle and Longford would have seen them disagree on anything. While it can be expected that Longford would downplay the supernatural themes in the film, it can also be equally expected that Doyle would overplay them as an excuse not to allow the film to be shown in any of the Union Theatres. Reading the transcript of the 1927 Royal Commission, it becomes clear that Doyle was careful not to display his personal dislike for Longford, but his testimony, littered with short, noncommittal answers betrayed him. On the other hand, Longford was very open with the Commission; he expressed nothing but contempt for both Doyle and The Combine.

Doyle's co-directors and those involved with

The Combine agreed with Doyle, and ran the film down. When also speaking before the Royal Commission, William Gibson, the then-General Manager of Australasian Films Ltd., had this exchange with the Senators:

"Quite a number of good Australian productions have cost less than £1000 to produce, pictures such as **THE MAN THEY COULD NOT HANG, SHOULD A DOCTOR TELL?, FISHER'S GHOST**, and others. I should not say they were good productions, although they might have caught the public fancy."[38]

FISHER'S GHOST and **THE MAN THEY COULD NOT HANG** were Longford-Lyell films. George Griffith, the Managing Director of Hoyt's, the cinema chain that had bought the film for a measly £30 *then* raked-in £1200 from it in a single week, described the film as being "Fair" when asked what sort of a picture **FISHER'S GHOST** was.[39]

Cecil Shannon, the manager of His Majesty's Theatre in Hobart, disagreed. He told the same Royal Commission that **FISHER'S GHOST** was, "...not a bad picture."[40] Bolstering the argument for the film being a success and not at all gruesome was Herbert Finlay, who, at the time, was a producer associated with Australasian Films, but who had been an exhibitor since 1898 when he began to tour films around the country. In 1926, he took a package out into the rural areas, telling the Royal Commission, "Only eighteen months ago, I traveled through the Riverina with the film **FISHER'S GHOST** and got ever so much better figures with it than with a double feature programme, **RIN-TIN-TIN** and Harold Lloyd in **GIRL SHY**."[41]

Reviews of the movie do not mention anything about it being gruesome, either:

"A splendid example of what can be done in Australia by Australians."[42]

"On a whole, the acting was very pleasing and some good comedy included. The photography of the Australian landscape and farms was a feature of the production."[43]

"This production not only proves that there are actors in Australia capable of appearing in the most pretentious film creations, but also that there are unlimited possibilities for really beautiful and artistic outdoor settings in the wild bush countries."[44]

"It is in no way morbid, but is relieved by an elevating love theme which runs the length of the film."[45]

"...A most interesting picture, which contains many humorous incidents, while the photography is a feature of the production."[46]

Numerous other reviewers praised the film, its usage of location shots being one of the particular appeals. Not one known review talks about it being too gruesome for anyone to watch, nor are there any reports of patrons becoming ill or otherwise distressed while watching it... which was the kind of thing that the newspapers would have picked-up on and run with, given the chance.

It's hard to know for sure, without seeing the film, if it was as gruesome as Doyle maintained, but all evidence points towards it not being so. It can, therefore, be deduced that Longford was probably right: that Doyle rejected the film purely on personal rather than professional grounds.

And so to the last question... Why did horror cease to be a valid genre for Australian filmmakers?

Following the troubled release of **FISHER'S GHOST**, no more silent horror films would be made in Australia. The problems that Longford-Lyell had experienced with The Combine had turned producers away from the genre, and the flood of American- and British-made movies, often boasting better production values, and the overall decline of the Australian film industry, meant that movies made locally would be more Australian in tone, and thus 'safer'. Action, romance and drama would become the norms and, outside of one pseudo-horror in the form of F.W. Thring's early talkie **THE HAUNTED BARN** (1931), no true horror movie would be made in Australia until as late as 1972, with Terry Bourke's **NIGHT OF FEAR**, a made-for-TV psycho thriller which was banned from that medium at the time on the grounds that it was too shocking.

It wasn't as if horror was ever a massively popular genre in Australia to begin with. Australian-made movies were mostly based on local stories, both factual and fictional. Classic bushrangers stories such as **ON OUR SELECTION** (1920, D: Raymond Longford; remade in 1932 by Ken G. Hall) and **FOR THE TERM OF HIS NATURAL LIFE** (1927, D: Norman Dawn), were known to almost every Australian in the early part of the 20th Century. Other than **FISHER'S GHOST**, there simply *weren't* any horror stories to speak of. When such a story arose, as with that of the Guyra haunting in 1921, it was either dismissed as a hoax or quickly made into a movie.[47] Even local legends that might be considered to fall into the 'horror' category—such as "Min-Min lights" (eerie illuminations in the sky) or "Bunyips" (mythical freshwater amphibious monsters), to cite two Australian examples—were largely ignored. Australians just didn't have the capacity to make a decent horror film, nor did they have the desire to, so it seemed. Even when they tried, the addition of comedy (e.g., **THE GUYRA GHOST MYSTERY** [1921]), romance (e.g. **FISHER'S GHOST**), guilt and redemption (e.g., **THE HORDERN MYSTERY** [1920]), crime and punishment (e.g., **THE FACE AT THE WINDOW** [1919]), or the classic damsel-in-distress predicaments (e.g., **THE STRANGLER'S GRIP** [1912]) were seen as essential elements to keep audiences interested. As was pointed out at the time, even the great horrors, such as Universal's imports **THE HUNCHBACK OF NOTRE DAME** and **THE PHANTOM OF THE OPERA**, and even their literary source material, possessed strong romantic overtones themselves.

When it came to literature, true horror came via works published by Europeans, and Britons such as Mary Shelley, John Polidori, H.G. Wells, Robert Louis Stevenson, M.R. James, Oscar Wilde, Bram Stoker and Victor Hugo, or from the Americans, Ambrose Bierce, Edgar Allan Poe, Henry James, Washington Irving and their contemporaries. These works weren't considered for adaptation in Australia, because the rights were long-gone. Australian authors, again, chose to write about Australian life, injustice and the ruggedness and harshness of the terrain, not horror fiction. It wouldn't be until well into the 20th Century before horror became a valid genre for Australian novelists.

But Australians loved a good horror movie, and a scary film was always guaranteed to good business, even if only for a week or two before it made the rounds in the country. Imported horror was far more accessible than domestically-made horror, and that was always the case until the beginning of the 1970s. When horror began to reemerge, it was Australian-based horror, such as the otherwise-without-dialogue-if-not-actually-silent **NIGHT OF FEAR** (1972) and **THE CARS THAT ATE PARIS** (1974, D: Peter Weir) through to the likes of **INN OF THE DAMNED** (1975, D: Terry Bourke), **PATRICK** (1978, D: Richard Franklin), **THIRST** (1979, D: Rod Hardy), **TURKEY SHOOT** (1982, D: Brian Trenchard-Smith), **RAZORBACK** (1984, D: Russell Mulcahy) and beyond.

Advertising also played a key role in the demise of Australian horror films. The producers of Australian content simply couldn't compete with the big—often times massive—budgets that American companies had on hand. A comparatively

Spooky denizens of a recent Fisher's Ghost Parade float shriek *"BOO!!!"*

The modern-day Fisher's Ghost mascot
[photo courtesy of ETB Travel News Australia's website]

thing to be avoided at all costs. It simply wasn't worth the trouble (i.e., financial losses) by attempting to resist The Combine.

Drama, comedy and romance were what Australians wanted from their local industry, along with social relevance. Horror was done better by foreign studios that had access to better-known source material.

All of these factors helped bring on the demise of Australian horror films.

In the meantime there were still plenty more such films to come and, although none of them were filmed in Australia, some of them did have a definite Australian flavor and connections.

(ENDNOTES)

1   Fisher's first name was also reported as "Frederic" (*sans* the 'k').

2   George Worrall's name has also variously been spelled "Worral", "Wurrell" and "Wurel". In most reports, it is spelled "Worrall", which is the spelling we will use here.

3   "Government Notice", *Sydney Gazette and New South Wales Advertiser* (NSW), September 21st, 1826.

4   *Monitor* (NSW), Saturday, February 3rd, 1827. Evidently nobody was alarmed that Gilbert knew what white man's fat tasted like!

5   According to author Robert Hughes, in his landmark work *The Fatal Shore* (1986), it wasn't uncommon for priests and reverends in colonial Australia to elicit such confessions from condemned men by telling them that they would go to Hell if they didn't bear their souls. No confession, no last rites, no salvation!

6   "Execution", *Sydney Gazette and New South Wales Advertiser* (NSW), February 6th, 1827.

7   "Fisher's Ghost", *Sydney Gazette and New South Wales Advertiser* (NSW), March 5th, 1836.

8   "To The Editors", *The Sydney Herald* (NSW), July 26th, 1841.

9   'Felix' was more than likely the pen name of one James Riley (ca.1795-1860), Irish-born ex-convict, "bush tutor" and associate of the Hume family, early explorers and settlers of the southernmost districts of New South Wales.

10 *Bell's Life* (NSW), June 27th, 1846.

11 "Advertisement", *The Sydney Morning Herald* (NSW), October 23rd, 1879.

12 Born Raymond John Walter Hollis Longford (September 23rd, 1878 – April 2nd, 1959).

13 Born Charlotte Edith Cox (February 23rd, 1890 – December 21st, 1925).

14 Longford-Lyell's first movie together was **THE FATAL**

humble film such as **FISHER'S GHOST** was promoted with relatively simplistic advertisements, as opposed to Chaney's **THE HUNCHBACK OF NOTRE DAME**, which was showing in cinemas at the same time and was promoted with full-page magazine advertisements in color, along with breathlessly hyperbolic text, photos and testimonials from famous people. At a time when studios were fighting for public money and cinema attendance, promotion was paramount. Many fine movies slipped through the gaps due to limited theatrical runs and/or poor promotion.

Star power and distribution also ranked high. As former reigning superstar Louise Lovely discovered when she returned to Australia to find that Lon Chaney had since outstripped her in popularity, the biggest names at the cinemas were generally American, or else Britons based in America (namely, the fledgling Hollywood). A movie starring Chaney or Chaplin could earn more in a week than most Australian movies could hope to make in a *year*. Exhibitors and theatre managers, when faced with taking-on an American production or an Australian one, would generally opt for the former.

The Combine also played their part in the downfall of horror. Witnessing the issues that Longford-Lyell had with **FISHER'S GHOST** would have been enough to cause any filmmaker to pause and consider their subject matter. The Depression was beginning as the 1930s came around, and losing money needlessly was some-

WEDDING (1911). The pair had performed the lead roles on stage. Costing an estimated £600, the film went on to gross £16,000 in both Australia and England.

15   *Smith's Weekly* (NSW). July 22nd, 1922.

16   Australia, Royal Commission on the Moving Picture Industry in Australia and Marks, Walter Moffitt, *Minutes of Evidence* Govt. Pr. Canb., 1927.

17   NAA: A1336, 12588

18   "Fisher's Ghost", *The Daily Telegraph* (NSW), June 18th, 1927

19   The first movie that is credited as being directed solely by Lyell was **THE BLUE MOUNTAINS MYSTERY** in 1921.

20   Later to become Greater Union Theatres.

21   Spencer's life had a bizarre end. He bought a ranch in Canada and settled down, but was financially ruined in the 1929 stock market crash. In September 1930, he went insane and shot and killed his storeman, Howard Smith, and wounded another man, Walter Stoddart, so severely that his arm had to be amputated. Spencer then vanished into the wilds of Vancouver, triggering a manhunt by a posse of an estimated 50 men. Six weeks after his disappearance his body was discovered in a lake where he had drowned himself. He left behind an estate valued at over £60,000.

22   Australia, Royal Commission on the Moving Picture Industry in Australia and Marks, Walter Moffitt, *Minutes of Evidence* Govt. Pr. Canb., 1927.

23   Ibid

24   Ibid

25   Ibid

26   Ibid

27   Doyle claimed, at the Royal Commission, that he had no idea how Hoyt's would have known about The Combine's rejection. He felt that Longford had told them.

28   Australia, Royal Commission on the Moving Picture Industry in Australia and Marks, Walter Moffitt, *Minutes of Evidence* Govt. Pr. Canb., 1927.

29   Ibid

30   "Fisher's Ghost in London", *Everyone's*, March 4th, 1925.

31   "Condescending, very!", *Everyone's* April 8th, 1925.

32   "Death of Lottie Lyell", *Everyone's*, December 23rd, 1925.

33   "The Man Who Met Raymond Longford", Tony Buckley, *Metro* #135.

34   Graham Shirley, "Doyle, Stuart Frank (1887–1945)", *Australian Dictionary of Biography*, National Centre of Biography, Australian National University.

35   National Film and Sound Archive Australia Title No 392164, Raymond Longford: Documentation: Assorted papers, including correspondence, invitations and unrealized scripts.

36   "The Man Who Met Raymond Longford", Tony Buckley, *Metro* #135.

37   "Worries of Movie Directors", *The Sunday Times* (NSW), April 29th, 1923. "For this particular scene it was necessary for Miss Lottie Lyell and Mr Raymond Longford, the **directors** to photograph Arthur Tauchert, who plays the Bloke." (emphasis added).

38   Australia, Royal Commission on the Moving Picture Industry in Australia and Marks, Walter Moffitt, *Minutes of Evidence* Govt. Pr. Canb., 1927.

39   Ibid

40   Ibid

41   Ibid

42   *The Herald* (Victoria), November 1st, 1924.

43   *The Brisbane Courier* (Queensland [Qld]), December 17th, 1924.

44   *The Daily Mail* (Qld), December 17th, 1924.

45   *Newcastle Morning Herald* (NSW), December 30th, 1924.

46   *The Mercury* (Tasmania [Tas]), February 10th, 1925.

47   **THE GUYRA GHOST MYSTERY** (1921), directed by John Cosgrove.

For another, more recent, lost ghost movie—this time from Malaysia rather than Australasia— see *Monster!*'s reportage on 1957's long-gone **PONTIANAK**, which can be found on pages 60-63 this very ish!

IF YOU THOUGHT WE ONLY PUBLISHED MOVIE MAGAZINES, THEN YOU NEED TO CHECK OUT THESE *ÜBER-COOL* BOOKS FROM WK BOOKS:

DRACULA DOWN UNDER!

WK Books proudly presents the newest tome from Rondo-nominated film historian Daniel Best: the nearly-forgotten history of the 1929-31 Australian Dracula stage tour!

Painstakingly researched and illustrated with numerous reproductions of original vintage newspaper ads, photographs, articles and reviews, Best has assembled as complete a picture of the legendary play's long-running journey through the Land Down Under as we are ever likely to get.

Every bit as fascinating a story as it is a piece of history, this is an indispensable volume for theatre and vampire enthusiasts alike...so grab a copy now and sink your teeth in!

WK Books
Books You Can Hold

AUSTRALIAN GOTHIC
UNTOLD STORY OF THE 1929 AUSTRALIAN DRACULA TOUR

BY DANIEL BEST

WITH A FOREWORD BY STEPHEN R. BISSETTE

UNLEASH THE BEAST!

From Rondo Award-nominated author Troy Howarth and WK Books, publishers of Weng's Chop and Monster! magazines, comes the ultimate guide to the films of Paul Naschy!

Featuring hundreds of stills, posters, behind-the-scenes and candid shots—many of which are provided by Naschy's family and presented here for the first time—this guide is an absolute must-own for Naschy fans, horror fanatics and cinema connoisseurs alike.

Available in both full-color and standard black-and-white editions.

WK

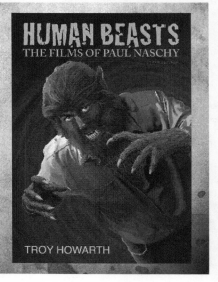

HUMAN BEASTS
THE FILMS OF PAUL NASCHY

TROY HOWARTH

PRINT IS NOT DEAD!

WK Books, publisher of *Weng's Chop* and *Monster!* magazines, is keeping cinema journalism alive and well and on printed paper!

Stop feeling like tangible cinema books are a thing of the past, and grab yourself a handful of of movie-book magnificence...

...Because nothing beats the feeling of a real book in your hand.

WK BOOKS
Books You Can Hold

WENG'S CHOP

REAL DEPRAVITIES
THE FILMS OF KLAUS KINSKI

MONSTER!

TROY HOWARTH

ISSUE 31
November 2016

FANGTASTIC!!

"Monsters for YOU to color" is our first coloring book with illustrations by MONSTER!'s Tim Paxton and his sister Heather

Monsters for YOU to COLOR

Art By Heather
THE HALLOWEEN PUMPKIN DIGEST

Art By Heather
A WORLD OF GOD AND MONSTERS

The title sez it all: "The Halloween Pumpkin Digest: 50 Jack-o-Lanterns" by Heather Paxton!

"The Gifted Toad Stool Swapper" is the perfect gift for that certain hard to buy for person. Over 50 pages of weird and wonderful artwork by Joel Paxton

Art work by Heather Paxton
Foreword by Stephen R. Bissette

"A World of God and Monsters" over 100 full color pages of Monster art by Heather Paxton with a foreword by comic legend Steve Bissette!

Background: *Not a Ghost of a Chance!* A rare glimpse at some ghastly goings-on from the long-lost Malay shocker **PONTIANAK** (1957), a film which is—sadly—likely never to be seen again

A Triple-Bill of Malaysian Macabre

Fentone

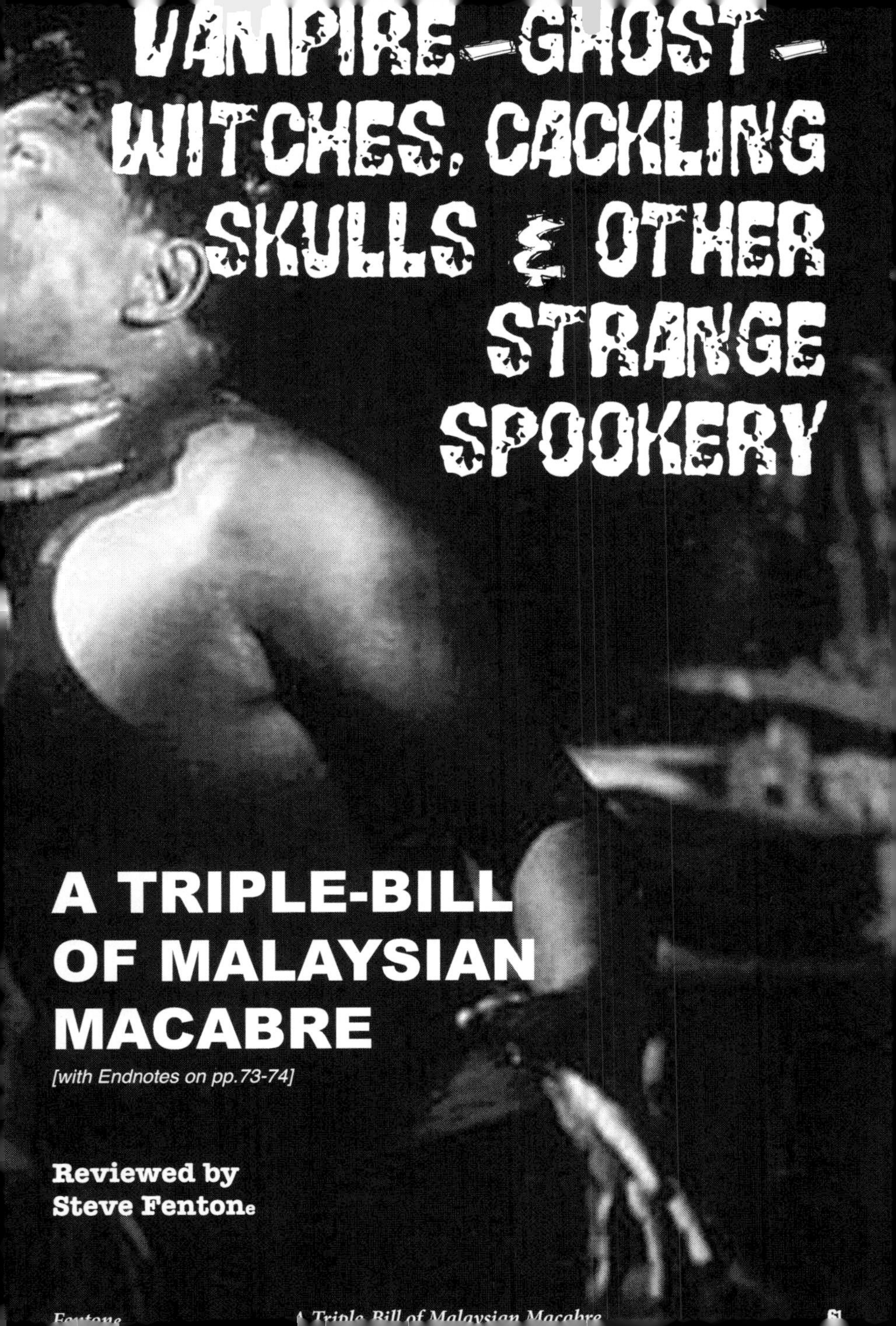

VAMPIRE-GHOST-WITCHES, CACKLING SKULLS & OTHER STRANGE SPOOKERY

A TRIPLE-BILL OF MALAYSIAN MACABRE

[with Endnotes on pp.73-74]

**Reviewed by
Steve Fenton**e

Introduction

If someone had told me way back in the '70s that one day I would get to see some bona fide Singaporean (etc.) creature features, I wouldn't have believed it. But that was then and this is now, the age of video streaming websites like YouTube, so things are entirely different than they were.

Now, call me a stodgy ol' codger who spends way too much time living in the past if you will, but there's something about real ancient spooky movies from Asia (as well as any number other countries besides) which creep me out—in a *nice* way—more than most other horror movies of much more recent vintage rendered in full-color and with all the other fixings to boot do. And *why* is it that so many producers seemingly think that ever-more-*ultra* 'ultra-realism' in SFX (i.e., CGI overkill) necessarily makes scary movies any the scarier? Sure, digital animation most certainly has its place, and can work damn fine when used well (i.e., judiciously and with artistry), and I really don't have anything against it at all, but dare I say that (at least in my eyes) sometimes much simpler and cruder— even downright *primitive*—effects can be *so-o-o* much more effective than all the hi-tech/state-of-the-art/top-of-the-line digital technology that 50- or 60-mill+ US dollars can buy. But let's get down to the nitty-gritty here, shall we…

Asian promotional materials for the lost horror film **PONTIANAK** (1957). **Above:** Malaysian newspaper ad. **Top:** Hong Kong ad

'57, the year that the below-discussed **HANTU JERANGKONG** was made, was also the year when the Independence Act of the Federation of Malaya (*Persekutuan Tanah Melayu /* ‏يالم هنات ناوتوكسرف‎; formerly British Malaya) first came into effect, so it was a historically noteworthy period in more ways than one. It also saw an unprecedented 'horror craze' (my words) occur in Malaysian cinema, one which lasted up until the mid-1960s or so. Now, being as I was born roughly two years after this movie was made (and actually lived in Singapore for several years as a small child in the early '60s), when I categorize it as "ancient", it's not because I feel that way myself simply by association; rather, since so many really old Asian movies have been lost in the mists of time due to being kept in improper storage facilities, as well as from neglect (etc.), there are relatively so few still extant in many Southeast Asian countries (including Malaysia, Indonesia, Thailand, the Philippines *et al*; a great many films have also 'vanished without trace' in subcontinental India over the decades too) that we should consider ourselves very lucky indeed that there are even *any* left at all. And I'm not just talking about monster movies here; I mean movies of all genres. But since horror-fantasy product was generally so vastly outnumbered in terms of production output by such more standard/'straight' mainstream commercial fare as dramas, comedies and musicals, this makes the odds of pre-'60 horror flicks surviving all-the-less-likely, simply because they were in such a distinct minority to begin with. A major cause of lost films in Asia is one which has caused the loss of countless cinematic offerings from around the world over the years: namely decomposition of the chemical components of the celluloid film

A Triple-Bill of Malaysian Macabre *Fentone*

on which they were shot, due to basic neglect from improper storage and the like. Because hot and humid climatic conditions—such as those commonly found in tropical Asian nations—only serve to accelerate the natural deterioration process of sensitive film elements, especially if they are inadequately or carelessly stored, the numbers of films lost to the ravages of time and the elements is that much greater than in cooler climes. But, added to this, there may well be any number other reasons why a film doesn't survive to entertain future generations, one of them being simple human indifference.

Case in point: the prolific Cathay-Keris Film Productions' shocker **PONTIANAK** (1957, D: B. Narayan Rao)—named for the creepy, long-fanged female vampire-witch of its title, played by local popular sex symbol Maria Menado, an actress with a knack for expressing the 'heart-wrenching torment' of her characters. This was one of the great many Malay films to be shot on Singaporean soil (Anglo Malay tagline: *"SEE: The Lovely Maria Menado transformed into a hideous Vampire!"*), and it was of considerable historical/cultural importance in the domestic film industry, yet 'legend' (or is it simply vicious rumor?) has it that the film ended up as good as tossed in the garbage by one of its co-producers/copyright holders *[see Endnote #1]*. Whilst the first *Pontianak* series entry presented Menado's accursed, pathos-laden Chomel character as an all-out vampiric villainess, by the third film she had spiritually redeemed herself to become a sympathetic and even heroic character and was performing deeds of social conscience rather than preying on victims in order to take their lives. Not only was **PONTIANAK** #1 a huge local hit, which, after its premiere on April 27th, 1957 ran for the better part of three months straight in local Cathay chain cinemas, but it even got exported into a few other Asian markets too, including being dubbed into Mandarin/Cantonese for 1958 showings (under the Cathay Organisation's banner) in Hong Kong *[see Endnote #2]*. Speaking of which, the film was such a success that it helped its production house Cathay-Keris break the local virtual monopoly/stranglehold on Malaysian movies by HK's Shaw Brothers megacorp, who bankrolled a great many productions in Malaysia (during that period, Malay movies were typically financed by Chinese producers, directed by Indians and cast from a ready talent pool of local Malays). For all its profits, however, **PONTIANAK** is now famously—and sadly—one of the nation's most-missed and sought-after 'lost' films of all. Another of the many cases in point is the Shaw

Top: Maria Menado *[center]* in her normal form, juxtaposed with her two, um, 'less-presentable' alter-egos *[left & right]* in **PONTIANAK** (1957). **Above:** Abdul Razak *[left]* and Ho Ah Loke, co-creators of the Cathay-Keris production house's profitable *Pontianak* trilogy, the first two films of which are now lost. The Shaw Bros. also made a cash-in trilogy of their own on the same theme

Bros.' later presentation **SITORA HARIMAU JADIAN** ("Sitora the Weretiger", 1964, Singapore/Malaysia [see *Monster!* #10, p.57]), a creature feature involving feline shape-shifters that was written/directed by and starred (etc., etc., etc.) late Asian superduperstar P. Ramlee; another film which has also disappeared with scarcely a trace other than for a handful of stills, some song recordings from its soundtrack and the faded memories of those moviegoers who were fortunate enough to catch it on its first-run, and is rumored by some to have suffered a similar ultimate fate as **PONTIANAK**. Ergo, if two such comparatively 'high-profile' films as that '64 one and the preceding '57 one can up and vanish virtually from the face of the Earth as though they never even existed at all (most typically in the cases of pre-1970 productions), just imagine how many 'smaller', lesser-known films (prints of which would have been produced in fewer quantities and received more limited distribution) might have done likewise. This sad state of affairs makes the survival/preservation for posterity of any 'moldy oldie' such a good thing... a very good thing.

HANTU JERANGKONG
(or *Hantu Jerangkung* / "Ghost's Skull")

Singapore/Malaysia, 1957.
D: K.M. Basker

Which brings us to the movie presently under review, **HANTU JERANGKONG** (produced by [the future Sir] Run Run Shaw [1907-2014] under the famous Shaw Bros. logo with Malay Film Productions), that dates from the selfsame year as the evidently long-gone-and-never-to-be-seen-again **PONTIANAK** (a hit which spawned a pair of quickie cash-in sequels, **DENDAM PONTIANAK** ["Revenge of the Pontianak", also from '57] and **SUMPAH PONTIANAK** ["Curse of the Pontianak", 1958], both likewise starring Maria Menado and directed by B.N. Rao; the sole surviving film out of the three is that latter-most one *[see Endnote #3]*). It's a crying shame about the first two films in the *Pontianak* trilogy going the way of the brontosaurus, but lucky for us, **HANTU JERANGKONG**—a product of the same local horror trend of the time—is still very much in existence, I'm happy to say. Very happy indeed, considering what a way-out wacky wonder it is!

Barring the actual film title, the entire opening credits are given in English. And unfortunately, while, like Hong Kong movies, many made-in-Singapore Malay productions were originally released theatrically with English subtitles, the print of **HJ** I watched for review purposes here doesn't come with any (not that I'm gripin', you understand. I was happy just to get to see it in *any* form!). Other than for whatever such indecipherable subtle details as might be present in the film's narrative, its rudiments of plot were fairly straightforward to follow, although I wouldn't be a bit surprised if I got my wires crossed somewhere along the lines over the course of the following synopsis, but I'm sure I got the basic gist of things fairly straight.

At an isolated hut late at night during the full moon, an old witch-woman (Habsah Buang) burns incense

---

Pages 64-65: *Bonehead!* Single-named Malay performer Zainon *[center 3 pics on both pages]* as "Ghost's Skull", the crazed, disembodied title character of **HANTU JERANGKONG** (1957), who can go from being a bare (if oddly hornless) skull to a full-fleshed noggin-with-horns seemingly at will. While he/it mostly just laughs—we can only assume there must be little else to do for fun when you're but a bodiless head!—his/its raucous scenes are among the most entertaining in the movie, which has numerous other oddball entertainments to offer besides

A Triple-Bill of Malaysian Macabre

Fentone

and wafts the pungent smoke in the direction of a bleached human skull sat upon an altar while making tributary offerings to it. No sooner has she done this than her whole trayful of proffered edibles is magically 'sucked-up' by the hungry skull, which—this sudden inrush of sustenance evidently having been the cause of this—promptly turns into the disembodied head of a hysterically laughing horned/fanged devil, the titular Ghost's Skull (portrayed by the mononymous performer Zainon). This living, laughing head (which he quite possibly laughed right off his now-nonexistent shoulders in the first place) laughs so much that it's a wonder he/it doesn't topple clear off the tabletop! Especially since he's in the habit of—*well*—throwing his head back and guffawing uproariously up at the rafters at least once every few minutes, often for quite lengthy stretches. Since his sole support (his 'one leg to stand on', so to speak) is the cleanly sawn-off stump of his neck, you'd think he'd overbalance and fall to the floor. And just how the hell does someone with no lungs laugh so damn *LOUD*—or even *at all*—anyhow?! (Okay, enough with the nitpicking already!)

Strange phenomena thereafter begin to plague the local *kampung*. After taking the form of a ghostly mist, the skull's spirit next assumes the shape of a black cat, then, having successfully snuck into a hut, turns into the old witch, who has the shape-shifting ability of a were-kitty, you see. Looking like some devil-possessed zombie, she prowls about the vicinity stiff-armed/legged. Bizarrely, just as a man is startled by the screechings of a pair of bickering giant fruit bats nearby outside the hut, the witch appears from around the corner and bites him (non-explicitly and out-of-frame) on his throat. She then stiff-legs it off through the dark forest until she encounters another man, whom she also kills in the same manner as before. His terrified shrieks alert his neighbors from their slumber, whereupon the townsmen discover the bodies of the vampire's two fresh victims. After surveying the scene and inspecting the corpses, the local shaman/medicine man (known as a *bomoh* or *hantu* in the vernacular) comes to the conclusion that it is the work of the horrible *hantu jerangkong*, much to the other men's fright (one of their number, the obligatory comedy relief character, is hilarious to watch as he stands shakily amongst the group of his fellows, violently quaking at the knees as though his legs might buckle right out from under him at any moment, while constantly looking all about him nervously. There are some real talented comic actors on show in this movie, without doubt!).

Almost spot-on the 13-minute mark (*oooooo*, eerie!), we are treated to our first song number. Yes indeed, international monster fans, not unlike Indian movies, Malay ones are also known for their

periodic, at-one-time-obligatory musical interludes. After all the spookery preceding it, we can only assume that, as with horror movies from India—as has been reported in these very pages by Tim Paxton—song-'n'-dance numbers, as well as comedy routines are used as a means of dissipating all the 'unbearable' psychological/emotional tension built-up by the more suspenseful/nerve-wracking scenes, which needs an outlet via which to vent itself lest a viewer might up and burst from all the pent-up pressure. The ditty heard here (entitled "Foo Kanan Foo Kiri", whatever that means) is a jolly, jaunty little number that begins with the phrase "*Ha-ha, ha-ha... La-la-la-la-la / La-la-la-la-la*", sung by the driver of an ox-drawn plow out in the middle of nowhere (with an 'invisible' entire orchestra backing him!). Because the former ominously moody nighttime setting has since suddenly switched to broad daylight in dazzlingly bright sunshine, this fact combined with the chipper chirruping of the cart driver immediately dissipates the dark mood of doom-'n'-gloom established so admirably prior to it. By the by, the fact that the farmer/singer ([Aziz Sattar] complete with pencil mustache) at first sight instantly reminded me of a young John Leguizamo for some reason only added to the song's entertainment value for me!

Thankfully, we don't have to wait very long before things dive right back into the spooky stuff once more. A young woman walking alone along a lonely jungle trail at dusk is startled by the appearance of the vampire-witch, who terrorizes her latest victim by distorting herself (much like an image in a funhouse hall of mirrors), wavering and warping grotesquely before the understandably screaming girl's eyes. While the vampire's newest victim remains rooted to the spot, unable to move—like a mouse frozen with fear by a cobra—the monstress slowly advances towards her with obvious evil intent. This time however, rather than kill her victim by drinking her blood, as before with the male victims, the vampire instead possesses the woman's body by inhabiting it with her own transitory spirit. Sensing the presence of supernatural evil, the village dogs start up a cacophonous chorus of baying/howling at her approach. She can appear and disappear at will simply by blipping out of sight

---

Hades Ladies! Frightful females abound in **HANTU JERANGKONG** (1957). The topmost two screen captures show Habsah Buang as the old vampire/witch. I was unable to identify the actress in the central pic (and also in the bottommost one on the preceding page), but she gives a convincingly creepy performance indeed. The bottom two images at left show **HJ**'s leading lady Hashimah Yon, the upper one while spiritually possessed and the lower one while her 'normal' self

then reappearing in a different spot, much to the horror of a lily-livered henpecked husband—none other than that singing farmboy—and his tubby bullying battleaxe of a ball-and-chain, who treats her spouse no better than a beast of burden. Using her powers of invisibility, the vampire treats this dysfunctional married couple to an all-night haunting by shuffling dishes around on the dinner table (via a pretty well-done 'stop-motion' effect) and making foodstuffs disappear into thin air. By dawn the haunted couple have been reduced to quivering bundles of nerves, huddled together under a blanket. As if you couldn't tell, this whole sequence is pretty much played for laughs, but the grotesquely grinning witch-possessed woman is pretty creepy-looking to behold nonetheless.

The next 'segment' of **HANTU JERANGKONG**, which isn't an actual anthology but is highly episodic in structure regardless, has the ghostly woman now appearing headless (her noggin simply matted-out of the frame rather than 'actually' chopped-off). In this new form, she creeps around the village after nightfall, fatally throttling whomever she meets. Musical number #2 comes just over another 13 minutes after the first one. This time we get a whole row of happily singing/dancing field laborers doing an 'inspirational' song which seems (?) to be somewhat along the lines of that "Whistle While You Work" jingle in Disney's **SNOW WHITE AND THE SEVEN DWARFS** (1937, USA). Then, ten minutes or so still further in, we get a velvet-smooth, really charming love song sung as a duet by a pair of attractive young sweethearts (the girl played by local hottie Hashimah Yon, the guy by her several-time co-star and frequent singing partner Aziz Jaafar) whose voices blend beautifully together and the sensual chemistry between them is so thick you can almost taste it. Born in Singapore, the smolderingly sultry Ms. Yon was the daughter of *Bangsawan* (نواسڠب [traditional Malay opera/theatre]) performers, who became a popular contract player in leading lady roles at Malay Film Productions Ltd. during the 1950s, including playing the heroine, Teratai, of director/co-star P. Ramlee's "Cinderella"-like fairy tale fantasy **PANCHA DELIMA** (1956)—which includes such supernatural elements as humans who transform into cobras—as well as appearing in other films with/for Ramlee.

Spurred-on by the ghostly voice of the devil/skull in her mind, the vampiress, still occupying the body of the young woman, sets her sights on *younger* victims. Yep, you guessed it: she's got a hankering for some kids' blood! Or so it seems, anyway, judging by the heavy implications while she leeringly spies on a group of tree-climbing young boys as though she'd like to have them all over to dinner then have them all *for* dinner. However, possibly due to certain inherent censorship restrictions which existed in Malaysia at the time (and do still, to this day, in the predominantly Muslim culture), her evident appetite for 'young stuff' is only implied rather than actually shown being sated.

At the tail-end of the 46th minute, after the witch-possessed chick sets up shop at a new hut in a new neighborhood and the devil's ever-laughing nut is reconstituted over its headbone on the altar, no less than Ghost's Skull himself goes off on a bodiless night flight, much in the manner of those Japanese folkloric flying heads—one of the teeming legion of fantastical spirit creatures collectively termed *yōkai*—known as *nukekubi* (抜け首 a.k.a. ぬけくび). It zooms up through the night sky to come hover larger than death outside the bedroom window of a young woman (none other than the lovely songstress from the lovers' duet, whose character's name is Ramla), there swelling to vast proportions like an inflating balloon. In its grotesqueness as well as content, this head-at-the-window scene totally reminded me of a similar image of a gigantic devil seen in Georges Méliès-influenced Spanish cinema pioneer Segundo de Chomón's eerie silent short *The House of Ghosts* (*La maison ensorcelée*, 1908, France).

The frightful sight of this 'bighead' lurking just beyond her windowsill not surprisingly sends the girl into total hysterics. She turns violent, attacking and attempting to murder members of her own family when they rush to her aid at the sound of her screams (which are shrill enough to shatter bullet-proof glass! Talk about a 'Scream Queen'!). The actress really gives her all—most convincingly indeed, I might add—while playing at stark raving mad, lashing-out viciously and realistically at her kinfolk without pulling her punches. And those *shrieks* of hers! It's hard to believe they could come from the same velvet throat which had warbled that liltingly sweet serenade we heard earlier. Fit to be tied, the screamer then has that very thing done to her at the express behest of the wise *kampung* headman, who rightly diagnoses her as a victim of demonic possession. Guess who shows up to perform the exorcism? None other than the woman previously possessed by the vampire-witch, who's in dire need of an exorcist herself! The plot thickens…

You'd never know judging by Music Valley's bland domestic Malaysian VCD insert for **HANTU KUBOR** (1958) that it's even a horror movie at all, and a comparatively lackluster one at that

When the headman presides over a ceremony during which the villagers burn the witch in effigy (i.e., a life-size wicker figure), much like happens in pop cultural depictions of voodoo dolls, the 'real' witch—who's really only occupying that other poor female victim's shanghaied body still—begins to go up in smoke. Just as she's starting to smolder, ready to burst into flames, Ghost's Skull obliges her by simply blowing the fire out with a puff of wind before it gets started. For his next trick, Skull turns the witch into an exact *doppelgänger* of the sweet songbird-*cum*-screaming mimi whom she had 'exorcized' (the real deal, meanwhile, has now become all sweetness and light again, with nary a scream to be heard out of her). Just as expected, her 'evil twin' (played by the same actress Ms. Yon, natch)

Hong Kong's Shaw Brothers very much had a hand in Malay Film Productions

substitutes herself for his real betrothed. While the real Ramla is away, the fake one then casts a spell over Abang her beau before spiriting him off to the witch's place (they vanish into thin air together).

What's next on Ghost's Skull's terrible to-do list, you may well be wondering? Why, it's off to the home of the parents of a newborn infant, where it huffs a cloud of black-magical smoke into the baby's room, causing the napping nipper to wake up screaming (yes, *more* screaming! And this is one baby that can really scream up a lung, believe you me! And every last scream 100% percent authentic, too. Man, never mind 'acting', this kid was *really* having a hissy-fit! Nowadays I suppose it'd be considered child abuse for working a poor tot into such an emotional frenzy, but what's done is done).

The film was scripted by Omar Rojik, who also functioned as its assistant director. Much of the technical crew appears to be Chinese (presumably from Hong Kong?). The monochromatic cinematography by N.B. Vasudev (a Russian?) really piles on the ominous mood, which fails to dissipate even during the numerous comic relief scenes. Performances by all in **HANTU JERANGKONG** are most proficient indeed, and the comedic scenes—of which there are a *lot*—are easier to take for this reason. For instance, a wiry, no-nonsense/take-charge midget with a big dopey fat guy for a sidekick provide some pretty amusing physical comedy (including a priceless joint 'double-take' at the witch—with the little guy jumping onto the big guy's lap in fright at the sight of her—which cracked me up and caused me to immediately replay the scene a couple more times in quick succession, that's how well-done it was; or maybe I'm just way too easily entertained).

Call me strange, but even though I couldn't understand hardly a single doggone word of it, I still found **HANTU JERANGKONG** exceedingly enjoyable regardless. The sequel was **HANTU KUBOR**, which is covered directly below…

HANTU KU:OR

(or *Hantu Kubur* / "Ghost's Grave")

Singapore/Malaysia, 1958. D: Chow Cheng Kok

Made the following year, this was the for-the-most-part highly underwhelming (and then some!) follow-up to the previously-discussed Malay *horor filem klasik* **HANTU JERANGKONG** (1957), for which much of the same principal cast returned, albeit under a different director (a behind-camera change which may go far in explaining the conspicuously lesser end results). At the outset of **HANTU KUBOR**, whose prologue takes up at the point where the preceding film left off (but, sadly, largely lacks its manic verve), the old vampire-witch (played by Habsah Buang once again)—shrieking madly all the while—is killed and her hut put to the torch by the *kampung*'s rightfully angry residents, but not before they safely spirit away her entranced captive, Ramla's beloved betrothed Abang (as replayed by Aziz Jaafar, who was likewise seen in the same role for **HANTU JERANGKONG**), who snaps out of his mindless, zombie-like trance and returns to his senses now that his former captor's evil spell has been broken by her death. *Roll credits!*

Shortly following this promising opener, we re-meet—if only fleetingly, for the time being—HJ's youthfully beauteous heroine Ramla, who is now fully back to her sweet, wholesome self once again, all cow-eyed in love. There then follows a whole lot of dialogue-heavy soap opera/character development and various comedic hijinks (plus the obligatory musical interlude), which goes on for well in excess of a half-hour with little of much visual interest happening; the total running time only being 83 minutes, this lengthy 'uneventful' section seems rather wasteful, to say the least. Again, the henpecked farmer played by Aziz Sattar is subjected to merciless finger-waggling / tongue-lashing tirades by his shrill ball-busting plumper of a wife, who would make a hearty meal for the vampire, if only he (and we!) could be so lucky.

Despite all appearances to the contrary, although believed conclusively destroyed, the witch is still very much alive (at least in spirit), and she returns to haunt Ramla's beau Abang by night, materializing and vanishing through window shutters that flap open and closed by themselves while a dog's plaintive baying is carried in on the midnight breeze. At long last, late into the 48th minute (only 35 more to go!), hideous shrieking banshee wails shred the night as the camera slowly pans across a miniature country landscape under an artificial full moon. However, just when things start to get promisingly spooky again, the action lapses back into yet another stretch of mundane drama and another sentimental romantic musical number care of reunited sweethearts Ramla and Abang. Right before minute 55 rolls around, the witch reappears in a puff of magical smoke and, robed in white, goes to pay a late-night visit on Abang amidst the frantic howling of the *kampung*'s dogs. She then proceeds to summon up from beyond the grave an *orang minyak* ("oily man") demon (a wiry black actor wearing dark swimming trunks!), that terrorizes locals and abducts screaming village women at the witch's behest *[see Endnote #4]*. When the creature is wounded by a machete-chop in the back, it flees into the darkness of the jungle, pursued by an angry mob of torch-bearing villagers. In a further development, the witchy vampiress turns our hero Abang to stone for a spell. Also, in an interesting moment of folkloric magic, the *kampung*'s wise *bomoh* ("shaman") uses the yolk of a raw egg as a 'crystal ball' to pinpoint the witch's whereabouts (her tiny image appears on its surface). Leave it to the shaman to blast the cackling crone back to the netherworld whence she came and rescue Abang from her clutches. He then performs a holy purifying ceremony to ensure that the *orang minyak* stays put in his grave. Cue Ramla's and Abang's joyous reunion… *Tammat* ("The End")!

Incidental music (probably 'recycled' tracks?) in **HANTU KUBOR** at times sounds like something out of a creaky Hollywood horror movie of the '30s or '40s. Despite momentary flashes of interest, quite frankly, this disappointing sequel can't hold a candle to its vastly more energetic and engaging forerunner, and its overly repetitive structure soon grows wearisome, despite occasional fleeting moments of interest. It's of note mainly (solely?) for some decent monochromatic atmosphere in some scenes, but that's about it, I'm afraid. Slim pickings, for sure!

Hashimah Yon, lovely leading lady of all three films under review, as depicted on a 1958 cover of the Jawi-language Singaporean periodical *Majalah Bintang* ("Star Magazine")

GERGASI
("Giant")

Singapore/Malaysia, 1958. D: Dhiresh Ghosh

Another **PONTIANAK**-era Malay horror outing produced by Run Run Shaw, this otherwise unconnected film again co-stars Aziz Jaafar and Hashimah Yon, the love-struck male and female leads of the above-covered *Hantu* duology (Aziz Sattar, the p-whipped farmer from those films, also reappears herein, this time playing a faithful domestic servant).

In the opening sequence, Rahman (Haji Mahadi), a hunter out after dark, is lured to a woodland clearing under a tree next to a footbridge by the entrancing singing of a beautiful woman (played by the actress known only as Rokiah). After momentarily repairing behind 'her' tree, she reemerges as her hideous *langsuir* alter-ego (c/o a schlocky fright-wig and greasepaint makeup). As Rahman rubs his eyes in disbelief at what he is seeing, the witch—cackling maniacally, natch!—transforms into a fanged, long-nailed, white-robed vampire, before

promptly reverting to her comely feminine form once more just as the man is raising his rifle to shoot her. After again unleashing her hellish cackle (a sure sign of evil intent in Asiatic horror movies!), she shortly vanishes into thin air right before his eyes, whereupon a violent nocturnal thunderstorm starts up. Upon later returning to the vampire's domain, Rahman ousts the occupying evil spirit from the lovely maiden's body by plunging a long iron nail into the top of her head (it's hard to tell that's what he does, as—evidently to avoid censorial cuts—it's shown only in murky long-shot and happens very quickly, almost off-handedly) *[see Endnote #5]*. This causes the monster to permanently revert to her attractive human form again, and, in gratitude, she goes on to marry and have a child with Rahman her savior. Their little daughter, named Mutiara, grows up to become a lovely young woman (now played by Yon), who, with her *bapa* ("father") and *ibu* ("mother")'s approval, is wooed by her childhood admirer Guntur (Jaafar), the *Penghulu* ("headman")'s son, who has been in love with her since he was a boy. Cue the first coyly flirtatious love duet sung by the two leads, which is much in the same vein as their sexy song in **HANTU JERANGKONG** and really emphasizes the stars' effortless chemistry once again.

Elsewhere, a Frankensteinian doctor (S. Kadarisman, with unkempt receding hair and pointy, curly-tipped whiskers) is conducting unorthodox 'scientific' experiments in his laboratory, which is kitted-out with all the standard 'mad scientist' accoutrements. After he doses it with his revolutionary growth formula, a baby white lab bunny increases in size to become a full-grown adult specimen within mere moments. His next experimental subject is a little boy (presumably a homeless orphan?), whom Doc takes back to his place and immediately begins covertly treating with his super-serum. Within no time at all, the lad has been transformed into the titular *gergasi* ("giant"), an XL adult male. Following this, the scientist attaches power cables to it and pumps electricity into the giant's body, evidently bent on turning his 'creature' into some sort of atomic age superman vaguely along the lines of Tor Johnson's "Lobo" from Ed Wood's **BRIDE OF THE MONSTER** (1955, USA). Complete with crazy long eyebrows, facial hair and a barbarian-style ponytail, he/it resembles some sort of deranged Arabian Nights genie, who soon busts loose of its bonds and rises from the operating table to go on a limited rampage before its creator authoritatively brings it to heel, then sends it out to pillage local livestock and generally harass the townsfolk. This whole sequence seems totally detached from all the earlier action leading up to it, as though it might have come from a completely different film. Once again, the sensible kampung headman takes charge of the situation by leading a torch-bearing throng of menfolk in search of the rampaging 'monster'.

Following a lengthy absence from the narrative, Ms. Yon as Mutiara the heroine reappears. When the girl 'accidentally' (!) removes the nail embedded in her mother's head, hidden under her hair—appearing not all that surprised to find it there, strangely enough—the older woman goes into screaming convulsions and turns back into her former monstrous self again, now that the iron spike is no longer in place to keep the witch's evil spirit at bay. But then, moments later, for no apparent reason, Mom returns to normal once more, without the nail being put back. During the community's celebration prior to Mutiara and Guntur tying the knot, the diabolical doctor sends his giant henchman to kidnap the prospective bride for himself, having long lusted after her from afar. As the big brute makes off with her daughter, Mom assumes her vampire form again to go off in pursuit, rescue Mutiara and avenge herself against the scientist, interrupting him in the act just as he is attempting to ravish her daughter. As she moves in for the kill with her knife-like (floppy) fingernails bared, the bellowing *gergasi* breaks free of its chains and slavishly lumbers to its master's aid. Having been repeatedly raked by the she-creature's razor-sharp talons, the he-beast, covered in blood (but with no actual contusions showing), weakens before succumbing to its wounds and kicking the proverbial bucket along with its creator (either this scene is missing some footage, or is so poorly directed that their deaths aren't conveyed very well, as they both just suddenly appear lying dead side-by-side on the floor, and that's it for the pair of them). As Guntur arrives to 'save' Mutiara—after Mom has already done most of the work—the girl's dear *ibu*, still in her monstrous form, wanders off dejectedly into the storm-tossed wilderness to return to her life of solitude as a hideous hell-hag. This seems to set the scene for a potential sequel, but your guess is as good as mine whether one ever transpired, although I assume that this is a stand-alone film.

Evidently shot on a very rushed schedule and mostly photographed in medium- or long-shot, **GERGASI** contains only very few closer shots, and no real close-ups. The director, Dhiresh Ghosh (from India?), also directed the mythological heroic fantasy adventure **TWIN PRINCES** (*Indera Bangsawan*, 1961, Singapore/Malaysia), another Malay Film Productions offering, which includes such wonders as a dwarfish ape creature, a lightning bolt-hurling humanoid deity atop a mountain and—best of all!—a horned devil that dwells in a cavern bedecked with giant flashing

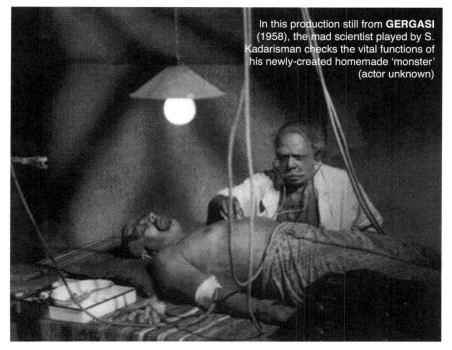

In this production still from **GERGASI** (1958), the mad scientist played by S. Kadarisman checks the vital functions of his newly-created homemade 'monster' (actor unknown)

eyeballs. Ghosh also directed Hashimah Yon in another mythological of the "Arabian Nights" type, **PUTERI GUNUNG BANANG** ("Princess of Mount Banang", 1959, Singapore/Malaysia), which, amongst other things, features a gaunt, ghostly he-demon, a creepy female apparition, a magic carpet and "Open Sesame!"-style sliding doors set in a wall of rock.

Although the present movie—which runs for the better part of two hours (i.e., a little over 110m) and is decidedly slapdash and choppy in spots—isn't as consistently entertaining nor quite as memorable as **HANTU JERANGKONG** is, in terms of garish thrills it at least offers quite a bit more in the way of entertainment value than **HANTU KUBOR** does. Fittingly enough, certain strains of music heard herein sound very much along the lines of those in the old Universal Monsters classics, as the surprisingly brutal closing brawl between the man-made monster and the *langsuir/pontianak*-like witch/vampire almost reads like an Asian variation of the eponymous critters' battle royal in Uni's **FRANKENSTEIN MEETS THE WOLF MAN** (1943, USA, D: Roy William Neill). Among other mandatory musical numbers, the P. Ramlee-penned song "Kenek Kenek Udang" is heard performed onscreen.

Afterword: And so ends my 'Malaysian three-pack'. It'd been a while since I covered any exotic Asian obscurities here in *Monster!*, so I figured it was high time I rectified that, and I intend to cover other similar (or maybe even wildly *dis*similar!) fare in future issues.

Left, Top to Bottom: Various screen captures of some of **GERGASI**'s relatively few close shots showing the hideous *pontianak*-like vampire crone, who may or may not (?) have been played by the actress Rokiah Jaafar in all the images seen here; but that's definitely her in the uppermost one, wherein she first reveals her monstrous visage. Since the continuity/appliqué of the character's special makeup is decidedly 'loose', we're hard-put to tell whether more than one actress performed the role

ENDNOTES:

1 According to the National Archives of Singapore (@ *http://www.nas.gov.sg/blogs/archivistpick/pontianak/*): *"Cathay-Keris partners Ho Ah Loke and Loke Wan Tho parted ways in 1960 when Ho decided to leave Singapore to set up Merdeka Studios in Kuala Lumpur. Before he left, Ho and Loke Wan Tho drew lots to divide the films that they had made together. Ho left Cathay and took his share of the films to Kuala Lumpur. According to his friend, film director Dato L. Krishnan, Ho possibly ordered removers to take 20 original film reels away in a lorry in a fit of frustration, these included* **PONTIANAK** *and its sequel* **DENDAM PONTIANAK**. *It is believed that the cinematic treasures were thrown either into a river or a mining pool. There are no known copies of the destroyed film reels."*

2 Without going into any detail, the Filem Klasik Malaysia blog (@ *http://filemklasikmalaysia.blogspot.ca/2012/10/pontianak-1957.html*) mentions that **PONTIANAK** was actually screened on US television at some point (presumably only in its native language?), but had no other information pertaining to this (to us) seemingly highly unlikely occurrence, but we thought we should throw it out there anyway.

3 In their efforts to cash-in on the hot new *pontianak* craze which was kick-started by Cathay-Keris' above-discussed first entry in '57 and continued with its two sequels, and presumably also in the process 'get their own back' for any lost revenue incurred by the upstart rival local outfit in town daring to give them some competition for once, the Shaw Brothers also made a largely only loosely-linked threesome of movies whose titles all contained the same trendy buzzword/prime selling point: **ANAK PONTIANAK** ("Son of the Vampire", 1958), **PONTIANAK KEMBALI** ("The Vampire Returns", 1963) and **PUSAKA PONTIANAK** ("The Vampire's Legacy", a.k.a. **THE ACCURSED HERITAGE**, 1965). Interestingly enough, no less than a Filipino director, Ramon Estrella—who was not normally known for making horror movies, but had a reputation for being a real fast worker, hence his hiring—was called in by Shaw Bros. to take the helm on the first pair of those latter three titles, the initial one of which even beat-out the final 'legit' Cathay-Keris series entry into local cinemas by two months (in February of '58). Indeed, such

was their all-fired eagerness to capitalize on the trend that the Shaws even succeeded in securing the services of Abdul Razak, author of the original *Pontianak* source stories—opportunistically luring him away from rival producer Ho Ah Loke in the process—to inject some extra B.O. clout into what was essentially the Shaws' blatant attempt to horn-in on and hog the action (as the Chinese brothers had very successfully been doing in the Malay market for quite some time up until that period, including producing/distributing a number of commercial hits starring ill-fated local mega-celeb P. Ramlee). Ironically enough, all three of the Shaw Bros. *Pontianak* series entries are still extant, while two-thirds of Ho's original Cathay-Keris trilogy that 'inspired' them have now gone extinct. But one sure beats none at all!

4 Other Malaysian films from the same period to utilize the *orang minyak* character were P. Ramlee's **CURSE OF THE OILY MAN** (*Sumpah orang minyak*, 1958), made for Malay Film Productions/Shaw Brothers, and R. Krishnan's **THE OILY MAN STRIKES AGAIN** (*Serangan orang minyak*, 1958), which was a Cathay-Keris production. Utilizing a far more outrageously fanciful variation of the 'same' monster—with garishly entertaining results—the frantic Hong Kong horror **THE OILY MANIAC** (油鬼子 / *You gui zi*, 1976, D: Ho Meng-hua), starred HK superstar "Danny" Lee Sau-Yin as the titular monster-man. Like the aforementioned **CURSE OF THE OILY MAN** and both this article's **HANTU JERANGKONG** and

The horned devil who, via an unholy pact, transforms P. Ramlee into the unsavory *orang minyak* in **CURSE OF THE OILY MAN** (1958)

HANTU KUBOR, THE OILY MANIAC was also a Shaw Bros. production. Much more recent Malay 'reboots' of this traditional supernatural entity from local lore (which also turns up in legends from Borneo and other countries in the Malay Archipelago too) can be found in **ORANG MINYAK** (2007, Ds: Jamal Maarif, C.K. Karan) and the spoof horror hybrid **PONTIANAK VS. ORANG MINYAK** (2012, D: Afdlin Shauki).

5 Iron (in the form of various [often mundane] objects) being used as an offensive/defensive weapon or immobilizing countermeasure against entities of the dark forces is common to folklores around the globe. For example, a later Asian film (yet another Shaw Bros. production, coincidentally enough) that features 'nailhead' monsters—in this case reanimated corpses—is "Homer Gaugh"/ Ho Meng-hua's **BLACK MAGIC PART II** (勾魂降頭 / *Gou hun jiang tou*, a.k.a. **REVENGE OF THE ZOMBIES**, 1976, Hong Kong). Its hideous undead creatures are either rendered dormant or else become active dependent on whether the six-inch spike (!) hammered into their skulls by the controlling black arts practitioner (Lo Lieh) is in the 'On' (i.e., in) or 'Off' (i.e., out) position.

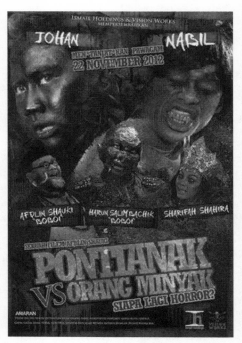

Below: A much-more-monstrous variation of the *orang minyak*, as seen in HK's nutty **THE OILY MANIAC** (1976)

THE GOOD, THE BAD, AND THE JUST PLAIN *UGLY*:

More-Recent Indian Ghostly Possession Films, Pt 2

reported by Tim Paxton

Without a doubt one of the best things about finding, watching, and eventually writing about obscure cinema is when something I have 'discovered' and experienced is totally new to me. For the most part, I don't have any prior knowledge of many of the titles I sit through. There are as many hits as there are misses, but whenever something does particularly strike my fancy, I feel both lucky and privileged to have seen it. When it comes to the Indian film industry, I don't listen to folks who trash horror films, new or old. The bigotry for most new horror films is strong with Indian fans, as I most often hear the deafening drone of comments like "It was a box office flop!" or "It's not as good as a Ramsay film!"—which tells me right away that, 1) they haven't seen the film or, 2) they are so closed-minded and living in the past that experiencing anything new is beyond their comprehension.

Come to think of it, kinda sounds a lot like movie fandom in the USA these days!

From this Westerner's faraway vantage point, it seems that much of what is considered a 'good' film in India happens to hinge on whether and where it was a success at the box office. There has been a literal plethora of horror films being churned out by the Indian film industries in recent years. So many, in fact, that it has been hard to keep up with all the recent releases. In typical Indian fashion, the films—be they shot in Hindi,

Tamil, Telugu, or whatever other language— there have been whole cartloads of promotional trailers flooding the internet promising new heights in terror to any unsuspecting theatregoer who just might happen to catch a title or two. Most make very bold, hyperbolic claims, boast fancy editing, show plenty of skin (or as much is allowable, anyway), and announce release dates that may or may not be very accurate. Some

Random "zombie" artwork used to used to promote numerous Indian horror films on YouTube

films, like the Tamil-made **YOOGAN** (2015, D: Kamal G.), did have all the trappings commonly seen in its trailer and online promotional artwork: a spooky corpse-like, messy-haired female spook with glowing eyes and cracked skin walking stiffly about a dreary landscape while terrified twentysomethings cower at the sight of her. The problem is that its announced release date of "April 2015" came and went without hide nor hair of a supernatural (or otherwise) nature making an appearance. As of this writing, according to a 2017 article by *The Times* of India,[1] this "Ghost story set in an IT company" seems to still be in production, and I have been waiting *three years* for **YOOGAN** to surface after reading a brief interview with its director Kamal G. online. In it, he touted the benefits of not using CGI to make a horror film. "To explore horror sequences, we avoided using VFX and instead shot everything with real makeup to make it an authentic experience for audiences. It's not that the end product looks bad in VFX, we just wanted it to appear realistic", he said. Oh boy, *that* bit sure made me sit up and take notice back in 2014! He then went on to add, "I believe this movie will set a different trend in the horror genre in Tamil cinema. I want to give audiences an overall Hollywood experience", he said.[2] Ahhhhh!

---

1 *http://timesofindia.indiatimes.com/entertainment/tamil/movies/news/Yoogan-is-a-horror-story-set-in-an-IT-company/articleshow/45004633.cms*

2 *http://www.bollywoodlife.com/south-gossip/real-make-up-over-vfx-in-horror-film-yoogan/*

Hmmmmm… Then, come 2017, my high hopes of seeing the film are once again dashed. Did it receive only a limited initial release and then get shelved, perhaps? No DVD, VCD or streaming release of the film that I know of has transpired to date. Maybe a dispute with the distributor was what caused it to get yanked from circulation? Or the producer for some reason put the kibosh on it? Who can say, as this sort of thing is a not-uncommon part of making films in any country, let alone within the notoriously fickle industries of the Subcontinent. For example, I was saddened to hear that, due to conflict with its producer/star (Rajasekhar), Ram Gopal Varma's recent Telugu horror film **PATTA PAGALU** (2015) has been indefinitely shelved.

STOP PRESS! Of course, right when I least expected it, what should I stumble upon to my pleasant surprise but a full-length upload of the (temporarily) 'lost' film **YOOGAN** available for viewing on YouTube! Yes indeed, it appears that, back in August of 2016, it received an official streaming release via Speed Video's YT channel (@ *www.youtube.com/user/SpeedTamilMovies*). However, I think I'll let that previous paragraph stand, if only because I sank too much research into it to simply let it fall by the wayside!

And now, without further ado, allow me to add this review of the film I thought I'd never get to see…

To put it bluntly, **YOOGAN** is a load of *rubbish*, which is probably why it got deep-sixed upon

In a move not unlike that of movies in the USA and other places worldwide, **YOGAN** *[sic]* played theatres for a brief period before being laundered out to satellite and streaming services in hopes of recouping its meager budget. Depicted above is one of the numerous promos for the film that popped up on the web via YouTube

As in many other countries' film industries, sometimes what might appear to be a surefire slam-dunk horror hit turns into a problem production that, for any number of reasons, winds up getting canned (if not in the good way!) and gets left unreleased. Trailers, pressbooks and posters might be prepared, all ready to go...and then, like Ram Gopal Varma's 2015 effort **PATTA PAGALU** *[above]*, the production is shelved, never to see the light of a projector

its first release in 2015. As the film plays out, we have a group of IT workers being stalked by a ghost associated with a deadly 'haunted' text message (*YAWN!*) that they each receive on their mobile phones. The film *stinks* to high heaven of Eric Valette's **ONE MISSED CALL** (2008), which itself was an inferior American remake of Takashi Miike's 2003 Japanese spook-shocker of the same Anglo title (a.k.a. 着信アリ / *Chakushin ari*). While any plot theft is not overly evident in the present film, there *is* also a(nother) deadly long-haired, sulking she-ghost who may (or may *not*) be responsible for the deaths of various characters in the film. As for the much-touted "*[we]* shot everything with real makeup to make it an authentic experience" claim by director Kamal G, all we get is a young actress with some white greasepaint slopped on her face, with nary even a *hint* of the classic albino eyes that are almost always associated with supernatural beings in these sorts of Indian films. And to make matters worse, it turns out that most of the killings in the film have actually been committed by a spiteful male character, and it isn't made clear if there ever even really *was* a ghost to begin with. There is absolutely *nothing* to recommend this film. I hate to trash any film in *Monster!*, and am always willing to try and find something positive to say about even the humblest cinematic offering, but **YOOGAN** really had it coming no thanks to all its advance cock-teasing—all come-on and no payoff—about a creepy ghost, which, ever-hopeful idiot that I am, I sat through two hours of absolute nothingness hoping to see…then, *phhhfffffttt!*

Director Kamal G., who wrote, directed, and produced **YOOGAN**, is not unlike many an indie filmmaker from other parts of the world. Reaffirming the old adage "Talk's cheap", they know how to hype-up their product, no matter how misleading and awful the end result turns out to be. (Bad Kamal G.! No biscuit!)

The blandness in Indian spook cinema continues with a string of Southern outings courtesy of Speed Audio & Video's YouTube channel (@ *www.youtube.com/user/SpeedAudiosAndVideos*]), where it seems that most of these films wind up unceremoniously dumped (no doubt saving on the cost of producing VCDs or DVDs of them). Titles including **THALAIYATTI BOMMAI** (Tamil, 2017; D: Bagavathy Bala) wherein a group of pals are tormented by a female ghost of the woman they *thought* they had killed and buried (another classy greasepaint ghost like the two that appeared in the 2012 Kannada Movie **NAGAVALLI** [see *Monster!* #32, pp.129-131]); **BOMMAI** (Tamil/Malaysian, 2017; D: V. Nagaraj) the ghost of a young girl possesses the young son of a terrified a couple by way of a blond-haired baby doll; the mind-numbimgly bad Tamil horror "comedy" **ADDAM LO DEYYAM** (2015; D: Satyanarayana Bachhu) **MOONDRU NAATKAL** (Tamil, 2017), in which a bus full of ghosts are on a mission to pick up, murder and then add living human passengers to their numbers (an interesting plot, if not all that well-executed); **PEI NADAMADUM PAGUDI** (Tamil, 2017), a film which offers some lush cinematography,

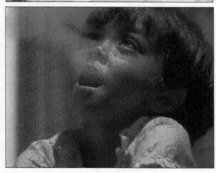

a fine score, and even believable effects work, despite the underwhelming directorial pacing by maverick Senkuttuvan (whose Anglo credit reads "Story, Screenplay, Dialouge *[sic!]*, Direction"); and **FEB 14**[TH] (Tamil, 2017, D: V.S. Phanindra). This latter title is a micro-budget ghost film involving three college-age friends who bed-down for the night in a dilapidated mansion, where they are soon terrified to discover that the ghost of a murdered child haunts the place, and it becomes up to them to put an end to the restless spirit's haunting. The film ends on an ambiguous note as the following words fade in after the closing scene: "Any doubts? Please wait... coming soon Feb-15" *Yeesh!* The, um, 'hideous' green-faced, bug-eyed ghost seen in **FEB 14**[TH] is played by Baby Prema, a young actress whose unsettling looks are possibly a result of some sort of real-life genetic disorder (such as Crouzon Syndrome, or maybe Graves' Ophthalmopathy, which is associated with thyroid disease, perhaps?). This would not the first time that a director (Indian, Italian, or otherwise) would utilize someone with a physical deformity in place of shelling-out for expensive practical or CG effects. (The shocking climactic scene where all the devils and demons—largely played by all-too-authentic human 'freaks'—convene in Michael Winner's occult shocker **THE SENTINEL** [1977, USA] comes to mind.) I must admit that, as distasteful as it may sound, the use of handicapped actors in lieu of special effects *does* work at a gut level, as an instinctive revulsion towards those 'unalike' us is deep-rooted in our human psyche, and it is this very same primal instinct that is often triggered when 'real' (i.e., fake) monsters show up on the screen to thrill and chill us.

Top: Tamil director Bagavathy Bala working the floor at the premiere event (held in Chennai, India) for his less-than-awesome 2017 ghostly possession thriller **THALAI-YATTI BOMMAI** (note poster), along with some of its cast and crew. **Center:** In the film, a greasepaint ghostess possesses a young man and goes on a vengeful rampage against the living. **Above:** A possessed child literally lets off some steam in the same Tamil/Malay co-production

As for the Southern shocker **BIDALARE** (Kannada, 2004, D: Ramana), it starts off promisingly enough when an amorous couple encounter a ghost during a thunderstorm. First the husband gets slaughtered by the unseen menace lurking outside their home when he goes to investigate a nocturnal noise. When he doesn't return to their bedroom, the wife also steps out into the rain, spots her late hubby's bloodied body, then herself also encounters the murderous creature (kept strictly *off*-camera, of course). She dashes madly back into the house, slamming the door behind her and using her body to bar it. We then see the monster's claw—which it rams clear through both she and the door—erupting from her belly, along with a vivid gusher of cheap CG gore. The police investigate, up pops some animated ghouls, and out of one of their maws comes the film's title. Cut abruptly to a song, and we're off and running!

If you're ready with your checklist of tropes, then sharpen-up your pencil and get ready to tick-off all that **BIDALARE** has to offer, cuz here we go…

A movie company decides to inject some local color into their production, so they send out a van filled with their most promising stars and best film crew to shoot a new musical production. Of course, their vehicle beaks down…near the site of the ghostly killings…so everyone piles out and they shortly 'happen upon' a local *baangla* to crash at. Subsequently, a member of the crew (Aravind Akash) meets and falls for a local beauty named Laxshmi (Keerthi Chawla) at the local village's Shiva temple, only to have the ghost kill the driver of the production company's van, whereafter everyone else in the party becomes suspect in his murder. However, there is always time for more songs and taking in the Southern atmosphere before the evil spirit decides it's time to possess Aravind and slaughter all the remaining folks in the village.

BIDALARE is made with surprising competence in spite of its micro-budget, with most of the production's finances seemingly funneled into the obligatory *filmi* sequences by K.M. Indra, aided by DP Babu Theja's rather lush cinematography. These are quite well-made toe-tapping ditties, ranging from the crowd-pleasing 'dance-off' numbers to Laxshmi's climactic sung pleas for divine intervention down at the local temple. This particular number is like many to be found in this subgenre of devotional horror, and similar acts of beseeching a boon from a deity can be seen in both Kodi Ramakrishna's influential

Top to Bottom: The evil spirit shows its ugly mug early on in Ramana's 2004 opus **BIDALARE**; the heroine of the film pleads to her god for the power to save her beloved from a ghost; the *aatma* in possession of a troubled young man; and finally, the ghost is separated from her victim once the local deity decides to bestow this boon

Yet another mindless YouTube promo banner, this one for **BIDALARE** (2004)

Telugu-language outings **AMMORU** (1995) and **DEVI** (1999), as well as in any number of other such films besides. **BIDALARE**'s equivalent is a rousing devotional hymn called "Sathyam Shivam", and it has the desired effects on the local deity (a Shaivist saint, I do believe [?]), which exorcises the *aatma* (roughly meaning "soul" or "spirit") of an angry wronged woman and sends her off for some much-needed *saṃsāra* (the cycle of reincarnation). If you happen to Google the English title of the film, **BIDALARE**, you may also find a link to another Kannada possession film called **NAANINNA BIDALARE**. That 1979 film by director Vijay is an early example of a Southern horror production which, along with A.E. Baby's **LISA** (Malayalam, 1978), helped pave the way for future Indian horror films in *all* of the indigenous industries nationwide.

And since we are currently down South, while we're at it we might as well take in Makam Manohar's **POURNAMI** (Kannada, 2007) which, despite sharing some of the same tropes as **BIDALARE**, lacks any real punch to its tale of a vengeful ghost. A(nother) van loaded with young college-age ladies are off on a botanical trip to the countryside. Wouldn't you know it—yep, you guessed it: the van breaks down!—and the girls have to seek shelter at an out-of-the-way village. Death soon descends on the students, and a ghostly "woman in white" appears to be the killer. To say the least, this dull dud's eventual wrap-up makes little sense, and it ends abruptly after our female *bhoot* ("ghost") possesses the body of a local police inspector, who then stabs the evil one with a special dagger. The film's odd post-dub, hackneyed editing and meandering storyline soured what could have been one of the more interesting entries in this subgenre of ghost films, but...*oh well*.

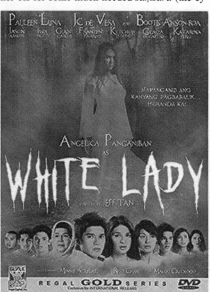

Spooks clad in white are a common motif in horror films and literature the world over. Jeff Tan's **WHITE LADY** (2006) is an example of the Filipino variation

As a bit of a historical side-note, some sources[3] point to Wilkie Collins' 1859 novel *The Woman in White* as having been an inspiration for much

3 For example, *https://in.bookmyshow.com/discover/movies/indian-cinemas-fixation-lady-white-saree-came-novel*

of what was to come later in Indian horror films featuring that quintessential "Indian ghost in a white *saree*". While this *might* well be the main inception point, ghost stories have always been popular within Indian literature (e.g., noted Bengali author Rabindranath Tagore penned quite a few before his passing in 1941), and I'm sure there are more-than-likely a whole assortment of urban legends that provided the *actual* source material. One of the earliest entries in the cinematic genre is Raj Khosla's 1964 **WOH KAUN THI?** ("*Who Was She?*"), a Hindi mystery thriller which is more psychologically-based than supernatural in content. In it, a young doctor (Manoj Kumar) is driving down a lonely stretch of road and offers a lone young woman (Sadhana Shivdasani) a ride. She asks to be dropped-off at a graveyard a short distance further onward, at which she exits the car then wanders through the tombstones singing a mournful love song. That pretty much sums-up many of the films to follow, no matter what Indian language they happened to be shot in. There is also a popular Southeast Asian ghost story about a scary hitchhiker which began to make the rounds in the Philippines during the 1950s, of which there are now innumerable regional variations all across the Islands.[4] While slightly different, and a heck of a lot less dreamily romantic than the usually beauteous Indian variant (in the Filipino version, the woman either has a hideous face, no face at all, or is entirely headless!), it does follow a decidedly similar pattern.[5] Made the same year as **WOH KAUN THI?** (1964), A. Vincent's Malayalam film **BHARGAVI NILAYAM** was India's very first ghost film featuring a highly self-aware spook. The ghostly white saree-draped spirit of a beautiful-but-sad deceased woman (Vijaya Nirmala) interacts with a young novelist staying at a haunted *mahal*. The film is based on the writings of noted southern author Vaikom Muhammad Basheer (1908-1994), who also penned its screenplay. In **BHARGAVI NILAYAM**, the audience not only witnesses a man watching spectral *bhoots*

Top to Bottom: A young man falls in love with a mysterious woman who turns out to be a ghost. A. Vincent's Malayalam film **BHARGAVI NILAYAM** was India's very first ghost film featuring a highly self-aware spook

mindlessly haunting a lonely location,[6] but the man can also communicate with the female ghost, and he eventually falls in love with her (and she him?), a timeless theme which has been enduringly popular in the movie industries of any number of countries/cultures from across the globe. For the Kannada films mentioned above, most especially in Manohar's **POURNAMI**), the 'singing-ghost-in-a-graveyard' motif has become all-too-familiar.

---

4 Filipino folklore and urban legends are full of monsters and ghosts, many of which have been turning up in their cinema since as at least as far back the 1940s (and even earlier). For more about the legend of the "White Lady" and the whole menagerie of other spirits that haunt the Islands, here's an interesting URL link: https://en.wikipedia.org/wiki/Ghosts_in_Filipino_culture.

5 Folktales and urban legends about spectral hitchhikers—primarily women, but not always—abound in other cultures, and have been especially popular in the US since the 1870s. – Fine, Gary Alan (April 1982), "The Vanishing Hitchhiker: American Urban Legends and Their Meanings", by Jan Harold Brunvand, Western Folklore, Western States Folklore Society. 41 (2): pp.156-157.

6 As seen in Tapan Sinha's 1960 Bengali film **KSHUDISTA PASHAN**, an adaption of Rabindranath Tagore's short story "The Hungry Stones". Said story would later be rehashed in the 1991 Hindi film **LEKIN...** which fleshed-out the tale somewhat—adding-in a reincarnation theme, for instance—but still managing to keep the central point of the spirit of a beautiful woman trapped in a cycle of what appears to be eternal spectral acts. Both these films are worth checking out if you are at all interested in the development of Indian ghost films.

But not *all* films from the Karnataka film industry share the same sort of classiness…

AA MARMA (Kannada, 2012. D: H. Madan) garnered some free publicity when its release was delayed by the regional Karnataka Film Chamber of Commerce (KFCC) due to the committee's claim that **AA MARMA** was dubbed into another language. The Indian state of Karnataka has strict and often confusing rules and regulations concerning the dubbing of Hindi, Tamil or Telugu films into Kannada. The KFCC and other "pro-Kannada organizations would join hands in opposing dubbing culture".[7] The film eventually made its way through the courts, however, and eventually got released theatrically in 2015. Not that **AA MARMA** had any noticeable positive effect on the box-office revenues of horror films for that year, mind you, as it floundered at theaters for a week before vanishing from the radar. The film is basically a crime drama with some black magic elements stirred into the mix. It includes scenes in which a ghostly woman sings, two guys sit around watching Sam Raimi's **THE EVIL DEAD** (1981, USA) on TV, and we also get a few exchanges between the angry female ghost and a crime-solving *tantrik*. The only real reason to watch **AA MARMA** is that it starred an ill-looking Rami Reddy, who appeared in more than his share of low-budget horror films from the 1990s until his passing in 2011 during the inauspicious present film's production. The monstrous ghost from Ram Gopal Varma's vastly superior Telugu horror film **DEYYAM** (1996) also makes an appearance, albeit via stolen footage, if that matters at all.

7 @ http://www.thehindu.com/todays-paper/tp-national-al/tp-karnataka/controversy-in-kannada-film-industry-over-release-of-aa-marma/article2317763.ece

As popular as Indian horror films still appear to be, the revenues from them do not seem to do so well beyond their initial theatrical runs once they have been released onto physical media. Sales of VCDs, DVDs and BDs just can't compare to the amount of films which are currently pirated or released directly to the web via YouTube (etc.) on select private and public channels (see this issue's editorial [p.6]). For anyone interested in catching a variety of Indian horror films, just Google "New Bollywood Horror Films" or "New Tamil Horror films" or what-have-you. Once you hit Enter, you'll virtually *drown* in all the online content!

And since I'm on the subject of new and *somewhat* new films here, **MAYA** (Tamil, 2015, D: Ashwin Saravanan) is a good-looking one both in cast and cinematography, but the tale tries to be much more complicated than it needs to be. *Still*, it remains one of the better Indian horror films to be made in the past few years. More importantly, it's one of the better Tamil productions that doesn't rely on idiotic humor to 'liven things up', nor a bad musical score to punctuate every moment of horror either (like all the usual Mickey-Mousing that goes on in much of the genre). The film also doesn't feature a "White Lady" from more traditional origins, and it is instead based more on folklore of the South (although the "Bloody Mary" reference is taken from a very old superstition here in the USA).

Films like **MAYA** are typically the exception to the rule in Indian cinema when it comes to the more recent popular box-office topic, ghostly possession. There are times when a novel approach is tossed aside for a bit of an amble down an old, familiar path, and the 2015 Hindi film **MAIN HOON EK RAAZ** is a prime example of

The black magic film **AA MARMA** features footage lifted from **THE EVIL DEAD** to spice things up

New Indian Monster Films, Pt 2 *Paxton*

what can be produced when the lowest common denominators of plot and budget are what's most important to a director and producer. In the case of Ravi Kumar Nivoriya's **MAIN HOON EK RAAZ**, it appears to be a film built by enthusiastic amateurs, which is not me being critical in a negative way, by any means.

As a point of context, the word *māyā* (माया) translates to "illusion", as in a power that Hindi deities and demons use in order to alter reality. The word has wiggled its way into Western consciousness by way of the New Age movement, a quasi, multi-faith belief system fabricated from various faiths, although its primary core is Hindi-based.[8] *Maya* figures heavily in New Age literature, and became increasing popular in the '70s as gurus and self-help philosophers worked the word into popular culture.[9] And in some cases this *māyā* is a permanent state of being. For devotional films, the word takes on an entirely different meaning, as it refers to the Goddess in any manner of Her aspects, although for the horror genre it is more in line with alternate reality or, as with Saravanan's **MAYA**, dipping into the fantastic world of folklore. *Māyā* can also be used as an alternate descriptor for *chudail* ("witch"), and has been utilized quite regularly over the years. One example of this form (which I covered in *Weng's Chop* #10 [pp.25-60]) can be seen in **MAYA MALIGAIL** (Tamil, 1980, D: Sajjan), a film which is a mash-up of the woman-in-white trope along with a crumbly-faced fanged corpse that kills whomever it wants to. It's also an exorcism film, which is based primarily on Christian practices (the Indian states of Tamil Nadu and Kerala each have sizeable Christian populations).

Then we have **NAAN MAYA** (Tamil, 2016, D: Vijay Surana). Not to be confused with the two previous films of similar title, this would-be spooker is a mediocre attempt at both titillation (due to a lengthy 'sexy' scene at the beginning of the film) and horror (the murder of a young woman during a lover's spat), leading to spectral rampage. Add in a jeepful of rowdy twenty-somethings out on a joyride in the country, the creepy caretaker of a local hotel and the ghost of a woman in a white *saree* singing sad songs, and you can pretty much guess what's going to happen next. The twist ending makes no sense, and I suspect that the producers wanted to wrap-up the production early and get **NAAN MAYA** into theaters for hit-and-run bookings as quickly as possible. The crystal-clear, utterly atmosphereless HD cinematography and flat direction make for an exceedingly *dull* 105 minutes indeed…but, looking on the bright side, at least that's quite a bit shorter than many Indian movies run for.

---

8   The New Age movement can be traced back to one individual, Ukranian-born "Bohemian" Helena Petrovna Hahn Blavatsky who, in the 1870s, along with American Henry Steel Olcott, formed the occult-based study group The Theosophical Society (roughly, "Divine Wisdom"). Much of her philosophy and occult knowledge came from her travels throughout India and Tibet, and that included the elements of *māyā* and—much-later-developed in the 1960s—a revival of the quasi-Mother Goddess-based Gaia religion through the "Wicca" movement, which seems to be a mishmash of Euro-Indo beliefs.

9   A good example of this is the slinky shape-changing humanoid femalien Maya (Catherine Schell), who appeared in the second season of Gerry Anderson's live-action UK sci-fi teleseries *Space:1999* (1975-77). I doubt many people who watched the show would associate her name to its actual meaning, and her 'magical' ability to morph into birds, monsters or other humans, which brought a weird paranormal aspect to the series.

Dramatic web promo art for the film **NAAN MAYA**

Promotional poster art for Prosit Roy's **PARI**

Just over the border to the north in Pakistan, we have yet another film with a similar name: Jawad Bashir's **MAYA** (a.k.a. **MAYA: A TRUE STO-RY**, 2017), which takes things in yet another di-rection… although it treads a path worn smooth by earlier filmmakers.

Despite all its promising prerelease promotion-al materials (various sneak-peek photos of the ghost, a nicely-put-together trailer on YouTube, etc.), this Urdu-language production turned out to be much like most of the other ghostly pos-session stories from that region of the world. The credits boast of its "Indie" cred and that the su-pernatural premise *is* based on proposed actual events (*YAWN!!*). As if the tagline "A True Story" will gull anyone into watching this painfully dull, drawn-out tale of an exorcism gone awry. As per the most popular genre trope—the same basic idea is common to horror fare from around the world—a group of friends (three men and two women) travel out to a remote vacation lodge, where they plan on kickin'-back, hangin'-out and chillaxin' a while. Of course, the lodge they have selected to stay at has a Christian cemetery located right next door (!), as well as a Catho-lic church with its resident priest. Seems that the recently-deceased Maya Joseph (this time a "Maya" in name only, with no apparent actual reference to the Hindi word intended) senses the group of twentysomethings partying it up next door, so she decides to rattle her chains, look sul-len and possess each of the humans that falls into her clutches. After a bit of spooky hanky-panky, the ghost proceeds to bump-off the kids one by one by way of violent possession.

MAYA: A TRUE STORY is not a *complete* waste of 90 minutes, as the image of the grimy ghost-in-chains with downcast, spooky-eyes makes for a strong visual (it's the only element in the film that was of any real interest to me). The mixture of Roman Catholicism in a predom-inantly Islamic film is interesting. But of course, the root of all the problems in it proves to be an RC exorcism which didn't turn out well. At one point, Ahmed, one of the young men in the group of friends, cries out, "*Bhoot! Djinn!* What *is* Maya?!" Clearly, she is a Christian ghost causing all their problems, and hence no one involved has any idea what to do about her.

Since we are on a roll with similarly titled films here, I will touch on two more. Both are called **PARI**, but that's where the similarities end.

The Hindi film **PARI: THIS IS NOT A FAIRY TALE** (talk about a godawful subtitle! But that's how Indian cinema rolls) is one of *the best* subcontinental horror films of the past ten years; heck, even since Ram Gopal Varma's **BHOOT** in 2003, for that matter! The film is given a lengthy review in *Weng's Chop* #11, but for the sake of this article (and its comparison to the Pakistani film) I'll briefly touch on its plot. A young man by the name of Arnab (Parambra-ta Chatterjee) encounters a dirty, near-starved woman named Rukhsana (Anushka Sharma) chained-up in a rundown hovel. He dutiful-ly releases Rukhsana and takes her home to his apartment to be cared for. Apparently, this doesn't sit to well with his fiancée, especially when Rukhsana decides that she has claimed Arnab as hers and sleeps with him. Strange things *really* begin to happen when Arnab uncovers the truth about his new ward/lover: that she is the offspring of an evil *shaitan*, the most powerful species of *jinn*. If that isn't bad enough, a demon-killer is hot on Rukhsana's scent, and he is determined to exorcise her… even if it kills her.

Prosit Roy's **PARI** is a decent film in more ways than one. Here we have a non-Hollywood pro-duction based more on local supernatural beliefs and folklore rather than the typical quasi-**EXOR-CIST** tropes that plague most of Indian horror cinema. It also lacks any song and dance num-bers, has little-to-no off-putting humor to lessen the mounting terror, and there is little in the way of histrionics when it comes to all the actors involved. A very solid effort!

Less can be said for its Pakistani namesake, as the entire budget for Syed Atif Ali's **PARI** seems to have been blown on its trailer and slick advertising campaign prior to its scheduled release on Halloween of 2017. However, the film was shelved and apparently recut for a later mid-Spring 2018 'rerelease'. I'm curious to know the what and why of it taking so long to get a release, but we will probably never know if the delay was intended to possibly save the film from becoming a total disaster. As it turned out, this **PARI** is about on par with Jawad Bashir's **MAYA**, in that it too only just manages to be interesting when the possessed little girl begins flexing her paranormal muscles. In both Hindi and Urdu, the word *pari* means "ethereal" (or "fairy" or "angel", depending on how it is applied). *Pari* is the diminutive form of the Persian name *Parisā*, which is a very old word indeed; pre-Islamic in origin and referring to a race of ancient malevolent fairy folk. One would think that, with this interesting bit of background, someone would be able to conjure-up a decent horror film about backwoods monsters taking-out a cabin full of unsuspecting teenagers or twentysomethings. Sound familiar? That could have been one way to approach the subject matter, no matter just how many times that particular plot has been recycled in the last thirty-odd years. Nope. Instead the film revolves around a couple, Mehwish (Azekah Daniel) and Shehram (Junaid Akhtar), and their daughter Pari (Khushi Maheen), who, after they move into a new house in the mountains, encounter a weird, *jinn*-like ghost. Of course, little Pari becomes possessed and must be exorcised by a decent Allah-fearing young man. For the majority of this micro-budget production we are exposed to serious overacting, a crappy musical score, mindless flat cinematography and sub-GameBoy CG. The film does eventually manage to shine for about two minutes during its drawn-out climax, though. The possessed little girl—now become a snarling, tangle-haired, ugly little monster—floats through the air in a weirdly cheap-but-effective manner. She glides through a dark foggy forest on her way to kill her father. This creepy sequence is the *only* bit of originality and funky coolness to be had in **PARI**. Sad to say, but true. So much potential, with little-to-nothing to show for it.

To wrap-up this article (oh, there will be *more* titles to explore next issue, don't you worry!), I present to you a *quadrilogy* of ghost films, all very different from one another, although all

four do approach classic themes of possession and exorcism. Despite some reservations, I can honestly recommend them all to anyone who is interested in seeing how good an Indian ghost movie can be when there is some actual money and creativity put into the production.

Only slightly less serious, but equally as fun, next up we have the romantic ghost film **PHILLAURI** (Hindi, 2017. D: Anshai Lal), a silly-but-sad tale of love, loss and longing. Goofball twentysomething Kanan has just returned home to India from Canada, and at long last he is expected to wed his exceedingly patient betrothed Anu. But before their marriage can proceed, Kanan must first get married to an, um… tree. *Why?* As is customary in some cultures around the globe, a man or woman born under an unlucky star sign, as Kanan apparently was, must undergo a magical ritual in order to be cleansed of any negative energy before they can marry an actual human spouse. By marrying the tree beforehand, Kanan can shed his *manglik* mantle.[10] Reluctantly, he follows through

10 From Wikipedia: *"There is a belief that the negative consequences for a single-*manglik *marriage can be resolved if the* manglik *first performs a ceremony called a* kumbh vivah, *in which the* manglik *"marries" a banana tree, a* peepal *tree, or a silver or gold idol of the Hindu God Vishnu."*

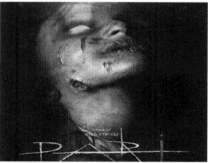

Promos for the Pakistani 'version' of **PARI** range from **EXORCIST**-based imagery *[top]* to something akin to Colin Hardy's 2018 hit **THE NUN** *[above]*

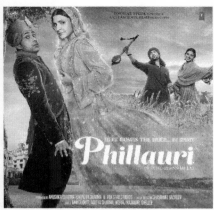

Cover for the CD soundtrack

look, originality and palatability. Even with its steady stream of comedic antics, **PHILLAURI** still manages to satisfy. One of the producers is Anushka Sharma, who also stars in the film as the restless spirit Shashi. Clean State Films has two additional productions in their new stable which are both very good. First is the grim possession shocker **PARI** (Hindi, 2018, D: Prosit Roy), one of the best Indian horror films to come along in the past year (along with U. Miliand Ru's 2017 **THE HOUSE NEXT DOOR**), which was reviewed in *Weng's Chop* #11. The other film on their roster is **NH10**, a violent 2015 thriller. Both films star Sharma and were 'inspired' by actual events. All three of these just-cited titles are worth watching if you get the chance.

with this ritual. However, unknown to he and the rest of this clan, the tree is home to the ghost of a woman named Shashi. And wouldn't you know it, after the simple custom is completed, the human and spirit are 'hitched'. Things gets weirder when Shashi realizes that only Kanan can see her, and she learns that he is about to be married *again*—this time to a mortal bride named Anu. Hilarity ensues, until we get the sobering backstory of how poor Shashi's spirit ended up stuck in the tree for more than a century. As these films go, there is a happy ending, so not everything is terrible in this world…or the next.

PHILLAURI is a good-natured supernatural comedy from Clean Slate Films, which, as of this writing, happens to be my favorite new Indian production company. Thus far their films have been top-notch when it comes to their overall

In a time when most new horror movies look as if they were just shat out of a digital camcorder, it's surprising to find one that is truly a joy to behold. **EZRA** (2017, D: Jay K) is a Malayalam-language ghost possession film which is just that, as well as being interesting culturally speaking, with a novel twist to its plot. I have written about the multicultural aspect of India in many of my past articles and reviews. For most of the past 2,500 years of its history, India has been—for the most part; every country has its dark periods of history—a country that is tolerant of its multicultural status. Christianity reached its southern shores in around 50 C.E. and established a congregation which is still active to this day. Prior to that in 562 B.C.E., it is believed by most historians that traders from Judea arrived in the city of Cochin, Kerala. There is also some evidence (although flimsy) that Jewish traders settled in India during the time of King Solomon

India's 'version' of **PARI** stars Anushka Sharma, who is seen here as the restless she-spirit Shashi in the 2017 Hindi spooky rom-com **PHILLAURI**

In 2017's **EZRA**, concerned husband Ranjan Mathew (Prithviraj Sukumaran) consults a Jewish mystic, Rabbi Marques (Sujith Shankar), about the possible possession of his beloved wife by an evil Semitic spirit known as a *dybbuk*

as far back as *circa* 970 B.C.E. Still more arrived around the same time as the first Christian wave when the Romans destroyed the Second Temple.[11] There were various waves of Jewish immigration from the 1400s into the early 1800s. Unlike in other parts of the world, there was and is very little anti-Semitism among most Indians, although due to modern world affairs, most Jews emigrated to Israel in the late 1940s, leaving only a tiny minority in Kerala and the city of Mumbai. History lesson aside, **EZRA** is unique in Indian cinema in that it is a multi-faith film which takes a somewhat intelligent approach to the age-old problem of exorcising ghosts from folks.

The fictionalized world of **EZRA** is set in Kerala, where the 'last Jew' of the city has died, and his passing is reported as important news. However, before the late Rabi's relatives can lay claim to his worldly possessions, many of his more valuable items are carted-off by an unscrupulous art dealer…including an odd locked box covered in Hebrew text and sporting a large Star of David on its facing. There is something highly *unusual* about this container, as one of the merchant's assistants discovers when he attempts to open it. He is attacked by a violent force…most likely a powerful ghost or spirit that dwells within the antiquated chest.

Yes, it's a "dybbuk box".

For those of you not in the know, the term *dybbuk* refers to a spirit or ghost of Jewish origins, typically that of a lover or loved one who refuses

to dissipate after death and "cleaves" itself to a living human being.[12] The classic tale of the *dybbuk* is based on ancient Jewish folklore, and was popularized when playwright S. Ansky penned his popular play "The Dybbuk" in 1920. The play was later made into a 1937 Yiddish-language Polish film entitled, what else, **THE DYBBUK** (רעד ‏קוביד‎ / *Der Dibuk*), directed by Michał Waszyńs-

12 A gross oversimplification of a complex theological thought; here's a link to a scholarly page that has a depthier explanation of just what a *dybbuk* is: *https://www.jewishvirtuallibrary.org/dibbuk-dybbuk*

Original promotional flyer for the 1937 Yiddish-language Polish film **THE DYBBUK**

11 @ https://en.wikipedia.org/wiki/History_of_the_Jews_in_India.

One of many such prerelease internet promotional ads for the Malayalam-language ghostly possession film **EZRA**

ki (see *Monster! International* #3 [1993], p.38). Many decades later, the Sam Raimi-produced horror film **THE POSSESSION** (2012, USA, D: Ole Bornedal) helped kick-start a mini "Dybbuk Box" boom on various blogs and sites such as Reddit. Sales of so-called 'authentic' wine cases or other antique containers allegedly housing dybbuks popped-up on eBay for a short while before the mini-craze abated.

Arriving late to the party, so to speak, one of these spiritual reliquaries is central to **EZRA**, and it represents the film's curious and somewhat respectful—albeit also highly theatrical—approach to Judaism as it is perceived in India. Ghostly possession is nothing new to Indian culture, as the god Hanuman is often called upon to lend an assist with the exorcisms of those unfortunate enough to have an unwanted spirit inhabiting their body. Like it was elsewhere, William Friedkin's **THE EXORCIST** (1973, USA) was a huge influence on the Indian horror genre, as its Catholic exorcistic rituals were as exotically alien as they were exciting. Hugely influential even to this day, the violent exorcism from the Friedkin classic is often coupled with images from Japanese ghost films (by way of their American remakes, no less!) and such recent entries as the *Conjuring* franchise. In the case of **EZRA**, we find out that the evil intent of the spirit released from the box is a lot more diabolical than merely its possession of a young woman, and the ultimate 'payback' planned by the *dybbuk* for an earlier injustice is truly monstrous in scope.

Traditionally, the Judaic method of expelling an ill-mannered spirit from an afflicted 'possessee' proceeds along similar lines to those often em-ployed by Hindu holy men—although very few Indian films opt to portray it, instead preferring the more dramatic and showy Christian variety. In most Jewish and Hindu traditions, the exorcist serves more as a simple spiritual 'counselor' rather than actually attacking the demon or ghost directly. As seen in the classic Indian horrors **JADU TONA** (Hindi, 1977, D: Ravikant Nagaich), **GEHRAYEE** (Hindi, 1980, D: Aruna Raje) and **AADIVARAM AMAVASYA** (Telugu, 1987, D: A.G. Baby), the presiding priest sits down with the possessed subject and begins asking the spirit within them a whole string of questions. In this manner, the priest hopes to eventually discover the reasons behind the possession. The marked difference between the antagonists of most Christian exorcisms and those rooted in the Hindu or Judaic practices is that the exorcist is dealing with a *ghost* rather than a demon or devil. A ghost possessing someone of the Hindu faith is not necessarily evil; it's just pissed-off and looking for answers, and the problems it causes for the living is just its way of getting attention. It's a bit different when Islamic exorcisms are in play, as many of these involve a very different kind of entity: the *jinn*. But discussing those films will have to wait for a future issue of *Monster!* (and, yes, I *do* have an article in the works!).

Another interesting note to the film is that three of its main characters are from different religions. While this is no major stunner (decades earlier in 1989, the Ramsays' **PURANI HAVELI** featured a Christian family confronting an Indian demon), mixed marriages are still a novel idea to Indian filmmakers, who seem to have a hard time passing-up all the emotional histrionics that can spring from inter-faith drama.[13] Still, the supernatural angle isn't new, as C.A. Kincaid's 1936 short story "The Old Graveyard at Sirur" weaves together an interesting tale of ill-fated love-gone-awry…and ghosts.[14] In **EZRA**, we have the protagonist Ranjan Mathew (Prithviraj Sukumaran), who is Hindi but married to a Christian woman by the name of Priya Raghuram (Priya Anand). Their union mirrors the troubled life of the exceedingly unfriendly *dybbuk* which, in the early 1940s, had been a Jewish man by the name of Abraham Ezra (Sudev Nair), who fell in love with a poor Christian girl (Ann Sheetal). Theirs was not a happy relationship, and it ended in tragedy due to bigotry and miscommunication, resulting in Ezra's soul being transferred into the *dybbuk* box by dark Kabbalahic magic (incidentally, Vikram Bhatt's Hindi exorcism thrillers **1920** [2008] and **1921** [2017] also deal with mixed marriages and ghosts).

LAKSHMI BOMB (Telugu, 2018. D: Karthikeya Gopalakrishna) is a Southern come-

13 A few choice examples includes the 1991 American/British co-production **MISSISSIPPI MASALA** (D: Mira Nair) starring Saritha Choudhury (Hindu), Denzel Washington (Christian), and Raj Kapoor's 1973 Hindi classic **BOBBY**, which stars Rishi Kapoor (Hindu) and Dimple Kapadia (Christian), as well as Mani Ratnam's **BOMBAY** (Tamil, 1995), starring Arvind Swamy (Hindu) and Manisha Koirala (Muslim).

14 C.A. Kincaid (1870-1954) was a British-born author who lived in India for most of his life. He penned a number of supernatural tales, some of which can be found in his collections *The Tale of the Tulsi Plant and Other Stories* (1908), *Deccan Nursery Tales; or, Fairy Tales from the South* (1914), *Tales from the Indian Epics* (1918), *The Tales of Old Sind* (1922) and other such books. I first became aware of his work via *Ghost Stories from the Raj* (2002) edited by Uttarakhand-based author Ruskin Bond.

dy which could have been *so* much better, but as these things go the end result is satisfying enough. Lakshmi (played by Lakshmi Manchu, an actress known in the States for her role on NBC's early 2000s TV show *Las Vegas*, as well as for appearances on ABC's *Boston Legal* and *Desperate Housewives*) is a tough-as-nails female judge who butts heads with a violent criminal mob boss named Vaikuntam (Prabhakar) and eventually gets him convicted on a numerous sex-trafficking charges. If life in the Indian judicial system isn't already tough enough for a single, sexy woman, Lakshmi must also deal with her parents (Posani Krishna Murali and Hema) at home, where she is constantly reminded by her folks that she is an unattached daughter who *should* go out and find herself a man. After some badgering from her parents, she agrees to meet up with an eligible bachelor at the local Shiva temple for a chaste late-night *randevú* ("rendezvous") There, Lakshmi—all dolled up to the nines in her best *saree*—meets a handsome young chap who (*D'OH!*) turns out to be an assassin for the mob boss, and he proceeds to stab her to death. But this wouldn't be a decent southern horror-comedy if there wasn't a sexy ghost on show, now would it?! Hence, the murdered Lakshmi returns from the grave to seek vengeance, hunting down and dispatching the evildoers one by one.

LAKSHMI BOMB was slammed (and even outright *hated*) by many critics, and some of it was with good reason. The negative reviews had less to do with the movie being a celebration of women's empowerment and dealing with worldwide issues like female dependency on men, corruption, gender bias, sex-trafficking and so forth, and more because the plot was just too *compli-*

Ghostly revenge is key in the horror-comedy **LAKSHMI BOMB**

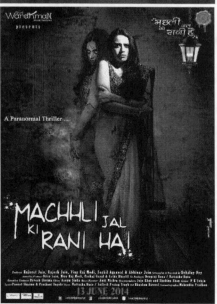

cated for its own good. There's a surprising twist to the plot, which I won't give away, and I must admit I was confused when it happened. It's a rather convoluted revelation, despite making perfect sense if you examine many of the *aatma* ("spirit")-based films made over the past 50-odd years in India. After the end credits had long since rolled, and I'd thought about the film for a couple of days afterwards, I came to the conclusion that, despite some of its silliness (and pretty *awful* comedy scenes), **LAKSHMI BOMB** just managed to squeak by onto my list of good ghost movies.

Another decent possession film which critics hated and I enjoyed was Debaloy Dey's **MACHHLI JAL KI RANI HAI** (Hindi, 2014), a neatly made production which, for our readers in the USA, is currently playing on Netflix. My major complaint was that the plot involves the possession of a young woman by *multiple* spirits, but I found this take on the entire subgenre refreshing, especially in scenes involving an obsessive *tantrik* by the name of Ugra Pratap Singh, who has been tracking the errant *aatmas* for decades. After losing sight of the ghosts during a harrowing battle with a possessed young woman, Singh is later arrested and found guilty of slaughtering his entire family. Of course, *we* know it was the ghosts that were actually responsible. A kind-hearted psychiatrist who suspects paranormal activity is afoot manages to get the court to send the *tantrik* to a psychiatric facility rather than sentence him to capital punishment. Years later, he has a chance to face the malevolent ghosts again when he is released on limited parole in custody of the doctor who had him committed. It seems that the evil *aatmas* have returned and are terrorizing another innocent family…

The Ugra Pratap character is brilliantly played by Deepraj Rana, who had appeared as Inspector Rana in Vikram Bhatt's **CREATURE 3D** (Hindi, 2014), as Dr. Saxena in Puja Jatinder Bedi's bloody good **GHOST** (Hindi, 2012), and as Inspector Sunil in Vinod Pande's 2007 Hindi female serial killer thriller **RED SWASTIK**).

Left, Top: Dramatic poster for **LAKSHMI BOMB**, which harkens back to the popular "Angry Goddess" films of the late '90s-to-mid-'00s (a subgenre of fantasy/horror cinema which I covered extensively in *Weng's Chop* #4 [pp.126-154]). **Left, Bottom:** Poster for the 2014 multiple-ghost possession film **MACHHLI JAL KI RANI HAI**

The Many Faces Of Evil: In Debaloy Dey's **MACHHLI JAL KI RANI HAI** (2014), heroic *tantrik* Ugra Pratap (Deepraj Rana) gets hot on the trail of a gang of errant ghosts that take up residence in unwilling living human hosts. He tracks down these evil spirits and lays them to rest with his portable mini-*trishula* ("holy trident")

It's a pity that **MACHHLI JAL KI RANI HAI** did so poorly at the box office, and that the tormented character of *tantrik* Ugra Pratap wasn't popular enough to warrant a sequel—nor even his own spinoff series on Netflix, either. (Now *there*'s an idea I can float out when I meet with some folks in India later this year. *Hmmmm…*)

Now, if there is one Indian supernatural thriller that you simply *must* see, then it is **TUMBBAD** (Hindi, 2018, Ds: Rahi Anil Barve, Anand Gandhi, Adesh Prasad), an Indian/Swedish—of all things!—co-production which, without a doubt and hands-down, is the *best* horror film in decades. That is, if you're like me and choose to lump it into that genre. The matter of genre is a funny thing for most Indian critics, it seems. Each one is a fundamental thing that should not be cross-pollinated with others. Most of what I review in *Monster!* falls into what I like to call the fantastic subgenre of non-fiction cinema, and it includes the Indian-approved genres of horror, fantasy, supernatural, fantasy, and in some instances devotional and mythological. **TUMB-**

BAD clearly straddles the horror and supernatural definitions simultaneously. The film is set in pre-Independence India at the rural town of Tumbbad, which is located just outside of Pune City. A young man obsessed with making a better life embarks on a deadly mission of enriching himself by stealing gold coins from a deathless creature that lives in the cellar of his ancestral *mahal*. Sounds rather like a Ramsay horror movie, doesn't it?! In a way, it is *sort* of like one of those classical hoary tales from Bollywood circa 1980s. However, in this case, there is precious little time wasted on slapstick humor or a rousing score by Ajit Singh or Bappi Lahiri. Instead we have a near-perfect folk horror tale of terror. More about this film in the next issue of *Monster!* For now, you'll just have to take my word on it: **TUMBBAD** is *not* to be missed, and it should be a prime contender for 2018's Oscar for Best Foreign Film.

LAST-MINUTE ADDITION...

UNAKKENNA VENUM SOLL
a.k.a. **PAAPA**
(Tamil, 2015. D: Srinath Ramalingam)

To put a new spin on an old adage, you can't always judge a movie by how its promotional department markets the product! That statement seldom rings truer than when it comes to Indian cinema. Honestly, I've often been baffled by how so many Southern Indian films are promoted, and it was purely by chance that I happened to luck upon some brilliant horror movies whose nondescript VCD covers were dominated by the broad grins or sexy smiles of their lead actors rather than highlighting any actual horrific elements. Had I not suspected they were ghost films simply by recognizing a telltale word or two in the title, I would have missed out on them completely. The same can be said about Srinath Ramalingam's **UNAKKENNA VENUM SOLL,** which, judging by one of its posters *[at right]* appears to be 'only' a romantic drama. However, had I not taken the plunge and checked the flick out on Netflix, I would have overlooked a fairly decent Tamil ghost yarn. Not a *great* one, mind you, but at least one that's different enough to be passably engaging. The film opens with a woman haunted by the ghost of a child who sings "Twinkle, Twinkle, Little Star" then giggles gleefully after slitting the woman's throat. *Not* a promising beginning, but I stuck with it anyway. The action then cut to a scene showing a street exorcism, and I was increasingly intrigued...

As the film unspools, we are introduced to a young couple, Pooja and her husband Shiva, who travel to Chennai seeking medical care for their gravely ill son Abhi. The couple stay at Pooja's ancestral *bangla* ("guest house"), and that's when the haunting begins. Toss in what I thought was a one-off comedic character who turns out to be the lynchpin of the movie (which has a highly satisfying and unusual ending), and **UNAKKENNA VENUM SOLL** manages to pull-off the impossible, emerging as a decent Tamil horror effort that doesn't rely on any witless 'humor' or horrible song-'n'-dance numbers to keep you entertained (not that I'm a fan of either of those two things, mind you). The ghost-girl injects some real pathos, and its Hindu

exorcist protagonist teams-up with a psychologist to straighten-out the whole paranormal mess. But there's a price to be paid...

This film was also released under the alternate title of **PAAPA**. The artwork *[at left]* for that release was much more in-line with what I would have expected from a ghostly horror film. Who knows *what* the distributors were thinking when they opted for that other totally bland and generic poster depicted above?!

CHANNEL OF DARKNESS

(CHAPTER 2)

by Stephen Jilks

[with Endnotes on pp.137-145]

Part I: Back to the Dark Ages | Ripping Yarns, Social Ruin & Hidden Agendas

"Fear is the mother of foresight." |– Thomas Hardy

"Doctor, witchcraft is dead*! And discredited. Are you bent on reviving forgotten horrors?"* |– Patrick Wymark as The Judge in **THE BLOOD ON SATAN'S CLAW** (1971)

Since the Whitechapel murders, what few facts of the case there are have routinely been shoved aside for the sake of lurid sensationalism. Over the not-really-so-very-many decades since the much-documented atrocities were committed, that horrible 'human monster' *[not* M!*'s favorite kind* ☺ *– ye eds.]* unpopularly dubbed "Jack the Ripper" has cast his (or, er…*her*?) foreboding shadow over countless films and television programs (etc.) which have largely been firmly rooted in one of the first-ever examples of lurid, sensationalistic tabloid journalism that appealed to the lowest common denominator. Plot devices are often conjure up out of thin air in the interests

of simple dramatic effect rather than for veracity's sake, though the firm facts are so thin on the ground that, for the purposes of obfuscation, any adaptation will out of necessity shroud them in dense layers of London fog which are not easily dissipated with a mere wave of the hand.

An enduringly popular misconception is that the killer was a royal surgeon who wore a top hat and cape, and carried a large black bag of shiny surgical instruments about with him. The Sir William Gull/Coachman Netley/Third Man Conspiracy has its origins in a 1970 article in *The Criminologist*, and despite Gull being a physician who

No Slashers Allowed? *(D'OH!)*: A vintage illustration of a pair of London bobbies discovering one of The Ripper's victims

never practiced as a surgeon—or indeed was ever a Freemason, either, contrary to common belief—threads were nevertheless woven into Alan Moore's centennial exploration for he and artist Eddie Campbell's hit graphic novel *From Hell* (1989-99), which was adapted for the big screen by The Hughes Brothers in 2001, starring Johnny Depp. In reality, the only known detailed description of the murderer said that The Ripper had "the appearance of a sailor", and actual evidence is limited to the findings in the murder cases of five prostitutes, all of whom were murdered within one square mile of Whitechapel between August 31st and November 9th of 1888.

Among the more fanciful and fantastical hypotheses to be posited regarding the perpetrator(s?) of the Ripper killings is that he, she—or even *it*—was impelled by supernatural forces… up to and including possibly even being a literal demon from hell rather than just a figurative one. At the other end of the scale, just for laughs in Joe Dante's "Bullshit or Not?" vignette of the multi-director schlock movie spoof **AMAZON WOMEN ON THE MOON** (1987, USA), stone-faced guest host Henry Silva—with tongue planted firmly in sinewy cheek—posits the question, "Was Jack the Ripper actually a sixty-foot sea serpent from Scotland?" to support his postulation ("…using undiscovered evidence" [!]) that perhaps "Nessie", the fabled Loch Ness Monster—as played by a 'life-size' animatronic amphibious saurian dressed in XXL Victorian gent's attire—might have been

responsible for committing the Whitechapel Murders. (We don't doubt there are even those out there—*waaaay* out there!—somewhere who would with a straight face blame the so-called Jack's dastardly deeds on Reptilians and/or extraterrestrials!) That said, in reality, some of the more amusingly far-fetched actual human suspects have included Charles Lutwidge Dodgson (the real name of author Lewis Carroll [1832-1898]) and Lord Randolph Churchill ([1849-1895] the father of Sir Winston). Carroll was thought to have had an unhealthy fixation with virginal purity—hence his reported unhealthy predilection for prepubescent girls—though it is unclear why this would have made him a viable suspect (unless perhaps he came to pathologically resent the lack of it in the "impure" fallen women who were The Ripper's primary prey?), and Churchill seems to be mentioned only because his political career was cut short by a fatal bout of neurosyphilis. American crime writer Patricia Cornwell "staked her reputation" by naming British artist and longstanding Ripper suspect Walter Sickert ([1860-1942] an *avant-garde* painter) as Jack. The authoress bought 31 of Sickert's works—even controversially tearing-up one canvas—and claimed that some contained visual references to the crimes; according to Cornwall, Sickert was impelled to become a killer due to having had a defective penis. (Presumably, according to Dr. Thomas Stowell, implicators of Randolph Churchill and Cornwall, afflictions of the genitals makes for a potential killer?)

Stowell's *Criminologist* article set in motion a frenzied flurry of Ripper activity in the early '70s. Hammer, for example, released not just one but two abstract Whitechapel tales simultaneously in October of 1971: Roy Ward Baker's gender-bending horror hybrid **DR. JEKYLL & SISTER HYDE** incorporates certain aspects of the case, albeit adding a science-fictional slant by simultaneously incorporating elements of R.L. Stevenson's oft-adapted novella *Strange Case of Dr. Jekyll and Mr. Hyde* (1886); while Peter Sasdy's **HANDS OF THE RIPPER** sees Jack's innocent adolescent daughter Anna (played by elfin Middlesex-born Welsh actress Angharad Rees [1944-2012]) carrying on the family 'tradition' by taking up where her dead daddy left off, and the narrative steers things in a potentially even more paranormal/supernatural direction ("She is what I would call *possessed*", opines a short-lived medium, rightly or not). But is it actually a case of spiritual possession by Jack's ghost, or only pathological/psychological in origin, caused by a deep-seated genetic mental disorder along the lines of schizophrenia…?

In his writings, the learned Stowell drew comparisons between The Ripper's ghastly evisceration of his female victims and the disembowelment of deer hunted by the aristocracy on their estates, and surmised that—although he was not named directly—Prince Albert Victor went mad after contracting syphilis in the West Indies, and was his Royal Ripper of choice.

Jack the Ripper (aired July 31st to August 17th, 1973) was a six-part BBC "documentary investigation" which intermixed period reenactments with contemporary sleuthing from fictional Detective Chief Superintendents Barlow (Stratford Johns) and Watt (Frank Windsor), characters who were popular on the police drama series *Z-Cars* (1962-78) and its spinoffs *Softly, Softly* (1966-69) and *Barlow at Large* (1971-75). This cross-pollination discusses suspects, forensic examinations and conspiracies in stuffy *ad infinitum*, and after five hours of milking the subject matter for all it was worth—which wasn't always very much—correctly concludes that there is insufficient evidence to determine who the murderer was. Despite this anticlimactic comedown—which should have come as no surprise at all to any viewers who were knowledgeable about the sparse actual known facts of the case—the experiment was deemed a success, and the formula was repeated in 1976 with *Second Verdict*, in which Barlow and Watt tackled various miscarriages of justice and more unsolved mysteries from the past.

Written by Elwyn Jones and John Lloyd, the 1973 *Jack the Ripper* laid the foundation for the alleged Masonic influence—after all, Supt. Watt *has* read Commissioner Warren's autobiography, and Warren was himself a prominent Mason—with an analysis of the misspelled/grammatically incorrect message scrawled on a wall that reads: "The Juwes are The men That Will not be Blamed for nothing" *[sic]*. With no substantiation of the Ripper crimes, let alone Freemasonry being involved in any way, this fixation with the wall-scrawl on Goulston Street is one of only many blind alleys which the program creates for itself (and of course for the viewer, too). And just when you think no more information could be squeezed in, the show's surprise witness is held back until the final moments: namely Joseph "Hobo" Sickert, the illegitimate son of aforementioned Ripper suspect/painter Walter. In a self-scripted sequence shot on Super-8, Joseph recalls his strange genealogy and supports Dr. Stowell's claims.

With this bombshell, the *East London Advertiser* sent young reporter Stephen Knight to interview "Hobo". Fleshed-out to become his bestseller *Jack the Ripper: The Final Solution* (London: George G. Harrap & Co. Ltd., 1976), in it Knight detailed an elaborate conspiracy theory involving both the British royal family and the ever-mysterious Freemasons. He concluded that

Looking Daggers: French *affiche* ("poster") for Hammer's 1971 cult 'split personality' shocker starring Ralph Bates and Martine Beswick(e) *[see pp.215-223]*

Rustic Gothic: In "The Withered Arm", the premiere episode of BBC's well-respected six-part series *Wessex Tales* (1973), a new bride (Yvonne Antrobus) suffers a strange, inexplicable blight *[above]* on her left forearm—that may or may not be the result of a witch's hex—for which a macabre supernatural cure is prescribed by a country bumpkin "conjuror" (Esmond Knight). **Next Page:** *Devilskin?* Four screen-shots from **THE BLOOD ON SATAN'S CLAW** (1971)

the victims were murdered to cover up a secret marriage between the then-second-in-line to the throne, Prince Albert Victor, Duke of Clarence and Avondale (1864-1892) and common working class Catholic shopgirl Annie Crook. Crook and the couple's daughter were consequently spirited away, and a quintet of Whitechapel prostitutes—who became privy to the information through the employment of one of their number (Mary Kelly) as the child's Nanny—were disposed of by a team of high-profile assassins. However, when Knight's misinformation went so far as to implicate Walter Sickert more than was to his descendent Joseph's liking, "Hobo" withdrew his cooperation and claimed he had only made everything up!

The mass-produced pulp "penny dreadfuls" of the late 19th and early 20th Centuries had a field day exploiting and capitalizing on The Ripper's abominable exploits, as well as those of the likes of Spring-Heeled Jack and Sweeney Todd, The Demon Barber of Fleet Street, irremovably ensconcing ghastliness, monstrosity and the macabre in the annals of human experience and helping found a long-lasting fascination for Horror Culture within us.

****

During the same year the Whitechapel Murders were committed, in his volume of collected stories *Wessex Tales* (1888), Thomas Hardy wrote of the true nature of 19th Century marriage and its inherent restrictions on both parties *[see Endnote #1]*, and a medical profession which could not cope with even the most minor diseases. Hardy did not explore the sensibility of Jane Austen or the caricatures of Charles Dickens; rather, his poems and novels are filled with characters that are as functional and rustic as their clothes, following the hardened edge of nature and the intractable workings of Fate. There is also a sense of enigma, that something beyond our physical appearance is guiding us into a relentless decline, and upon occasion, themes of the macabre, grotesque and monstrous found their way into Hardy's prose. For many Britons of a certain age, one *Wessex* tale in particular—"The Withered Arm"—is particularly remembered as an oddity of their school experience. Often included on English Literature syllabuses, it awkwardly straddles the wobbly divider between ambiguous morality tale and surreal horror.

Wessex Tales was adapted into a BBC anthology; the first episode shown was "The Withered Arm" (airdate: November 7th, 1973, D:

Desmond Davis), and it is a true masterpiece of the form. In a rural community, wealthy merchant farmer John Lodge (Edward Hardwicke) returns home with his new young bride Gertrude (Yvonne Antrobus). Gertrude awakes one morning to find a row of painful, sore-like welts on her left forearm ("It looks almost like *fingermarks*... It is as if some witch or the Devil himself had taken hold of me there and blasted the flesh!"), lesions which progressively worsen, lessening the young woman's desirability in her husband's eyes. Willing to resort to superstitious means if necessary in hopes of alleviating her chronic condition, out amid the wilds of local Egdon Heath, Gertrude consults Conjuror Trendle (Esmond Knight) with a reluctant assist from weathered milkmaid Rhoda Brook ([Billie Whitelaw] "Some do say she's a *witch*!"). Generally a specialist at clearing up more minor blemishes such as warts and the like, Trendle realizes that Gertrude's gradually withering arm is out of his league ("'Tis o' the nature of a blight, not a wound", he explains), and prescribes a ghoulish cure: "You must touch with a limb the neck of a man who's just been hanged, 'fore he's cold, just after he's cut down". It transpires that Rhoda's 18-year-young son Jamie (William Relton) is the illegitimate spawn of Lodge, and it is he who is hanged for a frivolous reason. The hangman (Paul Hardwick), who is sympathetic to Gertrude's plight and ready to give her aid— for a price!—arranges things so that the afflicted woman can attempt to affect a cure for herself as prescribed by the aging conjuror. However, more than one shocking revelation awaits her (and us!), in rapid succession...

Occurring in the wee small hours just as the clock strikes 2:00 a.m., Rhoda's unnerving dream of a grotesquely grinning Gertrude taunting her with her wedding ring sets the tale in motion, as Rhoda angrily grabs the new bride's arm before awakening with a start; the former character's performer Whitelaw holds the distinction of being perhaps the only actress ever to make milking a cow appear ethereally sinister! A mix of jealousy, a sense of loss and creeping body horror ("It is making me *ugly*!"), Gertrude is the 'Gothic Outsider', not just existing in an unfamiliar world, but an ultimately unwanted one: being barren, she cannot bear children. Dramatized by Rhys Adrian, who was greatly indebted, tonally speaking, to such period brutal rural horrors as Michael Reeves' **WITCHFINDER GENERAL** (1968) and Piers Haggard's **THE BLOOD ON SATAN'S CLAW** (1971, both UK), Gertrude wanders wearily through the bracken and over

ploughed furrows of earth, her physical affliction a close relation to that latter film's evil-afflicted characters' yearning for devilskin *[see Endnote #2]*. As well as dabbling in themes of witchcraft and folk medicine, the present program is also enveloped by the whole hanging ethic—unsurprising, as Hardy himself was an enthusiastic spectator of such public executions. This is illustrated by locals jostling for position to see the noose being tied, and an old man selling hanged figurines made of whittled wood as souvenirs of the event.

Stephen Jilks   *Channel of Darkness*   **97**

The final screened *Wessex Tale* (i.e., sixth of six) was "Barbara of the House of Grebe" (airdate: December 12th, 1973). In yet another Gothic tale of bridal torment and a pseudo-monster (this time of the quasi-'Phantom of the Opera' variety), Lord Uplandtowers (a very youthful Ben Kingsley) wishes to wed Barbara (Joanna McCallum); however, this willful daughter of Sir John Grebe (Leslie Sands) instead elopes with the handsome Edmond Willowes (Nick Brimble). Intent on marrying "beneath her", Barbara can only gain her parents' consent by having Edmond be formally "educated" in Italy for a year, while their lodge house is readied for the newlywed couple to move into together. During his stay in Europe, Edmond tragically becomes facially disfigured in an opera house fire while selflessly saving others' lives; upon his return to England, despite all her initial assurances to the contrary, Barbara ("I'm so horrified!") is repelled by his irreparably (quote) "scarred and shriveled flesh" and "forbidding appearance"—which he keeps tactfully hidden behind a blank, static flesh-tone mask that is a mere empty mockery of his erstwhile classical handsomeness—forcing him to do the honorable thing, in keeping with his innate heroic nature, and leave her a formal farewell letter. After learning of his death several years later whilst in a loveless 'second choice' marriage with Lord Uplandtowers, Barbara receives delivery of a commissioned statue in white marble of a pre-accident Edmond from a sculptor in Pisa. When his grudging new wife begins worshipping this idealized, Apollonian graven image of her deceased former love as a veritable shrine, indulging secretive 'trysts' with and whispering to it in the dead of night as though she might be in communion with her dead beloved's very ghost itself, Uplandtowers learns of the original's disfigurements and has the statue amended accordingly; only then, at long last (strangely enough), does the lovelorn lord receive Barbara's redirected (*mis*directed?) affections.

The (Pre-)Phantom of the Opera?
Edmond Willowes, the gallant-but-doomed hero of Thomas Hardy's magazine story (1890) and subsequent novel (1891) "Barbara of the House of Grebe", may possibly have partly-inspired the title character of Gaston Leroux's famous serialized 1909-1910 novel *Le Fantôme de l'Opéra*; either way, Nick Brimble *[top 3 pix at left]*, Edmond's portrayer in BBC's '73 TV version of "Grebe", definitely has a lot of Erik the Phantom in his characterization

Claw/Maw: The fabulously fearsome title beastie from **NIGHT OF THE DEMON** (1957). Can you believe that some detractors actually think its inclusion undermines the film's effectiveness?! ...We say— *"NAY!!!"*

However, after he achieves this ultimate conquest of Her Ladyship by forcibly driving-out all memory of the late Edmond from her memory and heart, His Lordship—evidently reaffirming the hoary adage "The chase is sweeter than the catch"?—grows increasingly bored with and tired of the 'new', obsessive/submissive Barbara, whose former haughty indifference to her husband has since been replaced by a weak, clinging dependency, possessive jealousy and advancing mental instability. In addition, the woman's infertility detracts still further from her desirability in the man's eyes. The overlying theme/image—that of the ill-fated Edmond's disfigured visage, both in the flesh and in stone—seemingly symbolizes in hysterically exaggerated terms the distaste (and even outright revulsion) felt by 'toffs' of the aristocracy for those whom they regard as their social inferiors. It is only after Edmond 'shows his true face' (so to speak) after it becomes permanently ravaged and ruined by flames that Barbara comes to see him for what he actually is: that is to say, unworthy of her. The shocking scarification which results from his burns serves as the catalyst that shows up the high-born female's superficiality in light of the fact that the man whom she had formerly desired primarily for his chiseled good looks now no longer has them, and thus she is able to finally accept—and *reject*—him as the low-born working class ruffian her father initially took him for. In this 'convenient' manner it is possible for the emotionally fickle Barbara to justify her change of mind (if not actually heart) in regards to Lord Uplandtowers—a highborn man equal to her own station—when she at last stoops to become his bride.

This social status has Barbara experiencing love and loss at every extreme level, from its initial blooming to isolation and despair. His horrible scars viscerally symbolize the young commoner's lesser social status in the eyes of the gentry, and the burned Edmond's big reveal (in some ways similar to Erik the Phantom's in the Gaston Leroux novel) is startling to behold: what appears to be just a simple unmasking turns into a full unveiling of face and wig, as if the voluntary exile is peeling an orange. Indeed, such is the overpowering intensity of her aversion to his new-found hideousness that Barbara very nearly up and vomits at first sight of it. While incarcerated together in their matrimonial hell, Kingsley and McCallum excel in their performances, with Barbara caressing her now-unattainable 'ideal man' (i.e., his graven image) as Uplandtowers simmers to his ultimate victory, only to then derive little in the way of real satisfaction from it.

Part II: The Legacy of Festive Frights | Ghost Stories as Christmas Tradition

"An idea, like a ghost, must be spoken to a little before it will explain itself."
|– Charles Dickens

An illustration by James McBryde *[see detail on next page]* for M.R. James' 1894 story "Canon Alberic's Scrap-book" (a.k.a. "The Scrap-book of Canon Alberic"; from *Ghost Stories of an Antiquary* [1904]); the author's first-ever dabbling in the kind of spine-tingling supernatural horror fiction for which he is best-known

In 1904, McBryde, the artist most-associated with MRJ's ghost stories, wrote in one of his many letters to the author, his friend: *"I don't think I have ever done anything I liked better than illustrating your stories. To begin with, I sat down and learned advanced perspective and the laws of shadows..."*

Set against backgrounds that are scholastic and/or ecclesiastic, often the apparitions found in the fiction of Victorian/Anglican/Medievalist/Etonian man of letters M.R. (Montague "Monty" Rhodes) James OM FBA (1862-1936) are connected with material objects, such as the bronze whistle from the ruins of a medieval Templars' preceptory in "Oh, Whistle and I'll Come to You, My Lad" (1904), and the trio of buried ancient Anglo Saxon crowns that purportedly prevent the invasion of England by interlopers in "A Warning to the Curious" (1925). There are also hints of bygone Satanism, such as the wicked warlock Karswell in "Casting the Runes" (1911)—which provided the basis, if heavily-elaborated-upon, for Jacques Tourneur's superior supernatural slow-burner **NIGHT OF THE DEMON** (a.k.a. **CURSE OF THE DEMON**, 1957, UK), wherein Karswell's character was played to excellent effect by Niall MacGinnis—for which James conjured up ancient manifestations into a more rational, decreasingly superstitious age (as exemplified by Dana An-

drews' staunchly realist/skeptic protagonist John Holden in said '57 filmic adaptation of "Runes" *[see Endnote #3]*). Horrors are set on the very outermost periphery of sight and understanding, or, to quote James himself, glimpsed only with "the tail of the eye"; even though his ghost stories are set within credible historic tableaux, they are also classics of psychological terror, too. For the son of a parson—and a lifelong member of the Church of England—James' phantasms are surprisingly outlandish, often wet-lipped, smelly, and all-too-tangible, even when lurking dimly (if by no means harmlessly) in the shadows.

Take, for example, James' following description of a demon illustration from the Testament of King Solomon that is viewed by the protagonist Dennistoun in "Canon Alberic's Scrap-book" (written in 1895; published in 1904), the lead-off story in the author's earliest collection of ghost stories, which represented the first time the author ever described such a horror in a published work:

"The hands were of a dusky pallor, covered, like the body, with long, coarse hairs, and hideously taloned. The eyes, touched in with a burning yellow, had intensely black pupils, and were fixed upon the throned King with a look of beast-like hate. Imagine one of the awful bird-catching spiders of South America translated into human form, and endowed with intelligence just less than human, and you will have some faint conception of the terror inspired by those to whom I have shown the picture. 'It was drawn from the life.'"

With its plot of an elderly alchemist seeking to attain immortality via taking the lives of children in order to preserve his own indefinitely, "Lost Hearts" (1904), James' next-published tale after the above-cited "Canon Alberic", amounts to one of the writer's absolute *grimmest* out of the over 30 classic tales of the supernatural he authored in total. "The Tractate Middoth" (1911) contains a spooky spectre with thick cobwebs—spiders included!—over its eyes; in "Mr. Humphreys and his Inheritance" (1911), there is a fearsome form (quote) "with a burnt human face" that emerges "with the odious writhings of a wasp creeping out of a rotten apple"; and, an unnamable *thing* in "The Uncommon Prayer-Book" (1921) resembles "a great roll of old, shabby, white flannel". Perhaps indicating that James had a bit of a phobia for fabrics in addition to a well-documented one for spiders, the nightmarish wraith of "Oh, Whistle, and I'll Come to You, My Lad" (1904) made its presence known via items of windblown drapery and possessed a horrific mockery of a face formed from (quote) "crumpled linen" ("…whitish, floppy…"), as of bed-sheets. It is after all our beds in which

"It is rather a nuisance of a thing to have round one's neck—just too heavy. […] He [Dennistoun] had taken the crucifix off, and laid it on the table, when…"

most of us experience dreams—and nightmares—so perhaps the covers that shroud us during sleep might be seen as having a kind of nightlife all their own. Because most of us tend to regard our bed as the ultimate place of safety and security in our lives, having those very comforting wrappings in which we feel safest and most secure turn on us in such a treacherous manner might be read as the ultimate height of horror.

Lawrence Gordon Clark, who directed a number of the BBC's 1970s tele-adaptations of James' works, had this to say about the author: "He has a great sense of *evil*. He's a great manipulator, like all great storytellers. To make people frightened when you want to, it's a wonderful power". In regards to James' manner in his supernatural stories, long-time fan Mark Gatiss remarked, "It sounded as if he knew whereof he spoke".

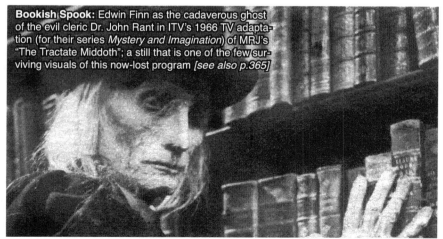

Bookish Spook: Edwin Finn as the cadaverous ghost of the evil cleric Dr. John Rant in ITV's 1966 TV adaptation (for their series *Mystery and Imagination*) of MRJ's "The Tractate Middoth"; a still that is one of the few surviving visuals of this now-lost program *[see also p.365]*

"[…] he is dead, these twenty years and more. He was a clergyman, though I'm sure I can't imagine how he got to be one […]"; from MRJ's original text

Three scenes from the non-BBC (i.e., ITV) adaptation of James' "Casting the Runes" *[see Endnote #3, p.137]*, a 1979 episode of the series *ITV Playhouse*. **Top to Bottom:** The rune of doom; the nightmarish spider-in-the-bed; and the show's equivalent of the demonic creature depicted on page 99

All this ultimately begs the question whether there had been some sort of epiphanous occurrence in the author's personal life—according to Gatiss in his below-discussed docudrama, James was a "notorious arachnophobe", for instance—that influenced such a well-educated man to look beyond our mere mundane existence into other, outer (and inner) realms. Events described in his short 'confessional', entitled "A Vignette" (first published in a November 1936 edition of *The London Mercury*), written shortly before his death, hint at an unnerving experience in James' childhood.

An all-new version of "The Tractate Middoth" *[see Endnote #4]* was broadcast on Christmas Day

of 2013, followed by its director/co-writer Mark Gatiss' engaging docudrama *M.R. James: Ghost Writer* (D: John Das), which was also written by Gatiss. This nicely-produced hour-long program explains how secondary in his life the ghost stories James (played in the doc by Robert Lloyd Parry, who gives spirited readings from the man's works) wrote were; they were almost just a hobby, a 'mere' casual recreational pursuit done in the 'off-hours' to all his astonishing achievements as a medieval scholar, for which he is arguably lesser-known today *[see Endnote #5]*. Gatiss paints a picture of a potentially sexually-repressed—and possibly latently homosexual—man who also viewed his tales as a social device, particularly for readings at King's College's Cambridge Chitchat Society (where James enjoyed sessions of "ragging"; essentially, floor-bound genital-grabbing! *[see Endnote #6]*). It is a compelling piece, where we follow James' infatuation with youthful illustrator James McBryde (who provided artwork for many of the author's stories), and his understandably increasing disillusionment with The Great War, which was a total horror of an entirely different sort.

Each Christmas from 1971 to 1978, the BBC broadcast late-night, self-contained dramas which would become known under the umbrella heading of *A Ghost Story for Christmas*. The first five were all based on stories by James: "The Stalls of Barchester", "A Warning to the Curious", "Lost Hearts", "The Treasure of Abbot Thomas" and "The Ash Tree". Charles Dickens' "The Signalman" was chosen for the 1976 episode, while the final two instalments were original teleplays laid in contemporary settings: Clive Exton's "Stigma" and John Bowen's "The Ice House". "A Warning to the Curious" was broadcast between 11.05 and 11.55 p.m. on Christmas Eve of 1972, and it attracted an astonishing-for-the-time (and most respectable even today) *nine-million* viewers. Because of its critical and public success, all subsequent entries were shifted from General Features to the BBC's Drama department proper, and as Lawrence Gordon Clark—who directed the first seven entries—has lamented, his personal vision was suddenly intruded/imposed-upon by screenwriters and script editors.

It might be argued that Christmas supernatural fiction can be traced back to the Victorian era, a time when magic lanterns and stage magicians milked the population's craving for thrills and sensation for all it was worth. With technology by then making printed matter cheaper and more widely accessible than ever before—not to mention his fascination with spiritualism and Egyptology—Charles Dickens (a favorite author of M.R. James') became the architect of things snowbound and spectral. But telling scary stories while huddling around a festively crackling fire can be traced back in several layers: English author, philosopher and cleric Joseph Glanvill's treatise on witchcraft *Saducismus Triumphatus* (published posthumously in 1681 and possibly edited by Henry More) had harsh words for those who dismissed the existence of unearthly powers as "meer Winter Tales, or Old Wives fables", and William Shakespeare had even titled his play about magic and transformation *The Winter's Tale* (1623). Looking back to the previous century, we find Christopher Marlowe using the same notion in his play *The Jew of Malta* (1589): "...now I remember those old woman's words, 'who in my wealth would tell me winter's tales, and speak of spirits and ghosts that glide by night'".

Although it was "The Stalls of Barchester" (airdate: December 24th, 1971, D: Lawrence Gordon Clark)—based on MRJ's 1911 story "The Stalls of Barchester Cathedral"—that started the BBC ghost story strand proper, a template had already been put firmly in place several years before with director Jonathan Miller's outstanding *Omnibus* episode (airdate: May 7th, 1968) adapted from James' "Oh, Whistle, and I'll Come to You, My Lad" (first published in the MRJ collection *Ghost Stories of an Antiquary* [1904]), here bearing the shortened/simplified title of "Whistle and I'll Come to You" *[see Endnote #7]*. Not so much an openly supernatural tale as an exploration of an elderly, too-long-alone academic's deteriorating faculties—a fate which such a studiously bookish and orderly personality as Monty James himself might well have rightfully dreaded—this dramatic adaptation plays much like a personal satire on James himself. Lost in his own carefully compartmentalized, apple-pie-order little world, the mind of aged, plucky but neurotic archaeologist Professor Parkins (Michael Hordern) steadily erodes like the slowly-subsiding rural graveyard where his troubles first really begin. An outspoken disbeliever in the supernatural (*uh-oh*...), obsessively fussy and orderly to the point of anal-retentiveness, has now become increasingly absent-minded in his dotage, the solitary old bachelor ("...I don't like careless talk about what you call 'ghosts'...") goes for a supposedly therapeutic stay at a small seaside hotel in the (fictional) town of Burnstow, Suffolk (on the East Anglian coast, facing toward Northern Europe across the North Sea and blown by wild incoming Scandinavian seawinds that carry who-knows-what primordial paganistic Norse forces with them). While out walking close along a desolate, lonely stretch of shoreline one afternoon, he picks up an ancient whistle ("...not

Coast Ghost? While out beachcombing along the windy shore alone, old Professor Parkins (Michael Hordern)—whose character is much older than he is portrayed in the source story—thinks he glimpses *something* in his peripheral vision and wonders if it's only his eyes (or his mind?) playing tricks on him; frozen moments from the frightening '68 Beeb dramatization of MRJ's "Whistle"

unlike a modern dog-whistle...") that he finds lying amongst the undergrowth over a Templar gravesite. That evening, after cleaning-up said instrument, he discerns a Latin inscription etched into the side of it—which translates to "Who is this who is coming?"—and proceeds to blow on it, much to his later regret. A mysterious wind comes in ghastly gusts from seemingly out of nowhere within moments after the whistle-blower has unwittingly summoned forth *something* ("...

the creature that came in answer to the whistle..."), and which continues to haunt the old man in his dreams.

With some individual moments stretched-out to a tortuous degree, "Whistle" is an affectingly effective mood-piece of psychological horror that constantly teeters precariously on the cusp of an all-out collapse into utter chaos. "Pagan, elemental forces are at work here", says Mark Gatiss of the tale in *M.R. James: Ghost Writer*. He then adds ominously, "*Purposeful* ones". A suffocating sense of isolation, alienation and rising dread permeates the proceedings, and eccentrically muttered/mumbled delivery of dialogue combined with bizarre, jarring sound effects add greatly to the off-kilter atmosphere as the narrative oversteps the dividing line separating reality and illusion—or *does* it?! Although the nightmare itself rapidly dissipates, its haunting presence lingers. Subtextually speaking, the story reads not so much as a warning to the curious (we all know what curiosity did to that darn cat!) but as more of a cautionary fable against succumbing to the prideful arrogance of human intellect itself ("I believe in hard facts, you know", states Parkins categorically with the utmost pride, not realizing he is tempting fate with this show of smug self-assurance). Prone to delivering pompously pedantic dissertations and impressed no end by his own wit and superior intelligence, Parkins expresses his disdain for paranormal phenomena by cockily 'repurposing' a famous Shakespearean quote as "There are more things in philosophy than are dreamt of in Heaven and Earth". His seeming encounters with the supernatural ultimately shake his perceptions of the world—and, more importantly, the *otherworld*—to their very core, leaving him emotionally shattered and in a state of denial in the aftermath, though now possibly open to changing his views on such things, which he had previously regarded as utter poppycock.

The best dramatic treatments of James' works register almost like silent Expressionist films, showcasing an elemental struggle that seeps into both the author's milieux and the characters who populate them. Director Miller's present well-remembered '68 work emphasizes Parkins as the Gothic Outsider by showing people around him conversing in incoherent mumbles and snatched words, as if the viewer is listening to others distractedly, the way the Professor has come to do out of habit due to his many years of self-sequestered scholastic solitude lost in his own thoughts. The creepy climax of the

"In a very few moments it seemed to know that the bed was empty, and then, moving forward into the area of light and facing the window, it showed for the first time what manner of thing it was." |– from MRJ's "Oh, Whistle, and I'll Come to You, My Lad" (1904); iconic artwork by James McBryde

waking dream, where Parkins is justifiably horrified to see his bedsheets billowing and rising-up eerily before him then attempting to form themselves into the vague shape of *something* (possibly human, but probably *not*), both mimics and mocks one's expectations of comical pretend 'ghosts' lurking under white sheets. Indeed, Hordern as Parkins' initial reaction—having been driven to the brink of all-out gibbering, thumb-sucking dementia by the frightening apparition before him—is so grotesque to behold that it almost registers as broad comedy (*à la* a caricature the likes of that seen in a parodic horror farce [**CARRY ON SCREAMING!** {1966, UK, D: Gerald Thomas}, say]).

James' aforementioned "The Stalls of Barchester" is the most overtly ecclesiastical of all the BBC adaptations. In 1932, whilst cataloguing the contents of the Barchester Cathedral library—the kind of work with which Monty James himself was highly familiar in real life—a Dr. Black (Clive Swift, later seen in "A Warning to the Curious" [1972], and as Lanyon in the BBC's 1980 adaptation of **DR. JEKYLL AND MR. HYDE** [D: Alastair Reid], starring David Hemmings in the title roles), to whom the librarian (Will Leighton) shows a sealed old chest containing a dusty diary that details the events leading up to the death of Archdeacon Dr. Haynes (Robert Hardy, star of the promising if failed 1972 BBC one-off *The Incredible Robert Baldick* [see Part 1 of this article in *Monster!* #33 {p.88}]). Dating from the late 19th Century, this handwritten record implies that the overzealously ambitious Haynes had willfully caused the 'accidental' demise of his 92-year-old predecessor Dr. Pulteney (Harold Bennett), and was thereafter haunted by two-century-old oaken choir stall carvings—of the Devil, Death and a black cat—made by an artisan name of John Austin ("They credited him with second sight..."). Adding to the air of mystery, the wood he used came from an ancient grove of oak trees whose history predates Christianity.

Filmed entirely on location at Norwich Cathedral, the broadcast hews to James' phrase "movement without sound", with its half-seen (or *un*seen) terrors and foreboding backstory. At other times sounds are heard—the plaintive mewing and angry hissing of a ghostly feline, for instance—whilst their source remains hidden from sight. Hardy gives a staunch performance as a guilt-ridden man trapped in increasing isolation ("I must be firm... I *must* be firm!"), whom the librarian suspects might have suffered from "incipient madness". Haynes himself, on the other hand, believed his uncanny visions were products of some undiagnosed phys-

"Ever since I touched this thing, I've never been alone..." l– Peter Vaughan as Paxton in the BBC's 1972 version of "A Warning to the Curious", regarding his discovery, one of the ancient Anglo-Saxon Royal Crowns

ical ailment rather than a mental one; in actuality, they are of a much more *spiritual* nature. Adding to the creeping sense of claustrophobic terror, contusions inflicted on him by a spectral clawed hand reveal that this is in no way merely an ambiguously abstract, unreal haunting that is only in his mind, but one with a very real if not necessarily corporeal nor entirely physical menace at back.

"A Warning to the Curious" (airdate: December 24th, 1972, D: Lawrence Gordon Clark) tells of one Mr. Paxton (Peter Vaughan), a clerk who has lost his job due to The Great Depression, so travels to the (real-life) village of Thruxton in Norfolk on the East Anglian coast—latter site a popular getaway spot for James protagonists—in hopes of discovering a legendary last surviving Saxon crown, one of three, the Royal Crowns of Anglia, that were put in place as a safeguard to supernaturally protect the English homeland from invasion by outside forces. Following in the footsteps of an archaeologist who was brutally murdered in the vicinity twelve years previously while on a dig at a local burial barrow, Paxton, whose hobby is archaeology, boards at a hotel which only has one other guest, Dr. Black (a returning Clive Swift, essentially reprising his same-named character from "The Stalls of Barchester"). Increasingly haunted by a mysterious figure—which may or may not be the ghost of one William Ager, whose job it was to stand endless vigil over the relics—Paxton is eventually bludgeoned to death right at the point of excavation.

Inspired by the bleak, desolate open beaches and dreamy isolation of Miller's above-discussed *Omnibus* entry, "A Warning to the Curious" is indeed an enduring drama. The chilling shot of a dimly-viewed man (?) hunched-over in Paxton's hotel room predates the similarly-motivated 'shock'

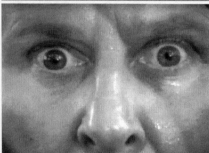

finale of **THE BLAIR WITCH PROJECT** (1999, USA, Ds: Daniel Myrick, Eduardo Sánchez) by close-on thirty years, and the sequence wherein Paxton encounters a (seemingly) sinister machete-bearing farmer well illustrates how an effectively-staged scene can win-out in its visceral impact over anything that is needlessly overly effects-laden. What makes Paxton's demise more startling still is that you really do *feel* for this 'average Joe Bloggs everyman', down on his luck and who just wants to make a name for himself, and is driven more by hurt pride and simple ambition for self-improvement rather than by any genuinely malicious intent. Having—he, a mere layman, yet!—only just recently succeeded in unearthing the Seaburg Crown of the Anglo-Saxons from within the barrow, Paxton comes to the realization that he must then do the right thing and put the sacred artefact back where he found it. This he proceeds to do, but this sudden change of heart will not save him from the dark forces that surround, manipulate and finally engulf him.

Based on one of James' earliest and least-subtle tales, "Lost Hearts" had first been adapted for the small screen by ABC (Associated British Corporation) as an episode of rival network ITV's *Mystery and Imagination* series (airdate: March 5th, 1966). Unfortunately, however, as with a number of other episodes in the series, all known copies of said episode have since been lost, although at least one privately made recording of its audio track alone is still *in esse*. In BBC's 'remake' of "Lost Hearts" (airdate: December 25th, 1973, D: Lawrence Gordon Clark), preteen orphan Stephen (Simon Gipps-Kent) is sent to live with his eccentric elderly cousin and benefactor Peregrine Abney (Joseph O'Conor). Stephen is there haunted by the spirits of two children—orphans who had briefly dwelled in the house some years before—and learns that Abney dabbles in ritual sacrifice in hopes of gaining immortality. Stephen's twelfth birthday is fast approaching, a date of great interest to Abney, who has planned a special ceremony ("A man's secret, between men…") involving the lad that must occur at precisely midnight on All Hallows Eve / All Souls Night. A dotty bookworm character, Abney lays down a smokescreen of jovial eccentricity and jollity so thick we peg him for being of sinister intent right from the get-go.

We learn that two orphans, an Italian boy named Giovanni (Christopher Davis) and Phoebe, a gypsy girl (Michelle Foster), had previously fallen afoul of Abney's evil machinations on the premises of his house, and their restless spirits still linger there. As if merely classifying just another part of the anatomy, the coldly analytical alchemist clin-

Above, Top to Bottom: *Lone Figure in a Landscape.* After making-off with the fabled crown, Vaughan as Paxton is later pursued by a distant figure—the ghostly guardian of the misappropriated artifact's haunted burial site—who, while evidently moving very fast, never seems to get any closer to him…*yet!*

ically refers to the spiritual remnants of his two prior juvenile victims as their "psychic portions". The ghostly children—with elongate fingernails that continue growing even after death—sway in hypnotizing unison to hurdy-gurdy music but, aside from the obvious Faustian element, there is a palpable subtext of child abuse herein that just *won't* go away, no matter how tactfully director Lawrence Gordon Clark tries to steer clear of making it obvious. "He may be an old bachelor, but he's very partial to children", says old Mrs. Bunch (Susan Richards), the household's head maid, evidently in all innocence as to how far her master's partiality extends. The scene of Abney forcing Stephen to imbibe some drugged wine prior to the proposed heart-removal ritual—the carving-out of that organ which James once poetically described as a "munificent engine"—makes for uncomfortable viewing, and the overall synopsis reminds one of the atrocities of French knight and lord Gilles De Montmorency-Laval—more commonly known to many as Gilles de Rais—who raped, murdered, and dismembered children in the furtherance of black magic. (Incidentally, that same year, Spanish horror icon Paul Naschy a.k.a. Jacinto Molina played the vile resurrected satanic sadist Alaric de Marnac, a thinly veiled variation of de Rais' character, albeit with an all-out genuinely supernatural slant, in Carlos Aured's gruesome period zombie shocker **HORROR RISES FROM THE TOMB** [*El espanto surge de la tumba*, Spain, 1973].) "No hearts! They had *no hearts!*" raves Stephen hysterically after sighting his ashen, smiling ghostly counterparts. Furtive whisperings from the shadows and deep gouges scored into the wooden paneling of a wall, evidently caused by the raking talons of some animal (shades of the murderous claw in "The Stalls of Barchester"), add to the mounting sense of foreboding that saturates the proceedings. "Lost Hearts" endures as one of the most effective dramatizations of James' writings, and still delivers chills to this day.

A slow-burning cryptography tale, again with strong ecclesiastic overtones, "The Treasure of Abbot Thomas" (airdate: December 23rd, 1974, D:

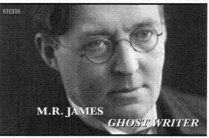

Top Right: M.R. James. The author's scholarly historical background lent extra depth and detail to his ghost stories, which far from represented his daily bread-and-butter; indeed, the writing of them was merely a sideline to his 'day job' of dedicated academician, whose contributions to art and culture run so much deeper than just his dabblings in literary fiction. The three other images at lower right are all from John Das' involving documentary, *M.R. James: Ghost Writer* (2013)

Lawrence Gordon Clark) transposes its Germanic origins to Wells Cathedral, in the South West English county of Somerset *[the place of my birth!* 😊 *– SF]*. The haughty arrogance of Reverend Justin Somerton (Michael Bryant [1928-2002], of Amicus' Robert Bloch horror portmanteau **TORTURE GARDEN** [1967, UK, D: Freddie Francis] and The Beeb's series *Spine Chillers* [1980]) cannot overshadow his thirst for the disgraced, alchemy-practicing titular cleric's secret stash of gold, which he transmuted from base metals—that literally brings about his sticky end ("It's a thing of *slime…* darkness and slime. It's an unholy thing"). Somerton is the archetypal James antihero: a character who gets punished in the worst way for his skepticism and disrespect towards the unearthly world (illustrating this aspect of his character, he soundly debunks a phony séance put on by an alleged clairvoyant named Mrs. Tyson [Sheila Dunn] and her husband [Frank Mills] early into the 36-minute runtime, much to the exposed charlatans' chagrin). Based on James' most intricate story, John Bowen's script opens this adaptation by including a young foil, Lord Peter Dattering (Paul Lavers), and includes some sly nods to the English fondness for comfort foods (in this case slab-cake and grilled chops).

With its uneasy ambience of dying curses juxtaposed with bleak moorlands, "The Ash Tree" (airdate: December 23rd, 1975, D: Lawrence Gordon Clark) has something of an air of Hardy's above-discussed "The Withered Arm" about it, albeit being ultimately far more grotesque in content and with a story that is unambiguously very much firmly grounded in the supernatural rather than ambiguity. 18th Century nobleman Sir Richard Fell (Edward Petherbridge) inherits a stately home whose grounds are dominated by an ancient Ash tree, the deeply embedded roots of which threaten the very foundations of the house itself. The family seat has been cursed since the day when his ancestor Sir Matthew (also played by Petherbridge in flashbacks) had condemned an earthy peasant woman named Mistress Mothersole (Barbara Ewing) to death for witchcraft. More a tale of resurrection and the aching loss of fertility than anything else, writer David Rudkin energizes James' prose by discarding the original tale's set of narrators in favor of but a singular descent into madness, also emphasizing sexual awareness with Fell's free-spirited muse Lady Augusta (Lalla Ward *[see Endnote #8]*). The Ash *[see Endnote #9]* is a tree that has inspired numerous cultural myths: in British folklore it is said that ill children could be cured by passing through a cleft in one; here it is a vessel that acts upon the sorceress' battle-cry ("Mine shall inherit!"), as its malformed branches unleash a brood of grotesque blood-suckling 'spider-babies'—disembodied, fanged humanoid infants' heads carried along on scuttling arachnoid legs!—into the sleeping Sir Richard's bedroom by night, making for what is arguably the most outrageous scene to be found in all of the James adaptations. Far from overstaying its welcome by dragging on too long, the tale is skillfully edited down to a concise and judicious (just under) 32 minutes.

"They found [...] below it a rounded hollow place in the earth, wherein were two or three bodies of these creatures that had plainly been smothered by the smoke; and, what is to me more curious, at the side of this den, against the wall, was crouching the anatomy or skeleton of a human being, with the skin dried upon the bones, having some remains of black hair, which was pronounced by those that examined it to be undoubtedly the body of a woman, and clearly dead for a period of fifty years." I– from MRJ's "The Ash Tree" (originally called "The Ash-tree", from *Ghost Stories of an Antiquary* [1904]); the scene's visualization from BBC's 1975 TV version

"The peaceful and retired seclusion amid which the honoured evening of Dr. Haynes's life was mellowing to its close was destined to be disturbed, nay, shattered, by a tragedy as appalling as it was unexpected…"
I– MRJ in "The Stalls of Barchester Cathedral" (from *More Ghost Stories* [1911]).

Above: In BBC's 1971 TV version (retitled simply "The Stalls of Barchester"), Robert Hardy as Dr. Haynes experiences a series of increasingly terrifying, seemingly supernatural encounters and begins to wonder whether he's gone insane or not. He hasn't—not *yet*, anyway! And by the time he *does*, he hasn't got time to worry about it, because he doesn't live long enough

Based on a Dickens story that was first published in the Christmas 1866 edition of the collection *All the Year Round*, "The Signal-man" (airdate: December 22nd, 1976, D: Lawrence Gordon Clark) is greatly infused with the author's own involvement with the Staplehurst rail crash of June 1865 *[see Endnote #10]*. For the dramatization, Andrew Davies' often in-limbo script creates a strong sense of foreboding, wherein the phantom—an unsettling blank-faced entity—appears via some sort of time displacement and which portends the impending death of a signal operator (Denholm Elliott, former star of ITV's 1968 *Mystery and Imagination* presentation of **DRACULA**). If James' ghosts aim to infiltrate and scar, Dickens' specter is one that personifies the overwhelming, inexorable forces of Fate.

"The attack is psychological, Damien. And powerful. *"* |– Father Merrin (Max von Sydow) in William Friedkin's **THE EXORCIST** (1973, USA)

"'Evil'?! No! No, I will not accept that. They are conditioned simply to survive. They can survive only by becoming the dominant species. When all other lifeforms are suppressed—when the Daleks are the supreme rulers of the universe—then you will have peace. Wars will end. They are the power, not of evil, but of good." |– Davros in "Genesis of the Daleks"

M.R. James' tales are self-contained, and they helped to transform The Gothic as being synonymous with the ghost story. Far simpler than earlier Gothics, the ghost story is also 'safer'; the reader enjoys being scared in a formulaic, straightforward manner, whereas traditional Gothics tended to be more innovative, elaborate and wholly unpredictable (and hence, tend to spend too much time beating around the bush rather than getting down to the nitty-gritty!).

The Gothic in *Doctor Who*'s mid-'70s serials runs deep through the British science fantasy tradition, releasing the exotic and eldritch into our stoic, repressed world. Britain is a land that, to a certain extent, still adheres to its ancient boundaries, pathways and quirky lore. Ever since Dr. Frankenstein travelled to Orkney (islands off Scotland's wind-and-surf-swept northeastern coast), Bram Stoker brought Dracula to Whitby (in the Northern England county of Yorkshire), and H.G. Wells deposited his extraterrestrial invasion down upon the outskirts of Woking (pronounced "Wooking"; a town in northwest Surrey), outlandish tales seem to have more ballast when played-out against the down-to-earth, upright/uptight backdrop of Britain. The United States can at times use its landmarks to startling effect—one need look no further than the climax to **PLANET OF THE APES** (1968, USA) for

evidence of that—but it doesn't have anywhere near Britain's dark oceanic history, and perhaps because of this it makes such stories as are discussed hereabouts resonate more subconsciously, at a more primal 'race memory' level that connects us to our ancient ancestors' instincts. It is largely about the power of contrast: in England, ancient horrors endure to envelop a restrained, civilized contemporary society; in the United States, horror films such as Tobe Hooper's **THE TEXAS CHAIN SAW MASSACRE** (1974, USA) play out against the beloved family unit of 'Mom and Apple Pie'.

Most hardcore fans of *Doctor Who* believe the early/mid-'70s period to be the series' Golden Era of sorts, a time when Tom Baker's goggle-eyed, good-humored eccentricity was married to contrastingly chilling stories. Producer Philip Hinchcliffe and script editor Robert Holmes plundered the likes of Universal Pictures, Hammer Films and 1950s science fiction movies for their inspiration, as well as famous literature, keeping the office of self-appointed moral watchdog/puritanical busybody Mary Whitehouse (1910-2001) constantly busy filing outraged letters of complaint to the BBC. *DW*'s take on Mary Shelley's *Frankenstein, or The Modern Prometheus* (1818)—"The Brain of Morbius" (discussed below)—predictably summoned-up her wrath once again, with Whitehouse declaiming that the story "contained some of the sickest and most horrific material seen on children's television". When the Corporation issued an unprecedented apology to Whitehouse over a drowning sequence in the four-part *Who* serial "The Deadly Assassin" (aired October 30th to November 20th, 1976, D: David Maloney), the repercussions were far-reaching: never would the show be as consistently absorbing again *[see Endnote #11]*.

****

Gothic as entertainment is usually traced back to Horace Walpole's *The Castle of Otranto* (1764), a novel which kick-started a darker supernatural literary genre that lived amongst decaying settlements, subterranean crypts and dark family secrets, with plenty of skeletons moldering in closets. Oscillating between romantic subplots and conventional reality, Gothic fiction places heavy emphasis on atmosphere and loss of humanity/identity; women are often cast in distress, but are typically heroines, while men frequently struggle with a Jekyll/Hyde-type duality of personality. The Gothic concept of The Sublime *[see Endnote #12]*—the vast grandeur of mother nature, at once beautiful and terrifying—is amplified by notions of time travel and alien civilization, and the other mainstay of the form, The Outsider, can be defined as The Doctor himself. A true Gothic surface must be expressive and immersive. "They call them the haunted shores" (so begins Ray Milland's voiceover for **THE UNINVITED** [1944, USA, D: Lewis Allen]), "these stretches of Devonshire and Cornwall and Ireland which rear-up against the westward ocean. Mists gather here, and sea fog, and eerie stories…" The wild, untamed coastline conjures the evocative landscape of the Gothic, with its proximity to the elements and history and transitory visitors.

****

When Hinchcliffe and Holmes took over on *DW*, there was a seismic shift away from what Holmes described as "straightforward, dull children's stories". In the seasons that followed, the cosmos-tripping Time Lord would experience more oppressive environments and, not just hauntings, possessions and torture, but also early trappings of that concept which would later become known as *body horror*. These tales also affected The Doctor himself, changing him from the adventurous-if-paternal/patriarchal aging dandy of Pertwee to the more unpredictable and unorthodox nonconformist Baker, a performer who embraced and embodied The Gothic Outsider's spirit, con-

stantly at odds with both himself and the universe. Together with his impractically overlong scarf and unruly mop-top (pseudo-Afro?), The Doctor was suddenly Melmoth the Wanderer *[see Endnote #13]* made flesh, yearning for a place in society but doomed never to find it (as the Time Lord states in "Pyramids of Mars" [aired October 25th to November 15th, 1975, D: Paddy Russell], "I'm *not* a human being; I walk in *eternity*").

Hinchcliffe's and Holmes' debut episodes (Season Twelve) saw them tackle a set of scripts that had already been commissioned during Barry Letts' time as producer. Although this featured reassuringly traditional elements, there was also a clear indication that the show was undergoing significant changes, particularly with the phasing-out of UNIT. But referring to Hinchcliffe's tenure on *Who* as simply "the horror era" detracts from and diminishes all the creativity, ingenuity and intelligence that was channeled into the show during this period. Writers, designers and directors were specifically briefed and consulted prior to production, and assigned according to their strengths—budget willing, of course—to best bring the Hinchcliffe/Holmes serial thrillers to life. Each story had to have emotional power, a good mix of rounded characterizations and a sense of atmosphere, plus adhere to more adult scientific concepts and convincingly realized worlds.

Holmes was in his element injecting a blacker, bleaker, more sardonic humor into the proceedings. In addition to the more mature and macabre approach, a great deal of the success can also be attributed to the naturalistic chemistry generated by co-stars Baker and Elisabeth Sladen (1946-2011). Baker was also creating a Who who was more overtly and fittingly *alien*, despite his all-too-human outward appearance and foibles; you

The Ark in Space": Infected by the insectoid Wirrn Queen, this poor human is being slowly eaten alive by the alien's broodlings

need only look at his 'homo sapiens' speech from "The Ark in Space" (aired January 25th to February 15th, 1975, D: Rodney Bennett) to see that he was taking things seriously, unlike in later seasons, when the actor's impulse to fool around was not addressed. "The Ark in Space" signaled a change to a more psychological danger. The last survivors of the human race are held in suspended animation on the space station Nerva, unaware that aliens are absorbing their bodies and memories. The insectoid Wirrn Queen is laying eggs inside the cryogenically-preserved crew; when the eggs begin to hatch, The Doctor, Sarah Jane and Harry (Ian Marter) work with revived humans to lure the pupae-busting Wirrn into a shuttlecraft and blast them off into outer space.

"The Ark in Space"'s trails of green slime are played out on Roger Murray-Leach's brightly lit, clinical sets. Noah (Kenton Moore)'s cell-by-cell mutation not only recalls Nigel Kneale's *The Quatermass Experiment* (1953/1955), but provides a bridging point for the kinds of bodily destruction explored in early David Cronenberg and Ridley Scott's **ALIEN** (1979, UK/USA); the shuttle craft finale also provides a precursive nod to Scott's film several years before it entered production. The voracious Wirrn grubs and the flesh of Noah's transforming hand were constructed

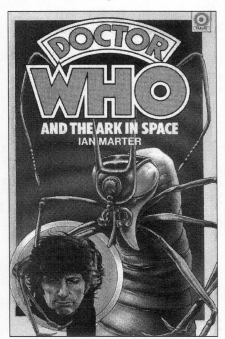

UK tie-in novel; art by Chris Achilleos

primarily from then-new bubble-wrap packaging and spray-painted green, and to further illustrate the show's queasy new hue—what better color for things alien?!—the opening titles to Part One were also green-tinted, although this idea was dropped for subsequent episodes.

This novel, more mentally-challenging edge is also played out in "The Sontaran Experiment" (aired February 22nd to March 1st, 1975, D: Rodney Bennett), wherein Field-Major Styre (Kevin Lindsay) is conducting tests on human physical and mental capabilities/limitations prior to an invasion. These include a shipwrecked astronaut being left chained-up to die of thirst, Sarah Jane getting subjected to doses of hallucinogens, and experiments to test human resistance (or otherwise) to "immersion in fluid".

With its overlying theme of racial hatred, "Genesis of the Daleks" (March 8th to April 12th, 1975, D: David Maloney) further enhanced a more realistic edge. For this serial, Terry Nation revisited early Dalek history, elaborating upon—and even contradicting—their backstory as established in "The Mutants" (aired April 8th to May 13th, 1972, D: Christopher Barry). Dramatic, gritty and uncompromising, "Genesis" pushed the show right to its creative boundaries in every sphere, as well as introducing a memorable new villain in Davros (Michael Wisher), the deranged and disfigured chief scientist whose genetic experiments gave rise to the Daleks. A megalomaniac who demonstrates a cruel eloquence and shares a cunning lack of empathy with the creatures he spawned, rarely has a Whovian villain been endowed with such depth of characterization, nor been played with such winning bravado either. Obsessed with the racial supremacy of his creations, Davros—a eugenics extremist—adheres to the Darwinian notion that evolution favors the strongest by modifying embryos to eliminate the weaknesses of conscience and pity. The Doctor's dilemma herein is whether destroying the Daleks—an act of all-out genocide—makes him every bit as immoral (or might it be *a*moral?) as the dastardly Daleks themselves. Talk about a quandary!

The weak link in this otherwise excellent season (#12, as you'll recall), "Revenge of the Cybermen" (aired April 19th to May 10th, 1975, D: Michael E. Briant) is nevertheless fondly remembered as the first Cybermen serial ever to be shot in color, as well as being the initial commercially available story arc to be released onto Beta/VHS videocassette in 1983. The Time Ring takes the

Sarah & The Sadistic Sontaran: Dome-headed hostile E.T. Field Major Styre (Kevin Lindsay) delights in torturing whatever puny humans he can get his mitts on! From "The Sontaran Experiment", the sole two-parter in Tom Baker's reign as/on *Doctor Who*

Doctor, Sarah and Harry back to Nerva (a.k.a. The Ark) in the Sol System, but to a period many thousands of years earlier than their previous visit in aforementioned "The Ark in Space" serial just a few months before. The space station is currently serving as a beacon, warning space traffic of the existence of a new asteroid orbiting Jupiter: Voga, also known as "the planet of gold". A plague has killed off all but a handful of Nerva's crew, and visiting civilian scientist Kellman (Jeremy Wilkin) is in fact a traitor working with a group of Cybermen, who want to reduce Voga to dust, for the simple reason that they can then use this gold dust to coat their breathing apparatus with (the plague being the result of a toxin injected by Cybermats). Kellman, however, is really a double agent, working with one faction of the Vogan race, whose plan all along has been to lure the Cybermen onto the beacon then destroy them with their Skystriker rocket, developed by the Voga scientist Vorus (David Collings) specifically for that purpose.

Scripted by Gerry Davis, the tale has long been a guilty pleasure for Whovians. It features an alarmingly high amount of off-color double *entendre*, which was knowingly enjoyed by cast and crew alike (and presumably viewers too). "Take the Cybermen from behind!" (*!*), "We're still heading for the biggest bang in history!" (*!!*) and "Pull it harder, it's coming!" (*!!!*) are typical examples of this, and the antics of the black-hel-

meted Cyberleader (Christopher Robbie) are hilarious to witness; often seen with his arms swishily akimbo, his would-be strangulation of

UK tie-in novel; art by Chris Achilleos

Stephen Jilks   *Channel of Darkness*   **113**

Sour-Puss! David Collings as Vorus, a Vogan with dreams of returning his dead empire to its former glory in "Revenge of the Cybermen"

The Doctor more resembles a Swedish massage than any sort of serious murder attempt! Sladen's experience of her attack by a limp, inert Cybermat—which had to be hugged to their bodies by the actors in hopes of making them appear even remotely threatening—led to her decision to quit the series, only to then reconsider and remain on-board once the show moved onto better realized stories once again.

The Vogans can be viewed as an allegory of '70s Britain—a power that was once great but is now bitterly divided over how to exploit its remaining resources. But the story is spoiled by the titular menace; it may have been a return for the Cybermen after a long hiatus (they were last seen in the eight-episoder "The Invasion" [aired November 2nd to December 21st, 1968, D: Douglas Camfield]), but they appear uncharacteristically emotional here. The idea of them being susceptible to attack with gold dust is also less-than-inspired; previous entries have shown them to be vulnerable to radiation, caustic solvents, gravity, low temperatures, electric currents, force-fields, emotional impulses and hand grenades, so the revelation of this latest comparatively rather mundane weakness—which isn't exactly as much of a threat to them as Kryptonite is to Superman!—only serves to further reduce their potency. Their ineffectiveness is further underpinned by The Doctor's contemptuous outburst, "You're nothing but a pathetic bunch of tin soldiers skulking about the galaxy in an ancient spaceship!"—a viewpoint that was reinforced by adventures yet to come *[see Endnote #14, p.141]*.

Metalheads: In the rinky-dink control room of the last surviving Cyber ship, The Doctor taunts his arch-enemies during "Revenge of the Cybermen"

Part IV: The Edge of Destruction | "Lucky 13" for *Doctor Who*

"Seems I've spent the better part of my life amongst the dead." |– John Banning (Peter Cushing) in Terence Fisher's **THE MUMMY** (1959, UK)

"Serve *you*, Sutekh?! Your name is abominated in every civilized world, whether that name be Set, Satan, Sedok…" |– Dr. Who (Tom Baker) in the *DW* serial "Pyramids of Mars" (1975)

Let Zygons Be Bygones! Horrible cephalopodic 'sucker'-aliens menace Baker as The Fourth Doctor in this promotional still from "Terror of the Zygons"

Not only did "Terror of the Zygons" (aired August 30th to September 20th, 1975) kick-off Season Thirteen of *Doctor Who*, but it saw the beginning of the Gothic Era in earnest. Written by Robert Banks Stewart and robustly directed by Douglas Camfield, this four-parter sees The Doctor, Sarah and Harry summoned by UNIT to The Fox Inn in the Scottish Highlands (actually Bognor Regis, a popular a seaside resort in West Sussex) while investigating the destruction of oil rigs in the North Sea. The so-called 'Loch Ness Monster' is revealed to be a giant Skarasen cyborg controlled by Zygons, organic shape-shifting aliens who plan to take over the Earth. When their craft emerges from Nessie's loch and The Doctor causes it to self-destruct, only the Zygon leader Broton (John Woodnutt) survives. Not to be put off, after assuming the identity of the Duke of Forgill, Broton then travels to London to destroy a World Energy Conference.

"Terror of the Zygons" features what are arguably both the *best* and *worst* monsters in the Time Lord's entire history. The bulbous-bodied, vaguely cephalopodic and fleshily fetishistic Zygons are superbly realized, their coarsely-textured rubbery bodies, suckers and throbbing veins bathed in red and green light. At the other extreme, however, their Skarasen / *faux* "Loch Ness Monster"—a creature design based on a dog's skull—is embarrassing to behold when seen rising from the Thames and moving across the moors (why, even the lowly **BEHEMOTH THE SEA MONSTER** [a.k.a. **THE GIANT BEHEMOTH**, 1959, UK, Ds: Eugène Lourié, Douglas Hickox] puts it to shame!). And, similarly to *DW*'s stereotypical depictions of Welsh folk in "The Green Death" (aired May 19th to June 23rd, 1973, D: Michael E. Briant [see Part 1 of this article in *M!* #33 {p.70}]), "Terror of the Zygons" stereotypically presents the Scots ("Can ye no' send over a few *haggis*?!") as bagpipe-blowing, kilt-wearing, superstitious loons. This 'local color' includes English-born character actor Robert **"WITCHFINDER GENERAL"** Russell (see Steve Fenton's lengthy 1991 interview with him in *Weng's Chop* #11 [pp.25-44]) affecting a broad "Scotch" brogue as a brawny, bushily red-bearded groundskeeper nicknamed "The Caber". Even though, being a

Mum(my)'s The Word! The Doctor and Sarah Jane, flanked by dour-faced undead Egyptologist Prof. Marcus Scarman (Bernard Archard) and a servile robot/mummy, inside the TARDIS; from "Pyramids of Mars"

'true' Scotsman—despite his dodgy ochcent—he presumably hasn't got any y-fronts on under his man-skirt, it is never revealed how or why he earned his impressive nickname!

A fusing of **FORBIDDEN PLANET** (1956) and *The Strange Case of Dr. Jekyll and Mr. Hyde* (1886), "Planet of Evil" (aired September 27th to October 18th, 1975, D: David Maloney) sees

UK tie-in novel; art by Andrew Skilleter

The Doctor and Sarah landing on Zeta Minor, where they discover that a Morestran geological expedition has fallen prey to an unseen killer, and only the group's leader, Professor Sorenson (Frederick Jaeger), remains alive. A military mission from Morestra has also arrived to investigate—at first suspecting The Doctor and Sarah—but the actual culprit is revealed to be a being from a universe composed of antimatter, retaliating for the removal by Sorenson of some samples from around a pit that acts as a crucial interface between two universes. This serial is brought to life by Jaeger's performance and Roger Murray-Leach's extraordinary jungle set, a vividly successful illustration of Hinchcliffe's desire to create ever-more-believable "elseworlds".

Intermixing Terence Fisher's Hammer classic **THE MUMMY** (1959, UK) and a metaphor for Colonial guilt—some of which had been present in said Fisher film—The Gothic is given its fullest expression in 1975's aforementioned "Pyramids of Mars" (aired October 25th to November 15th, 1975, D: Paddy Russell), that is ranked by many fans as not only the best *Doctor Who* story from the Tom Baker years (which extended from 1974-81), but also as one of the greatest *Doc* serials ever.

In 1911 Egypt, a British archaeological expedition led by Prof. Marcus Scarman (Bernard Archard) unearths a long-buried tomb dating from the 1st Dynasty. Boding badly, no sooner has Scarman entered than a red-glowing Eye of Horus emblem causes the native diggers to collectively bolt in fright, providing the requisite amount of ominous foreshadowing. Elsewhere in time and space at roughly the same moment, while traveling in the TARDIS, due to a freak energy surge in the cosmic continuum (or words to that effect), the title eccentric Time Lord and his plucky junior female sidekick Sarah Jane Smith find themselves precipitated back to Scarman's English country mansion in 1911. Here, in Scarman's absence, Egyptian fanatic Ibrahim Namin (Peter Mayock, sporting the usual scarlet fez, as per standard stereotype) serves the all-powerful extraterrestrial deity Sutekh a.k.a. Set (basically, Satan)—who isn't known as "The Destroyer" for nothing—from the planet Phaester Osiris. Having destroyed his own homeworld some 7,000 years prior and now fleeing the dread power of his ancient nemesis Horus, the evil alien god seeks to escape imprisonment from his Egyptian tomb, possessing and animating the deceased corporeal body of Prof. Scarman via (quote) "psytronic control" to help engineer his malevolent machinations. A sarcophagus serves as a 'time/space tunnel' leading directly to Sutekh's tomb, which he is unable to leave unless the title faraway Martian pyramid (note singular rather than plural) is destroyed. Plot-wise "Pyramids of Mars" likely sounds more than a little nonsensical on paper, but it's all done with such non-camp, straight-faced aplomb that you can't help but suspend your disbelief in due deference.

"I saw a mummy. A *walking* mummy!" exclaims Sarah not long after their arrival at the mansion (which in former decades had served as a priory); to which Doc replies, "Mummies are embalmed, eviscerated corpses. They *don't* 'walk'!" *Au contraire*, contained in oversized sarcophagi are three heavily built-up, barrel-chested mummies (Nick Burnell, Melvyn Bedford and Kevin Selway), which serve the alien intelligence and do indeed ambulate about while doing its bidding (including constructing an interplanetary ballistic missile; parts of said device are stored inside pottery canopic jars). Considering their oddly angular if neatly cloth-wrapped appearance, it comes as no surprise when it is revealed that these lumbering "mummies" are in actuality—yep, you guessed it!—inorganic servicer robots. Their bindings prove to be "chemically-impregnated in order to protect [...] against damage and corrosion". Amusingly (if absurdly) enough, at one point Dr. Who himself dresses up as one of the mock mummies in order to thwart a plot by Sutekh (Gabriel Woolf), the serial's primary villain, to launch the aforementioned nuclear missile to destroy a Martian pyramid (hence the slightly misleading title) in order to

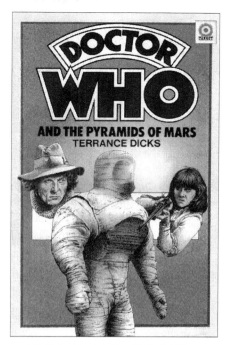

UK tie-in novel; art by Chris Achilleos

liberate Sutekh from captivity by blasting the Eye of Horus which holds him trapped (confused yet?!). Dr. Who reveals early on that the extraterrestrial Osiran culture was a direct influence on that of Egypt ("Egyptology and *Mars*?!" cries one character incredulously). The mumdroids in the present mid-'70s *DW* episode appear roughly equal parts ominous and humorous. Late in the fourth and final part, we are introduced to two more robomums, known as "The Guardians of Horus". These 'deluxe' models trimmed with what looks like gold-glitter duct tape (!), but are in actuality—illustrating yet another instance of the show's famed improvisatory economic ingenuity—just the very same costumes seen previously in the program, with slight added embellishments to make them appear different. To cut a long story short, one of these goodie mummies engages in an all-too-fleeting scuffle with one of the bad ones during the serial's somewhat-too-perfunctory climax, which results in Sutekh's grand scheme of universal domination being duly foiled.

There is a genuine feeling of dread conveyed by this serial's entombed ancient evil and walking mummies, with said 'creatures' being especially successful at projecting sinister intent in their simple yet hulkingly threatening appearance. Although modern readers have been conditioned by decades of stories and movies to expect a mummy to be a mindless evil monster, initial literature portrayed them as intelligent and even philosophical beings, such as in Italian writer Giacomo Leopardi's short work "The Dialogue of Frederick Ruysch and his Mummies" (1827; translated into English by Charles Edwardes in 1882 and published in London by Trübner & Co). It wasn't until later that the 'bad mummy' became a stock shock device, particularly in Arthur Conan Doyle's prototypical "Lot No. 249" (1892), which illustrates the shift in tone in the wake of important archaeological discoveries and the increase of Britain's involvement in and later occupation of Egypt. **THE MUMMY** continued Hammer's fascination with Gothic Romanticism, having John Banning (Peter Cushing) excavating the tomb of Princess Ananka, only to have the mummified corpse of her former lover Kharis (Christopher Lee) reanimated and instructed to murder the desecrators. A more sexual subtextual reading might view the men as weaklings, as either cripples or slaves; even in the afterlife, the female is still the one in charge. This particular subjective interpretation hits hard in the final confrontation, with Kharis being virtually reduced to a mere puppet, now become putty in the hands of a woman (Yvonne Furneaux) who simply *resembles* the princess to whom he's remained so devoted for several millennia rather than actually *being* her (other than in spirit, perhaps). This metaphysical charge is also channeled in the present *Who* serial by Sutekh: "I can,

if I choose, keep you alive for centuries, wracked by the most excruciating pain!"

For "The Android Invasion" (aired November 22nd to December 13th, 1975, D: Barry Letts) Terry Nation invents a new alien race, the rhinoceros-like Kraals, who go to finite trouble to create an exact replica of an English village and populate it with synthetic organisms for the purposes of rehearsing an invasion. Chief Kraal scientist Styggron (Martin Friend) also intends to release a deadly virus to aid in the elimination of resistance, but this is ultimately an unnecessarily convoluted serial. Themes of duplication and mind-draining are lost in a number of silly plot elements, most of all one in which the astronaut Crayford (Milton Johns) is duped into believing he has lost an eyeball, this by simply giving him an eye-patch to wear over his still-intact 'missing' one! On the surface this is a minor entry in the greater Gothic scheme of things, but it does cover the theme of interrogation (i.e., The Doctor's subjection to the Analysis Machine) and 1950s Atomic Age/Cold War sci-fi paranoia; Crayford may be a critical laughing stock, but he is a man in identifiable flux.

Originally scripted by Terrance Dicks under his alias of Robin Bland, "The Brain of Morbius" (aired January 3rd to 24th, 1976, D: Christopher Barry) was extensively rewritten by Holmes to up the horror quotient and remove Dicks' technically challenging notion of a scavenger A.I. The resulting story is a mix of Shelley's *Frankenstein* (1818) and Haggard's *She* (1886), set on Karn,

In a season full of truly *bizarre* stories, "The Android Invasion" turned out to be a goofy throwback to the days of needlessly convoluted plots and bumbling alien villains

Channel of Darkness Stephen Jilks

"The Brain of Morbius" turned out to be a gloriously *strange* neo-Gothic Horror full of macabre medical madness and Universal/Hammeresque nods and allusions

home-world to both a sorority of telekinetic priestesses known as The Sisterhood—whose sacred flame produces the elixir of life that gives the Time Lords their immortality—and a mad scientist named Solon (Philip Madoc [1934-2012], a prolific Welsh actor whose long CV includes memorably appearing as the reprehensible body snatcher Byker in Roy Ward Baker's aforementioned gender-bending shocker **DR. JEKYLL & SISTER HYDE** [1971, UK]), who is putting together a composite body in which to house the still-living cerebrum of the executed renegade Time Lord, Morbius (a classic glowing 'brain-in-a-tank' of bubbling lime-green liquid kept alive by nutrients and capable of rasping speech care of an attached microphone; sight unseen, actor Michael Spice—who later played the eponymous 'Chinaman' in the *DW* serial "The Talons of Weng-Chiang" (1977)—provides Morbius' electronically-synthesized vibrato voice). Having once again been thrown off-course from the time/space-lanes, when the Doctor and Sarah arrive in the TARDIS, The Sisterhood mistakenly believe they have been sent there to steal the last precious drops of elixir produced by their steadily dying Flame of Life, and Solon (pronounced "Soll-on") instead opts to use The Doctor's living brainbox ("What a *magnificent* head!") in which to install Morbius' disembodied mental organ and thus

complete his work; though it is left unclear why the industrious scientist doesn't just use the rest of Doc's body along with it rather than that of the grotesque and decidedly unwieldy man-made monster he has cobbled together seemingly at random off-screen beforehand. (But then again, one supposes that such a shortcut might defeat the purpose of his life's research. Besides, what would a neo-Gothic *DW* story be without a good old-fashioned, honest-to-goodness monster!)

Elsewhere, led by the crinkly elder Maren the High One (Cynthia Grenville) and her junior second-in-command Ohica (Gillian "Gilly" Brown), the ritualistic, coven-like Sisterhood (unflatteringly described by Solon at one point as "…that squalid brood of harpies…!") indulge in endless ceremonial chanting and arm-waving at their inviolable shrine, yet the serial's most ridiculous moment comes when Who—like a common plumber—rather-too-patly solves the problem of their extinguishing life-force ("…the impossible dream of a thousand alchemists, dripping like tea from an urn!") simply by removing some common *soot* clogging the gas-pipe that fuels the fire-fount, causing the flame to blaze back to its full former glory once more.

Ominously enough, the outlying environs of

Sarah Jane (Elisabeth Sladen) meets the brain of Morbius, a scene which harkens back to Felix E. Feist's **DOVOVAN'S BRAIN** (1953) and other such medical-themed horror/sci-fi films

Solon's lightning-wracked castle, set in a desolate, stormy mountainous landscape of everlasting night that resembles some 'alternate world' version of Transylvania, are littered with the wreckage of umpteen crashed space vessels supposedly brought down by the belt of deadly magnetic radiation that surrounds the planet, causing them to veer off-course. Too young to die ("I'm only seven-hundred-and-forty-nine!") and understandably eager to hang onto his head, brain included, our hero does his best to foil both The Sisterhood and Solon before the final fade of Episode 4 rolls around. In no time at all, the shrewd Who pegs the latter as being none other than a celebrated pioneering neurosurgeon who, prior to disappearing to parts unknown to engage

Timelord Face-Off: Baker as Doc taunts the piecemeal "Mr. All-Sorts" Morbius monster (played by Stuart Fell)

in dubious experimentations, authored the acclaimed textbook *Microsurgical Techniques into Tissue Transplant*.

In Episode 3, Solon's towering if mentally-challenged hooked/hunched henchman Condo (Colin Fay) carts off Sarah kicking and screaming ("Girl *pretty*! Condo *like*!") back to his master's dingy dungeon lab. Condo's pronounced Igorisms even include making like a butterfingers and dropping Morbius' freshly-detanked brain on the lab floor. After angrily shooting the big lummox repeatedly—if non-fatally—for this unforgivable blunder, without even bothering to rinse it off first, Solon promptly plops the damaged blob of mental matter into a spherical (quote) "braincase"—or "fishbowl", as Sarah describes it—molded from clear Perspex (with two goofy trumpet-shaped artificial stalked eye appendages attached!) prior to grafting it atop the prefabricated body. Stuart Fell (a frequent performer on *Who* and an alumnus of such other Brit SF telly shows as *Doomwatch* and *Blake's 7*) wore the suit, a delightfully outrageous chimeric mishmash—playfully dubbed "Mr. All-Sorts" by Sarah—that includes a hairy hide, an oversized clacking lobster pincer at the end of one arm and a normal human hand on the other, plus assorted mismatched bits and pieces of other species besides. The whole kit-and-caboodle now assembled, if severely compromised by its damaged brain, the thing's first order of business is to trash the laboratory in an insane-brained rage and terrorize poor Sarah, who has been temporarily blinded by a blast of dazzling blue light no thanks to Maren the High One's magical flashing thingamajig. No sooner has Sarah's vision returned to normal than she about-faces to find herself eye-to-eye-stalk with the newly-completed—and totally unhinged— Morbius monster. In classical Frankensteinian fashion ("Don't you recognize me?! I *made* you!"), it turns on its creator, KO'ing Solon and fatally clamping Condo in its crushing crustaceous claw before being taken out of commission (for now!) with a stungun.

Thankfully, Solon and his Igoresque, crook-backed/hook-handed assistant Condo make for some wonderful galactic Hammer Horror (with more than a few nods to Universal too), while the monster itself is so absurdly *weird* that it rivals even many a Japanese *kaiju* in the weirdness stakes. The lasting talking point of this serial is the mind-bending contest between Morbius and The Doctor, mainly because it seemed to contradict Whovian lore by indicating that there had been *eight* previous incarnations before William Hartnell (although an equally-viable explanation would be that the faces that appear—which include 'in-joke' photos of co-creators Hinchcliffe and Holmes themselves clad in stock costume— were actually Morbius' former selves rather than Who's). Unfortunately not dwelled-upon for very long at all and appearing only right at the outset of the serial's first instalment, a man-sized arthropodic critter known as a Mutt ("A mutant insect species," Doc explains) is on hand to further up the monster quotient. This marooned alien castaway, having recently made its escape from a stricken space cruiser in an emergency ejection pod, is shortly unceremoniously knifed and beheaded by Condo, only its inferior noggin proves unsuitable for his master Solon to use for anything other than some minor experiments.

"The Brain of Morbius" ends when, after pulling a fast one on Dr. Who that you'd think such a super-genius as our hero wouldn't be dumb enough to fall for in a million years, Solon repairs and resuscitates his Morbius monster and it engages Doc in a telepathic duel, very nearly fatally frazzling the latter's synapses in the process. In keeping with the numerous nods to *Frankenstein*, in place of a mob of torch-bearing villagers chasing down the monster in the last act, we instead get The Sisterhood bearing same. As the sisters close in, torches blazing, the malfunctioning Morbius stumbles and takes a looong plummet from a lofty precipice c/o the modern miracle of Chroma key.

UK tie-in novel; art by Chris Achilleos

For the final story of Season Thirteen, Robert Banks Stewart's six-part monster mash "The Seeds of Doom" (aired January 31st to March 6th, 1976, D: Douglas Camfield) draws on *The Quatermass Experiment* / **THE QUATERMASS XPERIMENT** (1953/1955, UK), Howard Hawks' and Christian Nyby's **THE THING FROM ANOTHER WORLD** (1951, USA) and John Wyndham's *The Day of the Triffids* (1951), but this is a strange serial because it could easily be played out *without* either The Doctor or Sarah being present at all. Two alien seedpods are found buried in the Antarctic permafrost, and the Doctor realizes that they are Krynoids; "I suppose you could call it a galactic weed", begins the Time Lord, "though it's deadlier than any weed you know. On most planets, the animals eat the vegetation. On planets where the Krynoid gets established, the *vegetation* eats the *animals!*" After an act of sabotage, one of the pods is delivered to eccentric plant collector Harrison Chase (Tony Beckley) at his English mansion, where his assistant Keeler (Mark Jones) becomes infected. Keeler—whose transformation is accelerated by Chase feeding him raw meat—subsequently goes on a rampage, rapidly growing to gigantic proportions before being destroyed by the good ol' RAF, who swoop to the rescue in the last act as reliably as the 7th Cavalry in a Hollywood western.

"Death, *always* death*! Do you think I* want *this carnage?"* |– Bloodthirsty French Revolution leader Robespierre (Keith Anderson) in the *Doctor Who* serial "The Reign of Terror" (aired August 8th to September 12th, 1964, D: Henric Hirsch)

The Master, in the late stages of Time Lord decrepitude, plans The Doctor's demise in "The Deadly Assassin"

Season Fourteen was the third and final block of *DW* on which Hinchcliffe would serve as producer, and Holmes would also move on midway through Season Fifteen. Hinchcliffe would be reassigned to the BBC's short-lived new police series *Target* (1977-78), devised by Graham Williams; by strange coincidence (or possibly design?), it was Williams who was to become his successor on *Doctor Who*.

The season opened with two stories of possession. "The Masque of Mandragora" (aired October 4th to October 25th, 1976, D: Rodney Bennett) is one of the most literate of all of the Time Lord's serials; not only is *Mandragora* Latin for the plant known in English as Mandrake (which in folklore is said to possess magical qualities), but the story has also been equated to Hamlet's discussions on the supernatural. This is a sumptuous costume drama set during Renaissance Italy (actually filmed in Portmeirion, a village in Gwynedd [pronounced "Gwyneth", North Wales), where the TARDIS lands, unwittingly carrying with it Mandragora energy that possesses an underground cult—the outlawed Brotherhood of Demnos—who are intent on dragging the world, kicking and screaming if necessary, back to the Dark Ages. This mixture of history

and the black arts uses the Mandragora Helix to symbolize the superstition that would become negated by science during the Age of Reason.

Disembodied hands have a long and grand tradition in horror. Amicus in particular employed the spine-tingling actions of more than one malevolently mobile severed mauler (e.g., in both Freddie Francis' **DR. TERROR'S HOUSE OF HORRORS** [1964, UK] and Roy Ward Baker's **AND NOW THE SCREAMING STARTS!** [1973, UK]). *DW* Season 14's second possession arc, "The Hand of Fear" (aired October 2nd to 23rd, 1976, D: Lennie Mayne), is set on contemporary Earth, and has Sarah getting possessed by the fossilized manual extremity of one Kastrian Eldrad (Judith Paris/Stephen Thorne), a criminal who was destroyed out in space as punishment for attempting to wipe out his own race. Sarah hijacks a nuclear reactor where radiation recreates the creature; now fully regenerated, Eldrad persuades The Doctor to take him back to Kastria, but the planet has since been destroyed in his absence, just in case Eldrad should ever return. At the serial's conclusion, Dr. Who has homeworld issues of his own: upon receiving an urgent summons from The Time Lords, he is forced to leave Sarah behind on Earth. This action resulted in the controversial 1976 story arc "The Deadly Assassin" (discussed below). In her female form, Eldrad presents a ruthless beauty, and Sladen is threatening while under the influence, then feistily accepting of her fate in her farewell scene. Sladen appeared in 80 episodes of the classic series between 1973 and 1976, and through subsequent audio dramas, reboot appearances and spinoffs, new generations could also fall in love with her grounded-yet-infectious charisma. Sladen's swift death from pancreatic cancer in April 2011 left the Whovian community in shock, and BBC Four fittingly reshowed "The Hand of Fear" as a tribute to the actresses' timeless appeal.

****

Producer Irene Shubik's book *Play for Today: The Evolution of Television Drama* (1975) is an account of her career that has become the standard reference work on the subject *[see Endnote #15]*. Shubik's influence on single play development encompassed *Out of the Unknown*, *Wessex Tales*, *The Wednesday Play* (and its transitional form *Play for Today*), as well as the BBC 2 equivalent *Playhouse,* which provided the eight paranormal tales discussed hereunder, most of which are now presumed lost from any archive.

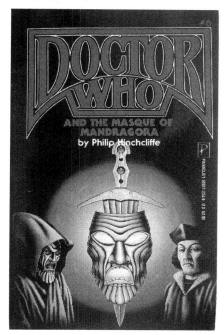

The less-than-amazing American Pinnacle edition; art by David Mann

The Corporation's weird one-tale wonders continued with two episodes of *BBC2 Playhouse*: "The Breakthrough" (airdate: January 8th, 1975, D: Graham Evans), an adaptation of Daphne du Maurier's tale about a scientist who builds a machine which can capture the life-force of a person after death, and also in the same year, "Mrs. Acland's Ghosts" (airdate: January 15th, 1975, D: Mike Newell).

Exhibiting some elements of Poe's famous short story "The Facts in the Case of M. Valdemar" (1845), Du Maurier's "The Breakthrough" tells of Saunders (Simon Ward), who is sent on assignment to a remote government lab to help prove the existence of a theoretical new form of energy. The experiment involves a subject close to death, as well as placed in a computer-induced hypnotic trance and telepathic communication. The person, a young girl, is a mentally-deficient but psychically-gifted child—possibly deeply affected by the death of her twin—who can report dying sensations posthumously. Lacking any clear resolution and suffering from limiting studio sets and stifled performances, there is too much speculation to enable the drama to breathe, even in its airy rural Suffolk exteriors. "The Breakthrough" is in some ways reminiscent of Glendale's **THE ASPHYX** (1973, UK, D: Peter Newbrook), which also documents spirits

and near-death experiences before similarly descending into absurdity. Far more melancholic is William Trevor's "Mrs. Acland's Ghosts", in which a tailor named Mr. Mockler (John Bluthal) receives a fateful letter from a stranger named Mrs. Acland (Sara Kestelman). The woman tells him of how the three ghosts of her deceased childhood siblings have continued to make appearances to her; Mockler discovers that Mrs. Acland is now in a mental institution—having been placed there by her husband—and was in fact an only child.

After these two try-outs, in 1976 *Playhouse* mutated into the six-story ESP-themed series *The Mind Beyond*. In the first three tales of this, "Meriel the Ghost Girl" (airdate: September 29th, 1976, D: Philip Saville) explores the contradictory nature of psychic experiences, opening with George Livingston (Donald Pleasence) witnessing a convincing séance, only for its authenticity to then be questioned in a *film noir*-style pastiche and subsequently being reevaluated by young reporter Robina Oliver (Janet Street-Porter, of all people); while "Double Echo" (airdate: October 6th, 1976, D: Alan Bridges) sees autistic teenager Alison Fisher (Geraldine Cowper) receiving treatment from Harley Street physician

A signed promo pose of Louise Jameson as fearless Sevateem she-warrior Leela, in her most iconic outfit

Dr. Mallam (Jeremy Kemp), only for the pair to develop a telekinetic bond; and finally, in "The Love of a Good Woman" (airdate: October 13th, 1976, D: John Gorrie), following the death of his first wife, Henry Ridout (William Lucas) remarries and builds a new life for himself in a harbor town, only to have his dead wife's restless spirit start communicating with him using his young daughter as a conduit from The Beyond.

The second half of the series starts with "The Daedalus Equations" (airdate: November 20th, 1976), wherein mathematical variables from a dead scientist are channeled into money-grubbing fraudulent psychic Eileen Gray (Megs Jenkins), yet the equations continue; "Stones" (air-

A purely gratuitous shot of ex-Who Jon Pertwee in his second-most-famous role: the loveable living scarecrow Worzel Gummidge!

date: November 27th, 1976) details an ambitious plan for the relocation of Stonehenge from the Wiltshire moorlands to London's Hyde Park in hopes of boosting tourist revenues (!), with Oxford academic Nicholas Reeve (Richard Pasco) realizing that the disappearance of three children is linked to their fathers' ownership of the last-known copies of *Stonehenge Defended*; while "The Man with the Power" (airdate: December 3rd, 1976) is a 'second coming of (a Black) Christ' story, with Boysie (Willie Jonah) embarking on a divine quest.

The opening titles of *The Mind Beyond* usher the viewer into a world of haunted faces and electrical impulses, a twilight domain away from the more rational human senses. *Playhouse* typified the giddy pseudoscientific air that was so prevalent in '70s BBC drama, but the center-staging of mentally disturbed characters—not to mention Livingston's mild if questionable interest in ghost girl Meriel's nakedness—clash with the more conventional yarns of mysteries better left alone; and, in "The Man with the Power", religious allegory quite frankly seems a leap way too far for the series to pull off.

****

While the earliest versions of Oscar Wilde's once-scandalous 1890 novel *[see Endnote #16]* date back as far as the early silent era of cinema (beginning *circa* 1910), it is Albert Lewin's ultra-classy 1945 Hollywood version of **THE PICTURE OF DORIAN GRAY**, co-starring Hurd Hatfield in the title role along with George Sanders and Angela Lansbury, that is debatably the best-remembered and highest-regarded adaptation, although numerous other dramatizations of *Dorian Gray* have been produced since then. Perhaps due to the fact that the 1970s decade was one of unparalleled permissiveness and hedonistic decadence—both of which are major thematic concerns within the story itself—there was a mini-resurgence of interest in the timeless (pun intended!) tale of the Adonis-like, ever-youthful immortal Dorian Gray during the so-called "Sexy 'Seventies", a.k.a. "The Permissive Era". First we got Sam Arkoff's and Harry Alan Towers' Eurotrashy 'Mod' multinational co-production **DORIAN GRAY** (*Das Bildnis des Dorian Gray*, 1970, West Germany/UK/Italy, D: Massimo Dallamano), starring Helmut Berger as Dorian, along with Richard Todd, Herbert Lom and Marie Liljedahl. Then there was Dan Curtis' slick tele-production of **THE PICTURE OF DORIAN GRAY** (1973, USA, D: Glenn Jordan), boasting a strong, primarily British cast that included the likes of Shane Briant (as Dorian), Nigel Davenport and Fionnula Flanagan. Fittingly, an "all-male" XXX parody of the story, naturally enough entitled **THE PORTRAIT OF DORIAN GAY** *[sic!]* (1974, USA, D: J.J. English) was produced at the height of the '70s so-called "Porno Chic" trend, and we can only wonder whether the openly, outspokenly and flamboyantly homosexual Wilde would have approved had he lived long enough to see it.

During the same period, also broadcast during the final Hinchcliffe/Holmes *Doctor Who* season was the *BBC Play of the Month* adaptation of **THE PICTURE OF DORIAN GRAY** (airdate: October 19th, 1976), as adapted by the playwright John Osborne. *Dorian Gray* was Wilde's only novel, and this Faustian Gothic, which many believe to be the finest adaptation made to date, explores the Aesthetic Art movement as drama— that is to say, elevating art over intellectualism. Dorian, the eponymous eternally youthful, undying character, enjoys the hedonistic pleasures of a double life while mixing high society with murder. Although such scenes are excluded from this quite conservative BBC version, Gray's frequenting of London opium dens equates crime with the so-called lower classes as High Art is to the upper class, a coarseness of comparison that acts as a direct thematic link to Stevenson's *The Strange Case of Dr. Jekyll and Mr. Hyde.*

While observing Basil Hallward (Jeremy Brett) painting a portrait of Dorian Gray (Peter Firth), Lord Henry Wotton (Sir John Gielgud) preaches his world view of beauty being the only aspect of life worth pursuing. This prompts Dorian to wish that his canvas likeness would age instead of he himself, and he consequently goes on to explore his appetite for sensuality, starting with a courtship of a beautiful actress named Sibyl Vane (Judi Bowker, the future Andromeda character in **CLASH OF THE TITANS** [1981, UK/USA, D: Desmond Davis]). Following a poor performance by her, however, Dorian rejects Sibyl, as to him the acting profession *was* her beauty; thus, when her sub-par acting skills are revealed to him, she suddenly becomes ugly in his eyes. On returning home, Gray notices that his painting has started to deteriorate. After receiving news that the grieving Sibyl has since committed suicide by swallowing prussic acid, Dorian begins to exploit his good looks by leading a debauched life. In self-pitying anger, he blames his fate on Basil, and stabs him to death. Deciding that only full confession will absolve him, Dorian destroys

Well past his expiry date, Hurd Hatfield in **THE PICTURE OF DORIAN GRAY** (1945) begins showing his age in a *bad* way!

the last vestige of his conscience, and the only piece of evidence remaining of his crimes. Upon stabbing his portrait, Gray recoils bloodied onto the floor, aging at a vastly-accelerated rate while the painting regains its original youthful form, silently mocking him in death.

Labeled the "most Wildean" adaptation, this feature-length *DotM* also includes definitive portrayals of the hedonistic Gray, aristocratic dandy Wotton, and infatuated artist Hallward. Although Wotton is the only one of the three main players without a character arc, this is more than compensated for by a channeling of Wilde at his most enchantingly deceptive. Lord Henry seduces Dorian through a poisonously irreverent wit that aims to shock, bait and test conventional truths; though naïve, Wotton's radical theories send Dorian into a tailspin, the fragilely vain Gray's early insecurities making him the perfect clay for the manipulative lord's willing hands to mold.

This particular take on the oft-told fable also accentuates the gay subtext more than most (especially in the relationship between Dorian and Alan [Nicholas Clay], when the latter is asked to draw on his experience in chemistry in order to dispose of the murdered Basil's body). Such homoerotica plays a large role, structurally speaking: the beauty of Basil's painting of Dorian depends entirely upon his adoration of him; similarly, Lord Henry is overcome with the desire to seduce Gray and mold him in his own misguided image. As a homosexual living in an intolerant society, Wilde asserted this philosophy partially in an attempt to justify his own lifestyle. For although beauty and youth remain of utmost importance, the price one must pay for them is exceedingly high. Indeed, Dorian gives nothing less than his very soul when opting to view Sibyl's self-administered death as the achievement of an artistic ideal rather than a needless tragedy for which he is at least indirectly responsible, if not more so.

The end-result when a Gallifreyan exceeds his or her regenerations...they turn into gloopy corpses!

Holmes' scripts for the *DW* serial "The Deadly Assassin" (aired October 30th to November 20th, 1976, D: David Maloney) take onboard Richard Condon's famed-and-acclaimed political novel about brainwashing, *The Manchurian Candidate* (1959). In "Assassin", Dr. Who is wrongfully accused of the assassination of the Time Lord President, but it is in fact only a frame-up plot engineered by a dying Master (Peter Pratt). Having used up all dozen of his regenerations, The Master now aims to control the hierarchy so he can obtain the Sash and Rod of Rassilon, keys to the Eye of Harmony, the source of all the Time Lord's power. When Who links his mind into the virtual reality of Matrix (a pretty novel concept for 1976!)—which has accumulated the wisdom of his race—he wins a struggle with a hooded opponent revealed to be Chancellor Goth (Bernard Horsfall), who has been used as a pawn. Having gained access to the Eye of Harmony, The Master now has aims to give new life to his withered, decaying, putrid husk of a body.

"The Deadly Assassin" provides a number of firsts for *Who*: a maximum regeneration number set at twelve (though perhaps a full baker's dozen might have been more apt?); no traveling companion; the portrayal of a layered society consisting of various ranks and chapters (very different from the glimpses seen in "The War Games" arc [a longer than usual ten-parter aired April 19th to June 22nd, 1969, D: David Maloney] and "The Three Doctors" [aired December 30th, 1972 to January 20th, 1973, D: Lennie Mayne]); and trivia such as the TARDIS being listed as a "Type 40" capsule. But for many, this spoiled the mystery of enigmatic The Time Lords' backstory, revealing Gallifrey as having a planetary power structure not so far removed from the doddering ol' House of Lords, or some crusty Oxbridge academic society (one decrepit Time Lord even

complains about having hearing and hip problems!). But within the Matrix, the adventure is irresistible, giving the show its most notorious and sadistically violent moment: the drowning of The Doctor at Goth's hands which gave Mary Whitehouse such palpitations. Providing this powerful, lingering image for *DW* kids to mull over for a whole week was too much for the National Viewers and Listeners Association linchpin to take, and after much whining-and-whinging from the censorious contingent, The Beeb caved under pressure and the scene was shortened/censored for repeat airings *[see Endnote #17]*.

Chris Boucher's "The Face of Evil" (aired January 1st to 22nd, 1977, D: Pennant Roberts) explores a different kind of horror. The TARDIS arrives on a planet where the savage Sevateem race worship Xoanon, "who" (i.e., *what*) is in fact a spaceship computer that The Doctor once inadvertently drove schizoid by endowing it with a multiple personality ("You can't expect perfection, even from *me!*"). Introducing the Time Lord to Sevateem wild-girl Leela (Louise Jameson)—and Jelly Babies!—here we have a fusion of the malfunctioning HAL 9000 from Kubrick's **2001: A SPACE ODYSSEY** (1968, UK/USA) combined with the generational degeneration/disintegration of William Golding's *Lord of the Flies* (1954).

Also written by Boucher, "The Robots of Death" (aired January 29th to February 19th, 1977, D: Michael E. Briant) is a "Deadly Assassin"-esque tale of deception ("...*nothing* is inexplicable, only unexplained..."). Mixing elements of Frank Herbert's *Dune* (1965) with Agatha Christie's *And Then There Were None* (1939), as well as in the process completely inverting the first and foremost of Asimov's "Three Laws of Robotics" (i.e., *"A robot may not injure a human being or, through inaction, allow a human being to come to harm"*), the TARDIS materializes aboard a sandminer that is combing an alien world for minerals to plunder. The massive vehicle is run by a small human crew who are aided by three classes of robots (Dums, Vocs and a Super Voc), and the Doctor and Leela come under suspicion when the crew are killed off by an unseen assailant. With the aid of undercover agents Poul (David Collings) and his robot associate D84 (Gregory de Polnay), the true culprit is revealed to be Dask (David Bailie), a scientist raised by robots who has been drastically reprogramming the automatons to commit murder and consequently form a superior order ("I see. You're one of those boring maniacs who's going to gloat, hmm?" smartasses Doc. "You going to tell me your plan

"The Face of Evil" is purely a technological tale of a computer gone mad

for running the Universe?!"). The program rises above its cramped 'people-killed-off-in-an-en-closed-environment' foundation by adopting a highly distinctive art deco design and treating viewers to some memorably—if contradictorily, for purists—lethal robots. Of all the numerous inspiration sources and influences that have been attributed to Ridley Scott's **ALIEN** (1979, UK/USA) over the years *[see Endnote #18]*, don't forget that the present Boucher story also involves a claustrophobic off-world mining setting and an undercover A.I. android. *Hmmm…*

The six-episoder "The Talons of Weng-Chiang" (aired February 26th to April 2nd, 1977, D: David Maloney) was Hinchcliffe's fog-laden series swansong, a throwback to the 'yellow peril' genre that was so prevalent in the 'Twenties and 'Thirties pulps thanks to the writings of Sax Rohmer and the like. "Chinese" magician Li H'sen Chang (English actor John Bennett [1928-2005], sporting now-decidedly-non-PC 'inscrutable Oriental' makeup and 'tong dragon lord' getup much along the lines of Fu Manchu) procures young girls for Magnus Greel (Michael Spice, provider of the titular evil Time Lord's voice in "The Brain of Morbius"), a 51st-Century war criminal who has come to 19th Century London to retrieve his lost time cabinet. Amateur sleuthing and a sinister living doll named Mr. Sin ("little person" actor Deep Roy) make this story an entertaining romp, despite the major flaw of the giant sewer rats, which Greel uses to keep people away from his Palace Theatre lair. But it

was also the first *Doctor Who* ever to depict the taking of illicit drugs (i.e., opium), and its violent use of nunchakus led to trouble with the censor for its first release on VHS. The most dominant controversy, however, was its uniformly *bleak* and surprisingly unflattering portrayal of the Chinese (e.g., "…inscrutable chinks…"), which led to a rebroadcast ban in Ontario after complaints from the Chinese-Canadian community.

UK VHS for "The Talons of Weng-Chiang"

Part VI: State of Decay | An Electric-Eclectic Mix of Success & Failure

"We must survive, all of us. The blood of a human for me, a cooked bird for you. Where is the difference?...I do not die like the bee when I sting once. I become stronger."
|– Dracula (Louis Jourdan) in **COUNT DRACULA** (1977)

"The dead and the living can never be one!"
|– Rose (Cheryl Kennedy) in "Schalcken the Painter" (1979)

In "Horror of Fang Rock", The Doctor comes face to, *uhh*, 'face' with a blobular alien villain.

Who: "Now I remember...
Reuben the Rutan!"
Rutan: "You know our form?"
Who: "Well, when you've seen
one Rutan, you've seen
them all!"

Hinchcliffe and Holmes had provided viewers with unprecedented levels of violence during their three seasons of *Doctor Who*. This reputation shadowed Hinchcliffe on *Target*, his new baby that was conceived in direct response to the rousing success of ITV's gritty coppers-'n'-villains show *The Sweeney* (1975-78). *Target* was also criticized for its excess usage of physical force, and to further mirror his time on *Doctor Who*, the BBC reportedly received some 5,000 letters of complaint from Mary Whitehouse's ever-watchful champions of moral decency, the so-called League of Light.

Incoming producer Graham Williams was under pressure from Beeb brass to tone-down the horror elements with his premiere block of serials. But right from the onset, Williams became embroiled in a number of tussles with the bureaucracy. His first intended serial, Terrance Dicks' "The Witch Lords" / "The Vampire Mutation", was vetoed late in the game because expenditures on it would undermine the lavish

production of Bram Stoker's *Dracula* (1897) that was then in preproduction (see below); Louise Jameson quit as Leela; and, in an attempt to reconnect with *DW*'s original intended audience as a children's show by upping the comedy quotient, the 'comic relief' robotic dog K9 became a regular companion—much to Tom Baker's entirely understandable chagrin *[see Endnote #19]*.

Against this backdrop, it's amazing that Williams' initial broadcast—"Horror of Fang Rock" (aired October 3rd to 24th, 1977, D: Paddy Russell)—became the absolute triumph that it is: one of the final genuinely scary classic-era adventures, it includes more inevitable nods to Nigel Kneale *[see Endnote #20]* as well as some discernible trace-elements of the Quatermass-esque Atomic Age Brit monster classic **THE TROLLENGERG TERROR** (a.k.a. **THE CRAWLING EYE**, 1958, D: Quentin Lawrence; based on the [unfortunately now-lost] 1956-57 ATV miniseries of the same name).

After arcing across the night sky in a blazing (quote) "fireball" (possibly an incoming meteorite), a shape-changing, tendril-trailing, amorphous, gelatinous mass—in actuality an advance scout for a hostile alien race from the planet Ruta 3, known as the Rutan—crash-lands into the sea nearby to an isolated English lighthouse during the Edwardian period. While the installation is initially only populated by its crew of three (one of whom shortly dies under mysterious circumstances), soon The Doctor and his 'new' female sidekick Leela (Louise Jameson, who both debuted on and resigned from the series in the same year ['77]) arrive in the TARDIS, plus four survivors (three gentry 'toffs' and an able-bodied seaman) from a steamship wreck further swell the numbers to a total of eight. The Rutan—engaged in a perennial war with the Sontarans (an epic conflict spanning more than 50,000 years!)—is killing in a quest to absorb life-giving electricity (explaining the creature's attraction to Fang Rock, the lighthouse's lamp is of the 'new-fangled' electric variety rather than an outdated oil-powered one, you see). It plans to use the absorbed electrical energy to power a spatial beacon with which to summon the Rutan battle fleet Earthward in order to use our world as a tactical stronghold against the enemy Rontaran ships… in a conflagration that will inevitably leave Earth a scorched cinder in its aftermath!

The realistically-cramped and claustrophobic lighthouse scenes were shot at Pebble Mill Studios in Birmingham, representing the only time to this point that the series had ever ventured out from its London studio base to other facilities. Boasting top-notch performances all-round, with the various characters moving back-and-forth to and from different floors of the lighthouse as required by the script, this is a tense tale that makes the most of its small cast and location, even if it is rather lacking in the kinetic intensity of a Hinchcliffe/Holmes entry. Perhaps feeding off of their reported off-screen personal tensions, Baker and Jameson are both outstanding; The Doctor at his unpredictable best, while Leela—here wearing a far-less-scimpy costume than her trademark animal-hide 'savage girl' outfit (perhaps at the behest of the censorial puritans?)—is typically fearless. This particular teleplay references real-life historical events surrounding the inexplicable disappearance of three lighthouse keepers from the Flannan Isles lighthouse in around 1900, a legend that is a mixed bag of hoax log entries, alleged sea monsters and a longboat full of ghosts heading to the Isle on the night the light went out. Alluding to similar such nautical

kinds of lore, in Episode 2 of *DW*'s "HoFR" serial, crotchety but goodhearted old dry-docked sea salt-turned-lighthouse-keeper Reuben (excellently played by Colin Douglas [1912-1991], a prolific player on innumerable British TV shows) ominously ascribes the night's troubles to the legendary "Beast of Fang Rock" ("There's no such animal," says Who skeptically in response to this claim. Not that he's by any means ruling-out the possibly of some unknown beast being involved, mind you!).

Electrically charged and giving off an emerald-greenish phosphorescent glow, the newly arrived extraterrestrial blobular glob generates its own artificial fogbank to serve as a smokescreen. The least-likeable of the shipwrecked toffee-nosed gits, Lord Palmerdale (Sean Caffrey [1940-2013], an alumnus of Val Guest's **WHEN DINOSAURS RULED THE EARTH** [1970, UK]) is a jumped-up bullying blowhard who arrogantly barks orders at his perceived social lessers ("Insubordinate ruffian!")—Dr. Who included—as though he has a God-given right to. No sooner has he opened his pompous gob than we peg him as prime disposable monster fodder (having had enough of his BS, even the hot-tempered Leela whips out her trusty stabber at one point and threatens to cut his heart out if he doesn't quit

AND THE HORROR OF FANG ROCK
TERRANCE DICKS

UK tie-in novel; art by Jeff Cummins

Stephen Jilks   *Channel of Darkness*

shooting his obnoxious mouth off!). Sure enough, he soon gets his c/o the alien, just as expected. After disposing of poor ol' Reuben off-screen, the green-glowing, jellyfish-like invasive lifeform assumes his shape ("...the Chamelon Factor," surmises Doc). Following this, it disposes of the insufferable Palmerdale character. (***Attention: SPOILER ALERT!***) As the death-toll rises, the following grim realization hits the Time Lord: "Leela, I've made a terrible mistake. I thought I'd locked the enemy out. Instead I've locked it *in*—with *us*!" When the jig is up, the Rutan ("We are specially trained in the new metamorphosis techniques") abandons its human simulacrum façade and resumes its normal form. Foiling the Rutan's master plan but good, Leela blasts the blobulous gobbet into a puddle of luminous snot using an improvised mortar, while Who jerry-rigs a large diamond (filched from the pocket of the late Palmerdale) so as to transform the Fang Rock lighthouse lamp into a powerful super-laser with which to knock-out the incoming Rutan mother-ship and thwart the invasion proper. Considering its minimal cast, "HoFR" racks-up quite the body-count (i.e., 6), with only our main hero and heroine surviving at the end.

Next up, "Image of the Fendahl" (aired October 29th to November 19th, 1977, D: George Spenton-Foster) was one last stab at Gothic horror for the Time Lord. In contemporary England, Professor Fendelman (Denis Lill) subjects a 12,000,000-year-old skull to the effects of his Time Scanner, thus providing a channel via which the malevolent Fendahl can terrorize the Earth once more. The skull's power also infiltrates fellow scientist Thea Ransome (Wanda Ventham, leading lady of **THE BLOOD BEAST TERROR** [a.k.a. **THE VAMPIRE-BEAST CRAVES BLOOD**, 1967, UK, D: Vernon Sewell] and periodic cast member of Gerry and Sylvia Anderson's live-action SF show **UFO** [1970-73, UK]), who is eventually transformed into the Fendahl core, mutating colleagues into snake-like monsters. Mankind being manipulated by an ancient alien once again draws from Nigel Kneale's *Quatermass and the Pit* (1958), but the story is let down by the Fendahl itself: an attractive woman with fake eyes painted on her closed eyelids doesn't exactly do justice to a "terrifying entity" that feeds on death. Nor does the climax, in which a powerful creature that has the ability to teleport itself clear across space is obliterated by a mere handful of rock salt (even if in occult lore common salt is said to possess powerful evil-defeating properties, it nevertheless registers as a too-simplistic solution in the present context).

Above: Ancient Nigel Kneale-style evil *à la* Doctor Who. An ancient skull is unearthed during an archaeological dig, and proves to have belonged to a long-dead alien evil which is bent on devouring the human race; "Image of the Fendahl" was a not a favorite of the critics, but co-editor Tim sure does love it! *["It's the bee's knees!" – TP]*

Late '70s *Ghost Story for Christmas* entries were also largely disappointments *[see Endnote #21]*. "Stigma" (airdate: December 28th, 1977, D: Lawrence Gordon Clark) concerns a family who remove an ancient stone—a Brittonic *menhir*—from their back garden. As this *menhir* is lifted from the earth, a curse is unleashed, causing the mother, Katherine (Kate Binchy), to bleed uncontrollably. "Stigma" might easily be interpreted as a meditation on male attitudes towards the female process of menstruation; the first image that we see—foreshadowing the blood to come—is an out-of-focus red dot, which then morphs into the ill-fated family's red Citroen 2CV.

If "Stigma" is mechanical in its execution, Derek Lister's "The Ice House" (airdate: December 25th, 1978, D: Derek Lister) is hazy, cryptic and pretentious. In this, the most experimental and maligned of all the episodes, Paul (John Stride) has recently parted from his wife and moved to live at a residential health spa. The disappearance of a masseur and the behavior of the brother and sister who run operations, Clovis and Jessica (respectively played by Geoffrey Burridge and Elizabeth Romilly), whose actions ("It is our pleasure to please!") seem to be governed by a strange vine growing in an ice house, also figure in the plot (such as it is). While the older residents go about their stately business, Paul is the center of attention, although *why* is never made clear. Perhaps he's just the latest in a long line of guests from whom they draw their vitality (Jessica enjoys "having people" around)? Clovis' and Jessica's otherworldly connection to the overpowering scent of the controlling vine is also open to interpretation…but many viewers might be hard-put bothering to try figuring it out come the conclusion, which settles very little.

A late '70s example of the BBC anthology-format series was *Supernatural*, devised by Robert Muller. With it, Muller intended to hopefully rekindle the flavor of early horror cinema by giving audiences subtle tales of fear based around The Club of the Damned. Each week, a prospective member will tell a true tale of terror. If successful at chilling listeners, they will be given a lifetime membership. However, if they fail to do so, murder awaits them. The most uneven of all anthologies, it was inexplicably broadcast on BBC 1 in the summer, oddly scheduled to clash with BBC 2's popular *Horror Double Bill*s. *Supernatural* was shot on industry-standard videotape, and suffers—fittingly enough!—from visible "ghosting" on the oxide (the gloomy castles and Victoriana add to the show's tired façade). The Club of the Damned is as dysfunctional as the stories:

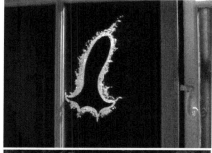

Top & Center: Two cryptic 'floral' images from the too-surreally-symbolic *AGSfC* episode "The Ice House" (1978), which is well-made and -acted enough, if ultimately not very memorable. **Above:** "What a *terrible* creature!'" John Justin as the undead and possibly vampiristic—at least in the spiritual sense—Vanderhausen, from *Omnibus*' effectively eerie and unsettling "Schalcken the Painter" (1979). *[check out p. 365 for a special Editors' Note]*

members are portrayed as stuffy armchair dwellers rather than as bloodthirsty Turks all-too-eager to literally wield an axe in the commission of murderous mayhem.

As adapted for the small screen by Gerald Savory, when the BBC's **COUNT DRACULA** (airdate: December 22nd, 1977, D: Philip Saville) finally arrived, it was rightfully considered

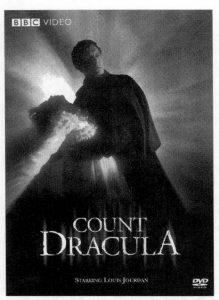

BBC VIDEO

COUNT
DRACULA

STARRING LOUIS JOURDAN

DVD

Louis Jourdan's excellent portrayal of The Count really makes this classy small-screen adaptation; UK DVD cover

the night. What music they make") in an almost casual, matter-of-fact and at times off-handed manner, devoid of any exaggeration or affectation, as though the actor were intentionally tactfully downplaying the role so as not to turn it into a broad caricature. This proves to be a wise strategy on Jourdan's part, as never does his performance veer into outright ham or camp, as might easily have happened in the hands of a lesser performer (picky purists may rest assured that there is nary a patented 'Lugosiism' on display anywhere throughout). At times the effortlessly charismatic star subtly punctuates his tastefully dignified reading with intense glowering glares/gazes or slight lip-curling sneers that give him a menacingly sinister air without being over-obvious about it. Arrogantly haughty and disdainful of humanity—perhaps understandably so, considering how much of its violent history he has witnessed first-hand over the centuries—to him the living are only a source of food at best ("You are nourishment to me…"), to be used and discarded as needed, as casually as empty bottles (he evens calls Mina "my beautiful wine-press" at one point). Early into the narrative, the plaintive nocturnal bleating of a sheep heard from off-screen echoes the ill-fated Harker (Bosco Hogan)'s symbolic 'lamb-to-the-slaughter' status. A known periodic sleepwalker as well as the more adventurous of the Westenra sisters, it is Lucy who is telepathically lured off into the cemetery by night to become 'turned' by the Count, who administers the fright-bite to her while she drapes moaning in pseudo-orgasmic ecstasy across a stone sepulcher. Despite the sudden (i.e., overnight) marked elongation of her eyeteeth afterwards, no one seems to notice!

one of the more faithful to its well-trod Stoker source material. It was certainly the first time on English screens that we got to see a literal (i.e., strongly-implied if non-graphic) depiction of the book's nastiest and least-often-dramatized incident: when the Count feeds his in-house trio of ravening white-gowned brides (played with frenzied eroticism by Susie Hickford, Belinda Meuldijk and Sue Vanner) a plump human infant *[see Endnote #22]*. Saville & Savory's '77 Beeb boob-tube version is also admired for its usage of some of the actual locations described within Stoker's original text, including St. Mary's Church in Whitby, Yorkshire and the decaying, ramshackle cemetery filled with lopsided, lichen-covered headstones that surrounds it; although it goes without saying that even this prestige production could ill-afford a working vacation for the cast and crew in the wilds of Transylvania for its early and latter-most sequences set outside England in the Carpathians and at Castle Dracula, so more local locales had to suffice, to more-than-adequate effect.

Neither the suave, otherworldly (literally) lady-killing Valentino nor the imperious, animalistic nobleman of either Universal or Hammer—despite his long, pointy fingernails and hairy palms!—Louis Jourdan's take on The Prince of Darkness has him speaking the familiar lines (e.g., "Listen to them, the children of

There is a pleasing cohesion and unity to all of the various elements that form **COUNT DRACULA**'s whole. The video optical effects work is inventive and effective without being overly elaborate, too flashy or overused, while any practical/physical effects (including the mandatory flapping rubber bat on a string!) are handled with considerable style and skill, as is the non-intrusive musical score by Kenyon Emrys-Roberts and the carefully-constructed, nuanced audio track. For instance, an eerie squeaking/twittering sound effect used during scenes involving bats harkens back to similar unearthly sounds heard in both Jacques Tourneur's aforementioned M.R. James filmization **NIGHT OF THE DEMON** (1957, UK) and Gordon Douglas' gi-ant attack classic **THEM!** (1953, USA); as a matter of fact, virtually the identical distinctive sound effect heard in **COUNT DRACULA** was previously used in a rival network's dramatization of *Dracula* some nine years previous *[see Endnote #23]*.

For all the faithful adherence to some aspects of the Stoker book—with a generous extended running time of 150 minutes to play with, this gave the adapters ample time for more plot elaboration than usual—there are at the same time also inevitable liberties/shortcuts taken with the source material: for example, the pert, prim and proper Mina (Judi Bowker again, from the above-discussed '76 small-screen version of **THE PICTURE OF DORIAN GRAY**, as well as the future heroine of **CLASH OF THE TITANS** [1981, UK/USA, D: Desmond Davis]) and Lucy Westenra (Susan Penhaligon, recently seen as Doug McClure's love interest in Amicus' dinosaur-filled lost world romp **THE LAND THAT TIME FORGOT** [1974, UK, D: Kevin Connor]) have been made sisters by the writer of the teleplay, while both the latter's suitors from the novel—Quincey P. Morris and Arthur Holmwood—are here combined into a single 'hybrid' in the form of visiting American diplomat Quincey P. Holmwood (Richard Barnes), to whom Lucy is devotedly betrothed…even after her undeath. Another change is that there is no playing around with the Count's age this time out, but this ensures a constant relevance, vitality and immediacy to Jourdan's performance. The rest of the cast is headed by the second-billed Frank Finlay (1926-2016) as Professor Abraham van Helsing. Affecting a non-emphatic Teutonic accent, he knows all the proper lingo ("…the undead… the *nosferatu*… the walking dead…") and astutely captures the tact, kindness and determination of a devoutly Godly vampire-slaying metaphysician. Jack Shepherd's Renfield, meanwhile, although kept in a padded cell, is (mostly) more introverted and restrained than the character is usually portrayed, and even expresses his penchant for a certain lowly winged insect by reciting verses from "The Fly" (1794), a poem by William Blake (*"Am not I / A fly like thee? / Or art not thou / A man like me?"*). It's only after the 'looney' deftly plucks a passing bluebottle out of the air and pops it into his gob that he allows his more unstable side to show, but despite his disordered mind he ultimately proves to be a decent, courageous and self-sacrificing sort far removed from Dwight Frye's unforgettably over-the-top characterization. When all is said and done, this handsomely mounted production ranks right up there with the very best adaptations of the oft-filmed *Dracula*, and has barely dated an iota.

To close out the BBC's long run of otherworldly tales from the '70s, director Leslie Megahey's

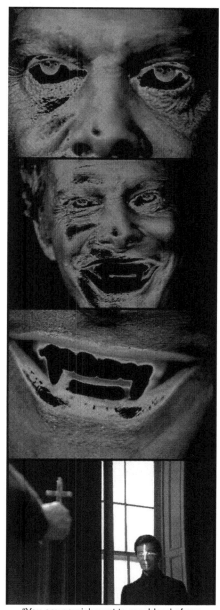

"You are nourishment to me; blood of my blood…" **Above, Top to Bottom:** 4 shots of Louis Jourdan as/in the '77 BBC **DRACULA**. In the top three C/U's, a simple-if-startling Chroma key 'negative image' effect endows him with an appropriately otherworldly aura. In the bottommost image, he is kept at bay by a reflection of the cross; the hand holding it belongs to Frank Finlay, as Abraham van Helsing

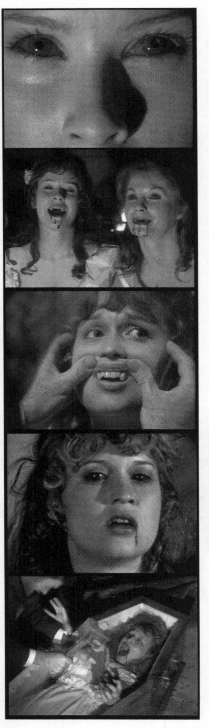

"Schalcken the Painter" (airdate: December 23rd, 1979) was screened as part of the *Omnibus* strand. A heavily-fictionalized tale about the real-life 17th Century Dutch artist Godfried Schalcken, this was adapted from *A Strange Event in the Life of Schalken the Painter* (1839), by Sheridan Le Fanu. Schalcken (Jeremy Clyde) is a student of Gerrit Dou (Maurice Denham) and an admirer of Dou's comely niece Rose (Cheryl Kennedy). As lifeless as the canvas he devotes his life to, Schalcken loses Rose's hand in marriage to the deathly, wealthy stranger Vanderhausen (John Justin), who is presented as a potentially 'undead' entity from beyond the grave (the program even includes a surprisingly graphic depiction—albeit within the framework of a nightmarish hallucination—of what is potentially an act of necrophilia, complete with fleeting full female nudity). If there is any 'moral message' to be had here at all, though, it is how females can often become regarded as objects of property by unscrupulous oppressors. The slow narrative and detached composition has been generously likened to Kubrick, and the story counteracts Jonathan Miller's "Whistle and I'll Come to You"; whereas Miller takes M.R. James and reflects the supernatural as mental breakdown, Megahey sees Le Fanu's tale as an artist's shattering loss of hope.

Above: The beefy Ilja Racek as Drac superimposed over Klára Jerneková as Mina Harker in the moody B&W Czechoslovak TV Stoker adaptation **HRABE DRÁKULA** ("Count Dracula", 1971) *[see Endnote #22, p.143]*. **Left, Top to Bottom:** From BBC's '77 televersion. Two shots of Dracula's vampirized 'brides', followed by three of Susan Penhaligon as Lucy Westenra, showing various phases of her vampirization—the beginning, midway, and the end. Her Hammeresque final staking is depicted in rather 'splashy' fashion for the time!

Part VII: Hiding Behind the Sofa | The Doctor Who "Fear Factor"

"[The] flak from Mary Whitehouse [...] was quite unwarranted. I think the kind of person who would have been upset by Doctor Who *would have been upset by anything."*
|– Elisabeth Sladen

Doc (Peter Capaldi) confronts a moldering monster—or is it the other way round?!—in the 2014 'New Who' episode "Mummy on the Orient Express"

Officious social activist and self-styled moral arbiter Mary Whitehouse, CBE frequently singled out mid-'70s *Doctor Who* as being (so she thought) particularly damaging to young minds due to its more shocking content. Yet the celebrated 'fear factor' and 'hiding-behind-the-sofa'-worthy mainstays of the program acted as a liberating and engaging, cathartic emotion for viewers, who always had the reassuring presence of the good Doctor to guide them through the scary spots.

Doctor Who in the 1970s played on people's real fears. Either reacting to social or political issues, or absorbing the darker aspects of living in that decade, the program's plotlines were big on themes of deception and duplication. It was as much a manipulation of the mind as a physical threat, illustrated by the qualities of *DW*'s leading and most enduringly popular foes, The Daleks (i.e., eradication of conscience) and The Cybermen (i.e., removal of all emotion). Aliens typically used infiltration/assimilation of bureaucracies and authority figures as tactics, also employing double agents to expedite their plans for conquest, and this overwhelming level of paranoia and mistrust was also applied to computers—which were then still very much in the

embryonic stage of their development—as well as the ever-ongoing battle between Science and Supernatural, Reason and Superstition.

Since its return in 2005, *Doctor Who* has continued to unsettle children with tales of gasmask zombies and Weeping Angels. These injections of the uncanny and macabre into familiar, homegrown surroundings mirror the classic era of Autons on Ealing High Street and Daleks emerging from the Thames. But by adopting a rapid-fire "edited highlights" cutting style and a super-slick, computer-graphics-heavy sheen that distances, distracts and detracts from what's occurring onscreen, the too-slick-sheened reboot has largely lost the gravitas of horrors steeped in the Gothic tradition, despite periodically utilizing supernaturally-created antagonists, even a traditional depiction of an Egyptian-style mummy (in the self-contained one-shot Peter Capaldi era episode "Mummy on the Orient Express" [airdate: October 11th, 2014, D: Paul Wilmshurst]), albeit one which only *appears* that way on the surface and is not what it seems to be. Consequently, for all its razzle-dazzle—and largely *because* of it— the newest incarnation of the 50+-year-old show struggles for emotional depth, with the protagonists and other characters crumpling under the

Above, Top to Bottom: Featuring creepy voiceover by horror king Donald Pleasence, while but a mere 90 seconds long, the 1973 British 'anti-drowning' safety TV spot *The Spirit of Dark and Lonely Water* (see text at above right) still haunts *Monster!* co-ed Steve F.'s memories to this day!

example, some of the most successful Public Information Films from during the Golden Age of *Doctor Who* drew on arresting and at times even all-out alarming images to amplify their points. Such as 1973's *Lonely Water* (also commonly known as *The Spirit of Dark and Lonely Water* or *I Am the Spirit of Dark and Lonely Water*, D: Jeff Grant), an 'anti-drowning' safety warning which aimed to scare children away from ponds and rivers by setting up a series of potential worst case scenarios involving a bank-haunting, hooded/monk-cassocked Grim Reaper figure (voiced in the short spot by no less than once-and-future horror movie kingpin Donald Pleasence ["I'll be back!"]).

It is the limbic Amygdala—within the temporal lobe of the brain—which hardwires this type of instinctual fear-conditioning for our self-preservation; the Amygdala also has a close association to memory, so shocks or scare tactics from our youth thereafter forever influence our behavior. Any moral guardian's intent to shield mental and physical experiences from the young consequently becomes a very important one.

As a special feature on the BBC's "The Deadly Assassin" DVD, released in 2009, a 16-minute documentary entitled *The Frighten Factor* aimed to answer what exactly *Doctor Who*'s all-important fear element entails, by interviewing a diverse panel of "experts", from an educational psychologist to a church minister. The show's ominous theme tune alone can be a frightening enough factor in itself to many. So, apparently, can The Doctor himself (as well as being a parent/uncle surrogate and role model to some). Although the program's visual use of everyday objects (dolls, dummies *et al*) and detrimental authority figures play with a child's conforming worldview, the juvenile attempts to play out these images within the comfort of their own homes, so it becomes an enjoyable experience for them. As the resident educational psychologist explains, it is this consumption of live-action visuals that makes the show resonate so effectively, as opposed to animated cartoons, which are too abstract to have the same effect. The "Hiding Behind the Sofa" mentality therefore projects the Gothic into a visual form of entertainment that can be played out in the comfort of your own home, epitomizing the "Pleasant Terror" coexistence of fright and delight.

****

Popular culture surrounds us in a whirlwind of nostalgia. Confusing the past with the present, and the real with the imaginary. A preference

exhausting weight of the visual onslaught, distractive bells-and-whistles/eye-candy, one thing piled on after another. But that is now.

This was then…

Inciting fear is one of the most effective ways of grabbing and holding audience attention. For

for the sights, sounds and scents of yesteryear often has its foundation in the carefree wonders of childhood. It was Immanuel Kant who stated that people who were steeped in nostalgia were triggered not so much for an actual place as for the lost time of their youth. David Lowenthal's *The Past is a Foreign Country* (1985) considers that nostalgia preys on the past to construct a form of escapism, and by savoring these ruins of artificiality, author Susan Stewart condemns the condition as a "social disease", maintaining that the past is something unspoiled, utopian and ever-unreachable to us. But perhaps that's as it should be.

During times of great social and political upheaval, the BBC television programming of the 1970s was a real Golden Age of Horror, and the key period for the last wave of genuine viewing gravitas. The Corporation embraced the Gothic, but also foretold how this portentously gloomy subgenre would mutate into pop-cultural visual art hauntology. Many lines feed into Gothic creation, such as a rise in scholarly antiquarian interest, an awareness in Eastern culture from colonial trade, et cetera. Ancient knowledge creates a detachment from latter-day convention, and provides a rich alternative to modern ostentatiousness. Through the political policies of '70s Britain, TV moved on to social commentary that could not help but be grotesque. The concept of "hauntology" was coined by philosopher Jacques Derrida in his work *Spectres of Marx* (1993), and was taken up by critics who referenced contemporary culture's persistent recycling of concepts and its incapacity to escape from old forms. If nostalgia is sentimental perspective, then hauntology bleeds into our psyche like a spectre that gestures towards an undefined future; towards what is now, inevitably, an intellectual abyss.

ENDNOTES: *(attributable to the author, unless otherwise indicated [i.e., "SF"])*

1 |- But lest we forget, the same antiquated English marriage laws which legally made a wife a man's (quote) "chattel" also just as surely made him her (quote) "beast of burden", so essentially both spouses became *one another*'s property. – **SF**

2 |- Piers Haggard's effective period horror film **THE BLOOD ON SATAN'S CLAW** (1971, UK) has pouting satanic neophyte Angel Blake (Linda Hayden) acting in league with a half-glimpsed, cowled Behemoth to tempt simple country folk over to the dark side. This particularly bestial incarnation of The Devil is regenerating his/its skin, with a coven of children in the beast's thrall from which to harvest the parchments. Inspired by the Manson Murders and child killer Mary Bell, the film stands as one of the keystones of the Folk Horror subgenre.

3 |- While it wasn't dramatized for the BBC as part of their classic *A Ghost Story for Christmas* franchise, a 'rival network' TV dramatization of the seminal 1911 James tale "Casting the Runes" (airdate: April 24th, 1979) was adapted by Clive Exton for *ITV Playhouse* (UK, 1967-), directed by Lawrence Gordon Clark. And who better to direct it but Clark, director of the best of The Beeb's earlier Yuletide terror tales? Julian Karswell, a.k.a. "The Abbot of Loughford" (Iain Cuthbertson) is an arrogant, megalomaniacal practitioner of the black arts—clearly modeled much along the lines of Aleister "The Wickedest Man Alive" Crowley—who seeks revenge in the worst way from those in the media who have slighted him by openly pooh-poohing his occult studies. Amongst other changes made to James' original story, the protagonist herein is female—in the form of investigating reporter Prudence

US one-sheet poster; artist unknown

Maximum Mummy Mayhem! In "Pyramids of Mars", Sarah Jane is about to be surprised by a robotic mummy *[top]*, and undead Prof. Marcus Scarman *[center]* transforms into the likeness of Sutekh *[above]*, an evil alien whose resemblance to the Egyptian god Bastet was more than mere coincidence

"The Ash Tree"). As of this writing, according to the IMDb, a new version of the oft-adapted "CtR" is reportedly in-development, but precise details are unknown. – **SF**

4 |- Produced as an episode of NBC-TV's adult-oriented thriller series *Lights Out* (USA, 1946-52), "The Lost Will of Dr. Rant" (airdate: May 7th, 1951, D: Laurence Schwab, Jr.) was a thoroughly Americanized version of James' tale "The Tractate Middoth" (first published in his 1911 collection *More Ghost Stories*), as adapted for television by Doris Halman. Starring Leslie Nielsen several years before his theatrical feature breakout role as the starchy space skipper in Fred McLeod Wilcox's SF überclassic **FORBIDDEN PLANET** (1956, USA), the story is here set stateside in Boston, Massachusetts and New Hampshire (albeit, this originally being "live" TV, entirely shot on interior sets). While compressed to a mere 22 minutes in order to fit into a tight half-hour timeslot, the rudiments of the story remain much the same, at least in content, although the show's brevity leaves little room for much in the way of character development or the building of any real atmosphere; in fact, the great writer's prose is virtually reduced to little more than a trifle. Aside from being briefly and indistinctly glimpsed as a crude lop-eyed prosthetic makeup applied to a short, stout actor, the 'undead' Rant's supposedly hideous deathly countenance is largely just hinted at by Nielsen's dialogue ("I saw that little old man, and he was *horrible*! ...His *eyes*—he didn't have real eyes, just this *spider*, and spider-webs...!"). A subsequent tele-adaptation, scripted by Dennis Webb, was made for *Mystery and Imagination* (UK, 1966-70): "The Tractate Middoth" (airdate: February 26th, 1966, D: Kim Mills), starring Giles Block, David Buck and Marian Diamond, with Edwin Finn as Dr. Rant. Sadly, this version, along with others in the *MaI* series (its '66 adaptation of James' "Lost Hearts" included) are no longer with us, although privately-made audio recordings of the program's soundtrack (with dialogue) alone are still extant to provide at least some non-visual hints as to its quality/effectiveness.

While an adaptation of the story wasn't mounted for BBC's 'first wave' (from 1971-78) of special Yuletide spook tales, M.R. James' "The Tractate Middoth" did finally reach the airwaves as an official entry in *A Ghost Story for Christmas* on December 25th, 2013, directed by Mark Gatiss (writer and host of the documentary *M.R. James: Ghost Writer* [D: John Das], which was aired immediately following his *AGSfC* episode on the same channel that same night). The sto-

Dunning (Jan Francis)—rather than male. Care of a hellish hex cast upon her by Karswell, the heroine finds a giant spider in her bed ("With *teeth*. Not an ordinary spider". Him being such an arachnophobe, perhaps understandably such arachnids or 'spiderous' imagery appear with some frequency in James' horror fiction, as well as in dramatizations of it). The cast of the present program also includes Bernard Gallagher, Joanna Dunham and Edward Petherbridge (previously seen in L.G. Clark's 1975 *AGSfC* adaptation of

ry's title—which for me has a distinct Lovecraftian timbre—is derived from "a collection of Hebrew writings", a.k.a. The Talmud. Just to be a total bastard to his few surviving family members, mean-spirited old misanthrope Dr. Thomas Rant ("Twisted, he was. *Twisted!* Where others had a soul, he had a *corkscrew*... He wasn't what you'd call Christian in his ways") hides his last will and testament from his expectant potential heirs by cryptically embedding the document amongst the title tome's Hebrew text, printed in reversed English characters. As his ex-housekeeper Mrs. Goundry (Eleanor Bron) describes Rant, her former employer: "Oh, I know he's a parson, but he's the very *devil!* ...Still, he's got a reckonin' comin' soon, I'nt 'e—with the Almighty! Or *[swivels eyes ominously downwards]* someone *else!*" This 2013 adaptation of "TTM" boasts a hypnotically eldritch and eerie texture; the musty, moldy air of the central library setting is speckled with innumerable drifting dust-motes, scintillating in filtered sunlight like so many tiny ethereal entities adding immensely to the atmsophere. While some might be of the opinion that it, uh, 'shoots its horror wad' a tad too prematurely, the episode has some wonderfully creepy—even *chilling*—moments that make it well worth a watch. – **SF**

5 |– M.R. James' other substantial attainments include the thorough cataloguing of the manuscript libraries of the University of Cambridge, and a translation of New Testament apocrypha. James also discovered a key fragment which led to excavations in the ruins of the abbey at Bury St.

Edmunds in 1902, in which the graves of several 12th-Century abbots were rediscovered.

6 |- The term "ragging" is more associated with the ritualistic bullying of new students in India and Pakistan. Sri Lanka has been especially affected as a result of British colonialism; soldiers returning from war reentered colleges and brought with them techniques learned in military camp, where people were made to fail as an individual, but succeed by working as part of a team.

7 |- Under a slightly shorter version of its original full-length title (i.e., "Oh, Whistle, and I'll Come to You, My Lad"), as "Oh, Whistle, and I'll Come to You", the story had a half-decade previous been adapted (co-written by Michael & Mollie Hardwicke) as a radio play for The Beeb, produced by Charles Lefeaux and broadcast on Christmas Eve of 1963. Future tele-adaptation star Michael Hordern also starred in that earlier audio-only version, which featured special sound effects—eerie whooshing wind very much included!—by the BBC Radiophonic Workshop that added immensely to the spooky proceedings. Audio would go on to play a vital role in the '68 TV version starring Hordern. (NB. Incidentally, those interested in hearing a fine sampling of said Workshop's output might want to lend an ear to their LP/cassette compilation entitled *Out of This World: Atmospheric Sounds and Effects from The BBC Radiophonic Workshop* [BBC Records & Tapes, 1976], which contains plentiful cool spacey synthesizer compositions and came in a cover whose suitably garish art featured a B.E.M. ["bug-eyed monster"]—a green

Tendril Loving Careless: The monstrous Krynoid alien in both its more human-sized mode *[right]*, and its XL edition attacking an English manor house; from "The Seeds of Doom"

Stephen Jilks   *Channel of Darkness*   **139**

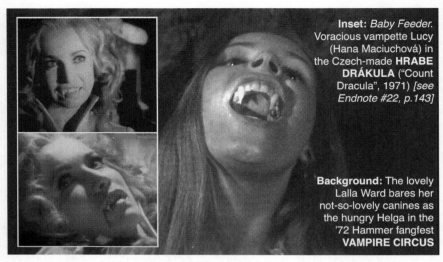

Inset: *Baby Feeder.* Voracious vampette Lucy (Hana Maciuchová) in the Czech-made **HRABE DRÁKULA** ("Count Dracula", 1971) *[see Endnote #22, p.143]*

Background: The lovely Lalla Ward bares her not-so-lovely canines as the hungry Helga in the '72 Hammer fangfest **VAMPIRE CIRCUS**

one, natch!—getting zapped by an astronaut's raygun.) In the spookiest scene of the '63 radio version of "OWAICTY", Malcolm Hayes played "The Thing", and his few lines were voiced in a suitably sinister otherworldly tone augmented by an electronic distortion effect which even today, more than a half-century on, is still quite unsettling to hear.

Not surprisingly, considering his seeming inextricable association with dramatizations of M.R. James' canon, celebrated stage/radio/TV/cinema actor, the future Sir (he received his knighthood in 1983) Michael Hordern (1911-1995), also narrated spoken-word recordings of many of the author's stories, including "Canon Alberic's Scrapbook" (1894/1904), "Lost Hearts" (1895/1904), "The Ash-tree," "Number 13", "The Mezzotint", "Count Magnus" (all 1904) "A School Story", "The Stalls of Barchester Cathedral", "Casting the Runes" (all 1911), "The Diary of Mr. Poynter" (1919), "The Uncommon Prayer Book" (1921), "The Haunted Doll's House" (1923), "A Warning to the Curious" (1925), and "Rats" (1929). All of said readings were collected into a now-OOP three-volume, six-tape series of audiocassettes (formerly available via EMI Records / Music For Pleasure / Decca Records / Argo): *Michael Hordern Reads Ghost Stories by M.R. James, Michael Hordern Reads More Ghost Stories by M.R. James* and *Michael Hordern Reads* Number 13 *and other Ghost Stories by M.R. James,* which may or may not (?) be currently commercially available on CD or some other digital format. All of the separate individual tales have been uploaded to YouTube, and as of this writing can collectively be found at the link entitled "Michael Horden *[sic!]* reads M.R. James", as well as numerous other audiobook readings of James' writings by other voices too. – **SF**

8 |– The daughter of the 7th Viscount of Bangor, Ms. Ward is also of pedigreed British cult movie heritage. Leaving quite an impression in her film debut—as the lithe and supple acrobat Helga in Hammer's **VAMPIRE CIRCUS** (1972, UK, D: Robert Young)—Lalla would also have a number of ties to *Doctor Who*; the actress, artist and author first appeared as Princess Astra in "The Armageddon Factor" (aired January 20th to February 24th, 1979, D: Michael Hayes) before becoming the second Romana and marrying Tom Baker in real life (their marriage lasted from 1980 to 1982, ending in divorce).

9 |- Also with strong links to Viking lore, the Ash is credited with a range of protective and healing properties frequently related to child health. Though there does not appear to be any religious reason why this tree should be associated with Ash Wednesday, the link is obvious, and in parts of England children used to bring a twig of black-budded Ash to school on this day. Any child who failed to remember this risked having his or her feet stomped on!

10 |– Killing ten passengers and injuring forty, this disaster occurred while the train was crossing a viaduct where a length of track had been removed during engineering works. Dickens was with his mistress and her mother in the first-class carriage, which did not completely fall into the river bed. He climbed out of the compartment through the window and, with his flask of brandy and a hatful of water, tended to the victims.

11 |– Ironically enough, the first issue of Marvel UK's *Doctor Who Weekly* (cover-dated October 17th, 1979), would see the start of a series of exemplary comic strip adventures far superior to the Time Lord's televised serials of the period. With the *Who* strip thankfully moved from its unnatural previous home at *TV Comic*, for the *DWW* strips artist Dave Gibbons and writers Pat Mills and John Wagner created sophisticated, emotionally engaging stories of a scale and substance that was only rarely attained on the telly series during the late '70s and '80s.

12 |– The Gothic Sublime is articulated by Immanuel Kant as the presentation of the unpresentable. Kant's colossal, the absolutely great, can occur only at that moment when reason gives way to imagination for a fleeting moment before it regains its power. What happened during this gap was the coming into being of the moment of the sublime. As stipulated by Schopenhauer and Freud, the oceanic sublime is the dissolution of self in death. This compulsion toward our own end helps explain the apocalyptic tendencies of The Gothic.

13 |– Charles Maturin's 'stories-within-stories' Gothic novel *Melmoth the Wanderer* (1820) sees the titular scholar selling his soul to the Devil for an extra 150 years of life. However, Melmoth fails to pass on his pact of damnation ("I have traversed the world in the search, and no one to gain that world, would lose his own soul!"). Like Faust, Melmoth must suppress his longings for a life of religion and love, becoming one of literature's greatest social outcasts.

14 |– If the Cybermen were becoming increasingly ineffective on screen, they were positively *pathetic* on the printed page! As a particularly

risible example, in one of John Canning's surreal Patrick Troughton-based strips for *TV Comic* ("Flower Power", #832-836, 1967), the silvery metallic 'menace' were even actually destroyed by the mere scent of *flowers*, of all things, in what was clearly intended as some kind of 'trendy' reference to hippies. In addition, the later (1985) Colin Baker story "Attack of the Cybermen" was particularly detrimental to both the Cybermen's mystique in particular and *Doctor Who* in general. By the mid-'80s point, the show's home network had become unnecessarily preoccupied with its back-catalogue, while the more obsessed fans were even acting as unpaid continuity advisers. This serial references earlier Cyber stories with the London sewers ("The Invasion"), a Cyber Controller and cryogenic chamber on their adopted planet of Telos ("The Tomb of the Cybermen"), and Mondas' imminent destruction in 1986 ("The Tenth Planet"). As for the "AotC" serial, out of this jumble comes a confused tale of the title robotoids trying to prevent the destruction of their homeworld in the past, while their domination of Telos seems assured in the future.

15 |– Other BBC anthologies that started in the early/mid-'70s were *Menace* (1970, 1973) and *Leap in the Dark* (1973, 1975, 1977, 1980). The latter changed format as many times as its stories did; initially featuring paranormal documentaries, the middle seasons (presented by Colin Wilson) consisted of reenactments, before the final season morphed into presenting original fiction dramas. While ordinarily its stories were laid in the mundane 'real' world, *Play for Today* also contributed tales of folk horror in "Robin Redbreast" (1970) and "A Photograph" (1977), meta-fantasies like "Penda's Fen" (1974) and "Red Shift" (1978), plus "Vampires" (1979), a popular entry about three boys watching **DRAC-**

British annuals from the original series (from the Saucerman Site Studios archives)

"Do I Have The Right?" Without a doubt one of *the* classic moments from any episode of *DW*, of either the original or reboot: caught in a serious dilemma, Baker as Who weighs the utter annihilation of the Dalek race against the moral implications of a future without them

ULA – **PRINCE OF DARKNESS** (1966) then coming to believe that a man in a local cemetery is one of the undead. Additionally, *The Omega Factor* was also screened in the final year of the decade. A clear forerunner to *The X-Files*, this ten-part BBC Scotland drama tells of journalist Tom Crane (James Hazeldine), who possesses untapped psychic powers. The show's fifth episode—"Powers of Darkness" (July 11th, 1979, D: Eric Davidson), in which teenagers hold a séance that unleashes the evil spirit of a dead witch—was labelled "thoroughly evil" by the ever-hyperbolic Mary Whitehouse, predictably enough.

16 |– First appearing in the July 1890 edition of *Lippincott's Monthly Magazine*, *The Picture of Dorian Gray* was presented in censored form, without Wilde's knowledge. After facing criticism for the work's homoeroticism, the writer subsequently expanded his characters' backgrounds so as to 'legitimize' the work, this in response to *The Scots Observer*'s question, "Why must Oscar Wilde go grubbing in muck-heaps?" In 2011, Belknap Press published *The Picture of Dorian Gray: An Annotated, Uncensored Edition*, which includes text that was deleted by Wilde's original editor.

17 |– The vigilantly meddlesome Whitehouse would also deplore "Genesis of the Daleks" for its (quote) "teatime brutality for tots," and remark on the close-up strangulations seen during "The Seeds

of Doom" (as well as the onscreen demonstration of how to make a Molotov Cocktail). During her endless censorial tirades—particularly against Johnny Speight, Dave Allen and Dennis Potter—she ran a successful campaign to ban Alice Cooper's hit single "School's Out" (1972) from being featured on the UK's top teen-oriented TV musical showcase show *Top of the Pops*. Cooper countered by sending Mary a bunch of flowers, believing the publicity helped the song to reach number one on the charts.

18 |– **ALIEN** screenwriter Dan O'Bannon would famously sum-up his various influences on the film by saying, "I didn't steal **ALIEN** from *somebody*, I stole it from *everybody*!"

19 |– K9 Marks I and II traveled alongside Tom Baker until 1981, when Mark III graduated to the one-off spinoff—pilot for an unsold series called *K-9 and Company* (1981, UK)—starring Elisabeth Sladen as Sarah, who gains a human companion of her own—her aunt's ward Brendan Richards (Ian Sears)—in a mundane tale of the occult, wherein it further transpires that K9 gets left for Sarah Jane by The Fourth Doctor. Entitled "A Girl's Best Friend" (D: John Black), this pilot episode was broadcast as a Christmas special and, despite strong ratings, the proposed series got vetoed by new BBC controller Alan Hart.

20 |– Nigel Kneale painted cynical landscapes of our future and developed into a genuine seer,

predicting the disintegration of broadcasting and society, as typified by his prediction/depiction of what would later come to be known as 'reality TV' in *The Year of the Sex Olympics* (1968). Kneale's arrival as a staff writer at the BBC coincided with television's post-Coronation mass appeal. Early drama was dominated by unambitious stage and literary adaptations, and there is some justification in Mark Gatiss' claim that the writer as good as invented popular television. Kneale's disdain for *Doctor Who* has been well-documented because of its wholesale 'homages' to Quatermass (to quote Kneale, "I once switched-on *Doctor Who*, and practically heard my own dialogue!"). But the writer's dislike can also be attributed to its treatment of children, or as Kneale put it, "bombing the tinies with insinuations of doom and terror."

21 |– The real "spirit" of the '70s *Ghost Story for Christmas* strand would have to wait until its belated short-lived revival of 2005 and 2006, with adaptations of M.R. James' "A View from a Hill" (airdate: January 2005, D: Luke Watson) and "Number 13" (airdate: December 22nd, 2006, D: Pier Wilkie). Both add a layer of weird science to their ghostly goings-on, and "AVfaH" (whose source story was first published in *The Living Age*, July 4th, 1925 and collected in the author's '25 collection *A Warning to the Curious and Other Ghost Stories*), particularly, evokes the washed-out landscapes and corner-of-the-eye creepiness so vivid in the early entries. The tale's protagonist, the youthful historian Dr. Fanshawe

(Mark Letheren), is yet another thinly disguised variant of the author himself. Central to the story is one Fulnaker Abbey, a no-longer-extant old building viewed by the young man as a 'mirage' through a pair of borrowed haunted binoculars. Long-destroyed, the rural abbey now only exists through the lenses of the field glasses and, on the aptly named Gallows Hill, ghostly figures attempt to hang Fanshawe from a gibbet... or is it all only in the protagonist's mind?

22 |- A similar scene had appeared—albeit shot in a restrained, non-explicit manner—some six years previously in **HRABE DRÁKULA** ("Count Dracula", 1971, D: Anna Procházková), a 76-minute B&W Czech made-for-TV adaptation of Stoker's novel starring Ilja Racek in the title role, who at one point provides his hungry brides with a 'midnight snack' in the form of a baby (that is implied rather than actually seen). The commanding, burly, heavily-bearded actor performed well in the part, even if he did differ quite vastly in appearance from the author's original conception of the Count. – **SF**

23 |- Adapted by Charles Graham, an earlier (B&W, 80m39s), often visually striking British tele-version of Stoker's novel from the BBC's rival commercial network was **DRACULA** (airdate: November 18th, 1968, D: Patrick Dromgoole), broadcast as part of Independent Television (ITV) / Thames Television's *Mystery and Imagination* series (Season 4, Episode 3). Sporting a rakishly devilish beardlet and affecting a

Skullfuckery: Baker as The Doctor confronts an ancient evil in "Image of the Fendahl"

New-Fangled: Denholm Elliott sported some atypical choppers as/in the non-BBC '68 TV **DRACULA**, and *[top]* his woodcut likeness from same

fairly subdued Slavic accent ("I do not drink... *wine*"), Denholm Elliott (1922-1992) stars to fine effect in the eponymous role. While many—especially the typical modern-day Emo/Goth teenybopper weaned on post-*Twilight* pretty-boy vampires!—might consider Elliott to have been miscast in the role, the seasoned actor acquits himself well in what might be regarded as an interestingly 'offbeat' portrayal of a much-stereotyped-to-the-point-of-caricature character. The biggest surprise of his performance comes when, immediately prior to putting the initial chomp on the slumbering Lucy's throat, he opens his mouth to reveal a pair of close-set, needle-sharp, rat-like fangs that rival Max Schreck's in the original **NOSFERATU** (*Nosferatu, eine Symphonie des Grauens*, 1922, Germany, D: F.W. Murnau) for sheer repulsiveness (see above). Despite this, however, the actress goes into paroxysms of orgasmic delight after being bitten! Professor van Helsing (Bernard Archard [1916-2008]) is called-in forthwith to diagnose the stricken girl's condition ("*Himmel!*" he exclaims in German, implying the worst), assisted by Lucy's dutiful fiancé, Dr. John Seward (James Maxwell [1929-1995]). Interestingly enough, Van Helsing's obligatory quickie seminar on vampirism for the skeptical Seward's benefit includes

(mispronounced) mentions of the Chinese *jiangshi* and the Malayan *penanggalan*, plus other international species of the blood-drinking undead.

At just over half the length of The Beeb's more ambitious full-color '77 mounting of the tale, the monochromatic '68 version—shot almost entirely on interior sets, unlike the later version, which often ventured out of doors—is obliged by necessity to condense the narrative to fit the tighter time constraints. Hence, the Jonathan Harker and Renfield characters are here combined into a single 'composite' character (named Jonathan Harker), played by Corin Redgrave ([1939-2010] complete with an unkempt mop of hair evidently turned white by fright), while a very young Susan George (then only 18) plays Lucy Westenra's part, her surname simplified to "Weston" for the occasion. Drac's bat-into-man transformations are much akin to those seen in Unipix's **HOUSE OF FRANKENSTEIN** (1944, USA) and **HOUSE OF DRACULA** (1945, USA) *[see p.347]*, featuring John Carradine as the Count, alias Baron Latos. Some of the moodily atmospheric imagery in the present production wouldn't look at all out of place in a Mexican or Italian vampire movie from earlier in the same decade. Interestingly enough for the time, one of the Count's briefly-seen triple threat of 'hopping' gossamer-draped vampire brides is played by a short-haired black actress (namely Nina Baden-Semper, of Trinidadian descent), postdating Jacqueline Sieger's appearance as "The Queen of the Vampires" in Jean Rollin's **THE RAPE OF THE VAMPIRE** (*Le viol du vampire*, 1968, France) by some six months. – SF

Works Consulted *(i.e., over the course of this entire article [Pts. 1 & 2])*

Books:
Condon, Paul and Sangster, Jim, *TV Heaven* (Collins, 2005)
Howe, David J. and Walker, Stephen James, *Doctor Who: The Television Companion* (BBC Worldwide, 1998)
Kerekes, David (editor), *Creeping Flesh: The Horror Fantasy Film Book Volume 1* (Headpress, 2003)
Kerekes, David (editor), *Creeping Flesh: The Horror Fantasy Film Book Volume 2* (Headpress, 2005)
Meikle, Denis, *Jack the Ripper: The Murders and the Movies* (Reynolds & Hearn, 2002)
Murray, Andy, *Into the Unknown: The Fantastic Life of Nigel Kneale* (Headpress, 2006)
Nevins, Jess, *The Encyclopedia of Fantastic Victoriana* (MonkeyBrain Books, 2005)

Octo-Men: The vaguely octopoidal Zygons rank among the very best of *Doctor Who*'s classic monster designs. **Inset:** Issue #93 (October 1976) of Marvel UK's tie-in periodical

Newman, Kim, *BFI TV Classics: Doctor Who* (British Film Institute, 2005)

Sleight, Graham, *The Doctor's Monsters: Meanings of the Monstrous in Doctor Who* (I.B. Tauris, 2012)

Turner, Alwyn W., *The Man Who Invented the Daleks: The Strange Worlds of Terry Nation*, (Aurum, 2011)

Magazines:

Inkol, Sheldon, "Where to Start with Doctor Who? The Best of the Third and Fourth Doctors" *Video Watchdog* #139 (Tim & Donna Lucas, 2008)

Meikle, Denis, "Time Travels in a Gothic Vein",

The Dark Side Presents: 50 Amazing Years of The Doctor (Ghoulish Publishing, 2013)

Warren, Nick, "A Ripper Who's Who", *Fortean Times* #155 (I Feel Good Ltd., 2002)

Online Sources:

Harris, Robert, "Elements of the Gothic Novel", @ *www.virtualsalt.com*, 2015

Kermode, Mark, "A Capital Place for Panic Attacks", @ *www.theguardian.com*, 2007

Lane, Anthony, "Fright Nights: the horror of M. R. James", @ *www.newyorker.com*, 2012

Pheby, Tom, "The Golden Era of Tom Baker", @ *www.warpedfactor.com*, 2014

YOU BETTER 'SQUATCH OUT!

From filmland's fear & fun-filled real & "reel" history, *Swamp Thing* artist & *Constantine* co-creator Steve Bissette spotlights select "Are They Real?" cryptids like the Yeti & Sasquatch, "They Can't Be Real!" critters from **THE KILLER SHREWS** to **THE GLASS-HEAD** to **CREATURE**, TV series from *One Step Beyond* to *Stranger Things*, and a menagerie of eccentric creators & creations from H.P. Lovecraft, Ron Ormond, and Janos Prohaska to Kevin Smith and the Duffer Brothers!

ENTER, IF YOU DARE, THE REALM OF CRYPTID CINEMA™...

the Movie-land of Sasquatch, Bigfoot, Bayou Beasts, Backwood Bogeymen and Bloodwater Brutes!

Available Now at Amazon.com

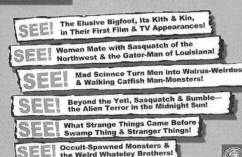

SEE! The Elusive Bigfoot, Its Kith & Kin, in Their First Film & TV Appearances!

SEE! Women Mate with Sasquatch of the Northwest & the Gator-Man of Louisiana!

SEE! Mad Science Turn Men into Walrus-Weirdos & Walking Catfish Man-Monsters!

SEE! Beyond the Yeti, Sasquatch & Bumble— the Alien Terror in the Midnight Sun!

SEE! What Strange Things Came Before Swamp Thing & Stranger Things!

SEE! Occult-Spawned Monsters & the Weird Whateley Brothers!

SEE! Sleepy LaBeef Beat a Man to Death With His Own Arm!

ANARCHY & MONSTERS

An Interview with Brett Piper
Parts 4 & 5 (of 6)

by Stephen R. Bissette

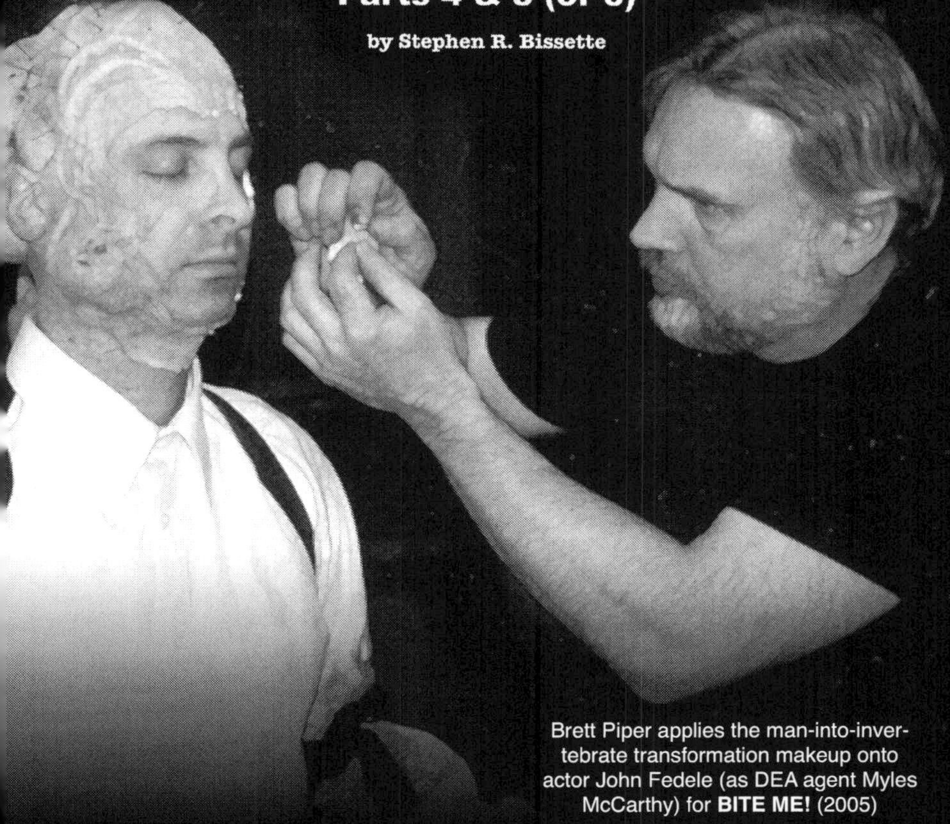

Brett Piper applies the man-into-invertebrate transformation makeup onto actor John Fedele (as DEA agent Myles McCarthy) for **BITE ME!** (2005)

> *"I'll tell you what the 'Brett Piper Universe' is about: anarchy and monsters. In all my movies the characters find themselves in situations, large or small, where they're on their own with no support from any kind of social structure... And there's* monsters. *"*

– Brett Piper[1]

---

1   Email from Brett Piper to the author, September 3rd, 2016; the full context of this quote is in Part 2 of this interview (the section on **DARK FORTRESS**), published in *Monster!* #33 (pp.134-145).

Part 4

Urban Blight! Between productions, Piper created his own *Monstro*, a "Crater Lake/Rhedosaurus type critter," in December 2016 to January 2017, redesigning the creature's head twice for the short

Let's cut to the chase, as I have done in the earlier instalments of this serialized interview: Brett Piper is the *only* American filmmaker who makes the kind of live-action-and-stop-motion-effects-creature-filled SF/fantasy/adventures films Willis O'Brien and Ray Harryhausen used to make.

Brett has done so, and continues to do so, since 1982, non-stop.

Full stop.

Brett accomplishes all this without major studio money or support—or, actually, *any* kind of Hollywood studio money or support, ever. In fact, in this portion of our career-spanning interview, Brett talks about the closest he's ever come to having even a modicum of "studio support," albeit that of Rutland, Vermont-based Edgewood Studios (now defunct) and Butler, New Jersey-based E.I. Independent Cinema.[2] As you shall soon see, attentive *Monster!* reader, "studio support" is

a decidedly mixed bag. Get ready to have your perceptions of how low-budget "studio" feature films are made shaken-up and shifted.

Brett has steadily kept making his kind of fantasy/SF/monster movies without the benefit of name stars (well, there was *one*: you can read about Brett's working one time with name-star Cameron Mitchell in Part 2 of our interview in *Monster!* #33, pp. 130–132). Brett has continued making his kind of fantasy/SF/horror features without teams of animators, without assistants or gofers, without CGI enhancements, and most definitely without breaking any banks. While today's brainless monster opuses like **RAMPAGE** squander the gross national product of multiple industrialized nations on their antics, Brett Piper always gets the job done without wasting time or money. His producers, on the other hand…well, read on.

If you want to know more, backtrack (or read for the first time) through the first three instalments of this interview in *Monster!* #32 and #33. As Brett succinctly puts it, "I just wanna make movies, you know?"[3] As I wrote in my introduction for the last instalments:

---

2 I visited and got to know Butler, NJ a bit during my own post-Joe Kubert School of Cartoon and Graphic Art, Inc. years, from 1978–1979; one of my housemates in the post-graduation period was from Butler, NJ, and it was my pleasure to get to know her and her younger brother. I'll leave this connection here, in this footnote; nothing more to say, though I do reference this later in the body of the interiew conversation with Brett, while discussing **BITE ME!**

3 Brett Piper, quoted in Kevin J. Lindenmuth's *The Independent Film Experience: Interviews with Directors and Producers* (2002, McFarland & Company, Inc.), p.150.

You name it, Piper has experienced it—shady business partners, short-sighted producers, broken promises, shaky deals, botched releases, shoddy handling of prints and video/DVD transfers—but he never gives up, and he still gives his all to every production. It's more a matter of absolute pragmatism than anything else, grounded in Piper's extensive knowledge of filmmaking and exploitation and genre film history. It is a track record precious few other living (or deceased) writer/director/effects artist monster-movie-makers can or ever will hold a candle to.

It's about time Brett Piper's story is told. Hence, this multi-chapter *Monster!* interview with one of our all-time favorite filmmakers.

OK, time to roll up our sleeves and dig in anew. For Part 1, get your hands on a copy of *Monster!* #32 (March 2017, pp.6-39), and Part 2 and 3 are in *Monster!* #33 (Spring 2018, pp.127-180). This 'monstrous' all-encompassing, career-length serialized interview will conclude with Part 6 in *Monster!* #35.

—but here we go, into the 21ˢᵗ Century with Brett Piper…

Having now covered the late 1980s (**BATTLE FOR THE LOST PLANET**, 1986, a.k.a. **GALAXY** a.k.a. **GALAXY DESTROYER** in foreign markets) and the 1990s, from **MUTANT WAR** (1987) to **DRAINIAC!** (2000), we're now into Brett Piper's last feature to be filmed in his home state of New Hampshire: **PSYCLOPS** (2002). Brett and I also work through (as best we can) the confusion over Brett's credits on movies made by others, which is a bit of a mess on *IMDb.com* and other online sites. Brett's account here is definitive, and should be taken as such, despite whatever dubious accounts to the contrary may exist online.[4]

I have to add that, back in 2002, I was particularly excited to hear through the grapevine at the time that Brett was moving to Vermont—*my* native state—to make monster movies.[5] It was, in a

way, a dream come true, or so it seemed to me. To those who were renting or buying Brett's new work at the time, it appeared that **PSYCLOPS** kicked-off two periods of what looked like a period of 'illusory stability' for Piper. The fact that *two* Piper features seemed to emerge from the same production house (as you'll see, they *didn't*, actually), followed by even *more* Piper features released one-after-another by what appeared to be an up-and-coming exploitation label—

—well, it was exciting. *Finally!* Someone recognized Piper as the filmmaker he is, and were getting behind him!

Dream on.

I use the term 'illusory stability' for a reason.

In the world of Anarchy & Monsters, there *is* no "stability," just survival.

———

ema.html#1cb82c3c2ccd50a6739348a92e167928 and other online venues.

Another filmmaker named Brett—Brett Kelly—used Piper's **DINOSAUR KIDS** dino footage to spice-up his own project, **SHE-REX** ([2009] OOP DVD cover art shown here)

---

4 We even clean up (pun intended) the messy lineage of—*wait for it!*—how **CA-CA CAVEGIRLS** became **LESBIAN LOVERS 2001 BC** became **BIKINI GIRLS ON DINOSAUR PLANET** …and you can take that to the bank!

5 I covered both **PSYCLOPS** and the then-forthcoming **ARACHNIA** in my book about Vermont filmmaking and filmmakers, *Green Mountain Cinema: Green Mountain Boys* (Black Coat Press, 2002), which is still available at *http://www.blackcoatpress.com/nonfiction-green-mountain-cin-*

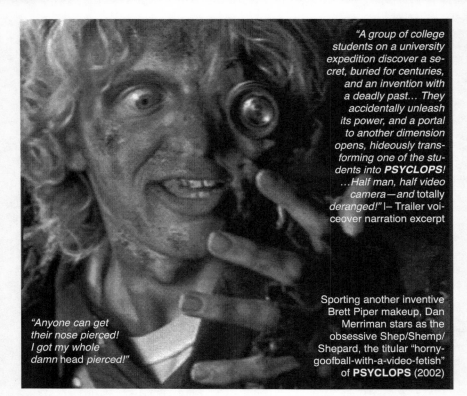

"A group of college students on a university expedition discover a secret, buried for centuries, and an invention with a deadly past... They accidentally unleash its power, and a portal to another dimension opens, hideously transforming one of the students into **PSYCLOPS**! ...Half man, half video camera—and totally deranged!" l— Trailer voiceover narration excerpt

"Anyone can get their nose pierced! I got my whole damn head pierced!"

Sporting another inventive Brett Piper makeup, Dan Merriman stars as the obsessive Shep/Shemp/Shepard, the titular "horny-goofball-with-a-video-fetish" of **PSYCLOPS** (2002)

PSYCLOPS (2002)

SRB: Your next two feature films as writer/director were presented direct-to-video as coming out of Edgewood Studios, in conjunction with producer David Giancola: PSYCLOPS and ARACHNIA. What was the groundwork you re-established with Edgewood before beginning production?

BRETT PIPER: **PSYCLOPS** was produced independently, with no input from Edgewood.

SRB: Sorry, my mistake on PSYCLOPS. We'll come back to the film; so, what brought you back to Edgewood eventually, then?

BP: I had stayed in touch with them and there had been much talk over the years about our doing something together, none of which led to anything. I did a few jobs for them. I wrote a script for a project they were trying to sell called **ILLEGAL ALIEN** *[2007].*[6] I was supposed to

be paid a token fee for the script and then I'd be hired to do the effects when the movie got made, but when the film fell through they stiffed me for the writing fee. I built several miniatures for their movie **ICEBREAKER** *[2000]*—a ski gondola, a plane, and a fairly large helicopter. I was only supposed to build the gondola, they had split the miniature work between three people presumably to speed things up, but I turned-out to be the only one who was competent, so I built all three. I got all kinds of praise for saving their ass, then found out the money for the last two models had already been given to the guys, who couldn't deliver, so I wound up with about a quarter of what was owed me. No discussion, mind you, just "Here you go, that's all we can afford." You'd think I'd learn, right?

Nicole Smith (just before her untimely death), from a script credited to Ben Coello, directed by David Giancola. Ben, who I knew at the time, abandoned filmmaking altogether after this debacle, which is a great loss to independent filmmaking. David Giancola subsequently directed the documentary **ADDICTED TO FAME** (2012; original title: **CRAPTASTIC!**, the title I saw it under at the Green Mountain Film Festival on March 19th, 2012), chronicling the making—and *un*making—of **ILLEGAL ALIENS**. **ADDICTED TO FAME** is essential viewing, and reveals much about Edgewood Studios' operations in its final years.

---

6   **ILLEGAL ALIEN** became **ILLEGAL ALIENS**, and was finally completed after absolutely insane production and post-production shenanigans involving in-part star Anna

So I gets a call from them, see, and we meet for lunch, and I get this pitch about how we ought to pool our resources and make some features together and do I have anything ready to go. By now I've finished shooting **PSYCLOPS** and it stills needs post. So the idea is I'll move to Vermont and be part of the Edgewood gang, we'll complete **PSYCLOPS** then move on to other great things. After a detour to Nova Scotia to help a friend with a project he was doing up there, I end up in the great town of Rutland. Biggest friggin' mistake of my *life*.

SRB: Let's focus on PSYCLOPS as your own independent production, pre-Edgewood-involvement. When did you first conceive of the film, and what was your process in working through the screenplay?

BP: Liz Hurley, who briefly appeared as Mom in **DRAINIAC!**, had recently sold some property and thought a movie might be a good place to invest some of the money. It almost *never* is, not anymore, but when she approached me about it I wasn't about to turn down the money. She wanted a nice part in it for herself, of course, but that was no problem.

SRB: Since you've cited the Asian ghost movie imagery and kinetics in DRAINIAC!, was that videotape transfer of old Artemis Winthrop (Phip Barbour) footage that plays such a key role in PSYCLOPS a riff on the Japanese RINGU [リング, TV movie, 1995; theatrical version, 1998]?

BP: Never seen **RINGU** (or its American remake *[2002]*).

SRB: Scratch that! I love how PSYCLOPS echoes H.P. Lovecraft (specifically, in some ways, his short story "From Beyond"), as well as the love/hate relationship with the camera and obsession with filming. There's an autobiographical component, maybe—or self-satire? In hindsight, watching it today, almost 20 years on, it's like a bridge between DAVID HOLZMAN'S DIARY (one of the first 'found footage' films, in which a young man played by L.M. Kit Carson is so obsessed with filming every aspect of his life that he drives everyone in his life away), VIDEODROME (the organic fusion of technology-with-flesh), and the entire YouTube and 'selfie' generation we're now in, but weren't at quite yet when you made PSYCLOPS.

BP: The main reason I created the video-obsessed

character of Shep/Shemp was so I could shoot sections of the film on tape and save money on film stock and processing. In fact, that was the genesis of the entire plot—saving a buck.

SRB: Necessity, the mother of invention. Correct me if I'm wrong, but it looks like PSYCLOPS might have been your last New Hampshire production. How did you pull everything together for the shoot, and what locations did you end up using?

BP: The usual story—scrounging everywhere for actors, writing scenes for locations I knew I could probably get. Much of it was shot at a house belonging to the parents of a high school friend, people who had always been extremely supportive of and patient with me. As a kid, when I wasn't allowed to shoot at my own house, they let me build sets in their barn and shoot there, even though it was sometimes a major pain in the ass for them. Bless you, Mrs. C! I also shot in my own apartment and at the local library. Finding an old barn was tough. It ended up being three hours away, which caused some major headaches.

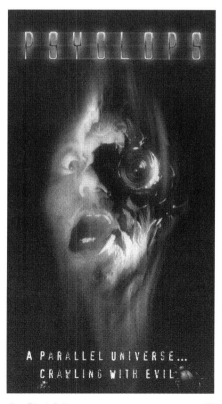

SRB: When the H.P. Lovecraft Historical Society filmed portions of their WHISPERER IN DARKNESS feature up in these parts, they had a hard time finding a suitable barn, too (and constructed a miniature for much of what they needed). What time of year were you filming PSYCLOPS? Was New England weather an issue for you on the shoot, as well?

BP: I ended up building part of the barn in miniature. The real barn we used was *huge*. To make it look small, I built a fake wall that could be moved in. I also used it for the shot where they peer through the hole that's been blown in the barn.

I seem to recall that the movie was made in the summer. We shot a lot at night, and I don't remember it being very cold.

SRB: Did the combination of videotape and film present any logistical problems during filming—and with your special effects creations (which included not just the elaborate makeup on Dan Merriman as Shep/Shepard, but also mechanical effects with the invented video technology, your stop-motion effects creatures, etc.)—or did it help? I imagine the faux-aged-videotape 'look' could help cover a lot of seams and such.

BP: The only snag to shooting scenes on tape was that I was editing on film so I had no way to cut those shots in. That had to wait until I could put everything on the computer and edit there. The faux-antique footage was actually shot on film. My Bolex was acting quirky, so I used that to advantage in giving the footage a primitive look. Then instead of transferring to video from the negative I transferred those shots directly from the beat-up black and white work print.

SRB: It's a great opener for the film.

BP: Another ignorant film critic story: in reviewing **PSYCLOPS**, one guy pointed out what he thought was a goof in the scene where the characters watch the antique footage. It was supposed to be archaic technology transferred to tape, but it had a film leader on it! "D'oh!" (His *d'oh*, not mine). I mentioned this to a fellow filmmaker, who immediately responded, "It was transferred to film before it went to tape." As anyone who knew anything at all about filmmaking could have figured out for himself. *D'oh* indeed.

SRB: Your scripting of the Shep character— who is meant to be as obnoxiously sexist as

possible—and Dan Merriman's performance took and takes a lot of critical abuse, but the fact is, the character is right out of the 1970s-1980s teen/college movie genre (from ANIMAL HOUSE to PORKY'S to PITCH PERFECT these days), and as the daily news demonstrates all too often, attuned to the stupidity of the current generation (many of whom have arrest records now due to their 'selfie' filming/videotaping of their own real-world misogynist antics).

BP: You know, words like sexist and misogynist have become essentially meaningless. They're simply applied to any man who, for whatever reason, does anything at all that rubs women the wrong way *(insert pun here)*. This in spite of the fact that there's an entire feminist subculture devoted to that idea that men are scum (Lifetime Network anyone?), which is considered entirely acceptable. You remember that diatribe Terry-Thomas delivers in **IT'S A MAD MAD MAD MAD WORLD** *[1963]* about how America is turning into an unbearable matriarchy? Well, it's here. So if anyone cares to refer to anything I've done as sexist and/or misogynistic (as they've done in the past, and will do in the future), then *fuck 'em*. In the words of Sam Goldwyn, it rolls off my back like a duck.

Getting back to the character of Shep: He's a horny goofball with a video fetish. Big deal.

SRB: —aaaaand he turns into a human camcorder. How long did it take to apply Merriman's "camera-faced Shep" makeup, and how was he to work with (since you brought him back for ARACHNIA, did all go well)? Coincidentally, I noticed Merman also appeared in another New England-set horror movie shortly after working with you (Michael Pleckaitis's TREES 2: THE ROOT OF ALL EVIL, 2004)…

BP: It took about 45 minutes to apply. That kind of makeup, with all that scar tissue, is very forgiving. Merriman was mostly good to work with, a good actor and really up for the part, but his one big drawback was that he never knew when to let go. He'd attach himself to you like a stray cat, and you couldn't make him go away. He showed up at Edgewood to see some of the footage, and literally stayed all night. He wanted to follow me home but I wouldn't let him, so he went back to the studio and slept on the couch, then he wanted to hang around all day until the Edgewood crew finally threw him out. The phrase "*Enough already!*" does not register in his consciousness.

SRB: Did all go well working with the rest of your cast—Robert Monkiewicz, Irene Joseph, Diane Di Gregorio, and Katie (a.k.a. Katy) Jordan in particular? Katie ended up doing a lot of direct-to-video horror/erotic features; you cast Irene again in ARACHNIA, and kept working with Rob (SCREAMING DEAD, BITE ME!). Jim Baker's small role (out to mug someone in PSYCLOPS) for you became the springboard for his doing a lot of acting work afterwards, and as an occasional producer.

BP: Mostly fine. Rob is a pleasure to work with, and I'd like to still be using him, but he's given up acting for civilian life. Some of the others drifted off to the oblivion of California. I never worked with Katy Jordan. Someone else shot that footage based on my script and sent it to me.

SRB: So it would have a different look from the rest of the film?

BP: No, because I couldn't find anyone locally to do it. That was the nudie footage Shep had supposedly shot of one of his girlfriends.

SRB: Got it. What was the last work you did on PSYCLOPS to wind-up the initial shoot—before any of the subsequent postproduction and such, outside of your NH base of operations?

BP: I had completed a first cut of the whole movie except for the video inserts.

SRB: The video inserts on PSYCLOPS—how quickly was that work completed? Did that include the stop-motion animation that's part of those sequences, or were you wrapping-up just the live-action elements of the video inserts?

BP: The only footage shot on video was Shep's POV, when he was behind his video camera or after he'd become the video cyborg. Everything else was shot on film. The video was shot concurrently with the rest of the movie.

SRB: What was "the detour to Nova Scotia"— was that to help someone on another film project? Anything you care to share on that?

BP: A good friend of mine, Danny Matmor, was making a shot-on-video feature called **SATAN'S PINOCCHIO**. Danny's mother is Kati Preston, who I mentioned as helping us with the casting of **DRAINIAC!**. Danny himself is a very talented and interesting guy—among other things, he had a fairly long association with the notorious Harry Alan Towers, and he wrote and co-

Skitter Critters! What's that under the table, skittering across the floor…? Meet the ominous, omnipresent stop-motion arthropodic invertebrates 'from beyond' of Brett Piper's **PSYCLOPS**

starred in **THE MANGLER** *[1995]*, although I wouldn't hold that against him. I was his DP on **PINOCCHIO**, did several makeup effects (including the nose) and generally helped out in any way I could. It was a tiring but interesting experience. By the way, Pinocchio was played by Danny De La Paz, who was in Edward James Olmos' movie **AMERICAN ME** *[1992]*.[7]

---

7 As best I can tell, the Canadian feature **SATAN'S PINOCCHIO** was never completed or released; see *http://www.imdb.com/name/nm0559169/?ref_=tt_ov_dr* and note on the Monster Kid Classic Horror Forum thread concerning "Films that never saw the light of day…,"

SRB: So, then, after Nova Scotia—the move to Rutland, Vermont, the Edgewood Studios 'gang,' and post work on *PSYCLOPS.* **Was the move to Rutland, VT a real pulling-up-stakes from your long-time NH home base? Was that a rough decision to move out of New Hampshire for you, personally?**

BP: I was planning to leave NH anyway. Enough was enough, I'd spent almost all of my life there, it was time to move on. Vermont seemed as good a place as any. I have some very good friends who live in Vermont and they tell me it's a nice place. My memories of it are perhaps a little skewed.

SRB: For those who'd never heard of (much less been to) Edgewood Studios, how would you describe the physical space and the setup when you began post-production work on *PSYCLOPS* **there?**

BP: It was a corner of one of his Daddy's industrial buildings.

SRB: Elizabeth Hurley, Jay Joyce, and Scott Jones—were they the original producers on *PSYCLOPS* **before the postproduction completion at Edgewood? You've explained**

'Madeleymade' posting, "Aside from his work with Harry Alan Towers, Daniel Matmor has a lot of unfinished work." (post #724, http://monsterkidclassichorrorforum. yuku.com/reply/1179695/Films-that-never-saw-the-light-of-day#.V909LTs4k_U).

Elizabeth's connection and funding; who were Jay and Scott?

BP: They ran Artist View, the company which distributed the movie. They had nothing whatsoever to do with the movie's production. Neither did many of the other people listed as producers, associate producers, or whatever. Actually, *I* was the sole producer of **PSYCLOPS**. Liz paid for it, and Edgewood fucked it up.

SRB: Postproduction wrap in Rutland: Edgewood's David Giancola and Peter Beckwith thus landed producer credits on *PSYCLOPS.* **Was that part of the deal?**

BP: I guess it was. As I said, all of **PSYCLOPS** had been shot and the first cut done on film before the movie went to Edgewood. It was essentially 90% finished. All that remained was to conform the video to the work print (which I did myself) and do the sound mix. They somehow decided that from that point on they would have complete control over the movie because "it was their money"; ironic, since they never put nearly as much money into the film as we did. I let them call the shots (while I did most of the work), hoping for a more finished product and maybe a decent distribution deal through their contacts. *Wrong* on both counts.

SRB: I've held onto the video trade ads and slicks (I was co-managing and the buyer for a

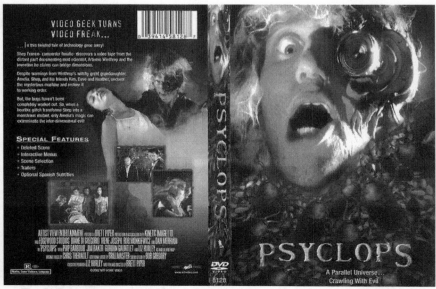

The DVD packaging for Artist View/MTI Home Video's New Year's Eve 2002 release

video superstore at the time): PSYCLOPS was released by MTI Home Video (who had also handled the direct-to-video release of THEY BITE years earlier) on December 31st, 2002; ARACHNIA followed from MTI on August 5th, 2003. That was obviously a package deal with MTI, for both films, most likely delivered to MTI just after the completion of ARACHNIA—

BP: It wasn't really a package deal. Artist View handled the distribution; they were the ones who arranged the video release through MTI. They were initially very pleased with the sales of **PSYCLOPS**—it did especially well for them overseas, although due to the usual creative bookkeeping, very little of that money filtered back to Liz and I. Because of the way **PSYCLOPS** was performing, they were anxious for a follow-up, which led to **ARACHNIA**.

SRB: For both films, what was delivered to MTI (16mm? 35mm? Who has the negatives?)?

BP: Both were shot in 16mm. Edgewood owns the negatives to **ARACHNIA**. I own all the elements to **PSYCLOPS**.

ARACHNIA (2003)

SRB: Given the MTI street dates for PSYCLOPS and ARACHNIA, it looks like you completed everything, including the extensive stop-motion animation and effects, in something like six months. That's extraordinary!

BP: You mean for **ARACHNIA**?

SRB: Yes.

BP: That's probably about right. I did everything as quickly as I could. I wanted to get the hell out of there as fast as possible.

SRB: How quickly did you move from completion of PSYCLOPS to starting production on ARACHNIA?

BP: As I recall, there was a bit of downtime between the two. We didn't discuss another movie until **PSYCLOPS** began generating sales. The original plan was that Edgewood, Artist View, and I would be equal partners, splitting the take equally. I specifically asked, "Are we talking gross or net?" because if the distributor gets to deduct his 'expenses' first, he basically has a license to steal. I was told gross. This seemed okay, so I agreed to it. When I finally

Above: No, it's not the climax of **THE EVIL DEAD**! Fire, death, decay, and **PSYCLOPS'** slithering stop-motion-animated creatures

saw a contract, my share had gone from an equal third of the gross to 17% of the net. I told Giancola I wasn't interested. He gave me a big sob story about how if I didn't do the movie Edgewood would have to close its doors and all my "friends" at Edgewood would be out of a job. This was pretty ironic, considering what transpired later. Anyway, for various reasons of my own I finally agreed to do the movie. I did talk them into paying me a small (very small) fee for part of my services. I said to Giancola, "This is the only money I'm ever going to see." He handed me a line of bull about how we were all going to make a pile off the movie, but needless to say I never saw a nickel beyond my up-front fee. For 90% of the work I did, I got *nothing*.

SRB: You also did some work (miniatures, second unit camera) for one of Edgewood's action-suspensers, TRAPPED: BURIED ALIVE (2002). Was that before ARACHNIA got underway, and what miniatures did you create for that production?

BP: That was before **ARACHNIA**. I was "officially" a second unit cameraman on that picture because Edgewood didn't want anyone to know I was doing miniature work—the powers

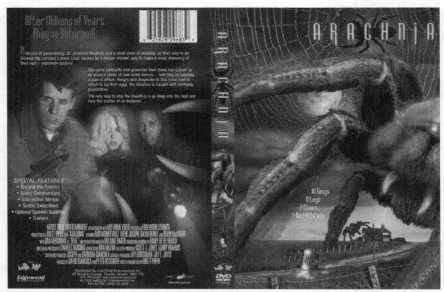

Eight-Legged Freaks: Packaging for kaBOOM! Entertainment/MTI Home Video's 2003 domestic Canadian DVD release. *[Scan courtesy of The Fentonian Institution]*

---

that were, whoever they might have been, wanted all CGI effects. I did all the miniature avalanche shots—the avalanche hitting the parking lot and tossing cars around, coming over the buildings, etc.

I had an "interesting" experience on that picture. They were shooting a full-scale effects shot, or at least that's what it was supposed to be—it was clearly something that wasn't going to work—and they had three or four cameras on it. I was running the A camera. I looked through the viewfinder and could see that the framing was wrong. It was supposed to be a master shot but it was framed as a tight close-up, the problem being that the director wasn't technically experienced enough to realize that, with that camera, you didn't get everything you saw, there are various cut-offs for different aspect ratios and such and a wide margin of "safety" outside of that. But it wasn't my movie, I'm very careful about not trying to direct someone else's work, so as tactfully as I could I called him over and had him look through the eyepiece and said, "Are you *sure* that's what you want?" And he said it was fine, so that's what we shot. When he saw the footage, he ran around telling everyone, eventually including me, that I'd screwed-up his shot. So that's what being tactful gets you.

SRB: What was the casting process on ARACHNIA, given the association now with Edgewood?

BP: Well, the leads were obviously carried over from **PSYCLOPS**, all except for Diane, who had moved to California. David Bunce was apparently someone Giancola knew and had worked with before. We had a casting call for the rest. Bevin McGraw was from upstate New York somewhere, maybe around Albany, a few hours away. She gave a quite extraordinary reading, although not actually for the part she played. She read fine for that role, but I had another woman auditioning for the female lead, Chandra, and no one to read opposite her, so I asked Bevin to read the part I'd written for Rob. And very subtly, with no exaggerated vocal mannerisms or anything, Bevin *became* the male character. The way she talked, the way she sat back in her chair, was totally convincing. It was quite remarkable.

The other girl was suggested by the editor of some film magazine. She was his little protégé. He was her Count Muffat. It was kind of weird. I think she's fine in the movie, but on set she was a handful. Like a six-year-old drama queen (or princess, I guess I should say).

SRB: Were you left alone to make ARACHNIA, or was Edgewood hands-on and micromanaging?

BP: They were hands-on but didn't interfere much in the creative process. Giancola was the DP, although I operated the camera. He was competent enough but bland. I kept telling him that the lighting was too flat, it had no character, and he would get upset and roll his eyes and gripe. He was a great eye-roller.

SRB: ARACHNIA makes extensive use of live-action models, the heads, pincers, limbs of the arachnids prominent among them. Did you sculpt and create the stop-motion models at the same time you were constructing the live-action full-sized props?

BP: I built *everything* in that movie, including the sets and the props. Since I had nowhere near enough preproduction time—Edgewood was desperate to get the movie started as soon as possible, to get some cash flowing—I was shooting all day and then staying up all night building things. I remember one morning Rob showed up on the set and found me working on something, I believe one of the full-sized spider heads. I'd been at it all night. He said, "Tell me you're just getting in now." I kind of shrugged, and he just walked away, shaking his head. At one point I was so exhausted, my brain froze-up in the middle of staging a shot. I simply could not think, at all. I had no idea what to do next. That's not exactly conducive to creativity.

SRB: What were you constructing the full-sized monster heads and limbs from? They outlived the production (they were still in the Edgewood Studio storage room last time I visited, before they shut it all down), and popped-up again in ILLEGAL ALIENS.

BP: They got used in **ILLEGAL ALIENS**? Oh, that's nice—not only did I not get paid for building them in the first place, they essentially stole them *twice*.

SRB: Sorry to deliver the bad news—

BP: What a swell bunch of guys. Anyway—they were mostly made of fiberglass, wood and latex. On the biggest one, the nearly-complete mockup, I didn't want to waste a lot of time on latex texturing it, so I found some rubber mats at Walmart with the right texture and glued them on.

SRB: The stop-motion monsters—arthropods which resemble giant versions of the tiny pseudoscorpions we find now and again in our bathroom, eight legs with palpal chelae [pincers] up front—are terrific, Brett. The only other film I've ever seen them in was in Willis O'Brien and Pete Peterson's stop-motion-animated underground sequence in THE BLACK SCORPION [1957]; one of them erupted

out of a subterranean 'trapdoor,' giggling like some demented hyena, in BLACK SCORPION. That always freaked me out as a kid when it was on Channel 8's afternoon movie!

BP: I love **BLACK SCORPION**. It was a great surprise the first time I saw it—it was on the Saturday night creature feature, and I didn't really know anything about it, but when I saw O'Brien's name in the credits I kind of perked-up. Then when all that great scorpion action started I was totally blown away. Needless to say, it's been a big influence on my own movies.

Top to Bottom (Pun Intended!): Day and night shots of **ARACHNIA**'s ravenous stop-motion-animated arthropods, plus James Aspden, Rob Monkiewicz, and... Bevin McGraw's butt!

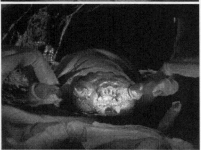

SRB: Like the feeding frenzies depicted in THE BLACK SCORPION, your ravenous pseudoscorpions really tear into their human prey. There's a matter-of-fact bluntness about the violence involving their feeding habits in ARACHNIA unlike anything in your earlier films; some victims are pulled limb-from-limb (though not in close-up, you don't wallow in gore). Why the intensified mayhem in this outing?

BP: It just seemed appropriate. That's what giant arachnids would do. Also, as you noted, there wasn't all that much gore. And I make a distinction between, say, Jason Voorhees slashing-up teens and animals killing because it's their nature. It's not the same thing at all.

SRB: Agreed—it's very effective. What was the toughest special effects shot or sequence to pull off in ARACHNIA?

BP: Hard to say. I'd built several small spiders and one big one, and the big one was always hard to animate. The shot where the spider gets the old man in the cave was tough because the puppets were hemmed-in by the miniature cave and it was hard to manipulate them. And the spider crawling up on the roof I never did get right. But by-and-large it was pretty straightforward stuff. I did get kind of a pleasant surprise a few years later when Jim Danforth commented on the movie on a stop-motion message board. He said he didn't like the movie, but it had some nice animation. Praise from a two-time Oscar nominee is always nice to hear.

SRB: Speaking of "the old man in the cave"—a moonshine-distilling old coot named Moses Cobb, whose cabin the plane-crash survivors move into before the action heats up—was played by James Aspden, who makes for an appealing character. Out of the entire cast, he and Irene Joseph (whose only other film credit was your PSYCLOPS) seem to be the two who 'got' the movie, and make their scenes work. How was Aspden (who only made one other film, Edgewood's ZOMBIE TOWN) cast, and how were these two to work with?

BP: Aspden was—a handful. He talked incessantly and couldn't remember his lines. I certainly don't

Left, Top to Bottom: Two iconic images from 1957's **THE BLACK SCORPION**. Wah Chang's drooling, roaring live-action scorpion head construction (used for close-ups); Willis O'Brien's & Pete Peterson's magnificent stop-motion arachnid charges toward an oncoming train; and three in-your-face C/U's of Piper's **BLACK SCORPION**-inspired stop-motion animation arthropods from **ARACHNIA**

want to bad-mouth the guy, he was a character all right, but his was definitely a performance made in the cutting room. Irene and I had worked on **PSYCLOPS**, and frankly on that movie she conducted herself like the total amateur she was, but by **ARACHNIA** she had decided to take acting seriously, and was much better to work with.

SRB: You've already noted you were happy working with Rob Monkiewicz (who plays the pilot/hero), and would have cast him again had he stayed with acting. How was it working with David Bunce (an actor/director, who later played Dr. Destruction on the TV series Super Knocked Up and on eScape, as well as an adaptation of H.P. Lovecraft's THE THING ON THE DOORSTEP in 2014), who played ARACHNIA's professor character, and Bevin McGraw and Alexxus Young (who appeared in a few more horror films after ARACHNIA)?

BP: Bunce was fine, a good actor, very cooperative. Bevin McGraw was excellent, a much better actress than you can tell from the movie, because that bimbette persona was all acting—too many people just assume she was playing herself, which couldn't be further from the truth. I would have loved to work with Bevin again, and in fact the lead in **SCREAMING DEAD** *[2003]* was written for her. She (alas) moved to L.A., and we gradually lost touch. Alexxus I've already mentioned. No point rehashing that.

SRB: ARACHNIA was filmed in Vermont, but it's set in Arizona. Were there any difficulties finding suitable locations to 'sell' the Arizona setting?

BP: I don't think it's set in Arizona. I think the plane was on its *way* to Arizona when it crashed.

SRB: My bad; point taken. ARACHNIA ended-up being a pretty polished-looking production that still hit all the exploitation beats—including some nudity (the washtub bath, and one sex scene between the female characters), Dan Merriman drawn-and-quartered by spiders, arachnid 'infants' bursting out of a character's chest, chainsaw vs. arachnid (with plenty of 'bug splatter'), and even red-tinted arachnid POV shots—and it's a fun ride. Despite all the shenanigans behind the scenes, were you happy with the final film?

BP: I've never seen the final film. I guess I was reasonably happy with my cut of it, which (from what I gather) actually played much better than

Edgewood's. It's hard to be happy with the fruit of such a miserable experience. "Aside from that, Mrs. Lincoln, how did you like the play?"

SRB: The full-sized mockups stayed with Edgewood; did the animation models and armatures stay with you? Did you use any of them in your own later films?

BP: Everything stayed at Edgewood.

SRB: When did you leave Vermont—and where did you move to from there, Brett?

BP: I left Vermont as soon as I finished the last shot of **ARACHNIA**. And I don't mean ten seconds later. It was *"Done!"* and I handed in my keys and walked out. I met Giancola in the parking lot and said, "I'm gone," and that was the last time I saw him until the lawsuit.

I went to NH and stayed with some friends, the Prestons, for a while, then it was down to New Jersey and E.I.

SRB: Wait a second: "the lawsuit"?? What was that, and what was the outcome?

Top: Another shot of a stop-motion-animated **ARACHNIA**. **Above:** The creatures swarm around the farmhouse during their nighttime siege

BP: You didn't know I sued Edgewood? Why did I think that was common knowledge in our circles? Anyway—yeah, after **ARACHNIA** came out and was all over the place, obviously doing well, and both Edgewood and Artist View refused to give me any information (although Artist View did let slip that they'd been sending Edgewood money), I'd had enough and filed suit. It was a mess. Edgewood had no defense except to get all of their people to swear I was a lousy filmmaker and an all-around shit, which (true or otherwise) had nothing to do with the case at hand. Ironically, most of the people they got to smear me were the people whose jobs I'd supposedly saved when I agree to do **ARACHNIA**. "No good deed goes unpunished"—did I already say that? My lawyer described Edgewood's statements as the biggest bunch of obvious lies he'd ever seen. And they couldn't even keep their lies straight—they'd make a statement on one page and contradict it on the next. They had people who weren't even around when the movies were made swear they'd produced them and recount totally imaginary conversations we'd supposedly had. It was unbelievable. Finally we had to go to mediation and Edgewood claimed that, because of fire, floods and pestilence, all their records had been destroyed, so they *couldn't* give me any information. Strange they'd never mentioned that during the year or so the preliminaries had dragged on. On the advice of my lawyer, I settled. I'm not allowed to discuss the details of the settlement, but it left me worse off than I was before.

SRB: As you say, "Aside from that, Mrs. Lincoln…" Thanks for being willing to talk about this phase of your career at all, Brett, very much appreciated.

ODD JOBS

SRB: You said earlier there are film titles and credits out there you have no recollection of, or may be the result of your having loaned a prop or mask or model to a production. For the purposes of 'cleaning-up' the filmography (and deep-sixing just-plain-wrong information out there on the internet), I'd like to preface talking about your most recent 15 years of work by hitting you with some titles and supposed credits. First off, when did you first meet and/or work with the Polonia Brothers, Mark and John, and John's compadre Jon McBride?

BP: I met the Polonias when they helped me out

with **DRAINIAC!**. I've never met Jon McBride.

SRB: Your name is cited in connection with special effects and/or monster or makeup work on a half-dozen of John, Jon, and Mark's films, TERROR HOUSE (1998), BLOOD RED PLANET (2000, and there is a cyclops in there that has the Piper 'look'), HELLGATE: THE HOUSE THAT SCREAMED 2 (2001), GORILLA WARFARE: BATTLE OF THE APES (2002), the anthology film NIGHTTHIRST (2002, comprised of four short films), and AMONG US (2004). Can you sort these out?

BP: A lot of those movies I've never heard of. What happened is that whenever I'd clean house and have a bunch of props or monsters to get rid of, I'd send them to the Polonias instead of throwing them out (as a matter of fact, I just gave them a van full of props and costumes yesterday!). They use them in movies and give me screen credit. I *did* work on **BLOOD RED PLANET**, creating and shooting some miniatures. The Cyclops creature was a modified prop from **DRAINIAC!**. I made the Bigfoot mask for **AMONG US**.

SRB: Thanks for clearing all that up. You've also been credited for doing effects on a Karl Roulston creature feature, CREATURE OF THE MIST (2002), which I've never seen, and from the same year, one of Donald Farmer's gore films, BODY SHOP a.k.a. DEADLY MEMORIES (2002, which some venues also credit you with photographing), made in Tennessee with an impressive cast [William Smith, Robert Z'Dar, etc.]. What's your recollection (if any)?

BP: **CREATURE OF THE MIST** was originally called "THE KELPIE." I did a lot of work on that, building and shooting the creature and a lot of miniatures, and actually editing the entire first cut. It dragged on forever. I don't think Karl wanted the movie to end. Finally I said, "That's it, I'm *done*." He continued working on it afterwards with Robert Gaffney, who'd made **FRANKENSTEIN MEETS THE SPACE MONSTER** (1965), who was running a postproduction company in New York. I'm not sure if I've ever seen the finished product. Karl did send it to E.I., who weren't interested.

BODY SHOP—*uh*—an interesting gig. Steve Williams introduced me to Phil Newman, who was producing. Phil had been in one of Don Farmer's movies and decided he would like to make a movie himself. He co-wrote the screenplay and raised the money then unfortunately he hired Farmer to direct. Don's approach to directing was, let's say, rudimentary. He liked to shoot everything, action scenes included, in a single static master shot as if it were 1903, and if anything went wrong he'd simply start over and redo the entire scene. In one case a fairly long scene went acceptably until the very end, when one of the characters, *who had his back to the camera*, flubbed a word. Don insisted on redoing the entire scene. I said "Don, you can just dub the word!" His response was "Dubbing costs money." So, in the interests of saving money, he blew our entire stock of film in a few days, doing take after pointless take. And it took forever—scenes that should have taken ten minutes would take *hours*, until we were working twenty-four hour days. It was one of those situations you could spend forever bitching about, things were so messed-up, but what's the point? Let's just say it's the only time I've ever chewed-out a director in front of his crew. Twice.

I'd been hired officially as DP and to do makeup effects, but I was actually there as back-up in case Phil had to fire Don. That never happened, but I did end up directing parts of it. Once when Farmer was sick with food poisoning, and again when he abandoned the movie with two days to go to catch a plane to Europe. The scenes he'd scheduled for two days I shot in one morning.

SRB: There was a 'special thanks' credit to you on one of the Misty Mundae films, Johnny Crash's SPIDER-MAN *riff,* SPIDERBABE [2003]. *What was that a nod to or for? Are we getting into the beginning of your E.I. period with this one?*

BP: Yes, while I was working on **SCREAMING DEAD** they were trying to finish up **SPIDERBABE**. The director, who was also editing (SOP at E.I.) was having trouble creating an effect he wanted, so I stayed late one night and did it for him. Interesting that it took them longer to edit **SPIDERBABE** than it took me to prep, shoot, and complete **SCREAMING DEAD**, yet Mike Raso was always bitching about how slow *I* was. Go figure.

SRB: Though we're now jumping our chronology, let's continue the credits 'housecleaning,' if you're up for it. During your E.I. tenure, you worked on the Misty Mundae/ Seduction Cinema vehicle BIKINI GIRLS ON DINOSAUR PLANET [2005]?[8] *If memory serves*

(I've seen a lot *of dinosaur and cavewomen movies!), you actually stop-motion-animated a defecating ceratopsian for that one.*

BP: Oh yes. And it was rather a nice piece of animation, if I say so myself. And it was, so the speak, the *raison d'être* for the movie. Here's the way I remember it: a guy named Bill Hellfire, a companion of Misty and sort of a filmmaker, was requesting ideas from 'fans' for his porno/ fetish movies, and someone said he'd like to see a cave girl thrown into a pile of dinosaur shit. So Hellfire got together some girls in furkinis and shot a bunch of stuff, including one of them being tossed in a pool of mud, meant to represent the aforementioned dino-feces. This epic ended-up in the hands of E.I., where it sat on the shelves for years[9] because no one could figure out how to add the dinosaurs to complete the film. Then I arrived, and between movies they hired me to create some dinosaurs. I was given carte blanche, with one proviso—there *had* to be a shot of a dino taking a dump. So I built three dinosaurs, a pterosaur, and a miniature volcano and spent a couple fairly happy weeks shooting footage for the movie, and that's how **BIKINI GIRLS ON DINOSAUR PLANET** came to be unleashed on the world.

fects in this movie are lifted from stock CGI frequently used in episodes of the TV series *Babylon 5*. Primarily used is the Jump Gate spiral, with a ship coming out of it." (*http://www.imdb.com/title/tt0447606/trivia?ref_=tt_trv_trv*)

9 True—it might have been shelved, incomplete, for as long as five years—hence, the Factory 2000 production credit on the film. The original short version of the film was from 2001, entitled **CA-CA CAVEGIRLS** ("custom video title"). It had been made for a specific client of Bill Hellfire: "The client had requested a non-violent film about a bunch of cave girls who stumble upon a large pile of dinosaur droppings... segments would be later inserted in and around the custom film. This extends the running time and also enables the film to be released under a different title (**LESBIAN LOVERS 2001 BC**), so as to generate two means of revenue...," quoted from David Kenny, "The Lost Weekend: On the road with Factory 2000," from the most complete in-print account of the Factory 2000 operation, "No Safe Words: The World of Factory 2000," in *Headpress 22: Bad Birds* (August 2001, pp.42-104), pp.101-102; filmography referenced pp.64-66. This means that **BIKINI GIRLS ON DINOSAUR PLANET** was a *third* edition, the most-extended revision of the original **CA-CA CAVEGIRLS**. Factory 2000 was launched in the late 1990s by William Hellfire, initially satisfying "ideas from 'fans' for his porno/fetish movies" with films like **I WAS A TEENAGE STRANGLER** (1997) and **THE BIZARRE CASE OF THE ELECTRIC CORD STRANGLER** (1999), both co-starring Erin Brown a.k.a. "Misty Mundae" and "Chelsea Mundae," Erin's sister. Erin/"Misty" starred in almost all of Hellfire's features, and her roles and perceived star value fueled the eventual alliance with E.I./Seduction Cinema, which began with E.I. distributing Factory 2000's **INTERNATIONAL NECKTIE STRANGLER** and co-producing and distributing **MISTY'S SECRET** (both 2000).

8 According to the IMDb, the outer space effects footage for **BIKINI GIRLS ON DINOSAUR PLANET** came from another source: "Some, if not all, of the space CGI ef-

BP: I did basically anything that looked like an effects shot. Any time you see a monster or miniature or composite, or anything like that, I created it. "John Bacchus" was someone Mike Raso hired to make a movie called **KINKY KONG**. Mr. Bacchus cranked it out in his usual who-gives-a-shit manner and handed in about forty minutes of badly-shot softcore footage with no title character. *How* badly-shot? At one point the DP, a very capable guy, was literally reduced to tears by the crap he was forced to shoot. Raso was horrified. He handed the movie to his editor, Brian McNulty, and me and said, "*Save it!*" Brian spent maybe six months performing a Herculean salvage job, banging the footage into shape, shooting new scenes, adding filters and effects so the movie didn't look quite so much like garbage. Then I built miniatures and monsters and an ape suit and shot all the effects, which I believe I helped Brian cut-in for technical reasons. Even in this, I was hampered by the fact that Mr. "Bacchus" directed the ape suit shots himself, so I didn't really have much to work with.

Here's the funny (*heh-heh-heh*) part. **KINKY KONG** was being shot around the time I was making **BACTERIUM**. I turned-in **BACTERIUM** finished and under-budget. **KINKY KONG** cost twice as much, and was essentially raw footage that took two other guys six months to turn into something like a movie. And yet Raso *still* held "John Bacchus" up to me as an example of how to make movies quickly and efficiently! "Why can't you be more like him?"

SRB: And here it looked like, from out here, E.I. was a bright spot for you to work within. There's a couple other E.I. credits I've caught over time. Did you do more than editing work on Justin Wingenfield's "witch's curse" horror film SKIN CRAWL [2007]?

BP: Oh, believe me, E.I. *was* a bright spot compared to what I'd been through! No complaints there. Regarding **SKIN CRAWL**, I shot some inserts and added a few effects (and I had a hand in the cover art—literally!) but it was primarily an editing job. It had been shot a few years before in Beta SP and left to sit on the

John Bacchus' Seduction Cinema opus
KINKY KONG (2006) prominently featured
a diapered gorilla suit (with moobs!) and
antic monsters created by Brett Piper

shelf. Brian McNulty had already done a first edit. Finally, Raso asked me if I would take a crack at reediting it and maybe adding a little pizzazz. He said I could do anything I wanted with it, but that the director, Justin, was not to be involved. I told him I wouldn't do that. I wouldn't redo another director's movie behind his back. "It's not Justin's movie!" Mike said, "it's *my* movie!" "You may own the property," I told him, "but Justin made the movie." Anyway, it turned-out to be moot at the time, because Justin was away on vacation, so while he was gone I made a copy of his movie and started re-cutting it. It was good material, but I thought it was redundant and dragged, so the first thing I did was slash everything I thought it didn't need. This left me with about a thirty-minute movie. Justin's original version had a straight linear storyline, so I came up with the idea of retelling the story three times, each from the point-of-view of a different set of characters. When Justin first saw it, he was horrified, but after the initial shock wore-off, he got to like it. Despite Raso's instructions that he not be involved, Justin and I would work together on it at night, and it's a good thing we did, because there was a lot of good material Brian hadn't used, and without Justin to point it out, I never would have known.

I think Justin told me he was about 80% happy with the finished movie. There were a few things he wanted me to put back in, but they were shots that he, as the director, was attached to that didn't really serve the movie (in my opinion, anyway). I've read reviews where Justin is praised for his clever "non-linear" story telling approach. Well, good for him. It's his movie, I just helped out.

SRB: You're credited with camerawork on the documentary MEDICAL RENAISSANCE: THE SECRET CODE **[2008]** *and second unit for a video game,* DARKSTAR: THE INTERACTIVE MOVIE **[2010];** *were you involved, and have you worked on any other documentaries or video games?*

BP: I don't know anything about those. Someone has suggested that there's another guy out there with the same name, and we're being confused.

SRB: OK, those are off *the filmography. What about Brett Kelly's* **She-Rex** *[2009]? It was a comedy short [37 minutes], not a feature; I mean, cave girls threatened by a Tyrannosaurus rex—sounds like your* **DINO BABES** *all over again!*

BP: Again, I have not heard of this.[10]

Above: KK, complete with Barbie doll 'victim' and diaper. **Top:** Brett Piper directing—or doing *something* for the cause, anyway—behind-the-scenes during the extensive 'rescue' of **KINKY KONG**

SRB: A subject for further research for me, then [see footnote]. *What about the "special thanks" extended your way in the credits for*

live-action model dinosaur test footage for Brett Piper's **DINOSAUR KID**, and a fleeting post-credits coda uses another **DINOSAUR KID** sequence featuring Piper's live-action baby dinosaur puppet interacting with one of the test footage child actors. Piper is credited for this footage, which frames the 37-minute comedy shot near Ottawa, Ontario, Canada, which otherwise uses a Tyrannosaurus rex hand-puppet for its titular menace. She-Rex was released on DVD in 2009 from Brett Kelly Entertainment, with a bonus commentary track and photo gallery; long out-of-print, at the time of this writing the film is still available via streaming on *amazon.com*. A December 9th, 2014 review by Gary Williams on *amazon. com*, "She-Rex Lacks Rex Appeal," notes: "This isn't one of Brett Kelly's better films, especially compared to the more recent Zom-Com **MY FAIR ZOMBIE**, which is drop-dead hilarious. She-Rex was obviously made on a shoe-string budget, more like the tips of the laces. The comedy just doesn't work—gags are stretched out waaaay too long, truth be told, most weren't that funny to start with. There is, however, a distinct plus to this movie for lovers of stop-motion dinosaur flicks (of which this writer is certainly one). The film's opening features numerous clips... of stop-motion dinos by Brett Piper... This featurette is worth purchasing just for this footage. Kelly could probably turn out a decent dino-com with a larger (much larger) budget than this effort. Still, I applaud him for making (to my knowledge) the first Ottawa area shot dinosaur flick—good deal!" (archived at *https:// www.amazon.com/She-Rex-Brett-Kelly/dp/B0032DGAHY/ ref=sr_1_4?s=movies-tv&ie=UTF8&qid=1474458224&s-r=1-4&keywords=She-Rex*). For more on Brett Kelly, see *https://brettkellyentertainment.wordpress.com/about-brett-kelly/* and *http://blog.canuxploitation.com/2013/11/can-film-five-my-fair-zombie-director-brett-kelly/*

10 Almost 90 seconds of *She-Rex*'s opening three-minute pre-title prologue comprised color stop-motion animated and

Buzz Cartier's *FILTHY RICH FILTHY UNCLE PHIL* **[2010]?**

BP: *Hah!* I didn't know about that, although in this case I have seen the movie. Buzz is a cool and very interesting guy. He had a small part in **BACTERIUM** and a fairly prominent turn in the opening scenes of **MUCKMAN**. But I have no idea why he'd have given me a "special thanks", unless he needed to pad his credits!

SRB: You were also credited with cinematography (videography?) on Seduction Cinema and Brian McNulty's LUSTFUL ILLUSIONS [2011]. Were you involved, and if so, any memories of that shoot?

BP: I helped Brian shoot some softcore action for something. I don't know what the title was. He wrote and directed the scenes, and I was his DP.

SRB: What was the scoop with Seduction Cinema—was that another one of E.I.'s labels?

BP: Yes, I believe they released their racier stuff under that label.

SRB: You corrected me when I erroneously cited your work in a print review in* Monster! *[#30, pp.40-41] of Sam Qualiana's shot-in-upper New York State SNOW SHARK: ANCIENT SNOW BEAST [2011]; my apologies, Brett. What did you actually have to do with that film?

BP: Mark Polonia did most of the work on that. He edited the first cut, then I came over and trimmed it some more—trimmed it a *lot,* in fact— and did some postproduction effects. I did the composites and cobbled-together a few new effects by combining and reworking existing footage. I had nothing at all to do with the shark except for comping it in. And they put back all the footage I'd taken out, so what you see now is essentially Mark's cut.

SRB: I'll save the rest of my questions on the Polonia Brothers films until we get to that period in your career, but one exception: I'm unsure about Anthony Palma's KNIGHTMARE [2014], which I've never seen. It appears it was shot in Pennsylvania—was this made among the Polonias' 'circle,' and what did you do for the film (if anything)?

BP: Tony Palma was an acquaintance of Ken Van Sant, who is a key member of the Polonia gang. I'm sure we'll talk about Ken a lot more later. Anyway, Tony had some money and an idea for a slasher movie, but he knew nothing at all technically about getting a movie made so he approached Ken. Ken suggested he basically hire the Polonia crew, which would have been Mark, Mark's son Anthony, Ken, Matt Smith (DP) and me. I was supposed to help with lighting and do makeup effects. Ken also found Tony his key location, a nice little rustic lodge.

The movie was originally called "RED REUNION," which I thought sounded like a bunch of ex-communists getting together. It was about a bunch of young people having a reunion out in the country who get killed off one-by-one … Oh, you know. The killer was supposed to be wearing a college mascot costume, an Indian or a chicken or something, but it got changed to a knight. We all got together at the location for what should have been a very simple shoot. The problem was that, in addition to knowing nothing about the technical end of filmmaking, Tony had no idea how to handle actors, and he communicated very, very poorly. To give you a very typical example: we were lining-up a shot by the front door of the lodge, and there was a garbage can in the shot. I asked Tony, "Do you want this garbage can moved?" So he opened his copy of the script and in a monotone drawl he began to read the entire scene to me. Very. Slowly. And that was how he responded to *every* question, from crew or actors or anybody. If you interrupted him, he'd start reading the scene all over again from the top. It drove the actors crazy. They wanted to quit by the first night. Mark finally ended-up directing most of the movie because Tony would be paralyzed by indecision over every question. One night we were supposed to shoot a death scene and Tony hadn't shown-up yet, so Mark, Anthony and I began blocking the scene. When Tony appeared he showed him what we'd come up with. He shrugged and said, "Whatever." It wasn't a fun shoot.

SRB: You're credited as a stop-motion consultant or supervisor on Greg Lumberton and Paul McGinnis' made-in-Buffalo, New York KILLER RACK [2015], which mixed surgical breast implants with the Cthulhu mythos. If you were involved, this would be your first horror/comedy/musical outing, yes?

BP: It was a *musical?* Yeah, that would make it my first one! I built the tentacles, both full-sized and miniature, that come out of the ladies boobs. I did the miniatures in stop-motion and my own variation of Go-motion, which has acquired the name "Piper-mation." I also drove up to Buffalo to supervise their green screen shooting.

They didn't really understand green screen. For example, they didn't know how they would shoot reverse angles because only one wall of the studio was green so they couldn't turn their cameras around. They didn't understand that you simply leave the camera where it is and turn the *actors* around. And out of everything they shot that night only one or two shots needed to be green-screen anyway. The rest could have been shot in the alley where they shot everything else. They could have saved themselves a lot of trouble by bringing me in earlier. *Hah!*—I sound like Jim Danforth!

SRB: You mentioned earlier having worked with Mark Frizzell on an animated TV spot; final question in this "Did you do this?" detour, Brett. Have you also done other TV promo or advertising work over the years? If

so, any memorable ones, involving stop-motion animation or your creature creations?

BP: The only one I can remember was a short series of TV ads for a chain of bookstores called Book Corner. (*"Book Corner, Book Corner, your own corner of the world!"*). They featured an animated book worm. Nothing very memorable.

Hooter Horror? Brett Piper's, um, 'teat-acles' bust from their cups and run amuck in Greg Lamberson/Paul McGinnis' made-in-Buffalo, NY horror-musical **KILLER RACK** (2015)

An Interview with Brett Piper, Part 5

Or; "E.I., E.I., O..."

The E.I. Independent Cinema Years (2004–2007)

Down Dark Corridors...Evil Awaits Mortal Flesh
SHOCK-O-RAMA CINEMA presents
MISTY MUNDAE RACHAEL ROBBINS a film by BRETT PIPER
SCREAMING DEAD

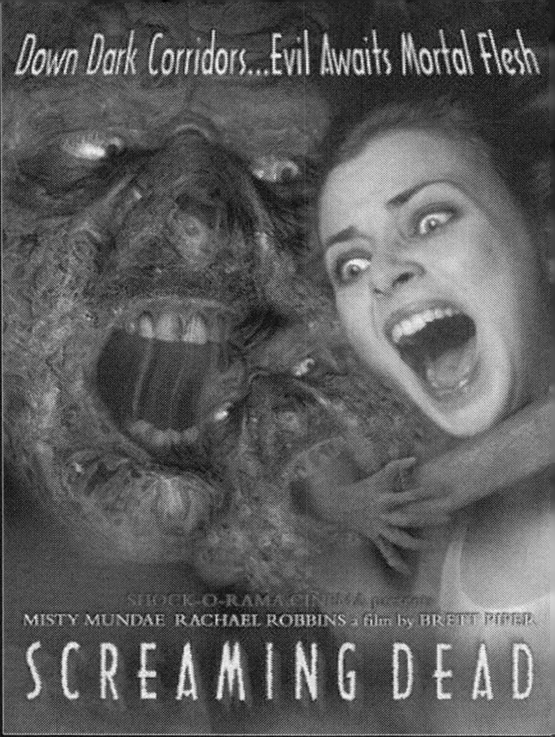

THE SCREAMING DEAD (2004)

SRB: What was your first brush with, and how did you firs connect with, E.I. Independent Cinema?

BP: I'd known about them for a long time. They had seen **DRAINIAC!**, and at one point when they were doing well they wanted to buy the movie outright. I mentioned the minimum figure I'd need to pay everyone off and turn a small profit, and *[Michael]* Raso said, "That's not out of the question," which would have been a better deal than we ever actually got for that movie, but it was tied-up by the California company. At any rate, over the years we'd talked many times about doing something together and finally, while I was staying in New Hampshire, post-Vermont Raso called me and asked if I had a story ready to shoot, and if so would there be a part in it for Misty Mundae? The answer to both was "Yes," so he invited me down to New Jersey to meet. It was pretty remarkable—normally these initial meetings are sort of empty chat-fests just to get acquainted, but in this case Mike and I and Jeff Faoro and Michael Weiss sat around a conference table and notepads came out, and before I knew it we had a deal for me to make **SCREAMING DEAD** (as it would come to be called).

SRB: Where was their setup in New Jersey?

BP: They rented space in an industrial park in Butler, NJ. They had a small suite of offices and editing rooms and a larger space which was used as a studio, although Raso hated it when we built sets there. He liked things tidy. Making movies is *not* tidy.

SRB: Where did you move to in NJ, come the time?

BP: I moved to Butler, right down the street from E.I.'s studio.

SRB: What were the initial plans with E.I.?

BP: At first it was just a one shot deal. I had written the screenplay for **SCREAMING DEAD** shortly before I got Raso's call. Jeff Faoro read it, told Raso it was fine, and we just proceeded from there. Raso never reads scripts himself. He didn't know what the movie was about until it was done.

SRB: "It was a modeling gig—with a director from hell!" – that *was one of the last lines in SCREAMING DEAD, and it had me thinking you might have been venting a bit about your previous 'studio' experience via this new film and horror story?*

BP: Well, let's just say that most of the elements that people dismiss as unbelievable in the movie—the behavior of the photographer, the willingness of the girls to go along with it—didn't require much imagination on my part, except to scale them back to make them *less* unbelievable. At least in the movie the villain is a successful and well-known artist. In real life almost anyone pretending to make a movie, no matter how flimsy his credentials, can get away with the same kind of crap. There are all kinds of stories about men pretending to be filmmakers shooting 'tests' of would-be actresses engaging in 'adult' behavior which only end up on private porno reels. People who watch **SCREAMING DEAD** and say "That kind of thing could never happen in real life" are just wrong. Period.

No one ever has a problem with the ghosts, though.

SRB: Why would we?! Let's talk about that lead ghost. The name of your spectral sadist in *SCREAMING DEAD* is Rossiter [Kevin G. Shinnick]—like the plastic surgeon/sadist played by Anton Diffring in *CIRCUS OF HORRORS (1960)*. It's what the maimed woman is screaming right at the beginning of *CIRCUS OF HORRORS*; me and my friends used to use that name as a reference for anyone who was "messed-up," which made me laugh when you

first dropped the name in SCREAMING DEAD.

BP: That's funny, I never knew that. I don't know where the name came from, although I suspect it might have been an unconscious reference to Leonard *[The Fall and Rise of Reginald Perrin[11]]* Rossiter.

SRB: There's also an early punk band from Cheltenham, in England, called Screaming Dead—they took their name from the Anglo retitling of a Jess Franco film. Any deliberate connection there?

BP: No, I'm afraid my interest in pop music began and ended with The Beatles. When I wrote the script I hadn't decided on a title. One of the ones I toyed with was "*House of the Screaming Dead*." I believe it was Mike Raso who decided to simply call it **SCREAMING DEAD**.

SRB: Oh, man, "HOUSE OF THE SCREAMING DEAD" is a terrific title—you should have used that! SCREAMING DEAD's screenplay demonstrated a far more patient, classical story structure than any of your earlier work. I dug how you set up your characters, the twisted 'employment' situation, and chose to build to the climactic horrors; it's 29 minutes before the first ghost (the eyeless victim) appears, and a full hour before your human villain Roger Neale [Joseph Farrell] discovers the subterranean torture chamber.

BP: I was trying for a more sedate, old-fashioned feel, more *[Val]* Lewton[12] than Hammer *[Films]*. Maybe it worked, maybe not. The "eyeless victim", by the way, was our producer, Rick Van Meter.

SRB: I think the slow buildup approach works in spades here. Was the prologue—with Neale photographing the simulated (but emotionally 'real') torture with the first model—an afterthought, or was that always how the script opened? It certainly establishes Neale's sadistic modus operandi and how close to the threshold he takes his models, without inflicting grievous lasting bodily harm.

---

11 Brett is referring to the actor Leonard Rossiter (October 21st, 1926–October 5th, 1984), who most famously played the Perrin character introduced in the novel series by David Nobbs (1975–78) for the British TV series (1976–79, 1996).

12 Surely every *Monster!* reader knows of producer Val Lewton, who produced a string of nine genre and borderline-genre gems for RKO, starting with **CAT PEOPLE** (1942) and ending with **BEDLAM** (1946).

BP: It was always the opening I'd planned. I wasn't sure it worked, but apparently so.

SRB: Your two male leads—Joseph Farrell and, returning as your hero, Rob Monkiewicz—are two of your strongest characters to date. Farrell really makes Neale a nasty piece of work onscreen; were you satisfied with his performance? Did they work well together?

BP: I'm satisfied with Farrell in the finished film but he was difficult to work with. Not in the sense of being hard to get along with, he was very cooperative, but he didn't take direction too well, I had to work on him a lot to get what I wanted, and then he didn't *retain* direction. I'd coax him along to the point where I was satisfied with his performance and then in the next take we'd be back to square one and I'd have to start all over again. I hope he never reads this! I remember shooting an over-the-shoulder of his dialogue with Rob and for once Joseph was spot on but *Rob* was having trouble with his lines, and I wouldn't call "Cut". Rob was furious, he thought I was making him look like a fool, but of course we only saw the back of his head so I could redub his lines later, whereas I didn't want to stop Joseph when he was on a roll. Fortunately when Rob gets mad he just goes away until he cools down and when he comes back he's fine. I would not like to have to deal with Rob when he was pissed.

SRB: The movie builds and builds Neale as the villain—and I loved how you staged his sudden (and hilariously brutal) comeuppance. How did that play with a live audience, in a theater?

BP: It played *great!* It was a very satisfying moment for me. The first time we showed it to an audience, they gasped, and then they *cheered!*

SRB: What was it like working with a 'studio troupe' for the first time, with SCREAMING DEAD's female leads? Misty Mundae was E.I.'s star attraction, and I recognized the other women from previous E.I. and Seduction Cinema productions.

BP: Misty, as I said, was on her best behavior and we got along fine. Same with Anju/AJ, although she only had a small part. In addition to her opening scene, she's also the model in the fetish photos hanging on the gallery wall. Shooting those stills was one of the first things I did for the movie, and that was the first time I met her. In one of the stills she's handcuffed, naked, with her head in a toilet. A spotless and unused toilet, I might add! And it's *supposed* to be gross

and misogynistic, that's the point. Anyway, the shoot went fine, but afterwards Misty said, "I'm surprised Anju went along with that. She's a very proud person." Well, maybe she realized there was actually a purpose to it all. Or maybe she just bit her lip and did the job. I've worked with her several times since then, and I *still* have no idea.

The only other "EI Babe" in the movie is CJ DiMarsico. When they suggested her, a couple of the guys said, "She's a beautiful girl, but she can't act." She came in to read for the part, and at first she was a little iffy, but with a bit of coaching she was fine. I think that was the problem—she'd never been *directed* before.

After the movie was shot I was working in the edit bay when Julian Wells came by—the edit rooms were all lined up in a row between the stage and the offices so people were always going back and forth through them—and she stopped and said "So you're the guy who didn't want me in his movie!" And she *kicked* me. Not hard, but still! Actually I had no idea who she even was. I'd have been happy to have her in the movie. I worked with her in two subsequent movies, and it was an absolute pleasure.

SRB: The film benefited enormously from location filming at New Jersey's abandoned Marlboro Psychiatric Hospital. There's a lot of production value right there, and it's onscreen. Did you have access to everything there, and what were the legalities of filming at the hospital five years after the facility's closing?

BP: Some of the buildings were off-limits, but many of them were empty. I think there were still some kind of rehab programs going on in certain locations. I'm not sure what the legalities were. Rick Van Meter handled that. I know we had production insurance.

SRB: Those kinds of buildings are often freezing in the best of seasons. How did you rig-up that basement shower setup, which also begs the question: what time of year were you filming there?

BP: I want to say we were shooting in March. And the room where we rigged-up the shower *was* freezing. The steam you see isn't because the water was so hot, but because the air was so *cold*. I'd rigged a shower head and some pipe to a five-gallon water jug to simulate the shower. We had a big propane heater that I was using to heat the water to make CJ as comfortable as possible, but it was still tough. Rick kept pushing us to shoot

4 FRIGHTFUL FILMS

SHOCK-O-RAMA HORROR COLLECTION

SCREAMING DEAD · SHOCK-O-RAMA
BACTERIUM · BITE ME!

Fearsome Foursome: If you're hankering for a complete E.I./Brett Piper smorgasbord, this is a DVD collection you need, featuring a whole quartet of "frightful" flicks!

faster, and at one point he said, "Okay, it's warm enough, it's warm enough, shoot the scene!" I got a little testy and said, "Rick, take off your clothes and I'll dump it on you, and if you *still* think it's warm enough, we'll shoot!" Which made him back-off a little. I mean, come on, if it's going to take two more minutes to make a poor naked actress a little more comfortable, he can damn well wait!

SRB: Given the sheer space of the facility— reportedly 400+ acres, over half-a-million-

Top to Bottom: Piper's **SCREAMING DEAD**. Sadistic photographer Roger Neale (Joseph Farrell) and his recently-published album *Face of Fear*, which tips us off to his **PEEPING TOM** (1960)-like obsessions; a shady individual reflects; to paraphrase Frank Zappa, "the torture never F-stops!"

square-feet of interiors—how did you settle on where you'd finally shoot, and was there any temptation to push that further? Were you tempted to return there for another film?

BP: We looked at all the available buildings and chose one with a big Hammer-esque entryway and a big wood-paneled "ballroom" (for lack of a better term) that we thought would look good on screen. It was such an amazing location. I think our production manager, Leonardo Baquero, found it for us. A lot of the cast and crew found shooting there creepy, and it was supposedly haunted, although I never got any such vibe. It did have some spooky places, including a morgue in the basement. There was some debate over whether the fetus skeleton we found there was real or not. But there was never any talk of shooting there again, because none of the features I did at E.I. called for such a location.

SRB: Just curious: had you seen Brad Anderson and Stephen Gevedon's SESSION 9 [2001], which was filmed at the abandoned Danvers State Mental Hospital in Massachusetts?

BP: I hadn't, although I didn't live all that far from Danvers, so I knew about the hospital. Media Blasters' **FLESH FOR THE BEAST** [2003], made around the same time as **SCREAMING DEAD**, used similar locations which gave it almost a "companion-piece" look, which was kind of ironic, since Raso saw Media Blasters as his chief competition at the time.

SRB: Was Neale's secret video surveillance studio set-up part of the Marlboro Psychiatric Hospital setup and shoot, or a separate set elsewhere? Was there any surveillance setup done in the Hospital rooms/hallways, or was that all faked?

BP: Everything that appears to be at the hospital was shot at the hospital except for the dungeon, which was a set built at E.I. We never did find a location suitable for that.

SRB: Where was the basement torture chamber constructed, and by whom? It's a great set, and you made excellent use of it.

BP: The set was constructed at E.I.'s studio by a local artist named Tom Taggert. He'd done some sculptures and paintings that had appeared in some of E.I.'s other movies. Very creative, neat-looking stuff. When it became obvious we weren't going to find a suitable location, I suggested that instead of hiring someone to do makeup effects,

I do them myself and we pay Tom that money to build our set. E.I. agreed to hire Tom, but insisted on hiring a makeup guy anyway.

SRB: That said, one question (well, sort of a question): the graffiti-stylized woman on the wall seemed anachronistic (to the timeframe we're told Rossiter did his dirty deeds there)— we're told Rossiter (like the infamous John Wayne Gacy) tortured boys, not women. I took it as, "Well, someone was down here at some point after Rossiter met his fate, and they painted that," maybe, suggesting earlier incursions into the chamber, earlier haunts; it did seem out-of-place, given what we're told earlier in the film.

BP: That was something Tom did on his own. He had pretty much a free hand. My only real contribution was to frame the doorway area, since Tom was an artist and not a carpenter. Aside from that, I just poked my head in now and then and said, "Lookin' good, Tom!" I don't regret it. The set was like something from a Corman movie, only weirder. I loved it.

SRB: Agreed! One last location query, Brett. Where was the sequence in the foyer of Neale's studio/gallery/office, and Neale's interview of Misty's character behind closed doors, filmed?

BP: Misty's interview was shot in the green room at E.I. The gallery was a real gallery on main street in Bloomingdale, NJ, just a few miles from the studio. The owner very graciously allowed us pretty much a free hand to move things around and replace her art with our fakes. It always amazes me when people do that.

SRB: In many ways, SCREAMING DEAD is your 21st Century revamp of those 1960s and 1970s European horror movies that were set in castles, where then-contemporary dancers ending up stranded where ancient horrors malinger and they become its prey. Your exterior shots of the hospital recall those films, too; very cool! It's closest to the 1970s Mario Bava movie BARON BLOOD—with the whole 'dead-torturer-back-from-the-grave' story, with the asylum instead of the castle, NJ instead of Austria—albeit relying on your own video era 'twist' for Rossiter's defeat.

BP: Yes, very much so in the final scenes. Kevin Shinnick commented that the movie starts out like a ghost story and ends up like Sax Rohmer.

SRB: Nice to know you had an actor who knew Sax Rohmer's work! According to your own statements, you had support on this production above and beyond that in all previous productions, including a fellow professional handling the makeup effects, Michael R. Thomas. Were you happy with Michael's work on the film?

SCREAMING DEAD hero Rob Monkiewicz and Rachael Robbins

BP: Ehhhhhh—yes and no. (I feel like Paul Stewart's character at the end of **CITIZEN KANE**—"Ehhhh—yes and no.") Mike's only job was to do the Rossiter makeup. He was obviously a talented guy who knew makeup, but I don't think we saw eye-to-eye on how the character should look. I wanted Rossiter to look more desiccated, bald and scaly with thin wisps of scraggly hair instead of the Harpo Marx wig he ended-up with. I had intended to do the makeup myself, but E.I. didn't want me spreading myself so thin. Actually, as it turned out, it would have saved time. Mike was recovering from surgery on his shoulders, and could barely move his arms. That and the fact that, bless his old vaudevillian heart, he was constantly interrupting his own work to share show business jokes and anecdotes meant that we sat around idle all morning and into the afternoon before Rossiter was ready. It took around four hours. It shouldn't have taken more than one.

SRB: How did the tech side of this production go for you, with this new team?

BP: It went very well. It was the first time I'd ever really had that kind of support group. Our DP was M.A. (Tony) Morales, a big bear of a guy from Patterson, who was great to work with. He knew all about the equipment and such, but I was more into the aesthetics of lighting, so it was an interesting collaboration, and I think we both benefited from it. Tony once paid me a very nice compliment. We were figuring-out a shot, and I was suggesting which lights to use and where to place them, and it suddenly stuck me that I might be getting in his face a little, so I said, "Tony, does it bug you having a director who's used to lighting his own movies?" And he said "Are you kidding? Most directors tell me they don't like a shot, but they don't know why. You tell me you don't like a shot, then you tell me how to fix it!"

SRB: Now, that's creative collaboration—

BP: While we were prepping the movie, I gave Leonardo, our production manager, a list of props we needed, and he said to me (very nicely—Leonardo was always nice), "Well, that's really not my department." Which kind of ticked me off. But then he said, "I know someone who can do it, though." And he ended up doing us a huge favor by introducing us to Christina Christodoulopoulos, who turned out to be one of the best people I've ever worked with in my life. When we interviewed her she had this wary look in her eyes, like she was the one sizing *us* up, but once we hired her she was invaluable.

Top to Bottom, Opposite Page:
SCREAMING DEAD again. Rob Monkiewicz ponders the painted portrait; Misty Mundae bleeds for Roger Neale's art; move over, Baron Blood! **SCREAMING DEAD**'s spectral sadist Rossiter (Kevin G. Shinnick) is present for the photo shoot— and your pain is his gain!

I've never met anyone who showed-up better-prepared and more ready to get the job done. On **SCREAMING DEAD** she did props and set decoration. On the next two E.I. movies she was doing almost *everything*. By the time we did **BACTERIUM**, she was the producer.

SRB: Who painted the oversized portrait of Rossiter for the film?

BP: I did. It's—adequate.

SRB: It's effective. This was the feature that marked your leaving 16mm behind, working exclusively with the new video camera and production technologies available by 2003. According to Bruce G. Hallenbeck's article on the film, you shot SCREAMING DEAD on 24p mini-DV; what was your experience with this transition, what were the benefits, the detriments?

BP: The benefits were mainly being able to work fast and cheap with smaller, more mobile equipment, and being able to review your footage immediately. The detriment, of course, is that the image was still inferior to film. It still has a "video" look, especially on a big screen. By the way, I didn't actually leave 16mm behind. **SHOCK-O-RAMA** was shot in 16mm. And not just 16mm, but *super* 16mm!

SRB: How different was this from shooting and working with the video inserts for PSYCLOPS?

BP: It was different because the inserts in **PSYCLOPS** were *supposed* to look like home video footage, whereas **SCREAMING DEAD** was shot the same way I would have shot any narrative feature.

SRB: Was it a relatively speedy shoot?

BP: I think the principle photography took about ten days, with a few days of pick-up shots after that.

SRB: It looks to me like Rob was doing all he could to keep the Budweiser logo invisible in the scenes where he's drinking and at one point offering beer to the women. A precaution you had to take?

BP: Probably. Between Rick and E.I.'s in-house legal counsel, Michael Weiss, someone was always worried about labels and such. I remember even after the movie was done Mike W. had me take the brand name off a close-up of a camera.

SRB: Speaking of which—how involved was post-production process? SCREAMING DEAD has

minimal effects of the kind associated with your work—and no monsters, save for the spectral materializations (those eyes!), and ultimately Rossiter's ghost. Was that stop-motion animation in close-up shots of the working torture devices, and when Rossiter's blown-off hand reconstitutes itself?

BP: Postproduction was certainly simpler than on most of my shoots. The simplest of any of my E.I. movies, really. The "buzz saw" devices in the torture chamber were stop-motion, as was Rossiter's hand, to some extent, although augmented by some morphs. There's one other stop-motion shot most people would never catch: an insert of the lock on a door turning. We didn't have a key to that door, so that was a quick bit of stop-mo. I think **SCREAMING DEAD** has less stop-motion in it than any of my other films except **BACTERIUM**, which has only a single shot.

Aside from that most of the effects were in the final sequence of the building on fire. Those were real smoke and flames matted in, not CGI as some people are quick to assume.

SRB: They looked like real flames and smoke. Back to the video format: what was your shooting ratio on SCREAMING DEAD, since you weren't dealing with 16mm film costs?

BP: I don't know. That's the great advantage to shooting on video—you don't even *think* about your shooting ratio! You still have to limit your number of takes because of time constraints, although shooting isn't usually what eats the time, it's preparing to shoot. And some of us don't like a lot of takes because it means a lot of footage to wade through during editing. (That's where Woody Allen and I think alike—at one point he was shooting everything in masters to speed up editing, which apparently he hates).

SRB: Were there any particular sequences where the freedom to do multiple takes paid off?

BP: I can't think any one example in particular, although it's certainly nice to have that luxury.

SRB: You were ahead of the curve with SCREAMING DEAD, which hit videostores March 30th, 2004, a month after the premiere

Misty Mundae and a Piper dinosaur in cover art for Seduction Cinema's 2005 DVD release of **BIKINI GIRLS ON DINOSAUR PLANET** (co-featured with **BIKINI GODDESSES**)

of Mel Gibson's THE PASSION OF THE CHRIST [February 25th, 2004]—which was a big-budget 'prestige' torture movie, the most vivid torture film ever made, whatever anyone says—and months before the theatrical release of SAW [October 2004]. I remember my filmmaking friend Lance Weiler telling me around the time he started working on HEAD TRAUMA (which was completed in 2006, but we had this conversation in 2005), producers were contacting him; they were looking for independent filmmakers to make what they were calling "contained horror" movies—what my son Daniel used to call "strap 'em to the chair" movies—based on the success of SAW [2004] and HOSTEL [2005].

BP: Honestly, I don't associate **SCREAMING DEAD** with any of those movies (which at one point were referred to as "torture porn"). I would compare it more to *Pit and the Pendulum* than any of the examples you cite, with a dash of EC Comics thrown in. Maybe I'm being naïve. On the other hand, maybe I appeared to be ahead of the curve because I was so far behind it. Same difference, geometrically speaking.

SRB: Understood—and indeed, it is very PIT AND THE PENDULUM [1961] and THE HAUNTED PALACE [1963]. But I was working in video retail at the time, and before the term you mentioned was coined, SCREAMING DEAD was one of the few direct-to-video offerings even close, when customers asked if we had "anything like SAW." But as your co-star said: it was very 'Sax Rohmer,' so what goes around, comes around! It appeared at the time that SCREAMING DEAD was getting the kind of push I'd never seen your films get. E.I. rolled-out their Shock-O-Rama label and line with SCREAMING DEAD— according to their own ballyhoo, the film was their fifteenth production, so they had a track record in the marketplace—with a Fangoria convention showing and panel, an NYC Pioneer Theater premiere, and heavy promotion to video retailers. Did they consult and involve you in the rollout, and was this heavier promotion than you'd seen before on any of your films?

BP: I was involved, if not consulted. I was on the panel at that *Fango* convention. I almost didn't make it. Misty's sister and I were walking toward the room where it was being held, and one of the 'security' people stopped us and wouldn't let us by. I tried to explain that

we were headed to a screening of my movie but he couldn't have cared less. Which put me in a quandary, because I didn't really care if I missed the screening, but I didn't want this twerp dicking me around, so things started to get heated. Fortunately Chelsea interceded and got things straightened-out. But there were a lot of complaints that year about how arrogant and difficult the security people had been, so this wasn't an isolated incident.

SRB: For what it's worth, the organizers of the Fango conventions used to run comics conventions in NYC, too. Security once kept writer Alan Moore—on his first and only appearance at a NYC convention—John Totleben, and me from attending our own Swamp Thing panel, too, back in 1984 or '85. It was only because one of the convention organizers came looking for us, and found us detained by security, that we finally made it to our own event.

BP: Well, you put a uniform on anybody, even if the uniform is only a blue blazer and a badge, and he becomes an asshole. It's a law of nature.

I also went to the Pioneer screening. That was kind of fun. Although, as I mentioned, on the big screen you could tell the movie was shot on video.

I don't know if it was the promotion or having Misty in it or what, but **SCREAMING DEAD** did very well. Mike Raso told me it was their most successful video release up to that time.

SRB: Had any previous distributor ever consulted or involved you with a film premiere of one of your productions?

BP: Nope, nobody before or since.

SRB: All I can ask at this point is, "How long did the honeymoon last" with E.I.?

BP: Until business started getting bad. Then panic set in, and everybody's honeymoon was over.

BITE ME! (2005)

SRB: I noticed the Stegosaurus head from BITE ME! in the shots of your interview on the extras for SCREAMING DEAD. How quickly did production on your next film for E.I., BITE ME!, begin on the heels of completing SCREAMING DEAD?

Above & Below: 'Life-size' saurian statuary standing behind the Go-Go-Saurus strip-club in **BITE ME!** (2005), 'modeled' after an actual NJ location which Piper wasn't allowed to use for the shoot—so he created his *own* miniatures and made them parts of the scenery

BP: We went into it right away. Everyone was happy, money was still coming in, so I was asked to do another movie immediately. The idea of a killer bug movie was Raso's. He had that and a title: **BITE ME!** "Whaddaya think?" he asked. "Sounds good to me," I said. Life can be very simple when things are going well.

SRB: Was it fun to write BITE ME!, Brett? BITE ME! is the polar opposite of SCREAMING DEAD: it kicks off with an action-filled prologue featuring an almost Cheech-and-Chong-worthy exchange between stoner driver and passenger carting the toxic marijuana crop central to the story and a glimpse of the stop-motion arachnids,

a strip club called Go-Go-Saurus headlining a lackluster stripper act [Misty Mundae] under the titles that's meant to be lackluster (building up to a real striptease extravaganza later in the film, for reasons I won't give away here), and more. No "slow and steady wins the race" Gothic story structure here!

BP: I'd gotten **SCREAMING DEAD** out of my system. It was back to fun and games. Actually, you'll notice that **SCREAMING DEAD** itself becomes much more "wild and woolly" as soon as Neale dies. I just had to kill the bastard off, if only in effigy.

I don't know that writing **BITE ME!** was actually *fun*. I rarely use the word fun in relation to making movies. Norman Mailer put it very well. "Making movies," he said, "is hard work. And I don't mean hard like writing a symphony. I mean hard like mining coal." That said, writing **BITE ME!** was no particular strain.

SRB: So, let's start with the setting—the strip club Go-Go-Saurus is a curious location you concocted with a real location, I presume different interior sets, and a combination of full-size dinosaurs and miniatures (the "dinosaur tower," which looks to me a lot like those knock-off oversized plastic faux-Godzillas they used to sell at the department and toy stores back in the

1980s and '90s). It's mentioned in the bonus materials you originally had a real *location with full-sized dinosaur replicas chosen. Can you tell us what happened here, and how you pulled together the strip club locations and sets we see in the finished film?*

BP: Most of the club scenes, interior and exterior, were shot at a real club in New Jersey. I can't remember the name of the place. The location we were *supposed* to use, the one the script had been tailored for, actually had full-sized dinosaur statues out back,[13] which I wrote into the script, but the owner reneged on our deal to shoot there not long before we were scheduled to start. Didn't even bother to tell us—I happened to call him about something at the last minute, and he said, "Oh, I've changed my mind, you can't shoot here." He thought it would be bad for his "image". I didn't want to rewrite the script, so I faked the dinosaurs with miniatures and a full-sized stegosaurus head. You're right, the big statue was a modified toy Godzilla. Jeff Faoro came up with the name "Go-Go-Saurus," which I thought was a clever semi-pun.

By the way, the idea for setting the movie in a strip club came from Rachael Robbins, who'd played one of the leads in **SCREAMING DEAD**. We were talking about the new movie, and she said, "I want to play a stripper before I get too old!" So the entire plot was concocted around that, then she ended-up not doing the movie.

SRB: As you say, the concept for BITE ME! *came from Mike Raso, and there's even a nod to* The Outer Limits *in the dialogue at one point.[14] If the Zanti Misfits had landed in a strip club instead of outside a military base...*

BP: That episode scared the hell out of me when I was a kid.

SRB: Me, too! It scarred our entire generation, one way or another. Your designs

Above, Bottom 2 Pics: Brett Piper's stop-motion arachnids for **BITE ME!** follow in the multi-legged footsteps of *[top]* the oversized arachnid created by Karl Hanoszek for **HORRORS OF SPIDER ISLAND** (*Ein Toter hing im Netz*, a.k.a. **IT'S HOT IN PARADISE**, 1960/1962/1965, West Germany) and *[2nd from top]* "The Zanti Misfits" on *The Outer Limits* (December 30th, 1963), animated by Jim Danforth

13 Might this have been in Haddonfield, NJ? See "World's First Dinosaur Skeleton Discovered Here," *Roadside America* (@ *https://www.roadsideamerica.com/ story/11155* and *https://www.travelthewholeworld. com/wp-content/uploads/2013/12/New_Jersey_Haddonfield_Dinosaur.jpg* @ *https://www.travelthewholeworld.com/traveling-new-jersey/*). Also see Monika Atkins, "Amazing Places to See Dinosaurs in New Jersey," *Mommy University*, April 20th, 2015 (@ *http:// mommyuniversitynj.com/2015/04/20/10-places-to-see-dinosaurs-in-nj/*) and Kelly-Jane Cotter, "Dinosaurs galore throughout New Jersey," Asbury Park Press, *Courier Post*, August 1st, 2014 (@ *https://www.courierpostonline.com/story/life/2014/08/01/dinosaurs-galore-nj/13496465/*).

14 "The Zanti Misfits," *The Outer Limits*, December 30th, 1963, stop-motion animation by Jim Danforth.

When **BITE ME!**'s suckers sup stripper's blood, their abdomens bloat like those of engorged ticks

for the arachnids—which are part spider, part tick (their abdomens grow massive after feeding on their victims), and part HORRORS OF SPIDER ISLAND (those mammalian faces, jaws and teeth)—are very neat. Did you go through more than one design before settling on the final? There's a minimum of texture, which means they 'read' clearly in all lighting setups, locations, and action; was that calculated?

BP: I was after a smoother, sleeker look than in my other bug movies, more like a black widow than a tarantula. The bodies were made out of resin for that reason. Only the movable jaws were latex. I didn't really 'design' them as such, just started building the prototype and kept puttering with it until it seemed to look right.

SRB: I hate to bring the title up once more, but was the Arizona connection mentioned in the dialogue as a possible source for the arachnid-tainted 'weed' crates a nod to ARACHNIA?

BP: No. I hadn't even thought of that!

SRB: The film builds to a final humanoid/ arachnid hybrid that begins as makeup on John Fedele (playing hyper-aggressive DEA agent Myles McCarthy), transforming into one of your stop-motion animated creations. With SCREAMING DEAD's makeup artist Michael R. Thomas playing an active role in this film [strip-club owner Ralph Vivino], did you design and execute the makeup effects this time around?

BP: Yes, I did the makeup effects this time (and on all my subsequent E.I. movies), although Mike Thomas happened to be around when we were shooting Fedele's monster scenes, so he gave me a hand applying it.

SRB: There's some bladder effects work on McCarthy/Fedele's transformation, and he sprouts the 'horns'/antennae stubs—but it looks pretty organic. What were you using?

BP: There are no bladder effects, I did those in post.

SRB: Whoa! You fooled my eye!

E.I.'s Shock-O-Rama Cinema DVD packaging

BP: All the transformation effects were done in post. I'm not sure if they count as CGI—I had pretty primitive tools, even more so than I have now, so nothing was actually 'created' on the computer, but I used what I had to manipulate the footage I shot and create those effects.

SRB: The final stage of the renegade DEA agent's transformation is all stop-motion, an impressive human/arachnid hybrid that loses an arm to Buzz [Rob's exterminator character] as they wrestle on high in the tower 'catwalk.' How did you go about designing and fabricating that creature, and how tough was it to orchestrate the live-action and animated elements?

BP: The puppet had a simple wire frame armature, and wasn't very difficult to make. Matching the action up to the background footage of Rob on the set was a bitch. That's one area where *[Ray]* Harryhausen's system, using process projection, is much better—you can see where the puppet is in relation to the background figures, whereas I was working blind. At one point I actually had to do a split-screen and matte the creature's claw in separately from the rest of the body, otherwise it wouldn't have lined-up.

SRB: The finale has Buzz's insecticide inadvertently causing eruptive growth in the arachnids, providing action set-pieces with people vs. giant arachnids—and the biggest mother of 'em all appears before the final credits. Were these all shot with the same models you'd created for the smaller arachnids, or did you construct one with more texture/detailing for the larger incarnation(s)?

BP: They were all shot with the same models.

SRB: By my eye, the only full-size live-action arachnid props in BITE ME! are the ones crushed or 'spiked' (on the high-heel shoe wielded by Amber [Caitlin Ross]), the pulped creature in the plastic baggie—or did I miss something?

BP: All of the little bugs were full-sized—that is, the puppets were the size you actually see them on the screen. This sometimes made things easier, because I could shoot them against real props and locations with no matting. The shots of the bug crawling around the bathroom floor, for example, were shot in E.I.'s bathroom on the middle of the night. Not the most pleasant of experiences, but what the hell.

Speaking of mattes—**BITE ME!** got mostly positive reviews, but the few who slammed it

Top 3 Pics: Stages in the transformation of **BITE ME!**'s overly-aggressive DEA agent Myles McCarthy (John Fedele), the final stage of which Brett Piper *[bottom pic]* realized using the stop-motion animation model seen in his hands above (see also p.180 for a shot of the creature in action)

tended to also trash the shoddy special effects, mentioning the "bad CGI" and the usual ignorant rubbish. One or two complained about the bugs being "pasted" onto the background footage, as if the images were actually cut out with scissors and attached to the background shots with glue (which I really believe is how some people think it's done). But in fact most of the mattes were front and back light composites, a tedious process which produces exceptionally clean mattes, and a few of the shots were fairly sophisticated—the low angle shot of the bug scurrying across the dance floor has interactive lighting and shadows, for example. "Cheap CGI pasted on." Sure.

It's funny—many reviewers, even now, assume most of the budget on my movies goes into the effects. In fact, the effects are the *cheapest* scenes for me to shoot. No actors, no locations, I don't even have to feed anyone during shooting except me, and I don't eat much. I spend more on gas getting actors to the set than I do on effects.

SRB: You mention in the DVD extras that this was the first film you'd done where the entire cast was pretty well in place before writing— that you were able to write for the actors you had in mind. Other than Rachel Robbins, how did the rest pan-out in terms of your ideal casting from the E.I. troupe?

BP: Well—the cast was all in place at the time I *wrote* the script, but after Rachael bowed-out,

I had to bump everyone up a notch. Misty went from being a secondary character to playing the lead, everyone else moved up a space, some of the smaller parts were played by people who weren't really actors at all, they were just roped-in at the last minute. The part that Caitlin played, the laziest stripper on earth, was written as a joke for Misty, who would joke herself about what a lazy actress she was. Caitlin was supposed to play the lady cop who shows up at the club. And so on. I think the only one who played a part originally written for her was Julian Wells. And again, as with Rachael, I wrote that part at Julian's suggestion. I said "What do you want to play?" and she said, "A tough Jersey broad." And she was great.

SRB: You noted earlier that "Rob is a pleasure to work with," and he really seems to be loosened-up and enjoying himself as the exterminator. Even his look—the beard, scruffier hair—is quite a change from his earlier macho roles for you.

BP: That's all his. The look, the voice, everything, Rob created that role. He told me before we started "I think I'm going to talk like Otto from *The Simpsons*." I love the scene where he and Misty are swapping urban legends about killer bugs. That scene wouldn't have worked at all if they both hadn't done such a great job with it.

SRB: The screen-test footage for the stripper characters on the DVD-R suggests there was

some musical chairs before everyone settled into their respective roles?

BP: That footage, I think, was test footage for another movie. Or maybe not. I don't know.

SRB: Misty had already been in a staggering 40 films by the time she appeared in SCREAMING DEAD, including eleven films released in 2003 alone (two of which—LUSTFUL ADDICTION and CONFESSIONS OF A NATURAL BEAUTY—she also wrote and directed). Was she flagging at all by the time she worked with you on BITE ME! and, shortly afterwards, SHOCK-O-RAMA?

BP: I'm not sure I know what you mean by "flagging." It was only my second time working with her so I didn't have much basis for comparison. As for her having done forty films by then, you need to bear in mind many of those movies only took a day or two to shoot, some of them probably no more than an afternoon. Not a lot of work involved.

SRB: Misty seems far more comfortable wielding camouflage, guns, and axes than being on that strip stage...

BP: I guess part of that might have been Misty's own attitude towards the kind of roles she'd been doing at E.I., but it's also there to serve the story. The idea that these girls are bored to death working in this tenth-rate dive. If Misty had looked at all excited or exciting doing the dance routines, it would have created the wrong atmosphere, and also lessened the contrast I wanted when she got pumped-up on bug juice and turned into Rambette.

SRB: I know New England, and NJ weather can change in a heartbeat, but I wanted ask about the shooting schedule(s), based on what we see onscreen: bare ground in some shots and scenes (the pre-credits sequence, the car crash, etc.), snow and ice cover on the Go-Go-Saurus' parking lot and grounds in others. It plays fine onscreen, for the casual viewer, but I noticed it. Was the shoot spread over more than a single stretch of time?

BP: It snowed during the shoot, creating some minor continuity issues. I matted-in snow falling during some of the transitional shots to try to smooth things out. It was Coffee-Mate!

SRB: Who did you work with to stage that impressive car stunt in the pre-credits sequence, and where was it shot? The DVD bonus features

Top to Bottom: Behind-the-scenes shots taken from the **BITE ME!** DVD's 'making-of' featurette. Michael R. Thomas as strip-club owner Ralph Vivino; BP shows how 'big' the behind-the-strip-club *kaiju* tower (note 'belly-window'!) is(n't) in real life; a pair of the film's full-sized prop arachnid claws

include a short overview of that entire sequence; the fellow behind the wheel seemed to know his business and enjoy doing the stunt, and it's cool to see you and your crew member(s) working it all out so efficiently.

BP: Chris Morena was the stunt driver on that. I think Jim Jankiewicz, who played one of the troublemakers in the club and had done stunt work and fight scenes for E.I. before, introduced him to us. The gag was shot at a farm just outside

Bite This! Smokin' stripper Amber (Caitlin Ross) nonchalantly 'spikes' one of the tick-like arachnoids with her high-heeled shoe as it scuttles along the bar-top in **BM!**; her boss Ralph Vivino (Michael R. Thomas) winces in disgust at sight of the bloody-bug-in-a-baggy

BP: I goofed big time when we shot the car crash. We were supposed to shoot with two cameras, but I forgot the second camera at the studio. We *did* use a second camera, but it was standard video. You can see the difference in the two formats in the finished movie. It's a quick shot, but it still bugs me. We all screw up now and then.

SRB: You mention in the DVD's bonus material on how the car crash was staged that you'd earlier worked on a film shot in Tennessee involving explosions and car crashes. Which film would that have been, Brett?

BP: That was **BODY SHOP / DEADLY MEMORIES**. Phil Newman arranged for a stunt coordinator who, I believe, used to work with the WWF. We got a lot of amazing shots, cars rolling over and blowing-up. I got to shoot explosions from a helicopter! We didn't have a helicopter mount, so I sat sideways facing out the side door, strapped in with my feet propped on the skids. It was great. The only good thing that came out of that movie.

SRB: How quickly did post-production go on BITE ME!, once you had everything you needed shot? Were you happy with the final results?

BP: Post took a long time, what with all the stop-motion and compositing and such. I think it came out okay.

SRB: How did E.I. proceed with the film—was there another premiere screening, convention appearances, etc., or was there less of a to-do about rolling BITE ME! out?

BP: They handled **BITE ME!** much the same as they had with **SCREAMING DEAD**.

SRB: How did BITE ME! do commercially?

BP: Not as well as **SCREAMING DEAD**. Last I heard, it came very close to showing a profit, but not quite. Apparently there was a mix-up in sales to the major video chains (remember them?)—instead of selling both DVDs and VHS, they sold only DVDs, which cut into the revenue quite a bit.[15] Also, the market was beginning to change.

of town. A lot of people think of New Jersey as all grimy, industrial slums. That's what they hear from New Yorkers who only know what they see across the river. Actually a lot of NJ would seem quite familiar to a Vermonter like you. Lots of farms and small towns. Very picturesque.

SRB: True enough. In fact, one of my cartooning school classmates (who I shared a house with after graduation) had a girlfriend who was from Butler, NJ, so I've been thereabouts.

---

15 I was still working in the video retail market when **BITE ME!** hit the market just in time for Halloween, 2004, and the market was indeed going through major upheavals (I left the business in March 2005). The major studios had pulled out of the video industry trade shows by that time (many moving all their money/muscle/promotions to large comicbook conventions, primary among them the San Diego Comicon), independent and chain stores had pretty much embraced DVD as *the* new format-of-choice for rentals and sales, ceasing VHS rentals (and, obviously, purchases). In 2003, Warner Home Video

Low budget movies were becoming harder to sell. By now I imagine the movie has broken even but you can't stay in business very long just breaking even.

SRB: One last question on BITE ME! Did you want the audience worried about the arachnid contagion spreading from the infected characters who escape in the van—Crystal [Misty Mundae], Gina [Sylvianne Chebance], Teresa [Julian Wells]? You'd already shown us how the creatures can spread after 'hatching' as young inside a victim, even passed mouth-to-mouth.

BP: I never gave it a thought. Maybe it's time for a sequel!

The Good Times! E.I.'s in-house Shock-O-Rama Cinema label

SHOCK-O-RAMA (2005)

SRB: One year (almost to the day) after BITE ME!'s video street date, SHOCK-O-RAMA was

became the first studio to release its new titles on DVD only, ceasing all VHS production; they'd already gone direct-only in August 2001 (cutting out the distributors, you could only buy WB product from WB), which created shock waves in distribution and retail that resulted in consolidation of distribution and threatened other studios also going direct-only (none did). Independent retailers were shutting down, crushed by the aggressive competition from the major video rental chains—Blockbuster Video, Hollywood Video, Movie Gallery, etc.—and mounting competition from satellite and Netflix (originally a rental-by-mail DVD provider, launched in 1998). Those that stayed in the game were increasingly dependent upon leasing rental product (VHS/DVDs) from Rentrak, a firm that specialized in providing titles to video stores "in depth" (i.e., multiple copies of new releases, to compete with the volume of a new title racked by the major chains), which further complicated revenues being paid to providers like E.I. (some whose product, if memory serves, was available via Rentrak). The chains were feeling the changes, too. Walmart became the dominant DVD sales retailer, replacing Blockbuster; DVD sales eliminated rental revenues, and family-friendly Walmart would not carry or sell titles like **BITE ME!** or any product from adult-oriented indy labels like E.I. The major expansions of the chains peaked in 2003-2004; Hollywood Video, the largest competitor to Blockbuster, was targeted by Blockbuster in a hostile takeover bid in December 2004, which Hollywood skirted in January 2005 by opting instead for a merger/buyout with/by their smaller competitor, Movie Gallery. The consolidation was completed by April 27th, 2005, but by September 2007 Movie Gallery had shut down over 500 stores and entered Chapter 11 bankruptcy reorganization soon afterwards. February of 2007, Netflix moved away from DVD-rentals-via-mail to VOD ("video-on-demand") streaming; Blockbuster filed for bankruptcy protection on September 23rd, 2010. Bear in mind, too, that all these consolidations, mergers, closings, and bankruptcies meant a lot of accounts—primarily independent retailers, providers, and/or studios, like E.I.—were paid pennies on the dollar on overdue or outstanding accounts, if they were paid at all (meaning their product had been "purchased" and shipped and placed in the retail/rental venues, but never actually paid for). All of this has had a most definite impact on the availability of, revenues streams from, and distribution of Brett Piper's films.

released by E.I. We've talked about some of the other E.I. productions you worked on; did you move right into SHOCK-O-RAMA after completing BITE ME!, or did some of the other E.I. productions you pitched-in on come between the two productions?

BP: It seems like we went into **SHOCK-O-RAMA** pretty quickly, but I may have worked on one or two things in between. I'm not very good with chronology, am I? Maybe I need to start keeping a diary. I remember the two Mikes, Jeff and I having dinner at a nearby Chinese restaurant and discussing what to do next and I happened to mention my earlier stab at an anthology called **SHOCK-O-RAMA**. Raso seemed intrigued, and he asked about using the already shot mummy segment, but due to Al Pirnie's unorthodox method of financing I thought that probably wouldn't be possible. So we decide to concoct all-new stories. I was headed back up to Canada for a little while and I wrote much of the script on the train up and back.

SRB: You said earlier that you'd had the idea for an anthology horror film for some time. What was the first portmanteau horror movie you remember seeing, and what was or remains your favorite anthology horror film? Any come to mind that just didn't work for you?

BP: The first one? That's hard to say. I don't think I caught **DEAD OF NIGHT** *[1945]* until I was maybe in my twenties. I think the very first may have been the TV movie **TRILOGY OF TERROR** *[March 4th, 1975]*. I didn't catch most of the Amicus movies until they started showing up on TV. To tell the truth, I don't much care for anthology movies. I like a sustained narrative, much as I prefer novels to short stories. Anthology movies feel like a series of digressions that don't go anywhere. The only one I think I

"Face Your Fears!" The garish 'get a-head' DVD cover art for Piper's 2005 frightfest

MISTY MUNDAE JULIAN WELLS AJ KHAN CAITLIN ROSS

FACE YOUR FEARS!

MICHAEL RASO PRESENTS

SHOCK-O-RAMA

A BRETT PIPER FILM

---

really enjoyed was **CREEPSHOW** [1982]. That doesn't mean I wouldn't *make* another one. The movies you like to watch and the movies you like to make can be quite different.

SRB: Did any particular previous horror anthology movie (or comic book) provide a template for what became SHOCK-O-RAMA?

BP: Well, the template is pretty standard, isn't it? A few short stories tied together with some kind of framing device. I'm guessing **DEAD OF NIGHT** established the formula.[16] **SHOCK-O-RAMA** is a little different in that one of the individual stories is also the framing story, but that was an afterthought. After the shooting was finished, E.I. decided it didn't want an anthology, so I had to try to tie everything together into a single storyline. The original framing device (a ghostly drive-in) was out, and Misty's zombie

---

16 This format in genre feature films dates at least back to the German silent era, when portmanteau features evolved, with Richard Oswald's **EERIE STORIES** (*Unheimliche Geschichten*, 1919), Fritz Lang's and Thea von Harbou's **DESTINY** (*Der müde Tod: Ein Deutsches Volkslied in 6 Versen*, 1921), Paul Leni's and Henrik Galeen's **WAXWORKS** (*Das Wachsfigurenkabinett*, 1924), etc. Prior to **DEAD OF NIGHT**, there were also compilation anthology horror films such as **DR. TERROR'S HOUSE OF HORRORS** (1943, USA), comprising condensed content from foreign feature films (including Carl Dreyer's **VAMPYR** [1932, Germany/France], Julien Duvivier's **THE GOLEM** [*Le golem*, 1936, France], etc.).

---

story became the linking device. It didn't hurt anything.

SRB: You also talked earlier about that footage you had shot for a planned anthology film (the one featuring a mummy that ended up, somehow, in someone else's unauthorized direct-to-video compilation). Had you scripted that earlier anthology concept beyond the mummy episode, and if so, did any of that end up informing SHOCK-O-RAMA?

BP: There was a full script written. Three stories and a framing story. One of the episodes, "The Wrong Crowd", about a young girl who falls in with a coven of witches to get away from her abusive father, was one of the better things I've written. I imagine the basic idea influenced the plot of **DRAINIAC!** a little.

SRB: Even if "The Wrong Crowd" might have influenced DRAINIAC!, is it a script you still might one day develop and film? It sounds like a solid story hook, for sure, and as timely as ever.

BP: I have such a backlog of scripts. I'll never live long enough to do them all! And there are others I'd rather do if given the chance.

SRB: What was the "ghostly drive-in" framing story you'd planned? Was that filmed as well, or did the "rethink" and change happen before you were in that deep?

BP: It was very simple. There was an actual abandoned drive-in not far from E.I. Old clunkers, ghost cars, would have driven up and the ghostly occupants would have bought tickets from a ghostly ticket seller. All the usual stuff at a drive in, kids playing at the little playground, people buying rotten food at a concession stand, but everyone was dead. There was no real story, just a quiet, spooky filler between 'features.' At the end the ghost cars would drive away as the sun rose. None of this was ever shot. The change of plans was handed down before we got to it. Extra 'studio-within-a-studio' stuff was shot instead.

SRB: Did you approach the making of SHOCK-O-RAMA as one production, or three (or four, given the initial planned drive-in framing story) separate smaller-scaled productions?

BP: It was basically broken-down into several productions. The first thing shot was the "Pit and the Pendulum" dream sequence *[for "Lonely Are the Brain"]*, which was done on the revamped

Godzilla *[tower]* interior from **BITE ME!**. Very simple, practically no crew, I lit and shot it myself. I don't think Raso even knew we'd started filming. Then that set was torn down and all the sets for the other nightmare scenes were built. Christina C laid it out so every inch of the studio space was used, there was barely room to squeeze through, which ticked Raso off considerably. It turned out, rather to my surprise, that shooting three short stories for an anthology was three times as hard as shooting a traditional narrative feature. You need three different casts, three sets of locations, three of everything. The only advantage was that after shooting an episode you could, if you chose, take time to regroup before starting the next.

SRB: What was your thinking on casting—a unique cast for each story, or moving some of the same performers between changing stories, in different roles?

BP: Misty was supposed to play the lead in all three stories (*à la* Karen Black in **TRILOGY OF TERROR**). But by the time we were ready to shoot, relationships had changed at E.I., and she was down to one. Obviously it had to be the zombie story, which was very much written for her. There was talk of her doing a small 'cameo' as one of the girls in the brain episode, but it never happened.

SRB: Was Misty's star status at E.I. the determining factor in making the zombie story the overall thru-thread for SHOCK-O-RAMA?

BP: No, it simply seemed like the most practical approach to integrating all the stories. The search for "Rebecca Raven"'s replacement became the excuse to include the other two episodes.

SRB: What order did you end up filming the stories in? It looks, in the film, like all exteriors were done in moderate weather; I only noticed seeing anyone's breath when the zombie [Duane Polcou] was approaching the window Misty was sitting next to in, before their first interaction.

BP: I'm reasonably sure that the zombie sequence was the first one shot, followed by the junkyard, followed by the brain, and finally the wraparound material shot in the studio. I'm basing this on the order in which we went through DPs. Excepting again the Pendulum scene, which was the first thing we shot, so we could tear down the set.

SRB: Let's discuss the individual episodes in order of their appearance in the film, then. Though "Zombie This!" opens the film, the first full narrative we get to enjoy is actually the science fiction spaceship-crash-in-a-scrapyard tale, "Mecharachnia." Were there any issues with that title?

BP: Sometime during production a certain Vermont would-be movie mogul got wind of it and sent an email threatening to sue if we used that title. Mike Weiss dropped a copy of the email on my desk and muttered, "Obnoxious little fuck, isn't he?"

Misty Mundae in **SHOCK-O-RAMA**'s "Zombie This!" episode. Note the mockup poster for "THE SCREAMING HEAD", a title concocted by producer Mike Raso that Piper took a shine to and later "wrote a movie around" (which was, alas, never filmed)

It's bulldozer versus the titular stop-motion-animated alien at the climax of
SHOCK-O-RAMA's "Mecharachnia" episode

SRB: You mention in the bonus extras on the DVD that you had total and free access to the location, no hassles: including use of equipment [the old bulldozer] and even crushing of bulky scrap—refrigerators!—as part of the action. Where was the scrapyard, what was the deal, and how long were you and the cast and crew filming there?

BP: It was a salvage yard in the Stroudsburg area. Just down the street from a small theme park called Wild West City.[17] I wish I could remember the name of the place—I feel bad about it, because the guy who ran it was just great to us. He literally handed us the keys and said go to it. We were only there three days and one night. It was the quickest of any of the segments to shoot.

SRB: Were all the office interiors also on site—the actual scrapyard office?—or was that a set you built at E.I.?

BP: Everything was shot there, interior and exterior. Except for the shot of the filing cabinet blowing open, I shot that at E.I.

SRB: Other than the eviction notices, there's some funny signage that pops up in some shots ("An 'X' Signature IS Legally Binding!").

Were those all 'found' props—signage and such that actually were on the grounds and in that cluttered office—that you just put to good use?

BP: The only signs I brought in were the big "Callahan Salvage" sign out front and the eviction notices. If I remember correctly we had to rig a front gate, I don't think they had one, or at least not one that was usable for our purposes. And we may have rearranged furniture and such to suit our blocking. But other than that, everything was there. An amazing place. Not just cars and appliances and such, but rows of airplane engines and things. Just a great location.

SRB: Rob Monkiewicz (as the down-on-his-luck scrapyard owner Jedd Callahan) and Caitlin Ross (as "where's the money I loaned you?" ex-girlfriend Linda) give great performances, and are a lot of fun. What was the chemistry on set? Were there any surprises?

BP: The main surprise was that Caitlin knew all her lines! Nah, I'm kidding. Sort of. For some reason, maybe because of the way we had to shuffle parts around, she'd sometimes been a little iffy on her lines in **BITE ME!**, so before the start of the "Mecharachnia" shoot I approached her and started to say something about it, and before I could finish talking she began rattling-off all her dialogue. She had it down pat. There were no actor problems at all. Caitlin and Rob seemed to get along great.

SRB: Did everyone do their own stunt work on "Mecharachnia"?

---

17 The closest-to-Stroudsburg, PA Wild West City theme park extant I could find online was actually on Lackawanna Drive in Stanhope, NJ; the closest auto salvage yard to Wild West City (50 Lackawanna Drive) is North Jersey Auto Wreckers (287 Lackawanna Drive), both are in the Byram Township. There is also an APS Recycling and Salvage on 2 Katz Road in Stroudsburg, PA. If any reader can correct this information, please, let us know!

BP: I don't think I remember any stunt work. Nobody was doubled for anything.

SRB: The opening in outer space has a splendid look and feel. As you say in the DVD extras, it was all done (per usual) 'old school'—models, animation, etc.—but it also has a bright color palette that immediately establishes the playful tenor and tone of the entire episode. How much of that was what you'd created for the camera, and how much was done in post?

BP: That was all done in-camera. The space background was a big painting and the planets and asteroids were models hung from strings. I was going for sort of an 'Antonio Margheriti' look, old-fashioned and colorful. I had a bitch of a time with the space ship mattes. I used blue screen instead of green because the background was primarily blue, but for some reason the film-to-tape transfers (shot on super 16mm and transferred to Digi-Beta) had a lot of "noise" in the blue, so the edges of the mattes were terrible. I had to clean them up by hand, so to speak (I also had to matte the "noise" out of the blue in Rob and Caitlin's jeans!).

SRB: Was there a miniature version of the crashed spaceship, or was there just the full-sized prop?

BP: There was a miniature about ten inches long.

SRB: Ah, I thought so! The first shot of Rob discovering the ship in the junkyard looked like it might be a miniature, then he interacts with a full-size 'ship'—

BP: The first shot when he sees the ship was the full-sized prop as well, but I tried to shoot it in forced perspective to make it look bigger—I didn't want the audience to realize how small it was right away—which is why it may have had a 'miniature' look. I built the full-sized prop first because it's always easier (for me, anyway) to copy a big prop in miniature than the other way around. I got some flack on the design of the ship—one 'critic' said it looked like something out of a cereal box—but I thought it was pretty obvious that I was going for an old-fashioned *Flash Gordon* look. I guess you can't be obvious enough for some people.

SRB: Oh, I got that! It adds to the fun. Though we never get a good look at it—due to the rapidity of its movement—the cyclops-alien creature looks pretty cool. What was the inspiration, and how did you settle on its 'look'?

BP: I can barely remember what it looked like! I guess I must have sketched it out first; I always do just to get the proportions right when I build the armature. I'm sure it was inspired by Charlie Gemora. He inspires a lot of my stuff. He was so much more than just a gorilla man—his aliens in **WAR OF THE WORLDS** *[1953]* and **I MARRIED A MONSTER FROM OUTER SPACE** *[1958]* are two of the best aliens ever put on film, and that Pompeian mummy in **CURSE OF THE FACELESS MAN** *[1958]*, which I just watched again the other day, is genius in its simplicity.

SRB: How did you maintain the dimensional depth of the paths of the ray blasts from the alien's weapon? Was that all done 'by eye,' or something you'd carefully calculated?

BP: Just by eye. If I were Jim Danforth I'd have figured it all out according to the laws of physics and spatial geometry and what not, but I'm only me and I just wing it.

SRB: Well, it looks ideal, to my eye. Well done! The alien's makeshift scrapyard robot is a terrific concoction. What did you build the model from, what make and model car was that dominating the upper section, and what size was the model?

BP: "Make and model of the car?" *Wow!* I have no idea, and I probably couldn't have told you at the time. I just wandered through the toy store until I saw something that looked right. I knew roughly the look I was after, that kind of '60s family sedan thing, but that's all. The robot model was built in proportion to the model car, so it was maybe a foot tall. It was basically made out of scrap, odd bits of metal and plastic hardware and old parts from other model kits—it there was ever a case where kit-bashing was justified this was it. Anything I had leftover was used in some of the junkyard backgrounds. I also bought a bulldozer which I customized to match the real one we shot on location but it ended up being used in only one shot, the pan over the miniature junkyard after the alien ship has crashed.

Interesting side note: **SHOCK-O-RAMA** was shot in super 16mm but all the stop motion was shot with my Bolex, which is standard 16mm. For the most part this worked fine because the animation models never had to fill the entire frame they were matted in to, but once in a while the corner of a model would "disappear" and I would have to tediously recreate the missing section in post.

SRB: *What did that recreation of missing imagery entail, Brett?*

BP: For example, the robot might turn and for a few frames one "arm" would pass outside the 4 x 3 frame of the Bolex, which meant that when I matted it into the wider aspect ratio of the background plate, that part of the arm would disappear. I would have to grab pieces from other frames which more or less matched the missing part of the image and matte them into the area of the frame where they should have been.

SRB: *Were there any other post-production issues with "Mecharachnia"?*

Top: BP's sto-mo "Mecharachnia". **Above:** Jack Kirby, Dick Ayers, and Stan Lee introduced "Fin Fang Foom!" with this spectacular splash page (from *Strange Adventures* #89, October 1961)

BP: Except for the huge amount of work for such a short episode (and the previously-mentioned snags), the post went pretty smoothly. I was still using front and back light mattes at that time which are kind of arduous, but it worked out fine.

SRB: *Who did the voices for the aliens (the scrapyard crash alien, and the one in the police ship that shows up in the finale)?*

BP: I believe Jeff Faoro did one of the alien cop voices, and either David Fine or Justin Wingenfeld did the other. The actual alien mutterings may have been me. I think so anyway.

SRB: *The ending of "Mecharachnia" is right out of an early 1960s Stan Lee/Jack Kirby or Lee/Steve Ditko pre-Marvel Atlas comic book.*

BP: Yeah, *Strange Tales* or *Journey Into Mystery* or something. More *[Steve]* Ditko than *[Jack]* Kirby, I would think. Someone needs to make a movie featuring Fin Fang Foom some time.[18]

SRB: *I'm surprised the Marvel franchise movies haven't tapped that vein as yet—give 'em time. "Zombie This!" is the next full story, though it technically frames the other two and pulls the whole feature together; the other two tales are showcased as 'audition tapes' for actresses being considered to replace "Rebecca Raven" [Misty]. You really pulled it all together nicely; did you have to retool the flow of the stories for any reason after the shoot was completed for "Zombie This!"?*

BP: Not really. I wrote some new connecting material (none of which involved Misty) but I don't think I had to alter any of the original stories at all except for breaking the zombie episode into three parts.

SRB: *Were the offices we see in the opening and coda of "Zombie This!" the E.I. offices, or a constructed set?*

BP: The office was a set. I'd wanted to just shoot it in Mike Raso's office but he wouldn't hear of it, so Christina said, "Don't worry, I can make you a set," and turned the Green room into an office. I'd also wanted Mike to play the producer but when I approached him about it he said "You'll have to coax me." I don't coax, either you're in or you're not, so that was that. Someone later

---

18 Brett is referring to the giant Chinese dragon in Stan Lee, Jack Kirby, and Dick Ayers' "Fin Fang Foom" in *Strange Tales* #89 (October 1961), and he's right.

suggested I should have asked Lloyd Kaufman to play the producer! I wish I'd thought of it at the time. I'll bet he would have done it, and then he'd have plugged the hell out of the movie! I'd planned to use posters from Misty's actual E.I. movies on the office wall, but for some reason Mike didn't like that idea either, so he came up with the 'fake' posters, "THE SCREAMING HEAD," and so on. Actually, I liked the poster for "SCREAMING HEAD" so much, I later wrote a movie around it.

SRB: Actually, the box art for SHOCK-O-RAMA prominently featured a screaming head (the zombie head, riffing on what Rebecca Raven delivers to her ex-producer's desk at the end of that episode). What would your future "SCREAMING HEAD" be about? Other than the obvious…

BP: I love that box art! I worked on it a little, by the way—I built the zombie head and helped with the set-up and lighting. My script for *Screaming Head* was sort of a parody of **THE BRAIN THAT WOULDN'T DIE** *[1959/1962]* type thing, as you might imagine, except that, in addition to a disembodied head, I had a headless body lumbering around. It was written for the usual E.I. regulars, Misty in the lead, Mike Thomas as The Head. I think it would have been pretty good.

SRB: Who is the fellow playing the editor Rebecca/Misty is first seen talking to?

BP: That was Mike Schuster, actually another editor who did some work for E.I. I forget how

we came to cast him in the part, but I thought he did a good job.

SRB: Your "Producers" (Mel Brooks reference intended) for "Zombie This!" were played by Michael R. Thomas and David Fine (I suppose Gaylord is a producer, yes?). They made a good onscreen comedy team—

BP: They both had a flair for that type of thing.

SRB: Not to jump ahead, but you also cast Michael as the slobbering brain-from-the-future in "Lonely Are the Brain." He was clearly up to the challenge!

BP: I cast him in that part because he had a life-mask I could borrow to build the giant brain! He actually did the makeup himself, blending in the Big Brain appliance I'd built. It was easier for him to do it once he was in position than for me to.

SRB: Did Michael create any other of the makeups for SHOCK-O-RAMA?

BP: Mike didn't actually create any makeups for the movie. He blended the brain 'head' to his face, but that was all.

SRB: Where was the location you filmed Rebecca/Misty's remote "vacation destination" at? Were the interiors and exteriors, including the toolshed, all shot at the same location?

BP: The tool shed was out behind Jeff Faoro's house. The rest of the scenes were shot at a bed-

David Fine and Michael R. Thomas as the producers in **SHOCK-O-RAMA**'s "Zombie This!" episode

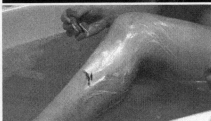

and-breakfast in upstate New York. We rented the whole place and stayed there for the shoot. As often happens, the owner got a little tired of having movie people swarming all over his property for days on end, but then when I began making-up Duane [Polcou] as the zombie, he stood there watching for a bit and finally said, "This makes it all worthwhile!" He seemed to be a fan of horror movies. He told us that not long before we arrived Sara Karloff had stayed there!

SRB: Hey, that's a cool connection-by-proxy, isn't it? "Zombie This!" reaches a sublime spot in which your zombie is being terrorized by Rebecca/Misty, and you made the most of that turnabout. You should do more comedy, Brett; the setup, dialogue, pacing, and timing was spot-on throughout this episode.

BP: *All* my movies are comedies! Duane made a great zombie. He's a comedian anyway (in addition to being a photographer—he shot most of E.I.'s "glamour" stills). I love his little jig of delight when Misty's chainsaw won't start. Like Walter Huston in **THE TREASURE OF THE SIERRA MADRE** *[1948]*.

SRB: "Lonely Are the Brain" is the final self-standing episode, and it's a pip. The cast of "Lonely Are the Brain" really delivered. A.J. Khan carries the lead as Naomi; she had fleeting roles in both SCREAMING DEAD (she was the model tortured in the pre-title opening) and BACTERIUM (as biker Rob/Jed's bed-mate who answers the phone), but she'd done a ton of work for E.I., including a role in KINKY KONG. What prompted your casting her for the lead, and were you happy with A.J.'s performance?

BP: As I mentioned earlier, Misty was supposed to play the leads in all three episodes, but when it was decided otherwise I had to scramble to find two other actresses. Caitlin was chosen right away for "Mecharachnia," but I didn't know who to get for the "Brain". Someone suggested A.J., whom I didn't really know very well, and I said fine, so she jumped into the part with only two days' notice. The first scene she did was talking with Sylvianne on the bench out back, and she nailed it, every line letter perfect and delivered just the way it should have been. Like a lot of actresses at E.I., she had talent she'd rarely been asked to use.

SRB: You brought A.J. back for one more role in your first film after the E.I. run, MUCKMAN [2009], where she was credited as "Anju McIntyre."

BP: Yes, her real name. "McIntyre"—I told her it was nice working with a fellow Scot. All the girls at E.I. had phony names, *noms de cinéma*. "Misty" is not really Misty, nor "Erin Brown," for that matter.

SRB: Ahh, I had heard or read that somewhere... Julian Wells seemed to relish her role as Dr. Carruthers, the somewhat shady, sexy scientist overseeing the dream and behavioral experimentation on the women in "the program" (under domination of the brain-from-the-future). What landed Julian this plum role, including her prominent nude role in almost all the dream sequences? Did she enjoy playing the part?

BP: The part was written for her. I'd enjoyed working with her so much on **BITE ME!** that I was happy to bring her back. In fact, for a brief time we considered her playing the female lead in "Mecharachnia" as well, but decided if the same actress wasn't going to play all three leads then they should all be different. We also discussed (very briefly) Misty playing a small cameo in the "Brain" episode, the part that Suzy Kaye played, but that never happened either.

I don't know how much Julian enjoyed playing Carruthers, we never discussed it. She was certainly never anything but professional and easy to work with, even on one occasion when I asked her to go way over the top and she was clearly embarrassed. That was the bit where she has her melt-down when confessing all to A.J. I kept pushing her to go further and further, and she gave me exactly what I asked for. Now I realize I went too far, and she's the one who looks silly for it. Sorry, Julian.

SRB: The rest of the all-female cast of "Lonely Are the Brain" (save for Michael as the brain) was led by Sylvianne Chebance [as Monique], Merav Tal [as Jessica], and Suzy Kaye [as Celeste]; given the talent pool at E.I., what landed this trio their roles, and how was it for you helming the ensemble?

BP: I think there may have been a desire at E.I. to separate their 'real' movies (which I was the only one making) from the T&A pictures that had been their mainstay, so except for 'The Big Three'—Misty, Julian, and A.J.—I don't think they wanted my movies filled with their regulars. It also may have been financial. Most of the usual E.I. girls were pros looking to make a buck, not aspiring actresses willing to take short money in return for the opportunity. I don't know. Sylvianne, of course, had already been in my two previous movies. The part that Merav played was originally written for Heidi Kristoffer, who'd told me she'd always wanted to play "a real bitch," but she turned it down as "Too E.I." Merav herself was concerned about the semi-nudity, and sat down with me to review the final sequence to make sure nothing was too revealing. Unlike some actresses, she was entirely reasonable about it, and even okayed a couple of shots I was sure she'd have a problem with. But the funny thing is, she had absolutely no problem with being naked in front of the crew while we shot. When we did the 'heart-ripping' sequence, she came onto the set without a stitch on (and looking fabulous), took her position, and then we fussed with her hair for a while to make sure her nipples didn't show in the shot. When I asked her later why, since she was obviously so secure with her body, she objected to any nudity, she shrugged and said, "I'm not ready for that yet."

Pages 190-191: Images from **S-O-R**'s "Zombie This!" episode, featuring Misty Mundae and zombie Duane Polcou

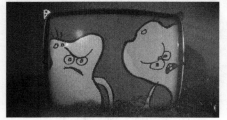

SRB: Each dream sequence has its own distinctive design and look—no two are alike—it's all very inventive, at times startlingly so, including the stop-motion animated 'pop' environments for one of them.

BP: I love dream sequences. There is absolutely no limit to the imagination you can bring to them, and I think we pulled most of them off pretty well.

SRB: The 'pop' dream is startling in the context of the rest of the film—as if "Penny" from Pee-wee's Playhouse *slipped into the E.I. universe—and unlike anything in any other of your films. Didn't that require a more intensive and exacting orchestration of all elements (color, costumes, makeup, etc.) than you'd ever tackled before?*

BP: Not more intensive or exacting, really, just different. Heightened colors and more extreme stylization. But the other sequences required just as much work.

SRB: Were you working with clay or plasticine for the stop-motion visuals in the 'pop' dream?

BP: The only stop-motion that I recall from that sequence was the car driving by. That was just a miniature that I built. It had different designs on each side, so that coming one way it was a car, the other way it was a cab. Saved building two of them.

SRB: The 'sacrificial dream' culminates in that graphic mastectomy image—essentially, the left breast replaced with a bloody cavity in its place—and more blood (including that covering the nude body of the dream-surrogate for the doctor) than you typically indulge in your films.

BP: But remember—*it was only a dream!*

SRB: Where were the exteriors filmed? That location presented as the clinic is an astonishing setup, with the elaborate exterior stairways (fire escapes?) and such—

Left, Top to Bottom: Wild imagery from **S-O-R**'s "Lonely Are the Brain" therapy and dream sequences, featuring Sylvianne Chebance, Merav Tal and Suzy Kaye, along with one of the few—actually, the *only!*—cartoon-animated sequences to be found in BP's body of work

BP: That was the York Street House in Lambertville, NJ. Christina had made up a list of houses that might be suitable for the episode, and we spent a day driving around looking at them. Most of them were nothing special. One of them, of which the owner seemed very proud, looked like a turn-of-the-century whorehouse. When we entered the York Street House, I said, "Oh, this looks like the place!" But here was the clincher—when I was writing that episode, I had (for no particular reason) imagined the two lead characters sitting in a corner at a small table with a chessboard inlaid on the top, and when I looked over in the corner of the main room, *there was the damned table!* Just as I'd imagined it. It was almost eerie.

SRB: Where did you film the interiors for "Brain," including the titular brain's base of operations?

BP: All the 'normal' interiors were shot at the location in Lambertville. All the dream interiors were sets at E.I. Christina mapped-out the studio space to use every inch to best advantage. When we started discussing how to build the 'brain room,' it quickly became apparent that there was going to be a lot more discussion than building, so I said, "Look, here's what we'll do—we'll split up, and I'll build this set and you build the corridors." This did not go down well, but that's what we did, and it worked out fine. Christina built the weird nightmare corridors and the cartoonish kitchen set for the 'pop' sequence, including the stove and the table. I did the brain room and the 'normal' corridor. The brain room, by the way, was reused in one of E.I.'s softcore quickies. I have no idea what for, but I insisted on

revamping it so it wouldn't look quite the same in both movies. Raso seemed to resent this, like I was somehow taking advantage of him.

SRB: "Lonely Are the Brain" culminates in all hell breaking loose—in reality, and in the dream realms—including the raving brain-from-the-future paying the ultimate price, and yet another explosive conflagration (hot on the heels of the one at the end of SCREAMING DEAD and BITE ME!). It's like the 1960s Corman and Hammer films all over again!

BP: *Yes!* Corman has said that, when he shot **THE TERROR** *[1963]*, he was so sick of his movies ending in flames that he decided to go the opposite way and end it with a flood. When we were planning **BACTERIUM**, Christina, who

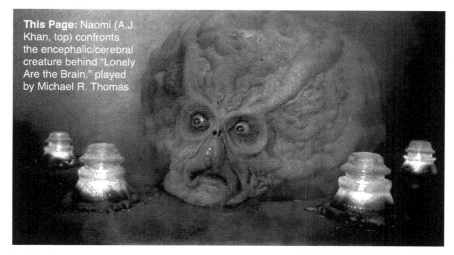

This Page: Naomi (A.J. Khan, top) confronts the encephalic/cerebral creature behind "Lonely Are the Brain," played by Michael R. Thomas

was producing, said, "I ask only one thing—don't end this movie with another explosion!" So we went for an *implosion* instead.

SRB: You earlier noted that SHOCK-O-RAMA was "basically broken down into several productions." That begs the question: Was the post-production and editing process on SHOCK-O-RAMA more time-consuming than any of your earlier features? You were, after all, seeing through three narratives, and the nuances of the wraparound story.

BP: No, editing was pretty straightforward. Once you sit down to edit these things all the heavy lifting has been done. Everything's been reduced to a stack of tapes. I've heard people say that editing is the most "creative" part of film-making. Bullshit. All the real creating has been done. Editing is merely the *most* creativity you can exercise for the *least* amount of actual work. It's a lazy man's idea of being creative.

SRB: Correct me if I'm wrong, but SHOCK-O-RAMA was your final feature shot-on-16mm or film, yes?

BP: It was. I shot a little bit of **MUCKMAN** on 16mm, a slow-motion shot of a miniature truck rolling down a hill and the stop-motion, but that was that. End of an era.

SRB: I've neglected to ask about working with the MPAA/CARA ratings board on the E.I.

films. Were the E.I. features the first time you had to deal with the ratings system?

BP: I didn't deal with them. That was E.I.'s concern.

SRB: Were there any issues with the ratings board on any of the E.I. films?

BP: Not that I heard about.

SRB: Did E.I. give SHOCK-O-RAMA the red carpet treatment, or was the market already flagging? How did SHOCK-O-RAMA do for E.I.?

BP: By the time **SHOCK-O-RAMA** was done, the market for these films was already dying. That and the fact that it went well over-budget meant that (as far as I know) it didn't make any money. Neither did *I*! I had tried to convince E.I. that it was too big a movie, that we'd be better off retrenching and doing something quicker and cheaper. I was told, as usual, "You make the movie, let us worry about the money." But I was getting the same deal to make it as I'd gotten for **BITE ME!**, which had cost about a quarter as much and been a much simpler picture. I was told, "Don't worry, if it becomes a problem, we'll adjust your deal." Well, it *did* become a problem, but I decided to be a team player and went for something like three months without a paycheck to keep the costs down. And as a reward, when it came time to make **BACTERIUM,** they initially offered me even *less!* We worked it out.

Quality Pictures: Nothin' but the best from **SHOCK-O-RAMA**'s fictional producers (David Fine and Michael R. Thomas)!

Brett Piper Interview Pts 4 & 5 *Stephen R. Bissette*

Much worse was the way they cheaped-out on the DVD master. After spending way more than they should have on the movie itself, they had someone with no experience make a crappy DVD master to save a few bucks. As a result, the movie is just a tenth-rate version of what it had originally been, the image pale and washed-out and the sound almost inaudible. I saw it at a *Fangoria* convention on a DVD made straight from the original and, if I say so myself, it looked and sounded like a *real movie*—like one of Corman's Poe movies or something. No one will ever see it like that again.

BACTERIUM (2007)

SRB: Your final feature for E.I. was BACTERIUM, which was a real change of pace from all the earlier E.I. films. It may end with an implosion, but BACTERIUM kicks off with a grim pre-title sequence worthy of George Romero's THE CRAZIES [1974], and a pretty spectacular fire sequence.

BP: It's funny you should mention that because one reviewer, in describing how "cheesy" the movie was, said the opening looked like it was shot "in someone's back yard." How perceptive. The opening is pretty much as I wrote it in the script, with the exception of the barn burning down, which was *not* stock footage—it was shot expressly for our movie. Johnny Sullivan, our stunt coordinator, arranged that. He called me up one day and said, essentially, "When we do the crash at the beginning, how about it sets a barn on fire and burns it to the ground?" And I said, "Uh, yeah—that'd be great." And he set it up for us. We had to drive down to Maryland, where he lived, to shoot it, but it was worth it. And it cost almost nothing. In fact, **BACTERIUM** turned out to be the cheapest of all my E.I. movies.

SRB: You also have fairly extensive use of Bell helicopters and, during the climax, motorcycles in the film; pretty extensive action that carries a lot of screen value. How did you manage that on a modest budget, and how intensive were the logistics involved?

BP: Not as intensive as you might think. The motorcycle scenes were the first things shot. My landlord, a very cool guy named Fred Bauer ("Panhead Fred"), was big into motorcycles, he used to do competitive motocross racing. He got a bunch of his buddies to show up with their bikes. In fact, he's got a big close-up himself. The only problem we had was

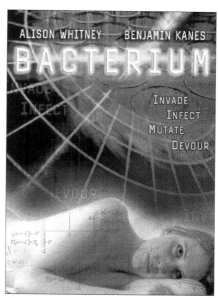

E.I.'s comparatively complacent DVD packaging/promo for **BACTERIUM** (2007) barely registered in the dwindling marketplace

that Rob couldn't ride a motorcycle. He can fly a plane or a helicopter, but he can't ride a motorcycle. He got a few quick lessons, but it was too tricky on that grass, so one of the other bikers doubled him. The helicopter (only one) was arranged by Christina. Those suckers are *expensive* to rent, but she found one relatively cheap, and by the time she got through charming the pilot, it was even cheaper. We got something like $2000 worth of services for a few hundred bucks.

SRB: In the DVD extras, you note that BACTERIUM began (if I heard you correctly) with your producer asking for a "traditional monster movie," but you wanted to do something you'd never seen—a bacterial 'monster.' What was your original conception of BACTERIUM?

BP: At the time, Raso was very high on the idea of selling features to the SyFy Channel (or whatever they called themselves at the time), and apparently they liked monsters that people could relate to, things that they might see in real life but, well, monstrous (this was before every other movie they ran was about some kind of mutant shark). So I tried to think of something we encountered every day that would be scary in monstrous proportions, and came up with idea of giant bacteria. I pitched it to Raso, he liked it, and away we went.

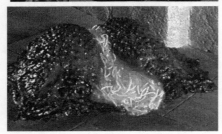

SRB: BACTERIUM, as you noted in the DVD bonus feature, ended up becoming your 'blob' movie instead. As such, it's a revamp of the 1950s-1970s 'contagion' movies—everything from THE QUATERMASS XPERIMENT a.k.a. THE CREEPING UNKNOWN to THE ANDROMEDA STRAIN, from SPACEMASTER X-7 to THE BLOB and CALTIKI, THE IMMORTAL MONSTER. Did you have any favorites of that genre you were consciously tapping into, or even recreating scenes from?

BP: Well, it's both—the blobs *are* giant bacteria. Actually, my real inspiration in writing the script was *The Avengers*—not the Marvel comic, but the TV show *[1961-69]* with Diana Rigg and Patrick Macnee. They would often have episodes that started with seemingly normal situations that led to government cover-ups of projects gone wrong or something. So I kept pretending I was writing an *Avengers* episode—with giant blobs.

My favorite blob movie, by the way, is one you didn't mention—**X THE UNKNOWN** *[1956]*.

SRB: I can totally see the Avengers influence, now that you say that—and I love X THE UNKNOWN, too! I think that was the first blob movie I ever saw (on afternoon TV, about age 5 or 6). I can see that, too—the melting faces (that was the first big 'shock' shot in X THE UNKNOWN), the military presence, and so on.

BP: Well, you can't do a blob movie without melting a few faces.

SRB: As you reveal in the DVD extras, the gruesome makeup effects were actually quite simple: dental supplies customized to your needs, flesh-colored gelatin, which you applied as necessary by hand. How quickly were those makeups accomplished, and how long would they hold up during shooting?

BP: They were quick to do, but wouldn't last long. I didn't use any kind of adhesive, so the gelatin tended to just fall off. Fortunately I only needed them for a few quick shots.

Left: Piper's progressive **BACTERIUM** 'blob' SFX creations include phases of growth/transformation, human meltdowns and mitosis division. The latter process had been depicted *[bottom]* via John Earl (a.k.a. John St. John Earl), Michael Albrechtsen, and W. T. ("Billy") Partleton's effects showing the life cycle of the Silicates in **ISLAND OF TERROR** (1966, UK)

SRB: The 'blob' effects are all pretty effective, and seem to involve a variety of techniques as they reproduce (via division, like one-celled organisms), sprout tentacles, feed, crawl up walls and across ceilings, and so on. Could you walk us through how you realized those effects? How many involved miniatures?

BP: There were three stages of blob. The small ones, the "babies," were just slime, made of very thick wallpaper paste with a little Ultra Slime added for cohesion. The next stage, the bigger organisms you see crawling all over the lab, were basically large half-filled water balloons covered with latex and spider-webbing (the kind you can buy in any store around Halloween) and foam tentacles. There were only one or two of them, multiplied through split-screens, and manipulated by hand. One of my favorite effects in any of my movies is a shot of one of these blobs dividing, which was done entirely live, with no optical work. The biggest blobs, the ones that looked sort of like paramecia, were made of gel wax, the kind you make soft candles with, tinted and embedded with various items, small pearl beads and glitter and such, to give them the right look, and fibrous tentacles attached. There was a bit of rod puppet-style manipulation, but primarily they were moved by gravity, similar to a way the original **BLOB** *[1958]* was brought to life. They were mostly shot on miniature sets, with the occasional green screen shot (very difficult, due to the translucent nature of the creatures).

SRB: They really look alive in the film—I love the discovery of them in the attic—

BP: The shot of them crawling all over the attic ceiling was interesting. I built a miniature of the room and a framework to attach the camera to it, so that, whichever way I turned the set, the camera stayed in the same relative position. Then I did several shots, with the set turned on one side, then another, and so on, so that the blobs were all moving in different direction in each shot. Then I used multiple split-screens to tie them all together. It was a little more complicated than it probably sounds—I had to rotoscope where they overlapped, for example—but I think it came off pretty well.

Did you notice the "SCREAMING HEAD" poster hanging in the attic?

SRB: Yes! And it wasn't the "SCREAMING HEAD" poster from SHOCK-O-RAMA, either. As you mentioned earlier, the climax involved

Top to Bottom: More **BACTERIUM** FX shots. In their earliest stages, the blob "babies" were composed of "very thick wallpaper paste with a little Ultra Slime". At top, a questing tentacle enters an experimental lab animal's cage, looking for a snack; miniatures played a part in the laboratory sets; an oversized 'blob' absorbs its human prey, in the form of a female scientist

an implosion rather than an explosion or fiery finale. How did you create the 'implosion' and 'wind' (actually, the suction/vacuum created by the implosion, drawing anything within miles of the center of the implosion into its 'ground zero') effects?

BP: I built a quickie miniature of a field, with some trees and a fence and a small tractor and such, none of it tied-down, just set up on a sheet of plywood. I mounted the camera to the same plywood and just tipped it sideways,

Blobular Beasties: Brett went back to "BLOB" basics for **BACTERIUM**'s monsters. "The biggest blobs… were made of gel wax… tinted and embedded with various items, small pearl beads and glitter and such… and fibrous tentacles attached…"

then added some wind and a 'stretching' effect in post. Raso wasn't happy with the mess it made. I don't blame him—there was dirt everywhere in the studio. and it took days to clean up. Maybe I should have shot it in the parking lot.

The effect of the General's face being warped and melted was done by making a soft gelatin face, mounting it sideways, then letting it melt. The shot was rotated ninety degrees so it seemed to drip sideways, then doing a soft matte to combine it with the actresses' features and stretching the combined shot.

The headquarters exploding was mostly a lot of miniature rubble (left over from the exploding building in **SHOCK-O-RAMA**) shot falling away from the camera, then run in reverse and matted over a shot of the actual headquarters which was optically tweaked to make it look like it was bursting. I'd have rather destroyed a real miniature, but aside from the expense, **BACTERIUM** (unlike **SHOCK-O-RAMA**) wasn't shot on film so shooting slow-motion miniatures was pretty much not an option.

SRB: Where did you shoot BACTERIUM? There's the forest 'paintball stalk' scenes, and two central standing structure locations—the house the scientist has set up his laboratory in, where your heroes and heroines are trapped, and the dilapidated structure the military sets up headquarters in.

BP: The paintball scenes were shot across the street from the house I was staying at. The scene of A.J. waking Rob up, for that matter, was shot in my bedroom (that's one of Fred's vintage bikes in the foreground). We'd wanted Caitlin back to be the girl in bed with him, but she was unavailable. All the other exteriors, and all the abandoned building interiors, were shot at Fort Totten in Queens. All except for the lab, which was a set at E.I., which I built mostly out of flats left over from **SHOCK-O-RAMA**. Christina kept insisting we didn't need a set, that she could dress one of the rooms at Fort Totten, but she didn't understand that I needed a lab I could continue to use for all the effects shots of blobs breaking loose and multiplying and such, which could (and did) take months. Anyway, it all worked out.

SRB: BACTERIUM had a pretty believable 'mad scientist' character, Dr. Boskovic; what did Chuck McMahon bring to the role, to your eye/mind?

BP: There's an unfortunate story behind that. Marc Gettis, who had played "Doc" in **SCREAMING DEAD**, had originally played that part. I thought he'd done a good job in the previous film and he had the right look, so I asked him to play Boskovic without a reading. We shot the entire thing, and he was just all wrong for the part. He wasn't crazy enough, he was much too laidback. I thought I could make it work in the editing, but it just wasn't there, so I had to call him up and tell him I was reshooting it with someone else. He offered to do it over, but there was no point, the performance I wanted just wasn't in him—it was my fault, I'd cast the wrong guy. He was very understanding but it was not a happy conversation. Actually, he is still in the film—most of the scenes with Boskovic in his Hazmat suit, outside the lab, are still Marc.

Oh, another bit of Boskovic trivia—at one point it looked like Reggie Bannister, from **PHANTASM** *[1979]*, was going to play the part, but we had a phone conversation where he expressed his enthusiasm but insisted that he could not be doubled in any shots, even where his face didn't show, because his fans would know it wasn't him. I explained we couldn't do that— we didn't have the money to keep him around for weeks when we only really needed him for a couple of days. He was adamant, so that was that.

So Chuck McMahon got the part, and he was very good. At first I thought we weren't going to get along because he was full of questions about the character's backstory and motivations, and such and I had my hands full just getting the footage I needed, so I didn't have much time for that kind of thing, but we quickly came to an understanding. He really got into the part, he gave me the 'crazy' I needed (in fact, I had to tone him down once or twice, but as Terence Fisher once said, it's easier to tone a "real actor" down than it is to boost one up) and I'm glad he's in the movie.

SRB: He does a terrific job. Two of your leads— Alison Whitney [as Beth] and Benjamin Kanes

[as Jiggs, the young hero]—were making their feature film debut in BACTERIUM, and both have gone on to bigger and better things, including a fair amount of television. How were they brought on, and were you happy with their performances?

BP: Oh, bigger and better, huh? Not just bigger, but bigger and *better!* You sure know how to keep a guy in his place.

SRB: Awwwwww, I didn't mean it that way—

BP: Hah, just kidding. I hope they do go on to better things. What's good for one of us is good for all of us! Alison in particular is very determined, very hardworking, she really wants to make it, and I hope she does. She almost wasn't in **BACTERIUM**. We had cast someone else in the part. We told the other girl about the nude scene, and she was fine with it, but she called us back a few days later and said she'd changed her mind, she couldn't do it. Alison had already read for the part, so we called her back, she came down and actually read again in the lab set, and we hired her. Then the first girl called us back *again* and said she'd changed her mind *again* and could she still have the part? Tough luck, kiddo, that ship has sailed.

Alison was amazingly cool about the rather protracted nudity, which some people have dismissed as *gratuitous*, but I don't think they actually know what that word means. It's certainly justified by the plot. Boskovic is nuts and doesn't want anyone around who hasn't been

As **BACTERIUM**'s blob-thing grows, it breaks out of the laboratory structure—a careful match of miniature work with real locations—

—and, once outside, it swells toward critical mass, engulfing everything within reach, in the grand tradition of its kindred in **THE QUATERMASS XPERIMENT, THE BLOB, CALTIKI THE IMMORTAL MONSTER,** etc.

decontaminated. Someone else wondered why Alison was the only one who was seen naked— well, bonehead, because by the time the other characters meet Boskovic, she's turned the tables on him and he's *her* prisoner and in no position to decontaminate anybody! *DUH!*

After we'd done that scene, we were driving together to a location and I thanked her for how well she'd handled it. I told her scenes like that can be a real headache if the actress decides to be difficult, and I appreciated how smoothly it had gone thanks to her. She shrugged and said, "I just didn't look down at my body. If I didn't see myself naked, I was fine." Later on I sent her a link to a review of the movie. It had a picture of her nude and the caption read "Best—boobs— *ever!*" I said "Come on, that's got to make you feel at least a little good!" and she admitted that yes, it did.

Boy, feminists (of both sexes) are gonna *love* this, aren't they? Screw 'em. It's funny, it's always the other actresses who seem curious to know how a girl looks in the nude scenes. Alexandra asked me on **DRAINIAC!** how Georgia looked, and Miya asked me on **BACTERIUM** how Alison looked. And I gave them both the same answer: "She looks gorgeous." Which she certainly did.

SRB: You also cast John Fedele as one of the key military outpost officers; he was in a colder mode than his hothead BITE ME! renegade Federal agent—but he appears here without

a screen credit, and the role isn't listed in any online sources, either. I noticed he worked behind the scenes on SHOCK-O-RAMA, and he has a lot of tech credits (cinematographer, special effects, etc.) and screenwriter, director, producer, and even musical score composer credits on a number of other films. What's the scoop with John?

BP: John doesn't have a screen credit for **BACTERIUM**? I almost find that hard to believe, but I'm sure you wouldn't lie about it. I would work with John in front of the camera any day of the week, and I would not work with him behind the camera ever again. I like John, let's get that straight, but it's like a Jekyll and Hyde situation. As an actor he is affable, capable, and easy to work with. On crew he is—not good. We hired him as DP on **SHOCK-O-RAMA** based on his work on **SKIN CRAWL**, which looked very good. He was supposed to shoot the whole movie. I had him canned after seeing the first footage, and I was sorely tempted even before then. Now, I don't think it was entirely John's fault—I think Mike Raso had a hand in it. I think Mike sat John down and said "Look, we're spending a lot of money on this thing, and I want it to look *perfect!*" And as a result John became so fixated on getting everything "right" that he became rigid and inflexible to the point where I couldn't get the shots I wanted. For example, there was close up of the zombie standing in front of a fireplace, and I wanted to move the light we were using for the fire effect to get a better rim light on the zombie's face. And John refused to do it. "That's not where the firelight is coming from," he said, "we've already established where the light is." Who the hell *cares?* Things like this are cheated all the time. In another case, we shot the zombie in a doorway and I wanted a light on one side of his face, and John said, "We can't, we haven't established a light source in that room." I said "John, we've never *shown* the room! The light could be coming from *anywhere!"* But he absolutely wouldn't budge. So he had to go. He ended up on the lighting crew, where he was the classic "bad filmmaker" with no respect for anyone's property. He'd be sawing limbs off a tree because they blocked a light, and I'd say, "John, you can't do that, it's not your tree!" and he'd shoot back, "So what, it'll grow back." There was another occasion, much worse, which I will not describe because if the property owners ever learned how close he came to trashing an irreplaceable fixture they would probably want to kill us both. So that was it. John the actor, a pleasure. John the crew person—somebody get me a gun.

SRB: This was your last film with Rob, whose role of Jeb is brief but vital (he basically comes to the rescue, leading the cavalry—of bikers). It was also his final film credit to date, period. What prompted Rob's decision to step away, do you know?

BP: We discussed it. I tried to get him back a few times, but he politely declined. He decided that the acting was never going to amount to anything serious and he'd be better off devoting his time and energy to his family and his job. I didn't see where it would hurt him to take a week, a few days every now and then to do another movie, but he decided to make a clean break. We stayed in touch for a while, but you know how that goes. He had, last I knew, a lovely wife and an adorable little girl. I'm certainly not going to say he made the wrong decision. But still...

SRB: This was your second feature with Marc Cavello [cinematographer], and your third with Jon Greenhouse [music] as part of your E.I. production team, and we've not talked about them as yet. How were they to work with? You came back to Jon for scoring three of your subsequent films, I noticed...

BP: It was my fourth with Jon, wasn't it? I'm pretty sure we used his music in all our E.I. features. I never really worked much with him per se, he simply rented his library to us to use in the movies (although he did write the great

opening title music for **SHOCK-O-RAMA**). He's a very talented guy, and very understanding of our low budgets (even more so now that I'm producing movies on my own and have even less money to work with than at E.I.). I would love to have the cash to hire him to write an entire score someday.

Marc Cavello was one of the DPs on **SHOCK-O-RAMA**, he lit most of the "Brain" episode except for a few pick up scenes I did myself. There's another DP credited, but he was somewhat less than useless, by which I mean he was a total fuck-up. Marc was supposed to be his assistant, but it quickly became obvious that he was doing all the work—the other guy literally did not know how to read a light meter! I remember the two of them coming up to me on the "Brain" set wanting to know who was getting screen credit for the episode. I guess there'd been an argument about it. I said, "Both of you." One of them said, "Who's name appears *first?"* and I said, "Marc's of course, he's doing all the work." Somebody stomped away angry, and it wasn't Marc.

Marc was very talented and good to work with but the last I heard he wasn't working as a DP any more. It may seem silly to say this, but he wasn't tough enough. You need a reasonably thick hide to work on movies. I made him cry once. I didn't mean to. We were shooting in the tunnel and there was only one electrical outlet so I reminded Marc we'd need cables. When we got there I found he had brought just one cable, not nearly enough to reach where we needed it. I was pissed and said something to the effect that he should have known better—I didn't explode or anything, but he knew I was angry—and a few minutes later Christina came over to me and asked "What did you say to Marc? He's crying!" I couldn't believe it. I felt like Tom Hanks in **A LEAGUE OF THEIR OWN** *[1992]*—"There's no crying in baseball!"

SRB: What kind of cameras were you and Marc working with on *BACTERIUM,* **given the variety of demands—helicopter POV shots, exteriors and interiors, miniatures, etc.?**

BP: All the same camera. It was a Panasonic, maybe a DVC-Pro or something like that, mini HD. A step-up from what **SCREAMING DEAD** and **BITE ME!** were shot on. I'm not really a gadget guy, so I'm hopeless with details like that. For years I thought my 35mm SLR was a Canon until I looked down and realized it was a Konica. Well, they *sound* almost the same.

SRB: The E.I. release of BACTERIUM seemed sadly perfunctory; the box art was pretty lackluster, lacking the eye-catching graphics of the earlier films, no interior booklet in the packaging. What was that process looking like on your end, Brett?

BP: The end was near. By the way, not only was **BACTERIUM** my cheapest E.I. movie, it was the only E.I. movie to *ever* come in under-budget! We'd had producer issues all through **SHOCK-O-RAMA**, so by the time we shot the wraparound sequence, Christina and I were pretty much on our own, and cut the daily expenses by 90%. As a result, we produced **BACTERIUM** ourselves and brought it in for 20% under the already low budget. So much for 'artistes' not being able to handle money.

SRB: BACTERIUM was your final E.I. production as a writer/director. Care to talk about how it all came to a close with the studio? Did you all part company on good terms?

BP: I was supposed to make two more movies for them after **BACTERIUM**. I pitched them all

sorts of ideas, but never got a definite go-ahead. After a while the two-picture deal became a *one-*picture deal. I started working on an old project of mine called *Cold Blood,* building creatures and such, and it started to look like that was going to be the next movie, when Mike called me into his office for a meeting. I thought, "Great, we're finally getting somewhere," and I sat down at the table across from him, and he pointed to a date on the calendar and said, "That's the last day you'll be here. We can't keep you after that." It was two weeks away. Whatever deal we'd had had been unilaterally dissolved. Now, I'd been a salaried employee of E.I. for six months, and the date they picked for my last day 'just happened' to be the date my benefits would have started. I thought that was kind of shabby, but maybe it was coincidence. You tell me.

SRB: That's—beyond "kind of shabby." Sorry, Brett, you deserved better.

In our book, Brett Piper always has deserved better…

Coming in *Monster!* #34: The Brett Piper monster madness continues with Piper's run of creature feature fearfests created in-part solo / in-part amid fruitful collaboration with Mark and John Polonia! Join us for Part 6, the final instalment of "Anarchy & Monsters," and meet **MUCKMAN**, **THE DARK SLEEP**, **QUEEN CRAB!**, **TRICLOPS** and more!

(©2019 Stephen R. Bissette, all rights reserved. Profound thanks to Brett Piper once again, for everything.)

Art by Denis St. John

THE HORROR OF THE UNSEEN: BBC GHOST STORIES

by David Flint

British TV in general—the BBC in particular—has changed a lot since the 1970s. These days, it seems oddly fixated on ratings and demographics; oddly, because the BBC is a public service broadcaster, paid for by an obligatory license fee that anyone with a TV connection has to pay, under threat of large fines or even imprisonment (and each year, a few people DO go to prison for non-payment. It's possibly this fact that makes the BBC feel it has to compete with independent broadcasters for who can dumb-down the most, or possibly because, increasingly, executives for all British TV channels all come from the same source—the head of ITV will move on to run a BBC channel, a Channel 4 programmer will become a BBC boss—and bring with them their obsession with appealing to the all-important youth demographic and the desire to be seen as doing something cool by their drinking club buddies. While 1970s British TV had its fair share of dumb game shows and audience-pleasing content, it was in many other ways a very different world.

There wasn't a lot of TV in Britain in the 'Seventies. We had just three channels, two of which belonged to the BBC and the third of which was a network of regional independent broadcasters, who didn't always broadcast the same shows. The BBC shut down for much of the day—apart from educational shows for schools, only ITV showed anything before about 3 p.m.,

and by midnight on most weekdays, everything had closed down (although at weekends, a late film might stretch things to as late as 2 a.m.)—24-hour TV was seen as a bit vulgar and American.

Throughout this period, the BBC—and even ITV, to a lesser extent—took its public service remit seriously. There were current affairs, news,

Michael Hordern plays Parkins, the almost-pathologically-eccentric, mumbling-and-muttering professor who unearths an old wooden whistle, unaware of the terror that will soon haunt him

Plagued with nightmares about being pursued by an unseen specter and waking to find the unused bed next to his in disarray, his fears increase until one night he awakens to be encountered by the ghost

& Co., 1931)—is one of the author's more powerful ghost stories: the tale of a strait-laced and rather pompous college professor who takes a holiday by the sea and encounters supernatural forces, it remains a potent scare story today. Miller's 1968 version of the story, shot in grainy, moody black and white, gets off to a bad start with a Miller voiceover needlessly setting the scene with talk about James, his work and the meaning of the story we are about to see—rather too much hand-wringing justification, I would suggest. That aside, this is a magnificently unsettling work. Michael Hordern plays the lead, far from the prim young professor of the original story—his character is almost pathologically eccentric, mumbling and muttering to himself and others, smugly self-satisfied and amused at his own ideas and yet hiding secret fears that come to the fore when he unearths an old wooden whistle near a gravestone ("finders keepers", he proclaims) that has a Latin inscription which translates as "who is this who comes?" He dutifully whistles, but then spends nights lying in bed worrying about who—or what—*will* come. Plagued with nightmares about being pursued by an unseen specter and waking to find the unused bed next to his in disarray, his fears increase until one night he awakens to be encountered by the ghost. Whether this is a literal supernatural figure or the manifestation of his own fears—well, that's for the viewer to decide.

In many ways, this production sets the template for later James adaptations; it's quiet, methodical and has a continual sense of unease which builds to a moment of terror that we experience as much through the reactions of the protagonist as through any onscreen horror. Hordern's professor, arrogantly dismissive of the supernatural but secretly terrified by it, is eventually reduced to a broken shell of a man—unharmed physically by the apparition in the room, his sense of reality and self-belief (or disbelief) have been so shattered that you know there is no going back. It's an extraordinary performance.

Miller gives a master class in creating terror from very little—that his ghostly manifestations are essentially moving bed sheets and yet still utterly terrifying is a remarkable achievement, but much of the horror comes from the close shots of Hordern's face, lying in bed in twitchy, terrified denial, and from the soundtrack, which is one of the most disturbing you'll ever hear. The combination of all these things makes this one of the most genuinely scary ghost stories you'll ever see on film.

science and arts shows throughout the week, as well as Serious Drama, both as series and one-off plays (we didn't do "TV movies"!). Yet interestingly, horror, science fiction and fantasy were not frowned on or dismissed in the way they would be in later decades, when, prior to the revival of *Doctor Who*, no producer wanted to touch such low-rent or juvenile fare.

One of the more unusual traditions that sprang up on the BBC in the 1970s was the idea of the Christmas Ghost Story. But then again, it makes a certain sense—ghost stories (not "horror films") had a certain respectability, and a Christmas connection thanks to the likes of Dickens. And so it made a sort of sense to have a creepy tale—one based on the work of a serious writer, mind, and a period piece to boot—as part of the festive schedule. Oddly though, it's proven one of the few BBC traditions that has stubbornly refused to die. Even at the lowest point for genre TV production in Britain, the Christmas ghost story never quite went away. And thanks to the efforts of the BFI, as part of their 2013 Gothic strand, a lot of this material is now available on DVD.

It all began quietly enough, with Jonathan Miller adapting M.R. James' 1904 tale "Oh, Whistle, and I'll Come to You, My Lad" (the broadcast title dropping the "My Lad") as part of the *Omnibus* arts strand. Miller was an intellectual heavyweight, James was respectable and *Omnibus* was a serious arts program, so this radical interpretation of the story was never going to be dismissed as mere spook stuff.

James' tale—taken from *The Collected Ghost Stories of M.R. James* (London: Edward Arnold

"He could not, though he knew how perilous a sound was—he could not keep back a cry of disgust..." I– M.R. James in "Oh, Whistle, and I'll Come to You, My Lad" (1904); Michael Hordern reacts at the frightful highpoint of the BBC's 1968 TV version

The success of this one-off inspired the BBC to do more James at Christmas, starting in 1971. This wasn't a series as such, but with Lawrence Gordon Clark writing the early episodes and producing and directing most of them, and all but two based on James' work, they have a definite connection running through them. An onscreen title of *A Ghost Story for Christmas* on some episodes gave the "series" its name, though each was actually produced as a stand-alone drama.

Based on the story "The Stalls of Barchester Cathedral" from the M.R. James collection *More Ghost Stories* (London: Edward Arnold & Co., 1911), "The Stalls of Barchester" is the first story adapted in this strand, and treats the original James story quite faithfully. It opens in 1932, with a Dr. Black (Clive Swift) cataloguing the collections of Barchester Cathedral and finding a box of secret papers and diaries belonging to former Archdeacon Haynes (Robert Hardy). The film then flashes back to 1872, where Haynes is waiting none-too-patiently for the aging Archdeacon Pulteney (Harold Bennett) to either retire or expire, neither of which he shows any sign of doing. Eventually, aged 92, Pulteney slips on a loose stair carpet and goes to meet his maker, allowing Haynes to take over his role. It soon becomes clear that the death might not have been entirely accidental, and Haynes finds himself subject to assorted supernatural events—voices in

the night, a wooden carving that seems alive and mysterious figures seemingly lurking in his home.

This is an impressive opening salvo in the series. Hardy is perfectly cast as the arrogant and ambitious Archdeacon who slowly falls apart as both his guilt and the supernatural events he finds himself subjected to take over his life, his nervous twitchiness and deflating pomposity all too convincing. Unlike Jonathan Miller's production, there's no hedging on the ghostly aspects here—while Haynes may be breaking down, he's definitely doing so under a genuine ghostly vendetta.

The film lets itself down in a couple of places—a signpost seen towards the end is all too clearly of 1970s vintage—and for a film that is making such an effort to keep its horrors unseen, there are a couple of overly crude moments—an unconvincingly ghostly hand rather too blatantly and slowly reaching out to grab Haynes is more likely to induce sniggers than shudders, although we should perhaps remember that these films were made to be seen on smaller, blurrier 625-line TV screens than anything anyone will be watching them on nowadays. And these are minor blunders in what is for the most part a very satisfying and effectively creepy ghost story.

Good as this first effort is, "A Warning to the Curious", broadcast a year later, is a considerable

A Warning To The Curious: Digging up forbidden treasure can cost you your life!

step-up—Clark seems more confident in his abilities ("The Stalls of Barchester" was the first drama from the usual documentary-maker) and his source material is more genuinely scary. With this adaptation, Clark is a lot looser—by necessity—with the source material (M.R. James' 1925 story of the same name), taking the main theme and crafting one of the most unsettling pieces of television ever broadcast around it.

Here, Peter Vaughn plays Mr. Paxton, a company clerk who has lost his job in the Great Depression and travels to the seaside resort of Seaburgh, hoping to make a splash in the archaeology world by discovering an ancient and magical Saxon crown, buried nearby to help keep the area safe from invasion. We already know this is a foolish pursuit after seeing another archaeologist hacked to death by the last surviving "guardian" of the crown in the opening scenes, and although the killer is now dead, Paxton's secretive excavations are watched by a mysterious figure—and once the crown is uncovered, Paxton finds himself relentlessly chased.

Quiet, steadily paced and moody, "A Warning to the Curious" lets its horrors build before unleashing them—but when it does, it does so very effectively. The scenes of Vaughn running, being chased by a black-clad figure, have an almost surreal atmosphere to them; they seem at odds with the steady realism of the rest of the film, and it's this weirdness which makes them so effective. Again, the film perhaps suffers a little from advances in TV technology, the ghostly figure sometimes seeming a little too up-front when seen on a big HD screen. This is a curse that sadly afflicts a number of old TV horror shows—watching the notorious 1993 show *Ghostwatch* (a precursor to mockumentary horrors that traumatized more gullible viewers into thinking it was real, thanks to a cast made up

of light entertainment presenters) on a big screen a couple of years ago, it was embarrassing to see a "shadowy" figure in the background looking all too clear.

In "AWttC", Clive Swift again turns up as Dr. Black—here, he is an observer who gets caught up in the events after Paxton prevails on him to help him to replace the crown and lift the curse around him. Ghost story enthusiasts will know that it's never that easy, of course. Swift's appearance suggests a character that will run through the film series, though the final scenes hint at a far worse fate for him, and sure enough, this was his final appearance.

Both these films—and this is true of the others in the non-serial series too—have an entirely unique feel. Shot on 16mm film, they don't look like TV shows (either of the time or of now) or movies; instead, their grainy appearance seems to add to the unique atmosphere of the films.

After these first two productions, the remaining shows in the "series" were produced under the auspices of the BBC's drama division and written by an assortment of writers. This change seems to have had a clear impact on the series, as these three stories lack the weirdness and sense of atmosphere that marked-out the earlier episodes. That's not to say that these are bad, by any means. The three stories here are still superior chillers, at least in comparison to more modern efforts, but they are also decidedly more "normal".

Adapted from a story in his collection *Ghost Stories of an Antiquary* (London: Edward Arnold & Co., 1904), "Lost Hearts", made in 1973, was one of James' more overt horror tales, and that is reflected here. This is certainly one of the least subtle of the stories in the series, going for full-blooded horror more than ghostly chills as it tells the story of Stephen (Simon Gipps-Kent), a young orphan sent to live with his eccentric relative Mr. Abney (Joseph O'Conor). As soon as he arrives, Stephen is haunted by the vampiric spirits of two children, both orphans like himself who had briefly lived at the house before mysteriously disappearing. As the story goes on, the truth behind their disappearance starts to emerge, leading to an act of vengeance that ultimately saves Stephen from the same fate.

With some surprisingly gruesome moments, "Lost Hearts" is an effective shocker, helped by O'Conor's excellent performance as the seemingly harmless but ultimately malicious guardian, whose evil is revealed slowly behind his omnipresent smile. The ghostly children, as grey as **DAWN OF THE DEAD** (1978) zombies, are genuinely creepy, and the story moves at a fast pace unusual for the series. What it perhaps lacks is the ambiguity and moodiness of the earlier stories, replacing them with less-subtle 'horror film' moments.

Also adapted from a same-named tale in *Ghost Stories of an Antiquary*, 1974's "The Treasure of Abbot Thomas", on the other hand, steps back from the horror, and for much of its running time is more of a period mystery, with the Reverend Justin Somerton (Michael Bryant) and his assistant Lord Peter Dattering (Paul Lavers) in search of the title treasure, belonging to a medieval cleric and alchemist. While claiming to only be interested in the treasure for historical reasons, Somerton is clearly arrogant (early on, we see him rather-too-smugly expose a fake medium) and greedy, both for wealth and glory. It's no surprise then that he eventually meets his downfall, having stubbornly ignored the increasingly supernatural clues. Encountering a strange (ambiguously- and creepily-shot) apparition when he finally finds the treasure, the Reverend is reduced to a shell of a man by the ensuing haunting—something that, in true Jamesian style, is not assuaged any by the return of the treasure.

More creepy than scary, "The Treasure of Abbot Thomas" is possibly the weakest of the original 'series', with no sympathetic characters and for being rather too-talky for its own good. Nevertheless, the final moments of horror (and the strange ghostly figure that guards the treasure) are impressive.

Monster Kids: With their eerie smiles and elongated fingernails, the pasty-faced ghostly children Giovanni (Christopher Davis) and Phoebe (Michelle Foster) profoundly affected—as in scared the bejeezus out of!—*M!* co-ed Steve F. when he (*sans* parental permission!) saw "Lost Hearts" first-run on the telly as a child in the UK during the '70s

David Flint   *Horror of the Unseen*   **207**

Above, Top to Bottom: Stripped to the waist, accused witch Mistress Mothersole (Barbara Ewing) is subjected to inquisitorial interrogation in "The Ash Tree"; a sinister silhouetted figure from the same episode; and a ghastly premonitory apparition from "The Signal-man"

as it turns out, actual) witch Anne Mothersole, whom he harbored secret desires for. Her curse eventually explodes from the tree in the shape of some remarkably effective creatures (the effects are crude, but that somehow adds to the creepiness of these little horrors).

"The Ash Tree" certainly doesn't hold back on the horror—alongside the monsters, there is a scene of the half-naked witch being interrogated that wouldn't seem out of place in **MARK OF THE DEVIL** (1970)—but it's the creeping sense of inevitable retribution that makes the story work, along with a strong sense of sexual repression. The vengeance begins with the return of the less-stuffy Sir Richard and his fiancée Lady Agatha (a small-but-notable role for **VAMPIRE CIRCUS** / *Doctor Who* star Lalla Ward), who is so effortlessly sexy it's no surprise that the free tree-spirit of Mistress Mothersole is revived!

Curiously, this would be the last M.R. James adaptation of the original run. While other stories of his were looked at, they were rejected as being too difficult to film, and so Clark turned to Charles Dickens—in many ways the 'father' of the Christmas ghost story—in 1976.

"The Signal-man", faithfully adapted by Andrew Davies from the Dickens story (first published in 1866), is probably the best of the whole series. Effectively a two-hander between Denholm Elliott and Bernard Lloyd, it drips with atmosphere and unease, as an unnamed traveler (Lloyd) comes across a signalman on a remote country railway line and listens to the man's stories of a ghostly figure that appears at the side of the tunnel entrance to warn of disaster. Naturally skeptical, the traveler is nevertheless drawn into the nervous signalman's tales as he reveals that the specter has recently been appearing again—meaning that death and tragedy is just around the corner...

Elliott dominates the story with a performance that is all nerves, paranoia and barely-contained terror, while Lloyd is solid too as the sympathetic ear who finally realizes the truth of what he's been told. With dialogue often lifted wholesale from the original story, the characters have an otherworldly formality about them, adding to the odd atmosphere. But it is the structure of the story that makes it so effective. There's a slow, creeping build-up of terror, from the silent opening titles (the words "A Ghost Story" appearing onscreen as a stark introduction) to the subtle, almost imperceptible music mirroring the vibrating sound of the bell that signals the arrival of the specter—a specter who is first seen as a

Still another one from *Ghost Stories of an Antiquary*, 1975's "The Ash Tree" is a considerable step-up. This tale offers a combination of subtle growing fears and outright horror—with an army of mutant fetus-like creatures emerging from the titular tree at the rather action-packed climax. The story follows Sir Richard Fell (Edward Petherbridge), a nobleman who returns to his family home, where an ancient ash tree towers over the house, and who is soon plagued with nightmares and memories of his ancestor Sir Matthew, who was responsible for the condemnation and killing of accused (and,

barely-visible character in black before we see a close-up of a genuinely horrifying face. Unlike the vengeful ghosts of James, the specter here is more of a warning—a warning of a fate that cannot be escaped.

The series took a major change of direction in 1977, with the first story that was both contemporary and an original work. Both "Stigma" and the following year's "The Ice House" have tended to be dismissed by critics as a result, which is a pity, because had either been part of any other horror anthology series—*Out of the Unknown* or *Dead of Night*, say—they'd probably have a much better reputation.

"Stigma", written by Clive Exton and the final *Ghost Story* to be directed by series veteran Lawrence Gordon Clark, is in fact very much within a supernatural tradition that was especially popular in the 1970s, where tales of pagan, druidic curses and strange events involving ancient stones were surprisingly big on TV in shows ranging from *Children of the Stones*, *The Stone Tape* (a Nigel Kneale story that was originally planned as part of this strand, and was broadcast on Christmas Day [see Stephen Jilks' "Channel of Darkness, Part 1" in *Monster!* #33 [p.90]), *Quatermass* and *Doctor Who*. In this story, a family who have recently moved into a country cottage and are renovating it come to regret trying to move a large stone from the middle of their garden. Katherine (Kate Binchy) suddenly finds herself bleeding extensively, even though she has no wounds, the blood-loss getting worse as efforts to move the heavy stone increase.

This is a slight story, but nevertheless an effective one. As the curse settles on Katherine, the tale takes on a surprisingly visceral level of flesh and blood—Binchy spends a fair amount of the story semi-naked and covered in blood as she tries to find—to no avail—where her injury is, and the story moves steadily towards an inevitably dark ending. There's a strong atmosphere of horror in this story, hitting us as it does with some of our deepest fears about the safety and frailty of our own bodies. There are no ghostly characters here, just the continual blood curse, which removes it firmly from the tradition of the series to date, but certainly doesn't make it an inferior work.

Things get *decidedly* stranger in 1977's "The Ice House", the final *GSfC* instalment until the 2005 revival. Written by John Bowen, this is again a modern-day story, though the events take place in a remote country health spa that could exist in almost any time. This is a very strange, rather unsettling story in which Paul (John Stride), a resident at the spa, is drawn into the bizarre world of sibling owners Jessica (Elizabeth Romilly) and Clovis (Geoffrey Burridge) who, despite having several other clients, lavish all their attention on him.

"The Ice House" lives in a world of hyper-reality. The acting is mannered, every line of dialogue carefully-constructed and slightly off-center, so that you find yourself continually aware that whatever is happening here, it's not 'normal'. There is a sense of eroticism (including a creepy moment of incestuous passion) that pervades the story, with strange, sexual flowers that give off a hypnotic, overwhelming scent, and the hints of seduction from both brother and sister, as well as moments of horror…but had this not been a part of this series, you might not even realize that it even *is* a ghost story. And you'll be left questioning who the 'ghosts' actually are.

In the end, this is a very daring piece of television. You can't imagine anything like this being made for British TV today. It's too strange to really work within the context of the series, but as a stand-alone piece is a remarkable and admirable work.

The Christmas Ghost Story 'series' came to a halt

Top: Ominous stones mar the otherwise idyllic rural landscape in "Stigma".
Above: A potentially homoerotic moment from "The Ice House"

Schalcken The Painter: At the instruction of Dutch Master Gerrit Dou ([1613-1675] played by Maurice Denham), two figure models strike poses as "The Temptation of St. Anthony" for a life-study drawing class that includes then-student Godfried Schalcken ([1643-1706] played by Jeremy Clyde)

with this story. But it wasn't to be the end of the line for festive fear…

In 1979, the *Omnibus* strand once again adapted a gothic tale, this time in the form of Le Fanu's "Schalcken the Painter" (first published in 1839), initially suggested as—and eventually shown in—the same slot that the *Ghost Story for Christmas* had occupied. A slow-moving, creepy, oddly erotic horror docudrama, again shot on film, this is a production I saw as a child on initial broadcast and which remained with me for decades afterwards, until I finally belatedly caught up with it again on its BFI release.

"Schalcken the Painter" occupies a curious if-not-exclusive genre of television that, even in 1979, was becoming a thing of the past. *Omnibus* was, after all, an arts documentary series, not a drama strand, and "Schalcken" is curiously both fiction and a documentary piece about the now-obscure artist. In this, it fits into the same strand as Ken Russell's increasingly-fictionalized 1960s and '70s 'biopics' of famous composers. Visually though, it is far removed from Russell. Instead, the clear influence is Walerian Borowczyk, or more specifically his classic film **BLANCHE** (1972, France). With his careful framing and visual style, Borowczyk's films have often felt like they were paintings made

reality, and that is very much the case here. Only fair, after all, in a film about a painter.

The plot, however, is based on a story by J. Sheridan Le Fanu, and presents a fictionalized account of the life of Godfried Schalcken (Jeremy Clyde), 17th Century Dutch painter, whom we first see as a pupil of artist Gerrit Dou (Maurice Denham). A voiceover from Charles Gray (**THE DEVIL RIDES OUT**, 1968, UK) fills-in the background and historical facts, while the drama plots its own course, based around Schalcken's barely-expressed love for his patron's niece, Rose (Cheryl Kennedy). This is a love doomed to be frustrated, however. A few centuries before Feminism, Rose is little more than the property of Dou, and when a mysterious stranger, the monstrous-looking Vanderhausen (John Justin) decides he wants her for his wife, he makes a financial offer that her uncle cannot (or at least will not) refuse. Schalcken too capitulates in the deal, effectively selling his soul in the process. Soon, the idealistic young art student is churning-out paintings on demand for cash, his ambition and ego outstripping his artistic and personal integrity.

But while this might make for a grand tragedy in itself, there is more to this story than simply lost love and self-destruction. For Vanderhausen is quite clearly less than human: he is, depending on how you interpret it, the Devil—or Death himself. When Rose flees from him, seemingly beaten and brutalized, she takes shelter with Schalcken and her uncle, but Vanderhausen will not be put off so easily, leading to a nightmarish, erotic and trippy finale where Schalcken fails to save her once again, and is instead plunged into a sort of madness.

There is much ambiguity and very little action in "Schalcken the Painter", which might make it seem like a difficult proposition. But this is a tale in which the atmosphere of the visuals is all. Writer/director Leslie Megahey sets out to create the televisual equivalent of a classical painting, and for the most part he succeeds brilliantly. This film has a look unlike any other TV production—it's incredibly dark, much of the screen disappearing into shadow (like Kubrick's **BARRY LYNDON** [1975, UK/USA], it was shot using candlelight and other limited light sources, to a large extent), and within that shadow lurk various mysteries, few of which are explained. This is a film that works by getting into your gut rather than your head. There's a continual unease and sense of 'not-quite-rightness' about it, while the pseudo-documentary presentation gives a curious reality to its more fantastical moments and the sense of helplessness and betrayal.

The film also plays with sexuality in a way that you would never see on British TV today. There's nothing gratuitous about the nudity—much of it is strictly functional, presented by the models that Schalcken paints. But the final vision of Rose, a sly smile on her face as she strips-off to mount the corpse-like Vanderhausen, is both erotic and disturbing; all the more-so for being left unexplained.

The next BBC foray into the world of the Christmas ghost story saw the return of M.R. James in the unexpected form of a children's TV series. The 1980 show *Spinechillers* was sold as a spooky version of the long-running children's storytelling show *Jackanory* (1965-96), aimed at slightly older kids and broadcast at 6 p.m. It consisted of 19 episodes, and these 11-minute stories featured the likes of Freddie Jones and Jonathan Pryce telling condensed and sometimes censored versions of classic ghost stories, without illustrations—gone are some of the more grisly descriptions as well as discussions of smoking, drinking and licentiousness. The recent BFI release *Classic Ghost Stories* features the three James stories as extras: "The Mezzotint" (1904), "A School Story" and "The Diary of Mr. Poynter" (1919) remain effectively creepy stories, even when edited.

The same format was revived in a 1986 series featuring Robert Powell reading James' stories. There's no series title, each episode is simply named according to the story being read (the BFI release is *Classic Ghost Stories*). The format sees Powell as the narrator in a cozy study, giving a dramatic reading of the short story in question, each enhanced by atmospheric music and brief dramatizations. These are probably most effective in "The Mezzotint", where the picture of the title is shown as it mysteriously alters over a couple of days to show the story of ghostly child abduction.

The other stories included are "The Ash Tree", "Oh, Whistle, and I'll Come to You, My Lad" (both already adapted for the *Ghost Stories for Christmas* series), "The Wailing Well" (adapted from a tale in *The Collected Ghost Stories of M.R. James* [1931]) and "The Rose Garden" (first published in *More Ghost Stories of an Antiquary* [1911]). The first two are potent, creepy ghost stories that even today still have the power to unsettle, while the latter two are somewhat less-effective. But regardless of the strength of the story, Powell does a fine job of bringing a sense of drama and horror to his readings.

The dramatic inserts are, thankfully, limited and don't upset the balance of the story. There's no dialogue to interrupt the flow of the story, for instance, and no important points are left to the visuals. In fact, depending on how you choose to consume these stories, you can easily ignore them

After being as-good-as shanghaied into indentured servitude as a life model by the painter Schalcken, a poor country girl (Val Penny) poses for him in various stages of undress, including as the classical Roman poetess Lesbia

Above & Below: John Hurt in the 2010 remake of "Whistle"

entirely—these readings work just as well sight-unseen simply as audio books, should you choose to disregard the visuals.

This would be the last BBC festive ghost story for some time, but in 2000, the idea was revived in the four-part series *Ghost Stories for Christmas with Christopher Lee*, which feature the iconic star as M.R. James (Lee denied that's who he's playing, but it's clearly supposed to be the author), reading his stories to pupils at Cambridge. The initial set-up aside, these are essentially spoken-word performances, with Lee reading the tale in his own inimitable manner. They are, therefore, similar to the earlier Powell series—and an oddly stilted concept to have made it onto TV in 2000—with "The Stalls of Barchester", "The Ash Tree", "A Warning to the Curious" and "Number 13" making

up the content. All but one are included as extras on the BFI's *Ghost Stories for Christmas* DVD collection.

It was a minor return to the classic Victorian ghost story for the BBC, but it turned out to be the start of a revival that, although frequently stalling, has continued to this day.

In 2005, the M.R. James Christmas ghost story drama finally returned, with two productions that are nice tries, but feel somewhat alien to the series as a whole. Shot on HD video rather than the 16mm film that made the 1970s productions seem so strangely alien to anything else out there, these two tales look rather like any contemporary TV drama, and that strange, grainy stillness of the original series doesn't translate to the sharpness of high-definition video. Yet on the other hand, these two films are as removed from the world they emerge from as any of the earlier programs. After all, single dramas—especially period pieces, and even more especially supernatural stories—are generally a thing of the past on British television these days.

First published in *The Living Age* in 1925, James' story "A View from a Hill" was considered for production back in the 1970s, but rejected as being unsuitable for TV (that decision brought us "The Signal-man", so we can agree it was a wise one). Watching this '05 version, it's hard to argue with that original thought, because, despite impressive efforts all round, the story is altogether too thin for TV drama. James could be a sparse writer at the best of times, and this is a particularly open story that doesn't translate entirely successfully.

"Well," Parkins said, [...] "I freely own that I do not like careless talk about what you call ghosts. A man in my position, [...] cannot, I find, be too careful about appearing to sanction the current beliefs on such subjects. [...] I hold that any semblance, any appearance of concession to the view that such things might exist is equivalent to a renunciation of all that I hold most sacred." l– M.R. James in "Oh, Whistle, and I'll Come to You, My Lad" (1904)

Horror of the Unseen   *David Flint*

Mark Letheren plays archaeologist Dr. Fanshawe, visiting the estate of cash-strapped Squire Richards (Pip Torrens) to evaluate the contents. After borrowing an old pair of binoculars made by occult dabbler Baxter (Simon Linnell), he finds that they give him a view into the past…and seemingly unleash dark forces.

"A View from a Hill" is a handsomely-mounted piece, but it lacks the creeping unease of the earlier stories, instead being an awkward mix of talkative exposition and sudden—perhaps too-blatant—shock scenes. It's by no means a bad work, but it does somehow feel inconsequential.

Based on still another selection from 1904's *Ghost Stories of an Antiquary* collection, "Number 13", made in 2006, is perhaps a more effective ghost story, even if it rather dispenses with much of the James original. Here, we have Greg Wise as stuffy, arrogant academic Anderson, investigating old church records and uncovering dark stories about a former bishop, even as his hotel room becomes the scene of strange events—mysterious noises coming from the room next door—a Room 13 that only appears at night.

Greg Wise as Prof. Anderson in "Number 13" (2006)

Among several tweaks and changes, the story ditches James' satanic, dancing shadow figure for a more moody (if somehow less scary) figure seen in shadows, swaps a skeletal arm for a black-gloved hand, and switches its location from Denmark to the more-affordable England. Some of these are improvements, to be honest: a final revelation about a missing guest is effective, as is the switch of Anderson from a rather affable fellow in the original story to the sort of pompous fool more often found in the writer's work. Certainly, this version of the story is much more suited to film than the James original, and the story builds a good head of steam as it goes along.

2010 saw a new version of "Oh, Whistle, and I'll Come to You, My Lad"—its title abbreviated to simply "Whistle and I'll Come to You"—which of course immediately suffers in comparison with Miller's version (the fact that both appear on the same BFI disc hardly helps matters). This new version (directed by Andy De Emmony; written by Neil Cross) takes its abbreviated title from Miller and the basic setting from James, but little else from either, instead taking the theme of James' story and working a new tale, with decidedly modern concerns, around it. In this version, the earlier dramatization's unnamed professor—known as Parkins in MRJ's original tale—becomes academic James Parkin *[sic!]* (John Hurt), who places his senile wife Alice (Gemma Jones) into

a nursing home and then heads off for a break at their favorite old haunt, a seaside hotel that has seen better days. A wedding ring—which again contains the haunting inscription—is found on the beach. But there, really, the connection to the earlier version ends.

By making its lead character a married man in mourning for his lost wife, this new version dramatically alters the nature of the character's isolation, and the extensive backstory that comes to play a major part in the proceedings—you won't be surprised to discover who the ghostly figure in this version is, given that the clues are sledgehammered home so heavily!—feels like a distraction. Everything about this version feels like a depressing statement on modern television; the idea being that the original story and TV adaptation are somehow too-subtle for modern audiences to grasp, and so need to be crudely spelled-out. The haunting of Hurt is louder and more blatant than Hordern's "corner-of-the-eye" ghosts, and far-less-effective, and his character—modest rather than smug, emotional instead of detached—might be more in keeping with our touchy-feely age, but is oddly less involving. This isn't to knock Hurt's performance, which is by far the best thing about this version, but his character's descent into mindless terror is less convincing than Hordern's simply because he is already gripped with so much guilt and self-doubt when we first meet him.

Having the new version take place in a contemporary setting also feels off, somehow. Perhaps we are too used to seeing James' work unfold in a Victorian world of repressed emotions, but the modern take simply doesn't seem convincing. And then there is the switch from the whistle to a wedding ring; necessary for this new story perhaps, but it immediately renders the title meaningless. Hordern summons the demons of his psyche by blowing the whistle found near a gravestone—Hurt simply finds a ring in the sand. Which makes no sense.

The current BBC *Ghost Story for Christmas* duties have been placed in the hands of Mark Gatiss, currently the corporation's 'go-to' guy for anything a bit "spooky" or "sci-fi". So far, the results haven't been spectacular: In 2008, he wrote a three-part series shown over Christmas called *Crooked House*, one episode of which—"The Wainscoting"—had a Jamesian feel, but not the sense of unease that made the original 'Seventies shows so impressive. This was followed in 2013 by an authentic James adaptation, "The Tractate Middoth" (a tale from James' *More Ghost Stories* [1911]). Marking Gatiss' directorial debut, this proved to be a rather weak affair, lacking the atmosphere, the creepiness and the visual style not only of the original 'Seventies shows, but also of the 2000s versions too. It was the worst of all things: a *bland* adaptation. None of the Gatiss productions have yet been released on DVD.

At least we can be sure that as long as Gatiss remains interested, the future of BBC's Christmas Ghost Stories remains assured. The quality might vary, but I'll take even the weakest of them over another tedious cop drama (modern British cop dramas are just the *worst!*). And the fact that the BBC are once again willing to produce horror television—even if they do still seem to be embarrassed by the fact, as their continuing description of *Being Human* as a "comedy drama" shows—is something to celebrate. Hopefully, they'll eventually remember how to do it *well…*

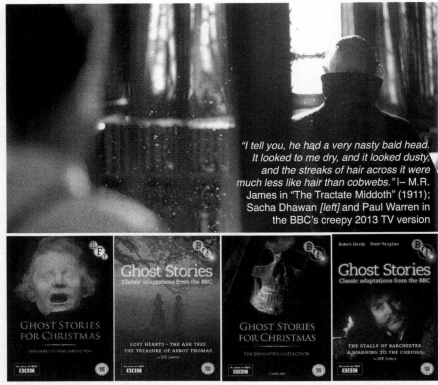

"*I tell you, he had a very nasty bald head. It looked to me dry, and it looked dusty, and the streaks of hair across it were much less like hair than cobwebs.*"I– M.R. James in "The Tractate Middoth" (1911); Sacha Dhawan *[left]* and Paul Warren in the BBC's creepy 2013 TV version

Top: A suspensefully tensile moment from Gatiss' "The Tractate Middoth". **Above, Left to Right:** Various covers from the BFI's must-have *Ghost Stories* DVD collection

Horror of the Unseen *David Flint*

THE HOUSE THAT JOSH BUILT

by Troy Howarth

Joshua Kennedy directs Martine Beswicke in a tribute shot to **DR. JEKYLL & SISTER HYDE**

Youthful indie filmmaker Joshua Kennedy is living 'The Dream'. Not only is he continuing to make films which pay homage to the movies that sustained him as a young(er) man, but he's now managed to make a film which unites four—yes, FOUR!—of the actors who actually appeared in some of those films. His latest homage to Hammer, **HOUSE OF THE GORGON***, assembles a dream cast headed by Veronica Carlson (**FRANKENSTEIN MUST BE DESTROYED** [1969, D: Terence Fisher]), Caroline Munro (**CAPTAIN KRONOS – VAMPIRE HUNTER** [1974, D: Brian Clemens]), Martine Beswicke[1] (**DR. JEKYLL & SISTER HYDE** [1971, D: Roy Ward Baker]) and Christopher Neame (**DRACULA A.D. 1972** [1972, D: Alan Gibson]). As is customary for young Master Kennedy, he not only wrote the script and directed, but he also plays one of the key roles as well. Having already interviewed Joshua for issue #22 of* Monster! *all the way back in the fall of 2015, it was inevitable that I would follow-up with him again, and the news that* **HOUSE OF THE GORGON** *is now officially "a wrap" provided as good an incentive as any for me to conduct...* "The New *Best Damned Joshua Kennedy Interview To Date"!*

---

1 In the 1980s, Martine Beswicke had the spelling of her surname legally changed to include the "e" at the end. Prior to that, she had used the shorter spelling "Beswick".

JK: I believe I have to thank Caroline Munro herself for a comment she made at the 2017 Chiller Horror Convention in New Jersey. Martine Beswicke, Veronica Carlson, and Christopher Neame were all together in a signing room, and she said something to the effect of: "We have quite the cast here, don't we?" And thus, the seed was planted in my brain.

The eagle-eyed Gothic Hammer Horror fan will find countless references throughout, but, being the ultimate film nerd that I am, the film is also awash in incredibly random tributes, angles, movements, and bits of dialogue from, among others, **20,000 LEAGUES UNDER THE SEA**, **THE PRODUCERS**, **THE ALAMO**, **CASINO ROYALE**, **THE TEN COMMANDMENTS**, **SLEEPING BEAUTY**… and those are just off the top of my head!

TH: How long does it take you to write a script, on average?

JK: Good question. It really depends: one-to-four months?

TH: You've been making films since you were a child, but this is the first time you've been in the position to hire 'professional' actors. What made you decide to go that route?

JK: In Christopher Lee's 'Dracula' voice: "IT WAS MY WILL!" The film was born from Caroline Munro's comment, so having these actors involved was always baked into the cake. Luckily, I've spent my life working with student actors looking to go professional, so it wasn't that much of a leap.

TH: Obviously being in the position of directing four actors who were a part of the films you know and love so much must have been a surreal experience. Can you tell us what sort of emotions you were feeling as the movie inched nearer and nearer to reality?

JK: Surreal is the definitive word. I do remember having a "What-is-happening?" moment when I was at the post office mailing them all the script. The first few phone calls/Skype sessions were stress-inducing, but after we all began to work with one another, discussing plot details and character motivations, nerves began to subside. I can never watch their movies the same way again because they are now people that I've worked with. It's crazy!

TH: You sought financing for the film through Indiegogo; do you think the campaign was a success, and is it something you are likely to continue using in future?

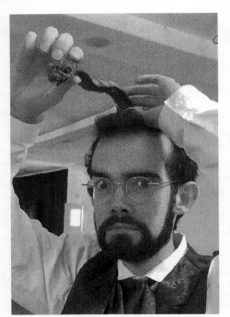

Joshua Kennedy with one of the snakes crafted by Mitch Gonzales

TROY HOWARTH: The last time we spoke, your newest creation was DRACULA A.D. 2015; tell us a bit about the projects you've been involved with since that time.

JOSHUA KENNEDY: Has it *really* been that long? *Wow!* I appreciate your interest in checking-up on me after all this time; it is always a pleasure and honor to talk with you. Well, since 2015 I have made six films: **THE NIGHT OF MEDUSA**, about a young girl in the present-day being possessed by the spirit of the gorgon; **THE RETURN OF SHERLOCK HOLMES**, my first period piece; **THE ALPHA OMEGA MAN**, my tribute to the Charlton Heston post-apocalyptic film **THE OMEGA MAN**; *The St. Augustine Monster*, a silent short dedicated to German Expressionism; **THE FUNGUS AMONG US**, a black-and-white 'Russ Meyer-meets-Roger Corman-meets-Ed Wood' heist/horror film; and **THESEUS AND THE MINOTAUR**, a tribute to the Ray Harryhausen sword-and-sandal films of yesteryear. I also graduated from Pace University and directed a stage production of *Frankenstein* with my good friend Marco Muñoz.

TH: I know Terence Fisher's THE GORGON (1964) is your all-time favorite film, so it may go without saying, but: what inspired you to write HOUSE OF THE GORGON in particular? Apart from the obvious, what were some of the other points of reference you put into the movie?

Joshua Kennedy Interview *Troy Howarth*

JK: Hey, I consider raising *$10* a success! And we ended-up raising about $14,000! It really helped cover certain aspects of the production, and I would love to be able to return to that site for future films.

TH: I'd like to talk a bit about your cast. I think I'm right in saying that your 'in' to the universe of Hammer stars was your friendship with Martine Beswicke? How did you first meet her?

JK: I first met 'Mrs. Kennedy' *[Joshua's "pet name" for Martine Beswicke, the lucky dog! – TH]* at a convention in the fall of 2013. Jeez, time flies! I was simply a fan who had idolized her since time immemorial.

Anyway, I had the insane idea of having her star in a quick music video with me: all she had to do was sit in a chair and react to me singing and dancing around her. I went for broke and asked her, she agreed, and we shot the entire thing in 15 minutes on her lunch break. The resulting video, "The Night is Young", can be found on YouTube, and the rest is history! Every time she was back at a convention in the states we made a video together, and we have since grown very close. And for the record, SHE was the one who started calling me her "Husband"... and who am I to argue with that?!

TH: So, to go from meeting and chatting with an actress like that—somebody you've admired

The poster created by Graham Humphreys

on screen for so long—to directing her... what was that like? I'm guessing you also shared scenes with all of them, as well. Did that make you nervous?

Joshua Kennedy directs Caroline Munro and Martine Beswicke

Georgina Dugdale and Veronica Carlson

JK: Not as nerve-wracking as one would think! Honestly, the entire cast of **HOUSE** was so kind, respectful, generous, and humble, I never felt nervous at all when sharing scenes with them. We all sort of became a big, happy family by the end of the week: eating together, talking together, going to bed at the same time. I've rarely seen such camaraderie among a cast before. It was marvelous.

TH: Now, I know Veronica and Martine and Caroline have all done the Monster Bash—I met them all there—but how did you come into contact with Christopher Neame? He doesn't seem to do the convention scene very much...

JK: Chris is actually quite new to the scene, and I believe Chiller was his first convention. I had a chance to spend a few hours working with him at his table, and we chatted about all sorts of things. He is such a quiet, hardworking and respectful gentleman: very much how I imagine Cushing or Lee were. It was a thrill to have him involved in the film. He comes from the Shakespearean theatre, and you could just *feel* that classical training in everything he did.

TH: One of Caroline's daughters is also in the film. How was it seeing two generations of the family at work on the same set?

JK: *Yes!* Georgina Dugdale was our leading lady, Isobel Banning, and she was an absolute delight.

We had many Skype sessions before her trek to the Lone Star State, discussing all aspects of the film. By the time she got here it was as if we had known each other for years! Caroline's other daughter Iona was actually on-set as well behind-the-scenes. To see them all working together towards one goal was such a delight. They all are such hardworking women, and I am honored to call them my friends.

TH: Did you actually write these characters with these specific actors in mind?

JK: Most certainly, and all of them have little tributes to their past roles for Hammer. For example, Veronica Carlson's character is named Anna, after her role in **FRANKENSTEIN MUST BE DESTROYED**, and Christopher Neame's character of Father Jonathan Llewellyn is a nod to the fellow who wrote the original story for **THE GORGON** and "Johnny" Alucard in **DRACULA A.D. 1972**. Caroline and Martine's are a little more subtle, but I would recommend paying attention to their dialogue—one might catch a familiar line or two.

TH: Tell us about some of your favorite moments connected with making the film.

JK: How *long* do you have?! The whole week was bursting with wonderful moments. However, for the sake of brevity, I will share two that immediately come to mind:

There is a scene in the script where Veronica Carlson's character is confronted by Martine Beswicke and Caroline Munro. As we were blocking the scene and rehearsing, Martine looked over at me and said, "This is the first time we three have ever been in the same scene together!" Then Caroline chimes in with, "This is the first *movie* we've all been in together!"

That really put a lot in perspective. I mean, no pressure right?!

The other moment I will never forget began as an idea to introduce Martine's character while she played a piano. The night before we shot the scene I was planning the setup, and realized it would be much more villainous if she played an organ instead of a piano.

While preparing the organ music we would play on-set for Martine, I instantly thought of "War March of the Priests", which Vincent Price plays in the opening of **THE ABOMINABLE DR. PHIBES**. I had a full circle moment right there: If we are playing the organ music from **DR. PHIBES**, we might as well have *MRS. PHIBES* playing it!

Caroline was game for the tribute—she truly is a fearless actress, and game for anything—and, as we were practicing the shot, she told me she was there on set the day Vincent shot his organ scene (!).

Then another full circle moment hit me: We should place the portrait of Vincent Price above the organ for Caroline to play to. Trying to be "Captain Continuity", I hesitated, as the portrait was already seen in the main castle dining room. I said it would stick out like a sore thumb if it moved into a different location. I turned to see Georgina Dugdale and her co-star Jamie Treviño staring at me with crossed arms. *Really?* I was going to let something as frivolous as "continuity" ruin this once-in-a-lifetime opportunity?! I ran to grab the painting, placed it on the organ, and readied the camera for the scene.

I called action, and as my sound man Julian played "War March of the Priests" on a loudspeaker, I saw Caroline look up at Vincent's portrait and whisper in that adorable, innocent voice of hers, "I think you would be so happy to see what's been going on here these past few days. I hope you like my playing". Tears burst from my eyes, and I became so overcome with emotion that I had to step away from the set for a few minutes. It was a really magical moment.

TH: And of course, not everything could have been sunshine and roses; tell us about some of the more trying moments.

JK: Actually, I hate to admit it for the sake of a good article; the production really WAS sunshine and roses! Easily the smoothest shoot I've ever been a part of. Everyone really went above-and-beyond the call of duty: Tami Hamalian, Jacob Ramirez on makeup, Martin Torres on camera, Julian Flores on sound, the enchanting Natalie Wise and her mother Christina, my parents, my sister, my friends Dan Day, Mark Holmes, Lauro Hinojosa, Michael Moralez… spirits were incredibly high, and everyone was a joy to work with.

TH: You filmed HOUSE OF THE GORGON in just six (6!) days; that's incredible to me. What sort of preparation do you do ahead of time? Do you storyboard, or do you prefer to let the actors do their thing and figure out blocking from there?

JK: A bit of both, actually. I am a huge believer in preparation, but I think a director should be ready, willing and able to adapt themselves to the climate of the day: the microphone is being buggy, so you rework the scene to be without dialogue; an actor is sick, so you have to shoot a scene that's not on the schedule; a costume is torn, so you come up with a way to make it part of the scene, etc.

With no offense to my Pace University professors, I'm also a huge believer in the auteur theory being a lot of hogwash. A film is a Frankenstein monster assembled by all sorts of different people: actors, writers, directors, sound people, costumers, makeup people, etc.

Caroline and Martine—devilish sisters!

Christopher Neame as
Father Llewellyn

I am the first to welcome actors coming to set with their own ideas; nearly all of the time their suggestions will be something I'd never even thought of.

For example, for **HOUSE** I did something I'd never done before: I storyboarded the entire friggin' film.

Anyway, I storyboarded a scene starting with Chris and Veronica's characters bursting into the church mid-argument, screaming at each other at the top of their voices. After seeing the story-boards, Chris very politely asked for permission to suggest an idea: "What if we started with Veronica walking up to the priest silently, and having the scene begin with a whisper, that would ultimately lead to an explosion of emotions?" I thought it was a marvelous idea, and I had no problem at all throwing away my six pages of storyboards and improvising shots on the spot.

This suggestion made for a much more dynamic scene, and if I had stuck to my storyboards wholeheartedly, there would have been no freedom for these ideas to grow and percolate amongst me and my actors.

TH: Making films can be physically punishing. John Carpenter has described it as being incredibly hard on the body—getting up when it's dark, coming home when it's dark and not having much time for anything else when you're in the midst of making a film. How long were your days on average? How did you tend to feel at the end of a given day?

JK: I completely agree with Carpenter on this: it really *IS* physically demanding. On a similar note, one of my favorite Mel Brooks quotes is his advice to directors: "Sit down!"

The days would range from 8-5... I think we had one late evening where we went until around 7... But no one (except me and my crew) worked that ENTIRE time. Even so, I was constantly in fear of pushing my actors too hard, but I was enthralled to hear one of them say late in the week, "Eight in the morning is pretty late, Josh. Are you sure you don't want to start earlier?"

TH: Compared to your earlier films, this was an expensive picture—did you feel any more pressure related to that?

JK: Hmmm... no, not necessarily. I've made no-budget movies for so long it was honestly more of a relief to actually have a budget this time!

TH: Your films typically have an absurdist sense of humor—but I never get the impression that you are playing-down to the genre. The humor just seems to be part of who you are. In other words, your movies never feel like they are trying to be 'cheesy', as if to suggest that the movies you're referencing deserve to be seen as such. Is this one in the same vein, or did you decide to go for a different approach this time?

JK: I'm glad you feel that way, haha! It's true: I never try to make fun of the films I am paying tribute to, and this one is no different. I like to think of the script for **HOUSE OF THE GOR-**

GON as one of those 'unfilmed Hammers' like "ZEPPELIN VS. PTERODACTYLS" or "THE DAY THE EARTH CRACKED OPEN": a film that Hammer never got to make but that is finally seeing the light of day now. That's how I envision it, anyway.

TH: I can't help but notice from some of the stills I've seen that the lighting is very 'Mario Bava'. What made you decide to go for that approach? Who did your lighting?

JK: All of the credit for that has to go to my ingenious lighting designer, Rosa Cano. She did the lights for my stage production of *Frankenstein*, and she is the hardest-working girl I know. In preparation for this film, I recommended she watch a few of the early Hammers, as well as Bava's **BLACK SABBATH**. I thought she would look-up a few Google images, but the girl watched all of them in their entirety, and looked-up a few on her own! She is fabulous, and her sense of color is exquisite.

She and I both believe that color is really a lost art in modern moviemaking: everything is so color-corrected, grey and dull. I wanted this film to swing in the completely opposite direction, and she agreed with me.

TH: Tell us about the portraits in the film—they seem to be specific references to specific films and/or characters.

JK: An extremely talented artist friend of mine, Hector Núñez, painted an entire slew of portraits for the walls of the castle: Sir Hugo Baskerville in **HOUND OF THE BASKERVILLES**, Vincent Price as Joseph Curwen in **THE HAUNTED PALACE**, Peter Cushing in **FEAR IN THE NIGHT**, and Ingrid Pitt in **THE VAMPIRE LOVERS**.

My Mom also painted a couple: Christopher Lee in **DRACULA A.D. 1972** and Michael Gough in **CRUCIBLE OF HORROR**.

Even I got in on the action, and I painted a portrait of my dear friend and muse Haley Zega. Haley played Medusa in my film of **THE NIGHT OF MEDUSA**, so it was nice to have all three gorgon sisters reunited cinematically in the same house.

TH: Were there any elements of the story or the overall concept that had to be dropped or altered due to budget or time constraints?

JK: I think the one thing that we had to drop was the use of a horse-drawn carriage (I can feel all Hammer fans hissing at me!). We were going to

build one, as it was crucial to the finale, but then the script shifted and it turned out we only needed it for the opening scene. The coach eventually transformed into a train that, believe it or not, was a lot easier to do... all we needed was some fog and an offscreen whistle!

TH: I know you graduated from PACE in 2016, unless I'm mistaken... You've elected to remain in Texas and continue to make films there, at least for the time being. Can you see yourself changing your home base and trying to break into the 'big leagues', or would you prefer to keep making films in your own way, on your own terms?

JK: I get this question a lot, especially from my fellow filmmaking friends, who are convinced that moving to Hollywood is the only route for movie directors. My answer is pretty much clean cut: I make the movies I want to see, and Hollywood, as a whole, doesn't make those movies anymore. Why should I go contribute to something that I don't enjoy?

Of course, having a multi-million dollar budget would be phenomenal, but would I sacrifice my family, friends, locations I am familiar with, and complete control over my films for that? I don't think so. Some of these privileges many Hollywood directors don't even have, so I think I'm doing okay right now.

Heck, I just completed a week of filming a tribute to my favorite movie of all time with my favorite actors of all time... I am far beyond "okay"!

Rosa Cano, ingenious lighting designer

The exquisite paintings of Hector Núñez

TH: Now that you have worked with some of these Hammer veterans, do you have any other actors you'd most like to work with?

JK: I am always game to work with people who are enthusiastic and willing to have fun—*any* actor that fits that description is welcome on my set, in my book.

TH: Do you read reviews? When you see a negative one, does it tend to linger, or are you good at letting it roll off your back?

JK: As an artist, you can't fully escape your reviews. A positive review by someone who "gets it" is such a great affirmation of your toils and hard work. A negative review will always sting; that's your baby they're bashing! But I always try to remind myself that I am not making these films for other people, I'm making them for me, because I love to do them. Kind of sappy to say, but that's what I believe.

TH: Can you tell us about any projects you have in mind, or are they top-secret for now?

JK: I'm honestly a little superstitious about announcing projects before they are fully prepared, so I will say what I've been saying for many, many years: I'd love to do Shakespeare's *Richard III*.

TH: Now that HOUSE OF THE GORGON is

finished filming, how do you feel about the experience?

JK: I can say this with no hesitation: It was the best week of my life, and I will probably never fully grasp what and how it happened.

TH: And lastly, do you have any distribution set up for the film?

JK: As of yet, no.

TH: You received a well-deserved nomination for Best Independent Film at this year's Rondo Awards for THESEUS AND THE MINOTAUR; here's wishing you all the luck in the world with that!

JK: Thank you, Troy! Best of luck to you as well!

****

*[But wait! There is more—if you can handle it! Joshua referred to his friend (indeed, our mutual friend), Dan Day, Jr., who came to Texas to assist behind-the-scenes and even ended up playing a small role in **HOUSE OF THE GORGON**. Dan is a fellow horror movie buff and all-around good guy—he writes about his obsession with vintage cinema on his blog The Hitless Wonder Movie Page. Interested readers are encouraged to check it out (@ https://dandayjr35.blogspot. com/). – TH]*

TH: How did you come to be involved in HOUSE OF THE GORGON?

DAN DAY, Jr.: Josh first told me about the idea for his dream project back when we were at the 2017 Monster Bash. He asked then if he was able to make a movie with some Hammer vets, would I be able to come to Texas? And I was like, "Are you kidding??!!"

TH: What were your specific tasks on the production? I know you acted in it, but did you also work behind the scenes?

DD: I basically was a key grip. I also gave Caroline and Martine a ride back to their hotel once.

TH: Working alongside the Hammer veterans was obviously an awe-inspiring experience for a fan... how much did you get to interact with all four of them?

DD: I interacted with all of them—but I tried not to overdo it. I didn't want to come off as a geeky fanboy. The ladies are wonderful; they'll talk to anyone at any time. Chris was approachable, but while preparing to go before the camera he definitely needed his space.

TH: I believe you shared some scenes with some of the Hammer veterans...how did it feel to share a scene with these people?

DD: I exchanged dialogue in a scene with Veronica—and that was an absolute dream come true. I stood next to Chris in another scene.

TH: Have you ever done any acting outside of the experiences of working on Joshua's movies?

DD: No.

TH: If you had to pick a favorite memory from the film, what would it be?

DD: Working with Veronica Carlson—she is probably the most elegant and gracious woman I have ever met.

TH: Now that the film is finished and you are back to 'the real world', how would you sum-up your experience on HOUSE OF THE GORGON?

DD: Simply incredible. I was a nerdy teenager watching all these folks on *Svengoolie*—and now I'm on a movie set with them. How can you top that?!

TH: Any parting thoughts you'd like to share?

DD: Just how everyone—the cast, crew—all worked together toward a positive common goal. And how I hope Josh gets as much out of this as he can. This young man made genre history—to quote *Death of a Salesman*: "Attention must be paid"!

[And attention is being paid, and will be at a peak just as soon as HOUSE OF THE GOR-GON is available for genre fans to experience for themselves. In the meantime, here's wishing Joshua Kennedy all the best on his next projects, and My Thanks to both Joshua and Dan Day, Jr. for taking the time to talk about their experiences on HOUSE OF THE GORGON. – TH]

NIGHT OF THE GORGON's cast and crew assemble for a group shot

SO... MANY... MONSTERS!

From acclaimed artist Denis St. John and WK Books, publishers of Weng's Chop Cinema Megazine and Monster! Digest, comes a new terrifyingly terrific tome of mad monster mayhem!

Jam-packed with over 100 pages of thrilling, chilling, creature-centric comics, this beastly book is guaranteed to fill your days with delight and your nights with terror!

GET YOUR COPY NOW, AND JOIN THE MONSTER REVOLUTION!

AVAILABLE NOW AT
amazon.com

ONLY
$7.95

FROM YER PALS AT
WK BOOKS

The Official
MONSTER!
T-shirt featuring the toothy Indian vampire from the cover of issue 19!

MONSTER!

FAST CUSTOM SHIRTS. COM

fastcustomshirts.com/monster-t-shirt/

All sizes; cuts for ladies and gents

妖怪シリーズ

YOKAI MONSTERS

Art by Marcio Costa

···Heed The Spirits Or Face Their Wrath!

by Michael Hauss

In issue #32 of Monster! *magazine, I covered the three Japanese* Kaiju *(怪獣 / kaijū) fantasy films in the* Daimajin *(大魔神) series. This fantastic trilogy sparked an awakening in my mind towards further, deeper exploration of the Japanese sci-fi / fantasy / horror film genres that has currently reached the point of fevered* obsession*! Now, I was not a total novice to these films—quite to the contrary, in fact; I had seen hundreds of them over the years—but I had previously viewed them strictly at the surface level only, then casually filed them away in my memory. That, in a roundabout way, means I watched these films purely for their superficial entertainment value, and looked for no further emotional connection or depth to most of them. With the* Daimajin *films, however, I was, cinematically speaking, 'reborn', if you will. I found the sincerity of their religious basis along with the unquestioned belief in the power of prayer and redemptive acts of self-sacrifice to be a refreshing cup of Kool-Aid, which I drank down with frenzied reverence. I felt for and* cared *about the characters in the films, and pained for them and all the hardships they incurred, typically through no fault of their own. I craved revenge and retribution for the oppressed, and had tears welling-up in my eyes whenever Majin reawakened to stomp the oppressors into the dirt and gravel whence he had come!*

Battle Of The Badasses! Long predating the Cinema era, samurai tangled with *yōkai*, as seen in this two-page spread from an antique manga on the subject, *circa* the late Meiji Era (1890-1912); other details are unknown. *[Imaged from the private collection of Tim Paxton's Saucerman Site Studios]*

So, when I approached this magazine's co-editor Tim Paxton with my proposal to do an article on Daiei Film's *Yokai Monsters* (妖怪シリーズ) trilogy (1968-69), I was both excited and apprehensive at the same time; apprehensive about the emotional bond I was about to reenter into with this series of flicks. I had seen all three before, many years back, on their initial domestic DVD releases in the early 2000s through ADV Films and, sadly, at the time of those viewings, I had glossed over them with an eye that then viewed them only superficially, following which I quickly dismissed them from my mind as just three more Japanese *daikaiju* monster flicks. An all-new excitement was generated for me by the fact that, if I could come to love and embrace the *Majin* series how I did, then, quite possibly, *Yokai Monsters* too might bring me just as much rubber-suited joy…if not *more*! And joy they indeed did bring to me. As I sat down to write the appraisals hereunder, the emotional depths each film delved into was enough to also emotionally impact my writing, much as the *Majin* films had done. The precise moment of realization that I was also entering into a profound, impassioned bond with this series of films came when two characters from the first film, the youthful hero Yasutaro (Jun Fujimaki) and the young common-er woman Osen (Mikiko Tsubouchi), are conversing, immediately following when Yasutaro has escaped from the town's various thugs, who want to question—or kill—him for interfering in their nefarious plans.; this after the brave Yasaturo has just given the beautiful Osen some of the dirty money (totaling 30 *ryo*) which he had made off with "Robin Hood"-style from the local corrupt developer, money intended to repay a debt and save the tenement house from destruction (which is the prime focal point of the whole story). As he does so, in the most touchingly simple manner, the two young people exchange smiles and words of comfort with one another in these tense times of hardship and tribulation. While misdeeds born from avarice are being committed all around them outside, Osen, her heart now filled with new hope thanks to his selflessly charitable gesture, says simply to Yasutaro, "Please be careful."

The strings of attachment in my heart were plucked by this moving moment, as was my desire for the oppressed residents of this humble tenement house to be saved from their enforced destruction, and for their sacred shrine to be rescued from demolition (so that a brothel, of all things, can be erected in its place). At this point

I stopped the DVD and, with a teary mist upon my tired eyes, I wrote in my notebook at that very next moment, "I *care* about these characters." I cared about the poor, put-upon people on various levels in all three of the *Yokai Monsters* films. I cared because, deep down inside, when my problems arise and the chains of oppression are at their tightest, I wish I could have a savior in any human or supernatural form to save me from the oppressiveness and rid my world of the oppressors. Alas, sadly this will never happen, but I do have these three beautiful films to thank for bringing me the simple joy of a basic belief in something greater than us, beyond our earthly existence, and also of the importance of preserving our hard-fought past and all our cultural legacies for the benefit of future generations.

While I had some basic prior knowledge of what a *yōkai* was and is, the time invested in researching this article really opened my eyes—and, quite frankly, my mind—to the beauty of these myriad mythical creatures and the philosophical/theological symbolism that surrounds them; especially the most-ancient ones, and the adoption of these beings as symbolic stand-ins for particular inexplicable happenings and phenomena that were indecipherable in literal terms to the minds of Japan's ancients. And thus, a system of fantastical spirit-creatures, collectively known as *yōkai*, were invented and entered into Man's lexicon (at least in Japan; but there were/are equivalents to be found in other such disparate places as the Aboriginal American, European and Filipino cultures, too), to help the less-sophisticated minds of the time better comprehend the various unexplained phenomena, natural disasters and sociopolitical injustices that shaped their daily lives, often completely against their will and beyond their power to control. While the *yōkai* are not actually *god*like beings, they do work within the ethereal realm of the gods' environmental and social provinces`, and are certainly not without arcane powers of their own.

Before we start, I should mention the following: I'd be remiss in my writer's duties if I failed to point out something about some of the actors and actresses I discuss in regards to these films. Many, many older Japanese films, especially those from some of the smaller production companies, have completely disappeared from circulation in any form, so, when I list details of any given performer's career, it was culled from what I sourced at the IMDb, along with whatever I managed to decipher from the Japanese Movie Database ([JMDB] 日本映画データベース / *Nihon Eiga Dētabēsu*). Another point to note as you read this article is that it is *not* a comprehensive piece on the myriad of Yōkai creatures

themselves, but rather a look at the three *Yokai Monsters* movies (as well as one of their key progenitors) specifically, although along with that I have included some capsule histories of the *yōkai* in the various media over the years, along with other relevant factoids. Expanding this article beyond its current roughly 10,000-word length would have pushed it beyond the scope and breadth of this magazine, and have me chasing my tail even more. The *yōkai* are many and varied, and they have been part of Japanese culture for centuries, and to do such a vast and variegated subject justice would require a whole book on just the creatures alone, plus another mammoth tome to cover them in all their screen, television, literary and manga (etc.) manifestations.

What are Yōkai?

Yōkai (妖怪; the same word is used as both the singular and the plural) are mythical, mystical beings from Japanese folklore and fairy tales. It is believed that these entities were most-probably largely introduced into Japan by the Chinese, via their religious and academic texts. But not all. Some *yōkai* were entirely homegrown in origin, and still more are relatively new additions to the virtually limitless horde of these supernatural characters, which continues to expand organically along with modern folklore as still more are

An *oni* (鬼 / "demon" or "ogre") pelting a human with *azuki* beans. Turnaround is fair play, as these same beans are also used by humans to banish demons; *circa* the late Meiji Era (1890-1912); other details are unknown. *[Imaged from the private collection of Tim Paxton's Saucerman Site Studios]*

Left & Above: Two more horned *oni* demons. **Facing Page:** A long-schnozzed *tengu* (天狗 / "heavenly dog") tangles with an elephant in what could be a case of, er, 'nose-envy'. All three images are circa the late Meiji Era (1890-1912); other details are unknown. *[Imaged from the private collection of Tim Paxton's Saucerman Site Studios]*

introduced into popular culture. The Chinese also introduced *Kanji* (logogram writing characters) into Japan, a written language that is still in use today, in a modified, congealed form combined with Japanese *hiragana* (平仮名、ひらがな) and *katakana* (片仮名、かたかな、カタカナ). Broken down into its two Japanese syllables, the word *yōkai* means—*yō*: "ghost, apparition, phantom, specter, demon, monster or goblin"; and *kai*: "mystery and wonder".

Yōkai can be roughly traced back to the 1st Century, originating from what is now China, and gradually became incorporated into the folktales of Japan. Legends about them would continue to proliferate through many different mediums, including: oral children's fairy tales, handwritten scrolls, *Ukiyo-e* (浮世絵) woodblock prints, *kamishibai* (紙芝居 / "paper plays" *[a subject discussed on pp.13-16 of Jolyon Yates'* Yōkai *article – eds.]*), and, much later, manga, television, movies, books, magazines and, more recently—yes—even video games too. The prominence of the Yokai would rise considerably in Japan during the Heian (平安時代) Period (794-1185) when, in literature, the *Mononoke* (モノノ怪),

which were introduced from China and considered a type of *yōkai*, were referred to as various types of evil spirits; vengeful dead or alive ones.

The most famous of the ancient *yōkai* artists would undoubtedly be Sekien Toriyama (1712-1788), whose book on the subject entitled *Gazu Hyakki Yagyō* (画図百鬼夜行 / "The Illustrated Night Parade of a Hundred Demons" or "The Illustrated Demon Horde's Night Parade") was published in 1776, and proved so popular that it was followed in 1779 by *Konjaku Gazu Zoku Hyakki* (今昔画図続百鬼 / "The Illustrated One Hundred Demons from the Present and the Past"), *Konjaku Hyakki Shūi* (今昔百鬼拾遺 / "Supplement to The Hundred Demons from the Present and the Past") in 1780, and the last in the series, *Hyakki Tsurezure Bukuro* (百器徒然袋 / "The Illustrated Bag of One Hundred Random Demons" or "A Horde of Haunted Housewares"), which was published in 1781. Toriyama Sekien was the pen-name of the 18th Century scholar and artist Sano Toyofusa (1712-1788), whose books on the *yōkai* were both rooted in tradition and also incorporated others which Sekien invented himself. The artist Katsushika

Hokusai (1760-1849), who is credited with coining the phrase *"manga"* (漫画); a word which is a combination of two *Kanji* characters: *man*, meaning "rapidly thrown off"; and *ga*, for "drawing". Hokusai, who is most-famously known for his landscape prints (including "Thirty-Six views of Mount Fuji" [富嶽三十六景 / *Fugaku San-jūrokkei*], 1830-32), would incorporate *yōkai* into some of his drawings of rural village life, including those of opium smokers and others depicting women with elongating, extending necks, such as those possessed by the type of *yōkai* called *rokurokubi* (ろくろ首, 轆轤首), along with many other works dealing with the supernatural, demons and ghosts. In literature, the list of *yōkai* tales is long and extends back thousands of years, with numerous mentions being made of them in mythic and religious texts and scriptures, as well as in folktales that were retold again and again from mouth-to-ear—ever 'evolving' in the process—by the common masses and higher classes alike. A massive amount of manga have featured *yōkai* in their pages, most famously in *GeGeGe no Kitarou* (ゲゲゲの鬼太郎), by the legendary Shigeru Mizuki ([1922-2015] see below).

Daiei Film

The *Daimajin* and *Yokai Monsters* series of films—both of which are formed along much the same basic 'crime-and-punishment' structural lines, dramatically speaking—originated at the famed Japanese movie studio Daiei Film Co. Ltd. Daiei was founded during WW2, when the Imperial Japanese government, in order to save on valuable resources and give them greater control over the films being made, combined all the domestic film studios into three national companies, with Daiei Film being one of them. Daiei's domestic and export hit **RASHOMON** (羅生門 / *Rashōmon*, 1950, Japan, D: Akira Kurosawa), starring Toshirō Mifune, would become the first locally-produced film ever to be screened internationally, and its smash success proved how the once-insular Japanese industry could be a major mover-and-shaker and force to be reckoned with on the world cinema's stage. Daiei would also produce their first color film—which was also the first Japanese color film to be exhibited outside Japan—with director Teinosuke Kinugasa's *jid-aigeki* (時代劇 / "era drama") entry **GATE OF HELL** (地獄門 / *Jigokumon*, 1953). In addition, Daiei produced both the long-running *Gamera* (ガメラ) and *Zatoichi* (座頭市 / *Zatōichi*) series, the *Yokai Monsters* and *Daimajin* trios, plus sundry other assorted fantasy/sci-fi film offerings besides, including: **WARNING FROM SPACE** (宇宙人東京に現わる / *Uchujin Tokyo ni arawaru*, 1956, D: Koji Shima), **THE SNAKE GIRL AND THE SILVER-HAIRED WITCH** (蛇娘と白髪魔 / *Hebi musume to hakuhatsu-*

ma, 1968, D: Noriaki Yuasa) and **THE OIWA PHANTOM** (お岩の亡霊 予告篇 / *Yotsuya kaidan – Owia no borei*, 1969, D: Kazuo Mori), among many others, all of which make for prime *Monster!*-approved viewing. But nowadays Daiei is probably best-remembered among genre film buffs as the company that introduced the giant flying, flame-throwing space turtle Gamera to the world in 1965, as competition for Toho's successful *Godzilla* series. To date there have been a total of thirteen Gamera films released, the latest being **GAMERA THE BRAVE** (小さき勇者たち～ガメラ～ / *Chilisaki yusha-ta-*

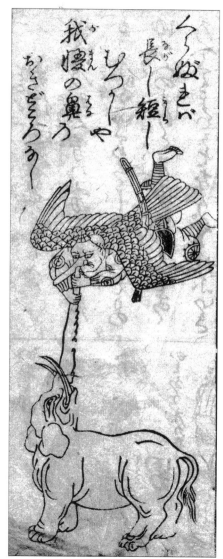

A deadly *onibaba* (鬼婆 / "demon hag"); art by Ian Coleman

TOICHI MEETS YOJIMBO (座頭市と用心棒 / *Zatōichi to Yōjinbō*, 1970, Japan, D: Kihachi Okamoto) and **THE INVISIBLE SWORDSMAN** (透明剣士 / *Tomei kenshi*, 1970, Japan, D: Tomei Kenshi), which are but a few of the more notable examples among his two-dozen writing credits. The director of **100 MONSTERS**, and co-director of **ALONG WITH GHOSTS**, Kimiyoshi Yasuda, is probably best known for helming several of the *Zatoichi* series, including **ADVENTURES OF ZATOICHI** (座頭市関所破り / *Zatōichi sekisho-yaburi*, 1964, Japan), **ZATOICHI'S CANE-SWORD** (座頭市鉄火旅 / *Zatōichi tekka-tabi*, 1967, Japan), **ZATOICHI MEETS THE ONE-ARMED SWORDSMAN** (新座頭市・破れ!唐人剣 / *Shin Zatōichi: Yabure! Tōjin-ken*, 1971, Japan/Hong Kong) and **ZATOICHI'S CONSPIRACY** (新座頭市物語・笠間の血祭り / *Shin Zatōichi monogatari: Kasama no chimatsu*, 1973, Japan), and for helming the first magnificent *Daimajin* movie. Yoshiyuki Kuroda, the director of **SPOOK WARFARE**, sadly only directed thirteen films, with **LONE WOLF AND CUB: WHITE HEAVEN IN HELL** (子連れ狼 地獄へ行くぞ! 大五郎 / *Kozure Okami: Jigoku e ikuzo!*, 1974, Japan), being his best-known project besides his *Yokai Monsters* work, and his CV also includes a co-directing credit along with Kimiyoshi Yasuda on **ALONG WITH GHOSTS**. The beautiful cinematography on the first *YM* film was by Yasukazu Takemura, whose fantastic work can be seen most notably in the *jidaigeki*/*chanbara* actioners **NINJA, A BAND OF ASSASSINS** (忍びの者 / *Shinobi no mono*, 1962, Japan, D: Satsuo Yamamoto) and **ZATOICHI'S FLASHING SWORD** (座頭市あばれ凧 / *Zatōichi abare tako*, 1964, Japan, D: Kazuo Ikehiro), among others. Hiroshi Imai was cinematographer on the final two *YM* films, and he brings an arresting visual style to both. Other noteworthy work by Imai in the field of cinematography can be seen in the outstanding **SATAN'S SWORD** (大菩薩峠 / *Daibosatsu toge*, 1960, Japan, D: Kenji Misumi) and **BUDDHA** (釈迦 / *Shaka*, 1961, Japan, D: Kenji Misumi), plus a whole host of other fine films.

The Yōkai *on Film*

This is a decidedly mixed bag. While references to the mythical creatures do pop up in any number of productions and throughout Japanese popular culture as a whole, films in which the main narrative is built around them are not all that plentiful; except, that is, in the case of one particular *yōkai* creature, and that would be the *Bakeneko* (化け猫 / "changing/changed cat"), which has appeared in more movies than any of its fellow *yōkai* have. Essentially, this is an ordinary mortal feline that has reached an advanced age and be-

chi: Gamera, 2006, Japan, D: Ryuta Tazaki), with another possible reboot of the franchise to be coming soon, according to some reports. Sadly, during the early '70s cinema slump in Japan, Daiei Film filed for bankruptcy in 1971, because of the sharp downturn in their fortunes, as 'free' television programming was drawing away ticket-buying cinemagoers in droves, with theatre attendance reportedly dropping a whopping 30% from 1959 to 1969. Daiei was revived as a production company only in 1974, and then, in 2002, it was merged with Kadokawa Pictures Inc. and the hybrid company was renamed Kadokawa-Daiei Film Co. Ltd.

Much as the *Daimajin* films had been, the entries in the three-film *Yokai Monsters* series were also produced and released in dizzyingly swift fashion by Daiei, with each consecutive entry seeing release within mere months of its predecessor: **100 MONSTERS** (妖怪百物語 / *Yōkai hyaku monogatari*) on March 20th, 1968, **SPOOK WARFARE** (妖怪大戦争 / *Yokai daisenso*) on December 19th, 1968, and **ALONG WITH GHOSTS** a.k.a. **JOURNEY WITH GHOST ALONG YOKAIDO ROAD** (東海道お化け道中 / *Tokaido obake dochu*) on March 21st, 1969. All three of the *Yokai Monsters* films were written by Tetsuro Yoshida (with an assist from Shozaburo Asai on **ALONG WITH GHOSTS**), who also wrote the *Daimajin* series, as well as **FIGHT, ZATOICHI, FIGHT** (座頭市血笑旅 / *Zatōichi kesshō-tabi*, 1964, Japan, D: Kenji Misumi), **ZA-**

Yokai Monsters ...Heed The Spirits Or Face Their Wrath!　　　*Mike Hauss*

comes transformed into a deathless *yōkai*, with shapeshifting abilities. In many of the Ghost-Cat (怪猫 / *Kaibyō*) or *bakeneko* films, of which there are many in Japan's *kaidan-eiga* (怪談) movie genre, the cat had been murdered, along with its human master, and thereafter returns from the afterlife to exact vengeance against the perpetrators of those earthly wrongs. (For a list of films featuring the *Kaibyō* and *Bakeneko*, please refer to Steve Fenton's select filmography in *Monster!* #10.) One particular film with a direct connection to the *Yokai Monsters* series is the Shintoho Co. Ltd. production **GHOST STORIES OF WANDERER AT HONJO** (怪談本所七不思議 / *Kaidan Honjo nanafushigi*, 1957, Japan, D: Gorō Kadono), which, it being so prototypical of its *kaidan eiga* subgenre, I will go into a bit more detail about below, just before I go on to discuss the *YM* trilogy proper.

Other notable and diverse films with *yōkai* very much in attendance include—but are by no means limited to—the international arthouse hit **KWAIDAN** (怪談 / *Kaidan*, 1964, Japan, D: Masaki Kobayashi), **HIRUKO THE GOBLIN** (妖怪ハンター ヒルコ / *Yōkai Hantā: Hiruko*, 1991, Japan, D: Shin'ya Tsukamoto), **KIBAKI-CHI** (牙吉 / *Kibakichi: Bakko-yōkaiden*, 2004, Japan, D: Tomo'o Haraguchi) and its sequel, as well as **THE GREAT YOKAI WAR** (妖怪大戦争 / *Yōkai daisensō*, 2005, Japan, D: Takashi Miike). The mythos also includes any number of anime, most famously in adaptations of the legendary manga artist Shigeru Mizuki when his *GeGeGe No Kitaro*—which first appeared serialized in *Weekly Shonen Magazine* from 1960 to 1969—was made into an animated series for Japanese television (that first ran from January 3rd, 1968 until March 30th, 1969). A number of other anime series related to or otherwise influenced/inspired by *GeGeGe No Kitaro* have appeared on TV in Japan over the last 40 years or so. More

A trollish *namahage* (生剥); art by Ian Coleman

recently, there was the *tokusatsu* (特撮 / "special effects") *sentai* (戦隊 / "superhero team") teleseries *Ninja Sentai Kakuranger* (忍者戦隊カクレンジャー / *Ninja Sentai Kakurenjā*, 1994, Japan), which abounded with a whole menagerie of villainous and exceedingly outrageous (and highly rubbery!) *yōkai*. Interestingly enough, because action scenes from *Ninja Sentai Kakuranger* were subsequently edited into Season 3 of *Mighty Morphin Power Rangers*, it represented one of the first times that *yōkai* (albeit exaggeratedly absurdist ones!) made appearances on mainstream American television, and they—as well as Japanese *kaijū* culture in general—have steadily

Great Gobbledy-Goo Goblins On The Loose! One of the weird *yōkai [left]* that populate **GHOST STORIES OF WANDERER AT HONJO** (1957), alongside *Monster!* co-ed Tim Paxton's Halloween 2011 variation on the theme

been gaining in prominence and popularity ever since, showing no sign of slowing down.

****

And now for a few paragraphs on the film that largely served as a prototype/blueprint for the *Yokai Monsters* trilogy…

GHOST STORIES OF WANDERER AT HONJO

(本所七不思議 / *Honjo Nanafushi-gi*; a.k.a. **GHOST STORY OF THE SEVEN WONDERS OF HONJO; SEVEN MYSTERIES**)

Japan, 1957. D: Gorō Kadono

A B&W production from Shintoho Co. Ltd., **GSOWAH** (as we will hereafter refer to it for brevity's sake), is the single film that can be said to have most directly influenced the *YM* series. (ATTENTION: The following two paragraphs contain spoilers, so be advised!)

The story concerns a kindly middle-aged noble-man named Sazen (Hiroshi Hayashi) who, on the anniversary of his wife's death, saves an imperiled she-*Tanuki* (狸 / "raccoon dog" [based on an actual species of canid mammal]) by paying for its life to the group of men who have captured it in its animal form, and have decided to kill it and turn it into soup (!) in payback for the pranks it plays on humans ("It is very bad! It always tricks people"). The *Tanuki*—colorfully described at the Tofugu website as "The Canine Yokai with Gigantic Balls!" in its male form!—is a supernatural-born trickster that possesses shapeshifting abilities and has a playful, mischievous streak that sometimes makes it the bane of humans. On the same day that Sazen pays tribute to his late wife Yone at her burial place, his disgraced-and-disowned ne'er-do-well nephew Gonkurō Komi-yaya (Shigeru Amachi) arrives, looking for an easy handout and secretly hoping to reignite an old flame with Sawa (Akiko Yamashita), Sazen's manipulatively coquettish new wife, with whom he'd once had a fling. A handsome and dashing if sly and unscrupulous roving *ronin* ("masterless samurai") with a wandering eye, Gonkurō is in urgent need of a large sum of money (i.e., 50 *ryo*) to pay off an outstanding debt and, after seducing Sawa—his own aunt-in-law!—once again for old times' sake (a dripping tipped-over *sake* bottle subtly symbolizes the unseen sex act), has her arrange for Sazen to be ambushed and killed by a band of hooded thugs, led by none other than

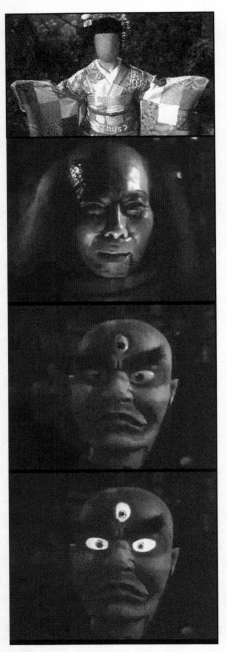

Above: A quartet of screen captures from **GHOST STORIES OF WANDERER AT HONJO**, depicting some of its frightful entities. Dating from '57, **GSOWAH** served as a direct influence on the *Yokai Monsters* series of a decade later

Yokai Monsters …Heed The Spirits Or Face Their Wrath!   *Mike Hauss*

Gonkurō himself, aided by Sazen's treacherous manservant Gosuke (Saburō Sawai).

The *Tanuki*, whose name is Tebeidanuki, now in female human form (Michiko Tachibana), had pledged to protect Sazen the good Samaritan in gratitude for him saving her life. However, on the night of his murder, Tebeidanuki was off dancing it up with her fellow Tanuki maidens, and thus her savior/master's life was taken, so the Tanuki swears to avenge herself on his murderers. Sazen's youthful son Yumenosuke Komiyama (Jūzaburō Akechi) has recently left his father's home to find his own way in life, and his faithful woman-in-waiting, the wholesomely virtuous and virginal Yae (Namiji Matsuura), is in dire danger of being ravished by the deranged (and way-oversexed!) swordsman Gonkurō, who has coarse and unchivalrous designs on her following the death of Sazen. Indeed, Gonkurō would have had his awful way with her already if Tebeidanuki hadn't shapeshifted into Yumenosuke to thwart his rape attempt. With the eventual return of the real Yumenosuke from his travels, the film plays-out to its bloody, retribution-filled conclusion, wherein the murder victims' ghosts, the Yokai and Yumenosuke take their revenge on the evildoers, the kill-crazy Gonkurō most of all...

An economical mere fifty-five minutes in length, **GSOWAH** unreels briskly and brilliantly, telling its tale in a well-executed fashion, propelled by Shigeru Amachi's arrogant, over-the-top performance as the wholly unethical Gonkurō. Despite the briefness of its running time, the film's various 'mundane' tangential subplots (involving cuckoldry, sneaky samurai subterfuge and other immoralities) are every bit as socially complex and convoluted as those found in the *YM* series, but this doesn't detract from the pacing any, and its acts of human mean-spiritedness are vital to illustrating and underlining the ultimate moral message of this "Aesop's Fable", Asian-style. The varieties of *yōkai* that receive screen time herein are introduced individually at the outset of the movie and, besides the protagonistic Tanuki, are gradually reintroduced later on, most prominently being shown at the conclusion, whilst they assist the mortal hero and the 'animal girl' heroine in exacting her revenge. The raccoon dog spirit's shapeshifting abilities include the power to transform into a miniature floating fireball, *à la* "will-o'-the-wisp" spirits to be found in the folklore and movies from all across Asia (largely in the southeast).

The action takes place in Edo along the river Sumida, where the ancient *Tanuki* played tricks on the locals, and what follows was based on the so-called *Seven Wonders of Honsho* (本所七不思議

/ *Honjo Nanafushigi*), a septet of ghost stories, whose various adaptations went from *Rakugo* (落語 / "fallen words") storytelling recitals to depictions on woodblock prints, and much later got adapted onto celluloid as well. Another, earlier film derived from *Seven Wonders of Honsho* was produced (in 1937), but this reviewer has been unable to acquire a copy of it to view.

Seen early into the narrative, the *Oitekebori* (置行堀 おいてけぼり), is a ghostly guardian that dwells within the vicinity of local bodies of water and puts the haunt on any intruders onto its territory. In **GSOWAH**, this apparition frightens off two illicit anglers when it appears in the form of a human woman (albeit *sans* any face!), commanding the unheeding men to "Leave the fish!" During a similar sequence in **SPOOK WARFARE** (*YM #2*), an Oitekebori likewise spooks two masterless samurais-turned-poachers, who, after being duly warned by an elderly monk not to take fish from the accursed body of water and contemptuously ignoring his warning, are ordered to "Leave it!" by an eerie disembodied voice. A one-legged (and armless, if by no means *harm*less!) *Karakasa-obake* (から傘おばけ / "umbrella ghost") joins the proceedings and hops around wildly, flapping its floppy XL tongue, as his kindred would do in the *Yokai Monsters* films a decade-plus later, joining in with *Okuri Chochin* (送り提灯), the "sending-off lantern" (which also made appearances in the *YM* flicks) to scare away the poachers and, later in the narrative, drive the

Preceding Page: A still from **GSOWAH**.
Above: Its Japanese B2 poster

main villain Gonkurō right off his rocker. The masterless samurai character—in this case the irredeemably villainous and vicious Gonkurō—became a heroic one for *YM* #2, **SPOOK WARFARE**. (Incidentally, the *ronin* [浪人] baddie in **ALONG WITH GHOSTS** [*YM* #3], in that case its evil lord's hired hitman, was also named Gonkurō, perhaps in a nod to the present story.) As would also be seen in the later *YM* series, a female *Rokurokubi* (ろくろ首 or 轆轤首), a species of *yōkai* with a grotesquely elongated, extendable neck, also puts in a brief appearance here.

The films in the *Yokai Monsters* trilogy are thematically and structurally similar to **GSOWAH** in many ways, borrowing and incorporating ideas from it, and—stagey, pantomime-style and simplistic though they are—the special effects work on all four films is outstanding. The ending of **GSOWAH** echoes that to **100 MONSTERS** (*YM* #1), where the eponymous creatures' group haunting of the corrupt land developer and shrine magistrate sends the men into a furious frenzy of fear, unleashing the raging wrath of the *katana* ("sword") against the *yokai*, who psych-out their villainous victims by disguising themselves as their human compatriots, driving the evildoers mad with self-realization, guilt and panic prior to dispatching them for their many misdeeds.

GSOWAH concludes on an optimistically upbeat note with the now-fully-redeemed humanoid *yōkai* Tebeidanuki joining her kimono'd Tanuki sisters for another joyous dance routine.

THE YOKAI MONSTERS TRILOGY

(***ATTENTION: SPOILER ALERT!*** The following reviews reveal synoptic details which may potentially spoil the viewing experience for first-time viewers. *Proceed with caution!*)

YOKAI MONSTERS 1:
100 MONSTERS
(妖怪百物語 / *Yōkai hyaku monogatari*; a.k.a. **THE HUNDRED GHOST STORIES**)
Japan, 1968. D: Kimiyoshi Yasuda

"Mr. Tajimaya will tear down this filthy shrine and build a brothel" – *"If you build a brothel here, it'll cause a lot of neighborhood disturbance!"*

It's difficult not to bring mention of the *Daimajin* series into the discussion of this kick-off *Yokai Monsters* outing. Like all three of those earlier films, **100 MONSTERS** is about defying/defiling the sacred and disregarding past traditions by not showing proper reverence to the ancient deities, resulting in dire ramifications for the serious missteps committed by the evil lords and their unquestioningly obedient underlings. While the *Daimajin* movies deal with a more universal religion—including elements of Shinto, and even Judeo-Christianity—the religious angle in **100 MONSTERS** revolves almost exclusively around Buddhism and the Shinto (神道 / *Shintō*) faiths. *"Shinto ('the way of the gods') is the indigenous faith of the Japanese people, and as old as Japan itself. It remains Japan's major religion alongside Buddhism. Shinto gods are called* kami. *They are sacred spirits which take the form of things and concepts important to life, such as wind, rain, mountains, trees, rivers and fertility. Humans become* kami *after they die and are revered by their families as ancestral* kami. *The* kami *of extraordinary people are even enshrined at some shrines. The Sun Goddess Amaterasu is considered Shinto's most important* kami.*"* ("Shinto". N.p., n.d. Web. March 21st, 2017.)

Now, I would be selling it short if I told you that **100 MONSTERS** is merely a straightforward escapist fantasy adventure, although it definitely *is*

Yokai Monsters …Heed The Spirits Or Face Their Wrath! *Mike Hauss*

that, too. But it's also a compelling mix of stylized samurai theatre and impassioned social drama.

With unchecked economic expansion and profiteering inevitably comes greed and corruption... Ambitious, unscrupulous local shipping magnate / land-grabber Reimon Tajimaya (Takashi Kanda) is permitted a certain 'under-the-table' concession by the corrupt, self-serving Shrine Magistrate Lord Hotta (Ryūtarō Gomi) which allows Tajimaya—and *himself*, of course—to profit and prosper greatly; this when a local zone ordinance is lifted so that more of the monopolistic Tajimaya's ships are free to carry cargo as they please without the hassle of bureaucratic interference. To further fill his already overflowing coffers, in another shady business deal, the bottomlessly greedy Tajimaya decides to tear down a local sacred Shinto shrine, planning to build a brothel on the land it occupies, which represents prime real estate to him, nothing more. Just for bad measure, he also plans to demolish a surrounding tenement house while he's at it, thus leaving all its needy residents without a roof over their head. As the builders arrive on the grounds to start the demolition, the shrine's outraged elderly longtime caretaker Gohei (Jun Hamamura), is brutally beaten up by Tajimaya's paid goons for his interference, and he dies as a result of his injuries. The deed of the tenement house was held by one Mr. Jinbei (Tatsuo Hanabu), who had put it up as collateral for the money needed to purchase expensive medicine for his wife, who suffered from a chronic illness, and Tajimaya, the man currently holding the deed for 'security' (pos-

session being nine-tenths of the law), now owns the property outright. Thus, with powerful and influential local officials in-on the corruption, the tenement house appears doomed to destruction, with all its poor lower-caste occupants seemingly destined for the streets.

Enter a good-hearted masterless samurai (*ronin*) named Yasutaro (Jun Fujimaki), who soon comes to the aid of the distressed tenants, and he infiltrates a get-together at Tajimaya's house, where an old priest presides over a ceremonial telling of the "one hundred stories," with a candle being ritually extinguished after each one is told. One story the old priest tells—dramatized in a 'flashback'-style sequence—tells of two drunken fishermen, who, desperate to find food, go fishing at "The Lake of Death", as an old Buddhist monk informs the two men it is called (and with good reason, we soon learn!). He warns them in no uncertain terms that they should leave the area as it was and depart immediately, because if they take a fish from the lake, they will be punished by a terrible curse. Arrogantly disregarding the monk's advice—one of the men actually threatens to kill him if he doesn't get lost—the samurai succeed in hauling a large Koi (鯉) carp from the lake and, just as they are triumphantly leaving with their catch, the sky ominously darkens and a fierce thunderstorm angrily starts up. A disembodied voice tells them to leave the filched fish behind, but they foolishly ignore this warning too, believing it to be some sort of trick. When the pair head off to one of the samurai's homes for some more *sake* and a hearty fish supper, his

Yōkai? *Yikes!* Woe betide any foolhardy humans who get caught out after dark on the night of **100 MONSTERS!** (Japanese lobby card for the film)

泥田坊

大首

カラー作品

ろくろ首

一本足の傘

からす天狗

和

妖怪百物語

よう

かい

ひゃく

もの

がたり

映倫

牛おに

ぬっぺほう

中村　水原　吉田　五味　神田　平　坪内　藤巻　嘉藤
村倉原田味龍平内ミキ田美
康浩義太　正　新　一子征　和潤
純子一夫郎隆蔵　二　子征　和潤

wife complains that—ominous foreshadowing alert!—the Koi's blood won't wash off her hands after she cuts it up for sushi. Evidently having been 'infected' with evil by the blood of the fish from the accursed lake, the wife shortly assumes the form of a neck-stretching *Rokurokubi yōkai*, causing both her husband and the other samurai to drop dead in fright at the sight of her.

The action subsequently switches back to the storytelling gathering, where the old priest says in summation after relating his latest cautionary fable, "For ignoring the curse's warnings, the two masterless samurai lost their lives." After concluding the one hundred stories, the priest is prepared to lead the assembled group through the formal, mandatory and *absolutely crucial* (note italics!) curse-eliminating ritual, so as to avoid any dire supernatural repercussions, only to be stopped from doing so by the haughtily realist / modernist Tajimaya, who is openly skeptical and contemptuous of such superstitious nonsense: "An apparition appears if the ritual isn't performed?" he asks mockingly. "That's just a superstition believed only by the weak-minded dregs. There's no need to go through with the ritual!" The old priest nevertheless pleads with Tajimaya to allow him to perform it, as this ritual has been done since days of old and passed down to successive generations with good reason. Instead however, Tajimaya casually dismisses the priest, then has his servants present a monetary gift to each of his guests in the form of personal packages of golden *ryō* (両) currency, which, the gifter says with much sarcasm, rather than the traditional curse-eliminating ritual, they can use as a charm to ward off any evil spirits. During the gift-giving of this ill-gotten money (unfairly earned by Tajimaya's criminal activities), none other than the wily and resourceful Yasutaro, who has been covertly posing as one of the party guests, is discovered by a guard and confronted by Tajimaya, only to make good his escape into the night. Alarmed by this intrusion, Lord Hotta believes—and rightly so, as it transpires—that Yasutaro might be a special investigator sent by the High Magistrate to dig up dirt on he and his criminal associates' unlawful operations. Thus, Tajimaya and Lord Hotta send out their henchmen in a concerted effort to find and dispose of Yasutaro. Having succeeded in scoring a sizeable share of the gift money at the party before making good his getaway, Yasutaro—Robin Hood style!—proceeds to give the entire sum to the beautiful maiden Osen (Mikiko Tsubouchi), who lives in the tenement. The money—30 *ryō* in all—is intended for Mr. Jinbei, in order for him to repay his overdue loan to Tajimaya, thus saving the tenement from destruction…or so they hope! However, poor Mr. Jinbei is stabbed to death by Tajimaya's head henchman Jūsuke (Yoshio Yoshida), who then disposes of his victim's body in a local lake. Following Mr. Jinbei's murder, the shrine does indeed get leveled and, as the holy structure crumbles to the ground and the skies overhead darken with the gods' rising wrath, all of henchman Jūsuke's thugs become blank-faced *Noppera-bō* (のっぺらぼう / "faceless ghost" *yōkai*), and this sends the fear-maddened Jūsuke scrambling back to Tajimaya's house in abject panic.

The *yōkai* are sparse until the final twenty minutes of the film. But in those final minutes, a whole plethora of the mythical creatures manifest themselves. Rather than cause any real damage, however, they only terrorize their intended targets, Tajimaya and the other evildoers associated with him. As they meet their fate, the villains realize that the curse-eliminating ceremony which they had chosen not to perform and disregard is the reason why these otherworldly beings are hounding them to their graves.

The Yasutaro character turns out to be something other than the masterless samurai he initially claims he is, and, as played by Fujimaki, he makes for a wonderful hero. The rest of the film's cast are also all outstanding. While it can be classified as a samurai film infused with elements of the supernatural and fantasy, its focus on human drama first and foremost endows it with a deeper emotional impact, while allowing its characters to be properly developed. It should be said that some viewers might be disappointed by the comparative shortage of monsters on view (despite the seeming promise of its title), but that isn't to say the *yōkai* don't play a key and central function in the film nevertheless. The narrative's emphasis on the social class struggle between the serfs and their supposed 'betters' allows the put-upon characters to be developed into individuals deserving of our sympathy, who need a helping hand (or *other* appendage!) from not only the *yōkai*, but also from the brave Yasutaro, in his secret identity.

In addition to the ones already mentioned above, some of the other notable *yōkai* that make appearances in **100 MONSTERS** include, but are by no means limited to, the following: *Burabura* (不落不落 or 不落々々): a floating, burning paper lantern. *Karakasa-obake* (から傘お化け / 唐傘お化け): a comical "umbrella ghost", with one leg, one eye, two spindly arms, and a long, waggling tongue, with which it sometimes licks its victims. *Ōkubi* (大首): a gigantic, detached, floating man's or woman's head. *Namahage* (生剥): a fearsome demonic ogre, the Namahage's duty is to chase after idle people, scaring them out of their wits. *[See artist Ian Coleman's pen-and-ink interpretation of such a creature on p.231 – ed.]* And, last but by no means least, the *Kappa* (河童), or "river-child" (a.k.a. *kawatarō* [川太郎 / "river-boy"], etc.): one of the most famous and beloved *yōkai* of all, this is a mischievous water-dwelling but amphibious imp, reptilian in appearance, with a plate on its pate (fringed with bristly hair) which serves as the source of its power.

100 MONSTERS is a beautifully-composed film, boasting assured direction, top-notch cinematography and a fun, playful score by Michiaki "Chumei" Watanabe. The cast is a wonderful collection of actors and actresses, who each perform their parts adroitly. They are led by the charismatic Jun Fujimaki as Yasutaro. In the first *Daimajin* film, Fujimaki had played Kogenta, a vassal of Lord Hanabusa, who, following the death of their parents, escorts the Lord's young son Tadafumi (Yoshihko Aoyama) and daughter Kozasa (Miwa Takada) into the forbidden mountainous area. The breathtakingly

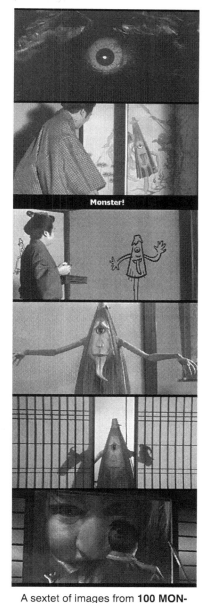

A sextet of images from **100 MONSTERS. Top:** Some giant hairy thing with a single eyeball. **Center 4 Pix:** The man-child Shinkichi (Rookie Shin-ichi)'s wall-doodles conjure up a not-so-imaginary playmate in the form of a mischievous *karakasa-obake* (から傘お化け / "umbrella ghost"). **Above:** An *ōkubi* (大首 / "giant head") says *"BOO!"*

beautiful Mikiko Tsubouchi plays Osen, who has amorous feelings for Yasutaro. This actress only appeared in a relatively small body of work (some twenty-five films in all), but a few notable titles do stand out, including the *chanbara* **NEW TALE OF ZATOICHI** (新·座頭市物語 / *Shin Zatōichi monogatari*, 1963, Japan, D: Tokuzo Tanaka), **ZATOICHI'S REVENGE** (座頭市二段斬り / *Zatōichi nidan-giri*, 1965, Japan, D: Akira Inoue), **ZATOICHI AND THE CHEST OF GOLD** (座頭市千両首 / *Zatōichi senryō-kubi*, 1964, Japan, D: Kazuo Ikehiro) and the *kaijū-eiga* **GAMERA VS. ZIGRA** (ガメラ対深海怪獣ジグラ / *Gamera tai Shinkai Kaijū Jigura*, 1971, Japan, D: Noriaki Yuasa). Takashi Kanda, who plays Reimon Tajimaya in the film, also played an equally evil bastard in **RETURN OF DAIMAJIN** (大魔神怒る / *Daimajin ikaru*, 1966, Japan, D: Kenji Misumi), wherein his sinister turn as Lord Danjō Mikoshiba is one of the highlights of the film, as is his demise at its end, when he is killed by the living stone god Majin! Some of Kanda's other noteworthy appearances include: the notorious sci-fi stinkers **PRINCE OF SPACE** (遊星王子 / *Yūsei ōji*, 1959, Japan, D: Eijiro Wakabayashi) and **INVASION OF THE NEPTUNE MEN** (宇宙快速船 / *Uchū Kaisokusen*, 1961, Japan, D: Koji Ohta), whose only point of interest *[Says you! ☺ – SF.]* is the inclusion in the cast of an early film appearance by the legendary "Streetfighter" himself, shitkickin' Shin'ichi "Sonny" Chiba. Kanda appeared in some 84 films, including the brilliant Yasuharu Hasebe's **MASSACRE GUN** (みな殺しの拳銃 / *Minagoroshi no kenjū*, 1967, Japan), and the following **SPOOK WARFARE** ([*YM #2*] as Hyogo Isobe) being only two of them.

The evil that stokes the fires of retribution in **100 MONSTERS** mostly revolves around the Lord Hotta figure, with his smarmy, sadistic rapist's attitude and his utterly corrupted character, willingly aiding and abetting the equally nefarious Tajimaya in his own dastardly deeds. The part of Lord Hotta, as interpreted by the fantastic actor Ryutaro Gomi, is a morally-bankrupt personage of elevated social class, thoroughly compromised and utterly dirty through-and-through. Answering directly only to the Shogun himself, being the Shrine Magistrate—despite his essential godlessness, ironically enough—his official duties include overseeing all things divine, including the region's Shinto shrines and Buddhist temples. Considering his governmental title, Hotta's allowing the destruction of the shrine temple reads very much like blasphemy (which it indeed very much *is* seen as in the eyes of both the tenement's devout residents and the shrine's guardian *yōkai*). Gomi had memorably portrayed the wicked aristocrat Samanosuke in **DAIMAJIN** #1 and, while he is much more reserved and pompous in his role as Lord Hotta here, his Samansosuke character therein was far more violent and vindictive, but was never turned into an all-out caricature, as might easily have been the case in the hands of a lesser performer.

As **100 MONSTERS** ends, the Yasutaro character tells the perplexed tenants of the tenement house, who are feeling the after-effects of the otherworldly night before due to the protective spirits' handiwork, "There are things Man just can't measure or understand in this world!" The "100" given in the title of the film is nowhere representative of the actual amount of *yōkai* seen onscreen, and is more of a symbolically significant number intended to connect the film to the folklore surrounding the so-called Night of One Hundred Demons. This, legend has it, occurs

The Gang's All Here!

Yokai Monsters ...Heed The Spirits Or Face Their Wrath! *Mike Hauss*

at the height of summer, when, come nightfall, a hundred *yōkai* are said to march, prance and dance across the countryside and through the streets. Anyone who crossed paths with these ethereal beings would be taken out of their earthly existence and transported over onto the astral plane. The best way for someone to avoid this happening to them is to simply stay home and not venture out during said event.

From what I can gather, this film did receive a very limited theatrical release in the States (probably subtitled for 'arthouse' screenings?), possibly playing some venues in west coast cities. However, upon revisiting **100 MONSTERS**, which is based on mythical creatures and religious beliefs that are so distinctively Japanese in origin, I find it hard to believe that it would have found its way into many outside markets. Unlike the *Majin* trilogy, all of which were dubbed into English, it appears (?) as though none of the *YM* entries ever were given the same treatment.

YOKAI MONSTERS 2:
SPOOK WARFARE
(妖怪大戦争 / *Yōkai daisensō*; a.k.a. **BIG MONSTER WAR; GHOSTS ON PARADE**)

Japan, 1968. D: Yoshiyuki Kuroda

"The struggle for the soul of one, and the fate of many!"

"If we leave the likes of him alone, shame will be brought on Japanese apparitions!"

The second *YM* film doesn't waste any time forging an emotional bond with the audience. It goes straight for the horror vein, and within its first twelve minutes or so, paints a horrific picture of rubber-suited possession and desecration of religious objects within a household controlled by a vengeful demon in human form. **SPOOK WARFARE**, starts with some brief narration, and scenes of Arabian looters raiding an ancient Babylonian (Iraqi) tomb beneath what looks like a decaying statue of Ishtar, the goddess of love, power, fertility, sex and war. A sinisterly-adorned, magical staff is unburied by one of the thieves, and this discovery brings on a violent seismic upheaval. As the two looters hurriedly make their way out of the crypt, the skies turn an ominous black, torn by lightning, then, at the opening of the passageway into the crypt, a shimmering mist appears floating in the air, whereupon a monstrous green-faced demon materializes before the men. With a flick of its staff, this mon-

Above & Next Page: Alternate Japanese poster designs for **100 MONSTERS** (1968). How many different *yōkai* can you identify?

ster brings down a wall of stone atop the men, crushing the life out of them (such ingratitude after they have brought about the creature's resurrection!). Daimon (from the Greek, δαίμων; a variation of "daemon"), as this demon is called, takes to the skies on bat-like wings and makes his way to Japan. The incoming foreign creature stops at a small village, where it attacks a beloved, fair-minded local magistrate named Lord Hyogo Isobe (Takashi Kanda, from *YM* #1, **100 MONSTERS**), sucking his blood in horrifying style and using his dead body as an earthly vessel so as to freely move around unnoticed by the general populace.

Upon returning to his home after being 'turned', the Lord—or rather Daimon, using his victim's body as a disguise—is met by his worried daughter Lady Chie (Akane Kawasaki), his trusted aide Shinhachiro Mayama (Yoshihiko Aoyama) and the family dog. When Hyogo crosses and pauses upon the small bridge in front of his home, his dog, sensing something is amiss, barks at its master, so, prior to entering the house, Lord Hyogo/Daimon kills the poor animal with a speedy slash of his *katana* ("sword"). To me, this scene resembled (albeit on a smaller scale) the homecoming scene in the "I Wurdalak" segment of the Mario Bava horror classic **BLACK SABBATH** (*I tre volti della paura*, 1963, Italy/France/USA), wherein the vampiristic patriarch Gorca (Boris Karloff) returns home to his family, is likewise

not recognized by his pet canine, so has his son kill the animal on his behalf. Both scenes have a similar sense of impending doom, and there are other similarities besides.

In **SPOOK WARFARE**, much as the dog had done, a canny *kappa* water imp (Gen Kuroki) that dwells in the pond of the house's courtyard sees through the interloper Daimon's human façade and attempts—unsuccessfully at first—to convince his fellow *yōkai* from elsewhere in the vicinity to believe his story that the formerly benevolent Lord Hyogo is now host to a vindictive bloodsucking demon (considering that they are themselves supernatural beings, it seems a tad odd that they're so skeptical of the existence of another such being). The *kappa* is vindicated in the eyes of his initially disbelieving fellows when a couple of kids, a brother and sister, while trying to evade the goons of the now-evil Hyogo after

Yokai Monsters …Heed The Spirits Or Face Their Wrath! *Mike Hauss*

Above: Japanese B2 poster for **SPOOK WARFARE** (1968)

their parents had been murdered, flee through the adjoining wooded area and find themselves at a *yōkai*-haunted Shinto shrine (their childlike purity protects them from being harmed by the resident spooks), where the children succeed in convincing the assembled *yōkai* doubters of Lord Hyogo's transformation into an inhuman despot.

Thanks to being bitten by Hyogo/Daimon, Sa- heiji Kawano (Gen Kimura), the steward of the magistrate's house, also becomes transformed into a blood-drinking demon; just as Hyogo's corpse is used as a shell for the malevolent power to dwell within, so too does another demon, a 'cloned' duplicate of the original Daimon (who consists of multiple ethereal entities contained in a single being), use Saheiji's. The *yōkai* elect to assist the humans in their patriotic battle against

Above: Japanese B2 poster for **ALONG WITH GHOSTS** (1969)

the vampire monster, as, it being a foreign entity, it will reflect badly on the local mythological characters otherwise ("We let that thing roam free, and our reputations as Japanese apparitions will be tarnished!"). It not being an indigenous supernatural species, Daimon isn't listed in either the *Apparition Social Register* or the *Japanese Apparition Picture Book*, a pair of *yōkai*-watch-

er's 'field guides' consulted by the domestic spooks in hopes of identifying the invading foreigner on their turf. Led by the globular-headed *Abura-sumashi* (油すまし / "Oil Presser") *yōkai*, the proudly nationalistic Japanese monsters prepare for battle against the dastardly middle-eastern demon. The fight will not be easy, though, as an early scene shows, when, using dark sorcery,

Yokai Monsters …Heed The Spirits Or Face Their Wrath! *Mike Hauss*

Daimon defeats a Buddhist monk (who chants the guttural prayer "*Onkirikiri basaranbatten!*" over and over again) and the *yōkai*'s initial disastrous skirmishes with the demon end in their resounding defeat.

Meanwhile, the brave samurai Shinhachiro—who happens to be the late monk's nephew—has also seen through Daimon's disguise and attempts to defeat him, but proves no match for the powerful demon...until, that is, he gorily punctures its right eye with a blessed arrow, causing the bodily form of Daimon to die. The fortuitous arrival of the replacement magistrate Iori Ohdate (Osamu Ōkawa) in his palanquin provides another handy body for Daimon to inhabit, and he promptly summarily frames and condemns Shinhachiro to death for allegedly killing the past magistrate. The local *yōkai* are at a loss how to defeat the demon but, in a last-ditch effort, they summon a whole army of spooks from all over Japan to serve as allies in the cosmic conflict and thus ultimately prove the superiority of Japanese apparitions to the world. A fierce battle royale is fought, as Daimon sends out his clones to engage the *yōkai* horde...

This second *YM* entry is more of a horror film than the first, and never really fleshes-out or builds its characters, although the *yōkai* monsters themselves are invested with at least some characterization so as to give them individual personalities. The first film founded its narrative on the put-upon people of the tenement house, but #2 opts to leave the world of the living for the

SPOOK WARFARE *sonorama*

majority of its runtime, concentrating instead on the *yōkai*-versus-Daimon conflict, which largely unfolds in the spectral dimension. All three *YM* films present distinctly different narratives, as opposed to those in the *Daimajin* trilogy, which, while beautifully done, do tend to get a bit repetitive plot-wise and follow much the same basic dramatic structure (i.e., oppression of the poor peons, their prayers for salvation and the title character's retributory ass-stomping of their oppressors). **100 MONSTERS** (*YM* #1) doesn't reach a crescendo until its finale, whereas the present film becomes a bit anticlimactic after

Japanese lobby card for
100 MONSTERS

the dizzyingly spooky opening twelve minutes, in which the Daimon creature is introduced and proceeds to take the magistrate's life and possess his dead body. Frighteningly enough, children are used for food by its evil monster, who, after whetting his appetite with a few adult kills decides he would like to take the blood of some tender younglings, so has his goons secure some by raiding serfs' homes.

Power to the creators of this film for opting to bring an outside entity into the Japanese mythology framework, which makes for an interestingly fresh tensile dynamic. The *yōkai* are given way more screen-time in this film than in the previous one. Presented as creatures who actively—and understandably—shun mankind, they are drawn into the fray for the common good (i.e., of both Japan's apparitions and its human population), and ridding their traditional territory of Daimon becomes a point of national pride for them. The yokai's collective 'xenophobia' towards the encroaching Babylonian demon might be interpreted to symbolically represent Japan's lingering post-WW2 paranoia about potential invasion and defeat by an outside power, although that might be reading too much into things.

In **100 MONSTERS**, the Yokai never openly associate with humans, preferring instead to remain ghostly apparitions. Relentless in their spooking, in this form they torment and drive the guilty persons they haunt to the point of madness… and beyond. In **SPOOK WARFARE**, the *yōkai* do interact with humans, and even need a human's help to release some of their kind who have become accidentally trapped and sealed inside an earthenware urn by a stray paper prayer (*à la* the kind later used with such aplomb by so many Daoist priests in Hong Kong/Taiwanese horror fantasies of the '80s). The *yōkai* and mortals are forced by circumstance to work together in **SPOOK WARFARE**, whereas in **100 MONSTERS** they worked independently of—if not entirely indifferent to—human beings.

Part bat, part reptile and part arthropod, the Daimon character is a wonderful design, and the vampire/demon angle is inventively realized. The *yōkai* are led by the aforementioned *Abura-sumashi*, who—despite his top-heavy big, round head—rather reminded me of Yoda from the *Star Wars* movies, as he is among the more thoughtful and intelligent of the many and variegated types of *yōkai* shown herein. He is assisted by other diverse specimens of his kindred, including, if not limited to: *Yujin ungaikyō*, a deep-voiced, pot-bellied ursine creature who can project images of events on his huge, inflatable gut (crystal ball-style), another *rokurokubi* (Ikuko Mōri), who at one point has her elongated extendable neck tied in a knot by Daimon, and a comically cute-but-useless *karakasa* parasol critter. Without doubt, the stars of this film are the *yōkai* and the Daimon character. The human actors are all fine in their parts, but their characters' development comes second to that of the otherworldly beings. Thus the humans' plight, while also an integral part of the narrative, is ultimately abandoned in favor of highlighting the *yōkai*'s contributions (it isn't called **SPOOK WARFARE** for nothing!), especially in their display of the Japanese apparitions' combined might when they band together in single-minded solidarity to trounce the green-skinned menace from abroad.

Chikara Hashimoto plays the part of the rubber-suited Daimon, and he also played Majin, the stone god brought to life, in all three of the *Daimajin* films. Hashimoto is probably best-known for playing the over-the-top villain who battles the great Bruce Lee in the 1972 Hong Kong 'fu flick **THE CHINESE CONNECTION** (精武門 / *Jing wu men*, D: Wei Lo). The benevolent Lord Hyogo Isobe was played by the great Takashi Kanda, fresh from his villainous role as the gluttonously greedy Reimon Tajimaya in *YM* #1 (more of his credits are listed above under the **100 MONSTERS** entry). Yosihiko Aoyama portrays the brave samurai protagonist Shinchiro Mayama, and the actor subsequently appeared in both the superb *kaidan-eiga* **THE**

Kappa (河童 / "river-child") Menko card

OIWA PHANTOM (お岩の亡霊 予告篇 / *Yot-suya kaidan – Oiwa no borei*, 1969, Japan, D: Kazuo Mori) and the *chanbara* actioner **ZATOI-CHI IN DESPERATION** (新座頭市物語・折れた杖 / *Shin Zatōichi monogatari: Oreta tsue*, 1972, Japan, D: Shintarō Katsu). In the original **DAIMAJIN**, Aoyama had played the part of the young Tadakiyo Hanabusa, who tries to help save his late father's village from the evil warlord Samanosuke and is saved from crucifixion by the advent of the mighty, miraculously-reanimated deity Majin.

This film was—loosely, and much more extravagantly—'remade' (or rather, entirely *reinvented*) by maverick moviemaker Takashi Miike as **THE GREAT YOKAI WAR** (2005, Japan), which was released in its homeland under the same Japanese title as **SPOOK WARFARE** (i.e., 妖怪大戦争 / *Yōkai daisensō*) *[see p.33]*.

YOKAI MONSTERS 3:
ALONG WITH GHOSTS

(東海道お化け道中 / *Tōkaidō Obake Dōchū*; a.k.a. **JOURNEY WITH GHOST ALONG YOKAIDO ROAD**) Japan, 1969. Ds: Yoshiyuki Kuroda, Kimiyoshi Yasuda

"It's never a good idea to gamble with the spirit world."

In my opinion, this film, emotionally speaking, is the strongest in the series. Its narrative is built upon the same basic lines as the first movie, but it really amps-up and emphasizes the classical horror elements even more than both the preceding *YM* entries do.

As with the third and final *Majin* outing **WRATH OF DAIMAJIN** (大魔神 逆襲 / *Daimajin gyakushū*, 1966, D: Kazuo Mori), this film places children in the lead protagonist roles, and it even sends the kids on a quest that sees them having to overcome hardships and much tribulation. In **ALONG WITH GHOSTS**, the epic journey undertaken by the seven-year-old female lead character Miyo (Masami Burukido) is not to free her father, as in **WRATH**, but to find her father, a man she has never met, as he had abandoned her as a baby. Miyo is forced to go down this figurative and literal road after her peaceful grandfather and sole custodian Jinbei (Bokuzen Hidari) is murdered by Kanzo, the leader of a group of

Top to Bottom: A string of non-consecutive screen shots from **SPOOK WARFARE**. The topmost three each depict Daimon the blood-drinking Babylonian demon, who—as per the title—engages in a battle royal with the film's fiercely patriotic *yōkai* for possession of Japan!

1969 Japanese publication hyping *YM #3*
ALONG WITH GHOSTS on its cover

bushers that those who don't heed his warnings to steer clear of Onizuka will become cursed by the spirits that dwell there and meet with a nasty end. That very night is the night that, once a year, not only the usual apparitions will gather there, but also those from deep in the mountains and swamplands, too. As Jinbei had forewarned the intruding miscreants immediately prior to being viciously cut down by Kanzo's sword, "There's an old saying which states Onizuka is a spiritual land where apparitions from all over Japan gather, because it is connected to the world where the apparitions live."

Having managed to crawl back to his hovel despite being mortally wounded, with his dying breaths Jinbei tells his granddaughter Miyo that she must go off in search of her father Touhachi. Believing that she has come into possession of the document that incriminates Kanzo, his hired goons endeavor to track down the little girl in order to get their hands on it. Along her trek, Miyo is aided by a young boy named Shinta (Pepe Hozumi), who feels pity for her and repeatedly tries to protect her from her adult pursuers, which include a shady character named Sakiichi (played by the actor known only as Mutsuhiro). On the road, the kids meet a skilled samurai named Hyakasuro (Kojiro Hongo), who becomes their protector for the duration of the narrative.

thugs, simply for being in the wrong place at the wrong time. Kanzo and his gang have chosen Onizuka, a sacred place that the old Jinbei serves as guardian over, as the ideal spot to bushwhack and assassinate the boss of the Nihei clan, who is in possession of a document which reveals all the crooked deals in which Kanzo has been involved. Jinbei duly warns the would-be am-

I would be remiss if I didn't mention that the storyline meanders at times. The emphasis of **ALONG WITH GHOSTS'** story is placed on the juvenile heroine, and the first supernatural sighting doesn't occur until shortly past the half-hour point. A crow encoiled by a snake and gnarled dead tree branches that turn into cadaverous clawed arms are just two of the horror stuff's more arresting images. This time out, the all-important *yōkai* are shown only briefly until their 'big scene' at the climax, but, their screen-time is well-utilized. Rather than being depicted as grotesquely comic, as they largely were in **SPOOK WARFARE** (*YM #2*), the *yōkai*—including a number of 'all-new' specimens not seen in the previous films—are instead used in a much more straight-faced manner, with the more frightening qualities of the scarier ones being effectively emphasized by well-placed mood lighting and shadow. While they come fewer and further between here, some of the monster scenes are among the most effective and memorable to be found in the *YM* series.

100 MONSTERS; Japanese tie-in book

At times the film's soundtrack (again by Michiaki Watanabe) has the feel of a spaghetti western to it, and even the various double-crosses and the duel between the samurai Hyakasuro and Gonkurō near to the conclusion is staged much

Yokai Monsters …Heed The Spirits Or Face Their Wrath! *Mike Hauss*

along the lines of a western standoff. This registers as a bit anticlimactic after all the continual build-up leading to it, as the two combatants' showdown is continuously put on hold until almost the end, when the *yōkai* beasties show up to steal their thunder…which is as it should be, I suppose.

Kojiro Hongo, who plays Hyakasuro, has many fine credits in his filmography, including such prime *kaijū-eiga* fare as **GAMERA VS. BARUGON** (大怪獣決闘 ガメラ対バルゴン / *Daikaijū kettō: Gamera tai Barugon*, 1966, Japan, D: Shigeo Tanaka), **GAMERA VS. GAOS** (大怪獣空中戦 ガメラ対ギャオス / *Daikaijū kūchūsen: Gamera tai Gyaosu*, 1967, Japan, D: Noriaki Yuasa), **GAMERA VS. VIRAS** (ガメラ対宇宙怪獣バイラス / *Gamera tai Uchū Kaijū Bairasu*, 1968, Japan, D: Noriaki Yuasa) and **RETURN OF DAIMAJIN** (大魔神 怒る / *Daimashin Ikaru*, 1966, Japan, D: Kenji Misumi). Bokuzen Hidari amassed many, many acting credits over the course of his career, and is most widely-known for playing Farmer Yohei in Akira Kurosawa's classic **SEVEN SAMURAI** (七人の侍 / *Shichinin no Samurai*, 1954, Japan). Pepe Hozumi, as Shinta, is probably best-remembered for appearing in the crazy *tokusatsu* sci-fi television series *The Super Robot Red Baron* (スーパーロボット レッドバロン / *Sūpā Robotto Reddo Baron*, 1973-1974, Japan, D: various) as the teenage character Daisaku Hori.

Conclusion

I invested myself deeply in all three *YM* films, and felt a great affinity with them! They present a mystical, mythical world in which the *Yokai* come vibrantly to life and help explain away some of the evils of the mundane world in which we live. The first and third entries are essentially samurai films with supernatural elements, but human drama is the main motive of their narratives. The second film is more of a full-on *kaiju* movie, and it plays-out as one along the lines of **DESTROY ALL MONSTERS** (怪獣総進撃 / *Kaijū sōshingeki*, 1968, Japan, D: Ishirō Honda) in its throwing of as many rubber-suited monsters into the action as it can possibly cram in. There is no continuing narrative between any of the *YM* entries, therefore any of them can be watched in random order, if the viewer so chooses.

This really is a great series, that sadly ended after the third instalment. There was so much more that these creatures had to offer, if only Daiei's producers would have afforded them more opportunities to work their cinematic magic!

Top to Bottom: Some of the scarier moments from **ALONG WITH GHOSTS**, which really ratchets-up the shock value, albeit showing less of its monsters overall

Above, Clockwise from Top:
Japanese newspaper *The Sun*'s
Yokai-themed issue (August
1974), art by Shigeru Mizuki;
a collectible bromide for **100
MONSTERS**; the oversized
disembodied head of the same
film's grotesque *Ōkubi* spook
terrorizes some folks out of their
wits; and a contemporaneous
SPOOK WARFARE tie-in vinyl
Ungaikyo toy. **Left**: Shigeru
Mizuki's take on the hideous
Kuchirake-onna (口裂け女 /
"Slit-mouth Woman")

[SECOND] SON OF MY MONSTER MOVIE MARATHON DIARY:
GODZILLA A GO-GO 2!

Or, how I spent Easter with monster movies and stopped worrying.

SIZE MATTERS!*

A newbie's overview of Toho's Godzilla films, Chapter II: the Hesei Era (1984-1995) and the Millennium Era (1999-2004), plus other assorted goodies!

by
Christos Mouroukis

* That is when we are talking about monster movies, because the multitude of these films forced your favorite column to a massive 10,000+ words in size this issue, and the previous one as well, and by the looks of it for every subsequent instalment too. This is also because your favorite magazine is now published more irregularly, and is extra-thick too, so naturally the Diary had to adapt and get rid of the old pint-sized 5,000-word style. And speaking of size, my wife tells me that a few inches more don't make a difference.

You-know-who does some, uh, 'exterior decorating' in **THE RETURN OF GODZILLA** (1984)

Preface

Before we proceed with our usual reviews of monster movie mayhem, allow me to speak a little bit about mainstream books, films, and television. This column *is* a forum of discussion of all things popular media, with a strong emphasis on monsters, after all…

In January 2017, I caught-up with **INFERNO** (2016, USA/Hungary, D: Ron Howard) which was much better than the two films that preceded it. I also saw executive producer Ovidio G. Assonitis' **PIRANHA PART TWO: THE SPAWNING** (1981, USA/Italy/Netherlands, D: James Cameron) featuring Lance Henriksen, and the second season of *Scream Queens* (2015-), which has to be the funniest comedy I've seen in ages (I literally had to force myself to stop laughing, in order to be able to listen to the next joke; I haven't come across such excellently-written one-liners since I-don't-know-when), and it also helps that both Jamie Lee Curtis and Emma Roberts are gorgeous beyond words. I also read Paul Auster's *The New York Trilogy,* which, although very atmospheric (in a 'neo-noir' way), was very boring indeed. And finally, I at last got around to reading quite a few of Lovecraft's short stories.[1]

In February of '17, I caught-up with Marvel's **DOCTOR STRANGE** (2016, USA, D: Scott Derrickson) which features the most impressive visual effects I've ever seen in my life; the extended cut of DC's **GREEN LANTERN** (2011, USA, D: Martin Campbell), which had me struggling to stay awake; the first (and simultaneously last!) season of the extremely boring *Limitless* (2015-2016), which I can imagine being real problematic to market to a mass audience—apparently, not too many people feel a need to see a TV series about drug addicts (although, it must be said that it is not without its merits—including the highly creative use of Black Sabbath's signature tune "Black Sabbath" [1970] to underscore the effects of psychedelic drugs, and the surprising-but-welcome use of X-Ray Spex's "Oh Bondage Up Yours!" [1977])[2]; the first—and probably *only*—season of *The Exorcist* (2016)—*Surprise!* It actually made it all the way to the end of Season Two, for a grand total of 20 episodes!—whose themes of disease, psychoanalytic issues, religious fanaticism and even feminism are brilliantly developed (and besides that, the end product is *very* scary indeed; possibly the only truly frightening series I've seen in ages); and the third season of *From Dusk Till Dawn: The Series* (2014-), in which many heads are blown-off amidst a lot of monster action that includes female vampires and other assorted abnormal beauties. I also read Gaston Leroux's *The Mystery of the Yellow Room* (*Le mystère de la chambre jaune*, 1907) and Wes Craven's *The Fountain Society* (1999), but both failed to keep my interest until the end. Other books I had the pleasure of reading recently include Patrick Modiano's *La Petite Bijou* (2001), Stephen King's *Carrie* (1974) and *'Salem's Lot* (1975), and Jay Bonansinga's *The Walking Dead: Search and Destroy* (2016). But the most interesting book I've read recently was by far Sasha Grey's *The Juliette Society, Book II: The Janus Chamber* (2016), which is a story about nothing, but is filled with endless Face-book status-like rants that give a new meaning to the word 'philosophy'.

In March 2017, I read Clive Barker's *Cabal* (1988). I also caught up with the unaired pilot episode of *Wonder Woman* (2011), which was as awful as I was expecting it to be (albeit in a very charming 'Roger Corman'-ish kinda way), but there was something sinfully great about seeing Adrianne Palicki in leather baring her deep cleavage; watched **BAD SANTA 2** (2016, USA, D: Mark Waters) which might not be as funny as the original (which is my *favorite* Christmas movie, by the way) but it is equally depressing, and therefore refreshing; struggled to stay awake through **ROGUE ONE** (2016, USA, D: Gareth Edwards), although the female lead (Felicity Jones) was outstandingly beautiful and somehow charismatic; and fell asleep during **THE GREEN HORNET** (2011, USA, D: Michel Gondry), although some of the dialogues in that one are really well-written.

But enough with that; I know that you are here for the *monsters*, so, without further ado, here's The Diary (Part 6) of those that have haunted me recently...

Introduction:
"Gee for God, Zee for Zilla"

THE RETURN OF GODZILLA (ゴジラ / *Gojira*, 1984, Japan, D: Koji Hashimoto), first instalment in The Big G's Hesei Era (1984-1995), ignores all of the previous sequels and works as a straight follow-up to the original (**GODZILLA** [ゴジラ / *Gojira*, 1954, Japan, D: Ishirō Honda]; see *Monster!* #33, p.210). Also, that first instalment's eventual sequels are set during the same lifetime, and make sense continuity-wise. What also makes sense is the introduction of several theories (as discussed by the performers on-screen) in regards to the monster's origins, as the audience had since matured; it seems as if Toho intended targeting the same people who were watching the old films, but by now were grown-ups. Original special effects director Teruyoshi Nakano was brought onboard for the initial movie, but was replaced for all the others by Koichi Kawakita. The Godzilla suit was always worn by Kenpachiro Satsuma.

The Millennium Era (1999-2004) films are mostly known for having little-to-no connection to any of the past films, and each instalment works on its own as a separate, stand alone story.

---

1   These would be "The Tomb" (1917), "Dagon" (1917), "The Transition of Juan Romero" (1919), "Beyond the Wall of Sleep" (1919), "The Statement of Randolph Carter" (1919), "The Nameless City" (1921), "Herbert West: Reanimator" (1922), "Hypnos" (1922), and "He" (1925).

2   Coincidentally, I recently read Steve Jones' autobiography *Lonely Boy: Tales from a Sex Pistol*, in which he made a point of explaining how pills helped him better focus on learning how to play the guitar. So much for rock stars regretting their drug abuse in their post-rehab days and trying to school everyone onto the right path, huh?!

THE RETURN OF GODZILLA
(ゴジラ / *Gojira*; a.k.a. **GODZILLA 1984**)

Japan, 1984. Director: Koji Hashimoto

Ad-lines: *"There goes the neighborhood."* – *"The Legend Is Reborn."*

In what is possibly the greatest introductory montage of scenes in Toho's history, we see volcanic action on Daikoku Island, and when reporter Goro Maki (Ken Tanaka) approaches the area in order to investigate, he is attacked by a gigantic sea-louse, only to be saved at the last moment by Hiroshi Okumura (Shin Takuma, mostly known for his TV work).

Back in Tokyo, by looking at some pictures the aforementioned duo realize that, aside from the sea-louse, the volcanic site also coughed-up the new Godzilla and, although the reporter wants to go public with the information, the Japanese authorities withhold his article. However, they are forced to reveal their secret after a Soviet ship is destroyed by Godzilla, leading the communist top brass to suspect that the Unites States was behind the attack, an event that almost started a nuclear war (the drastic measure of using nuclear weapons against Godzilla is even discussed by

Japanese B2 poster for **THE RETURN OF GODZILLA** (art by Noriyoshi Ohrai)

leaders, who seemingly don't much care about the consequences to the human population).

Godzilla eventually approaches Tokyo and havoc is wreaked, but the Japanese authorities have their recently-invented super-weapon "Super X" to defend themselves with—but will this be enough, and what will be left of the miniature buildings in the aftermath…?

Following the box-office failure of its last few *Godzilla* entries (see previous issue), Japanese production and distribution house Toho kept looking for the proper way to revive the series. The three such cases that went to press (meaning the projects were actually announced officially) were THE REBIRTH OF GODZILLA (which would be a remake of **GODZILLA** '54), GODZILLA VS. THE DEVIL and GODZILLA VS. GARGANTUA (in these two last cases Hollywood's UPA studios were also supposed to be involved in a co-producer capacity). Coincidentally, in 1979, on Godzilla's 25ᵗʰ Anniversary, Pennsylvania's Three Mile Island accident occurred. The most famous nuclear incident ever to occur on US shores, it made the return of Godzilla seem as relevant as ever, especially presented in a darker tone that would take the mighty monster back to its roots. Akira Murao (of **BRUTAL TALES OF CHIVALRY** [昭和残侠伝 / *Shōwa zankyō-den*, 1965, Japan, D: Kiyoshi Saeki]) wrote a story called *The Return of Godzilla*, but it wasn't realized onscreen. A few years later in the early '80s, as was famously reported by *Fangoria* and other periodicals in the fandom press, Toho started working on a new project in collaboration with writer Fred Dekker (future director of **NIGHT OF THE CREEPS** [1986, USA]) and director Steve Miner (who was fresh off the massive successes of the first two entries in the *Friday the 13ᵗʰ* movie series), but the proposed project was ultimately abandoned due to prohibitive production costs. Finally, the screenplay by Hideichi Nagahara (who is perhaps better-known for penning the yakuza drama **A COLT IS MY PASSPORT** [拳銃は俺のパスポート / *Koruto wa ore no pasupōto*, 1967, Japan, D: Takashi Nomura]) included bits and pieces from some of the aforementioned aborted attempts, but mainly focused on its clear message regarding the very real threat of all-out Atomic Armageddon.

What were the results, you ask? Well, for one thing, director Koji Hashimoto (who was assistant director on some of the entries in the original *G* series) delivered a film that is genuinely scary—and actually very serious overall—which was apparently what the franchise needed (To-

In **GvB** (1989), Biollante, one of the most spectacular monsters ever, literally dwarfs The Big G!

ho's failure to realize that long ago, when, instead of producing serious films, it instead delivered cutesy kiddie product for US TV, is beyond me. Also, everything herein is very '1980s' in style/tone, and this includes the cinematography by Kazutami Hara. Also, since you are probably mainly here for the special effects and the monster, rest assured that the work of Teruyoshi Nakano (returning from the originals) is totally state-of-the-art, and the most astonishing events actually look believable thanks to it. On a final note I should add that bringing composer Reijiro Koroku onboard made a world of difference, as his soundtrack is so bombastically over-the-top that it is actually my favorite of the series. So, you bet your ass I recommend this highly!

Produced by Kiyomi Kanazawa (**LESSON OF THE EVIL** [悪の教典 / *Aku no kyōten*, 2012, Japan, D: Takashi Miike]) and Norio Hayashi (**SUGIHARA: CONSPIRACY OF KINDNESS** [杉原千畝, 2000, USA/Japan, D: Robert Kirk]) on a $6.25 million budget, it grossed $11-million domestically. I had the pleasure of watching the original Japanese version (with English subtitles) in a gorgeous color, 1.85:1 print (this was the first *Godzilla* number to utilize this format, and the subsequent ones followed suit), but many US monster kids caught up with it via **GODZILLA 1985**, the heavily-altered Anglo theatrical reedit released by Roger Corman's New World Pictures which also included insert footage starring Raymond Burr (returning from

the original messed-about-with version, retitled **GODZILLA, KING OF THE MONSTERS**, Embassy Pictures' widely-seen 1956 stateside import version of the '54 Japanese originator).

Saturday, January 21st, 2017

GODZILLA VS. BIOLLANTE
(ゴジラvsビオランテ / *Gojira tai Biorante*)

Japan, 1989. D: Kazuki Ohmori

Ad-lines: *"The Super-Beast Battle of the Century"* – *"The most terrifying monster of all time is back in his greatest movie ever"* – *"The ultimate battle has only just begun."*

This movie continues on from where the previous one ended, and Godzilla's cells are studied by Saradia's top scientists in hopes of turning infertile ground into thriving farmlands, and boost the economy as a result. However, terrorists foil their lofty plans by destroying the project.

Fast-forward to five years later… The Japanese authorities are studying Godzilla cells in order to create a weapon they can deploy in case the monster ever returns (doesn't it *always*, after all?!). Following a series of interrelated events, we are also introduced to the other titular monster, Biollante—whose design, in all honesty, is *amazing* beyond words (just check out the pictures my dear editors have included). Eventually, Godzilla is unleashed as well, and, as per the title's promise, the duo battle it out in a lake. This particular sequence is among my favorites in the entire franchise. The battle will (*natch!*) end with Godzilla as the winner, but the duo will have an extra—this time final—duel at the end of the movie, at the Osaka Mountains. The question is obvious: which monster will win…?

Due to the previous film's only modest success, executive producer Tomoyuki Tanaka was hesitant about moving forward with the series, so he held a competition, in which people would come up with a scenario in which Godzilla would fight another monster. Among the around 5,000 submissions received, it was Shinichirō Kobayashi's story that won, and it was turned into a screenplay by director Kazuki Ohmori. The rest, as they say, is history, be-cause this is widely-accepted by fans as *the best* Godzilla film (although opinions were sorely divided upon its initial release). This was, after all, 1989, at the very height of special-effects driven cinema, and any monster movie with SFX of the caliber presented here was destined to become a classic. Simply put, the visuals are *breathtaking*! It amazes me that upon its original release **GvB** flopped at the Japanese B.O., and it went straight-to-video in the US (amidst much legal chaos with its distributors, Miramax) rather than securing a well-deserved theatrical release.

On a final note, the bombastic score by Kōichi Sugiyama does wonders here, but the show is really stolen by the reworkings of Akira Ifukube's classic original theme. You should watch this *immediately* (many times over), if you haven't already done so… no ifs, ands or buts about it!

Taiwanese newspaper ad for **GODZILLA VS. BIOLLANTE**

GODZILLA VS. KING GHIDORAH

(ゴジラvsキングギドラ / *Gojira tai Kingu Gidora*)

Japan, 1991. D: Kazuki Ohmori

Writer Kenichiro Terasawa (Kosuke Toyohara, from the Steven Seagal vehicle **INTO THE SUN** [2005, USA, D: mink]) is a failure, but he has high hopes for his new project, namely a *Godzilla* story. During his research, he discovers that, in 1944, a patriotic monster saved Japanese soldiers from the hands of the Americans, and he believes that this particular monster might have turned into the Godzilla we all came to know in the same-titled original '54 film (reviewed last issue by yours truly, in Part 1 of this very column [p.210]).

It's not too long before a UFO lands in Japan (resulting in some pricelessly Ed-Woodian dialogue exchanges between cast members!), and its passengers announce that they come from the future (2204, to be precise), explaining that, in their future, Japan no longer exists, because Godzilla finally destroyed it (it's no wonder, though, considering all the times he wreaked havoc in Tokyo; he was bound to succeed eventually!). So, the plan is really simple: go back in history and alter its course. Yes, it's all very **TERMINATOR 2: JUDGMENT DAY** (1991, USA/France, D: James Cameron), and it comes complete with a lengthy chase that includes a robot that can outrun speeding cars after emerging from the flames of an exploded vehicle. But this is *not* the only American/Hollywood film reference here, as one character exclaims, "*Make my day!*" in an obvious nod to Eastwood's **DIRTY HARRY** (1971, USA, D: Don Siegel).

Anyway, back to the present film... The main characters manage to go back to the future, but they return with the second titular monster (i.e., King Ghidorah), which the people from the future control and demand that Japan surrender to them, which it does not. In the meantime, Godzilla shows up and the expected wrestling match ensues between the two monsters. Which one will win, and whose politics will prevail...?

Executive producer Tomoyuki Tanaka was disappointed by the previous instalment's

Thai poster for 1991's **GvKG**
(art by Noriyoshi Ohrai)

only modest success, and didn't go with Kazuki Ohmori's plan of kick-starting a new film series that would be about Mothra (the first film was to have been called **MOTHRA VS. BAGAN**, but it never transpired). However, **GvKG** was manufactured instead, with hopes that the highly-Americanized themes would ensure it secured overseas sales. Produced by Shogo Tomiyama on an estimated $12-million budget, it didn't manage to create too much sensation, despite the minor controversy that it caused due to its false depiction of certain events of WWII, especially at a time when political/economic tension existed between Japan and the USA.

You're here for the special effects, though, and admittedly those are more-than-decent, but the problem is that the whole thing feels very irrelevant in 1991 (if you get what I mean). Also in regards to chronology (a prevalent theme here) the cinematography by Yoshinori Sekiguchi is dully '1990s' all the way. The war scenes are well-executed, though, and Akira Ifukube's soundtrack complements the action well, as always. I wouldn't say that **GvKG** is not without its merits, but with so many other, better instalments, I would advise you to give this one a pass, unless you happen to be an absolute completist.

GODZILLA VS. MOTHRA

(ゴジラvsモスラ / *Gojira tai Mosura*; a.k.a. **GODZILLA AND MOTHRA: THE BATTLE FOR EARTH**)

Japan, 1992. D: Takao Okawara

This one starts-out as randomly as they get, with the introduction of the Indiana Jones-like char-

acter of Takuya Fujita (Tetsuya Bessho, from the infamous SF megaflop **SOLAR CRISIS** [1990, Japan/USA, D: Richard C. Sarafian]), who gets himself in all sorts of trouble, including with the law. The authorities are willing to drop the charges, but he'll have to perform some research over at Infant Island for them first. After some hesitation, and with no other option available, he does just that with his motley crew. They are

quick to discover a gigantic egg, plus the Cosmos fairy twins (this time played by Keiko Imamura and Sayaka Osawa), who explain that the egg belongs to Mothra, and that another monster called Battra (バトラ / *Batora*) may also be on the loose. Add Godzilla into the mix as well, and you have a pretty awesome three-way monster mash! Which *kaiju* will win this time around…?

Special effects director Koichi Kawakita devised a screenplay that would have Mothra and Godzilla fighting against each other (in what was essentially a comeback vehicle for the former monster) entitled GODZILLA VS. GIGAMOTH, but that idea was scrapped by Toho. Executive producer Tomoyuki Tanaka and producer Shogo Tomiyama really wanted to do one more film with King Ghidorah (it would be called "GHIDORAH'S COUNTERATTACK"), but a poll taken amongst Japanese audiences which proved that Mothra was more popular forced them to go with a film featuring that monster instead, and they went with Kazuki Ohmori's screenplay (see the previous review), but handed the directing duties to Takao Okawara. Made on an estimated $20 million, **GvM** proved to be box-office gold domestically, as it was the highest-grossing film from the Hesei Era, but, once again, it went straight-to-video in the USA.

The cinematography by Masahiro Kishimoto reminded me a lot of the later **GODZILLA** (1998, USA/Japan, D: Roland Emmerich) and, surprisingly, the overemphatic score by Akira Ifukube fit rightly with these aesthetics. The special effects are a bit too 'family-friendly' for my taste this time out, but this could well be an impression I mainly got because the screenplay brought back a lot of elements from the 1960s films.

Thursday, February 2nd, 2017

GODZILLA VS. MECHAGODZILLA II
(ゴジラvsメカゴジラ / *Gojira tai Meka-gojira*)

Japan, 1993. D: Takao Okawara

Ad-line: *"After this battle, it will all be over."*

The United Nations, in what seems to be another groundbreaking action towards world peace (yeah, *right*!) forms the United Nations Godzilla Countermeasures Centre (UNGCC), whose main task is to protect us against the ever-impending threat of Big G (the monster had been a baddie

Pages 256-257: Japanese B1 posters for **GvM** and **GvMG** (art for both by Noriyoshi Ohrai)

in the last few sequels, after all), and to do so they create an all-new Mechagodzilla, along with a super-weapon called Garuda.

Fast-forward to a couple of years later, when a gigantic egg awakens Rodan and Godzilla, and, having nothing better to do, the two monsters lock horns for a tussle. Godzilla wins, but this is not a spoiler, as it happens very early on, so it comes as no surprise. It turns out, though, that a baby *two*-brained Godzilla comes out of the egg (as opposed to the too-cutesy-poo 1960s baby Godzilla, which was a total no-brainer!), and when it is stolen by Japanese scientists, it somehow calls upon its father, who in turn comes to Japan on a destructive spree. The authorities are prepared, though, and Mechagodzilla takes action.

A final battle ensues between a returned Rodan, Godzilla, and Mechagodzilla and Garuda. Which monster will win? What will be left of the miniature sets and will the CGI appear realistic? Will Godzilla finally get to connect and bond with its double-brained monster progeny…?

You are here for the monsters and the special effects, and you can take it from me that they look *gorgeous* (so much better than the US/Hollywood competition of the era), but unfortunately everything else is so *boring* (including the screenplay by Wataru Mimura) that I caught myself falling asleep on more than one occasion whilst watching the film. It was supposed to be the last film in the franchise, both in order to honor Ishirō Honda's recent passing, and to avoid competition with the 'reboot' **GODZILLA** (1998, USA/Japan, D: Roland Emmerich), which was already in the works. Unfortunately, this proved not to be the case, and the series continued on to further lows. Toho originally wanted to pair Godzilla with King Kong (again), but failed to secure the rights of the latter monster, so therefore they settled on another Mechagodzilla outing instead. Executive producer Tomoyuki Tanaka and producer Shogo Tomiyama also arranged a lot of marketing around what would be Akira Ifukube's last collaboration with the franchise. Made on an estimated $9.5 million budget, **GvMG2** grossed more than $18 million.

Saturday, February 4th, 2017

GODZILLA VS. SPACEGODZILLA

(ゴジラvsスペースゴジラ / *Gojira tai SupēsuGojira*)

Japan, 1994. D: Kenshō Yamashita

Ad-lines: *"A Supernatural, Super-Powered Intergalactic Epic!"* – *"Can Godzilla Save Japan from Intergalactic Evil?"*

Mothra and Biollante are transporting Godzilla cells into space, but when these are exposed to a black hole, the SpaceGodzilla is born! The first thing this monster does is attack Baby Godzilla (just when you thought we were rid of this annoying imbecile, he's back again, for further 'comedy relief'!). The wrath of the real Godzilla is awakened, and a fight between the two titular creatures ensues. Actually, the two monsters have a whole *lot* of fighting to do (including an epic one in the end) this time round, and the authorities will once again be involved (including the Japanese ones, along with NASA, the United Nations Godzilla Countermeasures Center and the Mobile Operation Godzilla Expert Robot Aerotype), along with the Cosmos fairy twins (Keiko Imamura and Sayaka Osawa), and—are you ready for this?—even the local Yakuza underworld lend an assist!

Okay, the screenplay by series semi-regular Hiroshi Kashiwabara and one-timer Kanji Kashiwa may be bordering on the idiotic (it was based on an idea Toho started developing back in the late 1970s), and legend has it that the series composer Akira Ifukube refused to do the film after reading the script (although, as mentioned in the previous review, he had already decided it to call it quits by this point), and it does indeed get incredibly stupid during its desperate attempts at serious

Above: A page and the front cover from a Japanese tie-in mini-book for **GvSG** (1994) that was brought back from Tokyo for Steve Fentone back in the late '90s by his buddy Jason *"Sub-Terrenea"* Gray *[Thanks, Jase!* ☺ *– SF.]*

drama (just wait for the unintentionally hilarious romance scene by the beach, under a sunset, no less!), but this is only one of the myriad of problems with director Kenshō Yamashita's movie (he was also second unit director on **TERROR OF MECHAGODZILLA** [メカゴジラの逆襲 / *Mekagojira no Gyakushū*, 1975, Japan, D: Ishirō Honda], reviewed last issue [p.232]). Said problems include some of the very *worst* special effects (including both practical and visual) you could possibly come across in a 1990s movie. **GvSG** is not without its merits, though, as all things robotic (and there are many of those here) do look particularly amazing, including my favorite: 'killer-driller' action!

Producer Shogo Tomiyama and executive producer Tomoyuki Tanaka made this on an estimated $10.3 million budget, and it grossed a modest $20 million, despite being promoted as Godzilla's 40th Anniversary film. As per usual, it was consigned straight-to-video in the USA with little fanfare.

Monday, February 6th, 2017

GODZILLA VS. DESTOROYAH

(ゴジラvsデストロイア / *Gojira tai Desutoroia*)

Japan, 1995. D: Takao Okawara

Ad-lines: *"It's a Major Monster Meltdown!"* – *"Get Ready for a Three-Way Monster Melee!"*

Birth Island, home of Godzilla and its littl'un, appear to be destroyed. However, making for a cinematic first, Godzilla shortly wreaks havoc in Hong Kong. Scientists theorize that, due to nuclear power absorbed by the beast, it has now become a powerful potential bomb, so they acquire the assistance of something called "Super-X III" in hopes of solving the problem. Meanwhile, the ol' "Oxygen Destroyer" wakes up and creates an army of evil minions that resemble mutated crabs. The potential explosion is averted by Super-X III, and Godzilla is lured from foreign waters back to Tokyo, in order to fight with Destoroyah (a.k.a. Destroyer), the secondary titular creature. Which monster will come out on top…?

Right, Top to Bottom: A pair of action shots of its star and the Japanese B2 poster for 1995's **GODZILLA VS. DESTOROYAH** (art by Noriyoshi Ohrai). Thee Almighty Godz has seldom looked more fearsomely ferocious than he does in that topmost shot!

After the only-modest success of the last couple of films in the series, executive producer Tomoyuki Tanaka and producer Shogo Tomiyama, decided that the film under review would be the final one in the series (and it was, at least for the Hesei Era, anyway) and employed the services of screenwriter Kazuki Ohmori, whose original idea was for a film that would set the ground for the Hesei Era Godzilla to battle the one from the 1954 classic (presumably in the form of a ghost, since it is made clear here that the original beast had actually died in the original film: something which the subsequent instalments couldn't agree on). Although this plot was not used, some elements can be found in director Takao Okawara's movie. The real surprise is Akira Ifukube's return as the composer for one final time, but his soundtrack here is a far cry from his previous bombastic works. The special effects look dated even for 1995. It was made on an estimated budget of $10 million, and it grossed a modest $18 million (in the US, it went straight to video yet again). I must admit that it had me struggling to stay awake, so you might want to pass on this one, unless your sedatives don't work.

Wednesday, February 8th, 2017

GODZILLA 2000
(ゴジラ2000 ミレニアム / *Gojira Nisen: Mireniamu*)

Japan, 1999. D: Takao Okawara

Ad-lines: *"Get ready to crumble." – "Godzilla returns – destroying the city of Nemuro in Japan."*

Japan is in crisis—*again!*—as a recently discovered UFO is after important governmental documents. Godzilla (who is now green for some reason) will have none of that he fights against the aliens, but will that be enough? Don't be quick to answer, as the aliens soon manage to reform into Millennian, which later becomes Orga (オルガ / *Oruga*), a demented monster.

Written by series semi-regulars Hiroshi Kashiwabara and Wataru Mimura, Godzilla's return (on its 45th Anniversary, no less) through this first film in the Millennium era may be impressive in terms of practical effects (what little of them are actually here), but it suffers greatly from laughable CGI that actually affects viewing and turn the end result into a joke, rather than quality entertainment. Takao Okawara's direction is invisible, in a Hollywood kind of way, and that is in the film's favour, as it is in perfect tune with

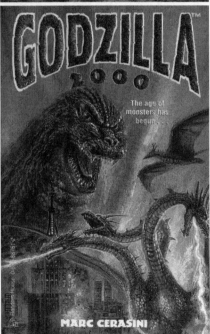

Top: US theatrical poster for **G2000** (1999); artist unknown. **Above:** This '97 Random House paperback novel, boasting dynamic cover art by Bob Eggleton, was unrelated to the later movie of the same name other than by its title

Godzilla A Go-Go: Part 2　　　　　*Christos Mouroukis*

the series' overall feel. Executive produced by Shogo Tomiyama on an estimated budget of $8.3 million, it grossed a modest $27.9 million, which was enough for the producer of the US version (which played theatrically, something that the franchise hadn't seen since 1984), Michael Schlesinger, to write a sequel called GODZILLA REBORN that he wanted Joe Dante to direct, but it failed to materialize. Five other sequels ensued, and they are each reviewed below…

Thursday, February 9th, 2017

GODZILLA VS. MEGAGUIRUS

(ゴジラ × メガギラス G消滅作戦 / *Gojira tai Megagirasu: Jī Shōmetsu Sakusen*)

Japan, 2000. D: Masaaki Tezuka

This entry kicks-off with a montage of images and narration that try to piece-together a map of the first films' timelines, yet it only manages to confuse things all the more (the most inventive aspect being that of Japan's capital city now having become Osaka!). Zoom ahead to 2001, and we are introduced to an ugly-looking egg that was deposited by a gigantic (Paleozoic Era) dragonfly through a wormhole. The egg spawns still more eggs, and a swarm of creatures called Meganulon (メガヌロン / *Meganuron*) are born, that in turn become larger creatures called Meganula (メガニューラ / *Meganyūra*). Godzilla shows up to take them on, but will he be able to win, and what will be left of the miniature buildings? The battle will be a really difficult one for your favorite monster, as we are introduced to the swarm's king, namely the gigantic Megaguirus.

Executive-produced by Shogo Tomiyama, on an estimated $8.3 million, it played theatres in Japan, but went straight to television in the US, essentially grossing a modest $10 million. Director Masaaki Tezuka's movie is letdown by laughable special effects (that often look straight out of a 1960s film—I kid you not!) and an incredibly uninteresting plot (the screenplay was written by Hiroshi Kashiwabara and Wataru Mimura) full of annoying characters. There is an outburst of violence that comes complete with a couple of gruesome deaths in the spirit of Roger Corman's dark 1980s sci-fi epics, but other than that this remains a SyFy-level affair. But (are you ready for this?!) I couldn't help but be surprised by how visually entertaining the whole thing was, and as such, it comes recommended.

Saturday, February 11th, 2017

GODZILLA, MOTHRA AND KING GHIDORAH: GIANT MONSTERS ALL-OUT ATTACK

(ゴジラ・モスラ・キングギドラ: 大怪獣総攻撃 / *Gojira, Mosura, Kingu Gidora: Daikaijū Sōkōgeki*; a.k.a. **GMK**)

Japan, 2001. D: Shūsuke Kaneko

Ad-lines: *"Who will be the last monster standing?"* – *"Battle On Fire!"*

Pretty much the same way as the previous film, this one also begins with an introduction covering Godzilla's doings in the first film (**GODZIL-**

Toxic Monsterlinity: The antsy combatants size each other up in **GODZILLA VS. MEGAGUIRUS** (2000)

Japanese BD of **G,MAKG:GMA-OA** (2001)

LA [1954]; see my review in the previous issue [p.210]), this time narrated by SDF Admiral Taizō Tachibana (Ryūdō Uzaki, from **THE LOVE SUICIDES AT SONEZAKI** [曾根崎心中 / *Sonezaki Shinjū*, 1978, Japan, D: Yasuzō Masumura]). Fast-forward to the present day (i.e., 2002), and we witness Godzilla demolishing a submarine. We are then introduced to Yuri Tachibana (Chiharu Niiyama, later seen in **THE GRUDGE 2** [呪怨2 / *Ju-on 2*, 2003, Japan, D: Takashi Shimizu]), who is the host of a *faux* 'reality' show about paranormal activities and other such happenings, including monster sightings. We are also reintroduced to the cool-looking monster Baragon (バラゴン). And you can take my word for it that the title is *not* a cheat, as Mothra is quick to show up as well (randomly attacking some youngsters, for no apparent reason). Godzilla is once again the baddie here, and the rest of the monsters appear to have formed some sort of alliance that goes by the name of "The Guardian Monsters", that protect the good people of Japan. So Mothra and Baragon fight against Godzilla, but they appear to be no match for fire-breathing legend, so King Ghidorah is also awakened, and joins the fray. Which monster/s will win and what will be left of Japan…?

The screenplay by Shūsuke Kaneko (who also directed),[3] Keiichi Hasegawa (writer of several *Ultraman* TV episodes) and Masahiro Yokotani (who also penned the same year's **OBORERU SAKANA** [溺水的鱼, 2001, Japan, D: Yukihiko Tsutsumi]) suffers from some very awkward comedy, but the state-of-the-art special effects elevate this to something more-than-decent (in comparison to the same year's CGI-heavy **JURASSIC PARK III** [2001, USA, D: Joe Johnston], which was the 'big' American monster-fest of the time, the film under review looks *so much* better). Also, the fact that Godzilla appears as menacing as he does here is quite refreshing (the film makes a point of showing us the deaths of many humans, and a number of the violent outbursts here look far too adult for a Toho film), so much so that the rest of the monsters are virtually extraneous (one character rightly exclaims that the situation has become like a "*kaiju* convention"!).

Sunday, February 12th, 2017

GODZILLA AGAINST MECHAGODZILLA
(ゴジラ×メカゴジラ / *Gojira tai Mekagojira*)

Japan, 2002. D: Masaaki Tezuka

Ad-line: *"The Battle of the Century!"*

Set in 1999, this film kicks-off with Lieutenant Akane Yashiro (Yumiko Shaku, from **THE PRINCESS BLADE** [修羅雪姫 / *Shurayuki-hime*, 2001, Japan, D: Shinsuke Sato]) losing a battle against a Godzilla descendant, and some scientific mumbo-jumbo explains to us that even the full might of Japanese firepower is useless against these superspecies, which means that Tokyo is under serious threat should the original Godzilla ever decide to make a comeback. What do they do? They create a giant robot that they name Mechagodzilla, which will now be controlled by Yashiro. A demonstration of the new robot's abilities is set for the public, and (what do you know?!) Godzilla shows up, and the two monsters—one of meat, the other of metal—fight

---

3 An earlier draft would have had Godzilla fighting against the gigantic mantis カマキラス / *Kamakirasu* a.k.a. Kamacuras (from **SON OF GODZILLA** [怪獣島の決戦 ゴジラの息子 / *Kaijū-tō no Kessen: Gojira no Musuko*, 1967, Japan, D: Jun Fukuda],which I reviewed in the previous issue [p.224]), and a later draft had Godzilla fighting against the giant 'spiny squirrel-lizard' Varan ([バラン / *Baran*] first seen way back in **VARAN THE UNBELIEVABLE** [大怪獣バラン / *Daikaijū Baran*, 1958, Japan, D: Ishirō Honda]), as well as Anguirus (アンギラス / *Angirasu*) and Baragon (バラゴン), but producer Hideyuki Honma (executive producer of **BE WITH YOU** [いま、会いにゆきます / *Ima, Ai ni Yukimasu*, 2004, Japan, D: Nobuhiro Doi]) and executive producer Shogo Tomiyama instead settled for Mothra, King Ghidorah, and Baragon (the latter being strangely absent from the title). It was made on a $9.4-million budget, and grossed a modest $20-million.

against each other. Mechagodzilla malfunctions and sows destruction in the city, in the most 'SHORT CIRCUIT' (1986, USA, D: John Badham) moment of the film. Fear not my friends, as the mega-mechanoid is repaired and sent to battle Godzilla in a second attack. Will the baddie Godzilla and its fire breath win, or will Mechagodzilla's super-weapon Absolute Zero deliver the goods and save the day...?

Series semi-regular Wataru Mimura's screenplay suffers from some exceedingly awkward comedy, but we're here for the special effects, and these look particularly amazing (especially the robotics action), so a good time is guaranteed. Series semi-regular Masaaki Tezuka's direction is invisible, as always, which is probably a good thing for such fare. This was executive-produced by Shogo Tomiyama (who also produced) and Takahide Morichi (who was production manager on **THE RETURN OF GODZILLA**, **GODZILLA VS. BIOLLANTE**, and **GODZILLA VS. MOTHRA**; all three reviewed above) on an $8.5 million budget, and it grossed a modest $16 million.

Monday, February 13th, 2017

GODZILLA: TOKYO S.O.S.
(ゴジラ×モスラ×メカゴジラ　東京SOS /
Gojira Mosura Mekagojira Tōkyō Esu Ō Esu)

Japan, 2003. D: Masaaki Tezuka

Ad-line: *"Terror Comes in Threes!"*

Set in the then-near-future (now long-past) year of 2004, this film kicks-off with the main human characters briefing us once again in regards to the events of some of the previous films. Once this is over, and following the events of **GODZILLA AGAINST MECHAGODZILLA**, we are told that the latter monster is going through repairs for the replacement of the Absolute Zero super-weapon, with a new Tri-Maser addition. The twin fairies (Masami Nagasawa and Chihiro Ohtsuka) explain that the Japanese authorities should refrain from using Godzilla's skeleton as a basis for Mechagodzilla's design, and that it should be returned to the bottom of the sea, otherwise the real Godzilla may get pissed-off again and return to stomp the shit out of Tokyo. What's more, if the monster's bones are not returned, the twins' flying monster boss Mothra will declare war on humankind. It's not too long before カメーバ / *Kamēba* a.k.a. Kamoebas is found dead (presumably killed by Godzilla?) and a battle royal between all the monsters mentioned above ensues.

Kaijū-Worthy Versus Cringe-Worthy:
The BigG goes tooth-'n'-nail to nuts-and-bolts on the cover of the Japanese DVD *[top]* for **GODZILLA AGAINST MECHAGODZILLA**. The film has everything a die-hard 'Zilla fan could need to get their fix of rompin', stompin' giant critter action—well, except for that damned horridly 'cute' baby Godzilla *[above]*, which has editor Tim P. cringing through every second of the li'l bastard's screen-time!

Japanese **G:T S.O.S.** DVD cover

Which monster will win and what will be left of the miniature buildings…?

Series semi-regular executive producer Shogo Tomiyama acquired several stories for series semi-regular director Masaaki Tezuka to choose from, but he rejected them all and proceeded to write his own screenplay with returning writer Masahiro Yokotani. The film was made on an estimated budget of $12 million. By this point the series had grown extremely tired, and the special effects were nothing to write home about, especially when compared with Hollywood product

Wanna Hug? The way-cool monster mantid of **G:FW** (2004)

from the same era. What was once-upon-a-time a series of monster spectacles that you could not see anywhere else had by this stage become decadent and formulaic (they almost seem to have no reason to exist at all in the modern world). I was struggling to stay awake, and you should definitely pass on this sad little chapter of monster movie history.

Wednesday, February 15th, 2017

GODZILLA: FINAL WARS
(ゴジラ　ファイナルウォーズ　/　*Gojira: Fainaru Wōzu*)

Japan/Australia/China, 2004. D: Ryūhei Kitamura

Set in (the not-too-distant future of) 2044, this finds a league of mutated superhumans, along with a league of extra-strong monsters (we've seen previous incarnations of most of them in the older films, but some of them are new, I think) battling against each other. The twin fairies (Masami Nagasawa and Chihiro Ohtsuka) and the aliens are also involved, in what is clearly the series' most confusing and chaotic plot. The screenplay by Ryūhei Kitamura (who also directed) and Isao Kiriyama (from Kitamura's **AZUMI** [あずみ, 2003, Japan]) is a case of 'let's chuck *everything* in, and see if it works'—or better yet, a case of 'let's throw a whole lotta shit on the wall and hope *something* sticks'—and unfortunately the end result (expectedly, I would say) is, um, problematic, to say the least. Will Godzilla, who is the hero this time around, manage to win-out against all the baddies? What do *you* think?!

The score by Nobuhiko Morino (**TERROR FIRMER** [1999, USA, D: Lloyd Kaufman]), Daisuke Yano (from Kitamura's **ALIVE** [アライヴ, 2002, Japan]), and Keith Emerson (no introduction needed), is as bombastic as they get, and sometimes it even borders on heavy metal. Fittingly, the editing by Shūichi Kakesu (who also cut together the anime **GHOST IN THE SHELL** [攻殻機動隊 / *Kōkaku kidōtai gōsuto in za sheru*, 1995, Japan, D: Mamoru Oshii]) is machine-gun like, so much so that it made me dizzy on more than a few occasions. If you like your monster movies to be extended music videos, this might be up your alley (although I doubt it, considering the amount of oldies usually reviewed in this magazine), but at over two hours long (it's the series' lengthiest instalment), I think it overstays its welcome. Executive-produced by Shogo Tomiyama on a whopping $19.5 million (the largest budget ever to be utilized by a Toho *Godzilla* feature), it grossed an embarrassing mere $12 million (the series hadn't seen such failure since 1975), becoming one of the long-running franchise's greatest flops; essentially putting an end to it, until the recent **GODZILLA RESURGENCE** (シン・ゴジラ / *Shin Gojira*, 2016, Japan, Ds: Hideaki Anno, Shinji Higuchi), which I shall be reviewing for this column in the very near future (see below).

Thursday, February 23rd, 2017

OUIJA: ORIGIN OF EVIL

Japan/USA 2016. D: Mike Flanagan

Ad-lines: *"When you talk to the other side, you never know who will be listening." – "No telling what you'll see."*

Korean poster

Set in Los Angeles (or the City of Angels, if you will, as it is appropriate in this context), in 1967, this is about con-artist Alice Zander (ultra-sexy M.I.L.F. Elizabeth Reaser, from **YOUNG ADULT** [2011, USA, D: Jason Reitman]) who makes her dough by staging phony séances, and manages to provide her daughters Lina (Annalise Basso from **OCULUS** [2013, USA, D: Mike Flanagan]) and Doris (Lulu Wilson from **DELIVER US FROM EVIL** [2014, USA, D: Scott Derrickson]) with a decent living. Problem is, the kids acquire a Ouija board (made by Hasbro, on whose game this franchise was based) which conjures-up a spirit called Marcus, that is quick to possess Doris. More strange events occur, including the random appearance of some much-needed cash and implications that the family can now communicate with Alice's dead husband. Soon the family acquires the help of Father Tom Hogan (Henry Thomas from **GANGS OF NEW YORK** [2002, USA/Italy, D: Martin Scorsese]). A lot of in-fighting between people, possessed humans and outright evil spirits will ensue, the latter depicted by terrible CGI that is supposed to look scary (the main attraction monster ghost looks particularly amusing and non-menacing, and although some sort of explanation is given at the end, you should wait until a post-credits sequence which connects this with another film by producer Jason Blum[4] (I can't tell

you any more, because I don't want to spoil anything in case you decide you'd like to see this).

I admit that I fell asleep during my viewing of the earlier film **OUIJA** (2014, Japan/USA, D: Stiles White), which is one of *the worst* ghost films of recent times, but I did not learn my lesson and came back for more, mainly because 'the horror critics' convinced me that this sequel is better than the first. Yes, that is absolutely right, but I don't think editor and director Mike Flanagan[5] had to put in too much effort to manage that feat. The production design by Patricio M. Farrell (art director of **BATMAN V SUPERMAN: DAWN OF JUSTICE** [2016, USA, D: Zack Snyder]) is top-notch, as this is a convincing period piece (e.g., attention to 'retro' detail includes the Universal logo at the beginning being the same one the company was using back in the 1960s), and

(**THE AMITYVILLE HORROR** [2005, USA, D: Andrew Douglas]; check out my article on the *Amityville* movies over at *Weng's Chop*), Brian Goldner (**JEM AND THE HOLOGRAMS** [2015, USA, D: Jon M. Chu]), and Michael Bay (no introduction needed!). It was co-produced by Phillip Dawe (postproduction executive on **UNFRIENDED** [2014, USA, D: Levan Gabriadze]) and executive-produced by Jeanette Brill (**THE TOWN THAT DREADED SUNDOWN** [2014, USA, D: Alfonso Gomez-Rejon]), Victor Ho (unit production manager of **THE NEON DEMON** [2016, USA/Denmark/France, D: Nicolas Winding Refn]), Trevor Macy (**THE STRANGERS** [2008, USA, D: Bryan Bertino]), and Couper Samuelson (**THE PURGE: ELECTION YEAR** [2016, USA/France, D: James DeMonaco]).

---

4   The other credited producers are Stephen Davis (**MY LITTLE PONY: THE MOVIE** [2017, USA/Canada, D: Jayson Thiessen]), Andrew Form and Bradley Fuller

5   Flanagan co-penned the screenplay with Jeff Howard (**BEFORE I WAKE** [2016, USA, D: Mike Flanagan]).

RESIDENT EVIL:
THE FINAL CHAPTER

USA/Germany/France/UK/Japan/Canada/
South Africa/Australia 2016. D: Paul W.S.
Anderson

Ad-lines: *"The journey ends." – "It ends where it began." – "Everything has led to this." – "Back to the Hive." – "Evil will end." – "Evil comes home." – "My name is Alice. This is the end of my story." – "Fight to survive." – "Finish the fight."*

although this was shot by cinematographer Michael Fimognari (**THE LAZARUS EFFECT** [2015, USA, D: David Gelb]) on video (although highly cinematic Alexa cameras were utilized), it doesn't look like it, but is that enough? I don't think so, but it grossed $81.7 million on a $9-million budget, so maybe I don't know jackshit about modern US ghost movies. There were some cool scenes in the trailer that didn't make it into the film, and famously so did loads of other material (the director went on record admitting the existence of an original cut that ran up to 40 minutes longer), and I can't help but think that maybe if we could see that, things would be better… then again, maybe *not*.

As always happens with this linear series, this film takes up immediately after where the previous instalment (**RESIDENT EVIL: RETRIBUTION** [2012, Germany/Canada/USA/France/ UK, D: Paul W.S. Anderson]) left off. **RE:TFC** finds Alice (the ever-returning Milla Jovovich, who, although no longer as young as she was, still looks gorgeous) somewhere near the destroyed White House, where she is digitally approached by her young self, the Red Queen (a debuting Ever Anderson), who tells her that she should go back to Raccoon City's Hive in order to find the evil Umbrella Corporation's vaccine elixir that has the ability—with just one drop, no less!—to kill-off all the zombies that have been walking the earth since the first film (that would be **RESIDENT EVIL** [2002, UK/Germany/ France/USA, D: Paul W.S. Anderson], which was made 15 years ago. My, how time flies!).

On her way to the Hive, Alice is stopped first by the evil Dr. Isaacs (Iain Glen, from **RESIDENT EVIL: EXTINCTION** [2007, France/Australia/ Germany/UK/USA/Canada, D: Russell Mulcahy]) and then by a group that survived the extinction of Arcadia. She escapes from the first baddie and joins forces with the latter group of survivors, to the extent that they will even fight against a zombie horde together. What's more, the group soon becomes the target of monster dogs as well. One great thing about this series is that we don't only get human zombies, but those of several other species as well, including canines, plus also several flying creatures that resemble mythical dragons from hell on acid.

Not too long after, when Alice is at the Hive, the Red Queen (via interactive video transmission, once again) tells her the backstory we've all wanted to hear since day one, and which was the well-hidden secret that made us stick with the

Defacement? An ugly-mug from **RE:TFC** (2016)

Godzilla A Go-Go: Part 2   *Christos Mouroukis*

series for a decade-and-a-half. I won't spoil it for you, but the explanation has a lot to do with modern Christian fundamentalist lunacy, which for once comes across as quite clever. What doesn't come across nicely though is the usual 'the rich are evil, the poor should resist' preaching, which although it is often correct, I couldn't help but think that this was a film that was made by the rich,[6] aimed at the privileged brats who frequent the multiplexes and can afford to play inflated prices for theater tickets, so isn't the whole thing just a bit hypocritical?

Once inside the Hive, Alice has to deal with a variety of booby traps, but unfortunately most of them look like upgraded ideas from **CUBE** (1997, Canada, D: Vincenzo Natali), only much less inspired. But anyway, will Alice manage to acquire the antivirus and save the world, or will the evil corporation win? It's badass female protagonist with guns against hordes of zombies and CGI, and you've seen it all before, but this time it's bigger and better, so why not give it a spin!

Although this comes with *tons* of digital FX (a staple for the series, really), it should be mentioned that a lot of the impressive stunts were done on set while on location in South Africa,

where unfortunately one stunt-woman (Olivia Jackson, who had also worked on **GUARDIANS OF THE GALAXY** [2014, USA/UK, D: James Gunn]) went into a coma after an accident and had to have a limb amputated, while a crew member (Ricardo Cornelius) died at the hospital following another accident.

Co-written by Paul W.S. Anderson (who also directed, of course, and also co-produced with Jeremy Bolt {**RESIDENT EVIL: APOCALYPSE** [2004, Germany/France/UK/USA/Canada, D: Alexander Witt]}, Samuel Hadida {**TRUE ROMANCE** [1993, USA/France, D: Tony Scott]} and Robert Kulzer {**RESIDENT EVIL: AFTERLIFE** [2010, Germany/France/USA/UK/Canada, D: Paul W.S. Anderson]}[7]), one thing that surprised me about this film, is that the screenplay doesn't follow the usual structural Hollywood approach, and goes off on a trip all its own. This is because the series is based on the same-titled video games, and the director does everything in his power for his movie to resemble one, but the fact that the story is anything but a traditionally-told Hollywood-style one surprised me in a positive way. Not that I like video games, but considering that even video games now follow the usual three-act baby-food approach, this

---

6 It was released by Sony in several territories. It was made on a $40-million budget. It grossed more than $307 million, which makes it the series' highest-grossing opus yet, so, although this is supposed to be a final chapter, the ending is left open, and, as of this writing, a TV series was in the negotiation stage.

7 It was executive-produced by Victor Hadida (**SILENT HILL** [2006, Canada/France/Japan, D: Christophe Gans]) and Martin Moszkowicz (**PERFUME: THE STORY OF A MURDERER** [2006, Germany/France/Spain/USA, D: Tom Tykwer]), and associate-produced by Bernhard Thür (**THE MORTAL INSTRUMENTS: CITY OF BONES** [2013, USA/Germany/Canada, D: Harald Zwart]).

It's Milla vs. Monsta—*again!*— in RE:TFC

can be considered somewhat innovative and daring. Although with the millions the series pulled in, I don't think that it would be difficult for Mr. Anderson to convince the suits to spring for pretty much anything he could think of, project-wise. One thing I could live without, though, is his **MAD MAX: FURY ROAD** (2015, Australia/USA, D: George Miller) approach to directing car chases, but I think that Oscar-winning extravaganza has set the template for what we'll be seeing for the next ten years at least, so I should probably learn to live with that. One thing I don't want to learn to live with is Anderson's obsessive use of hand-held camerawork, which may work wonders for young kids and may be essential for their short attention span generation, but it kept me feeling dizzy throughout.

Saturday, April 8th, 2017

GODZILLA RESURGENCE
(シン・ゴジラ / *Shin Gojira*; a.k.a. **SHIN GODZILLA**)[8]

Japan 2016. Ds: Hideaki Anno, Shinji Higuchi

Ad-line: *"A god incarnate. A city doomed."*

After a series of events of unexplained destruction in the broader Tokyo area, the authorities rightly believe that they have another in a long line of monsters to deal with, and soon, in the era of quickly-spread information, instant messaging, cell-cam video and photographs, this will indeed prove to be true, thanks to documentation that leaves no doubt. Further proof, this time of the scientific kind, confirms that the creature is in possession of nuclear powers, and it's not long before we learn that it is actually… *Godzilla!* Japanese leaders seem to be unable to deal with the gigantic creature's bad intentions for destroying Tokyo, and the help of the ever-reliable US forces is acquired in exchange for permission to study the beast if it is captured. The plan is really simple: will the humans be able to freeze Godzilla, or will the monster keep on destroying buildings and cars, as always…?

Speaking of cars, you will see a *lot* of these flying when the monster attacks, and you will also see many buildings getting destroyed, and for a (most welcome) change in the franchise, everything looks very convincing here (it's as if CGI were perfected with this film), much more so than in recent similar American films. Also, Godzilla itself looks better than ever, much more menacing than usual. This is *the best* Godzilla film of the last twenty years, but be aware that it is *not* the masterpiece that many claim will change the history of monster movies. What distinguishes it from the previous sequels is that most of the dialogue in Hideaki Anno's script (he also directed, with Shinji Higuchi) sounds totally 'scientific' and believable (I caught myself thinking that it all makes sense somehow), whereas in the last few movies even kids could tell that the actors were only spouting empty mumbo-jumbo. The top-notch cinematography by Kosuke Yamada makes this the most cinematic entry since the original, and I can see the great potential that this film has in turning young kids into monster movie fans. The original soundtrack by Shiro Sagisu reuses numerous elements from the first film's iconic score, but it stands well on its own as well and handles its high-flown nature particularly well, with real elegance.

Although there is no relation between this film and the timeline of Legendary Studio's Monsterverse **GODZILLA** (2014, USA/Japan, D: Gareth Edwards), it was that film's box-office success that inspired the business idea behind making the film under review (whose story and scenes of destruction were in turn inspired by recent real-world disastrous events, such as the tsunami). Produced by Yoshihiro Satō (**ATTACK ON TITAN II: END OF THE WORLD** [進撃の巨人 / *Shingeki no Kyojin*, 2015, Japan, D: Shinji Higuchi]), Taichi Ueda (**THE ETERNAL ZERO** [永遠の0 / *Eien no Zero*, 2013, Japan, D: Takashi Yamazaki]), Kazutoshi Wadakura (**THE WOLVERINE** [2013, USA/UK/Australia/Japan, D: James Mangold]) and Masaya Shibusawa,[9] on a $15-million budget, Toho went to great lengths in promoting this, and aside from the usual teasers such as trailers and posters it even included the creation of an actual theme park as a tie-in. They were right to do so, as the film enjoyed a lengthy worldwide release (both theatrically and on home video) and it ended up grossing almost $80 million, so therefore you

---

8　This is a capsule 700-word review by Yours Truly for the purposes of rounding-out the present article and being more thorough by bringing things as up-to-date as possible. For a more in-depth and analytical study of the film, please refer to my colleague Stephen R. Bissette's much lengthier article in *Monster!* #31 (pp.91-99), which I promise you will enjoy.

9　It was executive-produced by Akihiro Yamauchi (**DETROIT METAL CITY** [2008, Japan, D: Toshio Lee]), whilst Kensei Mori (Production Manager of **ZATOICHI** [座頭市 / *Zatōichi*, 2003, Japan, D: Takeshi Kitano]) is credited as the line producer, and Minami Ichikawa (producer of **13 ASSASSINS** [十三人の刺客 / *Jūsannin no Shikaku*, 2010, Japan/UK, D: Takashi Miike]) is credited as the chief producer.

The Great Profile: *Who says you can't teach old monsters new tricks?!* Everyone's favorite *kaiju* city-stomper got a drastic makeover and a fresh start yet again for his umpteenth comeback/reboot

should expect more of the same in future. However, the success was not strictly in numbers, ticket sales, clever merchandising and business planning, as the film was enjoyed as much by both old and new fans, and critics alike, and went as far as winning awards right, left and center. If *that's* not the most successful monster comeback in recent times, I don't know what could be!

Thursday, April 27th, 2017

INDEPENDENCE DAY: RESURGENCE
USA, 2016. D: Roland Emmerich

Ad-lines: *"They messed with the wrong planet"* – *"We always knew they'd come back"* – *"20 Years Of Evolution"*

Set exactly twenty years after the events (i.e., indescribable alien invasion) of the original film **INDEPENDENCE DAY** (1996, USA, D: Roland Emmerich]), it seems that now the powers-that-be (read: the United States Government) stands prepared, should the aliens ever feel like attacking us again. The problem is that alien leftovers from the first attack have sent signals back to their base, asking for revenge against we Earthlings. Now we'll see if we really *are* prepared! Fear not, my friends, after making a brief appearance, the aliens are made short work of by the humans. It's not long before we realize that

the defeated aliens were mere soldiers, however, and we now have to deal with a gigantic space-ship that begins destroying Earth at incredible speed. Are we going to survive this second and greatest attack, or is our dear home planet and all humanity doomed…?

This is one of those films which you just stare at and wonder how far CGI technology has gone, as visually it is indeed impressive. However, cinema is not only about how impressive your special effects are, and there needs to be a story as well (*usually*, at least), and the screenplay[10] here is a disaster. It works as a warning of the danger of the 'alien' (read: refugee), whilst the natives are presented as heroes. When the alien invasion stops at the White House, you will be absolutely sure that this is indeed a Republican manifesto. *["A Republican manifesto"? Out of modern Hollywood?! How rare is that?! – SF.]* There is nothing wrong for films to express views from either side of the coin, but what we have here is a naïve set of views that resembles the innocence of the 1950s sci-fi warning films, which would be great if it was only cheesy, but unfortunately it is not innocent at all.

Considering the amount of money that was spent on hiring the cast, the acting is nothing to write home about, and only the immensely beautiful

---

10 It was written by Roland Emmerich (who also returned to the director's chair), James Vanderbilt (**ZODIAC** [2007, USA, D: David Fincher]), Dean Devlin (producer of **GODZILLA** [1998, USA/Japan, D: Roland Emmerich], and actors Nicolas Wright and James A. Woods.

1979's one-and-only original **PHANTASM** was recently (2017) reissued in a deluxe restored edition, with brand-new artwork by Aaron Lea

Filmed on several locations throughout the whole wide world from April through to August 2015, it was quickly made apparent that this was intended as a major comeback film. Distributors 20th Century Fox were indeed firing on all cylinders, and, aside from the usual teasers and posters, the marketing included a trailer that featured famous football (a.k.a. "soccer") players from the English premier league team Manchester United. The end result was hated by the critics, and although it approximately doubled its money at the box-office[12], it did not become the phenomenon that the first film was. But what movie would be able to achieve such a feat in 2016 anyway?

Friday, April 28th, 2017

PHANTASM: RAVAGER
USA 2016. D: David Hartman

Ad-line: *"The Final Game Now Begins."*

Charlotte Gainsbourg (**ANTICHRIST** [2009, Denmark/Germany/France/Sweden/Italy/Poland, D: Lars von Trier]) and the always-likable Jeff Goldblum (**THE FLY** [1986, USA/UK/Canada, D: David Cronenberg]) deliver something that can be called decent performances. You are here for the monsters though, and I have to confess that these look amazing. Imagine a combination of an awesome and menacing creature with tentacles and the queen bitch from **ALIEN** (1979, UK/USA, D: Ridley Scott), and as such they should leave everyone satisfied (as they left me).

I saw the first film in a theater when I was only 14 years old. I have to tell you, it was an event movie, a blockbuster that everyone was talking about. Aside from its box-office success, it spawned a series of novels (*Independence Day, Independence Day: Silent Zone, Independence Day: War in the Desert, Independence Day: Crucible,* and *Independence Day: Resurgence* [the latter of which is a tie-in novelization of the film under review]). As in the early 2000s, there were discussions of a sequel, however the 9/11 attacks held the plans back. It was in the late 2000s that two sequels were decided upon; the present one, and **INDEPENDENCE DAY 3**,[11] which doesn't have a release date yet, but is set in stone after the box-office success of this **RESURGENCE**.

Reggie (the ever-returning Reggie Bannister) wakes up in a hospital, where he meets Mike (the also-returning A. Michael Baldwin), who tells him the following story: Reggie got back his car from a random man who was driving it out in the desert, and the first thing he did was pick up a hot chick named Dawn (Dawn Cody, from **PLEASANTVILLE** [1998, USA, D: Gary Ross]), to whom he, in turn, explains his story about The Tall Man (Angus Scrimm, who passed away on the January 9th, 2016, this being his swansong film appearance)[13].

Yes indeed, trouble is again at the door, complete with evil dwarf minions, silver spheres, and a full-blown alien invasion that is threatening to wipe the Earth off the face of the universe. But Reggie, being the ever-reliable, womanizing hero, arms himself with a big bag of guns and ammo and goes against The Tall Man in a final showdown.

Many reviewers have complained online (print is dead [yeah, *right!*], so where else could they take their venom out?) that, because director David Hartman (who also wrote this, with producer Don Coscarelli[14]) comes from a visual effects

11 The two of them would be shot back-to-back (the titles would be *ID Forever Part I* and *ID Forever Part II*), but the plans were changed, and only the one under review made it before the cameras whilst the other one was waiting for this one to succeed, which it did, in spades.

12 Produced by Dean Devlin, Roland Emmerich, and Harald Kloser, on a $165-million budget, it grossed $389.7-million. It was executive produced by Ute Emmerich, Larry J. Franco, and Carsten H.W. Lorenz. Volker Engel, K.C. Hodenfield, and Marco Shepherd are credited as co-producers, and Jeffrey Harlacker was an associate producer.

13 Head on back to *M!* #27 and refer to "My Monster Movie Marathon Diary Part 2", in which you can read my reviews of the first four films in the franchise (1977-1998).

14 It was co-produced by Gigi Bannister and Reggie Ban-

background, and because this was made on meager budget, the CGI FX are not good. And, gods forbid, they even used CG blood as well! Well, let me tell you something: I don't really know how else one could pull off such a demanding, high-concept story as this on such a modest budget. Wake up and smell the coffee! This is how low-budget filmmakers do stuff nowadays, and on this particular occasion, it is done well. Actually, if memory serves, I am pretty certain that this is the bloodiest *Phantasm* outing yet.

Another complaint I often came across in reviews is that the end result is too episodic, which couldn't be farther from the truth, as pretty much everything here stays consistent. Sure, the second half is more effects-driven than the first, but name one recent monster movie in which this

nister, while Mathias Dougherty and Cesare Gagliardoni are credited as associate producers.

wasn't the case. Also, one thing the *Phantasm* fans wanted for ages was to have a few plot-holes explained, and this film does just that in its first half, wherein a lot will be answered (if not always satisfyingly, it should be said).

It was in 2004 when Don Coscarelli first spoke of the possibility of doing a fifth film, and indeed the following year it was revealed that he and New Line Cinema were working not only on a new *Phantasm* entry, but a whole trilogy of 'em! Since then rumors were going on and off, until 2015 that the completion of **RAVAGER** was announced, and it was soon revealed that it was shot secretly in 2012 and 2013. The end product played at the Fantastic Fest in Austin, then enjoyed a brief theatrical release, which was followed by a full-blown home video campaign that included the rerelease of the four previous movies. It is essential viewing for fans of the series!

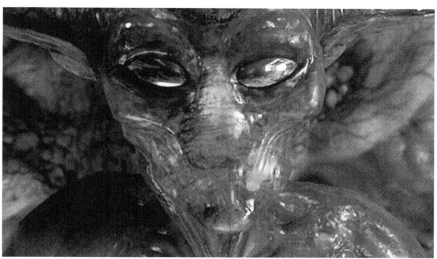

Ma, He's—Uh, *It's*—Makin' Eyes At Me! An inscrutable extraterrestrial invader from **ID:R** (2016) turns on the otherworldly charm

Postscript

The conclusion is really simple: Although I had a lot of fun reviewing all the *Godzilla* films, I came to the realization that *kaiju* cinema is simply not my cup of tea. The most positive outcome of this and the previous issue's marathons were the fact that I opened my horizons to Asian cinema for the first time in my life (and as a result I have scheduled to watch a couple of martial arts flicks). Steve Fenton knows that I was planning on tackling the *Gamera* series (1965-2006) as well, but I finally decided to pass on that idea. I even had plans of watching *Ultraman* (ウルトラマン / *Urutoraman*, 1966) too, but I had to pass on that one as well. Sure, I know that all these are classics, and I have the utmost respect for them, but my heart is devoted to US and European cinema, and I cannot be dishonest about that. So, I will proceed on doing what I do best, and you should be sure to come back for *Monster!* #35, for which, in Part 7 of your favorite column, I will be tackling more Western cinema-friendly monster romps.

Christos Mouroukis   *Godzilla A Go-Go: Part 2*

Anglo-Japanese export poster for **LATITUDE ZERO** *(reviewed on page 293)*

REViEWS:

The Eyes Have It!
Mahesh Balraj as *Ghoul*'s demonic terrorist leader, Ali Saeed

GHOUL

Reviewed by Kinshuk Gaur

India, 2018. D: Patrick Graham

Ghoul's opening blurb: *"Strike The Deal With Your Blood... And Out Of The Smokeless Fire... The Ghul Will Come..."*

Making a *good* horror movie or television show has always been an elusive objective for the Indian entertainment industry. Their explorations into the genre more often than not produce something quite lavish, yet with ridiculously-concocted plots which are hopelessly convoluted. Within India there have been a few memorable horror TV shows which managed to rise above the general mediocrity of their time period; The Ramsays' 1990s *Zee Horror Show* being a prime example.[1] Or, to make matters worse, Indian directors and producers seem to be in the habit of merely plagiarizing tropes from either/or/*and* Western or Asian sources (= Thai and Japanese, to be more precise). Horror is always done best when it is left unadulterated, but nevertheless our filmmakers are seemingly keen on creating something which has its very essence evaporate as they dish out their highly *damaged* product.

Case in point the new Netflix original show *Ghoul*, a three-part miniseries which reflects this rather confused current state of Indian horror. The series definitely has some money behind it, and it's curious that a British writer/director, Patrick Graham, was tapped to helm the project. Graham had previously directed a short film for Indian television, as well as various TV commercials, until he convinced someone at Phantom Films to green-light his *Ghoul* script.[2] He was also lucky enough to be able to direct the series as well. This three-parter is best binged all at one sitting, taking it in as if it were a full-length feature film; a *meager* one at that, but it's still better-paced than many Indian-directed horror films are.

The series' title references a supernatural being which originates from very ancient (i.e., pre-Islamic) Arabic folklore. A "*ghul*" is a subspecies of *jinn*, humanity's cousins, which were fashioned out of smoke rather than dirt, as were we, human beings, by the gods (or Allah, as Islam adopted the *jinn* into their belief system). *Ghuls* are horrid entities: malodorous monsters that are associated with skulking around graveyards, raiding burial sites for the consumption of corpses. For *Ghoul* (the anglicized variation of *ghul*), the eponymous creature instead feeds on living human flesh, with terrifying consequences.

The setting is the near future—or perhaps an alternate present?—wherein India appears to be an anti-utopia which closely resembles your typical xenophobic fascist state wherein the authorities' policies and laws resemble those of 1930-'40s Nazi Germany. The series' suffocating hyper-sociopolitical climate reflects the rise of the "Hindu Nationalism" movement in India,

---

1   As memorable as the series of weekly horror-based episodes was for those lucky enough to have watched it in the 1990s, *ZHS* also had its problems. I am currently working on an article about the show with *Monster!* editor Tim Paxton.

2   @   *https://nypost.com/2018/08/30/netflix-horror-series-creator-cant-speak-his-shows-language/*

coupled with the virtually worldwide criticism of Islam that is currently popular. That is the back story of *Ghoul*. And now, on with the show…

As the first episode opens, a group of military units trained to take down Islamic terrorists have tracked a known leader to a rundown apartment complex. Taking necessary precautions, they enter the building with weapons drawn, expecting the worst. What they find within is a lone man in a hallway covered in blood and with a strange symbol carved into his belly. All the suspects are discovered dead… except for one, their leader, Ali Saeed (Mahesh Balraj), who sits alone and unmoving amidst the carnage whispering the name of "Nida Rahim".

The script informs us how the nation of India has changed considerably in the not-too-distant future, when religious intolerance, fear and violence have reached catastrophic levels. In a bid to keep a lid on the mounting mania, the government has established undisclosed detention centers, and military suppression under martial law is in effect. Anyone (primarily Muslims) who is a dissident in any form is rounded-up and sent to these gulag-like centers for "reeducation".

A car containing a young woman—our protagonist—Nida Rahim (Radhika Apte), with her father Shahnawaz (S.M. Zaheer) at the wheel, is travelling by night. They are obviously nervous about being stopped, as they pass by a signboard proclaiming "*Terrorists are among us. Be vigilant*". The first dialogue between Nida and her father reveals that their community is being targeted by government and local officials: their ancestral artifacts and personal belongings—especially books—are systematically destroyed in huge bonfires fed by gasoline and flamethrowers. The pair witness their culture being obliterated because their beliefs may have an adverse effect on others (*most likely* Hindus). Also, when Nida says to her father, "Our community has been taught wrong things and misguided, but few do not get it" provides a direct reference to some of the series' underlying political concerns.

Her father, who is a college professor, is afraid that they will be caught with his incriminating lecture notes in his possession, and he is in a hurry to somehow escape all the madness surrounding them. Consequently, he is on his way to drop Nida off at "The Academy", an institution which we shortly learn is directly associated with the pogroms that are being committed all over the country. The car is stopped at a checkpoint and Nida's father is grilled by the military personnel

manning the post. However, they are left alone when Nida flashes her badge that identifies her as a member of the Advanced Interrogation Protection Squad. A patriot loyal to her country, Nida has no qualms about her father being interrogated and then arrested by The Academy. This is the last she sees of him, as he is taken away to be "reeducated" at an isolated detention facility.

While in the midst of her military training, Nida is ordered to report to a remote interrogation center called Meghdoot 31. It is here that we are introduced to the fierce interrogating team of Major Laxmi Das and Colonel Sunil Dacunha (respectively played by actress Ratnabali Bhattacharjee and actor Manav Kaul). The initial conversation between these two officers helps set the stage for much of the impending intrapersonal interaction between they and Nida, who is treated with obvious discrimination even before she is formally introduced to her superiors.

Cloaked in darkness, the detention center is at a military encampment where inmates are confined away from all contact with the outside world (they are even deprived of sunlight). We are given glimpses of various prisoners, torture chambers, and Nadia dreams of her father's death by execution. The twist arises when a new terrorist prisoner, none other than the recently-captured Ali Saeed, is led into the com-

Ghoul, Gal & Gun: Series heroine Nida Rahim (Radhika Apte), locked-and-loaded, does the Sigourney Weaver thang!

A Big Hand For The Little Lady: Italo starlet Antonella Interlenghi (1961-) gets touchy-feely with **YETI**'s mighty mauler. The love-smitten hirsute high-rise hominid spends much of his screen-time making cow-eyes at his diminutive human crush, the big sap!

pound, where his sinister presence generates a nightmarish ambience. Even the fiercely-barking army dogs go silent at his approach. Brutal interrogation techniques—such as extreme temperature variations, hanging him upside-down and blasting loud music at him for the purposes of sleep deprivation—are used to force information out of Saeed. Meanwhile, the captive plays 'mind-games' with his tormentors, gradually turning them against one another. Even while bound to a chair, the terrorist is able to manipulate and invoke guilty feelings amongst the interrogating officers. One man kills the other, and he is then driven mad and has to be physically restrained and removed from the cell. All the while, Saeed keeps a watchful eye on Nida, who witnesses everything.

Even after this first round of torture tactics fails, Col. Dacunha tries his luck by using his best technique: his own form of mind-games. However, by revealing damning personal truths about the officer, the whispering Saeed is able to turn the tables on him as well. Tormented by guilt, the enraged Dacunha attacks Saeed, inserts electric cables in his prisoner's mouth and kills the man with a massive jolt of electricity. (Or *does* he…?) Dacunha leaves the corpse in the cell and Nida examines the body. She experiences a few moments of terror as the electricity in the compound fails and she

believes she sees a monster in the darkness. As the power comes back on, Saeed is seemingly still alive, albeit very weak. What *did* Nida see? Might Saeed be something *inhuman*, perhaps…?

As a last resort, the colonel pulls his trump card of the interrogation: he calls in Faulad Singh (Surender Thakur), a vicious agent who arrives to interrogate Ali Saeed. And now the true horror starts, as Nida begins to unravel just what is happening at the compound. She figures out that an innocent man imprisoned with the guilty has called forth a supernatural entity to take revenge… in the form of a *ghul*, a shape-shifting supernatural monster that subsists on human flesh and can transform at will into anyone it chooses to impersonate.

Nida comes to this realization after Singh's corpse—its head ripped-off—is found hanging upside-down in the interrogation room. But wait. Why is the escaped Saeed unlocking the doors of all the prisoners' cells for? It is only then that Nida realizes the dreadful *ghul* has begun yet another orgy of slaughter, much like what had happened in an apartment at the beginning of the show. Everyone at the detention center is now fodder for the monster as it attacks and kills— and *feeds*—indiscriminately on both soldiers and terrorists alike.

A number of things work in *Ghoul*'s favor, mainly that it was made by a trio of big production houses: Hollywood's Ivanhoe Pictures, Blumhouse Productions, and the Indian-based Phantom Films. This really helped, as the production was certainly not short on finances. Jay Oza's dark and moody cinematography was key to pulling-off much of the tension in the series, and a decent background score by the duo Naren Chandavarkar and Benedict Taylor also helped considerably. But can all these qualities combined make for good horror? The answer is *no*. Now, if the genre is explored with style and substance, fine horror movies can be made on minuscule resources. We have had instances in the past where a good Indian horror movie didn't have an extravagant budget; Ram Gopal Varma's **RAAT** (Hindi, 1992) most immediately comes to mind.

As for *Ghoul*'s cast, leading lady Radhika Apte (who also appears in the Netflix-produced anthology film *Lust Stories* [Hindi, 2018, Ds: Directors: Zoya Akhtar, Karan Johar, Anurag Kashyap, Dibakar Banerjeeand] and the crime/action series *Sacred Games* [Hindi/Marathi, 2018, Ds: Anurag Kashyap, Vikramaditya Motwane], likewise for Netflix) has little more to do than look stern or shocked here. Maybe that is because Radhika, although a decent actress, is really not *that* versatile, and she was no doubt used mainly as eye-candy to offset all the horror and bloodshed that goes on in *Ghoul*. Manav Kaul is good in his part as the committed colonel overwhelmed by family grief, but he too is let down by a poor screenplay which doesn't properly explore the *ghul*'s folklore and its methods of supernatural subterfuge, although we eventually do discover the how and why behind what this particular subspecies of *jinn* is up to. In a way, its appearance is a retributory strike against acts of the inhumanity that both the Advanced Interrogation Protection Squad and the Islamic terrorists have been guilty of committing all along. Then we have the teeth-gnashing Ratnabali Bhattacharjee as Major Das, who is highly effective as a mean-spirited woman who has it in for Nida right from the beginning of the show. But just when you think director Graham might play the stereotypical predatory 'butch lesbian' card, he is smart enough *not* to, thankfully. Indian Horror fans will cheer Surender Thakur as Faulad Singh, who cuts a hulking figure, carrying-off his bad attitude and sheer meanness like he just stepped out of a classic Ramsay horror film.

That said, I feel that *Ghoul* ultimately fails as a horror series. For me it just did not go far enough in exploring what the *ghul* is (...or can be). All

disappointments aside, though, it is still one of the better horror series yet to be produced by Indians, although, probably because it was a co-production made for Netflix, it seems to have been skewed for the foreign market. But what seems to be the most interesting fact about *Ghoul* is that is easily one of the best adaptations of John W. Campbell's novella *Who Goes There?* (first published in *Astounding Science-Fiction* magazine in August 1938). Campbell's classic tale of science fiction horror and paranoia has been adapted at least three times to film: **THE THING FROM ANOTHER WORLD** (1951, USA, D: Christian Nyby), **THE THING** (1982, USA, Ds: John Carpenter) and **THE THING** (2011, USA/Canada, D: Matthijs van Heijningen Jr.), latter of which was a prequel to the Carpenter version. The third and final episode of *Ghoul* fits right into the framework of the '82 version, even going so far as aping parts of the famous Ennio Morricone/John Carpenter score, which *had* to have been a conscious effort on the director's part (the second episode's end credits track was even a straight-up rip-off!). But that's not a bad thing, considering how incredible Carpenter's film ultimately was/is.

YETI: GIANT OF THE 20TH CENTURY

(Yeti – Il gigante del 20° secolo)

Reviewed by Eric Messina

Italy, 1977. D: "Frank Kramer"/Gianfranco Parolini

The only thing I was aware about it before tucking-into this ape hair-encrusted plate of cinematic cannoli was that it once aired on *USA Up All Night* (1989-98). I'm always on the lookout for schlocky junk that was aired on that brilliant show, and have in the past done 'theme weeks' over at my blog *theaterofguts.com* dedicated to this program. I'm sure there was much guffawing and rib-jabbing from Gilbert Gottfried or that bubbly babe Rhonda Shear in regards to the present title under review. Online critics trashed the living shit outta this wacked-out Italian flick, saying that not even *MST3K* could handle this kind of punishment—but what do *they* know, anyhow?! Here at *Monster!* we don't subscribe to the notion of 'so-bad-it's-good'... we openly celebrate the (in this case mozzarella) cheese!

The cast all speak in a 'chop-socky movie'-style dubbed manner, though the voice actors who usually vocalize characters in Fulci films and

Italian *due-fogli manifesto* for **YETI: GIANT OF THE 20th CENTURY** (1977); art unsigned

other Italo exploitation fare are, oddly, not present here. However, there are a couple of choice in-front-of-the-camera gore film actors involved who'd worked with the maestro of maggots before, including Antonella Interlenghi from **CITY OF THE LIVING DEAD** (*Paura nella città dei morti viventi*, 1980, Italy), in which she played the zombie sister that kept on popping-up to scare the living shit out of her brother with that hideous orange face covered in wriggly meal worms and rice krispies courtesy of special effects wizard Giannetto De Rossi. One actor who I was stoked to see in **YETI** was Donal(d) O'Brien, a.k.a. "Dr. Butcher" himself, the vocal cord-severing, lobotomizing mad surgeon of "Frank Martin"/Franco Martinelli (a.k.a. Marino Girolami)'s **ZOMBIE HOLOCAUST** (*Zombi Holocaust*, 1980, Italy). A seasoned stalwart of Italian exploitation cinema, O'Brien last appeared in *M!*'s pages during my **FRANKENSTEIN 2000: AFTER DEATH** (*Frankenstein 2000 – Ritorno dalla morte*, 1991, Italy, D: "David Hills"/Joe D'Amato) review last issue (p.281).

Dr. Waterman (John Stacy), an Arnold Stang-type curmudgeon all decked-out in plaid, discovers the titanic Yeti frozen in glacial ice up in Canada, so they immediately get a team of dudes with flame-throwers to melt its icy tomb. Why are they so keen on releasing this tremendous cousin of Sasquatch? Perhaps they've all got a death wish? No, it's worse than that: they plan on exploiting him as an indentured corporate slave for Mr. Hunnicutt's

grocery store and gas station chains. Talk about unfairly capitalizing on an opportunity! That would be like if the Jolly Green Giant actually existed, and the frozen produce company for whom he served as mascot forced the big guy to submit to their devious business practices against his will.

YETI's crude production values are almost Ruben Guberman-esque, à la the guys responsible for *Johnny Sokko and His Flying Robot* (ジャイアントロボ / *Jaianto robo*, 1967-68, Japan); my brain just really responds favorably to this type of horrid ineptness that most would likely find an eyesore. The music by Santé Maria Romitelli and some funky studio musicians calling themselves The Yetians (get it?) for the gig is pretty rad, shifting from tripped-out psych to strains that wouldn't sound at all out of place on a '70s TV news show or as part of a ghastly porn score (this soundtrack at times reminded me of the satanic ritual music from **YOUNG SHERLOCK HOLMES** [1985, USA, D: Barry Levinson]). I actually mistook it for an even more famous piece of music—namely Carl Orff's "O Fortuna", from his cantata *Carmina Burana*, of all things—and there's a disco version on the soundtrack that's incredibly catchy.

"Operation Yeti" gets underway, and everyone kind of nods in unison to let us know that. Again, I'm not sure why they aren't all running and hiding from this humongous manbeast slathered in melted shaving cream that's supposed to look like melting snow. The sopping-wet million-year-old Yeti wakes up and bellows like a giraffe on PCP! The afro'd look of the beast is totally stolen from *The Six Million Dollar Man* (1974-78) episode co-starring Bionic Bigfoot. The late André the Giant portrayed that role and, later on when this character returned to the series, Ted Cassidy donned the costume in his stead. In **YETI**, Mimmo Crao looks like merely a cheap knockoff of Steve Austin's hirsute hominid foe, albeit on a far larger (if not necessarily *grander*) scale. As the beast herein, Crao resembles a sort of Cro-Magnon Barry Gibb and, just before this, the actor was seen in *Jesus of Nazareth* (1977, USA), a star-studded Biblical miniseries directed by Italian arty filmmaker Franco Zeffirelli. I guess the Italian producers weren't Bugs Bunny fans, because anytime I think of a Yeti, I can't help seeing that dopey giant snowman who squashes and pets Daffy Duck or Bugs while saying things like, "I will name him George and I will hug him and pet him!" in a goofy voice. In fact, somebody on YouTube took the time to compiled a video (@ *https://www.youtube.com/watch?v=X0D7iXCHfQA*) depicting all the *Bugs* Yeti's clumsily affectionate 'hugs and smothers', set to the disco track from this film. If you need cheering-up, might I suggest you check it out. I was actually *crying* from laughing so hard! For more Yeti-mania, there's the Paul

Spanish pressbook (*guía doble*) for 1977's **YETI**; art by "Joan" [*no*, not *Jano!* ☺]

Naschy train wreck **THE WEREWOLF AND THE YETI** (*La maldición de la bestia*, a.k.a. **NIGHT OF THE HOWLING BEAST**, 1975, Spain, D: Miguel Iglesias Bonns).

Dr. Waterman mentions how the titular—very 'tit'ular, as it happens! (see below)—Yeti is a descendant of *us*. OK, I took an anthropology course once, and there's no evidence of any mythical folkloric ape evolving into a supersized

bipedal apeman, just like regular horses don't evolve into winged Pegasus over time. The Yeti's appearance is *hilarious*! It's just this hairy dude Chroma-keyed in over the landscape. He carries Jane (Interlenghi) and her brother Herbie (Jim Sullivan) to his cave and becomes sexually aroused when one of them brushes their hand over his grotesque nipple, that pulsates in response. It's bizarre and obscene, and it made me scratch my head and wonder if I actually just

Spaghetti Yeti! Dino De Laurentiis' 1976 **KING KONG** spawned many imitations, including this Italian cheapie. **Top:** On the **YETI** set (note "snow"), regular-sized humans provide scale alongside the full-size mock-up of titular hairy monster. **Above:** German A1 poster; art unsigned

saw it! Turns out the lonesome, misunderstood Yeti's intentions are a lot more nurturing than we thought, and, like she's one of his young, he tosses a fishbone at Jane for her to munch on.

Meanwhile in Toronto, kids of all ages are clamoring to get a glimpse of the giant 'monkey'; they gots 'Yeti fever', you see. Only in the sleazy '70s would you see babes with handprint-shaped patches over their tits parading around a bunch of underage kids as a welcoming party for the monster's arrival. They basically shut down the town for Hunnicutt's grand store-opening festivities, and of course it rapidly shifts into panic mode as the big galoot proceeds to smash the shit out of the city. The way he kicks-in windows and bashes-in buildings reminded me of that awesome '80s arcade game *Rampage*, where you can take your pick as to what monster you want to wreak havoc with: the giant werewolf, lizard or Kong.

Towards the last half-hour, the Yeti falls over from getting lightheaded—maybe he's just all-tuckered-out from cutting so many ribbons for grocery store openings happening all over town? Finally, looking even more grizzled than usual, future "Dr. Butcher" O'Brien shows up wearing a tacky-looking cheap blazer toting a shotgun to ram the professor's head into a locker (he even calls him an "egghead"—too harsh!). These dime-store gangsters set him up in a cruel way, and not only that, they almost kill his dog on top of it. I love how Mr. Hunnicutt—who looks like a third-grader's drawing of a 'businessman', with frazzled hair, a beet-red face and a lightbulb nose—puts his head down and weeps for the gentle giant. I guess he had a lot riding on the poor (if highly-destructive) creature!

This film has been unfairly trashed and passed-off as having no redeeming qualities whatsoever. Well, I am here to tell you it's incredibly fun and I had a real *blast* with it. Highly recommended! (Just make sure you stock-up with a behemoth-sized supply of alcohol and/or other mind-altering substances beforehand.)

DEVIL FISH

(*Shark: Rosso nell'oceano*, a.k.a. **MONSTER SHARK; DEVOURING WAVES**)

Reviewed by Dennis Capicik

Italy/France, 1984. D: "John Old Jr."/ Lamberto Bava

'Dramatic' dialogue exchange: "God, what the hell is *that*?!" – "Whatever it is, I wouldn't wanna rub it the wrong way!"

Gianni Garko, as cowboy-hatted, white-shirted, gum-chewing secondary hero Sheriff Gordon: "...We are *not* talkin' about a little fish we can put in a fishbowl. We are talkin' about a *monster*, a monster that can wreck a twelve-ton boat!"

Dino Conti as marine biologist Bob Hogan, with maximum incredulity: "I can't believe it! Look at those tentacles! A shark with *tentacles*!"

In the wake of Steven Spielberg's enormously successful—and first-ever—summer box-office blockbuster, **JAWS** (1975, USA), it was inevitable that ever-opportunistic Italian filmmakers would eventually (*sooner* rather than later!) produce their own 'versions' of said film, a fact which is best-exemplified by Enio G. Castellari (= Enio Girolami)'s now-infamous **GREAT WHITE** (*L'ultimo squalo*, a.k.a. **THE LAST SHARK**, 1981, Italy/USA), which is a shameless combo carbon-copy of the first two films in the Universal Pictures franchise. Due to the rival producers' overt plagiarism, Universal filed a lawsuit against **GREAT WHITE**'s American distributor Film Ventures International and it got slapped with an injunction, keeping it out of both theaters and from securing a home video release stateside; a shame really, since, despite all its obvious similarities, it's an energetic and quite ambitious film in its own right (co-starring a slumming James Franciscus and Vic Morrow) that is well worth checking-out.

However, **GREAT WHITE** wasn't the first rip-off—and certainly *not* the last, by a long shot!—of Spielberg's film and, long before their litigious run-in with Universal, Film Ventures had also funded William Girdler's giant rampaging killer bear film, **GRIZZLY** (1976), a high-'n'-dry land-lubber variation of the Spielberg film which has sometimes been referred to (with good reason) as "JAWS with claws". Other producers having by no means been deterred by Universal's controversial litigation against **GREAT WHITE**, over the next few years, a veritable feeding frenzy of killer shark and other aquatic-based creature features splashed across cinema screens, including such titles as: **MAKO: THE JAWS OF DEATH** (1976, USA, D: William Grefé), which, in an attempt at injecting some novelty into its story, involved a man with a telepathic link to sharks; American International Pictures' star-studded if woefully flat and lifeless monster octopus film, **TENTACLES** (1977, Italy/USA, D: Ovidio G. Assonitis); United Film Distribution's **TINTORERA: KILLER SHARK** (*¡Tintorera!*, 1977, Mexico, D: René Cardona, Jr.]; ad-line: *"There's a monstrous killer churning up the sea..."*); American General Pictures' **BARRACUDA** (1978, USA, Ds: Harry Kerwin, Wayne Crawford), which concerned

pollution-addled specimens of the title fish putting the chomp on Pacific swimmers; one of the classier, more upmarket cash-ins spawned by the craze was **ORCA** (1977, USA/Italy, D: Michael Anderson), concerning a vengeful killer whale, starring respected thespians Richard Harris and Charlotte Rampling; and the wonderfully witty Roger Corman-produced / Joe Dante-directed cult crowd-pleaser **PIRANHA** (1978, USA), which took the basic **JAWS** template and successfully reworked it into something new, fresh and smart. Of all the marine monster movies made during the post-**JAWS** production proliferation, the present lowly entry shares perhaps most in common with the Rog Corman-exec-produced **UP FROM THE DEPTHS** (1979, USA, D: Charles B. Griffith), which concerns a gigantic, voracious prehistoric fish gobbling-up tourists down Hawaii way.

Drifting along nearly a decade late in the game, Lamberto Bava's cut-rate **DEVIL FISH** isn't the *worst* of the whole shoal of Italian "JAWS" knockoffs (that dubious honor is jointly reserved for Raffaele Donato's and Joe D'Amato's sluggish

Italian *locandina* for **DEVIL FISH** (1984); art by Enzo Sciotti

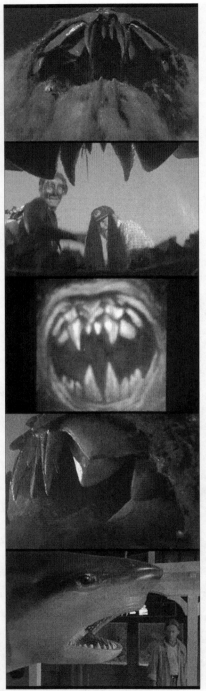

slogfest **DEEP BLOOD** [*Sangue negli abissi*, 1990, Italy] and "William Snyder"/Bruno Mattei's equally wretched **CRUEL JAWS** [*Fauci Crudeli – Cruel Jaws*, 1995, Italy]), but it's still a bottom-of-the-barrel mess, which at least has the unique distinction of featuring an intraspecies hybrid type of underwater 'Frankenstein monster' long before Sci-Fi/SyFy Channel trash flicks the likes of **SHARKTOPUS** (2010, USA, D: Declan O'Brien) and its sequels **SHARKTOPUS VS. PTERACUDA** (2014) and **SHARKTOPUS VS. WHALEWOLF** (2015, both USA, D: Kevin O'Neill), plus umpteen ever-more-fanciful variations/mutations, became commonplace Netflix chum.

Reuniting with his fellow **2019: AFTER THE FALL OF NEW YORK** (*2019 – Dopo la caduta di New York*, 1983, Italy/France, D: "Martin Dolman"/Sergio Martino) cast member actress Valentine Monnier, 'mini' action star Michael Sopkiw—whose short-lived career in Italo exploitation comprised a mere handful of movies during the early/mid-'80s—heads the once-popular cast of familiar Italian actors in this Florida-shot production. As expected, the basic premise follows the **JAWS** blueprint quite closely, so it's surprising to see that "Lewis Coates"/Luigi Cozzi's and "Dolman"/Martino's 'original' (we shall use that word with *caution* here!) story required fully four (4!) writers—including such diverse talent as Gianfranco Clerici, "Frank Walker"/Vincenzo Mannino and Dardano Sacchetti—to cobble it together, and it must have been a much more elaborate project on paper than what ultimately made it onto the screen!

When beer-guzzling marine biologist Bob Hogan (Dino Conti)—who *really* enjoys his Budweisers while on the job (!)—picks up a strange, deafeningly loud high-frequency aural disturbance off the coast of Florida through the submerged microphone of his floating laboratory, the Seaquarium, the sheer force of this heretofore unknown phenomenon very nearly capsizes his vessel ("*Holy Christ!* It's coming right at the boat!"). Meanwhile, further inland, his colleague, a peppy dolphin trainer named Stella (Monnier), witnesses her dolphins becoming severely agitated. Perplexed by this incident, Stella and Bob enlist the services of an expert electrical engineer named Peter (Sopkiw) to develop some sort of fancy sonar device, dubbed the "Pulse Generator", to help them track and locate the source of this (quote) "terrifying sound full of *hate*!" Elsewhere, the local Coast Guard recovers a limbless body from the water, a gruesome discovery which also attracts the attention of Sheriff Gordon (ex-spaghetti western superstar Gianni "Sartana" Garko, here credited under his frequent anglicized pseudonym of "John" Garko). However, complicating matters still further for the lawman—the plot thickens!—a low-rent hitman (Paul Branco) has been offing potential squealers associated with the hi-tech West Ocean International (W.O.I.) research institute run by Dr. West (William Berger)…

Top to Bottom: Five tooth-filled screen captures from **DEVIL FISH**

The spectacular French poster for **DEVIL FISH** (1984); art by Enzo Sciotti

Chopping and changing erratically between a scrappy monster movie and ho-hum tabloid TV-grade filler about corporate espionage and illicit office affairs, much of this back-and-forth genre-hopping was likely due to the strict budgetary constraints imposed on the production, whose script keeps most of the film's action safely—and, more importantly, *economically*—on dry land, with only minimal costly underwater cinematography being used. All things considered, **DEVIL FISH** (a title derived from a colloquial fishermen's term for a potential cryptid species of giant cephalopod, which gives you a clue as to its monster's mixed zoological origins) still remains a prime hunk of a stinkeroo, and it does have some nifty ideas in it, but unfortunately, many of them simply don't pan-out or else are jettisoned *en route* in favor of more conventional, predictable outcomes. In fact, upon closer inspection, Bava's decidedly humble wannabe **JAWS** rip-off has a fair amount in common with Dan Milner's poverty-row Atom Age 'sea serpent' snoozer,

THE PHANTOM FROM 10,000 LEAGUES (1955, USA), which is likewise marred by its zero budget and lifeless titlular menace, which (as here) gets supplanted at every turn by uninteresting subplots and extraneous dialogue. Late into **DF**, it's revealed that the film's generic genetic monstrosity is virtually invulnerable, since each of its individual cells is capable of spontaneously reproducing itself. Hence, the protagonists opting to blow it up (*à la* **JAWS'** now-iconic ending) with explosive buoys is out of the question, as each separate piece of tissue has the potentiality to grow into an all-new creature ("…we could find ourselves up to our asses with *monsters!*" exclaims Garko as Gordon). Naturally, as in so many no-budget Italian flicks, burning it to a crisp seems to be the optimal solution, so Peter, Stella and Sheriff Gordon try and lure it out into the everglades so that it can be torched into toast using flamethrowers, but how this ungainly creature manages to swim so far into such shallow inland waters is anyone's guess. Throughout the film, the monster is visualized by plentiful 'flailing tentacle' shots combined with unconvincing underwater glimpses down in the murky depths of the ocean. And even during the fiery, brief-to-the-point-of-perfunctory 'grand' finale amongst the Floridian mangroves, the nighttime photography leaves plenty to be desired, and is mainly intended to obscure the obvious sedentary-verging-on-static nature of Olivier Taito's clunky creature design. "It's *not* a shark! …I'll bet my ass it's not a shark!" exclaims Sopkiw at one point, and it certainly *doesn't* resemble any shark we've ever seen before. Its creator Dr. Davis Barker (Lawrence Morgant) describes the beast as "…a marine monster, almost indestructible, and whose genetic characteristics are as fearsome as the white shark's! A gigantic octopus, with the intelligence of a dolphin and as monstrous as a prehistoric creature!" Despite its nonsensically muddled origins, to be fair, a sequence involving an attack on a boat by floppy rubber tentacles is quite well-staged; no worse (and actually better) than similar scenes seen in any number other similarly-themed movies. Close-up 'gaping jaws' shots of the devil fish—which, despite its mouthful of stalactite/stalagmite-sized fangs, looks a lot more cephalopodic than shark-like—also fulfill their function adequately enough, but there are precious few decent views of the monster to be had and way too much time wasted on boring human subplots.

From right out of nowhere early into the narrative, we get the highly unexpected and decidedly sloppy strangulation/electrocution murder of a (topless) gossipy W.O.I. employee (Cinzia De Ponti, who was also viciously slashed to death in Lucio Fulci's **THE NEW YORK RIPPER** [*Lo squartatore di New York*, 1982], Italy), a scene which is more akin to something out of an American 'roughie' than the *giallo*-styled murder mysteries the Bava family is best-known for.

Shark, My Ass! The **DEVIL FISH** surfaces for a quick snack

His more straightforward approach to homicide here *might* have been a sly attempt by Bava junior to deconstruct the act of murder and show it for what it actually is, i.e., nasty and vicious… but then again (*wink*) maybe it's just plain old sloppy filmmaking. Soon after, it becomes abundantly clear that the rather shady and nebulous aforementioned W.O.I. organization is somehow involved in the creation of the titular 60-million-year-old, 40-foot-long so-called "proto-shark" (as a female ichthyology nerd explains, "…a living fossil"), albeit without generating even an iota of mystery or suspense in the process as it tries in vain to draw our attention to numerous distractive red herrings. The climactic reveal of the main human evildoer ("*You're mad!*") behind it all is akin to a third-rate *Scooby-Doo* villain unmasking, and is about as exciting as eating a tin of sardines sans tomato sauce.

Notwithstanding Lamberto Bava's stylish directorial debut, the languid, delightfully morbid horror film **MACABRE** (*Macabro*, 1980, Italy) or his Dario Argento-produced slambang occult gorefest, **DEMONS** (*Demoni*, 1985, Italy), Bava, Jr.'s career, has, for the most part, been an erratic jumble of work-for-hire projects and at times dire TV assignments (**GRAVEYARD DISTURBANCE** [*Una notte nel cimitero*, 1987, Italy], anyone?!). To be fair, though, at this point in time, due to Italy's failing economy, the Roman film industry was already beginning to implode on itself, so Bava surely shouldn't be expected to shoulder all the blame for the sub-par results here. **DEVIL FISH** (or, as per the film's original English export title, **MONSTER SHARK**) was made immediately after his "Rambo" / **FIRST BLOOD** (1982, USA, D: Ted Kotcheff) cash-in, **BLASTFIGHTER** (1984, Italy/France), which also starred Sopkiw and, truth be told, *that* imitatively exploitive shoot-'em-up actioner actually turned out to be one of Bava's better efforts, all told. **DF**, on the other hand, has all the makings of a fun monster movie… one which unfortunately never materializes. Flatly shot in the manner of a TV show by DP "John McFerrand"/Giancarlo Ferrando, it lacks any of the stylistic flourishes to be found in even some of Bava's sub-mediocre small screen work, and the sun-kissed tropical Florida location (a favorite shooting site of many Italian 'tourist' productions of the time) isn't taken proper advantage of. Hell, even "Antony Barrymore"/Fabio Frizzi's at times would-be 'jaunty' electronic score mostly just sounds uninspired, tired and by-the-numbers.

As with some of the other Italian films he starred in, Michael Sopkiw (adequately dubbed hereon by veteran Rome-based American voice specialist Larry Dolgin) is decent enough as the primary protagonist, who manages to keep the disparate elements of the film moving along passably well and, while the action scenes are far more limited in comparison to those in both the above-cited **2019: AFTER FALL OF NEW YORK** and "Michael Lemick"/Michele Massimo Tarantini's **MASSACRE IN DINOSAUR VALLEY** (*Nudo e selvaggio*, 1985, Italy), Sopkiw does pitch in by performing most of his own stunts. Both William Berger and Dagmar Lassander (as Berger's adulterous former wife) appear only in glorified cameos, but it's nice to see them just the same, especially when Berger and Garko get to share some screen-time for old times' sake, as they had done so memorably in earlier years for such notable spaghetti western pairings as **IF YOU MEET SARTANA PRAY FOR YOUR DEATH** (*Se incontri Sartana prega per la tua morte*, 1968, Italy/West Germany, D: "Frank Kramer"/Gianfranco Parolini) and **A BULLET FOR A STRANGER** (*Gli fumavano le Colt... lo chiamavano Camposanto*, 1971, Italy, D: "Anthony Ascott"/Giuliano Carnimeo). And not only that, but the underused Berger gets one of the present film's most memorable lines when his character proclaims that his oversexed ex (played by Lassander) has the "sensitivity of a slut!" Elsewhere, in an uncredited bit part as a fisherman, seasoned spagwest stunt-grunt Goffredo "Fredy" Unger (who also served as DF's AD) loses an arm—not a *leg*, as claimed at the IMDb!—to the monster. Having been hospitalized after suffering this physical trauma, he goes into a coma and then flatlines while the doctor unsuccessfully attempts to resuscitate him with adrenalin and a defibrillator ("It was fear. *Fear* stopped his heart!" opines Garko knowingly afterwards in a halfhearted attempt at generating suspense).

Even in these nostalgia-crazed times when virtually everything that ever saw the light of a projector bulb (and even some things that didn't!) is getting fancy-schmancy digital restorations in deluxe DVD and BD editions with all the bells and whistles, when all is said and done, despite its unrealized ambitions and eclectic cast, **DEVIL FISH** remains mere low-rent filler that is certainly worth at least one watch, but really doesn't warrant repeat viewings.

PLEASE DON'T EAT MY MOTHER!

(a.k.a. **SEX POT SWINGERS**; **THE HUNGRY PETS**; **GLUMP**)

Reviewed by Christos Mouroukis

USA, 1973. D: Carl Monson

Ad-lines: *"Pretty Young Ladies Make the Perfect Plant Food!" – "A Laugh with Every Burp!" – "The hilarious tale of a strange houseplant whose appetite grew from the neighborhood pets to more succulent dishes – and loved every piece!"*

One of the first comedies I fell in love with when I was a kid was **HONEY, I SHRUNK THE KIDS** (1989, USA/Mexico, D: Joe Johnston) and its first sequel **HONEY I BLEW UP THE KID** (1992, USA, D: Randal Kleiser), so it was

inevitable that I developed a soft spot for actor Rick Moranis (the Canadian comedian was a household name back then, starring in big-budget fare such as **GHOSTBUSTERS** [1984, USA, D: Ivan Reitman] and **GHOSTBUSTERS II** [1989, USA, D: Ivan Reitman]). Another film with him that made an impression on me was **LITTLE SHOP OF HORRORS** (1986, USA, D: Frank Oz). A few years later I found out that it was a remake of **THE LITTLE SHOP OF HORRORS** (1960, USA, Ds: Roger Corman, Charles B. Griffith, Mel Welles). Fast-forward to many years later, when I found out that director Carl Monson (writer/producer/director of **BLOOD LEGACY** [1971, USA]) had made an erotic version, which I finally got around to seeing…

Henry Fudd (Buck Kartalian, also in **THE ACID EATERS** [1968, USA, D: Byron Mabe]) shares a house with his domineering mother (Lynn Lundgren, who apparently had an uncredited part in William Castle's **STRAIT-JACKET** [1964, USA]). A frustrated bachelor, he seeks sexual escapism through skin-mags (hell, *I'd* love to get my hands on some of the now-vintage issues displayed in this movie!) and voyeurism (in typical **THE IMMORAL MR. TEAS** [1959, USA, D: Russ Meyer] fashion, but I think that this latter touch—right out of a nudie-cutie—was already dated even when the film under review was new). Henry finds friendship in the form of a plant, but it turns out to be a flesh-eating one that can talk, in a sexy female voice, no less! He starts by feeding it (*her?*) with frogs and other small creatures, but it eventually grows bigger (we never see the actual transformation—what happens is, we see it at one size in one scene, and then it is replaced by increasingly bigger and bigger versions in subsequent scenes). As its size increases, so does its appetite, forcing its owner to feed it a dog, then eventually moving on to feeding it humans. After one person too many goes missing in the vicinity, detective O'Columbus (producer Carl Monson, whose character's name was clearly a wannabe pun on that of then-popular TV gumshoe Columbo [as played by Peter Falk]) is assigned to the case, and when he visits Henry's room he gets gobbled-up by the monstrous plant, which apparently realizes that it doesn't like the taste of men (up to this point, all of its victims have been female, you see), so pukes-up his gun (the film is

Left: The opportunities for a tasteless caption here are virtually limitless, but we shall keep things out of the gutter by simply saying: '70s softcore/hardcore porn queen Rene Bond in the, um, clutches of **PDEM-M!**'s phallic plant-monster

PLEASE DON'T EAT MY MOTHER!

THE HILARIOUS TALE
OF A STRANGE
HOUSEPLANT
WHOSE
APPETITE
GREW
FROM THE
NEIGHBORHOOD
PETS TO MORE
SUCCULENT DISHES

—AND LOVED
EVERY PIECE!

A LAUGH
WITH EVERY
BURP!

RESTRICTED ADMISSION

© MCMLXXII

STARRING
RENE BOND · BUCK KARTALIAN · FLORA WISEL · ALICIA FRIEDLAND
PRODUCED & DIRECTED BY
CARL MONSON · JACK BECKETT · HARRY H. NOVAK · A BOXOFFICE INTERNATIONAL PICTURE
CINEMATOGRAPHY
EXECUTIVE PRODUCER
Color

Wannabe Jack Davis-style art (by one "CBS") adorns **PDEMM!**'s cute US one-sheet poster

full of similar vulgar gags, about the plant burping and the like). This leaves Henry with only one choice: to find a male specimen for the male victims, and for it to serve as a companion to the female plant, which has an appetite only for females. Say, might this be some kind of social commentary on gay plants we've got here?!

Okay, despite its epic title and potentially titillating premise, this is actually very boring stuff,

"Feeeeeeeeeeed Meeeeeee!"
Loud-sweatered nerdy nebbish Henry Fudd (Buck Kartalian) interacts with his 'unusual' potted houseplant in several consecutive scenes from **PLEASE DON'T EAT MY MOTHER!** that show its development from mere wee sprout to full-grown specimen. Any similarities to Seymour Krelborn and "Audrey" in **THE LITTLE SHOP OF HORRORS** are far from purely coincidental!

and is essentially merely an excuse for an amorous couple (I couldn't identify the man, but the woman is Flora Weisel, who debuted in **THE CLASS REUNION** [1972, USA, D: Stephen C. Apostolof]) to have a lengthy sex scene, which is split-up into smaller sections and scattered throughout the entire running time, and these scenes are largely unrelated to the rest of Eric Norden's (**A SCREAM IN THE STREETS** [1973, USA, Ds: Carl Monson, Dwayne Avery, Bethel Buckalew, Harry H. Novak]) screenplay, and appear to be present only because sleaze master Harry H. Novak (three years before executive-producing your favorite 'killer snake' guilty pleasure **RATTLERS** [1976, USA, D: John McCauley]) was its exec producer/presenter. Other than that, the monster plant—in all its sizes/incarnations—is as pathetic as it gets, and looks worse than what one might find in a toy store (the 'special effects' credit went to Harry Woolman, whose later **LASERBLAST** [1978, USA, D: Michael Rae] I reviewed over at "Greek VHS Mayhem Part 3: Charles Band" in *Weng's Chop* #7). If this magazine had some sort of a competition on worst-looking monster of the month, then the one here would definitely win this month's award hands-down.

Which isn't to say that **PDEMM!** is entirely without merit, though, as the soundtrack (I have no idea who wrote it, or whether it was 'borrowed' from somewhere else) includes playful nods to the theme tune of the TV classic *The Addams Family* (1964-66), plus much of the dialogue is incredibly quotable (there are some *amazing* one-liners to be heard!). I wouldn't say that the comedy here is smart (far from it), but it gets away with it most of the time, because it appears as though the filmmakers knew that, since they couldn't make a good movie with the limited resources at their disposal, why not make this work to their advantage by making an intentionally *bad* movie instead? Although, when the final title card asks if this is "The End????" (yes, with *four* question marks!!!!) it had me worried that I would have to suffer through a sequel. However, whilst this carnivorous plant idea might have worked well for a gruesome 'straight' remake, no follow-up ever transpired.

The cast is stellar for this sort of thing, and includes Art Hedberg (writer/actor of **BOOBY TRAP** [1970, USA, D: Dwayne Avery]), Alice Friedland and Dick Burns (both from **THE YOUNG MARRIEDS** [1972, USA, D: Edward D. Wood, Jr.]), plus Ric Lutze ('**NECROMANIA': A TALE OF WEIRD LOVE!** [1971, USA, D: Edward D. Wood, Jr.]), and everyone's favorite erotic film actress Rene Bond (who the next year found herself in the co-scripted-by-Ed Wood, Jr. sexploitation effort **FIVE LOOSE WOMEN** [1974, USA, D: Stephen C. Apostolof]).

HERCULES AGAINST THE MONSTER

(*Ursus il terrore di kirghisi*; a.k.a. **HERCULES, PRISONER OF EVIL**)

Reviewed by Steve Fentone

Italy, 1964. D: "Anthony Dawson"/ Antonio Margheriti

Although the title I'm listing this movie under here doesn't appear to have been an actual 'legit' release title, but rather was (evidently?) just an unused potential Anglo export handle dreamed-up by its Italian distributor's publicity department in hopes of generating outside sales, considering the name of this here mag and all, I couldn't resist using the film's **HERCULES AGAINST THE MONSTER** title instead of its better-known—if blander—stateside release one, **HERCULES, PRISONER OF EVIL**. Okay, now that we've got that minor point squared-away, let's get to it!

Feel free to correct me if I'm wrong, but to the best of my recollection, this review amounts to the first time to date that we've covered a '60s Italian "sword-and-sandal" (a.k.a. peplum) fantasy here in *Monster!* (though, under its more familiar title **HERCULES, PRISONER OF EVIL**, Tim P. did write about it 30 years ago in the original *M!* newsletter). Although the majority of *pepla* (= the plural), while 'epic spectacles'—or at least wannabe ones—don't overly concern themselves with the more fantastical aspects of classical mythology that many of them are (usually *very* loosely indeed) based on, and there are numerous other such epics which are generally lumped into the same category that are (again, usually loosely) more historically- rather than mythologically-based, there is definitely a prominent subgenre of Peplum cinema that are all-out fantasies—most typically derived from Greek myths and legends and/or characters from same—a goodly quantity of these (bless 'em!) even up to and including bona fide monsters or other imaginary creatures / supernatural entities that fall well within *M!*'s territory. For my money, while I'm not averse to watching a decent 'mundane' peplum once in a while (there are some real good ones out there with nary a lick of fantastic content in them), I generally gravitate more towards those that are fantasy-based, as they tend to boast more basic pulp entertainment value.

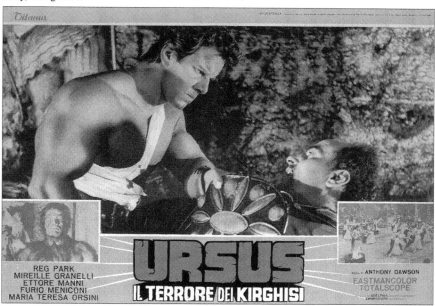

Italian *fotobusta* for **HERCULES AGAINST THE MONSTER** showing muscleman Reg Park strong-arming a puny foe. Inset at bottom left is a shot of the film's bestial eponymous menace

Such as the present title under review, for example. It was co-directed by prolific Italo fantasy specialist "Dawson"/Margheriti and his AD Ruggero Deodato, latter of whom at the time had several more years to go yet before making his solo directorial debut (incidentally, contrary to the IMDb's claim that Deodato goes "uncredited" hereon, his name is in fact very much visible in the film's Italian opening titles, which clearly credit him as its *aiuto regista* [= "assistant director"]). By '64, the year of this entry's production and release, the peplum genre as a whole was very much on its last legs, commercially speaking. With audiences and box-office takes having been steadily declining, budgets dropped-off accordingly. The new order of the day, imitative 007 clones ("Eurospy") and spaghetti westerns became bigger breadwinners for Roman producers (as well as those in Barcelona and Paris too) than the previous big trend to hit Europe, the costume spectaculars, and such productions began steadily eclipsing 'last month's flavor' (i.e., Maciste, Ursus and Ercole *et al* pictures) on Continental production rosters. And so to the present late-breaking example of the dying form…

A brutish and bestial, hirsute humanoid monster dressed in a flowing black cape has been terrorizing the countryside of the kingdom of Sura, wreaking general havoc by wrecking property and murdering whoever gets in its way; however, rather than killing-off the local Circassian populace, it known (logically enough!) as "The Monster" restricts its victims solely to fellow countrymen of the non-indigenous Kirghiz warriors who are currently occupying the region, both uninvited and unwelcome by the natives. The pugnacious Kirghiz are led by their ambitious warlord Prince Zara (played by the great Furio Meniconi, a 'baddie' specialist who appeared as memorable heavies in many a peplum and spaghetti western, in the latter often getting cast as blustering Mexican *bandidos* modeled along the lines of SW icon Fernando "*¡Vamonos, muchachos!*" Sancho), who believes that the monstrous murderous marauder is working in league with no less than the mighty Hercules ("…the man behind the monster"), attempting to incite a civil war between indigenous Circassian and non-native Kirghiz for the purposes of beating Zara to it by making his own power-play for the throne. Not only does the unscrupulously ambitious Zara proceed to prematurely crown himself Prince Regent of the territory, but he's such a dirtbag that he intends to force his own cousin Aniko (luscious blue-eyed Mireille Granelli, her hair dyed jet-black and her skin heavily darkened with bronzer for the occasion) to become his princess bride. Thing is, she's already betrothed to none other than Hercules himself, you see.

But what about the monster, you ask? For wont of a better description, the cry it makes sounds roughly somewhere between the trumpeting of

Above: German A0 poster for **HERCULES AGAINST THE MONSTER**

Creature Feature Reviews

an elephant and the cawing of a crow, a sound which does invest the creature with an extra layer of monstrousness when combined with its somewhat bat-like appearance as it swoops down out of trees or springs from thickets like a flying squirrel with its cloak spread out like wings. In the scene where it and Herc first come to grips, the monster attempts to bite him, possibly in order to simply kill him, but possibly because it has a vampiric thirst for blood; a potential aspect which is never made clear in the dubbed script.

As our he-manly hunksome hero Herc, Reg Park (whose best-known genre outings are inarguably Mario Bava's **HERCULES IN THE HAUNTED WORLD** [*Ercole al centro della Terra*], co-starring Christopher Lee, and Vittorio Cottafavi's **HERCULES AND THE CAPTIVE WOMEN** [*Ercole alla conquista di Atlantide*, both 1961, Italy]) definitely looks formidably-built enough, even if his post-ducktail/ pre-mullet hairdo seems a tad bit anachronistic for the period (although who can say for sure how ancient—*er*—"Greek" demigods wore their hair, I suppose. But since the so-called Hercules here seems to hail from the Northern Caucasus rather than Greece anyway, nitpicking about such 'factual' trivialities seems a tad redundant, so why bother). Appearing as Hercules' brother Ilo is the ill-fated Ettore Manni, another Italian performer who was active across the boards of genre cinema during the big Euro co-production boom of the '60s and '70s; although, that said, **HATM** is of strictly Italianate origin rather than a multinational joint-job, yet another indicator of producers' flagging interest in *pepla* as a going concern. In his younger days, Manni possessed the square-jawed good looks and heroic aura that saw him frequently cast as leading men (including in a number of 'straight' *pepla*), but gradual weight-gain eventually saw him filling character roles instead, if often quite substantial ones (notably during the spaghetti western cycle that was already getting underway during **HATM**'s production). In the present film we find him playing second male lead opposite Park's steely-thewed superman, and the two actors exhibit some decent chemistry in their scenes together.

Likewise appearing a good deal younger, trimmer and more chiseled than he would become later in his career—when he packed-on some extra beef (mostly around his midriff, rumor has it from drinking too much beer!)—future seasoned spagwest vet, burly-'n'-curly redheaded Claudio Ruffini, appears in an unbilled if quite decent-sized support part (with plentiful dialogue, even) as Frido. (***ATTN: SPOILER ALERT!***) Since

Top to Bottom: Three shots of spaghetti stunt-grunt Claudio Ruffini in monster make-up for **HATM**, plus a shot of María Teresa Orsini in a German lobby card for the film

Top: US TV title card for **HERCULES AGAINST THE MONSTER**. **Above:** Rough mock-up of an erroneous Anglo export poster, with messed-up English title

said actor was a trained stuntman and it is his character who is eventually revealed to be the monster—possessed of shape-shifting abilities—my educated guess would be that Ruffini, his face covered by a mask and with random patches of fur stuck all on his body, also played Frido whilst he was in monstrous form as well; in fact, it's a virtual *dead-cert* that he did. While minimalistic, crude and basically just an over-the-head rubber mask, the beastman makeup is pretty cool, rather reminiscent of a homelier/hairier version of Gomar the Gorilla (Gerardo Zepeda) from **NIGHT OF THE BLOODY APES** (*La horripilante bestia humana*, 1968/1972, Mexico, D: René Cardona, Sr.); actually, come to think of it, facially speaking it more resembles said actor's makeup as that 'same' character in **NOTBA**'s loose sequel, **THE**

WRESTLING WOMEN VS. THE MURDEROUS ROBOT (*Las luchadoras vs. el robot asesino*, Mexico, 1968, D: René Cardona, Sr.).

Make no mistake about it, this is assuredly one of Margheriti's humbler and more minor offerings as a cinematic fantasist, it must be said. To my way of thinking, while he is generally better remembered and more highly-regarded for his work within the horror/fantasy/sci-fi genres, some of his finest work as a filmmaker was actually done within the western genre. I'm thinking in particular of two often-macabre, horror-tinged ones: **VENGEANCE** (*Joko invoca Dio... e muori*, 1968), starring Richard Harrison, and **AND GOD SAID TO CAIN** (*E Dio disse a Caino...*, 1970), starring Klaus Kinski. Incidentally, at the very tail-end of the spaghetti western craze, Margheriti even made a 'spooky' western—albeit a strictly comedic one—entitled **WHISKY AND GHOSTS** (*Whiskey e fantasmi*, 1975, Italy/Spain [a follow-up to Margheriti's own hybrid martial arts comedy **HERCULES AGAINST KUNG FU** [*Ming, ragazzi!*, 1973, Italy]). However, it being yet another by-product of the *Trinity*-inspired 'spoof' oater period, **W&G** pales in comparison with those two earlier, straight-faced and decidedly grimmer Margheriti westerns I just cited. And not only that, but even to this day it's kept a decidedly low profile and remains notoriously difficult to see (although it was released dubbed into English on foreign videotape at some point back in the day).

Its dire dearth of budget is obvious all over **HATM**. Case in point, Prince Zara's 'horde' of mounted warriors, which numbers a whopping roughly ten (10) individuals. When these riders 'swarm' (forming a decidedly *thin* line, in single file, yet!) across the sward towards the Circassians' rickety-picket fort of sharpened wooden stakes, the effect falls far short of spectacular, to say the least. Sparsely-populated battle scenes are much thinner on the ground than was the norm for the genre, which routinely cannibalized footage (typically 'crowd' scenes, such as massed battles) from earlier, costlier productions in hopes of artificially padding-out production values some. That said, renting a few stock scenes seems to have even been beyond **HATM**'s budgetary scope, although Margheriti does manage to put together a passably exciting pre-finale by rallying every last extra he could muster for Park's Herc (whose woefully-mismatching stunt 'double' [*not!*] is glaringly obvious in one scene!) to hoist over his head and hurl around like ragdolls.

After he and his men nocturnally invade and

raze the Circassian stockade, laying waste to all within, Zara attempts to frame the monster for the atrocity in hopes that Hercules will also be blamed for being guilty by association. Star Park for some reason takes a temporary powder from the action at just past the halfway point of the movie, after being wounded during a *mano a mano* tussle with the monster and thereafter spending a spell laid-up in a mountain grotto while being tended by a hermit physician. Meanwhile, having understandably repeatedly spurned her uncle Zara's lecherous incestuous advances, our wholesome heroine Aniko winds-up trapped by him in the monster's cave lair. When Hercules shows up to rescue her, the film's 'startling' twist is casually dropped on us (one which, for what it's worth just in case you never saw it coming from a thousand leagues away, I shan't spoil by revealing). Much like the 'black-hats-for-baddies / white-hats-for-goodies' color-coding in old Hollywood westerns, in *pepla* it was oftentimes the females with jet-black hair who played the femmes fatale, while fair-haired actresses got to play the wholesome heroines. If you apply that bit of information here, it should provide you with a clue as to at least part of what said twist entails, although the 'big reveal' comes with such matter-of-factness that it scarcely causes a ripple of surprise, let alone actually throws us for any sort of loop.

The monster—well, *a* monster anyway (which is actually just one of three, none of which are ever seen sharing the screen together, more's the pity)—shows up one more time in the last reel, but nothing much becomes of its final appearance and, following a bunch of sound, fire and fury signifying not much of anything at all, the film simply ends (I hesitate to say runs out of steam and grinds to a screeching halt). While it's certainly no classic of its type, **HERCULES AGAINST THE MONSTER** is at the very least a mildly diverting minor timewaster, of some interest to fans of monster and muscleman movies alike.

Incidentally, the Cool Ass Cinema website includes this movie on their shit-list entitled "20 of the Worst Sword & Sandal Adventures" (@ *http://www.coolasscinema.com/2012/01/20-of-worst-sword-sandal-adventures.html*). Other titles listed therein/threat—prime 'monster peplum' fare all to varying degrees, in my opinion ("Worst", my ass!)—include **HERCULES VS. THE HYDRA** (*Gli amori di Ercole*, 1960, D: Carlo Ludovico Bragaglia), **ATLAS IN THE LAND OF THE CYCLOPS** (a.k.a. *Maciste nella terra dei ciclopi*, 1961, D: Antonio Leonviola), **MOLE MEN AGAINST THE SON OF HER-** CULES (*Maciste, l'uomo più forte del mondo*, 1961, D: Antonio Leonviola), **FIRE MONSTERS AGAINST THE SON OF HERCULES** (*Maciste contro i mostri*, 1962, D: Guido Malatesta), **VULCAN, GOD OF FIRE** (*Vulcano, figlio di Giove*, 1962, D: Emimmo Salvi) and **HERCULES AGAINST MOLOCH** (*Ercole contro Moloch*, 1963, D: Giorgio Ferroni).

LATITUDE ZERO

(緯度0大作戦 / *Ido zero daisakusen*)

Reviewed by Steve Fentone

Japan, 1969. D: Ishirō Honda

Anglo translation of the film's original Japanese trailer narration: *"Starring five of Hollywood's biggest stars, the world-renowned Toho presents the definitive version of a sci-fi film, which cost $1-million to make. Mystery of the unknown! An advanced scientific laboratory has been built 20,000 meters underwater: Latitude Zero. There lies a Utopia for the human race... Malik and his minions are trying to rule the world. Their submarine Black Shark and its opposing submarine, named Alpha. (Interspersed text blurb: An Evil Genius Is Proud To Present A Frightening Brain Transplant!) ...Unique weapons can be seen one after another! They arrive at the base of evil named Blood Rock Island and a great battle takes place! (Filled With Dreams And Adventures! A Spectacular Film! COMING SOON)."*

French *grande* poster; art by Constantin Belinsky

Above: Two intriguing stills for **LATITUDE ZERO**, the lower one a decidedly fanciful "cut-'n'-paste" composite job

if they didn't pan-out quite as originally planned on the production, which was severely compromised as a result—we Japanese monster fans can be grateful that we got at least one funtabulous flick out of it rather none at all!

Deep in the Equatorial South Pacific, whilst navigating the powerful Cromwell Current in Japanese waters, an exploratory bathysphere containing two top oceanographers (among them frequent face in *kaijū eiga* madness Akira Takarada [1934-] as Dr. Ken Tashiro) and a *gaijin* Trans-Globe News reporter named Perry Lawton (brawny American actor Richard "**GRIZZLY**" Jaeckel [1926-1997]) who is along for the ride tumbles out-of-control to the seabed—its mooring cable and airlines becoming severed from their support ship in the process—due to some serious turbulence from a violent seismic disturbance caused by an unstable underwater volcano. Although when it hits bottom it luckily lands right-side-up, just when things are looking real hopeless indeed for the men in the bathysphere (also including Masumi Okada (1935-2006), seen the previous year in Hiroki Matsuno's spooky J-horror **THE LIVING SKELETON** [吸血髑髏船 / *Kyūketsu Dokurosen*, 1968], here playing a very Eurasian-looking "Frenchman" named Dr. Jules Masson), along comes Joseph Cotten (1905-1994) as Capt. Greg McKenzie, an affable 204-year-old submariner/scientific genius who 'just happens' to zoom to the rescue in his massive sleekly-streamlined super-submersible, the Alpha (a vessel—which an inboard plaque proudly proclaims was launched way back in…1805!—that is quite obviously modeled after the Nautilus from Jules Verne's proto-SF novel *Twenty Thousand Leagues Under the Sea* [*Vingt mille lieues sous les mers*, 1869-1870], as is its skipper after that other sub's, Captain Nemo. In response to the Alpha's alleged vintage here, co-hero Takarada, who dubbed his own lines into thickly-accented English for the occasion, exclaims incredulously, "B-but, the first successful submarine wasn't built until the 1880s!").

Because Jaeckel also co-starred in another prime monster-filled Nipponese/American sci-fantasy, **THE GREEN SLIME** (ガンマー第3号 宇宙大作戦 / *Ganmā Daisan Gō: Uchū daisakusen*, 1968), the year previous to signing-on for the present gig, he isn't too surprised by all the weirdness to follow… He and his shipmates are fortuitously snatched from the brink of a watery grave by the ol' cap'n's crewmembers, including a bodacious bouffant blonde in a *très chic* mod low-cut gold lamé minidress and white go-go thighboots ensemble (who thereafter promptly politely introduces herself as Dr. Anne

And now for something, if not completely, then at least a little bit different from Toho, who here stepped outside their comfort zone somewhat to produce a one-off *tokusatsu* fest that stands completely separate from any of its then-ongoing kaiju series productions. That said, it's entirely feasible that the studio was hoping to kick-start an all-new franchise with **LATITUDE ZERO**, but for whatever reason, it didn't happen (actually, I do give a pretty good reason why below, but we'll get to that shortly…). However things might have been meant to ultimately go—even

Like A Bat Outta Heck! On the isle of Blood Rock, one of the malodorous Malik's batty hench-monsters imperils secondary heroine Mari Nakayama. Chances are that the stunt performer inside the bat-suit is either Haruo "Gojira" Nakajima, Harekichi Nakamura or Hiroshi Sekida

Barton ["She doesn't look much like a doctor!"] and is played by svelte, Floridian-born Linda Haynes [1947-], a kittenish Tuesday Weldesque actress whose none-too-prolific acting career included a decade later playing the heroine of the 'mock-horror' thriller **HUMAN EXPERIMENTS** [1979, USA, D: Gregory Goodell]. Then a budding starlet, Haynes celebrated her 21st birthday during the **LZ** shoot). Anyway, all safe and sound aboard the Alpha out of harm's way (for now!), the bathysphere's occupants are then spirited away to the wondrous, bubble-domed undersea community of Latitude Zero (so named after that point on the atlas where the Equator and International Dateline intersect), which is situated in a completely landless region right in mid-Pacific, hidden far below the surface (said ocean being the world's deepest, as you'll recall). LZ—informally known as "El Zee" for short by its inhabitants—is the adopted home to a collective of 'dropout' scientists, non-politicals ("Politics are only needed by those incapable of running their own lives," oversimplifies McKenzie in pat explanation) and various other voluntary defectors from the so-called 'civilized' capitalistic / imperialistic / militaristic societies that hold sway up on bad ol' *terra firma*. "Neither are we Russian, Greek, British or French, or any other nationality", explains the permanently self-scuppered skipper, who has no desire ever to return to the world above the waves. "We are *neutral*".

The bone of contention / thorn in the side of Capt. McKenzie's waterlogged Utopia is one ex-Lt. Hastings, alias Dr. Malik (TV *Batman*'s Cesar "The Joker" Romero [1907-1994], no less), who makes his initial appearance at almost exactly the 20-minute mark; tellingly enough, the first sound out of his mouth is a megalomaniacal laugh rather than an actual word of dialogue! Although, that said, the laughter sounds very unlike one of Joker's trademark maniacal cackles, so it wasn't *too* obvious of an attempt to call to mind his then-most-famous character. Reluctant to entirely let go of the upper world's influence and more of a semi-amphibious landlubber than his more idealistic nemesis McKenzie is, the gleefully evil Malik dwells on the nearby uncharted isle of Blood Rock (incidentally, Bloodrock, the Texas acid rock group of similar name, were formed the same year that this movie was released; we can't help wondering—and indeed, hoping!—that they got the idea from **LZ**), along with his ever-tippling, naggy GF Lucretia (occasional monster movie player Patricia Medina [1919-2012], who, ironically enough, was at the time married to her onscreen partner-in-crime's chief rival, Cotten, who only plays her 'old flame' in the film); oh, and last but by no means least, this villainous couple share their island with a wacky menagerie of enlarged Animalia, including giant rats (or 大ネズミ / *Oonezumi*), man-sized bipedal bat creatures (間コウモリ / *Ningen kōmori*; shades of the batty Berbalang and other similar

Chiroptera-based killer critters from Filipino lower mythology) and, most outrageous of all, a lion/condor composite lifeform possessed of a transplanted human brain. Malik's flagship is the sinister-looking Black Shark, a barb-finned, predatory supersub—a kind of ultramega über-U-Boat from Hell—skippered by the sultry Capt. Kuroiga (Hikaru Kuroki in her only known film role), a black-clad Oriental 'dragon lady', whose character's Japanese surname translates to "Black Moth". Complete with riding crop / swagger stick and a suitably dominatrix-like air, Kuroiga ends up, for her repeated failures, getting demoted by (involuntarily) 'donating' her grey matter to said lion/condor hybrid (which the *Toho Special Effects All-Monster Encyclopedia* [東宝特撮全怪獣図鑑 / *Tōhō Tokusatsu Zen Kaijū Zukan*, 2014] officially identifies as the Griffon [グリホン / *Gurihon*]; the same volume further informs us that said flyin' lion-beast is some 50 meters long and weighs-in at around 2,000 tons. So just how the hell it ever manages to get off the ground with its comparatively flimsy wings is anybody's business!). Gojipedia: The Godzilla Wiki (@ *godzilla.wikia.com*) credits busy monster suit performer Haruo "*Gojira*" Nakajima for playing not only the Griffon, but also a giant rat and batman herein too. His colleagues Harekichi Nakamura and Hiroshi "Yu" Sekida likewise performed onscreen as those lattermost creatures, of which there appear to be no more than a half-dozen in the film all told (*five*, tops?).

Elsewhere, we get oodles of submarine duels replete with whooshing heat-seeking torpedoes and zapping laser cannons shooting every-which-way that resemble something straight out of Gerry Anderson's "Supermarionation" teleseries *Stingray* (1964-65, UK). Fully-immersed in its own little world and seldom surfacing for air, as though its creators also much prefer what's Down There to what's Up Here (much as Capt. McKenzie and his followers do), **LATITUDE ZERO** gleefully thumbs its nose at both realism and logic, blowing loud and exceedingly moist raspberries at stodgy Cinema Critics in the process. It possesses a more-than-adequately fantastical look thanks to the lively SFX and nifty miniature work by the legendary Eiji Tsuburaya and his team (it repre-

Left, Top to Bottom: An alluring autographed cheesecake pose of the lovely Linda Haynes, one of **LZ**'s nicest "special effects" of all; *The Black Shark*; *The Alpha*; and a US lobby card showing the film's protagonists: *[left to right]* Richard Jaeckel, Ms. Haynes, Hiroki Matsuno, Joseph Cotten, Akira Takarada and Wataru Ōmae

sented said effects master's final assignment on a purely fantasy-based *tokusatsu* project), who give a whizz-bang, '60sesque *Dan Dare* comics style to the sleek designs of the underwater craft. These essentially resemble sub-oceanic space-ships, complete with rocket-like jet motors that leave wakes of fake 'bubbles'—actually smoky/steamy vapor trails—behind them (it rather goes without saying that most [if not all?] of the mini-ature sub scenes weren't really shot underwater at all. In actuality, the models were suspended by [*usually!*] invisible piano-wire out on dry land, with a 'shimmering' watery optical effect there-after superimposed atop the footage to make it appear to have been shot 'wet').

Temporarily capsizing the project if thankfully not succeeding in scuppering it entirely—its Jap-anese producers had already invested too much money in the production to allow it to sink with-out a trace now—according to August Ragone's mandatory tome *Eiji Tsuburaya: Master of Mon-sters* (San Francisco: Chronicle Books, 2007), **LZ**'s proposed American co-producer (Don Sharpe Productions) backed-out in the eleventh hour, yanking their half of the funding on what was supposed to be an even 50/50 split. Left in the lurch thus, Toho were forced to complete the film with their budget halved, meaning that many shortcuts had to be taken in order to salvage things. One result of this severe tightening of the

budgetary purse-strings was the FX dept. being out-of-necessity forced to skimp-'n'-scrimp on the creature suit designs, and in other areas too somewhat, although what made it to the screen is entirely acceptable enough to appeal to most kaiju geeks, I reckon (myself most definitely included!). Despite its failure to convince some-times—we prefer to blame this on those drastic budget cuts caused by that co-producer bailing on the project at such a critical juncture in its creation—the sheer enthusiasm and exuberance that went into the model work easily allows us to overlook all the numerous scientific bloopers and technical gaffes that are conspicuous behind some truly *unreal* Eastmancolor. But, what with all the colorful craziness that's going on, the last thing you'll be concerning yourself with is petty, nitpicky details like whether everything onscreen properly adheres to the laws of physics to the let-ter or not, right?

Largely relying on its lively visuals to tell the tale, the film's plot stays wafer-thin, as—in classic unilinear, myopic cliffhanger serial fash-ion—Malik seeks to kidnap a certain Dr. Okada (Canadian-born Japanese player Satoshi "Tetsu" Nakamura [1908-1992], the mad monster-maker from **THE MANSTER** [双頭の殺人鬼 / *Sōtō no satsujinki*, 1959, USA/Japan, Ds: George P. Breakston, Kenneth G. Crane]) in order to forci-bly extricate a top-secret formula for an "anti-ra-

With **LATITUDE ZERO** all in the can, its cast and crew pose for a group photo on the last day of the shoot

diation immunization serum" from him and put it to an improper use for which it wasn't originally intended by its inventor. **LZ**'s screenwriters (who notably included Ted Sherdeman, scripter of Gordon Douglas' 'gi-ant' bug classic **THEM!** [1954, USA]) bombard us with morally-simplistic juvenile-oriented thrills rapid-fire/non-stop, with the malevolently malicious Malik ("You're a *monster!*")—whose Kaiseresque costume includes jodhpurs and jackboots—surgically removing brains or whipping-up specimens of unnaturally-enlarged Mammalia on cue. Not quite as fanciful but close, taking a dip in a special chemical bath renders our heroes bulletproof (!?) for a 24-hour period, during which Cotten and the film's other protagonists conduct a commando raid on Blood Rock, fending-off malodorous mega-rats and creepy man-bats (latter of which—not at all a bad thing!—look like close kindred of those seen in Alfredo B. Crevenna's Mexi-monster *clásico* **ADVENTURE AT THE CENTER OF THE EARTH** [*Aventura al centro de la tierra*, 1964; see *Monster!* #16, p.6]. As per 'official' Toho-approved sources, the ones in **LZ** are around 7 feet tall and weigh about 200 kilos). According to the Toho Kingdom site (@ *www.tohokingdom.com*), the costumes worn by the "Bat Men" (as they are called in English in the book *Godzilla: Toho Monster Picture Book* [2005]) were reused on two different TV shows: "The first of these was heavily modified to create Alien Mechara for the Tsuburaya Productions' *Chibira-Kun* program [チビラくん, *1970-71*]. The second of these was an unmodified use, although the suit was in poor condition, to create Bat Man in the Toho

TV show *Go! Godman* [行け！ゴッドマン / Ike! Goddoman, *1972-73*]. The suit utilized in the *Go! Godman* show was the one with the curved-ear look. Teizo Toshimitsu modeled the head of the Bat Men. The body was modeled by Koei Yagi. In 2008, two toys of the Bat Men were released. Created by Tomohiro Sugita and released by Resin Chef & Team Ukeke, the models referred to the creatures as the 'Blood Rock Keepers'".

LZ comes with a twisteroo ending and some late-coming anti-war propaganda (again in keeping with staunch pacifist McKenzie's Nemo-inspired origins), and also—*ATTENTION: SPOILER ALERT!*—Mrs. Cotten (i.e., Medina) crumbling She-like to dust right before our eyes! That same year of '69, James Hill's British underwater fantasy adventure **CAPTAIN NEMO AND THE UNDERWATER CITY** (starring the mighty Robert Ryan as Nemo) explored some similar territory, albeit taking a considerably less-crazed approach to its material, although it memorably did boast a monster manta ray called Mobula, which might easily be the name of a Japanese kaiju. Both movies make for great Saturday matinees, so why not have yourself (and your kids, if you happen to have any) a double-bill sometime.

NOTES: After I originally saw **LZ** for the first time on Toronto late-night TV, a bare bones, no-frills version of this review (its 'foundation', if you will) first appeared in the final issue (#5, October 1990) of my long-defunct Xerox zine *Killbaby*; that review has been greatly revised / updated / expanded-upon for inclusion here. Whilst the IMDb and other sources spell Cesar Romero's character name as "Malic", the preferred spelling seems to be "Malik" (i.e., the one most-used at fan sites), so it's the one we went with ("He lives up to his name. In one archaic language, *malik* means 'murderer'", explains Cotten as the rather pedantic Capt. McKenzie, albeit without bothering to mention which language!). Supposedly the first-ever interview (dating from May 2016) that Linda Haynes ever gave specifically about **LZ** can be read via clicking on the link at the blog Sidelong Glances of a Pigeon Kicker (@ *http://sidelongglancesofapigeonkicker.blogspot.ca/2016/05/linda-haynes-interview-latitude-zero.html*). That will redirect you to the website Vantage Point Interviews: Conversations and Oral Histories (@ *https://vantagepointinterviews.com/2016/05/27/revisiting-latitude-zero-actress-linda-haynes-recounts-her-toho-experience/*). There you will find an illustrated item compiled/posted by Brett Homenick entitled "Revisiting Latitude Zero! Actress Linda Haynes Recounts Her Toho Experience!" Why am I listing

Above: The cuddly Griffon is one of Blood Rock's more spectacular denizens

Above: Obverse *[left]* and reverse *[right]* views of a Japanese Menko card depicting **LATI-TUDE ZERO**'s ferocious flyin' lion

both the blog and site here rather than saving you a step by pointing you directly to the latter and thus 'eliminating the middle man', so to speak? Because I'm sure Mr. Homenick would appreciate me giving shout-outs to both, that's why. It's the least I can do after 'borrowing' some factoids and images from his article! ☺ So by all means give both those URL addies some traffic, okay?!

INVISIBLE INVADERS

Reviewed by Christos Mouroukis

USA, 1959. D: Edward L. Cahn

Taglines: *"An unearthly enemy defying modern science in a war to the death!" – "How can you stop what you can't see?" – "A sci-fi shocker that'll keep you awake at night!"*

Atomic scientist Dr. Karol Noymann (John Carradine, who around the same time was doing voice-work for the English version of **INVASION OF THE ANIMAL PEOPLE** [1959, USA/Sweden, D: Virgil W. Vogel]) is killed in a laboratory accident in the opening scene, and his friend Dr. Adam Penner (Philip Tonge, who is mostly remembered for his TV work, but one year prior to this he was seen in William Castle's **MACABRE** [1958, USA]) thereafter resigns. At the funeral, an invisible (hence the title) alien takes-over and reanimates the late Dr. Noymann's corpse, which then informs Penner that all Earthlings must surrender, or else chaos will ensue via the mass-resurrection of still more dead bodies (you can see the similarities to the same year's **PLAN 9 FROM OUTER SPACE** [1959, USA, D: Edward D. Wood, Jr.], right? It's as though sci-fi filmmakers from the late '50s believed that the dead really would walk the earth, and I'm pretty sure hell wasn't even close to being full at that stage!).

The good doctor informs Dr. John Lamont (monster/horror movie regular Robert "**THE SLIME PEOPLE**" Hutton, later to be seen in the underrated Amicus anthology **TORTURE GARDEN** [1967, UK/USA, D: Freddie Francis]) about the impending menace, and Lamont in turn briefs Washington on the matter. The government ignores the signs and Doc Penner is branded a madman for his ravings, however. Thankfully, Penner has his daughter Phyllis (Jean Byron, who had a prolific career in television, but readers of this magazine may find it noteworthy that she also co-starred in the sci-fi'er **THE MAGNETIC MONSTER** [1953, USA, Ds: Curt Siodmak, Herbert L. Strock]) and Doc Lamont on his side, as the three of them have just witnessed another invisible invader (the fact that the aliens are kept mostly out of sight was a clever decision by producer Robert

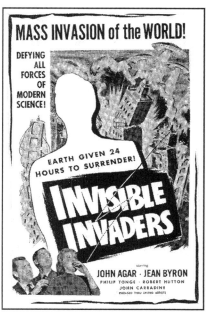

US pressbook ad

Mexican lobby card

E. Kent in order to keep the budget to a minimum; exploitation movie fans will be delighted to know that Kent's final film credit was as a writer and associate producer on the controversial 'sex-change' biopic **THE CHRISTINE JORGENSEN STORY** [1970, USA, D: Irving Rapper]).

Rough conceptual art for the US poster;
artist unknown

It isn't long before Lamont's theories in regards to the upcoming invasion prove correct, though, as an extraterrestrially-animated zombie (and a highly *visible* one at that!) wreaks havoc inside a hockey stadium. This creature is not one of the dumb living dead as we came to know them in post-'68 cinema, but is able to talk, and goes so far as making a public announcement over the airwaves. The invasion is now widespread (the headline of a newspaper clipping reads "First Photo of an Invisible Invader", but the image is blank) and the audience is subjected to several scenes of disasters, which are mostly depicted via stock news footage and miniature work (albeit nicely-rendered), but the occasional impressive stunt also pops up, including an awesome car-flipping (albeit borrowed from Robert Mitchum's 'moonshiners-vee-revenooers' classic **THUNDER ROAD** [1958, USA, D: Arthur Ripley]).

The U.S. Army wisely gets involved, and Maj. Bruce Jay (John Agar, who—just so you get an idea where his career was at this point—was also in the previous year's **ATTACK OF THE PUPPET PEOPLE** [1958, USA, D: Bert I. Gordon]) takes Docs Lamont and Penner, along with Phyllis, to a sanctuary, where they will shortly learn that the alien zombies are in fact radioactive (another cliché from the era, which be-

Creature Feature Reviews

comes apparent very early on when the atomic destruction of Hiroshima is mentioned). In order to find a solution to the menace, the protagonists conduct a series of experiments (mostly with an alien zombie they manage to capture, in a series of scenes that clearly inspired "Bub" [played by Sherman Howard] in George A. Romero's **DAY OF THE DEAD** [1985, USA]). Will they find a way to defeat the evil that threatens our planet, or will they all die in vain...?

Okay, the zombies herein are referred as "the walking dead", and there are a number of ideas that were later lifted for Romero's **NIGHT OF THE LIVING DEAD** (1968, USA), but the present film is mostly just silly fun that lacks the unsettling atmosphere and gruesomeness of **NOTLD**. Sure, most of the imagery (thanks to the cinematography by Maury Gertsman, who shot countless of your favorite genre movies, including the Sherlock Holmes epics **DRESSED TO KILL** and **TERROR BY NIGHT** [both 1946, USA, D: Roy William Neill]), while Paul Dunlap's soundtrack (which was recycled for **THE ANGRY RED PLANET** [1959, USA, D: Ib Melchior], **THE THREE STOOGES IN ORBIT** [1962, USA, D: Edward Bernds] and **DESTINATION INNER SPACE** [1966, USA, D: Francis D. Lyon]) is creepy as hell, and this could well be my 'new' fave moldy oldie (until I discover another one, that is!). It keeps things nice and simple overall, and—guess what?—it's all-the-more-entertaining for doing so.

Backed by Robert E. Kent Productions (under the Premium Pictures moniker), this was made as a package deal along with same director Cahn's spooky voodoo schlocker **THE FOUR SKULLS OF JONATHAN DRAKE** (1959, USA), and, contrary to popular belief, it received only a short run upon its initial June 1959 theatrical release, and became famous due to its subsequent TV airings (it gained more fame/notoriety after genre fans began to notice similarities between **II** and the aforementioned **NOTLD**). The film saw release onto VHS cassette in the '90s, but millennial monster kids can easily get ahold of an official DVD of it these days, as it was put out under MGM Home Entertainment's "Midnite Movies" banner as a double-bill with Sid Pink's **JOURNEY TO THE SEVENTH PLANET** (1962, USA/Denmark), which was the film that **II** was paired with upon its original release by United Artists. Its screenplay was written by Samuel Newman (who is mostly remembered for penning TV series and jungle movies, such as the *Jungle Jim* entry **JUNGLE MAN-EATERS** [1954, USA, D: Lee Sholem], starring Johnny

"Within three days, the dead will destroy all the living!" A triptych of scenes from the first massed zombie invasion flick ever made. **Top & Center:** US lobby cards. **Above:** US lobby still. Trailer narration excerpt: *"Living dead men threatening to destroy all life on Earth!"*

Weissmuller) and directed by Eddie Cahn (who directed more than a hundred films, among them such favorites of this magazine as **INVASION OF THE SAUCER-MEN** [1957, USA] and **IT! THE TERROR FROM BEYOND SPACE** [1958, USA]).

Brazilian DVD jacket for **LIGHTS OUT**

LIGHTS OUT

Reviewed by Christos Mouroukis

USA, 2016. D: David F. Sandberg

Ad-line: *"You were right to be afraid of the dark."*

One difference between the stuff that the esteemed Tim Paxton generally reviews and the stuff that Yours Truly reviews is that, typically, the films from the continent he usually discusses come with a distinctive cultural stamp (i.e., there are a great many folkloric legends in India about supernatural presences), and that element alone gives them a certain perspective and framework. On the other hand, what I usually watch (recent US stuff) largely depends on the imagination of the filmmakers at hand, as only comparatively rarely is a point made to connect the ghosts to, say, Native American legends—a common source for US-born-and-bred ghost stories—or some other such established mythos. This somehow makes the better entries in the recent wave of American-made cinematic ghost stories refreshingly unpredictable, and one such notable occasion is the film under review, which had me jumping off my couch, scared shitless!

In an extremely scary pre-credits sequence (especially for a movie opener), at a gloomy warehouse workspace after hours, an employee (Lotta Losten) worries about *something*—an indistinct shape, black as night—that she had seen lurking in the darkness when the lights were out, but her employer Paul (Billy Burke, from **RED RIDING HOOD** [2011, USA/Canada, D: Catherine Hardwicke]) thinks nothing of it, and tells her to punch-out for the evening and go home. After making the lights go out, the mysterious presence then finds its opportunity in the dark and savagely offs Paul, who—*too late!*—realizes his employee's frightened claim was all-too-real. With a prologue like this, filled with expertly-staged jump scares, I knew right from the outset that I was in for a real treat! And I was not disappointed...

Post-credits we are introduced to the first victim's stepdaughter Rebecca (Teresa Palmer from **WARM BODIES** [2013, USA/Canada, D: Jonathan Levine]), a high-maintenance drama queen with too much attitude who doesn't cut her boyfriend Bret (Alexander DiPersia, from **FOREVER** [2015, USA, D: Tatia Pilieva]) too much slack. Meanwhile, her estranged mother Sophie (Maria Bello, from David Cronenberg's **A HISTORY OF VIOLENCE** [2005, USA/Germany/Canada]) is suffering from mental illness (much ado is made of her being on antidepressants), and she even has an 'imaginary' friend, Diana; all of which are reasons enough for her young son Martin (Gabriel Bateman, from **ANNABELLE** [2014, USA, D: John R. Leonetti]) to feel unsafe living with Mom, so off he goes with his sister to stay at her place for a spell. The problem is that Diana *was* actually a real person: who as a girl was subjected by psychiatric practitioners to experimental treatments involving strong lights—which caused her to spontaneously combust!—and her lingering angry spirit was essentially what drove the family's late patriarch away. Diana's spirit lingers still, seemingly bent on tearing asunder the remaining remnants of the troubled family in her selfish eagerness to monopolize Mom's company for herself...

It's not always clear exactly what we see (or *don't* see) in the dark, but one thing is certain: it *is* a monster! And judging from the occasional flash-glimpse close-up we get of it, it's a dang scary one at that. This monstrous ghostess is rendered powerless and disappears when the lights are on (she goes to great lengths to prevent that from happening), but she is extremely powerful when they are off (hence the—*ahem!*—spot-on title); so powerful, in fact, that the creature's martial arts-like fighting skills surprised me at times. A ninja ghost? *Who knew?!*

Wisely for a film about a ghostly entity whose

powers depend on the absence of light for its effectiveness, both the cinematography and editing are expertly handled. Although **LO** is overall unnecessarily conventional with its settings, director of photography Marc Spicer (from James Wan's **FURIOUS SEVEN** [2015, USA/Japan]; Wan functioned as one of the many producers on the present title under review) really did miracles here by creating specific lighting themes and 'light-centric' visuals that will stick with you long after viewing the film. For the most part natural light was used (including candles and other authentic sources), but it's all so well-orchestrated that the results had me breathless.

Besides qualifying as an all-out ghost/monster movie, **LIGHTS OUT** raises a variety of questions, the most important of which being: what if the demons we all have in our minds could come out of our heads and materialize in physical form to hurt us and our loved ones? Sure, what we have here is a straight-on horror film (and a highly commercial one at that), but **LIGHTS OUT** is so much more than that: essentially a diatribe on Freudian notions of psychosis/shock therapy, albeit without belabouring the point. It was hands-down my *favorite* film from 2016! Plus, I can't remember *ever* being so scared of a PG-13 film, and a conspicuously goreless at that.

The young Diana was played by Ariel Dupin (**THE CHRISTMAS GIFT** [2015, USA, D: Fred Olen Ray]), teenage Diana was played by Ava Cantrell (**ONE UNDER THE SUN** [2016, USA, Ds: Vincent Tran, Riyaana Hartley]) and grown-up Diana was played by Alicia Vela-Bailey (a stuntwoman by trade, whose occasional acting credits include **HOSTEL: PART III** [2011, USA, D: Scott Spiegel]).

Director David F. Sandberg previously made the short subject *Lights Out* (2013, USA), which went viral online and made him a hot name in Hollywood virtually overnight. Not long thereafter, producers Eric Heisserer (who also penned the screenplay), James Wan and Lawrence Grey came onboard and—*voila!*—Sandberg had himself a bona fide feature film deal with the major players. Made for just $4.9 million, the feature-length version of **LIGHTS OUT** received its premiere at the 2016 Los Angeles Film Festival, going on to gross more than $148.9 million. As is to be expected after such commercial success, a sequel has been announced, but Sandberg's success story doesn't end there, as he went on to direct another genre effort, **ANNABELLE: CREATION** [2017, USA].

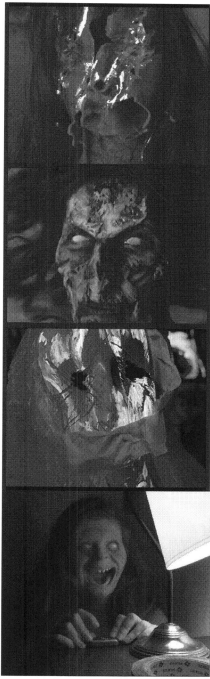

Top to Bottom: Three shots from the full-length feature version of **LO** and *[bottom]* the freaky punch-line from the original short

HOBGOBLINS X 2

A mini-monster twofer reviewed
by Christos Mouroukis

USA, 1988 + 2009. D: Rick Sloane

Ad-line: *"Be careful what you wish for... You just might get it!"*

Like all good monster kids, I too watched **GREMLINS** (1984, USA, D: Joe Dante) and **GREMLINS 2: THE NEW BATCH** (1990, USA, D: Joe Dante), but the pesky li'l creatures I *really* fell in love with were the ones in **CRITTERS** (1986, USA/UK, D: Stephen Herek) and **CRITTERS 2** (1988, USA, D: Mick Garris). I even tried awful hard to like **CRITTERS 3** (1991, USA, D: Kristine Peterson) and **CRITTERS 4** (1992, USA, D: Rupert Harvey), but it proved impossible. And don't even get me started on the ghastly *Ghoulies* franchise! Desperate for my 'little critter flick' fix, I then resorted to extra-low-budget fare the likes of **MUNCHIES** (1987, USA, D: Tina Hirsch). At long last I finally got around to watching **HOBGOBLINS** (1988), a justifiably much-ridiculed entry in the 'mini-monster' subgenre, and I can honestly say that it is virtually impossible to enjoy, because it isn't even "so-bad-it's-good"; it is just plain *BAD*, and (even worse) totally *boring* besides. So sue me!

An announced sequel, **LIGHTS OUT 2**, is due to see release soon

Pre-credits, in a movie studio, lowly security guard Dennis (Kevin Kildow, making his debut; his short career also included an appearance in **THE GIVING** [1992, USA, D: Eames Demetrios]) fantasizes about becoming and rock star, then he dies. Post-credits we are introduced to hero material Kevin (one-timer Tom Bartlett) and his conservative girlfriend Amy (one-timer Paige Sullivan), who appears to be impressed by Nick (Billy Frank, also seen in **NUDITY REQUIRED** [1990, USA, D: John T. Bone], but has since become a producer) who just came back from a stint in the Army, but Nick has eyes only for Daphne (Kelley Palmer, whose debut was in **THE VISITANTS** [1986, USA, D: Rick Sloane]). All these characters, along with nerd Kyle (one-timer Steven Boggs) are caricatures—and *pathetic* ones at that!—and they exchange dialogue that is supposed to be funny, but none of the intentional comedy works here… and there's precious little in the way of *un*intentional comedy either, for that matter. I think that jack-of-all-trades (master of none?) cinematographer/editor/writer/producer/director Rick Sloane (who made his inauspicious debut with **BLOOD THEATRE** [1986, USA]) believed that if he made his film 'knowingly self-aware', he could get away with how thoroughly rotten it is; but if so, he failed dismally in that aim!

Back at the aforementioned movie studio, Mr. McCreedy (Jeffrey Culver, later seen in the superior **BAD GIRLS FROM MARS** [1990, USA, D: Fred Olen Ray]; reportedly, John Carradine was in talks about the McCreedy part, but the paltry $15,000 budget couldn't afford him) explains to Kevin how, some 30 years ago, the titular varmints crashed their spaceship on the studio lot, and since then he has been trying to keep them under control, because they have the power— à la jinn (الجن) demons of Arabian/Islamic mythology—to force a person to dream about his (or her) wildest fantasies then turn them against their victims, bringing about their deaths. Well, the proverbial shit hits the fan, and the creatures escape. Their first order of business is to attack the aforementioned youthful protagonists' house party, but the pint-sized pests from outer space are so poorly realized that they are impossible to take seriously as a menace, despite the human performers' earnest attempts at trying to make it look as though they are fighting with them. A fun piece of trivia informs us that these puppets were created/operated by a mental patient, and the director hadn't seen them prior to shooting! An earlier draft of the screenplay had only the eyes of the hobgoblins appearing onscreen, and maybe they should have stuck with that idea. But then again, knowing how much monster kids love getting a good look at their monsters, perhaps that more 'demure' approach might not have worked very well either.

We shortly move to the Scum Club (actually shot at The Music Machine, a Los Angeles nightclub), which I think is *supposed* to be your standard discotheque, but instead comes across more like a whorehouse. Here, a lot of running time is padded-out when a new-wavey band of poseurs called The Fontanelles (including Cole Coonce, who scored **THE LIVING END** [1992, USA, D: Gregg Araki] and Patrick Dean, who now produces short films) performs what sounds like a Z-grade "Sisters of Mercy"-wannabe number. More time is then wasted when Amy performs a sexless striptease routine. It seems as though these two particular entertainments (i.e., the rock act and the 'peeler' [note quotes]) were supposed to be the main attractions here, which says a lot about **H1**'s lowest-common-denominator aspirations. Anyway, the protagonists decide that explosives will be the best method for getting rid of the hobgoblins, but will they go out with a bang or a whimper…?

Some of the soundtrack by Alan DerMarderosian (who since then scored **SAMURAI COP** [1991, USA, D: Amir Shervan], amongst other things) is reminiscent of Simon Boswell's score for the cyberpunk cult fave **HARDWARE** (1990, UK/USA, D: Richard Stanley), but this is where its merits end. Most of the spectacular scenes here (including a car explosion) appear to have been lifted from other movies (although I cannot confirm that), and a decently-staged 'man-on-fire' gag is not enough to save the day. Overall, I think that even Troma would be ashamed to release this pathetically unfunny comedy (as of this writing, it has a mere "2.3" rating on IMBb, which seems overly generous to me), but F.O. Ray's Retromedia outfit didn't mind releasing it on DVD!

H1 was shot on 'short ends' (i.e., scraps of unused film stock leftover from other productions) to minimize costs, and '80s action amazon Sybil Danning was approached for a part herein, but, as with Carradine, the production couldn't afford her minimum going rate. A sequel was planned by Rick Sloane as early as 1990, and he had even written a screenplay for it, but it would take him a 'few' more years—make that over *two decades!*—to finally get around to it (for what it's worth, the long-delayed sequel is reviewed below).

The present film also stars Tamara Clatterbuck (now famous for her TV career, she also showed-up in the same director's **VICE ACADEMY** [1989, USA]), Duane Whitaker (later seen in

German A1 poster; art unsigned

such high-profile fare as Quentin Tarantino's **PULP FICTION** [1994, USA]), Kari French (**ZODIAC KILLER** [2005, USA, D: Ulli Lommel]), Daran Norris (who also lent his voice to animated films, not to mention Trey Parker's infamous **TEAM AMERICA: WORLD POLICE** [2004, USA/Germany]!), James Mayberry (who filled a bit part in the big-budget dystopian SF disaster **FREEJACK** [1992, USA, D: Geoff Murphy]), Ken Abraham (now an editor of several hit TV series, but previously an actor in **CREEPOZOIDS** [1987, USA, D: David DeCoteau]), Don Barrett (who debuted in the shocker **SLAUGHTERHOUSE** [1987, USA, D: Rick Roessler]), and David Teague (who enjoyed a brief career in high-profile animation).

And so to **HOBGOBLINS 2** (ad-line: *"Don't Say We Didn't Warn You!"*), Sloane's exceedingly belated 2009 pseudo-sequel to the, er, original. We're guessing that the only reason this 20-odd-year-late self-cash-in even came about at all was because of **H1**'s newfound New Millennial popularity due to having been given the dubious *MST3K* 'treatment' in the interim. But such is life! Now, filmmaker Rick Sloane's humble output (his above-cited **VICE ACADEMY** [1989, USA] for example) didn't generate too much excitement even back during the boom years of home videotape (circa '80s/'90s). So can you imagine how dated and irrelevant it must seem today? See **HOBGOBLINS 2** if you're interested in finding out!

Kevin (Josh Mills, an executive producer of **DEATH HOUSE** [2016, USA, D: Harrison Smith]), Kyle (Josh Green, also seen in the same year's **SPICY MAC PROJECT** [2009, USA, D: Spicy Mac]), Nick (Jason Buuck, from **STAR PARTY** [2005, USA, D: Paul Curley]), Amy (Sabrina Bolin, also in the following year's **RICKY** [2010, USA, D: Kevin Wagoner]) and Daphne (Jordana Berliner, also seen in **CRUSTACEAN** [2009, USA, D: L.J. Dopp]) all return in this sequel, although it isn't clear when exactly it takes place, because, while on the one hand the lot of them don't appear to have aged any (although the characters are played by different performers), they now have all the modern amenities, including mobile phones and the internet. Anyway, this bunch heads off to the nearby psychiatric clinic, where they meet McCreedy (Roland Esquivel, from **SAFETY FIRST: THE RISE OF WOMEN!** [2008, USA, D: Greg McDonald]), who is now a patient there and who once again warns the youngsters of the hobgoblins that prey on their fantasies. Well, the so-called psychiatric clinic and its patients resemble what Troma's idea of a mental ward would be (complete with a "Do Not Disturb Further" sign), and as such it is more than a little offensive.

F.O. Ray's '00s stateside DVD edition, with bonus Bettie Page impersonator!

Yes indeed, it's business-as-usual, with still more immobile puppet nonsense. The critters do look a bit better this time out, as it appears as though Sloane learned a thing or two about creative camera angles when shooting things that don't have the ability to move by themselves. This time, Matt Berger (usually a gaffer on short films) was employed as the cinematographer (same as the original, this too was shot on economical 35mm short ends), but overall **H2** is far more polished (at least visually) in comparison to the original. Some minor details here and there also reveal that writer/director/producer Rick Sloane actually cares about the characters onscreen; despite how pathetic such an assumption might sound. As an unsubtle in-joke, a poster for **H1** is seen on a wall, adding further confusion to the films' timelines, as this indicates that the previous events were just a movie; but I think I'm probably the only person on Earth concerned with such trivial details.

Supposedly, in the tradition of **GRINDHOUSE** (2007, USA, Ds: Robert Rodriguez, Eli Roth, Quentin Tarantino, Edgar Wright, Rob Zombie), the present film promised us fake trailers, but all we get are glimpses of brief scenes with title cards. These include "CHAINSAW CHICKS" (supposedly co-starring Marilyn Burns and Linda Lovelace!), "NIGHTMARE OF THE LOST WHORES" and "AMPUTEE HOOKERS" (latter proclaiming that they charge an arm and a leg!), but you're better off watching Fred Olen Ray's **HOLLYWOOD CHAINSAW HOOKERS** (1988, USA) instead. Elsewhere, the opening scene from Wes Craven's **SCREAM** (1996, USA) is spoofed, and a closing title card 'wittily' assures us that no puppets were harmed during the making of **H2**.

The cast also includes: Chanel Ryan (**CIRCUS OF THE DEAD** [2014, USA, D: Billy "Bloody Bill" Pon]), Dan Glenn (**ALIENS VS. AVATARS** [2011, USA, D: Lewis Schoenbrun]), Ashley Ausburn (how *does* one pronounce her last name?!), Matthew Mahaney (**SAMURAI COP 2: DEADLY VENGEANCE** [2015, USA, D: Gregory Hatanaka]), Karen Knotts (**EXORCISM** [2003, USA, D: William A. Baker]), Derrel Maury (**MASSACRE AT CENTRAL HIGH** [USA, 1976, D: Rene Daalder]), John Grant (**BIRDEMIC: SHOCK AND TERROR** [2010, USA, D: James Nguyen]), Adrian Lee (**LOGGERHEADS** [2005, USA, D: Tim Kirkman]), and Joy Villa (**ZOMBIE ED** [2013, USA, D: Ren Blood]).

In summation, the *Hobgoblins* duology is for only the most forgiving, undemanding and easily-entertained monster mavens. All others beware! Consider yourself warned.

A hobgoblin says howdy-doody

LA HORA DE MARÍA Y EL PÁJARO DE ORO

("The Hour of María and the Golden Bird")

Reviewed by Martín Núñez

Argentina, 1975. D: Rodolfo Kuhn

Unfortunately, the Argentinean film industry seems to be sorely overlooked among film enthusiasts, but thankfully this mistake can be easily fixed thanks to the internet, which allows us to dive into the more obscure depths of its cinema (and the rest of the world's too!) at will…

Discerning cult film connoisseurs should already be aware of such Buenos Aires-born filmmakers as Armando Bo and/or Emilio Vieyra, while other Argentines such as Rodolfo Kuhn (1934-1987) still remain lost in the shadows on the darker side of the Latin-American film industry. We have to remark that Argentina used to have one of *the greatest* film industries on the American continent until the dawn of the big-budget productions that almost killed independent productions in the States, as well as other countries too.

In the 'Sixties, a sizeable number of Argentinean moviemakers started a sort of 'New Wave' that delved into 'depthier' concerns in order to express their views about society and politics

in those agitated days, as well as expressing their intentions to expose and erode the significant social barriers that then existed. In order to achieve this, they stripped-down film to the very basics. Thus, with relatively little in the way of budget/production values, a whole generation focused more on the core (i.e., *corazón* ["heart"]) of Cinema, distancing themselves from the star system and complicated camera tricks in order to let movies speak for themselves, organically, through new and particularly poignant poetics.

Argentine one-sheet poster; artist unknown

Among these directors, some got more attention than others. People like Leopoldo Torre Nilsson and Manuel Antín are considered among the greatest Argentinean filmmakers (with good reason, given their genius!), while others like Kuhn largely remained out of the limelight due to their obscure subjects and poor distribution deals.

Born in Buenos Aires on December 29th, 1934, Rodolfo Kuhn became fascinated with cinema in his childhood, and despite his father forcing him to study Medicine, the young Kuhn managed to secure a part-time job at an advertising company, which got him into contact with the world of documentary filmmaking, and subsequently with Cinema proper itself. Kuhn made his debut as a director in 1962 with the full-length feature **LOS JÓVENES VIEJOS** ("The Old Young Ones"), a movie that fell in line with the then-ongoing local new wave that focused primarily on societal problems. The film was heaped with praise by critics and audiences alike, scoring some decent exposure at various international film festivals that year. Also in '62, Kuhn directed **LOS INCONSTANTES** ("The Fickle Ones"), and in 1965 he premiered his most-acclaimed effort, **PAJARITO GÓMEZ** ("Birdie Gómez"), a tale of fame and its excesses that placed him at the very pinnacle of Argentinean auteurs. However, in 1967 he changed his artistic interests to make more commercial fare in order to be able to continue shooting movies on a constant basis, and that same year **EL ABC DEL AMOR** ("The ABC's of Love") got released. This was a multinational anthological drama co-produced by Argentina, Brazil and

The novel by Eduardo Gudiño Kieffer

Chile, with a director from each of those countries helming separate segments for their particular country of origin. Helvio Soto shot the Chilean segment, but its quality wasn't up to scratch, so his short story got trimmed for the film's Argentinean release. Sadly, the film remains lost to this day, so we are unable to discuss it further. This loss is unfortunate, because the Chilean segment starred and was photographed by two film icons in one of their earliest filmic efforts: respectively, Miguel Littín (director of **EL CHACAL DE NAHUELTORO** / "Jackal of Nahueltoro", 1969) and Patricio Guzmán, famous for **LA BATALLA DE CHILE** ("The Battle of Chile" [1975-79]), his epic three-part documentary on the Chilean Socialist era and its violent military aftermath.

In 1968, Kuhn got into action cinema with **HURACANES EN LA CARRETERA** ("Hurricanes on the Road", a.k.a. **TURISMO DE CARRETERA**), centering around the once-popular sport of auto-racing. That same year, he directed the comedy **UFA CON EL AMOR**, and a year later he got into politics once again with a multi-director sociopolitical documentary entitled **ARGENTINA, MAYO DE 1969: LOS CAMINOS DE LA LIBERACIÓN** ("Argentina, May 1969: The Roads to Liberation"), another title that seems to have become lost.

Following **ARGENTINA, MAYO DE 1969**, Kuhn had to wait six years before becoming involved with a new feature; that being the present film, a decidedly *weird* one which is extremely difficult to pigeonhole. Is it folk horror? About popular sorcery? A psychological drama? A coming-of-age tale? Arty, idiosyncratic cinema? ...*All* of the above, and yet *none* of them!

Based on a screenplay by celebrated Argentine man of letters Eduardo Gudiño Kieffer (1935-2002)—who also penned the movie's novelization—in 1975 Kuhn finally released **LA HORA DE MARÍA Y EL PÁJARO DE ORO**, a film that took so long to materialize due to his political exile, but it was worth the wait.

María Sepúlveda (Leonor Manso [1948-]) is a young country girl who dreams of leaving her rural life in the Northern Argentinean province of Corrientes, but she lives with her *abuela* (["grandmother"] Milagros de la Vega [1895-1980]), an old woman involved in popular witchcraft and ancient beliefs who dissuades María in her efforts to find liberation and emancipation by telling her about her own mother's fate when she headed off to the city. María's mother had left home right after noonday, in *la hora del sol* ("the sun's hour"), a time of day when, legend has it, a local monster known as Pombero roams the land ravishing innocent young girls, who become impregnated as a result. Another local being, the little blonde Yaciyateré, also goes out during the daytime, stealing babies.

María's life is simple and ruled by a fear that her granny inculcates within her granddaughter while the old woman keeps her busy with strange local black magic rituals. But at last the young girl manages to escape from her rude, rustic hovel at Sun's Hour, only to find herself haunted by visions of a humanoid bird-like being... Dracula (!). Terrified by these visions, she hurries back home, only to discover that Granny is dead, but in its death-grip her corpse clutches a voodoo-like periapt: a hand-carved, painted wooden skeleton ornament that will become María's personal protective amulet when she leaves her hometown and heads off to the city of Corrientes, attracted there like a moth to a flame. Upon her arrival, she secures a job at the estate of *doña* María (Dora Baret), a mysterious rich woman who also 'just happens' to be involved with black magic!

Argentinian filmmaker Rodolfo Kuhn (1934-1987)

Starting her new life will be difficult for our heroine, as she will need to get used to modern living and cultivating the social graces, which are in direct opposition to her previous life confined in a rural world filled with primitive pagan superstitions. María seems happy while discovering new kinds of friendship—and especially romantic love in the arms of a charming young Paraguayan peasant. However, the dread figure of Pombero haunts her still... (The folk horror elements can be appreciated here, despite the fact that we never actually get to see the Pombero or Yaciyateré monsters onscreen; they are very much present in a tacit—almost tactile—sense, however, much like myths are for us in 'real' life. Much more literally, we get to see firewalkers in action—María included—strolling over red-hot coals, and what resembles some sort of local variation of "Spin the Bottle", involving a drunken turkey [!?])

Wishing to at last live her life as she sees fit, María throws herself into work... and love (including feeling faint glimmerings of Sapphic attraction and temptation). This coming-of-age element of the story is one of the most assured aspects of the movie, as we witness María transforming from a scared, oppressed girl (although the actress was around 27 at the time) into a free-spirited young woman whose destiny will soon be bringing her into collision with that old black magic... again!

Newly-liberated in her adult life, María attends the local big Carnival, in which she sees her former childhood fears symbolized by that human-sized golden bird—which emits a shrill, *kaijū*-like squawk—and the Draculaic vampire she had sighted during the Sun's Hour earlier in the narrative. Along with an Igor-like hunchback and Dracula, who emerges from his coffin and bares his bloody fangs at her, she also sees a towering (roughly 15-foot-tall!) Frankenstein Monster figure and the troop of mad scientists who hastily construct him during this carnival, which resem-

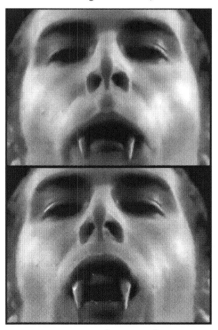

LA HORA DE MARÍA Y EL PÁJARO DE ORO's carnival vampire (actor unknown)

bles its more famous, gaudy costume-filled counterpart in Rio de Janeiro, Brazil.

Symbolically speaking, these monsters and the costumed carnival choreographies mark the end of María's innocence as she begins her struggle with adult life while dealing with her new boss, *doña* María. This enigmatic older, far worldlier woman seems to be hiding an obscure truth which María will try to uncover after discovering weird offerings—including a girl's photograph stuck with pushpins stuffed inside a shoe—buried on her boss' property, and it is at this point that the movie takes on a rather disturbing tone; this because María learns that these buried offerings belonged to girls who had formerly worked in the *doña*'s house. It is this unnerving discovery which causes María's irrational superstitious fears to return with a vengeance, leading her to see strange reflections in the mirror. In one scene, as she looks into said mirror, our heroine's reflected face is momentarily juxtaposed with that of the lady of the house (shades of a similar scene in Nobuhiko Obayashi's later **HOUSE** [ハウス / *Hausu*, 1977, Japan]; see *Monster!* #33 [p.317]). These eerie visions—such as one of her sinister boss holding a baby—take on strange and scary psychological ramifications, much like what happens in one of the greatest Argentinean psychodramas ever filmed, **LA MARY** (1974, D: Daniel Tinayre), in which a looking-glass is able to reveal the inner demons of those who look into it. Elsewhere in the present film, while covertly looking in through her employer's bedroom window one night, the young María, much to her disturbance, witnesses the older María sensuously caressing a large snake in a provocative manner. She subsequently sights the ghostly inverted image of a white-clad young woman on the reflective surface of a pond, and finds a wee 'voodoo' doll with black pins stuck in its eyes.

Simultaneously attracted to and repelled by the beautiful but mysterious and exploitative *doña* María, the younger María (the film's principal

Left, Top to Bottom: "Dracula" at the carnival (this is the same character that haunts María early in the film); Leonor Manso as María; her grandmother's magical skeletal amulet; Milagros de la Vega as María's granny, whose after-death influence stays with her granddaughter, whose inbred beliefs in folk superstition run too deeply to be forgotten. **Next Page:** Argentine newspaper ad for the film's premiere on August 28th, 1975. *[Image courtesy of Dario Lavia]*

Creature Feature Reviews

female characters both sharing the same Christian name is far from mere coincidence!) seeks advice from a local witch-woman. Frightened, the old witch tells María she must retrieve her granny's skeleton amulet from her boss, who has been keeping it in her possession since the day they met as a means of exerting an influence over our heroine. In order to get her precious protective periapt back, María must make tributary offerings to the local patron, Saint Antonito. Such regional saints are commonplace in Latin America. Homemade altars (or *Animitas*) devoted to dead 'regular' folks who are believed to have the power to perform miracles are to be found in the streets and on paths or rural roads all across South America, where such beliefs are deeply-rooted. Despite being a 'supernatural' element, these local altars are very much a part of the real-life landscape for Latin-American peoples.

In order to have a miracle performed on their behalf by one of these popular saints, a devotee has to offer them something in exchange: in this case, María's own hair. But what she doesn't know is that she has been made pregnant after being raped by a lustful middle-aged landowner. Nine months later, she gives birth to a blonde boy-child, just like the aforementioned Yaciyateré. This leads María deeper into supernatural autochthonous beliefs about Life and Death, culminating in madness and murder.

LA HORA DE MARÍA Y EL PÁJARO DE ORO is a solid, non-explicit and often decidedly cryptic effort that straddles the shaky fence between mundane social drama and horror movie, getting the best of both worlds thanks to Rodolfo Kuhn's abilities as a pure cinematic storyteller who focuses more heavily on the story rather than relying on flashy visual gimmicks. This results in a compelling drama of great universality, which uses the supernatural and mythological beliefs inherent to any country as a cultural backdrop. The omnipresence of folk mythology is felt throughout Kuhn's film, which is thoroughly *steeped* in it; indeed, while nebulous, it is as crucial to the thrust of the narrative as one of its actual physical actors or sets.

Much like any classical moral fable, the story is circular in structure and ends with a message (or more specifically, a *warning*). Ultimately, everything María was afraid of at the start of the film ends up rematerializing deep within her psyche, causing the 'ignorant' peasant superstitions she has tried so hard to escape from to impose themselves on her once again. Her rationality collapses, trapping poor María in an inescapable downward spiral of pain and, ultimately, death…

RAKKHOSH

RAKKHOSH

Reviewed by Tim Paxton, with Steve Fentone

India, 2019. Ds: Abhijit Kokate,
Srivinay Salian

Ad-line: *"You are never alone."*

Perception is a tricky thing. Most people would
consider that "what they see is what they get".
Cut-and-dried. However, this is not always the
case. In fact, since the early '00s, there has been
a rising consciousness in the scientific world that
each person on this planet of ours may have their
own unique perspective on it. For example, recently I was seated at a restaurant with a good
friend in Mumbai, and we both commented on
the floral centerpiece at our table. Since we are
each individuals, what we experience through
sight (etc.) and the cognitive process as a whole
might very well differ distinctly from that of another person. So, when are the leaves on the centerpiece green, and when are they *blue*? Another
example is the popular 2015 meme involving a

striped dress: some saw this garment as blue/
black while others saw it as gold/white. Using
our perceptions—i.e., the organization, classifi-
cation and interpretation of sensory information
in order to identify and understand the presented information or the environment[1]—is how we
interact with the world around us, and there is
oftentimes (if far from *always*, lest we forget) no
'correct' way of perceiving reality, and this holds
especially true for those individuals who share
multiple 'truths' within their own mind (who,
according to variable technical assessments, may
or may not be mentally unbalanced, according
to the perceptions of those assessing them). And
sometimes, these individuals' 'truth'—or rather,
their personal perception of it—can seep through
into our own, blurring that sometimes fine line
(and at other times distinct, unyielding boundary)
between what *is* and what *is not* real. Because,
of course, regardless of anyone's subjective personal interpretations of truth and reality, despite
what some misguided so-called "Postmodernist"
might wish to incorrectly believe just because it
suits them and their feelings take precedence over
actual facts, there *are* other inherent, unavoidable

---

1   Thank you, Wikipedia!

Creature Feature Reviews

and at times *absolute* cosmic realities ("laws", if you will) that—whether we like it or not (such as gravity and death [fuck taxes!], to cite but two inarguable examples)—transcend and override humans' own flawed interpretations, and over which we have no control whatsoever, however much we might wish to bend them to our will and force them to conform to our (mis)perceptions. (Howzat for a run-on sentence?!) Hence, while one observer might well view a particular object as blue while another perceives it as green, simply because the two colors are so closely related on the spectrum and thus share similar hues in their mix, so there can be subtle variations in each that might make them appear to be *either* color—and even *both*—in certain instances and under certain conditions (such as how the light-source hits them and whether individuals happen to have subtle differences in their sense of vision, say), *both* observers can rightly be considered correct in their opinions. However, if while they are both observing the exact same object or phenomenon at the same time and one person sees bright yellow with purple polka-dots while the other sees it as deep red with lime-green wavy lines, chances are that one of the observers (or, in rare cases, perhaps *even* both simultaneously) is entirely *wrong* in their perception—or else is possibly perceiving things on a whole other plane of existence entirely.

And so to **RAKKHOSH**…

In this new Indian film, we view the world through the eyes of Birsa, a young man who has (possibly?) suffered a severe psychotic break and has been institutionalized as a result. The film's narrative is viewed entirely through his eyes alone, and we the external viewers, by 'borrowing' his eyes, so to speak, are left to vicariously interpret our own opinions of what's what—is it actually 'reality', a mere approximation, or something entirely removed from it?—by assessing at secondhand everything that Birsa experiences in the first person. In this case, Birsa is *apparently* given the typical bored psychologist's broad diagnosis of "schizophrenia" (or so we are led to believe, anyway) and, following a brief-but-violent internment at his home, he is placed into a severely-underfunded/understaffed mental institution for prolonged observation. Life at this hospital is unpredictable and fraught with violence, as it is in many such places the world over; where people are all-too-often prone to dumping or hiding-away unwanted members of society—those who don't 'fit in', for one reason or another—within such institutions, for 'safekeeping'. We see many acts of inhumanity occurring in the hospital as patients are variously abused, up to and including being beaten, by the stressed-out, overburdened staff. Don't forget, though, that we are seeing it exclusively from the point-of-view of Birsa, who *may or may not be* (?) a paranoid schizophrenic prone to hallucinations.

As film genres go, the "POV" (i.e., shot-in-the-first-person or with a subjective camera) aspect of **RAKKHOSH** is similar in some respects to that of the still-relatively-new—if already over-tapped to the point of being worn-out!—"FF" (found footage) subgenre. In both the POV and FF subgenres, we are treated to a highly personal and direct visual interpretation of what is occurring to the main characters. While FF films have been around for at least the better part of 40 years now (with Ruggero Deodato's **CANNIBAL HOLOCAUST** spearheading the form in 1979)[2],

2 The two entries that took the "Found Footage" concept by the horns and most helped to popularize it with today's audiences are, of course, Lance Weiler & Stefan Avalos' **THE LAST BROADCAST** (1998) and Daniel Myrick & Eduardo Sánchez's **THE BLAIR WITCH PROJECT** (1999, both USA). While, more recently, the genre has faltered with some serious missteps (e.g., **DAY OF THE MUMMY** [2014, USA/Venezuela, D: Johnny Tabor], to cite just one), FF subgenre outings in recent years have included Koji Shiraishi's **NOROI: THE CURSE** (ノロイ / Noroi , 2005, Japan), Jaume Balagueró & Paco Plaza's **[REC]** (2007, Spain), Matt Reeves' **CLOVERFIELD** (2008, USA), the *Paranormal Activity* series (2007-), André Øvredal's **APOLLO 18** (2011, USA/Canada), Allyson Patel & Yash Dave's **?: QUESTION MARK** (2012, India [Hindi]), Sebastián Cordero's **THE EUROPA REPORT** (2013, USA), Bharat Jain's **6-5=2** (2014, India; a Hindi remake of Swarna

Promotional poster art for the film

the origins of POV films are much older (and oftentimes *odder*) in their depictions of action occurring within a filmed narrative.[3] While films in the FF format are a supposed post-chronicling using mechanical means (i.e., a camera) of some particular already-occurred event, POV films instead unfold in 'real' time, presenting events 'as they happen' as opposed to those that are in the past. In **RAKKHOSH**'s case, as already mentioned, we see the world—or rather, his potentially 'wonky' interpretation of it—through Birsa's eyes and, due to his diagnosed mental illness and the fact that our eyes are connected to our brain, what he sees aren't necessarily actual events but may only be, to varying degrees, the delusory imaginings of his disordered mind which are being transmitted to us via our own ocular/cerebral mechanisms.

During the film's opening, we are introduced to Birsa (voiced by Namit Das), who has been placed in an asylum on account of his detachment from reality and violent tendencies. While imprisoned in this misrun mental institution, he interacts with other inmates and sinister staff members. For most of the film Birsa's closest friend is his cellmate Kumar John (noted actor Sanjay Mishra, one of whose earliest roles was in Ram Gopal Varma's crime actioner **SATYA** [1998, Hindi/Urdu/Marathi], before he attained fame by starring in Rohit Shetty's goofy action-comedy **GOLMAAL: FUN UNLIMITED** [2006, Hindi]). Birsa interacts with John, and

it appears that through him Birsa connects and communes with an unearthly being known as a *rakkhosh* (which literally means "demon" in Bengali). While it is a well-known and extremely ancient folkloric entity from West Bengal, the *rakkhosh* does also figure in the folklores of other parts of India, where they typically appear as hideous monstrosities that feed on humans, often calling-out to their prey beforehand, "*Hau-mau-khau... Manusher gondho pau!*" (translation: "I can smell a human!" [which may bring to more Western minds the human-gobbling fairytale giant of "Jack and the Beanstalk" [c.1734], who, while sniffing-out wee Jack the daring protagonist, famously boomed, "Fee-fi-fo-fum, I smell the blood of an Englishman!"]).[4] During **RAKKHOSH**, victims are selected by Kumar John through his usage of a set of *dashavatar ganjifa* cards (a deck of ten suits of twelve cards apiece, each suit illustrates one of the ten incarnations of the great god Lord Vishnu, who is believed to reincarnate whenever there's too much evil, as per Hindu mythology); the unlucky chosen individual then suffers the brutal retributory wrath of the *rakkhosh*, which we perceive only through Birsa's (possibly delusional) eyes.

For much of the film's first part, Birsa is forced to contend with abusive asylum staff (including a sadistic head nurse *à la* Louise Fletcher's cold-hearted 'caregiver' Nurse Ratched from Miloš Forman's classic **ONE FLEW OVER THE CUCKOO'S NEST** [1974, USA]), meddlesome family members (for instance, his sister, played by Tannishtha Chatterjee), as well as Dr. Idris Shah, the head of the asylum (Barun Chanda), an investigative reporter and Kumar John's daughter (Priyanka Bose, who starred in Garth Davis' biodrama **LION** [2016, UK/Australia/USA]), plus other inmates besides. It isn't made clear until the climactic reveal just what the *rakkhosh* might possibly be, although the pedantic Dr. Shah believes he has unlocked in Birsa a deadly form of autoscopy (more commonly called "out-of-body experience"), which Shah refers to as "transcendental experience". It is during this paranormal autoscopic state that Birsa's spiritual alternate form, the rav-

Latha's lesser-known Kannada-language originator **6-5=2** [2013, India], and Eduardo Sánchez's bigfoot thriller **EXISTS** (2014, USA).

3   Although, on the other hand, it might well be argued that the form—of a sorts, anyway—actually originated as far back as virtually the dawn of cinema itself in another scenario involving a mental institution, namely Robert Wiene's silent Expressionist masterpiece **THE CABINET OF DR. CALIGARI** (*Das Cabinet des Dr. Caligari*, 1920, Germany), POV films—i.e., those not based around 'preexisting' found footage material—'officially' first came into being in 1946 with director/star Robert Montgomery's groundbreaking *film-noir* **LADY IN THE LAKE** (based on the hardboiled gumshoe novel by Raymond Chandler, and two-fisted private dick Phillip Marlowe [played by Montgomery in the film]). Much more recently we've gotten Gaspar Noé's French-German-Italian-Canadian-Japanese fantasy coproduction **ENTER THE VOID** (*Soudain le vide*, 2009) and Ilya Naishuller's gonzo Russian-American cyberpunk actioner **HARDCORE HENRY** (2015), which further sought to reinvent and innovate the POV prototype. The creative potentials of the POV 'gimmick' seem a good deal less-restrictive than FF, latter of which is hampered by far stricter—if by no means always adhered-to!—restrictions on what can plausibly be done within its narrower framework, often resulting in implausibilities that sometimes verge on outright impossibilities (as in the case of Richard Raaphorst's interesting-but-severely-flawed WW2-era 'Nazi experimentation' shocker **FRANKENSTEIN'S ARMY** [2013, Netherlands/US/Czech Republic], for instance, to cite just one example among many that take far too many liberties with the FF form).

4   (*https://www.vagabomb.com/12-Bengali-Ghosts-and-Their-Fascinating-Backstories-to-Keep-You-up-at-Night/*). By the by, a *rakkhosh* of sorts—if not identified as such—makes an appearance in the "Horror in the Heights" episode of the 1974 US teleseries *Kolchak: The Night Stalker*. Penned by Hammer Studios alum Jimmy Sangster (1927-2011), this tale of a human-flesh-eating monster represented the first-ever appearance of an Indian monster on a Western-made TV show. Providing food for thought, interestingly enough, while serving in the Royal Air Force (R.A.F.), Sangster was stationed for a tenure in India, which we like to think was where he got his idea for the murderous monster that menaces Carl Kolchak in said "HitH" episode… stranger things have happened!

enous avenging *rakkhosh*, is able to explode forth and unleash its mayhem; this theory also explains some of the wild, swooping point-of-view cameramatics used at such times as the creature attacks.

RAKKHOSH had two directors: one (Abhijit Kokate) for production and another (Srivinay Salian) for postproduction. It represents Kokate's first theatrical feature, having had prior experience working on the TV miniseries *Off Road with Gul Panag: Ladakh* (2015, Hindi/Tamil/English), and as editor on Ram Gopal Varma's gangster thriller **DEPARTMENT** (2012) and Vikas Bahl's dramedy **QUEEN** (2013, both Hindi).

Salian, who is credited for **RAKKHOSH**'s screenplay, began his career as the writer of an animated TV show called *The New Adventures of Hanuman* (2009-2010, Hindi).[5] He also scripted two episodes of Zee TV's horror series *Fear Files 2* (2015, Hindi), so you could say that he came to the present project fully-vetted. *Monster!* caught up with Salian recently and asked him about his stint on *FF2* (in particular the episode entitled "Manglik"): "With Horror, the idea was to link it with some-or-other prevailing superstition. Since the story was meant to be set in Kolkata, I researched on the place and the culture, and from that found the seed of the story. Again, being a horror genre fan, it was critical that, as much as possible, to be one-step-ahead of the audience."

For **RAKKHOSH**, Salian recalls how he approached writing the screenplay. The film is loosely based on "Patient No. 302", a short story by Narayan Dharap (1925-2008), the late Marathi language horror writer whose work was the basis for the fabulous—and frightening!—recent folk-horror film **TUMBBAD** (2018, Hindi. Ds: Rahi Anil Barve, Adesh Prasad).[6] "In fact, I *didn't* read the short story", Salian recalls, "I tried

Top: Head of the asylum Dr. Idris Shah (Barun Chanda) has plans for Birsa's newfound powers. **Above:** Kumar John (Sanjay Mishra) and his daughter (Priyanka Bose) uncover what—accent on *what*—is behind the killings

to follow the style of my idol Gulzar, a renowned poet and writer in Bollywood. He had avoided reading any material when he adapted a story for his film titled **MASOOM** *[1983, Hindi. D: Shekhar Kapur]* … (The producers of **RAKKHOSH** and director Abhijit Kokate and) I had a brief discussion on the central theme of the story, then we brainstormed how it would be if we incorporated the video game-styled narrative to it. On that basis, I first wrote the story and, when we locked on it, proceeded with the screenplay." It was

---

5 When asked about this mythologically-based kidvid gig, Salian replied, "The idea around '*Bal*' or '*Chotta*' ('Kid') in India is that we can give them a mischievous shade. So, Bal Hanuman, Chotta Birbal, Bal Ganesha, all are basically carved-out of the same rock: naughty-yet-cute heroes. Being a kids' show, we had to keep action to bare minimum. Also, there was no scope for dialogue scenes. So, we had a clear plan of weaving a series of gags that added the humor and yet led to the climax. We already had a bratty hero [a young, scrappy Hanuman], then we created goofy villains. Rest just *flowed...* You pick the two conflicting characters, put them in a situation, the story just falls into place automatically."

6 To clear up some confusion which is rampant on the internet concerning the film **TUMBBAD**: Rahi Anil Barve's film is called **TUMBBAD**, but is *not* related to the work by another late Marathi author Shripad Narayan Pendse. According to a recent interview, he states *"My film is not based on the novel* [Tumbad che khot]. … *After his death, I was looking for an apt title for my film. I first borrowed it as a working title. It has simply stayed on"* (https://indianexpress.com/article/cities/mumbai/touching-indifference/)

Above: Screenwriter/co-director Srivinay Salian *[left]* and creative producer Prashen H.Kyawal *[right]*

Bed-Dread: Kumar John (Sanjay Mishra) encounters the demonic **RAKKHOSH**

Srivinay Salian who adapted the story for the big screen before handling directorial chores during postproduction on the film. "There was a narrative of how the story flowed in the short story", Salian continued. "But we knew, when it comes to cinema, we have to make sure the protagonist has more to do. So, we had to drop certain aspects *[of the original story]* and add new plots. The entire 'whodunit' plot of the movie *isn't* part of Narayan Dharap's story."

RAKKHOSH is a *very* different horror film from any that has previously been made in India, primarily because of the subjective camera aspect of its storytelling. The film's unique mixture of the paranormal with the all-out supernatural, in combination with the main character's diagnosed schizophrenia—a mental disorder that in its severest form can result in uncontrollable hallucinatory lapses further compounded by extremely disordered thought processes, along with disassociated time perceptions and apparent shifts in reality. This makes **RAKKHOSH** a less-than-linear tale for the audience to follow (or *try* to!), but also allows us to experience some sense of the madness that is affecting Birsa in such extreme ways. The added horror elements of brutal murders, a mad scientist and the mysterious otherworldly force referred to by everyone in the film as a *rakkhosh* places the film well outside the ordinary (i.e., same old/same old) Indian horror genre. The climax especially recalls the wild final minutes of both Brian de Palma's telekinetic thrillers **CARRIE** (1976) and **THE FURY** (1978, both USA), David Cronenberg's psychic killer-thriller **SCANNERS** (1981, Can-

ada), Kuei Chih-hung's black magic mindblower **THE BOXER'S OMEN** (魔 / *Mo*, 1983, Hong Kong) and Vinod Talwar's impressive horror shocker **HATYARIN** (1991, India [Hindi]), when all Hell—*literally!*—breaks loose.

The film's cast is uniformly exceptional in their performances, and help keep things firmly grounded in believability when it comes to the characters' interpersonal interactions. Most notable are the roles played by Sanjay Mishra, Tannishtha Chatterjee and Priyanka Bose. That said, the *least*-effective role—it being my personal biggest caveat about the film—is that of Birsa himself, whose plaintively-pleading voice-over by Namit Das generated less pathos for me than it did plain annoyance; then again, the central character *is* a poor, tormented soul trapped in an exceedingly hellish situation, after all, so his emotive plaints and bewilderment are to be expected, I suppose. Speaking of which, this is one of only very few films that would seem bent on giving audiences a realistic view of what conditions are like inside an Indian 'insane' asylum. While Hollywood has produced in-some-ways similar—albeit over-glamorized/homogenized—films set in similar milieux, such as **BEDLAM** (1946, D: Mark Robson), **THE SNAKE PIT** (1948, D: Anatole Litvak), **SHOCK CORRIDOR** (1963, D: Samuel Fuller), **THE NINTH CONFIGURATION** (1980, D: William Peter Blatty) and the aforementioned **ONE FLEW OVER THE CUCKOO'S NEST** (not to mention the horrifying and highly-recommended—long-banned—documentary **TITICUT FOLLIES** [1967, D: Frederick Wiseman]), I don't recall ever seeing or knowing of any Indian-made film set in such a place, let alone one that is as realistically-depicted as the institution in **RAKKHOSH** appears to be.

The overall steady POV footage seen throughout the film was thanks to the DP's use of a Red Epic Dragon camera equipped with a special stabilizing custom-made POV rig (rather than the Go-Pro rig used for films like 2015's above-cited **HARDCORE HENRY**). This impressive feat, along with accomplished and at times sweeping cinematography by Basile Pierrat, makes for a visually involving end product.

Creative producer Prashen H. Kyawal, who spearheaded the project for the producers Santosh Deshpande and Sayali Deshpande, adds "then because the story was written in first person, we brainstormed how it would be if we incorporated the video game-styled POV narrative to it."

Producer Santosh Deshpande recalls, "We were looking for a simple movie, and were thinking of making it a POV movie. I came to the conclusion it was going to be a very difficult task. Then we discovered a music video called 'Varanasi' on YouTube." This is a trippy hit electronica dance track by DJ Kalki that was set to visuals in 2016 by future **RAKKHOSH** DP Pierrat. Opening with the tatted-up POV protagonist blazing a bowlful of an indeterminate narcotic substance, the viral video for the tune is a wild, often-ecstatic ride through various parts of India, that highlights not just people, animals, non-living objects, landmarks and landscapes—all of which are seen through the eyes of the 'day-tripping' protagonist—but is augmented by occasional subtle 'psychedelic' computer-animated touches and momentary distortions of the image that endow the proceedings with a fantastical, otherworldly air (although the bulk of the five-minute video is very much grounded in HD hyperrealism rather than fantasy). "We discussed our project with him *[Basile Pierrat]*. We shot some experimental footage under his supervision, and we were very enthusiastic. After some discussion, we decided to proceed for the movie."

Creative producer Kyawal also helped arrange for the film's visual effects work. Unlike many other Indian horror films which rely on their overuse of unimpressive (not-so-)special effects, **RAKKHOSH** manages to sidestep that issue to deliver a brief-but-effective rampage by Birsa's psychical/demoniacal alter-ego. The realistic effects seen during the rampaging *rakkhosh*'s explosive climactic assault on the hospital staff were created by Q-Lab, a local postproduction

visual FX company that has been around since the 1970s.

Adding the proverbial cherry—and a big blob of whipped cream!—on top of the film's yummy supernatural sundae is its innovative score by Ashim Kemson. The composer's incidental music[7] deftly fuses traditional and electronic motifs, a blend which further helps in keeping **RAKKHOSH** well above the quality of your typical dreadfully dull horror film soundtrack... the kind filled with tasteless squawks, bleeps and other oddball/off-the-wall sound effects.

Well worth your time (as it was mine), **RAKKHOSH** is currently playing the festival circuit around India, expecting soon too be part of few International Film Festivals.

---

7   The background score, as opposed to the soundtrack which, in Indian cinematic terms, is typically the musical aspect of a film. India is a country where a film's soundtrack is still a large draw. This is something that used to be important for Hollywood in pre-digital times, but has more-or-less fallen by the wayside as the consumer tastes of Western audiences have changed, and now a Hollywood film's soundtrack isn't as important to a film's success as it once was; gone are the days when box-office receipts were equally tied-into record sales. In the case of the Indian audience, what is generally more important is *who* writes and performs the soundtrack. In the case of **RAKKHOSH**, the songs were composed and performed by Ashim Kemson & Swati Marwal, with lyrics by Ashim Kemson, Swati Marwal & Abhijeet Joshi.

RAKKHOSH producer Sayali Deshpande *[right]* at the 2019 Rajasthan International Film Festival with festival director Ansh Harsh. **RAKKHOSH** received the Special Jury Award for Best Director

Above, Clockwise from Top: Toronto Chinatown bootleg DVD-R for **GVB** *[p.253]*, reusing the Hong Kong cover art with telltale added Triad pirate 'product' number (printed at the base of its spine); Finnish videocassette box for the 'spaghetti yeti' flick *[p.277]*, which comes with oodles of mozzarella cheez whiz; Daiei Video's Japanese DVD cover for **SPOOK WARFARE** *[p.239]*; and Sinister Film's **INVISIBLE INVADERS**' *[p.299]* Italian DVD artwork

MONSTER! #34 MOVIE CHECKLIST

MONSTER! Public Service posting: Title availability of films reviewed or mentioned in this issue of MONSTER!
Information dug up and presented by Steve Fenton and Tim Paxton.

Addendum & Et Cetera: Although we neglected to mention it last issue (for the simple reason that we didn't find out until after we went to press), **THE CURSE OF THE BLUE LIGHTS** (1988) was evidently released on domestic DVD by Code Red at some point, presumably in a very limited quantity. Also, in unrelated business, simply because Stephen Bissette has gone into some detail about the video availability of the films discussed within it over the course of his epic, career-spanning *Monster!* interview/article about "D.I.Y." cinema pioneer Brett Piper (which concludes next ish), we haven't bothered running separate entries hereunder in these our 'vid info' pages. However, to coincide with the sixth and final instalment of Steve's long-running piece, in *M!* #35 we'll be including an overview of whatever of Piper's canon has been released on home video over the decades, with the primary focus being his personal 'pet' projects as writer/director/FX artist (etc.) rather than his 'work-for-hire' assignments in the employ of others (although, if these 'side projects' happen to boast monster content—as many of them do—we will definitely be listing them). If all goes well, we hope to have some input from Mr. Piper himself on the subject, in order to make our videography as accurate and comprehensive as possible for future reference.

Doctor Who and Other Brit (Mostly BBC) TV Sci-Fi / Horror Series *[pp.93-145 & pp.203-214]* – Not that The Beeb's 6-part 'true crime' docudrama miniseries *Jack the Ripper* (1973) *[p.95]* is the kind of fare we usually approve of in these monstercentric pages (older readers may remember *Monster!*'s longstanding motto: "NO SLASHERS ALLOWED!"; not that we're slasherphobic, you understand), but since, purely in the interests of providing some pertinent 'historical color', the monstrous Jack's legend—which has transcended mere history to become the stuff of folklore—is given several paragraphs of coverage in Stephen Jilks' broader article this ish, we figured we should at least include a video source for the program he discusses. It appears as though *JtR*, surprisingly enough, hasn't been made available on disc yet (?), but there are uploads of all six parts, evidently ripped from old videotape copies (complete with a time-counter constantly visible onscreen throughout in three of them) to be found on YouTube at a group link headed "Jack the Ripper (1973 TV series)" (@ *https://www.youtube.com/watch?v=ffMg-T27ZS6E&list=PLlaGf2Zg8gscTVob5e_LMcy-dcUICysFbV*). Also initially broadcast by the BBC in '73, another 6-parter, the literary-based *Wessex Tales [p.96]*, was decades later (in 2009) released on British Region 2 DVD by Acorn Media. Those wishing to view only the two *WT* episodes out of the total half-dozen that might be of most interest to Gothic horror buffs may access fair-quality uploads of both "The Withered Arm" *[p.96]* and "Barbara of the House of Grebe" *[p.98]* on YT, at the links titled "Wes Tales (1973) S01E01 - The Withered Arm" (@

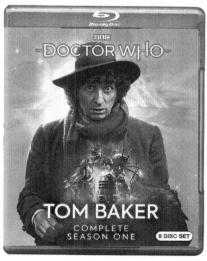

Who on Blu. *WOW!*

https://www.youtube.com/watch?v=e2RvrlpX-dRU) and "Wes Tales (1973) S01E06 - Barbara of the House of Grebe" (@ *https://www.youtube.com/watch?v=6Vg3ELYW1mE*). All of the following are available on disc from BBC Video: the full-length features **THE PICTURE OF DORIAN GRAY** (1976) *[p.125]* (included as part of 2008's *The Oscar Wilde Collection* box set) and **COUNT DRACULA** (1977) *[p.131]* and the *Doctor Who* serials "The Deadly Assassin" *[p.126]*, "The Ark in Space" *[p.112]*, "The Sontaran Experiment" *[p.112]*, "Genesis of the Daleks" *[p.112]*, "Revenge of the Cybermen"

NIGHT OF THE DEMON: Alternate-titled advance trade ad *[top]* from *Variety* (Wednesday, January 9th, 1957); the new BD

Face of Evil" *[p.126]*, "The Robots of Death" *[p.126]*, "The Talons of Weng-Chiang" *[p.127]* (voted Best Story in a 2003 poll), "Horror of Fang Rock" *[p.128]* and "Image of the Fendahl" *[p.130]*.

Relatedly to Mr. Jilks' and David Flint's M.R. James coverage herein, in late 2018, **NIGHT OF THE DEMON** (1957, a.k.a. **CURSE OF THE DEMON** stateside) *[p.100]*, the most-famous adaptation of James' enduring fan favorite "Casting the Runes" *[pp.100+137 {Endnote #3}]*, was put out as a superlative 2-disc "Limited Edition" BD—a larger-than-usual run of 10,000 numbered copies—in its country of origin, the UK, by Powerhouse Films / Indicator. Not only does this greatly-anticipated high-watermark release compile together no less than *four* (4!) different UK/US versions (i.e., two 96m prints and two 82m prints) of this undisputed occult horror megaclassic, but it's also cram-stuffed right to the bat-filled rafters with bonus goodies to boot, including such delectable delicacies as: a rare 10-minute 1972 audio interview with star Dana Andrews about the film; a 1984 audio recording of the then-recently-knighted (in '83), now-deceased Sir Michael Hordern reading the MRJ source story, "CtR" in his familiar engaging style; a quaint novelty in the form of **NOTD**'s drastically-abbreviated (200ft, 7m) Super 8 home movie cutdown reel; plus a wide array of other supplemental featurettes, interviews, commentaries and documentaries besides. Also in '18, this timeless film was issued on European (i.e., Brit) All-Region Blu-ray by Feel Films, complete with English, French and Spanish audio options. As far as the *A Ghost Story for Christmas* franchise *[p.102]* is concerned, the optimal option on digital disc thus far released is BBC's expansive—if relatively inexpensive—2013 6-DVD collection *Ghost Stories for Christmas*, which compiles a whole macabre myriad of ghostly goodies into a single convenient package (total runtime: a whopping 670 minutes [that's over 11 hours!]). In addition to both the outstanding 1968 *[pp.103+204]* and debatably inferior 2010 *[p.213]* adaptations of "Whistle and I'll Come to You", the set also includes the following series episodes: "The Stalls of Barchester" (1971) *[pp.105+205]*, "A Warning to the Curious" (1972) *[pp.105+206]*, "Lost Hearts" (1973) *[pp.106+206]*, "The Treasure of Abbot Thomas" (1974) *[pp.107+207]*, "The Ash Tree" (1975) *[pp.108+208]*, "The Signal-man" (1976) *[pp.109+208]*, "Stigma" (1977) *[pp.131+209]*, "The Ice House" (1978) *[pp.131+209]*, "A View from a Hill" (2005) *[pp.143+212]* and "Number 13" (2006) *[pp.143+213]*. (The

[p.112], "The Invasion" *[p.114]*, "Terror of the Zygons" *[p.115]*, "Planet of Evil" *[p.116]*, "Pyramids of Mars" *[p.116]*, "The Android Invasion" *[p.118]*, "The Brain of Morbius" *[p.118]*, "The Seeds of Doom" *[p.121]* (not to be confused with "The Seeds of Death", a Troughton-era Ice Warriors story), "The Masque of Mandragora" *[p.122]*, "The Hand of Fear" *[p.122]*, "The

far-from-ordinary "Schalcken the Painter" {1979} *[pp.134+210]*, meanwhile, is conspicuous in its absence due to its inevitable long-time association with the series, although, since it was initially aired, not as an *AGSfC* episode but as part of BBC's higher-brow *Omnibus* thread, its non-inclusion herein isn't surprising. It is, however, available as a stand-alone combo Region B/2 Blu-ray/DVD release from BBC Video / BFI Flipside, and is oddly engrossing and unsettling enough to warrant a viewing [or two, or three].) Amongst many other extras in the *GSfC* box set, such luminaries as Lawrence Gordon Clark (director of all the best *AGSfC* episodes), Jonathan Miller, Sir Christopher Frayling and Ramsey Campbell each provide audio and/or video input on the subject, while, in his characteristically charismatic, authoritative stentorian tones, playing no less than M.R. James himself, fellow superb storyteller Sir Christopher Lee reads aloud a quartet of MRJ's classical spine-tinglers on-camera in 'from the fireside' episodes of *Ghost Stories for Christmas with Christopher Lee* (originally aired one-by-one on The Beeb in the days leading up to Christmas and the New Year of 2000) *[p.212]*. This must-have British *GSfC* set can be ordered from Amazon.com as a PAL All-Region import at the page titled "BBC Ghost Stories for Christmas". While it doesn't appear to have been given a legit home video release (not even, surprisingly enough, as a special bonus feature with The Beeb's above-discussed ram-jammed *GSfC* box set), a decent "HD" (i.e., 720p) rip of the informative Mark Gatiss-hosted hour-long doc *M.R. James: Ghost Writer* (2013) *[p.102]* is accessible on YT at the link "MR James: Ghost Writer" (@ *https://www.youtube. com/watch?v=JOGZ4WQT2vg*), and it's well worth the time of anyone looking for a handy primer on the author's life and works to serve as an introduction.

Imprinted with digital time-counters, random episodes of the hard-to-see BBC paranormal series *The Mind Beyond [p.123]* on YouTube include "The Daedalus Equations" *[p.124]*, co-starring Peter Sallis and George Coulouris, which is uploaded at the link "'The Daedalus Equations' by Bruce Stewart" (@ *https://www.youtube.com/ watch?v=Fp_Me5O3h4Y*) and "The Man with the Power" *[p.124]*, co-starring Willie Jonah and Cyril Cusack, at the link "'The Man with the Power' by Evan Jones" (@ *https://www.youtube.com/watch?v=dmONaK5ZSE0*). The rare *BBC2 Playhouse* Season 2 episodes "The Breakthrough" *[p.123]* and "Mrs. Acland's Ghosts" *[p.123]*, complete with blacked-out time-counter on view throughout in the upper left corner

of the screen, may also be viewed at said site at the pages titled "BBC2 Playhouse - S2 Ep1 - The Breakthrough" (@ *https://www.youtube. com/watch?v=VqsPHu84fdo*) and "BBC2 Playhouse - S2 Ep2 - Mrs. Acland's Ghosts" (@ *https://www.youtube.com/watch?v=b9gxu-Za7mKg*). With sinisterly soft-spoken voiceover by Donald Pleasence as titular "Spirit", the grim 1½-minute 'anti-drowning' public information TV spot *Lonely Water* (a.k.a. *The Spirit of Dark and Lonely Water* or *I Am the Spirit of Dark and Lonely Water*, 1973) *[p.136]* may be accessed for viewing on YouTube (@ *https://www.youtube.com/watch?v=XNPMYRlvySY*). *Mystery and Imagination*'s handsomely-mounted ITV (i.e., non-BBC) tele-version of **DRACULA** (1968) *[p.143]*, starring Denholm Elliott in an 'offbeat' portrayal of the Count, is comped together with the spotty remainder of *MaI*'s surviving episodes in the Network (UK) company's 4-disc, 540-minute Region 2 DVD set, which also comps the following feature-length *MaI* adaptations in the same package: **FRANKENSTEIN** (1968, D: Voytek), starring Ian Holm as both the title scientist and the monster he creates; **UNCLE SILAS** (1968, D: Alan Cooke), adapted from the 1864 Gothic novel by Irish author Sheridan Le Fanu (1814-1873); **THE SUICIDE CLUB** (1970, D: Mike Vardy); **SWEENEY TODD** (1982, D: Reginald Collin); and **CURSE OF THE MUMMY** (1970, D: Guy Verney), this being a fine version of fellow Irishman Bram Stoker's (1847-1912) 1903 novel *The Jewel of Seven Stars*, which predated Hammer's more-famous 1971 theatrical adaptation **BLOOD FROM THE MUMMY'S TOMB** by roughly a year. It's interesting—as I (i.e., SF) did—to watch the '68 ITV and '77 BBC versions of **DRACULA** back-to-back for the sake of comparison, as both are very respectable, worthwhile adaptations with plenty going for them. As a bonus, ITV's *MaI* DVD set also includes the sole two remaining Season 1 episodes, including **THE OPEN DOOR** (1966, D: Joan Kemp-Welch). Audio-only recordings are all that now remain of a number of the missing earliest (shorter, 50m) episodes, all dating from 1966: "The Lost Stradivarius" (D: Bill Bain), "The Body Snatcher" (D: Toby Robertson), "The Tractate Middoth" (D: Kim Mills), "Lost Hearts" (D: Robert Tronson), "The Canterville Ghost" (D: Kim Mills) and "Room 13" (D: Patrick Dromgoole). We're only mentioning all this, *MaI* being a 'rival network' show, because a number of its episodes—particularly the lost M.R. James adaptations—in some fashion or other interconnect/intersect with certain of the BBC productions discussed in Mr. Flint's and

Mr. Jilks' articles.

Godzilla Movies: "The Hesei Era" (1984-1995) **and "The Millennium Era"** (1999-2004) *[pp.249-268]* – Since all of the entries in these two most-recent Big G "eras," we're going to give precedence to that format in our listing hereun-

Top: Sony's **G:FW** Blu-ray. **Above:** Found down in Toronto's Chinatown by Steve F. years ago, this Triad bootleg DVD-R of the Hong Kong edition of **GODZILLA AGAINST MECHAGODZILLA** came with both Japanese audio and Chinese or English subs options—for a mere 2 bucks Canuck, yet!

der. **THE RETURN OF GODZILLA** (1984) *[p.252]* is out on Region A Blu-ray from Section23 Films. **GODZILLA VS. BIOLLANTE** (1989) *[p.253]* can be had in the same format from Miramax-Echo Bridge. Back in 2014, all of the following were made available on Blu via Sony Pictures, paired-up in reasonably-priced 'twofers': **GODZILLA VS. KING GHIDORAH** (1991) *[p.255]* and **GODZILLA VS. MOTHRA** (1992) *[p.256]*; **GODZILLA VS. MECHAGODZILLA II** (1993) *[p.257]* and **GODZILLA VS. SPACEGODZILLA** (1994) *[p.258]*; **GODZILLA VS. DESTOROYAH** (1995) *[p.259]* and **GODZILLA VS. MEGAGUIRUS** (2000) *[p.261]*; **GODZILLA, MOTHRA AND KING GHIDORAH: GIANT MONSTERS ALL-OUT ATTACK** (2001) *[p.261]* and **GODZILLA AGAINST MECHAGODZILLA** (2002) *[p.262]*; **GODZILLA: TOKYO S.O.S.** (2003) *[p.263]* and **GODZILLA: FINAL WARS** (2004) *[p.264]*. So far as we can tell, **GODZILLA 2000** (1999) *[p.260]* hasn't been released on BD in a double-bill, but it is available singly as a stand-alone title in that format and was subsequently rereleased by Sony in 2015 as part of a 7-title Blu-ray set that also includes a half-dozen of Sony's other Millennium Era releases listed above. As for the latest live-action reboot, **GODZILLA RESURGENCE** (2016) *[p.268]*, it was released on Region A/1 BD+DVD stateside by Funimation! in 2017. In even-more-recent Big G movie news, via Netflix we've gotten Toho Co.'s feature-length computer anime spinoff **GODZILLA: PLANET OF THE MONSTERS** (*GODZILLA* 怪獣惑星 / *Gojira: Kaijū wakūsei*, 2017, Japan, Ds: Hiroyuki Seshita, Kōbun Shizuno, a.k.a. **GODZILLA: MONSTER PLANET**), and more recently still, the likewise-animated sequel, **GODZILLA: THE PLANET EATER** (*GODZILLA* 星を喰う者 / *Gojira: hoshi wo kū mono*, 2018, Japan, Ds: Hiroyuki Seshita, Kōbun Shizuno), which only just opened in Japanese theaters this past November 9th, so don't be expecting an English-friendly release for at least a little longer (although, now we're into the New Year of 2019, perhaps it might be available by the time this long-overdue ish [finally!] goes to the printers?).

"Malaysian Macabre Triple-Bill" (1957-58) *[pp.60-74]* – **HANTU JERANGKONG** (1957) *[p.64]*, **HANTU KUBOR** (1958) *[p.69]* and **GERGASI** (1958) *[p.70]* are all available on VCD ("video compact disc") from Malaysia/Indonesia's prolific Music Valley (a.k.a. MVM Home Entertainment) audio/video company, based in Malaysia's capital city of Kuala Lumpur. It goes without saying that none of the films come with

English subtitles! Fortunately, due to the difficulty of acquiring them via an online retail source (if westerners even *can* order them outside Southeast Asia [?]), as of this writing—they've been up there for years already, so there's no risk of them getting taken down anytime soon—all three films can be viewed on YouTube at the links "Hantu Jerangkung HQ (1957) Full Movie" (@ *https:// www.youtube.com/watch?v=hWOLAt_7yj8*), "Hantu Kubur (1958) Full Movie" (@ *https:// www.youtube.com/watch?v=HCjUuni-5R0*) and "Gergasi (1958) Full Movie" (@ *https://www. youtube.com/watch?v=rqhl1m1-V4E*). Evidently due to sloppy digital compression on the original VCDs the films' YT uploads were presumably ripped from, image quality of each upload fluctuates from pretty crappy to quite watchable, with **HANTU JERANGKONG** (my personal fave of the three) having the nicest and most consistent picture by far. As for consistency of image quality-wise, **HANTU KUBOR** (my least-fave) looks about the worst of all, while **GERGASI** (my second-fave) is an erratic, constantly-fluctuating mix of watchable and horrible. Needless to say, all are in their original Malay, without English subs, but their imagery often speaks for itself anyway, so you shouldn't have too much trouble deciphering their plots. Those wishing to pick up legit original copies might want to try a page I found on the website The Latarnia Forums (@ *https:// www.tapatalk.com/groups/thelatarniaforums/ turkish-dvd-thai-malaysian-indonesian-vcd-for-sale-t13991.html*), where, as of May 17th, 2018, a user named *jnfernal* was offering a limited assortment of 'exotic' foreign (i.e., Malaysian, Indonesian, Cambodian, Thai and Turkish) DVDs/ VCDs for sale; among the short list of titles posted there were **HANTU JERANGKONG** and **HANTU KUBOR**. Incidentally, the same person runs the Jnfernalworld blog (@ *jnfernalworld. blogspot.com*), one of whose archived posts (@ *http://jnfernalworld.blogspot.com/2013/05/old-*

As far as *M!* knows, this must-see monster movie is currently streaming on AmazonPrime in India

movies-from-indonesia-pt-1-horror.html) is entitled "Old Movies From Indonesia - Pt. 1: Horror" (2013) and includes sundry scans of Indonesian VCD inserts. Check it out and broaden your horizons! (If you haven't already.)

New(ish) Indian Ghostly Possession Films (*circa 2004-2018*) *[pp.75-92]* – While a number of the films cited/discussed in Tim Paxton's article are already viewable in some form on YouTube and many others will surely also be uploaded there sooner or later—though be advised that whether they'll come with English subs or not is an entire-

Music Valley's Malay VCD insert (note Shaw Bros. logos at top left & bottom center)

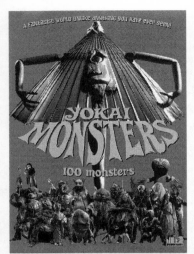

ly hit-or-miss proposition!—readers looking for original above-the-counter 'white market' copies of particular titles might want to browse any of the various 'Indiacentric' commercial retail websites to be found online: for example, Induna (@ *www.induna.com*), which is the site most-frequently patronized by our Tim, as well as Ultra (@ *http://www.ultraindia.com/products*), both of whose movie media (etc.) seems to primarily be marketed towards a Hindi-speaking audience. Because Tim P. cites it as a key prototype of many modern-day horror movie themes, India's included, we should mention that an English-hard-subbed upload of the seminal Yiddish-language Polish spiritual-possession film **THE DYBBUK** (1937) *[p.87]* can be viewed on YouTube at the page titled "DER DYBBUK 1937 - FANTASY FILM" (@ *https://www.youtube.com/watch?v=tjy7O9sA1TQ*), and it's well worth a watch by anybody interested in the deepest roots of horror-fantasy cinema (and folklore) in general. As for genre films of specifically Indian origin, may we wholeheartedly recommend Rahi Anil Barve's, Anand Gandhi's and Adesh Prasad's **TUMBBAD** (2018), an exquisitely-mounted—and at times scary as hell!—multilingual (i.e., Marathi/Hindi/Tamil/Telugu) 'folk horror' masterpiece with weirdness, wonder and (*of course!*) monsters to spare. While the film is still 'doing the rounds' (theatrically, VOD streaming, etc.) and it has yet to be released on home video media, chances are it'll be a cinch to find at either of the above sites when it does see a disc release. Trust us when we say that fans of international creature features regardless of their sociocultural origins won't wanna miss it! As far as Tim knows, as of this writing, **TUMBBAD** was playing on AmazonPrime in India.

The *Yokai Monsters* **Trilogy** (1968-1969) *[pp.225-248]* **and** *21st Century Yokai* **movies** (2000-2008) *[pp.31-36]* – Back in 2003—has it really been *15 years* already?!—**100 MONSTERS** (1968) *[p.234]*, **SPOOK WARFARE** (1968) *[p.239]* and **ALONG WITH GHOSTS** (1969) *[p.245]* were all released separately on domestic Region 1 DVD by ADV Films (@ *www.advfilms.com*), in their original Japanese subtitled in English but sans any English audio tracks, which is by far the preferable option of the two anyway. The same label later (in 2008) reissued the entire trilogy together as a 3-disc set. On a related note, the *YM* series' spiritual 'prototype' **GHOST STORIES OF WANDERER AT HONJO** (1957) *[pp.25+232]* was at one point viewable on YouTube complete with much-needed English subs,

Left, Top to Bottom: ADV Films' 2003 domestic R1 DVD editions of the *YM* trilogy, depicted in chronological order

but that upload seems to have since been removed from the site. (NB. Japanese rights-holders of intellectual properties—most famously Toho, Godzilla's long-time legal owners/handlers, who guard his trademark and copyrights jealously— seem especially intolerant of any unauthorized usage of their product.) As for official releases of **GSOWAH**, it has been put out in its country of origin at least twice on DVD (firstly in 2002 and again in 2004) by Tec Communications / Kokusai Hoei. Those editions presumably did not include English subtitles, as I'm pretty sure the now-'disappeared' rip of the film I viewed on YT had been fan-subbed by some private individual (perhaps the copy originated at Cinemageddon or someplace?). On a related *YM* note, Takashi Miike's phantasmogorically fantabulistic cinematic feast **THE GREAT YOKAI WAR** (2005) *[pp.25+33]*—which utilizes roughly 50/50 practical and computer-generated FX to tell its outrageously flamboyant tale about a whole multitude of mad, mad, mad, mad monsters—the maverick director's heavily-elaborated-upon 'reboot' (read: all-out reimagining) of **SPOOK WARFARE**, is also extant on domestic DVD from the USA's Tokyo Shock company in a "Double-Disc Special Edition" put out by them in 2006. TGYW was also issued on the same disc format down under in Australia that same year by Siren Visual Entertainment / Madman Entertainment, as were its '68/'69 inspiration sources, the *YM* series. Incredibly enough, there's a used copy of Tokyo Shock's now-OOP (?) edition of **TGYW** currently on offer at Amazon.com for a mere (!?!?) $741.49— *dream on!*—but thankfully there are numerous other copies (both brand-new/still-sealed and 'previously enjoyed') to be had at the same site for up to around 680%-or-more cheaper than that unrealistically astronomical sum. As for other New-Millennial *yōkai*-themed movies, amongst other home video editions (which also included an R2 German DVD from Warner Bros., sans any English option), **SAKUYA, SLAYER OF DEMONS** (2000) *[p.31]*, another turn-of-the-millennium movie containing affectionate nods to Daiei's *YM* series, was released in Japanese with English and Chinese subtitle options on Region 3 Hong Kong DVD by Universe Laser & Video Co., Ltd. Additionally, in '05 and '06 respectively, both **KIBAKICHI** (a.k.a. **WEREWOLF WARRIOR**) *[p.32]* and its same-year sequel **KIBAKICHI 2** (both 2004) *[p.33]* were released on domestic R1 DVD by MTI Home Video/Saiko Films (**K1** tagline: *"Half Man, Half Werewolf, One Deadly Samurai!"* – **K2** tagline: *"The Beasts Have Been Unleashed!"*). Each of these MTI editions included both English-dubbed and Japanese-language/English-subbed options,

plus a limited array of special features. **KITARO** (2007) *[p.34]* was issued on Region A/1 Blu-ray/ DVD by Navarre Corporation in 2008; in '09, Manga Entertainment released its sequel, **KITARO AND THE MILLENNIUM CURSE** (a.k.a. **KITARO 2**, 2008) *[p.35]*, on Region 2 (UK) DVD.

DEVIL FISH (1984) *[p.280]* – Considering this cinematic small-fry's general low profile in the great scheme of things, it received some pretty wide-scale distribution either in theaters or on home videocassette back in the day. For instance, it was released theatrically in France as both **LE**

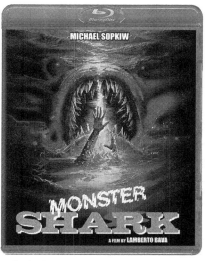

Code Red's optional BD covers for the same film

HERCULES AGAINST THE MONSTER
Italian DVD cover

MONSTRE DE L'OCÉAN ROUGE ("Monster of the Red Ocean") and, more sensationally still, on French video as **APOCALYPSE DANS L'OCÉAN ROUGE** ("Apocalypse in the Red Ocean"), in Turkey as **ÖLDÜREN DALGALAR** ("Killing Waves"), as well as on both Finnish and Hispanic video as, respectively, **SYVYYKSIEN TAPPAJA** ("Killer from the Depths") and **EL DEVORADOR DEL OCEANO** ("The Ocean Devourer"), to name only a few disparate releases from around the globe. **DF** was apparently at some point released theatrically in the USA by Cinema Shares International Distribution Corporation, a small outfit which seemed to specialize in releasing low-rent foreign imports. In 1998, the film received what was probably its greatest exposure ever on Season 9 of the long-running *MST3K* series. This heavily-edited version of the film was subsequently released on DVD via Shout! Factory's *Mystery Science Theatre 3000 – XIX* (1990-98) collection in both a standard edition boxset and as a spiffy Limited Edition, which also contained a "Gypsy Figurine". However, it's safe to say that most who saw it first caught this flick in the States and Canada via Vidmark Entertainment's big box clamshell VHS (*"Sink your teeth into pure terror!"*), which boasted a pretty good-lookin' transfer for the time. **DF** first hit DVD in 2000 via Japan's Magnet label under the somewhat misleading Anglo title of **JAWS ATTACK 2**. In 2002, Germany's Marketing

Film released it onto Region 2 DVD under its English export moniker, **MONSTER SHARK**, in a decent 1.66:1 (if non-anamorphic) transfer, which also included both German and English language options. A year later, Marketing Film decided to rerelease the film as part of their *Das Grauen aus der Tiefe Film Box* ("The Horror of the Deep Film Box"), that also included "Al Passari"/Massimiliano Cerchi's hilariously hysterical **CREATURES FROM THE ABYSS** (*Creature dagli abissi*, a.k.a. **PLANKTON**, 1994, Italy) and "Anthony M. Dawson"/Antonio Margheriti's **ALIEN FROM THE DEEP** (*Alien degli abissi*, 1989, Italy). In July of 2018, Code Red, along with Kino Lorber, decided to give Lamberto Bava's film a new lease on life in separate Blu-ray and DVD releases, both of which house the uncut version in a (quote) "brand new scan with extensive color correction done in America". Their All-Region BD is presented in a very handsome 1:66:1 anamorphic transfer, and it looks absolutely terrific given the inconsistent, low-budget nature of the film. The DTS-HD MA English track also sounds perfectly fine despite most of the actors being post-synched; and yes, that *is* actor Edmund Purdom's voice dubbing the beer-swilling Bob Hogan character, as played by Dino Conti. As far as extras are concerned, actor Michael Sopkiw (along with Code Red head honcho Bill Olsen in his "Banana Man" get-up) provide the film with a brief intro (1m54s), while Sopkiw is joined by Olsen and Damon Packard for a feature-length audio commentary. Sopkiw has plenty to discuss about his brief tenure working on Italian films during this period in his life, but at the same time he's also surprised to learn that directors Luigi Cozzi and Sergio Martino each had a hand in the script ("It's one helluva a story!" he remarks facetiously). He goes on to discuss his four-picture contract with Luciano Martino's National Cinematografica and Nuova Dania outfits, and how he got paid just $3500.00 for his first picture; he also discusses **DF**'s rather lengthy principal photography, which, according to Sopkiw, took six weeks (a virtual *eon* for a quickie Italian exploitation outing!), how each of the films were shot MOS (= "motor only sync", i.e., without direct audio), and that the Italian film industry's (quote) "dubbing capabilities were phenomenal". Even though the three participants admittedly do find plenty to snicker at, the commentary remains an interesting, easy listen nevertheless. The disc also contains trailers for Bava, Jr.'s mock-"Rambo" macho combat actioner **BLASTFIGHTER** (1984, Italy/France), Umberto Lenzi's *giallo* **SEVEN BLOOD-STAINED ORCHIDS** (*Sette orchidee macchiate di rosso*, 1972, Italy) and another for Sergio

Martino's superb *poliziotteschi* **THE VIOLENT PROFESSIONALS** (*Milano trema: la polizia vuole giustizia*, 1973, Italy). – **Dennis Capicik**

GHOUL (2018) *[p.274]* – This series is available for streaming on Netflix.

HERCULES AGAINST THE MONSTER (1964) *[p.289]* – Originally released in North America under its better-known if more nondescript Anglo title **HERCULES, PRISONER OF EVIL** in '64 by American-International Television (AIP-TV), this was subsequently made available on Beta/VHS cassette from the USA's Sinister Cinema circa 1990 under the same title. Again bearing the same title, rumor has it that English dubs of the film have also been released by any number of budget vidcos in cheapo "sword-and-sandal" movie box sets, in scrappy/scratchy full-frame versions 'digitally remastered' (*NOT!*) from old TV prints. Again under the **"PRISONER"** title, both Retromedia Entertainment and Image Entertainment (in 2007 and 2009 respectively) issued it on domestic DVD. It was formerly extant on VHS via Something Weird Video, who still carry the title in their catalogue for purchase on DVD-R (for $10.00) or as a direct download (for a mere penny less at $9.99) from their website (@ *www.somethingweird.com*), presumably in a 1.33:1 ("fullscreen") format. On YouTube, a quite nice "HD" English-dubbed, widescreen version of the film (running 87+ minutes) can be found at the link "HERCULES - PRISONER OF EVIL - Reg Park" (@ *https://www.youtube.com/watch?v=4UtHg6hL9w4*). A slightly longer if lesser quality-wise (and only fullscreen) upload is alternately available on YT at the link "Hercules, Prisoner of Evil 1964 Reg Park, Mireille Granelli, Ettore Manni Sword and Sandal" (@ *https://www.youtube.com/watch?v=iw-8v9asbnc*), but the former version cited here is by far preferable and seems to be about the best option currently available in English-friendly form. The film was put out on Italian DVD (via the Hobby & Work label in 2012) under its original Italo title of **URSUS IL TERRORE DEI KIRGHISI**, widescreen but only in Italian, with no special features and amateurish cover art. As **URSUS EL TERROR DE LOS KIRGUISES**, the film was released on DVD in Spain circa 2011 as part of the "*Grandes Clásicos Épicos & Colosal*" series (video label unknown), presumably dubbed into Spanish and without any English soft-subs option.

HOBGOBLINS (1988) *[p.304]* – Trailer narration excerpts: "*The hobgoblins are back, and they're ready to party! ...No one's safe from these cagey critters! ...And when your wildest dream*

is about to come true, these gruesome gremlins turn it into a nightmare!*" I seem to remember this flick getting resoundingly trashed/torn multiple extra assholes in the fanzines of the time (the more things change, the more they stay the same!). Now, general rule of thumb here at *Monster!* is that our contributors (we ye co-eds included) should kindly try not to focus too much on any negatives to be found in the films they review within our pages, no matter how much of a sub-cinematic craptastrophe it might be, and to accentuate the positive (if any) wherever even only remotely possible (like yo mama says, "If you haven't got anything *nice* to say, don't say anything at all", and all that). However, there are times—as in the case of the present title under discussion—when the 'accentuate-the-positive' approach is a virtual impossibility. That said, here goes nothin'… While watching this minor and exceedingly moronic (it had to be said!) **GREMLINS** rip-off, you can actually feel your brain-cells dying off in droves due to the extreme levels of sheer, unadulterated *STOOPIDITY* involved. Totally cringeworthy moments come thick and fast rather than few and far between. In fact, I don't think I've *ever* cringed so much while watching a movie before, of any genre. While apparently hoping for punkish 'hipness', the aimless central "Club Scum" sequence goes on and on (*and on and on and...*) without any real rhyme nor reason for being other than to kill time (and more brain-cells), with the immobile sub-John Carl Buechler-level knobgobblin' hobgoblins serving little more than a peripheral

South Korean VHS jacket for
HOBGOBLINS

and purely token function throughout, observing the human 'action' from the sidelines like so many inert stuffed animals sat atop a dresser. The pointlessness of it all is exceeded only by the utter ineptitude on display across the boards (although, in all fairness, I should at least give a shout-out/thumbs-up to the stunt crew and pyrotechnical technicians for making the best of a bad situation by providing some decent gags). About the only positive takeaway I got from this sorry excuse for a moncom (= "monster comedy") was the song "Love-Me-Nots" by The Fontanelles, which—if mostly by simple contrast—is a passably listenable Gothy *nuevo wavo*/power-poppish number, utterly unrelated to the movie's contents, that's far better than **HOBGOBLINS'** soundtrack deserves. But anyway, for better or worse, this celluloid stinker/steaming turkey turd was first issued on domestic Beta/VHS videocassette by Trans World Entertainment and subsequently reissued in the same tape formats (maybe VHS only?) but in totally different packaging by lowly sell-through label Star Classics (who usually put out shitty LP- or SLP-speed copies of PD ["public domain"] titles but in this case scored themselves an, er, 'exclusive'). New Video Production (NVC) released it on tape in South Korea, presumably in its original English dialogue with Korean subs (?). It was put out on Spanish cassette (presumably dubbed into *español*?) under its original English title by Quintovision. For its (Spanish-dubbed?) 1990 Argentinean videotape release by American Video / Magnetic Video, its title was shortened to simply **HOBLINS** (presumably for easier pronunciation by Hispanic tongues?). It was first (?) put out on domestic DVD in the late 2000s by Retromedia in a no-frills "20th Anniversary Special Edition". It was also issued in another Region 1 DVD edition by MicroWerks in 2009, again as a "20th Anniversary Special Edition". For its, uh, 'reworked' (i.e., further bowdlerized) release as part of the *Mystery Science Theater 300 Volume 8* DVD set, it was disparately quadruple-billed with **THE PHANTOM PLANET** (1961, USA, D: William Marshall), **MONSTER A-GO GO** (1965, USA, Ds: Bill Rebane, Herschell Gordon Lewis) and the '50s-style B&W *noir* retrofit **THE DEAD TALK BACK** (1993, USA, D: Merle S. Gould). We can only hope that, in the hands of the *MST3K* crew it actually—for once!—proved more entertaining for viewers than in its 'unadulterated' original version, which is about as funny as a stubbed toe. In 2014, VZ-Handelsgesellschaft / Ascot Elite / Shamrock Media released it in Germany as a PAL Region 2 DVD which offered viewers both English and German audio options; one can only

wonder how the witless lowbrow humor translated into *Deutsch*?! (Or better yet, Korean!) Most recently (2016), Vinegar Syndrome (@ *www.vinegarsyndrome.com*) released **HOBGOBLINS** as a Region-Free Blu-ray + DVD combo edition, "scanned and restored in 2K from the 35mm original camera negative" (and at a full 1.85:1 widescreen aspect ratio) that came loaded to da max with special features. These included an archival commentary track with director (etc.) Rick Sloane; an all-new "making-of" featurette, *Hobgoblins Revisited*; two more featurettes, *Hobgoblins: The Making of a Disasterpiece* and *Hobgoblins Invade Comic-Con*; a brand-new on-camera interview with hobgoblin creature creator Kenneth J. Hall; a trailer; and, last but by no means least, reversible cover artwork. As for **H1**'s decidedly tardy 30-years-late sequel **HOBGOBLINS 2** (2009) *[p.305]*, it was released on DVD by Infinity Entertainment / MicroWerks the same year of its production. BTW, if it sounds like I'm being unduly harsh/hard on this flick, that's because I *am*! But everything has its place, and it isn't to say that someone else might not derive immense entertainment value from **HOBGOBLINS**. Different strokes for different folks, and all that. So by all means give it a spin and make up your own mind.

LA HORA DE MARÍA Y EL PÁJARO DE ORO (1975) *[p.307]* – Audio plays a vital role in this film's effectiveness. Setting the tone early on, during the opening credits a naïve folk song/nursery rhyme sung in a delicately childlike voice by an unseen little girl on the audio track becomes gradually drowned-out by increasingly unsettling 'experimental' music. Symbolizing how much the 'innocent', rustic milieu in which she lives dominates her life, ambient sounds of nature in the raw—including a cacophony of animal calls, such as the seemingly gay (but actually fearful) twittering of songbirds and the chirruping of crickets—at times attain virtually deafening proportions in María's ears, while the nocturnal braying of a *burro* sounds like laughter to her (or so it seems). While we were unable to track down either a current or OOP legit video source for this unique Argentine obscurity, there is—at least as of this writing—a passably watchable rip of a fuzzy old videotaped version (taken from a TV airing of indeterminate date and filled with video dropouts, if bearable enough to those used to watching third- or fourth-generation VHS dubs), in Spanish with no subtitles, can be accessed at the lesser-known (at least stateside) Russian streaming website OK.RU (@ *ok.ru/video*). Simply key the following link name into the search field there: "La hora de maría y el pajaro de oro 1975" (@ *https://ok.ru/ video/42847767106*). The identical rip can also be found on YouTube at the page called "la hora de maría y el pajaro de oro" (@ *https://www. youtube.com/watch?v=whv4cM4RX6w*). While there are lengthy stretches of silence broken only by the ambient sounds of nature, the narrative becomes quite dialogue-heavy at times, and with so much of a subtly symbolic nature apparently going on beneath its surface, this is a film that demands literate subtitling—or a far greater knowledge of Spanish than I possess!—to help one get the most benefit from it, although the lush, lyrical cinematography and eye-catching visuals alone do speak for themselves upon occasion.

HOUSE OF THE GORGON (2018) *[p.215]* – Described by its creator as a "Gothic Fairytale", this as-yet-unreleased film's total doozy of a trailer can be viewed on YouTube at writer-producer-director-actor (etc.) Joshua Kennedy's channel (@ *https://www.youtube.com/ watch?v=5O4YT_M-iRs*), and it really makes you wanna see the full movie! **HOTG** is set to have its world premiere in June 2019 at Monster Bash in Pittsburgh (see *http://www.monsterbash-news.com/bash-June.html* for details). While you're at Joshua's YT channel, which has quite

a lot of funky content at it to browse, why not check out the trailers for his other Gooey Film Productions too, including: **THE FUNGUS AMONG US** (2018 [promo hype: *"A group of angry women, a kidnapping gone wrong, a house on the Mexican border, and a monster growing in the attic"*]); **THESEUS AND THE MINO-TAUR** (2017 [*"The classic tale of Theseus and the Minotaur comes to life on screen"*]), featuring stop-motion animation of the fearsome bull-headed beast by Ryan Lengyel; **THE ALPHA OMEGA MAN** (2017 [*"A Pace University Honors Thesis by Joshua Kennedy paying tribute to the science fiction classic"*]), starring Joshua K. himself in the equivalent role previously made famous by Will Smith, Charlton Heston and Vincent Price; **THE NIGHT OF MEDUSA** (2016 [*"There is something very* strange *about new student Elaine Carlisle..."*]); **THE VESU-VIUS XPERIMENT** (2015 [*"When a diabolical experiment goes awry, Doctor Vesuvius and his team must find the creature that escapes from his New York City laboratory before it murders again"*]), a B&W ode to the Quatermass series; as well as **THE MENACE WITH FIVE ARMS** (2013), **VOYAGE TO THE PLANET OF TEENAGE CAVEWOMEN** (2012), **CURSE OF THE INSECT WOMAN** (2011), and **AT-**

We're not sure if you're gonna be there, but there's a good chance Troy Howarth and Steven Ronquillo will be!

Video Availability Information

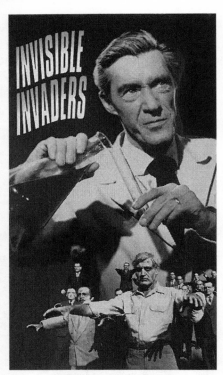

MGM/UA's 1996 US VHS

TACK OF THE OCTOPUS PEOPLE (2010). Some of JK's films—namely the above-cited **COTIW**, **VTTPOTC** and **TVX**—are available for purchase domestically from Alpha Video Distributors (@ *www.oldies.com*). For a fun sampling of this energetic young filmmaker's style, check out **DRACULA A.D. 2015** (2015), a loving hour-long pastiche/tribute to classic horror movies that is legally viewable gratis at Joshua's aforementioned YT channel (hype: *"In this love letter to Hammer Films, Count Dracula returns from the grave to wreak havoc on a New York City college"*).

INDEPENDENCE DAY: RESURGENCE (2016) *[p.269]* – Available on Region A/1 BD and DVD from 20th Century Fox Home Entertainment.

INVISIBLE INVADERS (1959) *[p.299]* – Opening with—*what else?!*—an authentic A-bomb blast, ("Radioactive particles have been blown into space! Who can tell when those particles will come down to Earth again…?"), for all its endearing qualities—or lack thereof!—**II** surely amounts to one of its prolific director Ed-

die Cahn's (1899-1963) *least* efforts; this in a star-spangled, AAA-grade B-movie career that encompasses such stellar schlock sci-fi/horror humdingers as **CREATURE WITH THE ATOM BRAIN** (1955), **THE SHE-CREATURE** (1956), **ZOMBIES OF MORA TAU** and **INVASION OF THE SAUCER-MEN** (both 1957), **IT! THE TERROR FROM BEYOND SPACE** and **CURSE OF THE FACELESS MAN** (both 1958), and **THE FOUR SKULLS OF JONATHAN DRAKE** (1959, all USA), among others (including, lest we forget, a number of gritty non-fantasy movies [e.g., the fast-paced JD crime actioner **RIOT IN JUVENILE PRISON** {1959, USA}]). As for **II**, on the other hand, among other things it is conspicuously marred by a number of poorly-thought-out plot developments that were seemingly made up on the spot as required rather than scripted beforehand. A quickie even by legendary swift-worker Cahn's whirlwind get-'er-in-the-can-ASAP standards, its corner/cost-cutting is for whatever reason far more apparent than in much of the filmmaker's quick-'n'-cheap canon. While we can only assume it's because they're all wearing their formal burial clothes, it's never explained to us why virtually all the zombies seen onscreen (i.e., ten or a dozen, tops!) are middle-aged white guys in business suits (with white shirts and neatly-knotted ties to boot). As for the principal performances, Philip Tonge as Dr. Penner is the only cast member who attempts to inject any real life into his role, leaving younger fellow male protagonists John Agar and Robert Hutton—neither of whom were the most expressive of actors even at the best of times, it must be said (bless 'em!)—to as good as sleepwalk through their parts, as if they've been partially zombified by the outer-spatial radiation themselves. Much as he had previously done a lot more literally earlier that same year in another modest sci-fi'er, **THE COSMIC MAN** (USA, D: Herbert S. Greene), in his character's alien-possessed form here—albeit being a good deal more menacing and openly hostile about it—guest star John Carradine essentially plays a variation of Michael Rennie's benignant humanoid extraterrestrial emissary Klaatu from Robert Wise's SF superclassic **THE DAY THE EARTH STOOD STILL** (1951, USA); that is to say, a representative of an alien race bent on dissuading Humanity from its foolhardy warlike course, albeit in the present film via violent means rather than through simple stern cautionary measures and 'tough love' diplomacy. JC's temporarily reanimated undead self delivers a dire warning: "Unless Earth surrenders in twenty-four hours, we will begin a mass invasion! …The dead will kill the living, and the people of Earth will cease to exist!" (Consider yourself warned, foolish humans!) Suggesting they are some sort of composite entity of a single collectivist mind, whenever an alien vocalizes his race's demands to the living humans via a taken-over human mouthpiece, it is Carradine's familiar booming speech pattern we hear, even though the actor's earlier-seen Dr. Karol Noymann character is no longer alive.

After being unavailable other than in scrappy bootleg form from various 'under-the-counter' dealers for years prior to then, in 1996 **II** finally hit legitimate home vid on Beta/VHS tape courtesy of MGM/UA Home Video. The film was later (in 2003) made available (now OOP) in a highly presentable digitally-remastered DVD edition as part of Metro-Goldwyn-Mayer's essential "Midnite Movies" series, double-billed with Sid Pink's hallucinogenic sky-high sci-fi space-trip **JOURNEY TO THE SEVENTH PLANET** (1962, USA/Denmark). Licensed from 20th Century Fox/MGM, **II** was more recently (in 2016) issued singly in a pristine Region A Blu-ray edition by Kino Lorber as part of their state-of-the-art "KL Studio Classics" line, boasting a *superb* brand-new transfer remastered in sharp/crisp HD (1920x1080p) and glorious B&W (at the original 1.66:1 theatrical aspect ratio). Besides a trailer gallery, the Kino BD's sole other special feature is a joint audio commentary by cinema experts Tom Weaver and Dr. Robert J. Kiss. This edition—which leaves all previous editions eating its proverbial dust!—is now the one to beat, and chances are it won't be getting topped anytime soon… if ever. For those so inclined, KL also released a DVD edition of **II** simultaneously (if separately) with their Blu. In 2010, under the title **ASSALTO DALLO SPAZIO** ("Assault from Space"), the film—featuring a special on-camera introduction by cult Italo filmmaker Luigi **"STARCRASH"** Cozzi—was put out on DVD in Italy by Sinister Film (ad-blurb: *"I primi zombie della fantascienza!"*). That fullscreen edition came with an English audio track and Italian soft-subs, although this only 64-minute Italo cut runs several minutes shorter than the original (67m) American release print, just so you know. – **Les Moore**

LATITUDE ZERO (1969) *[p.293]* – Formerly (in 1994) available on videocassette in the USA from Hellfire Video Inc., **LZ** was first issued on domestic R1 DVD by Media Blasters in 2007. As of this writing, there's also a Region 2 DVD edition (by one Creative Films) from Spain up for sale on eBay (@ *https://www.ebay.co.uk/ itm/LATITUDE-ZERO-1969-Dvd-R2-Joseph-*

Cotten-Cesar-Romero-/302318086808*); entitled **LATITUD CERO – DONDE EL MUNDO ACABA**, it comes in Spanish but with an English audio option too. **LATITUDINE ZERO**, the official, Toho-approved/certified 2007 Italian DVD release (from Password / Eagle / Pulp Video of Italy), likewise comes with an English audio option, and as of this writing at least two copies were orderable—one for 8,99 € (i.e., euros) and another for 11,69 €—from the retail website DVD.it (@ *www.dvd.it*). Several copies of the same edition, which comes in both single- ("Edizione Disco Singolo") and double-disc ("Edizione Doppio Disco") versions, were also being sold on eBay at reasonable prices ranging from around €7 to €12. So shop around and take your pick! The Italian DVD is presented at a 2.35:1 aspect ratio and includes both the Japanese-language (89m) and Anglo-dubbed international (105m) versions of the film, although I'm assuming both versions are paired-up with one another only in the 2-disc edition and that the single-disc edition only contains one version (?).

LIGHTS OUT (2016) *[p.302]* – **LO**'s gnarly, ghastly ghostie turns up in the closet, under the bed, down in the basement… in fact, anywhere she/it damn well wants to, just so long as it's good and dark (the title implicitly explains the creature's supernatural aversion to illumination of any sort, be it a candle, a flashlight or the screen of a smartphone, et cetera). This ban-

Toho Video's Region 2 Japanese edition

YETI German 8mm film box (Pt.2)

shee-shrieking harpy from Hades is largely seen as a spindly, spiderleg-fingered, jet-black silhouette punctuated by twin points of white light (its eyes) and topped with an unkempt ebony tangle of hellish hair. Sure, the too-cutesy-poo juvenile protagonist (a prime 'Spielbergian' casting choice if ever there was one!) has one of those annoyingly much-too-pouty lower lips that make you wanna grab hold of it, stretch it out about a yard then let it twang back into his face like a rubber band (*BOINGGG!!!*), but don't let that stop ya. Ignore any illogicalities in the script—and there are many (par for the course in horror flicks)—and just sit back and enjoy the shivers and shocks, which are delivered by-the-numbers and (surprisingly enough) with zero gore, but with some gusto. Hell, even Yours Drooly (i.e., LM) jumped in my seat a few times. Does it ever piss me off, getting manipulated so obviously like that! **LO** is available to stream in HD as a rental (for $3.99) or to buy ($14.99) via Amazon Prime, or it can be purchased on Blu-ray or DVD via Warner Brothers Home Entertainment both domestically and elsewhere around the globe. Even if, when all is said and done, it's nothing overly original, you could do a whole helluva lot worse, for sure. Those wishing to check out the roughly 2½-minute viral short film that started the whole **LO** 'phenomenon' may do so on YouTube. Simply key-in the link name "Lights Out - David Sandberg (2013)" (@ *https://www.youtube.com/watch?v=pmq9mOi94n4*). – **Les Moore**

OUIJA: ORIGIN OF EVIL (2016) *[p.265]* – Available on Region A/1 BD and DVD from Universal Pictures Home Entertainment.

PHANTASM: RAVAGER (2016) *[p.270]* –

Available on Region A/1 BD and DVD from Well Go USA Entertainment. The entire *Phantasm* series was recently put out in both current commercial disc formats by Well Go in the US and by Arrow Video in the UK, complete with plentiful special "pheatures" (*[sic!]* in-joke alert!).

PLEASE DON'T EAT MY MOTHER! (1973) *[p.286]* – This thinly-veiled, nudified impersonation of Roger Corman's **THE LITTLE SHOP OF HORRORS** (1960, USA) was issued as a "Special Edition" DVD by Something Weird Video (SWV) in 2001, and the same label also put it out on VHS too. Video Dimensions likewise released it on tape stateside at some point.

RAKKHOSH (2019) *[p.312]* – This just in from Tim (@ 5:01 p.m. on January 24th, 2019): "**RAKKHOSH** is playing the film festival circuit at the moment. It is scheduled to be released theatrically sometime in February."

RESIDENT EVIL: THE FINAL CHAPTER (2017) *[p.266]* – Available on Region A/1 BD and DVD from Sony Pictures Home Entertainment.

YETI: GIANT OF THE 20TH CENTURY (1977) *[p.277]* – Australian daybill poster taglines: *"From The Frozen Arctic, The Gigantic YETI ...So Big, So Strong, But So Gentle You Will Learn To Love Yeti!"* This dopey 'spaghetti yeti' opus was released by a whole plethora of home viddy labels around the world back in the day (*circa* the '80s), including on French SECAM Beta/VHS cassettes by Les Productions du Tigre/CDI as **YÉTI – LE GÉANT D'UN AUTRE MONDE** ("Yeti – The Giant from Another World") and on German Beta/VHS by Atlas Videothek under the title **YETI – DER SCHNEEMENSCH KOMMT** ("Yeti – The Snowman Comes"); also receiving a Super 8mm home movie release in Germany under that same main title, broken-up into two (?) 110-meter reels (the second reel subtitled *"Das Monster aus der Kälte"* ["The Monster from the Cold"]). The film was available dubbed into Spanish in the same two aforementioned standard tape formats of the period (i.e., Beta/VHS) from PAT Filmica/New Line in Spain as simply **YETI**, under which shortened title it was also issued on Finnish tape by Videocassettes/Techno Film (amusingly, that release's wonky small-print Anglo back-cover hype describes titular beastie as "a halph-man halph-animal *[sic!]* creature"!). As far as Anglo releases are concerned, Miramax put it out (as just plain **YETI**) on full-frame/pan-'n'-scan tape stateside in 1983, while Fletcher Video and K&C Video did likewise, respectively, over in the United Kingdom and down in Australasia. The USA's BijouFlix Releasing outfit issued the film in English-dubbed form on domestic DVD in 2008. It is currently available for rent or purchase (starting at a measly buck-99) from YouTube Movies at the page called "Yeti: The 20th Century Giant" (@ *https://www.youtube.com/watch?v=3oHGdowQUYQ*), but it's also up-for-grabs gratis— only full-frame, if English-dubbed and of average VHS-level picture quality—on the same site, at the link titled "Yeti: Giant of the 20th Century" (@ *https://www.youtube.com/watch?v=Mh7rKslDbb4*). Relatedly, a temporary fuck-band calling themselves The Yetians—including Santé Maria Romitelli, composer of **YETI**'s score—recorded a goofy, ultra-tacky disco track entitled—*what else?!*—"Yeti" as a 7" 45 rpm tie-in with the movie. It was released by Italy's Aris label (#AN 448), a record company co-owned by music/movie producer Aldo Pomilia (1933-1986) and his then-wife, dancing/acting Cuban bombshell/living love goddess Chelo Alonso (1933-); talk about a *lucky* fella, that Aldo! Among the many other records

produced—on good ol' vinyl (a.k.a. "hot wax"), natch!—by Pomilia during the '70s were electronic soul-funk act Red Blood's horror-themed novelty numbers "Soul Frankenstein" (1976) and "Soul Dracula" (1977), both recorded, not on the aforementioned Aris but on the Maximus label (that latter ditty was evidently a cover version of a same-titled song put out in 1975 by the similarly-named group Hot Blood [confused yet?!]). Complete with picture sleeve art that included a crude drawing based-off a famous, oft-used shot of Germán Robles as blood-sucking Count Lavud/ Duval in Fernando Méndez's Mexi-monster *clásico* **THE VAMPIRE** (*El vampiro*, 1957), Red Blood also released a Maximus single called "Dracula Disco" in '77... But I (i.e., SF) digress! ☺

NEW ON BLU

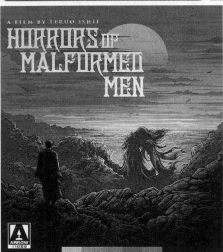

NEXT ISSUE:

The 6th and final part of Steve Bissette's "Anarchy & Monsters"; *M!* co-grammar nazi and cruel taskmaster Tony Strauss' eloquently literary treatise on the woefully-underappreciated 1981 cartoon creature feature **GRENDEL GRENDEL GRENDEL**; "Taylor-Made in Mexico & Spain", a belated reprint of a vintage 1991 interview (conducted by Michael Ferguson & Steve Fentone) with he who is arguably Spain's *second*-biggest Horror Movie icon, Jack Taylor; a rare interview (*circa* 1970s), translated from the Spanish, with Mexi-wrestling superstar *El Santo*, about his monster movie career; plus oodles of monstrous reviews, fab artwork and who knows (at this early stage) what else!

MIDNIGHT

Tasty Monstrous Munchies in More Bite-Sized Chunks!

SNACKS

*[Editor's Note: The following entries are credited with the monograms of their contributors, as follows: **LM** (Les Moore), **TP** (Tim Paxton) and **SF** (Steve Fenton)]

ALIEN OUTPOST (2014, USA, D: Jabbar Raisani) |– Clearly to better emphasize/exploit the content, this IFC Midnight acquisition's original more nondescript title **OUTPOST 37** was perhaps understandably changed to the more exploitable **ALIEN OUTPOST** instead. Filmed in a semi-mockumentary style and set in the not-too-distant future—2033, to be precise—at a time when the stubborn remnants of an extraterrestrial invasion force of monstrous beings nicknamed "the Heavies" by humans ("They're *big* fuckers. *HUGE!*") are kept at bay by a small-but-crack force of USDF ("United States Defense Force") soldiers manning the isolated titular stockade ("OP 37") out in the back end of beyond (in an, um, backward pro-Islamic country teeming with AK47-toting extremists, let's say). Amusingly enough, in the film's "Goofs" section at the IMDb, some 'know-it-all' who obviously wasn't paying proper attention when they watched the movie (assuming they even *did*!) wrongly 'corrects' the synopsis' setting of the story to "Iran", when in actuality—as is clearly stated more than once in **AO**, including via an on-screen title printed in HUGE BLOCK LETTERS—it is set in <u>Pakistan</u> in a DMZ located nearby to its neighboring nation Afghanistan… geesh, talk about being stuck in the asshole of the world! (Speaking of which, **AO** was actually shot in the increasingly-turbulent nation of South Africa, out-

Top & Above: A formidably brutish "Heavy" alien takes aim against human-kind with its zapper; design by Eddie Yang

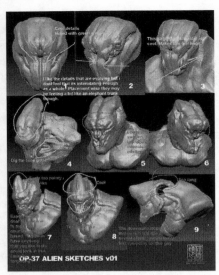

Digital designs for some of **ALIEN OUT-POST**'s monster FX

side Johannesburg, on various privately-owned farms.) Specially-developed high-impact phosphorous rounds (HIPRs) are one of the few terrestrial munitions that can penetrate the massive aliens' heavily-armored hides, and the genocidal brutes are running roughshod all around the territory, eliminating enemy humans with extreme prejudice. On the good guys' side there's a 'Jap-

US poster

anese-American' grunt character named Zilla (South African-born actor Kenneth Fok), presumably after "The Big G", plus other clichéd characters from a million war movies. Director Raisani (a former Stan Winston Studio employee) usually works in the visual effects arena, and, had he been allotted a somewhat bigger budget and a longer shooting sked for this outing—which has downscale 'mockbuster' (of the wannabe **MONSTERS** [2010, UK, D: Gareth Edwards] or **BATTLE LOS ANGELES** [2011, USA, D: Jonathan Liebesman] school) written all over it—he might have come up with something a whole lot more substantial, but points for trying. As it stands, though, while **AO** is far from totally satisfying—for instance, its faux documentarian framework, which, while preferable to the overused FF ("found footage") gimmick, tends to distance viewers from the action somewhat—it does have enough good things going for it to make it worth watching at least once, just for shits-'n'-giggles on a slow night. Sad to say, while the human protagonists are fleshed-out somewhat and given more than their fair share of screen-time, the so-called Heavies, while quite well-designed (Eddie Yang served as production designer hereon), are unfortunately pretty lightweight, uninspired and stilted computer-generated creations, for the most part. Thankfully, however, there are some very decent practical monster effects (c/o Alliance Studios and Steve Wang, another ex-Stan Winston associate) mixed-in, as in the all-too-brief sequence wherein a stray Heavy is wounded and taken prisoner by the Earthlings before being curtly shot dead in the head—not just once, but *four* times!—by the heroes' bullets-for-breakfast CO. In these scenes, the monster makeup really does the trick (veteran suit performer Doug Tait—who isn't nicknamed "The Monster Man" for nothing!—played the principal Heavy), but for the bulk of the action, clunkier CG versions take over. Any scenes (the not-so-'grand finale' included) involving supposedly 'spectacular' digital/optical FX fall short of being spectacular, it must be said, and might be considered below-par even by SyFy Channel (sub)standards. But all-in-all, not bad for a production whose total cost (under $5-million) was a mere pittance by today's standards, so you takes what you can get. Hell, my Mom liked it! For those who want to own it rather than just watch it on cable (as I did) or stream it online, **ALIEN OUTPOST** is available on Region A/1 Blu-ray/DVD from Shout! Factory. – LM

AMPHIBIOUS CREATURE OF THE DEEP (2010, USA/Netherlands/Indonesia, D: Brian Yuzna) |– Trailer copy: *"Deep In The Ocean A Creature Has Been Awoken By An Ancient Ritual. The*

Curse Must Be Broken." Tagline: *"You Are What It Eats."* Michael Paré as Jack Bowman, wryly: *"Twenty-thousand fuckin' leagues under the sea! It's a goddamn scorpion!"* Also known more succinctly as **AMPHIBIOUS 3D** and even more succinctly still as just plain **AMPHIBIOUS** (in plain ol' 2D) on British DVD, the present more sensationalistic/exploitative **ACOTD** title was applied to the film's 'flat' (i.e., only two-dimensional) version in some markets and, for obvious reasons (this being *Monster!* mag and all), is our preferred title. Although I was interested in seeing this 'old school' creature feature for the simple reason that it was directed by Mr. Yuzna (who partially co-wrote the script with Thai-born author/filmmaker "S.P. Somtow"/Somtow Sucharitkul, best-known [if at all] to Western horror fans as writer-director of the Mexican-set, Aztec mythology-based demons 'n' zombies weirdie-cheapie **THE LAUGHING DEAD** [1989, USA]), I was doubly curious, me being a big fan of movies from that general neck of the woods (i.e., Southeast Asia), due to the fact that this Dutch/British/Indonesian co-production was shot on location entirely in Indonesia (home to all sorts of weird and wonderful horror-fantasy flicks, mostly from the 1980s and often starring local 'scream queen' Suzzanna [1942-2008]). As Bowman, **ACTOD**'s down-on-his-luck charter boat skipper hero, 'name-brand' Yank lead Paré still looks in remarkably fine repair indeed some 15+ years on from his memorable turn as a tormented boy-next-door lycanthrope in Eric Red's sturdy shocker **BAD MOON** (1996, USA [see *Monster!* #33, p.260]). It must be said, however, that he sometimes appears far from fully-engaged in or committed to the present film, performance-wise; in fact, with his flippant air here, while apt to his stereotypical 'devil-may-care' sailor character, the actor at times seems to be expressing open scorn for the material (which is entirely his prerogative, if he wishes to, and I may only be projecting here anyway). But when all is said and done, it's the monster we're here for, of course. This, pleasingly enough, turns out to be a giant prehistoric water scorpion of the *Eurypterid* type ("Probably a *Mixopterus*," surmises our marine biologist heroine Prof. Skylar "Sky" Shane [Dutch leading lady Janna Fassaert]), a creature whose earliest evolutionary ancestors originated an estimated 430-million years ago, during the Silurian Period of Earth's genesis, complete with an agile stinger-tipped tail that sees plenty of usage, as well as being featured prominently in much of **ACOTD**'s promotional artwork internationally. Now, I must confess to loving (*adoring*, in fact) the concept of a gargantuan marine scorpion let loose in Asian waters, and I suppose you could say I had unrealistically high hopes for this flick, although

Above, Top to Bottom: *Everybody scream "AAAGGHH!"* A trio of garishly gory demises from Brian Yuzna's **AMPHIBIOUS CREATURE OF THE DEEP**, a lovably schlocky '50sesque critter fritter with an offbeat Asiatic angle

I presumed sight-unseen of it that its waterlogged arthropodic menace (part lobster-like crustacean, part *Scorpione* order arachnid, and all mean!) was, this being the computer age and all, going to be rendered almost entirely via digital means, which kinda put a damper on the idea for me. In fact, at the time of its initial release, if I'd found out it contained an all-practical megascorp—or better yet, a stop-motion-animated one—I would have gotten around to seeing it a whole lot sooner than I did. While the well-put-together trailer I previewed on YouTube didn't show *too* much of the creature, it showed enough for me to be able to spot the obvious prevalence of CGI—and from the looks of it, decidedly *crude* CGI, at that—which only made me less eager to see the full film, suspecting the

While mostly rendered in CGI *[top & center]*, **ACOTD**'s giant water scorpion also appears as an inert full-size prop *[above]*

of it occurring either on or above the surface. A post-opening titles sequence showing a topless bikini bimbo and her wimpass BF getting bloodily offed by some sort of sea monster proves to only be phony footage staged for a fictional 'reality' TV show called *Real or Fake?* which segues into the story proper. Depicted via some at times awkward second-unit direction, the local color of a frenzied pagan festival at a coastal village adds further visual interest ("Well, *I* think it's barbaric," opines pampered whitegirl Skylar snootily), even if its unflattering presentation of Indonesian tribal folk as gyrating, wailing, leering 'savages' is rather a throwback to the stereotyped Skull islanders of **KING KONG** (1933, USA); speaking of which, Paré even cracks a throwaway 'Kong' joke in regards to **ACOTD**'s monster at one point. But since the westerners played by the stars—who are equally as stereotyped as everyone else, I might add—are the least-interesting characters anyway, it would have been nice to have the story focus more centrally on the more interesting secondary/tertiary 'foreign' characters (I'm tempted to think that the film's Indonesian release version might be markedly different in both its editing and dialogue, but it remains to be seen). As was indicated right at the outset, we learn that young Tamal—by means of an ancient amulet—is in some way mystically/spiritually connected to the titular sea beast, which has been brought up from the depths by a recent catastrophic tsunami that devastated the region. It isn't until the final third of the movie that we are finally treated to a full-frontal shot of the complete monster, but even then it's largely presented with still more CGI (although a couple of its appendages—namely the pincers and stinger—are sometimes depicted via full-scale prop mockups). Thankfully, a practical (if utterly inert) full-size model—which *kind of* matches the animated version—was also constructed for one sequence, but this is shortly replaced by the CG version once more for the climactic concatenation. The rather startling and unsettling closing twist reveal is about the closest this film ever gets to the sorts of queasy body horror often found in more '80s-style Indonesian horror-fantasy fare, but the grim mood this evokes is lightened by a cute, cartoonish sight gag just before the final fade to black. As can sometimes happen, having recently watched **ACOTD** for the second time, now I knew what to expect I was able to enjoy it more than I did the first time (the IMDb's low ["3.6"] rating be damned!). Who knows, maybe 30 or 40 years from now—assuming this big blue marble is still spinning in space by then, and human beings are still the dominant lifeform—there will be as much love shown for **ACOTD**

worst. But anyway, on to the film… No thanks to his late father's uncle, young Tamal (a supposed tweenage boy actually played by a female actor, Monica Sayangbati), the grand-'nephew'—actually niece!—of an aged, ailing local *dukun* (["shaman"] Bambang Budi Santoso), winds up being sold into slave labor on an offshore fishing platform (known in Bahasa as a "*jermal*")—which fronts for a smuggling operation—out in the north Sumatran Sea. Isolated miles from land, this rickety wooden structure sits on bamboo stilts in the shallow waters and is ruled over with an iron hand (with billy-club) by cruel adult taskmasters, led by Boss Harris (Francis Bosco, an apparent East Indian) and Jimmy Kudrow (Irishman Francis Magee, an actual former real-life fisherman, aptly enough), who exploit and abuse Tamal and the other youths forcibly employed there.

Despite the title, only very little of the film's action actually takes place underwater, with most

as so many of us current aging monster kids in retrospect lavish on **THE BLACK SCORPION** (1957, USA, D: Edward Ludwig), a film that also went largely unappreciated in its time but is now rightly regarded as a B-movie classic. While ACOTD thus far doesn't appear to have been issued on Region A Blu-ray (?), it's available in Germany on Region B/2 Blu/DVD (in both 3D and 2D versions) from Projektor Film, in English but also with a German audio option. The film has also been released in a domestic (?) 2D DVD edition by Gaiam Americas, plus on countless other labels throughout the world (including in Australia, from Eagle Entertainment). For those so inclined, composer Fons Merkies' soundtrack—most of which isn't really very noticeable in the actual film itself, so might bear a listen independent of it—is up for grabs as an entire mp3 album (for $8.99), or as individual track downloads (at 99¢ a pop), via Amazon Digital Services LLC (on Amazon.com). – SF

ARBOR DEMON (2016, USA, D: Patrick Rea) |– Originally more nondescriptly titled **ENCLOSURE**, which doesn't really reveal anything about the film's contents in advance, the new title is a whole lot more self-explanatory, if not really revealing too much (might it be another bigfoot, perhaps?). The film stars Brad Dourif's daughter Fiona as Dana, who heads off into the bush on a camping excursion with her hubby of two years, Charles (Kevin Ryan), in hopes of reinvigorating their flagging relationship (or something like that). Once out in the woods, as expected, strange and scary things start to happen... Playing a baseball-cap and plaid-clad, trigger-happy yahoo who objectifies women and sneers his every utterance with a barely-repressed snarl, whilst his incidental character of Sean is every bit a clueless millennial city slicker's worst stereotype of everything a common-and-garden-variety "redneck" (a.k.a. "deplorable") should be (at least in their narrow minds), for all his so-called 'toxic masculinity', guest star Jake Busey plays the micro cast's most entertaining character... other than for those titular skin-crawlingly creepy bush-dwelling critters, that is (which is as it should be in a monster movie, of course). The main "demon"—in actuality a demon*ess*, just for the record—is performed by male actor Bruce Williamson. While it's far from a masterpiece of modern horror, **AD** does generate some unnerving atmosphere and at least deserves props for trying something a little bit different in the well-tapped 'people-stalked-in-the-bush' creature feature subgenre. It's available both on domestic DVD from Gravitas Ventures and undoubtedly via any number of streaming websites. – **LM**

THE ATONING (2017, USA, D: Michael Williams) |– Dialogue: *"Do you think there's a hell...?"* Spookery and babadookery collide and shakily cohabitate in this initially seemingly none-too-interesting haunted house tale that, following a quite startlingly 'twisty' plot development midway—whose reveal I shan't even *hint* at, for what it's worth—suddenly draws the viewer in and holds us for the duration... well, up until just before the supposed climax, anyway. But two-thirds of a decent film are better than none at all, I suppose. A semi-normal / semi-dysfunctional (i.e., typical) family unit consisting of a mother, father and their young son (respectively played to largely-understated effect by Virginia Newcomb, Michael LaCour and juvie actor Cannon Bosarge) find themselves caught-up in a decidedly *odd* predicament which becomes increasingly eerie and eventually all-out frightening—for a *little* while, at least—as more is revealed to us about their darkly dire shared situation. At first the fractured familial trio seem strangely detached and distant, even all-out alienated from one another, but as the plot thickens so too do their familial bonds, although a constant state of vague 'offness' seems to exist between them, as though they're desperately trying to reach out to one another across the small gulfs that separate them but can't quite come together completely as a unified whole. A couple of the much-too-sharp-focus 'shocks' (involving sightings of haunting spirits that are all-to-clearly played by solid human actors) early into the film aren't really all that effective, and seem to bode poorly for what's to come (...if anything. More on that below). But stick with it, as **THE ATONING**'s interestingly offbeat—and decidedly downbeat—premise makes this one—for the large part—stand out from the throngs of virtually interchangeable ghostly-themed 'nuclear-family-in-paranormal-peril' horror flicks being produced these days in the wake of the likes of the *Conjuring* and *Sinister* franchise entries. We do get some spine-tinglingly spooky chills here and there which are largely kept quite low-key rather than being over-emphatically in-your-face about it. And thankfully enough, that way-overused/abused genre trope known as the "jump scare" (*EEEK!*) is kept to a relatively tasteful minimum. Well, up till the closing act of the film, that is. Then the carefully-built-up suspense and air of slow-creeping creepiness is all frittered away to nothing, for the simple reason that the malevolent supernatural entities—identified by a clairvoyant as "lost souls"—behind all the weird goings-on are suddenly presented in a far-too-literal manner (i.e., as constantly-leering 'naked' white people smeared with all-over, um,

'90s UK double crown poster

resisted allowing it to sour me on the movie as a whole (sometimes I'm able to be quite objective about such things, even if they do kinda piss me off!). So, if you've got nothing better to do with your time, by all means give **THE ATONING** a watch and judge for yourself; although, at risk of damning it with faint praise here (*c'est la vie!*), I'm sure there are plenty of better things worth prioritizing over it in your viewing queue. – **LM**

BIG MEAT EATER (1982, Canada, D: Chris Windsor) |– Ad-line: *"Pleased To Meet Ya! – Meat To Please Ya!"* A movie that definitely isn't for vegetarians, the mere sound of **BME**'s meaty title alone is enough to trigger a devout Vegan to the point of hyperventilation. Made at the height of the era when "Golden Turkey" (thank you, Medved Bros.!) movie mania was at an all-time high and psychotronic 'cult/trash/sleaze/cheese/kitsch/camp/schlock' flicks *(bless 'em!)* were experiencing a theretofore unprecedented resurge in popularity, this Canuck tax shelter production (budgeted between $150,000 to $175,000 according to its producer/co-writer Laurence Keane himself) was shot in White Rock, British Columbia from late 1980 into early '81 (it's set in Burquitlam, an actual 'one-horse town'-like district of the BC city of Coquitlam which I'm betting has changed immensely since then thanks to that modern blight, 'urban sprawl'). XXL black jazz/blues belter Clarence "Big" Miller stars as Abdulla, a "Turkish" ex-janitor-*cum*-butcher whose words of dialogue come few and far between but whose larger-than-life screen presence is always most imposing indeed, especially when he lets loose the formidable (g) rumble of his baritone singin' pipes (a force of nature on a par with those of the mighty Howlin' Wolf or Screamin' Jay Hawkins), such as when performing the movie's title song while bare-fistedly splatting (tenderizing?) various types of squishy meat products atop a countertop, much to the wide-eyed horror of a group of shopping biddies stood agog across the counter from him. Forget such niceties as coherency of plot, dramatic continuity and realistic staging, as **BME** flies in the face of such minor concerns as those! Part musical comedy, part sci-fi satire and all eccentric, this one-of-a-kind wonder draws from an assortment of inspiration sources, creature features very much included. Robotic aliens from outer space—played by battery-powered 'Made in Hong Kong' toy robots—are out to tap Earth's supply of "Balonium", a powerful energy source derived from rotting animal flesh. As well as piloting a wobbly flying saucer *à la* Ed Wood's immortal **PLAN 9 FROM OUTER SPACE** (1959, USA)—although the one seen in the present film

blackface, for wont of a better description) that irreparably shatters much of the creepy effect of earlier scenes. The film isn't a total write-off, by any means, but it ultimately reads more as some sort of pretentious wannabe artsy allegory/metaphor for a seriously-troubled marriage than as a true horror/monster movie. The predictable twist reveal—that (*GASP!*) the husband/father is *not* as good of a person as he mostly seems to be, albeit with some issues—struck me as a gutless cop-out rather than a surprise. Wouldn't it make a nice change to see the wife/mother depicted as the hateful villain for once, just to at least crack the mold a little, if not actually shattering it into a million shards? But instead, after outed moderately abusive Hubby/Daddy sincerely tries to make amends for his not-really-so-awful wrongs and literally *begs* his immediate kinfolk in tears for forgiveness, only to then fall fatally afoul of the murderous restless souls lurking in the house, his widow and now-fatherless son simply indifferently shrug him off for the 'they-all-lived-happily-ever-after (minus Dad)' ending, as though he had never even existed at all, with the single mother now set to 'bravely' forge ahead and raise 'their' (i.e., her) son alone, without a father figure in the picture, presumably with all the resources of Big Mother's nanny state at her disposal to serve as a safety net in the absence of a second actual parent and paternal role model. There was a coldly mean-spirited, mercenary quality to this supposedly 'positive', 'inspirational' resolution which I must admit left me cold, but I grudgingly

is an actual off-the-shelf / over-the-counter plastic model kit UFO, albeit suspended wonkily on a string like the infamous repurposed spinning hubcaps in **PLAN 9**—**BME**'s invading E.T. bots (whose 'eyes' flash sparks and who converse in electronic tonalities translated by English subtitles) possess the technology to temporarily morph earthlings into mutant monsters, and they can also raise the dead at will, resulting in a couple of zombies who are subservient to the aliens' sinister cause (Burquitlam's skeezy Italian mafioso mayor Carmine Rigatoni [Howard Taylor] included). Much like the costumes and the rest of the production design, **BME** is set firmly in a throwback pseudo-1950s 'Middle America' milieu—which kind of prefigures the 'alternate reality' setting of a future Canuxploitation classic, namely Andrew Currie's brilliant zombie satire **FIDO** (2006), starring Scottish comedian Billy Connolly as the titular 'domesticated' undead character—and it's said decade from which it draws much of its cinematic influences (e.g., from the likes of **PLAN 9**, Bruno VeSota's **THE BRAIN EATERS** [1958] *et al*). This film was formerly (in 2005) made available domestically on Koch Vision DVD and before that on Canuck Beta/VHS tape by both Astral Video and HGV Video Productions, as well as in the USA by both Media Home Entertainment (cover-blurb: *"A Musical-Comedy That's a Cold-Cut Above the Rest..."*) and Video Treasures. A British tape edition was put out by Palace Video sometime in the (mid/late?) '90s. In an insightful 11+-minute on-camera interview posted at YouTube (@ the link titled "Big Meat Eater Interview Laurence Keane Feb 25, 2013" [*https://www.youtube.com/watch?v=vQI-w7ksWQo*]), co-creator Keane mentions that a Blu-ray release of **BME** will hopefully someday be in the offing; an eventuality which seems highly likely in these fruitful days when virtually every obscure movie ever made seems to be coming out on BD in pristine HD editions with all mod cons. But until then, the film can be ordered on plain ol' DVD-R, or otherwise streamed VOD in HD (for $2.99) or downloaded in the same quality format (for $9.99) via its official website (@ *bigmeateater.com*) through Utopia Pictures / Distrify; as an extra post-Christmas treat to myself (not that I deserve it after that dirty great lump o' coal I got from Santa, mind you!), I ordered a copy of the latter option, which is downloading even as I type these words. Those interested—and if you're in any way, shape or form a lover (or even just a liker) of wigged-out flicks, there's no reason why you shouldn't be—can check out this classic 'retro' Canuxploitation flick's Facebook page (@ *www.facebook.com/BigMeatEaterMov-*

ie). Better you do that than become embroiled in another no-win argument about politics there! – SF

DEATH BY INVITATION (1971, USA, D: Ken Friedman) |– US one-sheet poster tagline: *"Between Them Were A Thousand Years Of Witchcraft And An Axe!"* UK videotape tagline: *"She's the reincarnation of evil and she wants revenge."* This once-long-forgotten-and-recently-rediscovered diamond-in-the-rough fits neatly into the popular horror subgenre involving 'vengeful witches' epitomized by the likes of Mario Bava's **BLACK SUNDAY** (*La maschera del demonio*, 1960, Italy), John Llewelyn Moxey's pre-Amicus Productions studio kickstarter **THE CITY OF THE DEAD** (a.k.a. **HORROR HOTEL**, 1960, UK), Chano Urueta's **THE BRAINIAC** (*El barón del terror*, 1961, Mexico [see *Monster!* #32, pp.229-256]), "Robert Hampton"/Riccardo Freda's **THE WITCH'S CURSE** (*Maciste all'inferno*, 1962, Italy) and Michael Reeves' "Ernst von Theumer"/Mel Welles' **THE SHE BEAST** (*La Sorella di Satana*, 1966, UK/Italy), among others. Having largely begun in the early '60s, said subgenre had a bit of a 'resurgence' during the so-called "Satanic 'Seventies", when interest in fare concerning witches/witchcraft and the occult had risen to an all-new high among consumers of popular culture across all media. During the same general period as **DBI** was produced deep down within the bowels of the regional US indie film industry (it was shot on Staten

The mesmerizingly charismatic Shelby Leverington as **DEATH BY INVITATION** (1971)'s undead witch

the accursed Vroot clan as she can sink her hex into. Delicately pretty, lissome of form and fascinating to behold in the central (indeed, pivotal) role, such is her deftness of characterization that the highly viewer-friendly Ms. Leverington—the camera literally *loves* her!—virtually seems to *glide* across the screen and is suitably beguiling as the hauntingly haunted Lise, who at first kills her assigned victims with carefree callousness and icy detachment, but later comes to rue her murderous actions when she begins falling in love with one of their number (the *hunkiest*, natch!). Elsewhere in the small-but-strong cast, despite (even *because* of) his propensity to drift towards the hammier side of acting, movie one-timer Aaron Phillips is refreshingly offbeat and oddly engaging as Peter, the Vroot family's strict, bossy patriarch with one lazy eye (or possibly a glass one?). Norman Parker (billed hereon as Norman Paige) plays Jake, Lise's manly, forcefully persistent lust interest, who simply won't take no for an answer when she repeatedly—if clearly with reluctance—spurns his romantic advances, evidently because (rightly, as it happens) she fears her softened feelings towards him will interfere with her quest for vengeance/justice on the Vroots. Despite revealing not even so much as a *lick* of actual nudity anywhere throughout, some scenes (all of which involve the mesmerizingly photogenic female lead, whose lovely visage is periodically shot in extreme close-up in order that the cinematographer's lingering lens can catch every subtle nuance of her facial expressions) are imbued with an intensely powerful eroticism; as in the scene wherein Lise furthers her seduction of a virginal, nerdy youth (i.e., Peter Vroot's eldest son) at her apartment by recounting to him an ancient legend involving a tribe of sexually ravenous, blood-drinking/flesh-eating female jungle women, fierce amazonian huntresses whose menfolk were kept in enforced servitude by them (it was only still early into the so-called "Women's Lib" era, after all, so such 'innovative', 'non-traditional' concepts as a female-dominated society were then more trendily topical than ever before [even if most anthropologists worth their salt would scoff at such feministic wish-fulfilment utopian nonsense!]). Gore is kept to a tastefully judicious minimum too, and this is much more of an ambient mood-piece than it is 'right-in-your-eyeball'-style exploitation viewing, although it is nevertheless still low-budget and ragged enough around the edges in spots to qualify it as skid-row grindhouse/drive-in fodder. Fascinating viewing for sure, this! Don't believe the IMDb's measly "3.8" rating!

Island, NY), similarly-themed creepy-cheapies like **MARK OF THE WITCH** (1970, USA, D: Tom Moore) and **HAUNTED** (1977, USA, D: Michael A. DeGaetano) further exploited much the same thematic territory with varying degrees of success. The kernel of the present title's plot—the reincarnated spirit of a beautiful Dutch witch (Shelby Leverington) executed in the Netherlands three centuries before returns from beyond the grave to avenge herself on the American descendants of those who systemically murdered her via lynch-mob way back when—is as old as the hills, and little is done to flesh-out the backstory behind it without harming the simplicity of the main narrative whatsoever: basically, the witch is back from the dead and out to off as many members of

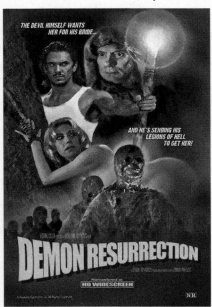

Poster for the SD 2008 flick's 2017 HD reissue

DBI's patchy and erratic home video history includes being issued on British PAL Beta/VHS tape by Market Video sometime in the '80s. It was once again salvaged from the unforgiving purgatory of obscurity in 1994 by Frank Henenlotter and Something Weird Video (SWV) as a VHS release—albeit containing only a B&W print—in their "Sexy Shockers" series, before the film returned to languish in little-seen limbo once more; SWV subsequently (in 2006) reissued the title on DVD-R in a proper color print, as per **DBI**'s original theatrical release. Having been previously (in 2013) released on DVD by the ever-surprising Vinegar Syndrome (double-billed with the outdoorsy survivalist thriller **SAVAGE WATER** [1979, USA, D: Paul Kiener]), the film has more recently been made available on domestic disc by the same company as the 'bottom half' of a discount twofer with the even older if better-known poverty row brain-boggler **THE DUNGEON OF HARROW** (1962, USA)—moonlighting broadcasting veteran-*cum*-Charlton Comics artist Pat *"The Peacemaker"* Boyette's threadbare, amateurish-if-ambitious wannabe imitation of an entry in Corman's AIP/EAP series—**DBI** is a 'lost treasure' that is well worth rediscovering (it can also be streamed online via Amazon Prime in HD or SD [@ $1.99 for a rental and $4.99 to purchase in the former quality format]). Like its just-cited VG co-programmer **TDOH**, it's destined to become a true cult favorite, and I became an instant fan after laying eyes on it for the very first time shortly prior to writing these words. Warts, jagged corners and all, it's a semiprecious gem that is definitely worth repeat viewings! – **SF**

DEMON RESURRECTION (2008/2017, USA, D: William Hopkins) |– Trailer narration: *"They're at the windows. They're at the doors. They may even be... inside you. They're back! Reaching out from the pits of Hell, clawing at innocent young flesh, devouring and destroying in a rampage of evil."* Here's another of the seemingly gazillions of low-budget, lower-profile regional horror flicks—in this case shot in Long Island, New York—that get released on a yearly basis but that I inadvertently overlook, for the simple reason that I don't have a clue they even exist at all until I stumble upon them whenever I happen to at a later date (what with the sheer volume of product being produced nowadays of every genre and description from all over the globe for every one of the innumerable media platforms that's out there, it's harder than ever to keep up with even a fraction of everything that gets made, so don't even bother trying. Just check out what you can when you can, that's my motto!).

Will McDonald—who I'm guessing might be more

Above, Top to Bottom: Talented FX artiste Ashley Benatar-Dargham designed/created **DEMON RESURRECTION**'s wicked demon-zombies; some of the coolest *Monster!* has ever seen from this side of the big soup

of a semi-pro actor (?) in fringe theatre or the like, for the simple reason that his IMDb filmography numbers just two titles, this film included—plays sinister cult-leader and practitioner of the black arts Mr. Toth (pronounced "Toath"; roughly [and aptly] rhymes with "loath"), who is out to recapture a defected former forcibly-inducted neophyte cultist named Grace (lead actress Alexis Golightly) for an evil purpose (more trailer hype: *"The Devil himself wants her for his bride, and he's sending his legions of Hell to get her!"*). You see, after having been branded over her left breast with the Devil's mark and forcibly impregnated by him during a satanic rite (that includes full-frontal female nudity, although the actual impregnation occurs off-screen), the AWOL heroine—whose actress Ms. Golightly was evidently replaced by a body double for the ruder nude scenes, but who does some of the milder ones herself—thereafter becomes targeted for retrieval so that the gestating fruit of the human mother and demonic father's loins can be reaped for the cult's benefit. This base premise leads into the group of young(ish) protagonists being besieged by dark forces at the isolated country manor of John the youthful hero (Damian Ladd), a scholar of white magic who pits his wits—and spells—against those of Toth the wily warlock for the very souls of he and his chums, numbering one ballsy black dude, name of Denton ([Bashir Solebo] who, for a change—*surprise!*—isn't the first to get killed-off) and a handful of white folks, including three chicks (Golightly, Laurie Miller and Amanda Renee Knox) and the token gay guy (Eli Kranski), who's pretty, um, ballsy too, in his own (non-'gay') way. Oh yeah, and there's also this total obnoxious a-hole of a honky gangsta/cracka dudebro (Chad Kessler) too, who not surprisingly doesn't survive till anywhere even close to halfway through the movie, not that anybody cares, least of all we the viewer.

Nicely put together for an SOV production of such lowly 'underground' origins, **DR** boasts a decent script (complete with mandatory nods to H.P. Lovecraft, including a *Necronomicon*-like ancient grimoire) and adequate performances, especially by senior actor McDonald as the glassy-eyed, stone-facedly / soft-spokenly menacing Toth. The real stars here, though, are the 100% all-practical prosthetics and special effects (the work of dishy makeup artiste / occasional actress Ashley Benatar-Dargham, whose latest FX credit is for the yet-to-be-released indie horror **ZOMBIE WITH A SHOTGUN** [2018, USA, D: Hilton Ariel Ruiz]), top attraction among these being the squad of walking corpses that the villain ritualistically summons forth from their shallow mass-grave to do his bidding (i.e., "*Kill them! Kill them all!!*"). As zombies go—even if the IMDb's cast listing does instead identify them as "demons"—these things really are something else to see! Upon first clawing their way up from out of the ground—wherein they have been buried for two centuries, preserved by the evil-purging salt that was mixed-in with the dirt to keep them at rest—they proceed to rip a couple of incidental dudes to bits before settling-in for a prolonged **NOTLD**-style nocturnal assault of the hero's home. Deathly dull grave-grey in tone from head to foot, dressed in timeworn, ragged shrouds and lugubriously slow-moving whilst getting from Point A to Point B, but fast-on-the-uptake when they want to be—such as raking victims' faces with their razor-sharp talons, for instance—these cadav-

erous, dirt-encrusted boneyard creepers, whose bodies give off visible wafts of putrid vapor, have a lot of the Italianate brand of undead shamblers about them, only they're a good deal more dehydrated-looking than your usual moist 'n' runny post-Romero / Fulci-style specimen. (Rather than crawling with maggots and oozing the putrescence of decomposition, **DR**'s appear almost ossified/mummified, endowing them with a distinctive look unto themselves which ties-in with the fact that, as opposed to being allowed to naturally rot, they were interred in a grave lined with a preservative agent [i.e., salt], which served to dry them out rather like salted meat.) No sooner has one of the girls trapped in the house peed herself in fright—as an emphatic close-up of her jeans crotch reveals—than she is dragged-out through a smashed window by the zombie attackers, but not before being disemboweled in passing by a projecting shard of glass during a queasily drawn-out Fulciesque moment. And speaking of gruesome moments (***ATTENTION: SPOILER ALERT!***), the scene in which Grace our disgraced heroine goes into labor and her far-from-virginal nether regions projectile-vomit forth a grossly-misshapen, vaguely caterpillar-like larval demon-spawn is—to use the quaint regional American colloquialism—enough to turn a hound from a gutwagon. But, while the film definitely has its splattery inclinations, it doesn't dwell overlong on the guts 'n' grue, showing us just enough to evince a "*Yuck!*" response without needlessly going into outright overkill. For the grand finale, Solebo as the heroic Denton, making like Duane Jones in **NOTLD** and Ken Foree in **DOTD**, does his best to fend-off the walking dead men using a short length of blunt-ended 2x4 (*not* the most effective weapon for combating *any* monster with, let alone never-say-quit zombie demonoids!). Just as he is about to get swarmed and swamped by the buggers and we're expecting a classical 'collective gut-ripping' *à la* Geo. R to occur, director Hopkins dispels our expectations by springing his big 'twist' on us. Not that it comes as any sort of a surprise, mind you, as (without going into any of the specific details here) we've been expecting it all along. Before you can say, "Too bad someone doesn't show up in the nick of time to blast all the zombies back to Hades in puffs of CGI smoke with a blessed wooden staff", the reanimated corpses are no more, leading into the final showdown with primary heavy Mr. Toth and ending things on a fittingly ironic EC Comics-style note that has one more unpleasant surprise in store… for *him*, not us.

While **DR** was originally released a decade ago back in '08, it has recently (in '17) been rereleased proudly "Remastered in HD Widescreen" (as for that "HD" claim, the image isn't exactly 1080p or

Blu-ray quality, but is still highly presentable regardless; only completely anal-retentive nitpickers will be complaining). This spiffy new edition—which I can't compare with the original, as I haven't seen that version—is only a lousy $1.99 to watch (a one-time-only deal) or a measly $4.99 to buy outright (i.e., download and/or stream anytime you want) via Vimeo (@ *https://vimeo.com/ ondemand/102966*). Honestly, after first laying my rheumy ol' ocular orbs on this movie's truly *awesome* zombie makeups in the trailer at said site (it's also viewable on YouTube), I literally *immediately* thereafter clicked on the "Buy" button without hesitation (thanks, PayPal!), and would have considered it a bargain even at three times the price! <u>Note To Self</u>: Now if only I could score myself a legal VOD download of James Sizemore's reputedly impressive **THE DEMON'S ROOK** (2013, USA), which from what I've seen of it—including all the trailers and supplemental materials officially posted on YouTube—seems to only be available for streaming online, but unfortunately not as an actual download. Since that latter option is my preferred format of choice these days and I no longer bother buying physical media when it can be avoided, I haven't bothered picking-up **ROOK** on DVD, but maybe I might have to, as I've long been wanting to see it. Why it is that more home video distribution companies don't get in the habit of offering 'soft' copies of titles in their catalogue rather than forever pushing plastic media and packaging on customers is beyond me. I guess maybe it's because, either 1) they get to charge a whole lot more for all the bells-'n'-whistles—such as fancy boxes, special features and reversible cover artwork, etc.—and/or, 2) they figure it'd be too easy for pirate mp3/mp4 copies to get passed around 'under-the-table' between fans via Dropbox, WeTransfer and the like? (Which, now I think about it, seem like fairly sound reasons, at least in regards to the latter one.) – **SF**

DON'T GO NEAR THE PARK (1979, USA, D: Lawrence D. Foldes) |– US one-sheet poster tagline: *"The entrance is the gateway to Hell!"* Trailer narration: *"Since the dawn of time, Man has been plagued by the evil curse of the lusting vampires! The living dead have risen again! ...KEEP OUT! This park is* not *for playing! The horrible truth will curdle your blood! They rise from the grave to wreck [sic] their ritualistic vengeance on the living! Zombies on a rampage of blood and terror! ...The gruesome reality more shocking than your most horrifying nightmares! There is no escape from the supernatural fiends that stalk your soul! BEWARE! You have been warned! KEEP OUT! This park is* not *for playing!"* Another true jaw-dropping offbeat novelty, is this one, and one which I'm real happy I stumbled across quite by

accident just the year before last. Despite how its title makes it sound—i.e., like just another formulaic slasher flick of the "Don't" do this-or-that horror subgenre—it surprisingly and thankfully turns out to be an all-out supernatural shocker about (among a *whole lot* of other things) the quest for eternal life, with pronounced vampire/zombie/cannibalism overtones plus some bona fide splattery ultraviolence and gratuitous T&A to boot (that said, the print reviewed here is obviously cut in places). Ergo, an easy fit for some down-homey *M!* coverage, just like Mamma Monster used to make! You know you're in for something a bit on the 'offbeat' side when a teenage boy gets garroted and has his guts ripped open and chewed on by a cannibalistic immortal named Gar ("Crackers Phinn"/Robert Gribbin) right in the prologue, reducing the kid to a wrinkly, grey-haired husk! For whatever reason, the cannibals' periodic ingestion of their victims' intestinal blood restores them to youth (something to do with an ancient curse ["You are condemned to perpetual dying, but never death!"], but the minutiae of the overcomplicated backstory behind these immortals is too confusing to bother explaining here). Although she was around 21 at the time, petite future Scream Queen Linnea Quigley only looks around 16 (while the credits claim to be "introducing" the budding actress, she'd actually already been in a handful of movies by this point, usually in uncredited bit-parts purely in the interests of adding T&A value). Typically enough,

shortly after being introduced she gets hazily nude in the shower—shot through the steamed-up glass door—only to then not show anything at all in a subsequent scene in which she makes as if to doff her negligee, then doesn't (here's where one of those apparent cuts I mentioned happens!), but there are some booby shots on view for "Celebrity Skin" enthusiasts to drool over. The oddly-named 'heroine' Bondi (played as a pert, precocious teenybopper by Tammy Taylor, who is very much in the Linda Blair genre of impish button-nosed girl-next-door cuteness) is the illegitimate love-child of the immortal Gar and his mere mortal mate Linnea (whose character herein doesn't even warrant a name). No sooner, to cut a long story short, has Bondi hit the road due to her incompatible parents' unbearable constant marital strife than she gets abducted by a vanload of stoner party animals. After only narrowly escaping a flaming auto-wreck, she winds up at an old western ghost town (scenes shot at Paramount Ranch) in the title park, where she meets two young male runaways, the rebel teenage rich kid "Cowboy" (Chris Riley) and 8-year-old smartass Nick (Meeno Peluce). If not for the kids' occasional profanity, pot-smoking and blatantly sexualized dialogue—even from Nick the nipper!—these scenes might almost have come from a family-oriented 'coming-of-age' drama. While **DGNTP** sometimes registers much like a '70s made-for-TV movie, especially on its soundtrack, there's *no way* this could ever have aired uncut on network television!

Confusing editing/continuity make an already muddy plot even muddier, but these periodic lapses into incoherence only increase the film's cryptic charm, in my opinion. The 'key' subplot concerning a 12,000-year-old race of immortals reminded me of a similar tribe in another work of wonderment from the same decade, 1976's **CRYPT OF DARK SECRETS** (see last issue [p.355]). Long after you've forgotten his name was even listed in the opening credits, slumming guest star Aldo Ray appears at just past the 50-minute mark, as Taft, a writer character of no real relevance to the, uh, plot other than to provide some expository dialogue and serve as a potential paternal surrogate for little 'orphan' Nick (and no, Taft *doesn't* have pedophiliac aims on the boy, as he would likely be depicted today). Of course, all this hogwash masquerading as plot development would be unendurable if this was just some mundane drama, but, after slowly-but-surely losing its mind even more following the halfway point (for all its futile attempts to tie-up the various trailing loose ends of plot by adding still more to the already muddled mix), this flaky flick loses all its marbles completely, spiraling into an incomprehensibly chaotic climax involving en-

coffined vampires, a certain alignment of planetary bodies, a too-cleancut caveman in warpaint, attempted incestuous rape, deadly eye-beams, a cavern cave-in of Styrofoam boulders, Bondi abruptly turning into a wizened old crone ("She"-like, care of stop-motion makeup FX), a blazing inferno, and, most randomly and unexpectedly of all (even in this wildly unpredictable context), a bunch of rotting human corpses come to life and swarm the evil immortals.

While **DGNTP** depicting cannibalism were cut from original theatrical prints so as to secure the film an "R" rating rather than an "X", Thriller Video's 1986 stateside VHS release contained a complete, uncut print. In 2006, Anchor Bay Entertainment released a fully-uncut edition as part of their compilation DVD set *Box of the Banned*. Circa the 1980s, the UK's Intervision outfit put **DGNTP** out on Beta/VHS tape there, where it was banned (in 1984, appropriately) as a so-called "Video Nasty" (it's featured in a number of docs on the subject, including both parts of *Ban the Sadist Videos!* [2005/2006, UK, D: David Gregory]). At some point during the '80s, it was released on home videotape in Finland (under the same native title) by at least two different labels—Magnum Video and Dollarvideo—as **PIMEYDEN PUISTO** ("Park of Darkness"), with English audio and Finnish subs. Amusingly enough, while each of those Finnish versions were packaged inside totally dissimilar cover art, both loudly-'n'-proudly claimed on their fronts in block caps that "ALAN ALDA" [sic] was the star! Unless you happen to be seriously dyslexic (or possibly half-blind), there's no mistaking the *M*A*S*H* star's name for that of **DGNTP**'s actual (if only nominal) 'star', the top-billed Aldo Ray—any more than you could possibly mix up their vastly dissimilar faces—so we can only assume that using the former of those two actors' names instead of the latter's was done either purely by accident or with the express intention of misleading potential customers into believing that the world-famous "Hawkeye" performer had somehow found his way into an obscure low-budget horror exploitation flick right at the very peak of his mainstream fame. Elsewhere in Europe, under the native title **NO VAYA CERCA DEL PARQUE...** (an exact translation of the original American title, albeit with an added ellipsis at the end), the film was put out on videocassette in Spain by Inter Video Española / Home Video International, whose frontal artwork misspelled the director's surname (as "Folbes" [sic]), but at least they got the star's name right. They even also spelled the director's name correctly on the cover to Carrère Vidéo's 1986 French-dubbed SECAM Beta/VHS tape version, which was retitled **LA MALÉDIC-**

TION DU FOND DES TEMPS ("The Curse of the Ages"). **DGNTP** provides further proof positive that numerical qualitative ratings don't mean shit. IMDb's for this is a mere "3.5", but in terms of entertainment value, I'd give it at least three times that much…if I gave a shit about such meaningless twaddle, that is. Yes indeed, this here oddity is one I shall be revisiting again in future… more than once, if I live long enough. – **SF**

HOUSE OF DRACULA (1945, USA, D: Erle C. Kenton) |– You may well wonder why I would bother writing about some hoary ol' Universal monster movie, when by now every single "monster kid" zine out there has covered all three of the studio's top creative periods (i.e., the 1920s, 1930s-'40s and 1950s) *ad nauseam*. I do have my favorites, including **THE MUMMY** (1932, D: Karl Freund) and **THE BRIDE OF FRANKENSTEIN** (1935, D: James Whale), but those are generally considered to be the absolute *classics* of the classics. I admit I am no big fan of Béla Lugosi, me being a die-hard Karloff kid since day one, so **DRACULA** (1931, D: Tod Browning) doesn't even crack my top ten. That said, **HOUSE OF DRACULA**, the final bona fide horror movie in Universal's second monster cycle (I *don't* count any of the Abbott & Costello 'meet-ups' as horror movies, by the way), also ranks highly on my list. Its director Kenton was an interesting guy. His 1932 Paramount Pictures production **ISLAND OF LOST SOULS** (whose rights eventually shifted to Universal, ironically enough) is a truly sumptuous piece of pre-Code divergent cinema, what with Kathleen Burke's smolderingly animalistic panther girl Lota and Charles Laughton's sweatily slimy and sadistic Dr. Moreau. Not to mention the incred-

1950s Realart US reissue pressbook ad

ibly, appropriately organic cinematography by Karl Struss, who was also responsible for the beautiful look of Paramount and Rouben Mamoulian's innovative **DR. JEKYLL AND MR. HYDE** (1931, USA), starring Fredric March in the title roles. Kenton's later Universal horror outings were far-less-artistic pieces of work, albeit no doubt largely due to the studio's tighter budgets during the wartime era, while horror movies had been Universal's bread-and-butter in the early/mid-'30s. However, by the time that era—which is typically considered by fans to be Hollywood's "Golden Age of Horror", both at Universal specifically and in general—came to a close, the studio shifted-down in their productions due to a change in the company's leadership and some bad financial moves, to concentrate on westerns, cliffhanger serials, light musicals, romantic melodramas, whodunits and also more

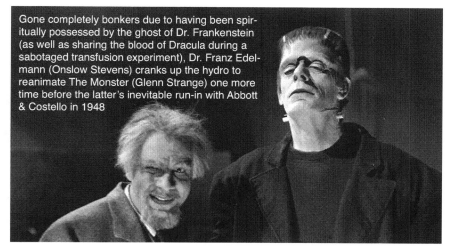

Gone completely bonkers due to having been spiritually possessed by the ghost of Dr. Frankenstein (as well as sharing the blood of Dracula during a sabotaged transfusion experiment), Dr. Franz Edelmann (Onslow Stevens) cranks up the hydro to reanimate The Monster (Glenn Strange) one more time before the latter's inevitable run-in with Abbott & Costello in 1948

Not only did iconic scream queen Barbara Steele's famous highly-photogenic facial features provide inspiration for "The Apparition of the Mill" in Kevin McTurk's wonderful rod-puppet horror short *The Mill at Calder's End* (2015), but the actress actually also provided voiceover for the character too; just one of the many ingenious little creative touches to be found in the film

Note: In its entirety, *TMaCE* was included as a segment of the multi-director horror anthology **MINUTES PAST MIDNIGHT** (2016, Canada)

horror films, albeit ones of a generally lighter/lesser tone than much of their genre fare from the 1930s. These more-formulaic and conservative '40s horrors relied heavily on preexisting sets and locations, second-tier stars, and established prequels, so why sink a ton of cash into what were considered B-pictures, when they already had a readymade audience anyway; thus, fast(er) 'n' cheap(er) became the studio's new MO. 1942's **THE GHOST OF FRANKENSTEIN**, which I consider to be the second-best of the series after **BRIDE**, was really the last entry that had any kind of decent production values and prestige. It was also the entry which could have been the savior of the waning series had someone actually bothered putting some serious thought into the direction it and its potential sequels might take (something I went into more deeply in *Monster!* #13's editorial about my favorite *Frankenstein* flicks).

Erle C. Kenton also helmed another personal favorite of mine, **HOUSE OF FRANKENSTEIN**, which was to follow in 1944, and it was the first major monster romp after the abysmal **FRANKENSTEIN MEETS THE WOLF MAN** (1943, Roy William Neill), a film which for me fails on many levels. This failure was neither screenwriter Curt Siodmak's nor director Neill's fault, rather it was due to in-house bickering at the studio and the insistence that all the dialogue spoken by the Monster (who could now talk, since having been installed with Ygor's cunning and intelligent brain) be chopped-out. This 'creative' decision ultimately neutered the Monster's

role as being pivotal in any way, shape or form for both that film and the remainder of the series (when he should rightly have been its central character, of course). What might have been a brilliant move on the franchise's part—imagine all the possibilities of an intelligent Monster bent on revenge and world domination!—instead nonsensically reduced him to no more than a clumsy lump, a mere shambling shadow of his former self. **HOF** didn't advance matters in the series' development of the Monster much, but it was still a very entertaining film nevertheless. Its monster mash-up of Dracula, The Monster, The Wolf Man, a hunchback (every mad scientist in a Frankenstein film has to have one, don't you know!) and Boris Karloff as the maniacal Dr. Gustav Niemann set the stage for the similarly monster-packed **HOUSE OF DRACULA**, and even **ABBOTT AND COSTELLO MEET FRANKENSTEIN**, one of Universal's biggest commercial successes during the waning years of the 1940s. For Kenton, with only pennies to work with, **HOUSE OF DRACULA** was a major, if still somewhat overlooked and underrated, horror classic. Needless to say, it, as with all the other Uni titles mentioned above, is presently (as always!) available on home video—both Blu-ray and DVD—from Universal Pictures Home Entertainment. – **TP**

THE MILL AT CALDER'S END (2015, USA, D: Kevin McTurk) |– Promotional materials describe it as "a Victorian ghost story puppet film in the tradition of Edgar Allan Poe, H.P. Lovecraft, and the gothic horror films of the 1960s.

This film utilizes 30-inch tall *bunraku* puppets and traditional in-camera practical effects." This 13¾-minute short is a truly remarkable accomplishment, for sure. Indeed, it's so well-done that I could quite happily sit through a feature-length effort from Mr. McTurk & Co.; or at least a considerably longer short than the present one, which goes by so quickly that it leaves you wanting more. One is left wondering what wonders the creators might come up with if they allowed themselves a full half-hour runtime, say (or better yet, a whole hour or more!). Having left there as a child, Nicholas Grimshaw returns to the title location, bent on its total destruction in order to put an end to the centuries-old curse that hangs over the place. Our young hero learns that "The Apparition of the Mill" (her dubbed voice provided by former Euro "Scream Queen" Barbara Steele) isn't the only horrible haunter of the site, which also harbors a monstrous great beast known as "The Bramblegor"... The Grimshaw character was voiced by one-time (in 2005) Quatermass performer Jason Flemyng (1966-), son of director Gordon Flemyng (1934-1995), whose directorial credits include both of AARU / Amicus Productions' mid-'60s *Dr. Who* theatrical features, starring Peter Cushing in the title role. The roughly half-scale puppets' faces are amazingly detailed and lifelike, and, while they mostly remain totally static—except for a couple of key moments when their mouths are animatronically animated to 'speak'—atmospheric lighting and camera angles endow them with great expressiveness regardless of their facial features' general immobility. If you go to the filmmakers' official website, The Spirit Cabinet (@ *http://www.thespiritcabinet.com/films/*), it provides a direct link to Vimeo, where you can purchase a hi-def download of *TMaCE* for $9.00 (US). Well worth it at thrice the price! While I was there, I also ordered myself a VOD download of McTurk's earlier quarter-hour horror-fantasy short, *The Narrative of Victor Karloch* (2012, USA), which reads rather like an extended trailer and features the voices and rod-puppet likenesses of Christopher "Dr. Emmett Brown" Lloyd and Elijah "Frodo Baggins" Wood, respectively voicing the title character and William Merriwether. After daring young adventurer Merriwether's deep-diving bathysphere is torn loose from its mooring cable by a giant squid, the man experiences a ghostly encounter on the sea-bottom... – SF

SHADOW CREATURE (1995, USA, D: James Gribbins) |– VHS cover blurb: *"A 50's feel... with a 90's flare..."* Set and shot partly in Buffalo, New York and partly in Cleveland, Ohio—home of such personal-fave-of-mine punk acts

as The Dead Boys, The Pagans and The New Bomb Turks, not to mention only a relatively short jaunt from my long-time zining *compañero* Tim P's hometown of Oberlin—here's another one of those 'from-right-out-of-nowhere' titles I stumbled across quite unexpectedly without ever having seen or heard hide nor hair of it before. Don't you just *love* it when that happens?! Especially when such unexpected finds prove to be actual tasty treats rather than intolerable trials of patience (after all, if you're gonna treat yourself to a midnight snack, you don't wanna have something that'll give you indigestion before you go back to the sack, right?). Garish crudely-hand-printed red lettering is slashed/splattered onto a plain black background for the opening titles, setting an appropriate 'horrory' if tongue-in-cheek tone for this fun, good-naturedly comedic creature feature, which not even plentiful hilariously hammy acting can spoil (in fact, it rather adds to the overall charm. Funny how things sometimes go like that, eh?).

Eager to be given more action-packed assignments, after hotheaded, rule-bending plainclothes street cop Detective Brighton (spit-curled brawny bodybuilder, former "Mr. U.S.A." / "Mr. World" / top ten *Playgirl* model and only occasional actor Shane Minor, whose IMDb

Other familiar faces turn up in puppet form in *The Mill at Calder's End*, including these two gentlemen above. Any reader who doesn't recognize them must give up their entire *Monster!* collection immediately!

Top: Chaparral Video's mid-'90s US VHS.
Above: Scott Heim as the marauding 'mussel-man'! **Next Page:** The original monster mask

filmography totals a mere three titles, this being his first role) discovers the butchered body of a man down on the waterfront while working the night beat with his partner Deputy Carla (African-American actress Kathy Imrie), and demands that his boss assign him to the case of tracking down the murderer. In his spare time when not lecturing about genetics on the local university campus, eccentric research scientist Professor Melvin (Dennis Keefe, hamming it up eccentrically, complete with all sorts of weird mannerisms and kooky gesticulations) works to create a 'miracle' hair-restorative called Hairgrow, in hopes of raking in a mint for he and his shady off-the-record 'partner', corrupt mob-affiliated Mayor Greenspan (Caribbean-accented Afri-

can-American actor Anthony Chrysostom), who has invested $100-grand—possibly of the taxpayers' money?—in the project. The supposed hair-restorer is made from an extract taken from the rare (i.e., utterly fictitious!) South American *"Envelopus"* plant, which, according to the dotty Doc Melvin, "possesses extreme mutanogenic qualities" and can alter the human DNA structure. After Len (John Hunt), the dopey proprietor of a bait-shop (whom one of his regular angler customers calls a "master-baiter"!) inadvertently pours some of the experimental Hairgrow tonic into his tank of live zebra mussels, mistaking it for fish-food, one of the li'l buggers—evidently suddenly thinking it's a piranha—shortly 'bites' him on the hand. Later that same day, not only does one of poor Len's ears fall off during some sub-Cronenbergian *(à la* **THE FLY** '86) scenes of body horror worthy of a Troma "Toxie" production, but the forearm attached to his shellfish-bit hand begins to pulsate horribly and leak greenish pus (c/o pneumatic condom bladder FX by makeup artist Rick Pawlewski, who also served as the film's creature designer). As the ill-fated baitman's condition steadily worsens, he transforms into the titular monster. After this point, movie one-timer Scott Heim, energetically doubling for Hunt as Len, dons the partial 'pants-and-shirt' monster suit (which, barring some more elaborate modern animatronic actions and various spiky appendages, isn't too far removed from that worn by director/star Robert Clarke in his classic 'solar lycanthropy' tale **THE HIDEOUS SUN DEMON** [1958, USA]). Consisting of a headpiece, clawed mitts and oversized feet, the rest of the stunt performer's body is covered by regular human clothing so as to obviate the expense of a full costume (as well as expedite the makeup-application process too, of course). Its performer Heim gives the beast some extra character by adopting an animalistic hopping, loping mode of locomotion. Due to the toxicity of its mutated body chemistry, Doc Melvin fears the worst: that, if it is shed and scattered due to gunshots or an explosion, the creature's virulent blood might well go on to infect others with its mutation ("First Cleveland, then Toledo and, quite possibly, the *world*!" he raves. He later deduces, "It's a cross between a man and a zebra mussel!" [?!?] but since when have impossibly mixed-up zoological origins ever been a problem in creature features?). While the human characters mostly play it for easygoing laughs, the monster attacks—such as when it slaughters and chews-up a couple of dope-smokin' morons—and other horror sequences are played straight, including some rather *squishy* gore scenes which ought to do the trick for splatter geeks. Right at the outset of **SC**, no sooner has one of Prof. Melvin's students, a nerdy science major / amateur inventor, revealed that he has created a D.I.Y. electrical weapon dubbed the "RBTG", whose acronym stands for "Really Big Taser Gun" ("It's big enough to stun an elephant!"), than we just *know* it's going to wind up being deployed against the monster—described by hero Miner as "...a seven-foot, slug-like lizard"—at some point later into the narrative. It's muscleman versus, um, musselman for the action-packed climax!

The musical score—which, to be frank, is more tasteful than such silliness as this warrants—was provided by Buffalo-based underground traditional/experimental/exotica jazz act David Kane's Them Jazzbeards, whose lushly evocative and esoteric music is tailor-made for movie soundtracks, even if they do 'only' (note quotes) happen to be of the low-budget / 'lowbrow' psychotronic trash type like the present one, which appears to be their sole movie assignment to date (those interested in lending DKTJ's ultra-classy music an extra ear might wish to check out the YouTube channel "Buffalo Music Archive - Promoting and Preserving Indie Music from Western New York" for a large sampling of their back-catalogue). As for **SC**'s limited video history, it was formerly available on domestic VHS tape (starting in '95) from Chaparral Video and was subsequently apparently (?) reissued on videotape stateside (in '96) by a certain Leo Films. It was also released on both German Region 2 DVD (cover-blurb: *"Das Experiment des Grauens"* ["The Horror Experiment"]) by one Great Movies, and in the same format on French video (cover-blurb: *"Leur objectif: Détruire l'espèce humaine..."* ["Their Goal: Destroying the Human Species..."]) by one ESI Video, release years for either indeterminate. Neither disc evidently came with an English track (?), only those in their respective native languages. Since this looks to have had only a limited life on home video and is a pretty hard-to-find title on physical media unless you really wanna dig around for it, for those wishing to view it before trying to track it down on tape or disc (try eBay), there is currently a very nice (if only SD [480p]) video rip of it on YT at the page entitled "Shad-

ow Creature (1995) full movie" (@ *https://www.youtube.com/watch?v=-Ptlu32PgAQ*), which is the very version of this quirky quickie I watched for the purposes of this review.

Note: Just to provide some backstory and help explain why the makers of **SC** evidently chose a lowly bivalve mollusk—*not* the most cinematically dynamic or menacing of aquatic creatures!—as the basis for its monstrous mutant, I should mention that the Zebra Mussel (*Dreissena polymorpha*) is an invasive species not indigenous to the Ohio River basin that, possibly sometime in the 1980s, is believed to have found its way there via the Caspian Sea (the world's largest landlocked body of water, situated between Europe and Asia), quite likely finding their way into the river system due to being expelled with dumped ballast water from visiting transatlantic ships. The species thereafter became a substantial threat to the local Ohioan ecosystem, as well as spreading to other freshwater ecosystems in the United States and Canada. Some theorize that these hardy mussels may have first found their way into the Ohio River circa the early '90s by 'hitching' rides on the hulls of barges incoming from the Lake Erie region. According to the U.S. Fish & Wildlife Service, this fast-proliferating mussel is the worst pest ever to invade American waterways, and it continues to overwhelm and decimate the some 127 species (of the 297 known freshwater mussel species native to North America) that are indigenous to the Ohio River, many of which are now on the endangered list as a result (a reported 11 species have already gone extinct, though not necessarily solely due to the zebra mussel invasion). Interestingly enough, as if presenting the hypothesis that this was how the infestation happened in real life, **SHADOW CREATURE**'s rather bizarre twist ending shows consumers flocking to their local pet-shop in order to buy their kids—you guessed it!—zebra mussels, this after mad scientist Dr. Melvin has first imported a batch into the USA from Europe in order to utilize them in his experimentations that resulted in the mutant 'musselman' (not that the monster suit in any way brings to mind a human clam, mind you! But it is nonetheless a pretty decent

Hyde Nor Hair: If only Louis Hayward actually sported this cool makeup in **THE SON OF DR. JEKYLL**, then it might actually be something, but... *MEH!*

old school-type spiny humanoid/reptilian critter anyway). – **SF**

THE SON OF DR. JEKYLL (1951, USA, D: Seymour Friedman) |– Dialogue: *"Come see young Jekyll... or young Hyde?"* After first seeing a garishly colorful reproduction of a Belgian poster for it way back in an issue of the UK's *World of Horror* mag in the mid-'70s, I'd often wondered about this long-unseen (at least by *me*... till now!) Columbia Pictures re-run-through of Robert Louis Stevenson's justifiably oft-adapted cautionary horror story; not that I was in any real urgent hurry to see it, mind you, as I'd read here and there that it was supposedly quite dull and undistinguished. However, after unexpectedly happening across a fuzzy, often-pixilated rip from videotape in English uploaded to the online streaming site Dailymotion (@ *http://www.dailymotion.com/video/x2276u8*), I figured why not give it a belated spin. TSODJ was made during one of Horrorwood's post-war 'lull'-years—when the recent all-too-real horrors of World War II (and to a lesser extent those of the then-ongoing Korean conflict) were overshadowing reel ones, which paled in comparison. That said though, plenty of horror pictures, and often quite lurid ones at that, were produced in America during wartime, although the '40s fare was generally a lot less contentiously controversial than many of the pre-Code '30s ones were, now that (starting in 1934) puritanical authoritarian head censor Will Hays

had long-since imposed his myopic "Moral Majority" view of what was too horrific (or too sexy, etc.) on American moviegoers. If anything, late '40s/early '50s US horror movies were for the most part even duller—as in generally more staid and stodgy—than a lot of those from the early/mid-'40s were; although, me being such a Classic Horror lover and all that, I do usually manage to find at least something to like in even the dullest and most dismal '40s so-called "horror" effort (case in point the generally much-reviled killer kitty-critter flick **THE CREEPER** [1948, USA, D: Jean Yarbrough], which I reviewed at ridiculously loving length way back in *M!* #9 [September 2014, p.42]. Within the same period as when the present entry **TSODJ** was produced by a rival outfit whose cinematic horrors had always been overshadowed by Universal's, even that same pioneering studio churned-out a number of lesser, lamer genre productions (including, for instance, their non-monster Gothic melodramas **THE STRANGE DOOR** [1951, USA, D: Joseph Pevney] and **THE BLACK CASTLE** [1952, USA, D: Nathan Juran], both of which—mainly because they each co-star Karloff—aren't entirely bereft of entertainment value for those willing to look for it, but can't hold a candelabra to Unipix's gothic classics from the '30s). And so to **TSODJ**...

Edward Huebsch's stuffy, stiffly-starched script was based on a story by Mortimer Braus and Jack Pollexfen (latter of whom later tackled the theme of Jekyll's progeny once again—this time of the female persuasion—in his far-livelier screenplay for Edgar G. Ulmer's much-cheaper-but-more-engaging/endearing **DAUGHTER OF DR. JEKYLL** [1957, USA], starring Gloria Talbott in the title role, which is a lot more entertaining than **SON** is[n't]); tellingly enough, R.L. Stevenson's name is nowhere to be seen in the present film's credits. **SON** begins promisingly and energetically enough in 1860, with Jekyll, Sr., in the form of his murderous alter-ego Mr. Hyde, being chased through benighted London streets by an angry torch-bearing mob howling for his blood. After being run to ground and cornered at the Jekyll residence, which is then put to the torch by his pursuers, trapping their quarry inside, both Jekyll/Hyde together as one perish during a plunge from the blazing building's rooftop while attempting to escape the flames. In the immediate aftermath of his father's demise, Dr. Jekyll's infant son Edward is taken into foster care by a philanthropic family friend, the lawyer John Utterson (Lester Matthews). The action then abruptly shoots ahead 30 years to 1890, shortly before the now-adult Jekyll, Jr.

(in the form of Louis Hayward) is obliged to re-sign from his scientific university studies after being accused of (quote) "violating the laws of nature" while conducting experiments intended to benefit humankind. Having been made aware of his lineage and late shape-shifting forebear's notoriety, Edward Jekyll not only hopes to live down the shame but in the process clear the family name ("Legends don't die. They have to be *killed*!"). To this end, having been presented with his father's journals—or so he thinks (*Hint-hint! Wink-wink!*)—he endeavors to prove that Jekyll, Sr.'s formula did indeed work, and can be a boon to rather than a curse on humanity. He then plunges into a series of new experiments using a freshly-mixed batch of the infamous transformative agent in hopes of repeating the startling results of his pops' work. Following his initial downing of the contents of the obligatory smoking beaker-full of formula, although one of Jekyll, Jr.'s hands is shown (seemingly) trans-forming into a hairy, long-nailed claw (or might it only be occurring in his imagination?), his face remains entirely unchanged… and it stays that way throughout, more's the pity. Despite that aforementioned 'monster mitt' teaser, which strongly implies that further monstrousness will shortly be in the offing, all our expectations are dashed, as the expected usual split personality / identity crisis / physical metamorphosis themes common to virtually every other *J/H* adapta-tion ever made are barely even alighted-upon, let alone actually dramatized to any satisfying degree. Instead, we learn that long-time family confidant Dr. Curtis Lanyon (Alexander Knox) is out to get his needy/greedy hands on the Jekyll estate, and will go to any lengths—up to and in-cluding posing as "Mr. Hyde"—in his efforts to frame Jekyll, Jr., have him institutionalized as a nutter and thus rendered ineligible to inher-it his late pater's property. (Don't all groan at once over this hoary plot-twist, whose clichés had whiskers on top of their whiskers even back when Stevenson's original story was first pub-lished in 1886!) All-in-all, this is deadly-dull stuff indeed, enlivened solely by the spectacular pyrotechnical effects sequences that open and close the movie. Ergo, it behooves me to say that it's small wonder at all why the largely-forgot-ten **TSODJ**, has remained so seldom-seen for so long. Not surprisingly, it's apparently never received any sort of official video release that I could find record of. Sad to say, some mov-ies are made to be forgotten, and better this one than a more worthy effort. I highly doubt that **SON**, for all its basic competence of construc-tion and decent production values, could ever be made to look good, even if given the deluxe

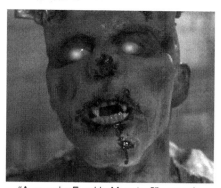

"A *vampire* Frankie Monster?" you ask. YES! (see below **TOF** entry)

Blu-ray treatment with all the fixings. But then again, it *could* happen, and I'd love to be proven wrong… – **SF**

TALES OF FRANKENSTEIN (2018, USA, D: Donald F. Glut) |– Trailer narration: *"Two-hundred years ago, a legend was born. Written by a teenaged girl, it is the one story that has constantly horrified the world with one name: FRANKENSTEIN! Now, four tales of ter-ror emerge from the past in an anthology film unlike any other…"* Very much one of the first generation of American "Monster Kids", au-thor-actor-filmmaker (etc.) Don Glut made his first short 8mm fan film *Diplodocus at Large* (1953) when he was but a wee lad of just 9 years young, and he's been a dedicated filmmak-er (etc.) virtually ever since, piecing together such labor-of-love patchwork creations—start-ing out with many more short subjects before moving on to feature-length projects—as *The Teenage Frankenstein Meets the Teenage Were-wolf* (1959), *Revenge of the Teenage Werewolf* (1960), *Dragstrip Dracula* (1962), *Spy Smash-er vs. The Purple Monster* (1964), *Atom Man vs. Martian Invaders* (1967), **DINOSAUR VALLEY GIRLS** (1996), **THE EROTIC RITES OF COUNTESS DRACULA** (2001), **DANCES WITH WEREWOLVES** (2016, all USA) and the present title on a semi-regular/irregular basis. As if you couldn't tell from the small sampling of titles given above, "homage" and "pastiche" are very much parts of DG's MO, and I by no means mean that as any sort of negative criticism. According to promo ma-terials, **TOF** the present title was based upon, not just one but fully *four* of Glut's 'unofficial' spinoff *Frankenstein* pulp short stories taken from his collection *Tales of Frankenstein*.

This is a true D.I.Y. epic at a total runtime of just over 1 hour and 52 minutes. In the first 25-minute segment, "My Creation, My Beloved", Gregore (Buddy Daniels Friedman), a hunchbacked descendent of the original Baron Victor Frankenstein, brings back his long-deceased fiancée Irma (whose unseen character's voiceover was provided by Monique Marissa Lukens) from the grave by installing her preserved brain inside the skull of a female 'monster' dubbed Helga (Lilian Lev), who he has lovingly assembled from all the best bits of a bunch of dead prostitutes (the victims of a brothel blaze). No sooner has he brought his shapely blonde creation—the top of whose tenuously-attached white rag bikini appears about ready to pop clear off at any moment!—than a shocking surprise awaits her creator, shortly followed by another one (neither of which shall be revealed here, for what it's worth). In "Crawler from the Grave", another of the infamous family's line, Helmut Frankenstein (Len Wein), much to the surprise of his much younger wife Lenore (Tatiana DeKhtyar), kicks the bucket due to a plague called The Grey Death before he has a chance to make himself immortal with his newly-perfected elixir of life. Eager to get his hands on the late scientist's fabulous ruby ring, an obsessive gem collector named Vincent (John Blyth Barrymore, Drew's senior half-brother) digs up the freshly-interred Helmut's grave in order to steal the gaudy bauble he craves. When the 'corpse' proves not to be *quite* as dead as expected

According to Pulp 2.0, this graphic novel cover isn't the final art

due to the lingering effects of the life-preserving elixir—Helmut had managed to take a small swig of the mouthwash-blue potion before succumbing to the plague, you see—the grave-robber chops off its forearm with the ring-hand attached, takes the ring for himself, then presents the severed arm to his friend Johann Veidt (Jerry Lacy), who collects strange artifacts (the monkey-like monster mask from Glut's cheesecake vampire/mummy flick **BLOOD SCARAB** [2008] makes a cameo appearance as a background prop in the collector's study). Before you can say "Gimme a hand!" the late Helmut's disembodied mauler proceeds to make like Thing from *The Addams Family* and crawl about independent of its body, bent on getting back its missing item of jewelry… "Madhouse of Death", meanwhile, contains nods to both the *film-noir* genre and the plot of more than one Three Stooges and Bowery Boys outing in its tale of mad medico Dr. Mortality (Mel Novak), a (quote) "bargain-basement Karloff" who is bent on installing the pea-brain of gormless gumshoe Jack Anvil, P.I. (ex-Foster Grant shades spokesmodel Jamisin Matthews, whose character at one points quips, "I always thought Frankenstein was just some guy in the movies who got mixed-up with Abbott and Costello!") into the skull of Gargantus, his in-house gorilla (a fabulous Rick Bakeresque suit, complete with animatronic facial movements, worn by Adam Meir). Fourth and finally, we get "Dr. Karnstein's Creation", set in Transylvania in 1958, during the Atomic Age, in which the eponymous doctor (Jim Tavaré) plans to recreate his Frankenstein ancestor's original patchwork creation ("The perfect superhuman slave!") using a combination of vintage and nuclear technology ("Maybe they're building an atomic bomb," gossips a local barmaid). To this end, Karnstein and his leather-jacketed JD assistant Carl (Justin Hoffmeister) go about procuring the necessary dead body parts. However, one of the graves they rob contains a dormant vampire, parts of whose undead corpse are utilized in creating the new monster. This segment gives us what may well be a movie first: a blood-drinking Frankie Monster (played by frequent creature player Douglas Tait [see also **ALIEN OUTPOST** {2014} entry above]) who is part-vampire, complete with elongated eyeteeth! *[See still on p.353.]* A more traditionalist Karloffian conception of The Monster (Scott Fresina, wearing John Goodwin makeup) is seen in the quartet of tales' linking scenes, which were shot in B&W. Another recurrent visual link seen periodically throughout is a painted portrait of the late Baron Victor F. (rendered by Pete von Sholly). While its ambitions do upon occasion overstep its budgetary limitations—better that than not even trying!—you've got to admire the amount of TLC that went into this homemade-right-from-the-ground-up production, which was released in time for Halloween 2018 (to jointly coincide with the 200th Anniversary of Mary Shelley's source novel) and is available on DVD from Leomark Studios or Barnes & Noble (@ *www.barnesandnoble.com*) for $19.99, as well as streamable VOD via all the usual online platforms. Info pertaining to **TOF** and other Glut projects can be found at Pecosborn Productions' website (@ *http://pecosborn.com/news/*). Amongst other tie-in merch being offered is *Tales of Frankenstein: The Book of the Movie* [see p.366], which, as well as going behind-the-scenes on the film, also includes the script and the four original stories it was based on, a special essay by director Don Glut, plus oodles of production stills and other extras besides. Available in both a "Deluxe Color Edition" and a "Black & White Edition" (the latter 'no-frills' edition lacking any bonus picture gallery), this book is published by the Cinexploits! offshoot of Bill Cunningham's ambitious Pulp 2.0 imprint. – **SF**

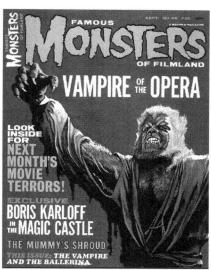

THE **VAMPIRE OF THE OPERA** (*Il mostro dell'opera*, 1964, Italy, D: Renato Polselli) |– If they were a regular reader of Warren's *Famous Monsters of Filmland*, any "Monster Kid" from the 1960s and '70s worth their garlic and stake should recall this film's memorable Anglicized title, which was prominently featured on the cover of issue #46 (September 1967) next to a striking illustration (artist unknown) of Oliver Reed in snarling wolfen form from Hammer's **THE CURSE OF THE WEREWOLF** (1961, UK, D: Terence Fisher). If you were like me, and had not yet seen either film, then you may appreciate the utter confusion that set in when I added that issue to my checklist of *FM* back issues. "'**VAMPIRE OF THE OPERA**'... with a *werewolf?*" (*FM* covers did that to me sometimes.) Issue #29 (July 1964) was another classic such example which caused me some preteen perplexity: on its cover (art by Basil Gogos?) we had a man screaming for his life while squiggles of what is apparently something akin to electrical energy crawl all about and over his head—looking like some electric monster's attack—while the words of the nearby cover-blurb "JERRY LEWIS ATTACKED BY MONSTERS" popped out at me, rather than the nearby title **THE FLESH EATERS**, a creature feature about human-devouring microbial organisms (see *Monster!* #33, Spring 2018 [p.276]), with which the illustration was actually intended to be associated. There were other such 'head-scratcher' *FM* covers, but for this quickie review (Dennis Capicik covered **TVOTO** at greater length from a different angle way back in *Monster!* #4, April 2014 [p.29]), I'll

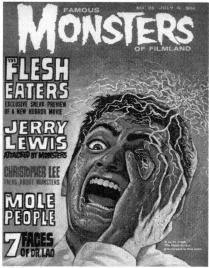

stick with the advance misconception I had regarding the film, which turned out to be, *not* an English one about a rampaging wolfman, but an Italian vampire flick whose original title was **IL MOSTRO DELL'OPERA**.

Post-credits, the film opens with one of the finest bits of '60s horror titillation I have ever seen. A young woman in a highly revealing sheer nightgown is seen fleeing through an old opera house with a vampire in hot pursuit. She dashes, jiggling, up and downstairs, screaming and bumping into objects out of sheer panic, all the while being strategically backlit so as allow the audience to ogle her near-naked body. This rather lengthy sequence ends as she escapes from the opera house, only to then be chased down a dirt road by a horse-drawn carriage. She manages to elude the carriage and stumbles into a near-by brook, where she momentarily rests, breast-deep in the cool water... that is, until the vampire catches up with her, and it's all over. Well, *not really*, because, you see, it has all only been a bad dream! The 'victim' turns out to be Giulia ("Barbara Hawards"/Marisa Barbaria), an as-piring young *danseuse* with a theatre group that has taken-up residence in an old theatre. She had merely fallen asleep and had a nightmare. Or so we are led to believe...

We shortly meet the dancers' brash young direc-tor Sandro ("Marc Marian"/Marco Mariani), who is trying his best to win-over the theatre's dour, elderly caretaker, Achille ("Albert Archett"/Al-berto Archetti). However, the latter man is most insistent that the troupe vacate the premises at once. Ignoring this cantankerous old fart—who babbles on about evil, mediums, curses and women who have vanished without a trace—Sandro introduces us to the rest of the female lineup, comely ingénues all: there's Manuela (the 'brainy' one), Roberta (the "vestal virgin"), Rossana ([Vittoria Prada] "...sensual lips..."), Yvette ("...born in the city of Lesbos, province of Sappho" [you get the idea!]), as well as Hilda,

Aurora (Carla Cavalli), Conga, Marta, Gabriella and Carlotta ([Milena Vukotic] who laughs like a hyena). Last but by no means least, Sandro in-troduces Julia, for whom he has a major case of the hots. The male troupers include Troy (the "to die for" gay dude), Filippo (a shy dancer), Aldo ("the romantic"), and one unnamed other. After a few lively instances of *almost* pansexual hook-ups (e.g., a chaste kiss shared by Rossana and Aldo; a titillating but equally-innocent 'three-some' between Yvette and two other women) and an improvised dance number, the bloodsucker Stefano ("John MacDouglas"/Giuseppe Addob-bati) eventually shows up, which sends Achille the caretaker—the vampire's faithful servant of over a 100 years—into a frenzy. We learn that Giulia is in fact the reincarnation of The Count's long-lost love Laura, and that she was a medium who came to the theatre to... (no spoilers here!).

Renato Polselli's **THE VAMPIRE OF THE OP-ERA** was initially conceived as a sequel of sorts to his **THE VAMPIRE AND THE BALLE-RINA** (*L'amante del vampiro* / "The Vampire's Lover", 1960), another Italian vampire melodra-ma that I had seen mentioned in the pages of *FM*, but never got around to actually watching until, decades later, it showed on TNT's "Monstervi-sion" back in the late '80s *[That was when/where I first saw it too! – SF]*. Not coincidentally, it also possesses a more-than-passing resemblance to

This Page & Next: *Out for The Count.* "John MacDouglas"/Giuseppe Addobbati as the fero-cious Stefano in a triptych of amazingly crazed stills from **THE VAMPIRE OF THE OPERA**!

Piero Regnoli's **THE PLAYGIRLS AND THE VAMPIRE** (*L'ultima preda del vampiro* / "The Vampire's Last Victim", 1960, Italy). Il **MOSTRO DELL'OPERA**'s Anglo working/export title **THE VAMPIRE OF THE OPERA** is what must have prompted that mention on *FM*'s cover for issue #43, as, so far as I know (as with any number of the more obscure foreign flicks featured in the mag's pages), the film was never released in the US under that title, and I have never found a copy of it dubbed into English. The copy I have is a composite version spliced together from two different prints, an inferior Italian print and a superior French one (hence the Francophonic title I have it under: *L'orgie des vampires* / "Orgy of the Vampires"), including some rather grungy inserts of what must have originally gotten excised by Gallic censors or editors.

The similarities between all three films are obvious, made more-so considering the confusion that I and other monster kids had with the names of the two primary creators behind them. To this Anglo, the names Renato Polselli and Piero Regnoli looked enough alike at a casual glance to get them mixed-up. Polselli wrote and directed both **THE VAMPIRE AND THE BALLERINA** and **THE VAMPIRE OF THE OPERA**, while Regnoli not only wrote and directed **THE PLAYGIRLS AND THE VAMPIRE**, but he also had a hand in the screenplay and assistant direction of the seminal Italian vampire gothic **THE DEVIL'S COMMANDMENT** (*I vampiri*, 1957, Italy, Ds: Riccardo Freda, Mario Bava). As well as each featuring actor-producer Walter Brandi in roles of varying prominence, all three films deal with vampires and reincarnation and include nightclub-style dance numbers that often verge on all-out burlesque, so they can almost be considered a loosely-connected trilogy of sorts, with the first two being more tightly-constructed and the third, **TVOTO**, wallowing in total chaotic bedlam. The film has the feel of a madcap stage play *à la* Moss Hart's and George S. Kaufman's manic *You Can't Take It With You* (1936) about it. Characters buzz around in their own minor orbits of lust and nonsense, with Giulia and The Count at the center. The count lives in his own magical world, hiding behind an old painted portrait of himself in a weird chamber swathed in fog that is also occupied by a quartet of scantily-clad vampiresses, chained to the dungeon walls (we don't ever find out *why* they are in chains, although the main reason was clearly for the purposes of injecting a bit of pulp-style B&D+S/M kink to the proceedings). And even though they want to nibble on Giulia or Aurora, these vamp chicks, like their master, flash their fangs a lot but never leave bite-marks or any traces of blood. The frenetic, feverish final twenty minutes are what makes the film. As the vampire chases the troupe through the theatre, everyone else is up on the main stage, where a wild Bohemian free-for-all modern dance number is being performed. It's utter lunacy, and utterly brilliant, in its own totally-fucked-up way. During the confusion, Count Stefano run off with Aurora and Giulia follows. She runs towards and disappears *into* the old painting of the Count. Meanwhile, the vampire entertains himself by torturing Aurora with a pitchfork (!). Sandro and the girls set fire to the cursed painting, forcing-out the Count for a final confrontation... All the while, the rousing orchestral score swells and ebbs on the audio track, with a spooky Theremin punching through now and then to let you know that this is very much a horror film, through and through... and a real *eerie* one at that. Long-unseeable in any form, **TVOTO** eventually found its way onto DVD in France via Artus Films as part of their "*Gothique Italien*" series. Unlike many a French disc release, it came complete with English subs (although the sparse supplemental materials, including an in-French-only interview with filmmaker/scholar Alain Petit, aren't subbed). – **TP**

THE RITUAL (2017, UK, D: David Bruckner) |– The woods. The deep, dark forest. There's good reason why so many horror/monster movies are set in this timelessly primal milieu, brimming with the long-lingering genetic race memories of our more feral and instinctively-attuned primordial ancestors, to whom terror and potential violent death constantly lurked behind every tree. Because, especially to greenhorn city slickers to whom 'getting closer to nature' means grudgingly leaving their omnipresent smartphones and laptops at home and not having access to social media for a week or two, it can be a truly frightening place to be stranded, especially at night. And *extra*-especially when some sort of raging psycho-killer or ravening monstrous beast—*Monster!*'s preferable option being that latter kind of menace, natch!—is out and about on the prowl there. Following a senseless, random tragedy—the murder of one of their tight clique of buds during an armed robbery by junkies at an urban convenience store gone very awry—in hopes of unwinding in its aftermath, four young Englishmen (convincingly played by Rafe Spall, Arsher Ali, Robert James-Collier and Sam Troughton [the grandson of Doctor Who #2 Patrick Troughton]) head off to 'rough it' out in the rugged bush country of Sweden (the film was actually shot on wild rural locations in Romania, which stand in passably well for Swedish forestlands, although some of the tertiary supporting players [cast as inbred hillbilly Swedes, apparently] do sound a lot more Slavic than Scandinavian, it should be said). However, no sooner have the quarreling quartet arrived than strange and terrifying things begin to happen, starting with several unnerving incidents of a seemingly ritualistic occult nature. Sure, what with its **BLAIR WITCH PROJECT**-type setup and other familiar genre tropes, **THE RITUAL** is as derivative (if not completely slavishly so) as they come, but it also has some great stuff going on in it too. For one thing—and it's an important one—its monster, which is most impressive indeed (no, I shan't give the game away by describing it in any way, shape or form!). Suffice it to say that this beast, which is tied-in with Norse legend in only the most superficial and throwaway manner, presumably just to further justify the 'exotic' Swedish setting, is nicely rendered, often via practical effects, although even at such times as CG does take over (mostly in the film's latter stages), it still registers pretty impressively, for the most part. The action gets quite grisly at times, although its splatter is usually more of the 'after-the-fact' variety as opposed to being shown in all its gory glory whilst it is occurring. While, unlike in our below entry **THE VOID** (2016), the debt to H.P. Lovecraft here isn't quite so obvious, the present film does have at least a few classically Lovecraftian elements, although they aren't overly pronounced (I mainly spotted it in the theme of the backwoods cultists worshiping

and making sacrificial offerings to an incredibly ancient demonic deity lurking in the darkness, although this creature doesn't really come from 'the other side' or wherever, but is already actually right here among us on the earthly plane of existence, big as life… and *death*, of course). – SF

SUPERBEAST (1972, USA/Philippines, D: George Schenck) |– H.G. Wells' classic mad monster-maker novel *The Island of Dr. Moreau* (1896) was mined for ideas a lot more than just once in the Philippines, most obviously that same year of '72 in Eddie Romero's fun multi-monster mash **THE TWILIGHT PEOPLE** (see *Monster!* #6 [June 2014, p.21]), as well as more than a decade previously in co-directors Romero and Gerardo de Leon's moodily monochromatic **TERROR IS A MAN** (1959); latter being arguably the finest, most-atmospheric American/Filipino horror co-production of all. Less-obviously so, Romero/de Leon's *Blood Island* trilogy likewise borrowed liberally from Wells' book, albeit more generally. It is said, logically enough, that you can't miss what you've never had, but for the longest time, the present Yank/Pinoy joint-job (which is less-influenced by *Dr. Moreau* than those other titles I just mentioned, yet stills bears detectable trace elements of it, if largely only unwittingly) was quite the elusive bugger to lay eyes on, and for this reason—as so many a little-seen film (etc.) does over time—it acquired a special sort of desirability in my mind, for the simple fact that, while I had never seen it, I'd read snippets and seen the odd image from it enough over the decades since it was made to be interested in seeing more. During the opening ten minutes of **SUPERBEAST**, the scene shifts locations (each one formally identified by an on-screen title) so frequently that your head starts to spin. At Manila Airport, a man with abnormally brutish/bestial facial features runs amuck aboard an airliner, terrorizing passengers before getting curtly gunned-down on the spot by the authorities. Globetrotting Anglo-American female pathologist Dr. Alix Pardee (prolific actress Antoinette Bower [1932-]) is thereafter dispatched out into the surrounding rain forest country of Pangan in hopes of discovering the origin of the unidentified deceased beastman (informally dubbed "Mongo"). Incidentally, a goodly portion of the dialogue is delivered in untranslated Tagalog by native actors. During one scene early into the narrative, a woman fleeing her village along with a throng of other justifiably frightened refugee residents superstitiously makes mention of an "*aswang*", not just once but twice; a word which is translated for Dr. Pardee's benefit as "an evil spirit or something" by her native colleague Dr.

Raul Rojas (Manny Ojeda, later seen in another US-Filipino horror effort, the much-maligned 'monster-mermaid' outing **THE DEATHHEAD VIRGIN** [1974, D: Norman Foster]). The tell-tale Tagalog word "*halimaw*" (meaning "beast", "monster" or the like) is subsequently heard uttered by a badly-mauled victim of the creature, adding to the foreshadowing. By dugout, Drs. Rojas and Pardee paddle ever-deeper downriver into the jungle. After their canoe gets caught in rapids and goes over a cataract, only the woman survives. Having been rendered unconscious as a result of the accident, the doctress comes-to in a bed at the disused plantation owned by youthfully handsome Dr. Bill Fleming (the at times rather Robert Woods-like Craig Littler, future star of the landmark post-**STAR WARS** serialesque Saturday morning kids' sci-fi show *Jason of Star Command* [1978-79, USA], no less. Interestingly enough, said show co-starred the great Sid Haig, who had appeared in a number of Filipino flicks himself, if not the present one). Whether consciously or not, **SUPERBEAST** derives the basics of its plot from Jack Arnold's 'man-into-caveman' classic **MONSTER ON THE CAMPUS** (1958, USA), which, like the present title, was itself a derivation of both Wells' above-cited novel and R.L. Stevenson's 1886 novella *Strange Case of Dr. Jekyll and Mr. Hyde*.

In **SUPERBEAST**, no sooner has Doc Pardee arrived at Doc Fleming's jungle hangout than she hears unsettling screams in the night, as of someone crying-out in agony... like a patient in Moreau's operating theatre-*cum*-torture chamber The House of Pain might whilst undergoing enforced surgery without any anesthesia, perhaps? Turns out, to nobody's real surprise—least of all ours!—that the not-so-wholesome-as-he-at-first-seems Doc Fleming has been irresponsibly mucking-about with things which Man (and Woman) were meant to leave well enough alone. Using convicts 'donated' to him as experimental subjects by the local sleazy, sweaty police constable (played by—*who else?!*—obligatory '70s Pinoy exploitation fixture Vic Diaz, here playing a character named Mondo), the doctor has been attempting to pacify their violently antisocial criminal tendencies by treating them with a special formula, whose effects unfortunately only last for less than a fortnight before wearing-off. The subjects then (quote) "...revert to the primitive. It's as if they've taken an evolutionary step backwards", to become animalistic beasts with Neanderthal-like features, albeit while still retaining all their human intelligence and cunning. These failed experiments are then hunted-down and destroyed "The Most Dangerous Game"-

Top: Shout! Factory's long-overdue Blu.
Above: Harry Lauter *[left]* hunts the most dangerous game—now more dangerous than ever!—in **SUPERBEAST**. Hiding behind the tree is Craig Littler, all-monstered-up

style by Fleming's in-house not-so-great white hunter ("...gun freak...") henchman Stewart Victor (super-prolific "heavy" specialist Harry Lauter [1914-1990], whose vast array of film and TV roles included bit-parting in Fred F. Sears' Atomic Age lycanthropy thriller **THE WERE-WOLF** [1956]). ***ATTENTION: SPOILER ALERT!*** Before you can say "Alley Oop", Dr. Pardee secretly treats Fleming with an overdose of his own formula, whereafter, completely bypassing the initial 'passive' stage in the pro-

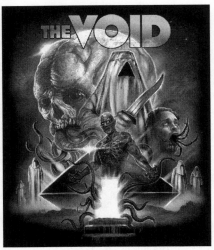

(are they ghosts, time/space-hopping satanic cultists, or maybe some horrible combination of *both?*) at the behest of powerful supernatural forces beyond their (and our) ken, the hapless humans must barricade themselves inside the building in hopes of fending-off and surviving the terrifying assault by some very ancient—and exceedingly EVIL—beings, and by no means necessarily *human* (nor even vaguely human-*oid*) ones at that. I really can't say too much else about the story without running the risk of spoiling the numerous scary and squishy surprises in store for potential viewers, but I will say that it definitely does have a pronounced Lovecraftian feel through-and-through, and its truly *monstrous* monstrosities from beyond are quite inspired in their realization—and mostly rendered all-practically yet, which is another big plus, say no more. Just *see* it for yourselves! **THE VOID** was released on Region A/1 Blu-ray/DVD by Diabolik-DVD in 2017, and on Region B/2 discs in the UK by Signature. – **SF**

cess, he begins to swiftly retrogress into an aggressive caveman-like brute (c/o effective if uncomplicated prosthetic makeup) and lurches off into the forest, hotly pursued by rifle-toting Victor, who has suddenly gone all trigger-happy and is eager to add another trophy to his collection. The movie's title is dropped in passing by him in sarcastic reference to the "superbeast" Fleming has become… evidently permanently. As the film ends, the fully-retrogressed Fleming—albeit still wearing his blue-denim street clothes to minimize the need for extra makeup FX—severs all ties with civilization and goes into voluntary exile out in the wilderness, alone. While it's nothing to get overly excited about, I was glad to finally get to see this minor if passably engaging creature feature at long last. Chances are I may even watch it again someday, although I'm not in any big hurry to. This long-hard-to-see flick was released on domestic Region A Blu-ray early last year by Shout! Factory, ensuring that it will never again be lost in that unforgiving no man's land of forgotten films. – **SF**

THE VOID (2016, USA/UK/Canada, Ds: Jeremy Gillespie, Steven Kostanski) |– Ad-line: *"There Is A Hell. This Is Worse."* I gave this well-worth-your-while effort an optimistic spin expressly on the recommendation of stalwart long-time *M! + WC* contrib Christos Mouroukis, who pretty much gives it a glowing appraisal in our meaty, beaty, big and bouncy 'big sister' magazine *Weng's Chop's* "2017 Holiday Spooktacular" (Volume 5, Issue 2, #10.5, p.44) the December before last. After a small, generic group of Joe/Jane Blows get inexplicably besieged at an inconveniently out-of-the-way hospital deep in the boonies by sinister, monk-robed ethereal beings

THE WASP WOMAN (1959, USA, D: Roger Corman) |– Newly-released as a positively *stunning* Region A/1 Blu-ray and DVD by Scream Factory. Since it's one of the first '50s monster schlockers I ever saw (sometime back in the late '70s, as I recall), I've since had a sweet spot for this humble-if-effective Corman B—or rather, *wasp!*—flick, so I wanted to 'shoehorn-in' a mention of its landmark new BD release, which includes not just Corman's original 61-minute '59 theatrical cut, but also the film's considerably longer (73m) *circa* mid-'60s TV version, which was padded-out to better fit its timeslot with a 12-minute prologue sequence directed by an uncredited Jack **"SPIDER BABY"** Hill. This latter longer print was the one that first introduced me to the film all those decades ago and, while the 61m cut plays just fine without it, I must admit I've come to prefer the 73m one out of simple habit by this point. As 'tacked-on' footage goes, it is handled better and blended more smoothly than that seen in many lesser 'doctored' movies. As well as providing textural contrast, it adds some picturesquely quaint rural color to a film which afterwards unfolds entirely within a more constrictive concrete-and-asphalt cosmopolitan urban setting. While Hill's 'all-new' prologue was clearly shot a number of years after-the-fact, as 'guest star' Michael Mark—best-known to many as Ludwig, the iconic grieving father of poor little drowned Maria in James Whale's original Karloff **FRANKENSTEIN** (1931, USA)—appears noticeably older and greyer than he does in Corman's original director's cut, the fact that he looks more aged at the outset than he does later in the movie proper seems entirely fitting to the context (at least to me): after all, since he's shown to already be obsessively working on his elixir of youth (derived from the queen's jelly of wasps) in the added opening scenes, something which he continues doing throughout most of the bulk of the action, who's to say he didn't simply use himself as a human guinea pig early into his experimentation, and that the partial rejuvenating effects of this treatment stayed with him for the remainder of the narrative? At least that's the way I like to rationalize it away, anyway. For my money, the prologue also contributes a good deal more pertinent backstory regarding Mark's endearing-albeit-misguided Dr. Zinthrop by fleshing-out the character and revealing him to be much more of a truly dedicated scientific researcher than merely the opportunistic hack/ quack charlatan that aging cosmetics magnate heroine Janice Starlin (Susan Cabot)'s dutifully protective employees (including those played by Barboura Morris, Anthony Eisley and William Roerick) peg him as. There's loads to love

about this B&W classic, not the least of which is an all-too-brief appearance by the talented if ill-fated Frank Wolff, here making his cinematic debut in just one scene—which he steals effortlessly—as a smartass deliveryman who takes a too-high-tone receptionist down a peg or two with just a few choice words and a cocky smirk. Talk about make the most of a thankless bit-part! No wonder Corman, impressed by Wolff's acting chops and 'offbeat' charisma, hired him to star in other films (**BEAST FROM HAUNTED CAVE** [1959, USA] very much included; it's another long-time favorite of mine). A wonderful slice of psychotronic movie history, this, now made all the sweeter by this optimum new presentation! Chances are most older *Monster!* readers know the film well, but now they can become even better-acquainted with it than ever before thanks to Scream Factory's state-of-the-art, pristinely crisp and crystal-clear edition. Never before until now have those infamously *LOUD* print PJs of Doc Zinthrop's popped off the screen quite as loudly as they do on Blu! – **SF**

WHITE TIGER (Белый Тигр / *Belyy tigr*, 2012, Russia, D: Karen Shakhnazarov) |– Excerpt of evocative dialogue: *"Do you know that he prays to the God of Tanks? ...He's got his own god, you understand: a Tank God"*. The IMDb categorizes this utterly enthralling film under three different generic tags: "Action, Adventure, Fantasy", none of which really sum it up very well, although it does contain elements of all three things. While it definitely fits under those first two descriptors, that third one is a much more subtle fit. Indeed, those not openly seeking-out more fantastical elements in the film might not even notice them at all, that's how understated, vaguely expressed and ambiguous they are, although potential supernatural content *is* present, albeit handled adroitly and without needless overemphasis. In fact, we are left miles of slack to play with in regards to whether or not the protagonist's confidently-stated perceptions are real, or—as Tim P. philosophically discusses in his review of the brand-new Hindi psychological horror film **RAKKHOSH** (2019, Ds: Ds: Abhijit Kokate, Srivinay Salian [see p.312])—if they're simply the fanciful fabrications of a disordered mind (in this case suffering from "shellshock" or "battle fatigue", outdated terms for a complex condition that is now properly known as Post-Traumatic Stress Disorder, or PTSD).

WT's action—and there's a *lot* of it!—is set on the Russian Front in 1943 in the months leading up to the final massed Soviet offensive against Berlin and, ultimately, Nazi Germany's humiliating defeat and surrender (key scenes of which are memorably dramatized herein). All the best war movies—from Milestone's timelessly poignant **ALL QUIET ON THE WESTERN FRONT** (1930, USA) to Spielberg's shockingly frank **SAVING PRIVATE RYAN** (1998, USA) and beyond—are almost invariably first-and-foremost staunchly *anti*-war in their attitude, which is as it should be, of course. And this one is no exception, as, despite being set to a stirring (if thankfully judiciously used and not bombastically overwhelming) Wagner score and boasting scenes of great excitement and heroism, **WT** certainly far from glamorizes or (overtly) glorifies the brutal conflict it portrays, and frequently displays its horrors in an unflinchingly graphic, matter-of-fact manner which would never have been allowed in some erstwhile Soviet propaganda piece laid in a similar milieu that was intended to prompt as many voluntary new recruits as possible for the once-mighty Red Army (after all, recruiting willing volunteers rather than forcibly inducting recruits against their will is far better for the morale). Speaking of which, said massive military force—which was so much more formidable in terms of sheer numbers under the Communist regime than it is today—frequently served as 'extras' in big-budget Soviet-financed wartime dramas (for example, some 15,000 active-duty troops were famously recruited to play members of the British, Prussian and French armies in Sergei Bondarchuk's vast Napoleonic Wars epic **WATERLOO** [Ватерлоо, 1970, USSR/Italy], starring Rod Steiger as the doomed Bonaparte). Red Army servicemen were also cast to pad-out largescale crowd scenes in other 'cast-of-1000s' Soviet cinematic epics, including some of Aleksandr Ptushko's majestically-mounted magical mythological adventures produced by/for the state-run Mosfilm company, such as **THE MAGIC VOYAGE OF SINBAD** (Садко / *Sadko*, 1953) and **THE SWORD AND THE DRAGON** (Илья Муромец / *Ilya Muromets*, 1956).

Albeit by then no longer under communistic governmental control, Mosfilm also bankrolled this much-more-recent film, which is as far removed from those two just-cited earlier heroic fantasy spectacles as you can get, if in some ways sharing some of their quintessential spirit. After miraculously surviving and fully recovering when his tank gets destroyed in combat and he suffers severe burns over 90% of his body, Naidyonov (Aleksey Vertkov ["He got burned and then he was reborn!"]) defies all odds to rejoin his tank battalion in active duty. At a time when every available able-bodied man and tank is vitally needed for the war effort, his commanding officers don't feel inclined to question the strange circumstances surrounding Naidyonov's near-death and unheard-of return to fight the hated Nazis once again. As for the deadly White Tiger of the title—a reported new, one-of-a-kind experimental model, spoken of only in hushed tones—it becomes the newly-"reborn" tankman's entire *raison d'être*, and he dedicates all his energies to destroying it. Apt to its ghostly-greyish/whitish coloration, it can seemingly appear and disappear at will, like a phantom. In this way, it makes surprise hit-and-run appearances to bushwhack and obliterate unsuspecting Russkie armored battalions before inexplicably up and 'vanishing' to parts unknown afterwards, like it hadn't even been there at all ("He disappeared. Like he fell through the earth"). Rather than sink like a stone to the bottom of a swamp due to its massive weight (in excess of 70 tons), this virtual wraith—albeit one heavily armored with reinforced steel plating—can apparently simply glide to the other side of it as lightly as Jesus walking on water. If not for all the carefully built-up, tactically understressed ambiguity in the script surrounding whether the Tiger is actually "real" or not, or merely a figment of more than one person's overactive imagination—it obviously *does* exist, as the narrative clearly and repeatedly depicts it in deadly action, but whether it's manned by actual living human crewmen or is otherwise powered by some supernatural force from beyond is left so wide open to conjecture that we're never entirely sure it isn't, and strongly tempted to believe it *is*—without ever even coming close to overstepping the fine line between the passably plausible and the utterly unbelievable. "I don't think there is a crew in it," remarks Comrade Major Fedotov (the charismatically intense Vitaliy Kishchenko), who gradually begins to suspect that *tovarisch* Naidyonov isn't anywhere near as much of a crackpot as everyone but his fellow crewmates think he is. Regarding the true origins of the Tiger, things stays very vague and well within the realm of possibility, with the gritty ultra-realism/authenticity of the production design, staging and performances adding to (by simple contrast) rather than detracting from the potential 'paranormal' aspects of the plot.

With its demonically roaring/rumbling engine, unstoppably advancing tracks and thundering cannon, the titular metal monster—which I prefer to think of (simply because we're given ample leeway to believe is so if we wish) as a supernaturally-powered machine from Valhalla rather than one manned by a mere mortal human crew—has an ominous air of the alien-possessed, caterpillar-tracked eponymous earthmover of **KILLDOZER** (1974, USA, D: Jerry London) about it, or that of the grim-grilled black 'driverless' automobile in **THE CAR** (1977, USA, D: Elliot Silverstein); although, it being a heavily-armed vehicle that was expressly designed to kill with devastating power and precision, it exudes a vastly more fearsome aura of motorized menace than its two just-cited metallic kindred. Like Captain Ahab with the elusive and possibly illusory great white whale of Melville's *Moby Dick* (1851), our main protagonist's driving obsession becomes stopping the Wehrmacht's seemingly unstoppable mechanical dreadnought at all costs. There's even a suspenseful "western"-style tank-to-tank gun duel staged in the muddy main street of a shell-pocked old ghost town that ends in a stalemate after the Tiger's turret becomes jammed due to a lucky shot and the protagonists' smaller, much-thinner-skinned tank accidentally spikes its own gun due to getting its overheated barrel clogged with mud while moving in to administer the coup de grace on their temporarily disabled foe. (***ATTENTION:

SPOILER ALERT!***) The closing implication, impressed upon his superior officer by devoted tanker Naidyonov (who, now that the war is over, believes he no longer has a purpose in life), is that the White Tiger has merely gone to ground for the time being... but should it ever come back, Naidyonov will be ready to do battle with it again (implying that, like his nemesis the mysterious monster tank, the film's human hero has himself become some sort of immortal being? His miraculously fast, almost 100% recovery from his horrific wounds at the outset seems to reinforce this possibility).

By the way, if you're interested in seeing **WHITE TIGER**, best you seek out the English-subbed version with the original Russian dialogue rather than the English-dubbed version that was prepared (which I haven't seen, and don't wish to. I heard more than enough of the Anglo dubbing track during the few seconds of the trailer for the English dub that I watched on YouTube before stopping it in contempt only partway through! I'm sure the redubbed dialogue could only serve to severely compromise—or even utterly demolish—the finely-tuned tone of the subtitled original, so I want no part of it). This remarkable piece of cinema must have been all the more amazing to behold on the big screen, and, if you'll excuse me for saying, it makes Brad Pitt's recent embarrassingly unconvincing ego-wank **FURY** (2014, USA/China/UK, D: David Ayer) look like some desperate WW2-era Hollywood U.S. Army recruitment commercial by comparison. – **SF**

YOUR HIGHNESS (2011, USA, D: David Gordon Green) |– Most eminently quotable line of dialogue: *"Prepare to be fist-fucked by two brothers at once!"* I first became a fan of comedic Hollywood actor Danny McBride after my hip-to-the-scene—if, I should stress, by no means 'hipster'!—20something son Chaz first introduced me to McBride's at-times-hilarious sports-based dramedy/sitcom *Eastbound & Down* (2009-2013) a few years back, but I never got around to checking-out the present epic S&S ("sword-and-sorcery") fantasy spoof starring/co-written/co-exec-produced by him until just recently. McBride has this natural-born knack for playing things both completely straight-faced *and* knowingly tongue-in-cheek simultaneously, and even in such scenes as his gags aren't as funny as in others, IMO he always makes for a likeable screen presence regardless, simply for being so gleefully and impishly impudent and irreverent. As for **YH**, bawdily raucous slope-foreheaded dudebro (and playfully non-PC homoerotic) humor, periodic

The horny Minotaur from **YOUR HIGHNESS** (2011) sez: *"Cut the bull! Buy every issue of* Monster! *...or else!"*

over-the-top smutty dialogue—often verging on all-out 'aural porn'—reams of irresponsible random profanity, plus gruesomely gory violence and some gratuitous T&A abound in it. We also get a tribe of nude cannibalistic/amazonian jungle women, a huge, acid-spitting five-headed 'hand dragon' (or words to that effect; it's too difficult to explain here!), a cadaver-strewn stone maze whose guardian is a Minotaur-like humanoid bovine monster (done all-practical rather than with CGI), plus a trio of demonic, magic fireball-flinging witchy hags (known as "The Mothers", and they're muthas alright) right out of *Hamlet*. And also, looking and sounding very much like something that might have been—but *wasn't*—created by the Jim Henson Creature Shop (it's actually the Spectral Motion company's work), there's this weird, purple 'glans'-headed gnome/seer/perv known as the "Great Wize Wizard" (voiced by Mario Torres) that puffs on a hookah pipe like the caterpillar in *Alice in Wonderland* and demands (thankfully sight-unseen) perverted sexual favors from those who call on him seeking his sage advice. Clearly inspired by Bubo the Owl from Harryhausen's **CLASH OF THE TITANS** (1981, UK/USA, D: Desmond Davis), there's even a cutesy chirruping mechanical bluebird named Simon herein that succeeds in being a good deal less irksome than its R2D2-based clockwork Strigiforme 'inspiration' source. Sure, the plot's the usual token fantastical gibberish/mumbo-jumbo about an impossible heroic quest—this time hinging on a prophesized impending major cosmic event called "The Dragon Eclipse"—but don't let that stop ya. As the main villain, the sorcerer Leezar, Justin Theroux really has a time of it, uttering some outrageous dialogue (e.g., "I'm *not* stiffening! I'm just not attracted to you!") through his gnarly upper set of prosthetic false teeth with

admirable aplomb; the cutely girl-next-doorish Zooey Deschanel—to whom that unflattering just-quoted line is addressed—co-stars as the bosomy-but-ditzy Princess Belladonna, McBride as the bumbling, ne'er-do-well Prince Thadeous' onscreen big brother the dashing Prince Fabious (James Franco)'s damsel-in-distress-to-be-rescued, who is the main baddie's chosen virgin bride for a little climactic altar-top fornication ceremony pricelessly known as "The Fuckening" (!!); while Natalie Portman plays the secondary female lead Isabel, a kickarse sword-and-longbow-slinging quasi-barbarian babe with an impeccable upper crust Brit accent and posture. The always-entertaining Charles "**SPACE TRUCKERS**/*Game of Thrones*" Dance guests as Thadeous' and Fabious' no-nonsense kingly sire, who sends them off on their mutual noble quest to better bond them in brotherhood, as well as get the ne'er-do-well former out of his hair for a while and hopefully make a man of him. More recently seen in Matteo Garrone's lavish, exquisite Italian/French/British medieval monster-fantasy spectacle **TALE OF TALES** (*Il racconto dei racconti – Tale of Tales*, 2015), 'oddball' English character actor Toby Jones here plays a sexually androgynous/asexual (?) mixed-gender (*no*-gender?) turncoat character named Julie. For all its (intentional) super-silliness and dumbness at times, I found **YH** impossible to dislike, and it's definitely one to watch again. Too bad this estimated $50-mill production was such a major box-office bomb, but oh well; you win some, you lose some. If mega-flop '80s schlock like, say, Hal Needham's oft-maligned **MEGAFORCE** (1982, USA) can go on to become hailed as a cult classic 30-odd years after it was made and bombed big-time, there's still plenty of hope for **YOUR HIGHNESS** yet. Its original theatrical version runs 102 minutes, while the somewhat raunchier unrated edition clocks-in at some 3½ longer and includes a scene in which the lonesome, horny Minotaur 'anally rapes' (?!) Thadeous' geeky, much-abused sidekick/squire Courtney (played by the po-faced Rasmus Hardiker), somehow managing to do it while its victim is still fully-clothed, and with his pants up, yet; about the only really 'racy' aspect of the scene is a fleeting (CG) shot of the bullish monster's still-erect-if-fast-waning male member (much was made of the 'anatomically-correct' bullhead's pelvic horn for publicity purposes at media photo-ops; there are even photos of the monster—schlong, bull-balls and all—on Alamy, FFS). No sooner has its dick nodded-off and gone flaccid than McBride as Thadeous shows up to post-coitally slaughter the rapey brute with a magical sword called the Blade of Unicorn. Afterwards, because he is unable to chop off one of its horns as a trophy, he instead severs its penis (off-screen) and thereafter wears it on a string around his neck for the duration of the runtime... well, up until the closing scene when he unsuccessfully tries to present it as a tribute/keepsake of him to Portman's ever-roving, restless loner she-warrior character, anyway (she declines his kind offer in no uncertain terms, needless to say). Like I said, I found this movie impossible to dislike, so there's no reason why you shouldn't too... assuming you're as sometimes fond of low-brow—if at times quite clever—stupidity as I am, that is. Amongst other sources, it's available on both Blu-ray and DVD from Universal Pictures Home Entertainment. – SF

BONUS STUFF

Preserved Parson: Because so little still remains of *Mystery and Imagination's* lost adaptation of M.R. James' "The Tractate Middoth" (1966) *[see Endnote #4, p.138]*, we figured we might as well fill up the very last empty space left in *M!* #34 with another shot of Edwin Finn as the ghastly, ghostly Dr. Rant!

Editors' Note from page 131:

As so many British television programs of the '70s did (non-Britishers aware of the '80s "Video Nasties" witch hunts who think that the UK government has *always* been so starchily stuffy and censorious in the media might well be surprised), "Schalcken the Painter" really pushed the envelope of what was acceptable to be shown on the idiot box by depicting not just full-frontal female nudity but even implied—or possibly actually *outright*, if the implications are to be believed—necrophilia! Indeed, mainstream Brit (and Canadian, for that matter) television often went way beyond the pale of what was allowed to be shown on American network TV of the time, especially when it came to horror and/or sexual themes. While America made such a big hullaballoo about seeing Dennis Franz's ass on that infamous 1994 episode of *NYPD Blue*—the first time an actual naked 'naughty bit' had (however belatedly) appeared in a commercial mainstream program to that date—full nudity and often quite frank depictions of sexuality were also fairly commonplace on Britain's (often aptly-named) boob-tube. Hell, as a kid from 12-to-16 or so living in Wales *circa* the early/mid-'70s, I saw more than my fair share of T&A (and even [*GASP!*] pubic hair) on the telly, and not always on late-night programming, either. Though it was the exception rather than the norm, such content was far from unheard of then, despite all Mary Whitehouse's whinging. As for today, though... – **SF** (*So true!* Although, the first time I saw a nekkid lady on US TV was in an episode of *Monty Python's Flying Circus* aired on PBS in the '70s, a time when nudity of sorts could be shown on public access stations... Then, when that same *MPFC* show was rebroadcast in the '80s, that scene was fogged out for, um, 'more sensitive' viewers, when more open attitudes towards sexuality became increasingly under attack by 'moral censors'. Similar censorship occurred with the rebroadcasting of shows such as *I, Claudius*, and various episodes of *Nova*. – **TP**)

YOU SCRATCH OUR BACK & WE'LL SCRATCH YOURS DEPT.

The ever-energetic and affable Bill Cunningham, owner-operator of the ambitious and ever-expanding cult cinema / comics / fiction (etc.) imprint Pulp 2.0 Press, out of CA, was kind enough to not only buy our zine (and some of WK Books' other quality print products besides, bless 'im! *[see selfies nearby]*), but he also posted the following much-appreciated rave review of *M!* on Amazon.com at the page headed "**Monster! #33: Spring 2018 Paperback – June 5, 2018**" (@ *https://www.amazon.com/Monster-33-Spring-Tim-Paxton/dp/1987723279/ref=sr_1_1?ie=UT-F8&qid=1548472985&sr=8-1&keywords=tim+paxton+monster*):

⊞ View Image Gallery

Monster! #33: Spring 2018

⭐⭐⭐⭐⭐ A MEGA MONSTER ISSUE!
By William Clark Cunningham on Jun 11, 2018
A MEGA MONSTER ISSUE!

I love everything about MONSTER no matter what size it is. This issue is a mega-sized 370 pages and well worth the read. It's the kind of fanzine they don't make anymore, and everything about it - the information, the format, the fun - makes it a must-have for fans of fantastic films. A terrific lineup of writers provide book designer TIM PAXTON and Editor STEVE FENTON with the raw clay they need to mold monstrously great pots. Don't miss out. Order this and other back issues today. I just ordered issue #32 and I can't wait!

Images in this review

Pulp 2.0 Press' website is @ *pulp2ohpress.com* (check it out for a catalogue of their way-cool products), and their Facebook page is @ *https://www.facebook.com/pulp2ohpress/?modal=ad-min_todo_tour&notif_id=1533233518754837&notif_t=page_invite*

Bill's a real friendly guy, so send him a friend request, why don'tcha! Amongst (many) other things he's got on the go—including a proposed-but-still-in-the-planning-stages, as-yet-untitled, full-color "Nunsploitation" movie book by *M!* co-editor Steve Fentone (a belated follow-up to his once-controversial, now long-out-of-print FAB Press tome *AntiCristo: The Bible of Nasty Nun Sinema & Culture* [Guildford, Surrey, UK: 2000])—includes publishing fully-licensed tie-in publications pertaining to Donald F. Glut's recently-released labor of love T.L.C. / D.I.Y. creature feature **TALES OF FRANKENSTEIN** (2018, USA), of which funtabulous monsterrific movie you can read more about in our "Midnight Snacks" entry for the film in our back pages (on p.353, to be exact).

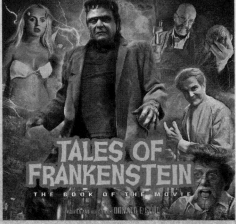

Pulp 2.0 Press' tie-in **TOF** "making-of" (etc.) book *[see p.353]*

ENDBITS...

***WANTED!* More Readers Like...** Who (or *what*)ever *this* might be! *[mask and photo by Joel Paxton]*

New—*VERY* new!—reader Leo William Capicik (born September 15th, 2018) with *Monster!* #32 and his fave BD box set of bedtime movies!

Valued *M!* contrib Martín Núñez *[right]* and his *hermanito* Thomas Byrén on a recent (2018) trip to Scandinavia!

Rough sketch from thesubnatural (a.k.a. Marcio Costa)'s Deskgram page; see the finished piece on p.225!

***WANTED!* More Readers Like...** Pulp 2.0's Bill Cunningham!

Toshirō the Friendly Umbrella-Ghost says:

さようなら！次の問題を参照してください！
Sayōnara! Tsugi no mondai o sanshō shite kudasai!

("BYE! SEE YOU NEXT ISSUE!")

Made in the USA
Middletown, DE
19 September 2023

38719843R00220